FRENCH DESTROYERS
Torpilleurs d'Escadre &
Contre-Torpilleurs
1922–1956

FRENCH DESTROYERS
Torpilleurs d'Escadre &
Contre-Torpilleurs
1922–1956

John Jordan and
Jean Moulin

Seaforth
PUBLISHING

Overleaf: *Chacal* arriving in Portsmouth with her sister *Léopard* on 26 August 1936. The ships had recently been assigned to the Officer Training School, the *Ecole Navale* (see Chapter 11), and were conducting a series of visits to major European ports as part of the training programme.

Copyright © John Jordan & Jean Moulin 2015
Watercolour paintings © Jean Bladé 2015

First published in Great Britain in 2015 by
Seaforth Publishing
An imprint of Pen & Sword Books Ltd
47 Church Street, Barnsley
S Yorkshire S70 2AS

www.seaforthpublishing.com
Email info@seaforthpublishing.com

British Library Cataloguing in Publication Data
A CIP data record for this book is available from the British Library

ISBN 978-1-84832-198-4

CONTENTS

Preface	6
Acronyms and Abbreviations	7
Conversion Tables	8

PART 1: TECHNICAL SECTION

Introduction		9
Chapter 1	The *Jaguar* Class	20
Chapter 2	The *Bourrasque* Class	41
Chapter 3	The *L'Adroit* Class	60
Chapter 4	The *Guépard* Class	75
Chapter 5	The *Aigle* Class	93
Chapter 6	The *Vauquelin* Class, *Milan* and *Epervier*	108
Colour plates		129
Chapter 7	The *Le Fantasque* Class	137
Chapter 8	The *Mogador* Class	160
Chapter 9	The *Le Hardi* Class	180
	Appendix A: The 600-tonne Torpedo Boats	205
Chapter 10	Paint Schemes and Identification Markings	197

PART 2: HISTORICAL SECTION

Chapter 11	The Period 1926–1939	206
Chapter 12	The Period 1939–1943	222
	Appendix B: *Léopard* FNFL 1940–1943	251
	Appendix C: *Le Triomphant* FNFL 1940–1944	253
Chapter 13	The Period 1943–1945	257
	Appendix D: *Le Fantasque* Modernisations USA 1943–1944	268
	Appendix E: Modernisation of the Older Destroyers 1943–1945	276
Chapter 14	The Period 1945–1956	279
	Appendix F: *Albatros* as an EATM Ship 1948–1955	287

Sources	292
Index	293

PREFACE

THIS BOOK IS EFFECTIVELY THE SEQUEL TO *French Battleships 1922–1956*, written with Robert Dumas, and *French Cruisers 1922–1956*, with Jean Moulin, published by Seaforth Publishing in 2009 and 2013 respectively. The authors thought long and hard about the coverage of the book. It would have been easier in many respects to focus exclusively on the more glamorous *contre-torpilleurs*, the development of which spanned little more than ten years and marked a clearer and more coherent progression than that of the French 'fleet torpedo boats' (*torpilleurs d'escadre*), which fell into two distinct groups with very different characteristics; it would have also greatly simplified the service histories of these two categories of ship, which were deployed for quite different tasks, particularly during the early part of the Second World War. However, a follow-on book dealing only with the *torpilleurs d'escadre* would have been difficult to justify in commercial terms, so this would have remained a significant gap in English-language coverage of the type. More compellingly, the technological and developmental links between the *contre-torpilleurs* (CT) and the *torpilleurs d'escadre* (TE) of the interwar period were closer than has been acknowledged: the TE of the *Bourrasque* and *L'Adroit* classes were designed by the same 'small ships' department of the Service Technique des Constructions Navales (STCN) which designed the CT of the *Jaguar* class, and had similar propulsion and common weapons systems, while the later TE of the *Le Hardi* class had many of the design characteristics of the last of the *contre-torpilleurs* of the *Mogador* class, of which they were close contemporaries. The late Henri Le Masson recognised these close developmental links when he wrote his seminal *Histoire du Torpilleur en France*, published by the Académie de la Marine in 1967.

French Destroyers 1922–1956 follows the same approach and organisation as the authors' earlier book on French cruisers. A general introduction is followed by nine chapters detailing, in chronological sequence, the conceptual development, construction and characteristics of each of the nine classes of *torpilleur* and *contre-torpilleur* covered in the book. This 'technical' section of the book covers the period 1926–1942 and is largely the work of John Jordan with the support and advice of Jean Moulin. The second part of the book, which is divided into four chapters, is a detailed account of the service lives of the ships during the four periods covered by the book: the prewar era (1926–1939), the early war period (1939–1943), the late war period when French naval forces rejoined the Allied cause (1943–1945), and the postwar era (1945–1956). Jean Moulin has again provided this 'historical' section, which has been translated from the French by John Jordan. One significant change to the format adopted for the cruiser book has been the insertion between the technical and historical sections of a new chapter dealing with paint schemes and recognition markings, which were an important recognition feature for both types of French flotilla craft; this chapter is a collaboration between both authors. Another is the provision of appendices at the end of the historical chapters dealing with the extensive modifications made to some ships during their service alongside the Allies from June 1940 to late 1945, and the conversion of the *contre-torpilleur Albatros* to serve as a gunnery training ship after the war; these are primarily the work of John Jordan.

The present book aims to summarise for English-speaking readers the considerable quantity of information, backed up by recently-released official documentation, made available in a series of monographs on the *torpilleurs* and *contre-torpilleurs* published in France since the mid-1990s (see Sources p.292). In addition to the technical and historical aspects of destroyer development in France between the wars, the book focuses closely on issues of infrastructure, tactical organisation and even national culture, which are not always well understood on this side of the Channel. It is hoped that this book will give the reader a better understanding not only of the design philosophy and technical characteristics of these ships, but also of the history and traditions of the Marine Nationale during the twentieth century.

THE DRAWINGS

The line drawings and labelled schematics by John Jordan, most of which have been specially prepared for this book, are based on official plans and other documentation currently held by the Centre d'Archives de l'Armement (CAA) at Châtellerault; many of the plans have been openly published on the website of the Service Historique de la Défense. Some of these plans and documents have only recently been made available as part of the *Fonds Potsdam*, an archive of material assembled by the German *Kriegsmarine* during the Occupation and transferred to Berlin, where it was seized by the Russians in 1945; the materials were returned to France after the fall of the Berlin Wall and have now been reclassified and distributed among the various French national archives. Unfortunately only partial documentation concerning the *torpilleurs d'escadre* of the *Le Hardi* class has survived, and much of this dates from 1936, before the final 'as-fitted' plans were drawn up by the shipyards. However, by piecing together the information available and by extrapolation from other contemporary projects, notably the *contre-torpilleurs* of the *Mogador* type and the battleships of the *Richelieu* class (which introduced the revolutionary Sural forced-circulation boiler), the authors are confident that they have produced the most complete study yet of these ships, even though some detailed aspects of the design must remain a matter for conjecture.

The colour section again features the work of marine artist Jean Bladé, formerly the Surgeon General for the French armed forces. These beautiful watercolours, which were painted during Jean's time in the Navy (1922–1965), constitute a valuable record of the destroyers and their activities, and provide a comprehensive illustration of the paint schemes and tactical markings of the ships at the various stages of their service lives.

ACKNOWLEDGEMENTS

The authors would like to express their thanks to the following organisations which have assisted them with their research:

The Service Historique de la Défense:
Centre d'archives de l'armement et du personnel civil (CAA) at Châtellerault
Département Marine at Vincennes, Paris

One of the highlights of the book is the section on the modernisations of the *contre-torpilleurs* of the *Le Fantasque* class, which corrects a number of errors in both English- and French-language secondary sources. This was possible only with the considerable help and support of A D Baker III, who was kind enough to lend his copies of the original BuShips plans and supplied many photos from his personal collection; Rick E Davis, who has conducted extensive research into the archives of the Charlestown Navy Yard, Boston, and Norman Friedman also provided many interesting photographs of the ships during their time in the USA, many of which are previously unpublished. Marc Saibène, author of the two French monographs on the *torpilleurs d'escadre* (see Sources), generously supplied photographs from his personal collection not only of the TEs of the *Bourrasque* and *L'Adroit* classes, but of the early *contre-torpilleurs*. Philippe Caresse, Robert Dumas, Leo van Ginderen, Jaroslaw Malinowski and Peter Cannon also contributed photographs, which have been duly credited. The remaining photographs are from the private collections of the authors; it has not always been possible to trace the precise origin of these, and all rights are reserved.

Sincere thanks are also due to Dr. Jean Bladé, who supplied the watercolour of *Volta* which illustrates the jacket as well as the colour artwork in the centre section of the book, and to his son, Jean-Sébastien Bladé, who was kind enough to provide high-resolution scans and photographs of his father's paintings. The authors also wish to extend their thanks to Rob Gardiner (Seaforth Publishing), who has offered support and advice throughout the project, and to Steve Dent, both for the intelligence and creativity he has displayed in designing the layouts and for the infinite patience with which he has accommodated the inevitable last-minute amendments. Without the collaboration of these people this book would not have been possible.

John Jordan & Jean Moulin
October 2014

ACRONYMS AND ABBREVIATIONS

ORGANISATIONS

CAA	Centre d'Archives de l'Armement (at Châtellerault, SW France)
CFLN	*Comité français de libération nationale* (French Committee of National Liberation)
CPE	*Commission permanente des essais* (Trials Commission)
CSM	*Conseil supérieur de la marine* (Navy Board [advisory])
DCAN	*Direction centrale des armes navales* (Ordnance Department)
DNL	*Division navale du Levant* (Levant Division)
EATM	*Ecole d'application du tir à la mer* (gunnery school ship)
EALM	*Ecole d'application du lancement à la mer* (torpedo school ship)
EMG	*Etat-major general de la marine* (Naval General Staff)
FMA	*Forces maritimes d'Afrique* (African maritime forces)
FMF	*Forces maritimes françaises* (French Admiralty September 1939 to 1944, at Maintenon & Vichy)
FNFL	*Forces navales françaises libres* (Free French Naval Forces)
MDAP	Mutual Defense Assistance Program (US)
NGS	Naval General Staff
STCN	*Service technique des constructions navales* (Constructors' Department)

TECHNICAL

ACAD	*automatique contre-avions double* (automatic AA twin mounting)
AMC	armed merchant cruiser
APV	auxiliary patrol vessel
CAD	*contre-avions double* (AA twin mounting)
CAQ	*contre-avions quadruple* (AA quad mounting)
CAS	*contre-avions simple* (AA single mounting)
CT	*contre-torpilleur*
CV	*chevaux* (horsepower: 1CV = 0.98632shp)
DA	*disponibilité armée* (care & maintenance)
DCT	depth charge thrower
DF	direction finding
D-P	dual-purpose
FPB	fast patrol boat
FTP	follow the pointer
GA	general arrangement
HA	high-angle (guns)
HE	high explosive
HF	high frequency
HP	high pressure (turbines)
IP	intermediate pressure (turbines)
LA	low angle (guns)
LP	low pressure (turbines)
MF	medium frequency
Mle	*Modèle* (model)
MG	machine gun
OEA	*obus explosif en acier* (HE shell)
OEcl	*obus éclairant* (starshell)
OI	*obus incendiaire* (incendiary tracer shell)

OPFA	*obus de perforation en fonte aciérée* (SAP shell)
OPf(K)	*obus de perforation* (armour-piercing shell)
OTC	*ondes très courtes* (VHF)
psi	pounds per square inch
p&s	port and starboard
p/w	passageway
RF	rangefinder
RPC	remote power control
rpg	rounds per gun
rpm	rounds per minute
SAP	semi-armour piercing (shell)
shp	shaft horsepower
S/L	searchlight
TE	*torpilleur d'escadre* (destroyer)
TS	Transmitting Station
TT	torpedo tube(s)
u/s	ultrasound
UTS	ultimate tensile strength
VTE	vertical triple expansion (reciprocating engine)
W/T	wireless telegraphy

RANKS

CA	*Contre amiral* (Rear-Admiral)
CC	*Capitaine de corvette* (Lieut.-Commander)
CF	*Capitaine de frégate* (Commander)
CO	commanding officer
CPO	chief petty officer
CV	*Capitaine de vaisseau* (Captain)
EV	*Enseigne de vaisseau* (Sub-Lieutenant)
LV	*Lieutenant de vaisseau* (Lieutenant)
PO	petty officer
VA	*Vice amiral* (Vice-Admiral)
VAE	*Vice amiral d'escadre* (Squadron Vice-Admiral)

NAVAL FORMATIONS

DC	*division de croiseurs* (cruiser division)
DCL	*division de croiseurs légers* (light cruiser division)
DCT	*division de contre-torpilleurs* (scout division)
DCX	*division de croiseurs auxiliaires* (armed merchant cruiser division)
DL	*division légère* (light division)
DSM	*division de sous-marins* (submarine division)
DT	*division de torpilleurs* (torpedo boat division)
EL	*escadre légère* (light squadron)
FHM	*Forces de haute mer* (high seas forces)
FI	*Force d'intervention* (intervention force)
FNI	*Force navale d'intervention* (Naval Intervention Force)
FNTF	French Naval Task Force
GASM	*Groupe d'action anti-sous-marine* (Anti-Submarine Group)

FOOTNOTE REFERENCES

CM	*circulaire ministérielle* (ministerial circular)
CN	*constructions navales* (construction dept.)
DM	*décision ministérielle* (ministerial directive)
EMG	*état-major général* (general staff)
/1	personnel
/2	intelligence
/3	operations
/4	support
FMF	*forces maritimes françaises* (French admiralty replaced EMG during Second World War)
PM	*préfecture maritime* (maritime district)
/1	1st Region (Cherbourg)
/2	2nd Region (Brest)
/3	3rd Region (Toulon)
/4	4th Region (Bizerte)
/5	5th Region (Lorient)

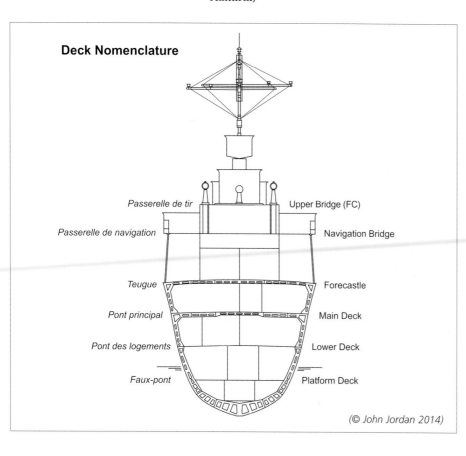

(© John Jordan 2014)

CONVERSION TABLES

Length

m	ft
95	312
100	328
105	345
110	361
115	377
120	394
125	410
130	427
135	443
140	459

Beam

m	ft
9.5	31
10.0	33
10.5	34.5
11.0	36
11.5	38
12.0	39.5
12.5	41
13.0	42.5

Guns

mm	in
75	3
100	3.9
130	5.1
138.6	5.5

Torpedoes

mm	in
381	15
450	17.7
550	21.7

Boiler working pressure

kg/cm²	psi
18	255
20	285
27	385
35	500

Notes: Length to nearest 1ft, beam to nearest 0.5ft; guns & torpedoes to one decimal place; boiler working pressure to nearest 5psi.

INTRODUCTION

THE FIRST FRENCH TORPEDO BOAT DESTroyers were built as a response to the British boats of that type, the first of which ran trials in 1893–94. When completed at the turn of the century they were referred to as *contre-torpilleurs* (lit. 'anti-torpedo boats'), and this would continue to be the official designation for the first series of 300-tonne boats and for their larger successors until 14 March 1913, when the designation was amended to *torpilleurs d'escadre* ('fleet torpedo boats').

Subsequent French destroyers (projects and ships) would continue to be officially designated *torpilleurs d'escadre*. The term *contre-torpilleur* would be revived in 1921–22 to describe a new and completely different type of large fleet scout unique to the interwar Marine Nationale with which the name has become synonymous. And the *torpilleur* ('torpedo boat') designation, previously used for small coastal torpedo boats intended for *défense mobile*,[1] would be revived for the 600-tonne torpedo boats built following the London Treaty of 1930, which set no quantitative or qualitative limits on ships displacing less than 600 tons standard.

The present book aims to cover the classes of *torpilleur d'escadre* and *contre-torpilleur* designed and built for the Marine Nationale during the interwar period, some of which continued to serve after the Second World War.

THE EARLY DESTROYERS

The characteristics of the earliest French destroyers were suggested by Jacques-Augustin Normand, whose Le Havre shipyard (the Chantiers Normand) had been particularly prominent in the construction of the *torpilleurs défensifs*.[2] Normand proposed a ship of 300 tonnes, with a speed of 25 knots to enable it to accompany the battle fleet, armed with two torpedo tubes and four 381mm torpedoes (the reloads were to be stowed in lockers on deck), together with quick-firing (QF) guns capable of penetrating the machinery spaces of an opponent.

The first four ships (*Durandal* class) were laid down from August 1896 and were launched and completed in 1899–1900. They were considered a success; a total of 55 ships of the 300-tonne type would be built for the Marine Nationale, together with 20 for foreign navies. In the last two classes the 381mm torpedo was replaced by a new 450mm model with greater power and range. However, this exacerbated the topweight problem which had long been considered the only negative feature of the ships

The 450-tonne type which succeeded the *300-tonnes* aimed to correct this deficiency. The mixed armament of a single 65mm and six 47mm guns of the latter was also regarded as a weakness, and the 47mm was now

---

[1] Essentially the protection of French ports; the concept of *défense mobile* was a key element in the defensive strategy promoted by Admiral Aube of the *Jeune École* during the early 1880s.

[2] Also known as *numérotés*; these small torpedo boats, none of which displaced more than 100 tonnes, carried only numbers, not names.

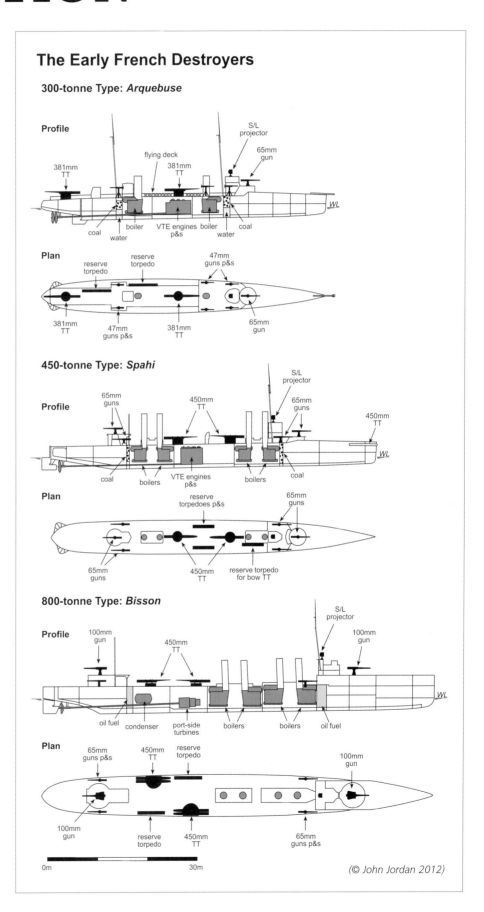

(© John Jordan 2012)

Top: The 300-tonne destroyers *Branlebas* and *Fanion*. Note the single trainable torpedo tubes above the stern. *(Philippe Caresse collection)*

Above: The 300-tonne destroyer *Mousqueton* at Toulon. Abaft the second funnel are the two after 47mm guns and the tube of the reserve torpedo for the after mounting. Note the pronounced tumble-home of the ship's sides. *(Philippe Caresse collection)*

considered too lightweight to be effective. The latest British destroyers of the 'River' class displaced 550 tons and were being rearmed with four 12pdr (76mm) guns. Normand proposed a homogeneous armament of six single 65mm guns and three 450mm torpedo tubes, again with reloads. It would be the last time he exerted an influence on French destroyer characteristics; he died shortly afterwards on 11 December 1906.

The first class of seven ships (*Spahi* class) had a similar machinery arrangement to the *300-tonnes*; there were boiler rooms fore and aft of a central engine room with conventional vertical triple expansion (VTE) reciprocating engines side by side. The *Spahi* type was generally regarded as successful. However, the next two units introduced an experimental mixed propulsion system on three shafts, with a VTE engine driving the centre shaft and steam turbines on the two outer shafts. This was an arrangement common in contemporary liners; it had the theoretical advantage of economic steaming using the reciprocating engine, while the thirsty turbines provided sustained high speed.

The experiment was not a success: the reciprocating engine had forced lubrication, which resulted in regular breakdowns before the technology was mastered; and both boiler rooms were now forward of the engine rooms, which unbalanced the trim of the boats. Coal was generally stowed adjacent to the boiler rooms, and the transfer of these considerable weights forward resulted in sea-keeping problems.

The last four ships had turbines only on their three shafts, and the last three had oil firing. The experimental nature of much of their machinery and the lack of uniformity between individual ships complicated training and maintenance. However, lessons were learned: subsequent destroyers would be powered by turbines alone, auxiliary machinery by electricity rather than steam, and oil would be preferred to coal, not only for ease of refuelling but because of the reduction in the physical exertion required by the stokers at the high speeds at which these ships were intended to operate.

THE 800-TONNE TYPE

The final type of destroyer built for the Marine Nationale prior to the First World War was the 800-tonne type. The fleet wanted bigger ships with better sea-keeping, able to maintain speed in rough weather; a raised forecastle was considered essential. Improvements in the performance of torpedoes meant that engagements between destroyers would take place at longer range; the 65mm Mle 1902 was considered effective only to 1000m, whereas a 100mm gun could reliably hit at 2500m. This would put the new ships on a par with the latest British destroyers of the 'Tribal' class, which displaced 850 tons and were armed with two 4-inch guns. The 65mm was retained, however, as its high rate of fire (12/13rpm) was liked, so the ships ended up with a mixed battery of two 100mm Mle 1893 (disposed fore and aft) and four 65mm guns. Four 450mm torpedo tubes in twin trainable tubes (each with a single reload locker) completed their armament.

A class of twelve ships (*Bouclier* class) was authorised under the 1908 and 1910 estimates and completed before the outbreak of war, followed by a class of six (*Bisson* class: authorised 1910–11, four in service by August 1914), and a final class of three (*Enseigne Roux* class: authorised 1913), two of which entered service in 1916 with the third suspended.

Despite a relatively mature technological base there were major differences in configuration, equipment and performance between individual ships, which in accordance with previous practice were allocated to no fewer than nine different private shipyards in addition to the two naval dockyards at Rochefort (3 ships) and Toulon (3 ships). Two ships had three shafts, the others two; some had cruise turbines, others did not. Most had four evenly spaced funnels but one ship, *Casque*, had the two central boilers mounted back to back and had a broad central funnel flanked by two slimmer funnels. *Bouclier* had a length overall of 72.3 metres; the other ships were between 74m and 78.3m; beam varied between 7.6m and 8.1m, and power between 13,000CV and 14,000CV. Unsurprisingly, performance was uneven: the three-shaft *Bouclier* achieved 35.3 knots on trials, the two-shaft *Dehorter* only 29.3 knots; in service *Casque* made 29 knots, *Bory* only 24 knots. This, together with the vibration suffered at different speeds, made tactical grouping of

INTRODUCTION

Left: The 450-tonne destroyer *Lansquenet*. The first seven ships of this type had a similar machinery arrangement to the 300-tonne destroyers, with reciprocating engines side by side in a single engine room and the boiler rooms fore and aft. They could be distinguished by their two widely-separated pairs of funnels. *(Philippe Caresse collection)*

the ships difficult. The heavy fuel consumption of the entire class drove the French inexorably towards reduction gearing. The first British geared turbines entered service aboard the destroyers *Badger* and *Beaver* in 1912–13,[3] and it was decided that the third ship of the *Enseigne Roux* class, the *Enseigne Gabolde*, would be completed as a test platform for Parsons geared turbines.

A document outlining tactics for the fleet dated 1910, and which was still in force in 1914, makes clear the influence of the Russo-Japanese war with regard to the deployment of the French *torpilleurs d'escadre*. It stated:

> The flotillas can act only in conjunction with the battle fleet ... Their intervention will be most effective during the exploitation phase of the battle, once the big guns have prepared the ground by disrupting the cohesion of the enemy battle line. In particular, they should take every opportunity to separate ships which have fallen out of the line or to inflict further damage on a crippled opponent. However, their key role begins at sunset and during the pursuit which will follow the battle...[4]

Although the flotillas would accompany the fleet into battle, the document suggests that they would be kept on the disengaged side of the line until 'opportunities'

arose; they would not attempt to launch an attack on the enemy line when the latter was still formed and engaged. Torpedo ranges were still in the region of 2000–3000m,[5] and torpedo-armed craft attempting to close the enemy line would be greeted by a hail of medium-calibre shell. This view would change as gun engagement and torpedo ranges increased.

The 'flotillas' of the elite force of the French Navy in August 1914, the *Armée Navale*, comprised six *escadrilles* ('flotillas') each of six *torpilleurs d'escadre*, led by the 800-tonne *Bouclier*: two comprised 800-tonne ships, two 450-tonne ships, and two the early 300-tonne type. The other major light formation, the *Division des flotilles* of the 2nd Squadron, operated in the Channel area and comprised three *escadrilles* each of six 300-tonne destroyers, and three *escadrilles* of submarines.

---

[3] *Badger* and *Beaver* were given 'part gearing' as an experiment; full single reduction gearing was first installed in the *Laforey*-class destroyers *Leonidas* and *Lucifer* in 1913.

[4] Quoted in Le Masson, *Histoire du Torpilleur en France* (Académie de la Marine, 1967), p.176; translated into English by the author.

[5] The newest French torpedo, the Modèle 1909R, the first to employ a reheater, had a range of 2000m at 33 knots and 3000m at 28 knots.

Below: *Voltigeur* and her sister *Tirailleur* (450-tonne type) had an experimental mixed propulsion system on three shafts inspired by that of contemporary passenger liners, with a reciprocating engine (for endurance) driving the centre shaft and steam turbines (for high speed) on the two outer shafts. The relocation of all four boilers and their associated coal bunkers forward adversely affected trim. *(Philippe Caresse collection)*

THE *STATUT NAVAL* OF 1912

The *Statut Naval* (Naval Law) of 30 March 1912, which was intended to arrest the decline of the *Marine Nationale* in relation to the other major European powers, established the fleet structure to be achieved by 1920 as: 28 battleships, 10 scout cruisers, 52 fleet torpedo boats, 94 submarines, and 10 vessels for distant stations.

The imbalance between the number of capital ships and the number of torpedo boats intended to accompany them is striking. The low priority accorded to flotilla craft in the programme would become alarmingly apparent in the following months. The year 1912 saw the authorisation of no fewer than twelve 'super-dreadnought' battleships of the *Bretagne*, *Normandie* and *Lyon* classes. In contrast, the number of fleet torpedo boats ordered in 1913 was cut to three (in previous years an average of 6–7 boats had been ordered).

In December 1913 Vice-Admiral Le Bris, Chief of the Naval General Staff (NGS), submitted a lengthy report in which he proposed the construction of 58 new destroyers for a total force of 115 in 1920 – he estimated that Rochefort and private industry could easily deliver nine hulls per year. The Navy Minister disagreed; there was limited funding available for new construction and he was of the opinion that this needed to be concentrated on the capital ship programme.

The NGS was not to be deterred. In successive reports submitted to the Navy Minister during 1914 it opposed the inclusion of the 450-tonne destroyers and the ten most modern 300-tonne boats in the figure of 52 destroyers projected for 1920.[6] It questioned whether the 300-tonne type could be classified as 'high seas destroyers' under the terms of the Naval Law, as their limited sea-keeping and endurance would inevitably place constraints on the deployment of the battle fleet. Even when the twenty 800-tonne destroyers completed or building were added to the 23 smaller ships, there remained nine new destroyers to be laid down by 1917 at the latest (for entry into service during 1920). The NGS therefore proposed the construction of nine destroyers of a new, more powerful 1500-tonne type under the 1915 estimates (to complete the force of 52 *torpilleurs d'escadre* enshrined in the Naval Law), a further ten of the same type (to replace the *300-tonnes*) in 1916, and thirteen additional ships (to replace the *450-tonnes*) under the 1917 and 1918 estimates. This would create a modern force of fleet destroyers comprising:

4 *escadrilles* each of eight *1500-tonnes*
2 *escadrilles* each of eight *800/900-tonnes*
4 x *800-tonnes* as replacements or for the Channel Fleet (2nd Squadron)

The 450-tonne and 350-tonne destroyers were to be transferred to anti-submarine defence duties.

By this time tactical thinking had moved much closer to British and German practice. The new destroyers would need to be able to protect their own battle line against attack by torpedo boats, hence the increase in size and power. (The latest British destroyers displaced close to 1000 tons and had a uniform armament of three 4-inch [102mm] guns.) Each *escadrille* would now have eight, rather than six destroyers, in imitation of the German flotillas and the British half-flotillas.

M89 AND M90

The year 1913 saw the publication of a report by the Comité Technique on the *torpilleurs d'escadre* built from 1908 onwards, which in addition to reviewing the ships in current service also pointed the way forward.

When considering armament, the report stated that the instability of the platform, together with the relatively small size and high speed of the targets – the enemy's own destroyers – meant that gunfire was effective only out to 3000m. The targets were completely unprotected, so a non-capped shell with a comparatively large bursting charge of picric acid (*Mélinite* – 15% of shell weight) was recommended; ideally this needed to penetrate the hull below the waterline in order to incapacitate the ship, so it should have a flat nose (*cône tronquée*) fitted with a light ballistic cap which detached when it hit the water; the shell would

Below: *Commandant Bory* had the classic 800-tonne configuration with four evenly-spaced funnels and the twin torpedo tubes *en echelon* abaft the fourth. Note the large 100mm guns fore and aft; the remaining four guns were 65mm. (Philippe Caresse collection)

Bottom: There were considerable variations in appearance and performance between the various ships of the class. This is *Casque*, which had her two middle boilers mounted back to back and the second and third funnels combined. (Philippe Caresse collection)

---

[6] The thirteen 450-tonne destroyers had entered service between 1909 and 1912, the 330-tonne ships of the *Branlebas* class between 1908 and 1910; they were therefore relatively modern units when the *Statut Naval* was promulgated in 1912.

require a very sensitive fuze to ensure detonation. Given an inherently unstable platform, a fast, manoeuvrable target and rudimentary fire control, it was thought that very few hits would be obtained, so the largest possible calibre was desirable to ensure maximum damage from a single hit. The report recommended a uniform armament of at least six 90mm guns or four 100mm guns; however, an even larger calibre of 14cm[7] was the committee's preferred option, even if this meant a reduction in the number of guns to two. The Comité Technique also wanted a doubling of the number of torpedo tubes from four to eight: two triple 450mm mountings abaft the funnels would be complemented by two single torpedo tubes abeam the bridge which would be capable of launching torpedoes within 20 degrees of the ship's axis. The boilers were to be designed to make smoke; geared turbines were preferred to provide improved fuel economy, giving a range of 2600nm at 10 knots.

Studies were produced and an *avant-projet* submitted by the STCN on 29 January 1914 and approved by the NGS on 9 June. The new destroyer would have a displacement of 1530 tonnes – almost twice that of the previous *torpilleurs d'escadre* and 50% greater than the latest British ships. It was estimated that 25,000–30,000CV would be required to drive the ships at the required speed: 33 knots on trials for 30 knots service. (This was over-optimistic; judging from contemporary British practice c.38,000CV would probably have been needed for a

SCHNEIDER 14CM/25 PROPOSAL

Breech:	SA horizontal sliding
Length in calibres:	25
Weight of mounting:	6.65t
Weight of shell:	36kg
Weight of charge:	3.9kg
Type of ammunition:	fixed
Pressure at breech:	2400kg
Elevation:	-1°/+20°
Muzzle velocity:	550m/s
Recoil force:	23.56t
Range:	6000/6500m effective (but excessive dispersion beyond 5000m)
Firing cycle:	15 rounds per minute

Note: This would have been the first gun with a sliding breech in the Marine Nationale.

---

[7] The precise calibre was 138.6mm.
[8] The flotilla leaders of the *Lightfoot* class (1914-15 Estimates), which displaced 1440 tons, needed 36,000shp to achieve their designed 34.5 knots.

Below: *Enseigne Gabolde*, the last ship of the 800-tonne series, was completed as a technology demonstrator for Parsons geared turbines and the new 550mm torpedo, which was carried in two twin mountings. Unlike her half-sisters she had a uniform armament of 100mm guns: two forward of the bridge, one aft. She is seen here shortly after completion in 1921. *(Marius Bar)*

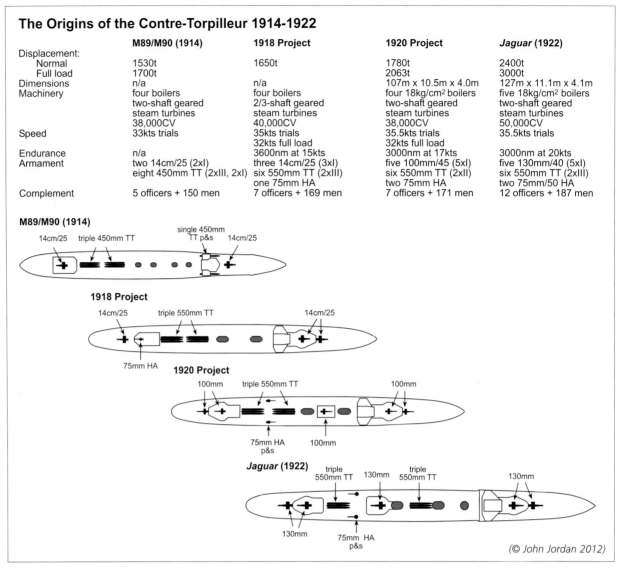

(© John Jordan 2012)

ship of this size.8) Armament would be that proposed by the Comité Technique, and the complement was fixed at 5 officers and 150 men. In the spring of 1914 a proposal was received from Schneider for a lightweight 14cm/25-calibre gun; the characteristics are in the accompanying table. A longer 45-calibre 14cm model derived from the 55-calibre secondary guns of the new dreadnoughts would arm the proposed scout cruisers (*Lamotte-Picquet* class).

Two ships, designated M89 and M90,9 were pencilled in under the 1915 estimates; they were to be in service by 1917. In the interim the last unit of the 800-tonne series, the *Enseigne Gabolde*, would trial the geared turbines and the triple torpedo tubes intended for the new ships. However, in the spring of 1914 the Navy Minister refused to incorporate M89 and M90 into the 1915 programme, much to the surprise of the Navy, which had already ordered torpedoes for them in anticipation. Studies continued until August 1914, but the outbreak of war put an end to any hope of completing them and the project was revived only in the spring of 1917.

---

9 The 300-tonne series had received the designations M0 to M54; the 450-tonne and 800-tonne destroyers M55 to M88.

THE ARGENTINE AND JAPANESE DESTROYERS

In 1910 Argentina had ordered twelve destroyers from Europe to accompany the two dreadnoughts *Rivadavia* and *Moreno* building in the United States. The Argentines wanted to sample the latest destroyer technology and therefore divided their order equally between Britain, Germany and France. The four French ships were designed and built by Ateliers et Chantiers de Bretagne, Nantes; they were launched in 1911. Construction times in the French shipyards were still notoriously slow, and the destroyers were still in the final stages of fitting out when they were requisitioned for the Marine Nationale on 9 August 1914.

Designed for operations in the South Atlantic, the Argentine destroyers were large, seaworthy ships which displaced close to 1000 tonnes on trials. They proved underpowered, and although some ships achieved their designed speed of 32 knots in early sea trials, 27 knots was a more realistic figure in service. The Argentine Navy had intended to arm them with 4-inch (102mm) guns and 18-inch (457mm) torpedoes, but in French naval service they received four 100mm guns – initially of an old and obsolete model – and four single 450mm torpedo tubes. They subsequently served with the Channel Fleet (*2ᵉ Escadre*

Légère), and *Intrépide* had the distinction of flying the flag of the British Rear-Admiral Horace Hood on one occasion.

The cessation of all new destroyer construction following mobilisation in August 1914 left the Navy seriously short of destroyers to counter the growing menace from German and Austro-Hungarian submarines, and in 1916 the French were compelled to consider having destroyers built in Japan, the other Allies being unwilling or unable to deliver sufficient hulls within the desired time-frame. Twelve 2nd Class Destroyers of the *Kaba* class were duly ordered in December 1916. Construction times were impressive by French standards, and all twelve ships were delivered to Port Said on 26 October of the following year. These comparatively small ships (displacement was 685 tonnes) were unremarkable, and their Japanese 4.7in (120mm) and 3in (76mm) guns created supply and maintenance problems for the Marine Nationale, but armed with depth charges they did the job they were required to do, serving as escorts for convoys and troop transports in the Eastern Mediterranean for the final 13 months of the war.

The ex-Argentine and Japanese-built destroyers had little influence on subsequent destroyer designs. However, the French were impressed by the sea-keeping qualities of the boats built for Argentina, and by the simple, robust machinery of the Japanese-built ships. The homogeneity of the latter was also seen as a significant advantage when compared with the diversity of the French 800-tonne type.

THE STUDIES RESUME

Studies of the new destroyers to be laid down once war had ended resumed in 1917. A note dated 20 April[10] reiterated the staff requirements for the 1914 design, but with a renewed emphasis on sea-keeping which reflected war experience. There were now to be three (vs. two) of the proposed Schneider lightweight 14cm guns and two 75mm HA guns. The triple – but not the single – torpedo tubes were to be retained, and these were now to launch a new heavyweight 550mm torpedo with much-increased explosive power and range. It was hoped that the adoption of single reduction geared turbines would deliver an increase in endurance from 2600nm at 10 knots to 3000nm at 16 knots. French familiarity with the Italian Navy during operations in the Adriatic suggested the 'light

---

[10] EMG Note 97.

France was allocated nine former German and Austro-Hungarian destroyers as war reparations, and following refit and refurbishment these served in the Atlantic during the 1920s before being replaced by the new 1500-tonne destroyers. The French were impressed with their military capabilities, their robust machinery and their well-designed command spaces, but considered their freeboard inadequate for operations in the Atlantic swell. All but one of the ex-German torpedo boats had a uniform armament of three 105mm guns and six 50cm torpedo tubes: two twin mountings abaft the funnels and two single mountings abeam the bridge. This is *Delage* (ex-*H.147*), which had been completed only just before the end of the war and was delivered minus her artillery. Because of a shortage of copper in Germany, much of the pipework for the machinery was of steel and soon had to be replaced due to corrosion. *(Courtesy of A D Baker III)*

scouts' (*esploratori leggeri*) of the *Aquila* class as a possible model.[11]

However, the Italian Navy was not the only one to influence French thinking during this period. A later note dated 24 September 1917 proposed the construction of two distinct types of destroyer following British practice: a *torpilleur d'escadre* of 1530 tonnes, and a larger *conducteur d'escadrille* ('flotilla leader'). The *torpilleur d'escadre* was to have a designed speed of 33 knots and an armament of three 14cm guns and six 550mm torpedoes in two triple mountings; the flotilla leader a speed of 35 knots and an additional 14cm gun. An EMG report dated 22 December of the same year broadly endorsed this proposal, but required the standard destroyer to make 35 knots on trials. Endurance was to be 3000nm at 14 knots for the destroyer and 3500nm for the leader. Both types were to have a tight turning circle and a reinforced bow for anti-submarine operations.

During the last months of the war the NGS was contemplating a force of 100 *torpilleurs* similar to the British 'V' class (1300 tons, 35 knots), following favourable reports by Captain Vandier, French liaison officer with the Grand Fleet. The Chief of the Naval Staff also wrote to each of the naval attachés in Rome, London and Washington asking them to supply details of the latest destroyer construction.

Work on plans for the new ships resumed in earnest after the Armistice of 11 November 1918. On the 28th of that same month the Constructors Department (STCN) wrote to the NGS asking for confirmation of staff requirements, which they understood to be: 1650 tonnes, four boilers in two boiler rooms, turbines on two/three shafts for 40,000CV, a maximum speed of 35 knots and a cruise speed of 17 knots. In its reply the NGS insisted on: three guns of about 14cm calibre with 30-degree elevation, firing a 30kg shell to a range of 15,000m; a single 75mm HA gun; a speed of 32 knots at deep load, and flexible machinery with an endurance of 3600nm at 15 knots or 2800nm at 17/18 knots. It also wanted a flared bow with sheer, and a spacious, 'comfortable' bridge. Complement was to be 7 officers, 19 POs and 150 men.

This was a bigger ship than the 1914 project, with an extra gun, fewer but more powerful torpedoes, and greater endurance. There was a renewed emphasis on seaworthiness, but arguably the greatest difference in requirements was for a gun engagement range out to 15,000m, which reflected both the longer distances from which the latest torpedoes could be launched and war experience. In being less than specific about the calibre of the main guns the NGS was recognising a problem with its previous assumptions. The lightweight 14cm/25-cal. gun proposed by Schneider had too short a barrel to deliver accurate fire beyond 5000m. In specifying a minimum 30kg shell the NGS was opening the door to a slightly smaller-calibre gun.[12]

In a note dated 25 February 1919 Admiral de Bon, Chief of the Naval General Staff, pointed out to the Minister that the Italian Navy had completed or laid down no fewer than twelve flotilla leaders and 40 torpedo boats during 1914–18, and that the corresponding figure for the Marine Nationale was three. He proposed that the new priority for construction be as follows: 'destroyers' (British terminology was adopted to denote the entire category of flotilla craft), followed by light cruisers, and finally capital ships. These suggestions were accepted by the new Navy Minister, Georges Leygues, on 4 March.

The Naval General Staff followed up this submission by a more detailed '*Note sur les destroyers*', which was approved on 12 March 1919. This was the most significant submission yet by the NGS, as it attempted to define the missions and capabilities of the larger ships now contemplated.

The double role of the *torpilleur d'escadre* had been clearly set out in a study dating from 1914: its primary mission was to attack the enemy battle line with torpedoes; its secondary role was to disrupt by torpedo and gunfire the attacks of enemy flotilla craft against the French line.

The larger vessel described in the note of March 1919, however, and which would subsequently become the *contre-torpilleur*, had a triple role, with a markedly different set of priorities. Its primary mission was scouting, followed by the protection of its own battle line against enemy flotilla craft. Torpedo attacks against the enemy line of battle were relegated to third place, and were circumscribed by constraints on approaching the enemy ships too closely.

The qualities required for the first two roles were stated to be: high speed, endurance, a large radius of action and a powerful armament. When scouting for the battle line these ships would be expected to hold a contact and to be capable of engaging not only destroyers but small cruisers. This implied a speed and armament superior to current flotilla craft, light protection, and a displacement of at least 2000 tonnes.

The Naval Staff considered that torpedo attacks on the enemy battle line with torpedoes would no longer be launched at the close ranges accepted before and during the war. Torpedo technology had progressed to the point at which attacks could be launched at 12,000–15,000 metres. While accepting that the percentage of hits obtained at such distances would be small, the solution was seen to lie in combining multiple torpedo firings with superior fire control.

The French considered torpedo reloads impractical under action conditions, even at these longer ranges. In the European theatre ships would normally return to their home port after each engagement, and it was important to maximise the number of torpedoes immediately available in the tubes; the Pacific powers, faced with longer campaigns over vast expanses of ocean, would fit their destroyers for at least two torpedo engagements.

Close combat was envisaged by the report as being

---

[11] As completed in February 1917 the *Aquila* displaced 1600 tonnes, had a designed speed of 34 knots, and was armed with three 150mm guns, four 76mm guns and four 450mm torpedo tubes. The armament was later amended to four 120mm guns and two 76mm HA guns.

[12] The Schneider 14cm gun fired a 36kg shell; the weight of the shell fired by the 130mm gun on which development work would soon begin, and which would eventually be adopted both for the *torpilleurs d'escadre* and for the early *contre-torpilleurs*, was 32kg. Note that the shell fired by the contemporary British 4.7in (120mm) gun would have been considered too light; it weighed less than 23kg.

most likely at night, when hostile forces might stumble into one another. In these conditions ramming might still be possible; ramming was also considered important for the effective prosecution of submarine contacts, so the bow would need to be reinforced. Both the scouting role and night combat would require propulsion machinery which was flexible and responsive.

In the context of the above considerations the following detailed recommendations were made:

A – Hull
To be designed for strength and speed; reinforced bow; a 'clean' hull, with anchors in hawsepipes; bridge to be protected from wind, sea and spray to ensure comfortable command spaces in all weathers; greater draught to ensure good sea-keeping (earlier French flotilla craft had been designed with shallow draught in order to minimise the threat from mines and torpedoes).

B - Armament
Guns: Need for compromise between weight of shell and rate of fire; largest practical calibre 138.6mm (need stressed for high level of reliability of loading mechanisms and fire control to achieve acceptable rate of fire); four semi-automatic 138.6mm proposed, disposed as superimposed single mountings fore and aft; all guns to have shields to protect their crews from splinters and spray; each gun to be provided with 150 rounds, including some ready-use rounds stowed close to the gun (an innovation attributed to British practice); anti-aircraft protection to be provided by one of the 138.6mm guns on an HA mounting plus four machine guns; fire control to be provided by a director[13] incorporating a rangefinder.

Torpedoes: Two triple mountings for 550mm long-range torpedoes on the centre-line with good arcs, especially forward; torpedo sights to be located on bridge.

Depth charges: Although not primarily anti-submarine vessels, might need to use depth charges in the event of a hostile submarine being present, or against enemy flotilla craft in the event of a failed ramming or close encounter(!); eight 100kg DC to be carried for this purpose; study proposed for laying mines in the path of the enemy battle line, ten mines being carried by each destroyer; depth-charging and minelaying also to be controlled from bridge.

Illuminating shell: Searchlight projectors to be replaced in their traditional role of illuminating enemy ships at night by starshell in order not to provide a point of aim for an opponent; one 60cm projector to be fitted for long-range signalling, plus a 30cm projector for signalling in formation (the stress laid on power and reliability of the electrical circuits suggest that these were particular failings of earlier French models).

C – Speed
To be capable of 40 knots at full load displacement for six hours in order to ensure a comfortable 35 knots in normal service; boilers and auxiliaries to be robust and reliable (rough weather speed trial proposed).

---

[13] The British term 'fire-director' is used in the Note.

D – Radius of Action
Must be able to accompany the battle line in all weathers.

E – Wireless Telegraphy
Main W/T office to be close to the bridge with direct communication.

F – Aeronautics
Winch for balloons.

G – Making Smoke
By direct injection of fuel oil into funnels.

H – Protection
Sides of boiler and machinery rooms to be protected by 5cm gratings with a height of three metres (one metre above, two below waterline), with transverse end bulkheads of same composition; protective deck of 4cm plated gratings over the same area; protective mattressing around the bridge, torpedo tubes and guns to absorb splinters; paravanes against mines; comprehensive damage control arrangements employing hand-operated steam pumps, and powerful ventilators to disperse gases.

I – Compartmentation
Ship to be divided into three sections for damage control purposes, of which central section to comprise boiler and machinery rooms; ship to be able to steam with either of outer compartments flooded.

J – Pumps
Each of the three sections to have two powerful independent pumps per compartment.

The above proposals are reproduced in detail because of the insight they give us into French technical and tactical thinking of the period. Some of that thinking is retrospective and analytical, reflecting on lessons based on hard wartime experience (cf the observations on hull-form, the reliability of machinery, and on damage control). However, the document also shows an acute awareness of the tactical possibilities opened up by new technology (lightweight large-calibre guns, long-range torpedoes, starshell). Of particular note is the emphasis on superior battle control from a capacious, comfortable bridge, with centralised director fire control and long-range torpedo sights.

Such was the philosophy which was to underpin not only the *contre-torpilleur*, but also the new *torpilleur d'escadre*, the design of which would also incorporate many of the above features.

TOWARDS A NEW *STATUT NAVAL*
Given the disruption to French industrial infrastructure resulting from the war there was still little chance of laying down a new ship for at least two/three years. Serious consideration was given to an offer by the British Thornycroft company to complete two of the cancelled destroyers of the 'W' type for the French government, but in June 1919 the proposal had to be rejected due to a dramatic fall of the franc against the pound sterling.

Work on the new generation of French flotilla craft continued, however. On 1 April 1920 the *Conseil*

THE SHIPS WHICH INFLUENCED THE FRENCH *CONTRE-TORPILLEUR*

	Leone (It)	*Scott* (GB)	*S.113* (Ger)
Built:	3 ships 1921–24	1917–19	1917–18
Displacement:	2000t	1625t	2060t
Dimensions:	109.5m x 10.4m	97.5m x 9.7m	105.5m x 10.2m
Machinery:	2-shaft geared turbines; 42,000shp = 34kts	2-shaft geared turbines; 40,000shp = 36kts	2-shaft steam turbines; 45,000shp = 36kts
Armament:	8 – 120mm/45 (4 x II) 2 – 76mm/40 (2 x I) HA 6 – 450mm TT (2 x III) (70 mines)	5 – 120mm/45 (5 x I) 1 – 76mm/45 HA 6 – 533mm TT (2 x III) (40 mines)	4 – 150mm/45 (4 x I) 4 – 600mm TT (2 x II)

Notes:
Length is waterline (*S.113*) or between perpendiculars (others).
For comparability, data for *Scott* are metric equivalents.

Above: The Italian *Tigre*, one of a series of large, fast and powerful *esploratori leggeri* ordered in 1917 and completed postwar. With a displacement of 2000 tonnes (normal), a speed of 34 knots and a main armament of eight 120mm guns in twin mountings, these ships had a major influence on the design of the French postwar *contre-torpilleurs* of the *Jaguar* class. (Leo van Ginderen collection)

Supérieur de la Marine formally proposed a *torpilleur d'escadre* with the following characteristics:

Displacement: 1350 tonnes
Armament: 4 – 100mm (4 x I), 2 – 75mm HA (2 x I), 4/6 – 550mm TT (2/3 x II)
Speed: 33 knots
Endurance: 3000nm at 15 knots

The proposal was approved by the Minister on 28 April. On that same day he agreed to include two new destroyers of the larger type, variously referred to as a *torpilleur-éclaireur* (lit. 'torpedo scout') or *contre-torpilleur*, in the next naval estimates; they were to bear the names *Lion* and *Guépard*. The characteristics of these ships were as follows:

Displacement: 1780 tonnes
Armament: 5 – 100mm (5 x I), 2 – 75mm HA (2 x I), 6 – 550mm TT (2 x III)
Speed: 35.5 knots
Endurance: 2800–3000nm at 17 knots

The key differences between this type and the proposed *torpilleur d'escadre* were higher displacement, an additional 100mm gun (to be located between the funnels), higher speed and greater endurance.

The *Comité Technique* was unhappy because the 100mm gun failed to meet the Navy's requirements. Not only was shell weight (16kg) only half that recommended by the NGS, but the 100mm was outclassed by both the British 4.7-inch and the Italian 120mm guns now being fitted in their destroyers. In order to avoid any delay in ordering these vessels, the *Comité Technique* was prepared to accept that the first two ships, which would effectively be the prototypes, would be armed with the lightweight 100mm weapon, but envisaged that their successors would be armed with four 138.6mm guns.[14] In the event the French Parliament, equally unconvinced by the design in its current form, refused to sanction the Minister's request.

The need for a larger-calibre gun would be underlined by the resumption of building on the Italian *esploratori leggeri* of the *Leone* class,[15] which displaced 2000 tonnes and were armed with four twin 120mm guns, and by French acquisition of the ex-German 'super-destroyer' *S.113*, displacing 2060 tonnes and with an armament of four 15cm guns.[16] A further meeting of the *Comité Technique* on 3 July 1920 determined that 100mm was too light a calibre and the 138.6mm gun too heavy for a destroyer, and that the 130mm currently under development represented an effective compromise. The committee, no doubt influenced by the Italian *Leone* design, proposed that a twin mounting be developed alongside the current single mounting to give maximum flexibility in the armament of the new ships.

By September 1920 requirements for a war against Italy were calculated as nineteen ships of the *contre-torpilleur* type: six for blockade and thirteen for the fleet; all were to be at least as powerful as their Italian counterparts. A total of 146 *torpilleurs* would also be required in the event of a war against Italy and Germany.[17]

New proposals considered on 14 January 1921 by the Naval General Staff showed a major jump in displacement for the *contre-torpilleur*, from 1780 tonnes to 2310–2400 tonnes. Steam was to be provided by no fewer than five boilers, and the turbine machinery would deliver 50,000CV for a top speed of 35.5–36 knots. Endurance was to be at least 3000nm at 15 knots. Six alternative armament layouts were presented:

---

[14] From about 1920 the Marine Nationale used millimetres rather than centimetres; the 14cm gun of the Great War period became the 138.6mm gun.

[15] Five ships had been ordered from Ansaldo, Genoa, on 18 January 1917, but a shortage of steel and other materials meant they could not be laid down during the First World War. Three were reordered on 30 October 1920. The first class of French *contre-torpilleurs* would be christened with the same 'big cat' names.

[16] *S.113* was ceded to France on 5 May 1921, and entered service with the Marine Nationale as the *Amiral Sénès* in May 1922. Her main guns had a horizontal sliding breech which made a considerable impression because of its speed and simplicity of operation; it was subsequently adopted for the models of 138.6mm gun which armed the later French *contre-torpilleurs*.

[17] It was envisaged that the *contre-torpilleurs* would operate only in the Mediterranean, where they would be opposed by the Italian *esploratori leggeri*.

A: four 138.6mm guns in single mountings.
B: eight 130mm in twin mountings.
C: five 130mm in five single mountings (two forward, two aft, one amidships).
D: six 130mm in single mountings (three forward, three aft).
E: six 138.6mm in two twin and two single mountings (two forward, two aft, with the twin mountings superimposed).
F: six 138.6mm in four single and one twin mountings (superimposed singles fore and aft with the twin mounting amidships).

Design 'A' was rejected because of the height of the 138.6mm mountings, and 'D' because of the triangular arrangement of the guns fore and aft – a feature of the prewar French destroyers. The Naval General Staff was inclined towards 'F', despite the mix of twin and single mountings, with design 'C' – which could be realised immediately – as the 'safe' option. Provided the twin 130mm mounting was successful, 'B' could then form the basis of the design for ships laid down after 1921.

A Note of 20 January 1921 (137 EMG 1) proposed a powerful anti-submarine outfit for these ships, comprising:

- stern rails for launching 200kg depth charges or mines
- depth charge throwers mounted on either side of the ship
- ultrasonic submarine detection apparatus
- an SC listening tube[18]
- provision for Walser listening apparatus and an associated cabin

The definitive project was outlined in Note 1062 EMG 1 of 25 May 1921. The new *contre-torpilleur* would displace 2360 tonnes and would be armed with six 130mm guns: a single mounting with a twin superimposed forward, a single amidships, and two superimposed singles aft. The new *torpilleur d'escadre* would have a normal displacement of 1455 tonnes, and would have only four single 130mm guns, superimposed fore and aft.

---

[18] The SC listening tube was conceived by US, British and French scientists in 1917. The tube contained two air-filled rubber balls, each connected to the listener's ears via a stethoscope. The listener turned the SC tube until the sound was the same in both ears, which gave the direction of the contact – although it was impossible to tell whether it was to port or starboard, ahead or astern. Range could be estimated by the intensity of the sound. The original device was considered primitive, and was usable only at short ranges and at low speeds. For the Walser listening apparatus see Chapter 1.

Below: Another important influence on the French *contre-torpilleur* was the German 'super-destroyer' *S.113*, which served with the Marine Nationale from 1922 until 1936 as the *Amiral Sénès*; she was employed for much of that time as the leader of the Atlantic flotillas. Displacing 2060 tonnes (normal), she was designed for a speed of 36 knots, which she achieved on trials. The French were particularly impressed with the lightweight (8.5-tonne), fast-firing 15cm gun, of which she mounted four. The German 15cm L/45 C/16 gun featured a sliding breech, and would influence the design of the later models of 138.6mm fitted in the French *contre-torpilleurs*. The Germans destroyed all examples of their new 60cm torpedo before the ship was handed over, and the tubes were modified to fire the standard German 50cm type. (*Courtesy of Marc Saibène*)

CHAPTER 1

THE *JAGUAR* CLASS

INTRODUCTION

The tortuous route to the *contre-torpilleur* of the 1922 Programme has been outlined in the previous chapter. In April 1921 an *avant-projet* was adopted by the Technical Committee (*Comité Technique*). Characteristics agreed on 12 May were as follows:

Displacement: 2360 tonnes (normal)
Horsepower: 50,000CV for 35.5 knots (normal displacement)
Endurance: 700nm at 35 knots (main turbines); 3000/3500nm at 15 knots (cruise turbines)

Note that the horsepower required for 35.5 knots was calculated to be 31% greater than in the 1920 design (38,000CV), and displacement had risen accordingly by 33%.

The draft plans were drawn up by the STCN under the supervision of *Ingénieur principal* Garetta. Six units were to be ordered and, in a break from previous practice, these were to be identical. In particular, commonality of machinery and shaft layout would ensure that they could operate together in a six-ship *escadrille* without allowances having to be made for optimum cruise and flank speeds, as had been the case with the destroyers of the 800-tonne type.

The Washington Naval Arms Limitation Conference intervened in November of that year, effectively putting plans on hold. Faced with Anglo-Saxon insistence that France should be limited to 175,000 tons of capital ships – a third of the total tonnage allocated to Britain and the United States – a meeting of the National Defence Council (*Conseil de la Défense Nationale*) on 28 December proposed that France should opt for a purely defensive fleet, and it was suggested that for the not-unreasonable sum of 500m francs per year, 330,000 tons of light surface ships and 90,000 tons of submarines could be built over a period of ten years. The Washington Treaty was duly signed on 6 February 1922, and little more than a month later (28 March) a new naval programme was adopted, authorising the

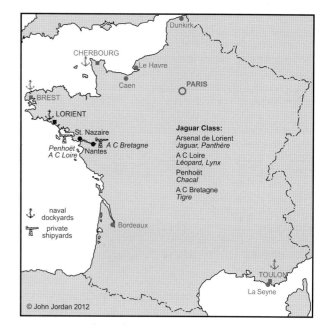

construction of three cruisers (*Duguay-Trouin* class), six *contre-torpilleurs* (*Jaguar* class), twelve *torpilleurs d'escadre* (*Bourrasque* class – see Chapter 2) and nine sea-going submarines (*Requin* class)[1] over two financial years.

A sum of 156 million French francs was allocated to build the six *contre-torpilleurs*. The Navy Minister decreed that two would be constructed in the French Naval Dockyards; the remaining four hulls would, in conformity with the wishes expressed by the lower house of parliament, the *Chambre des Députés*, be ordered from private shipyards. This arrangement would ensure quality control on the one hand – by effectively making the *arsenaux* the lead yards responsible for coordinating the project – and on the other a broadening of the industrial base, thereby

---

[1] In addition, twelve small 600-tonne submarines would be authorised under the Coast Defence budget.

BUILDING DATA

Name	*Jaguar*	*Panthère*	*Léopard*	*Lynx*	*Chacal*	*Tigre*
Programme	1922	1922	1922	1922	1922	1922
Prog. no.	4	5	6	7	8	9
Project no.	–	–	–	–	–	–
Builder	Lorient	Lorient	ACL St-Naz.	ACL St-Naz.	Penhoët St-Naz.	ACB Nantes
Ordered	18 Apr 1922	18 Apr 1922	26 Feb 1923	26 Feb 1923	26 Feb 1923	26 Feb 1923
Laid down	24 Aug 1922	23 Dec 1923	14 Aug 1923	14 Jan 1924	18 Sep 1923	18 Sep 1923
Launched	17 Nov 1923	27 Oct 1924	29 Sep 1924	25 Feb 1925	27 Sep 1924	2 Aug 1924
Manned for trials	1 Jun 1925	12 Apr 1926	20 Sep 1925	4 Aug 1926	10 Nov 1925	10 Jun 1925
Acceptance trials	14 Sep 1925	9 Sep 1926	14 Dec 1926	7 Feb 1927	26 Feb 1926	15 Sep 1925
Commissioned	25 Jun 1926	1 Nov 1926	15 June 1927	1 Jun 1927	1 May 1926	5 Dec 1925
Completed	7 Oct 1926	4 Jan 1927	13 Oct 1927	18 Oct 1927	28 Jul 1926	1 Feb 1926
Entered service	19 Nov 1926	4 Feb 1927	15 Nov 1927	15 Nov 1927	23 Dec 1926	7 Feb 1926

DESTROYER BUILDING DURING THE INTERWAR PERIOD

BETWEEN THE WARS FRANCE HAD NUMEROUS NAVAL CONSTRUCTION facilities. There were state-run naval dockyards at Cherbourg, Brest and Lorient on the Atlantic coast, and Toulon in the Mediterranean; the naval dockyard at Rochefort, which had built destroyers before and during the Great War, was closed in 1928. There were also numerous privately-owned shipyards capable of building naval vessels. These were subject to several reorganisations involving buy-outs, mergers and closures during the period in question; the reorganisations were often due to social changes and had a major impact on the local community.

The list of yards involved in the construction of *contre-torpilleurs* and *torpilleurs* between 1922 and 1940 follows. The abbreviation in square brackets is the one used in the Building Data tables:

– Arsenal de Lorient [Lorient]
– Anciens Chantiers Dubigeon, Nantes [Dubigeon Nantes]
– Ateliers & Chantiers de la Seine-Maritime Worms & Cie, Le Trait (between Le Havre and Rouen) [Worms Le Trait]
– Ateliers et Chantiers de Bretagne, Nantes [ACB Nantes]
– Ateliers et Chantiers de France, Dunkirk [ACF Dunkerque]
– Ateliers et Chantiers de la Loire, Nantes [ACL Nantes]
– Ateliers et Chantiers de la Loire, Saint-Nazaire [ACL St-Nazaire]
– Ateliers et Chantiers de Saint-Nazaire Penhoët, Grand Quevilly (near Rouen) [Penhoët, G Qu.]
– Ateliers et Chantiers de Saint-Nazaire Penhoët, Saint-Nazaire (Penhoët is a district of Saint-Nazaire) [Penhoet, St-Naz]
– Chantiers Navals Français, Blainville (near Caen) [CNF Caen]
– Dyle et Baccalan, Bordeaux (renamed *Ateliers et Chantiers Maritimes du Sud-Ouest et de Bacalan Réunis* in 1928) [D&B Bordeaux]
– Forges et Chantiers de la Gironde, Bordeaux [FC Gir Bordeaux]
– Forges et Chantiers de la Gironde, Harfleur [FC Gir Harfleur]
– Forges et Chantiers de la Méditerranée, Graville (a district of Le Havre from 1919) [FCM Graville]
– Forges et Chantiers de la Méditerranée, La Seyne [FCM La Seyne].

Key Dates in the Construction Process
The different stages in the construction of warships were defined by decrees published in the *Bulletin Officiel* (BO). The baseline publication was that of 17 June 1925, subsequently modified 19 Aug 1929, 10 July 1933 and 13 March 1937. An explanation follows:

– *Mise en chantier* [Ordered]: for the dockyards the date of the official instruction to lay the keel; for private yards the official notification of the order.
– *Mise sur cale* [Laid down]: first steel laid on the slipway (or in the construction dock).
– *Lancement* [Launched]: date of launch (or floating out); followed by fitting out (*achèvement à flot*).
– *Armement pour essais* [Manned for trials]: command of the ship at this point passes from the builder to the Navy and its nominated CO; the ship is partially manned for her initial trials.
– *Présentation en recette* [Acceptance trials]: the official acceptance trials; the turbines and gearing, together with other items of auxiliary machinery are partially dismantled towards the end of this stage and all components inspected (*les démontages*).
– *Armement définitif* [Commissioned]: from this date the vessel is fully provisioned and receives her full complement; this is effected during the period of inspection of the machinery and before reassembly prior to the final machinery trials (*les essais de bon fonctionnement*), conducted to ensure that all machinery is in fully working order. [After 13 March 1937 this would become the completion date – *date d'achèvement* – in order to conform to the provisions of the London Treaty of 25 March 1936.]
– *Clôture de l'armement* [Completed]: follows successful completion of the *essais de bon fonctionnement*; it is generally marked by an inspection visit from the Trials Commission, the *Commission supérieure d'armement*. [Before 10 July 1933 this was also the official completion date – see above.] The *Clôture de l'armement* was followed by an endurance cruise, which had to be for a minimum of four days for large surface warships and 24 hours for smaller vessels, called the *traversée de longue durée* (TLD).
– *Admission au service actif* [Entered service]: the subject of an official pronouncement by the Navy Minister, this date often coincides with the attachment of the ship to a specific squadron/division/flotilla. [Before 10 July 1933 the date of 'entry into service' was that of the *Clôture de l'armement*; between 10 July 1933 and 13 March 1937 it was the date of *Armement définitif*; from 13 March 1937 it became a date in its own right.]

laying the foundations for the major programme of construction anticipated.

In July the ships were given the names of predators: *Jaguar, Panthère, Léopard, Lynx, Chacal* and *Tigre*.[2] The names previously proposed for the two 1920 ships, *Lion* and *Guépard*, would be revived for the second series of *contre-torpilleurs* (see Chapter 4). At the same time the first two units, allocated the programme numbers 4 and 5[3] were ordered from Lorient Naval Dockyard. The other four ships were put out to tender, and following a lengthy tendering procedure contracts were awarded on 7 March 1923 to three experienced private shipbuilders. Ateliers et Chantiers de la Loire of Saint-Nazaire received the orders for *Léopard* (6) and *Lynx* (7), Ateliers et Chantiers de Bretagne of Nantes for *Tigre* (8), and Penhoët-Saint Nazaire for *Chacal* (9). All three of the private shipyards were geographically close to Lorient, on the west coast of Brittany (see map), and the four privately-built ships were to be delivered on completion to the naval dockyard, which was to be the *port d'armement* for all six units of the class.[4]

The name-ship, *Jaguar*, was laid down on the Lorient no.7 slipway (see map) on 22 August 1922, a full year before the second ship of the class. *Léopard* (A C Loire) was laid down on 14 August 1923, closely followed by *Chacal* (Penhoët) and *Tigre* (A C Bretagne) on 18 September. *Panthère*, the second ship assigned to Lorient, would be laid down on 23 December 1923 on the slipway vacated by *Jaguar* at her launch, and *Lynx* (A C Loire) would be laid down on 1 January 1924 on a different slipway to her sister *Léopard*, which would be launched only on 29 September of the same year. From laying down to launch took an average of 12–13 months per ship; however, fitting out and completion took a further 2–3 years, due largely to the novelty of the design, the late delivery of equipment from sub-contractors and, in particular, teething troubles with the new propulsion machinery, which considerably delayed the entry into service of the lead ship, *Jaguar*.

Despite the desire for conformity, there would be numerous detail design differences between the ships

---

[2] The influence of the Italian *Leone* class is readily apparent in the choice of names; the four sisters of *Leone* were to have been named *Tigre, Pantera, Leopardo* and *Lince* (the last two were cancelled).

[3] The cruisers *Duguay-Trouin, Lamotte-Picquet* and *Primauguet* were nos.1, 2 and 3 respectively.

[4] The *port d'armement* was responsible for all except the initial machinery trials, and provided the ships with their full statutory complement.

GENERAL CHARACTERISTICS

Displacement:	2126 tons standard; 2380 tonnes normal; 2980–3075 tonnes full load
Dimensions:	Length 119.7m pp, 126.8m oa; beam 11.1m; draught 4.1m
Machinery:	Five Du Temple small-tube boilers, 18kg/cm² (216°) Two-shaft geared steam turbines 50,000CV for 35.5kts (designed)
Oil fuel:	530 tonnes; radius 3000nm at 15kts, 700nm at 35kts
Armament:	Five 130mm/40 Mle 1919 in single mountings (132rpg) Two 75mm/50 Mle 1924 HA in single mountings (150rpg + 120 starshell) Two 8mm Hotchkiss MG Mle 1914 in two single mountings Six 550mm torpedoes Mle 1919D in two triple mountings Two DC chutes each for six 200kg depth charges (+ 4 reloads) Four Thornycroft depth charge throwers Mle 1918
Complement:	10 officers + 187 men peacetime 12 officers + 209 men wartime

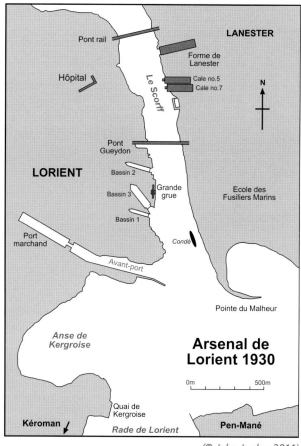

(© John Jordan 2011)

built in the various yards. The Marine Nationale divided the six ships into three pairs for reference purposes: *Jaguar* and *Panthère* (Lorient NDyd) were referred to as *Arsenaux*, *Chacal* and *Tigre* as *Industrie A*, and *Léopard* and *Lynx* (A C Loire) as *Industrie B*. These differences are readily apparent in the official plans. Variations in the layout of the accommodation spaces are evidenced by the number and spacing of scuttles fore and aft, and the configuration of the bridge structure, the centre deckhouse and the gun deck for no.3 mounting was quite different in the *Industrie* ships. These detail differences extended to much of the equipment and fittings, which were generally sub-contracted by the shipyard.

HULL AND GENERAL CONFIGURATION

Longitudinal framing was adopted for all the new flotilla craft – it had previously been employed only for larger vessels. The transverse frames, 58 in number, had a spacing of 2.1 metres, reducing to 1.4 metres at the ends of the ship, and were numbered from the aft to the forward perpendicular. Eleven main transverse bulkheads (*cloisons principales*) extended from the ship's bottom to the upper deck and divided the hull into twelve watertight compartments designated A–L (see drawing), penetrated only by cables and pipework.

The *Contre-Torpilleur Jaguar* 1926

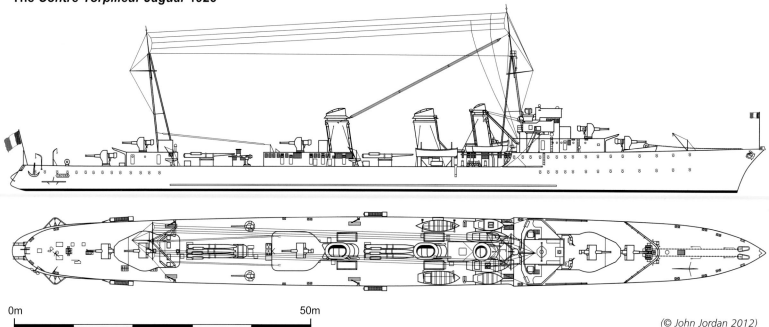

(© John Jordan 2012)

The profile and plan drawings are based on 'as fitted' plans for *Jaguar* and *Panthère* drawn up by the STCN and dated Paris December 1926. They show the ships broadly as completed, with a 3-metre base rangefinder atop the bridge. In the plan view, note the configuration of the centre deckhouse abaft the funnel which distinguished these ships from their 'industry' counterparts.

THE *JAGUAR* CLASS

Jaguar: General Arrangement Plans

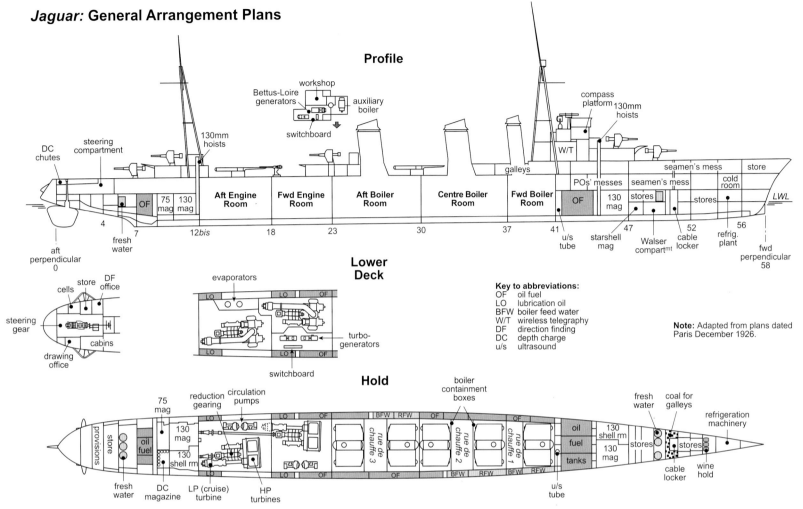

Fourteen pumps rated at 100 tonnes of water per hour were provided – two in each of the larger spaces – plus two portable 30t/h pumps for the two *arsenaux*.

The double bottom extended for most of the ship's length. Abeam the machinery spaces a continuous longitudinal bulkhead rose from the double bottom to the Main Deck to enclose the main oil fuel and boiler feed water tanks and to provide some protection against flooding for these large compartments. There were additional transverse fuel tanks forward and aft of the machinery spaces.

The slim hull, which had a length/beam ratio of 10.8:1, was designed for high speed. For the first time in a French destroyer there was a prominent raised forecastle (*Teugue*) with pronounced sheer and flare, combined with a 'clipper' bow. The Main Deck (*Pont Principal*) was the only continuous deck apart from the Hold (*Cale*) and was the strength deck; abaft the forecastle it was the weather deck. The Lower Deck (*Pont des Logements*, lit. 'Accommodation Deck') was interrupted by the five large machinery compartments, which extended to the Main Deck. At its forward end were the messes for seamen and petty officers while the officers' cabins were, according to tradition, located in the after part of the ship, forward of the steering compartment (see Inboard Profile). A second seamen's mess, the *Poste supérieur de l'équipage*, was located in the forecastle, together with the sickbay.

There was a large, capacious bridge structure of broadly square configuration to house the compass platform, chart house, main W/T office and signal distribution centre. Abaft the break in the forecastle

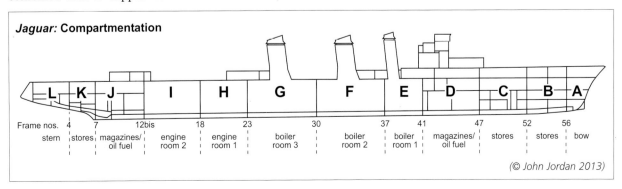

there were three deckhouses: the forward deckhouse (*roof avant*) housed the uptakes and ventilation trunking for the first two boiler rooms, as well as the bakery and the main galleys; the centre deckhouse (*roof milieu*) the uptakes and ventilation trunking for the after boiler room, the machinery workshop, the auxiliary boiler and emergency generators, as well as the CO's galley; the after deckhouse (*roof arrière*) the secondary W/T office and the after ammunition hoists. The ship's boats were grouped around the forward deckhouse, while the centre and after deckhouses each supported a gun mounting; the third of the upper guns was mounted atop a deckhouse which extended from the lower level of the bridge (*roof supérieur avant*).

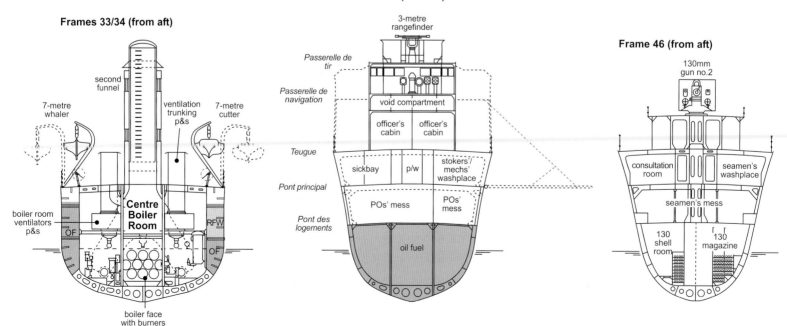

Jaguar: Sections

Note: Adapted from plans dated Paris December 1926.

(© John Jordan 2012)

THE *JAGUAR* CLASS

There were two light tripod masts. The mainmast was offset to port of the ship's axis. Between the masts were suspended the main W/T aerials.

The six *Jaguar*s were of riveted steel throughout; electric welding was introduced in the French shipyards and dockyards only from 1930. The steels used for construction and protection were classified according to their Ultimate Tensile Strength (UTS), the maximum stress a material can withstand while being stretched or pulled before 'necking' (when the cross-section begins to contract significantly). The unit of measurement used by the French was kilogrammes per square millimetre (kg/mm^2, often shortened to 'kg'). The mild steel used for the construction of these and other contemporary French flotilla craft was rated at 50kg (= 32 tons/psi).[5] Total hull weight for the *Jaguar*s was approximately 813 tonnes, representing 37.5% of standard displacement.

GROUND TACKLE AND NAVIGATION

There were two bower anchors in hawsepipes. These were of the 2360kg Hall stockless type, and were attached to seven shackles of 42mm chain cable. They were handled by a 30CV windlass located on the forecastle.

Two further anchors were provided on either side of the stern. To starboard there was a 910kg anchor, lowered by gravity. To port was a 570kg anchor – that of *Tigre* was to starboard, forward of the stern anchor – which was moored using a launch. Both anchors were raised by a 7.2CV stern capstan. A second 910kg anchor was stowed on board.

The single suspended, balanced rudder had a surface area of $14.44m^2$ ($14.13m^2$ in the two *Industrie A* ships). It proved too small, and the servo-motor too feeble, for a ship of this size and speed. At 30 knots it took 25–30 seconds for the rudder to move through its maximum 35-degree angle. As a consequence the turning circle was excessive: 525m at 20 knots, 570m at 25 knots were the figures obtained on the trials of *Tigre* in 1925.

---

[5] High-tensile steels used for protective plating in French cruisers were 60kg, and later 80kg.

MACHINERY

Much of the internal hull of the ships was occupied by their powerful propulsion machinery; the machinery compartments occupied 50% of the ships' length (between perpendiculars) and the propulsion machinery alone accounted for 35% of standard displacement.

Steam for the turbine machinery was supplied by five small-tube boilers of the Du Temple type: those for the four *Industrie* ships were provided by the builders; those for *Jaguar* and *Panthère* were subcontracted to the A C Gironde shipyard at Bordeaux, the order being placed on 31 January 1923. Robustness and reliability were prioritised over performance, and the boilers were rated at a conservative $18kg/cm^2$ (260psi), giving a saturated steam temperature of 216°C. Each boiler, together with its auxiliaries, weighed 74 tonnes.

The five boilers were disposed 'in line' on the ship's axis in three boiler rooms. Boiler Room 1 (Section E) housed a single boiler, with the exhaust uptake being led into the smallest of the three funnels. Boiler Rooms 2 and 3 (Sections F and G) each housed two boilers face to face, with a single *rue de chauffe*[6] between them, the uptakes being combined into two broader funnels (see General Arrangement plan). Each boiler was housed within a gas-tight containment box so that the *rue de chauffe* remained at atmospheric pressure and the stokers could work in a well-ventilated space with moderate temperatures.

The turbine machinery was in two separate, albeit adjacent engine rooms. Each set of turbines was completely independent of the other, with its own pumps and other auxiliary machinery, and comprised two high-pressure (HP) turbines working in parallel (main turbines), and a separate low-pressure (LP) cruise turbine with an integral reverse turbine. Single-reduction gearing was located between the paired HP turbines and the cruise turbine. Each set of turbines, including gearing and auxiliaries, weighed 193.2 tonnes. The forward set of turbines (Section H) drove

---

[6] The working path which ran across the boiler faces and was the domain of the stokers.

Left: *Tigre* running trials on 14 October 1925. She was the fastest of the class, achieving an impressive 36.7 knots with 57,200CV, which was widely reported and had a considerable impact abroad. (*US Navy NH 88960, courtesy of A D Baker III*)

Below: A fine stern view of *Tigre* as completed in 1926; she still has the original half-shields on her main guns, which would be replaced in early 1928. Note the distinctive stern, with the doors for the depth charge chutes and the rails fitted to ensure that the charges did not strike her hull when dropped. Note also the height of the tripod mainmast, which is offset to port. *(US Navy NH 88960, courtesy of A D Baker III)*

the port shaft; the after turbines (Section I) the starboard shaft. Each shaft was fitted with a bronze outward-turning three-bladed propeller with a diameter of 3.6 metres.

Considering that this was the first installation (with the *Bourrasque*s) of reduction gearing in a production destroyer design,[7] it proved remarkably problem-free and delivered substantial benefits in endurance. This was less true of other components of the propulsion machinery. Four of the ships received Rateau-Bretagne impulse turbines, which were generally successful after the initial 'teething' troubles were resolved. However, the two *Industrie B* ships built by A C Loire, *Léopard* and *Lynx*, were fitted with reaction turbines from Breguet-Laval which gave enormous problems (sheared blades, ingress of seawater into the condensers). Considerable additional work was necessary before they were passed fit for service, and *Léopard* was delivered to Lorient two years late. Following this experience Breguet-Laval turbines would never again be fitted in French destroyers.

All six ships sustained speeds of around 34.5 knots with 52,200–56,000CV at normal displacement over their 8-hour trials, and a mean average of 35.3–35.6 knots with forced draught over the ninth hour (see table). *Tigre* was the fastest, with an impressive 36.7 knots on 57,200CV, which was widely reported and had a considerable impact abroad. In service the ships comfortably sustained 30 knots on main turbines with all five boilers on line, even in their later years.

There were four main fuel tanks with a capacity of 530 tonnes of heavy oil. Thirty-five tonnes of lubrication oil were carried, plus 100 tonnes of reserve feed water for the boilers, in side and bottom tanks. There was also 12 tonnes of fresh water for sanitation and 4 tonnes of potable water for the crew in separate tanks fore and aft (see plan).[8] Following trials, endurance was calculated at 3300nm at 13 knots on cruise turbines with just two boilers lit. These figures were within the original parameters specified. However, the high fuel consumption of the boilers at maximum power meant that when the main turbines were engaged, range was only 600nm (vs 700nm) at 35 knots, and 1000nm at 28 knots.

The engine rooms were on two levels, with platforms at the upper level to starboard and to port of the turbines respectively. The upper platform of the forward engine room was occupied by two 60kW (80kW max.) Fives-Lille turbo-generators, which used the steam from the turbines to produce on-board electricity to power the searchlight projectors (circuit no.1), the ammunition hoists (2), the torpedo tubes (3), the ventilation for the machinery (4), the electrical motors for various items of equipment (5), and the port and starboard lighting circuits (6&7). Electricity was distributed through the ship via the seven 115V circuits, the main switchboard being adjacent to the turbo-generators (see GA plans). The platform in the after engine room was occupied by the evaporators which provided distilled water for the boilers and fresh water for the crew.

The fore and after capstans and the steering motors were powered using steam from the auxiliary boiler, which also provided services for the crew. The auxiliary boiler was located in the centre deckhouse abaft the third funnel. Also located in this deckhouse were two Bettus-Loire oil-fuelled generators, which in theory could provide sufficient electrical power when the ship was alongside without having to light one of the main boilers. The larger of the two generators, rated at 30/36kW, comprised a four-cylinder, four-stroke diesel and a six-pole 110V, 254A (305A max.) dynamo. A second, smaller generator rated at 15/18kW was added as emergency back-up following a ministerial instruction dated 11 September 1926.[9] The modest

---

[7] Parsons reduction gearing had first been trialled in the 800-tonne *Enseigne Gabolde* from 1923 (see Introduction).

[8] Under the Washington Treaty, neither the fuel oil nor the reserve feed water were counted in 'standard' displacement, but although Washington standard displacements were calculated (retrospectively) for these ships, these considerations had no impact on French destroyer design during the period 1922-1930.

[9] DM 15417 CN/4.

MAXIMUM NORMAL POWER AND FULL POWER TRIALS

The Maximum Normal Power (*puissance maximum normale*, or PMN) trials were over eight hours. The Full Power (*feux poussés*, or FP) trial normally followed on from the 8-hour PMN trial and was run for one hour. All the trials were run on the Iles de Glenans/Ile de Groix range; three successive runs were made, and the results of the best recorded. The trials for the *Jaguar* class were to be run at a mean displacement of 2,404.73 tonnes; adjustments (parentheses in the table) were made for ships which displaced in excess of this figure at the start of the trial.

	Jaguar	*Panthère*	*Léopard*	*Lynx*	*Chacal*	*Tigre*
Date of trial:	18 May 1926	16 Sep 1926	12 May 1927	20 Apr 1927	18 May 1926	3 Oct 1925
Displacement:	2574t	2576t	2642t	2630t	2628t	2564t
Average over 8 hours						
Shaft revolutions:	353/341rpm	357/352rpm	345/343rpm	343/342rpm	349/349rpm	358/354rpm
Horsepower:	53,050CV	56,000CV	n/a	55,470CV	52,192CV	55,200CV
Speed:	34.75kts	35.22kts	34.86kts	34.50kts	34.60kts	35.80kts
(corrected)	(–)	(35.30kts)	(–)	(–)	(34.70kts)	(35.93kts)
Fuel consumption:	28.01t/h	28.39t/h	29.10t/h	29.78t/h	28.93t/h	27.09t/h
Average 9th hour						
Shaft Revolutions:	364/349rpm	365/356rpm	357/351rpm	353/348rpm	356/355rpm	371/360rpm
Horsepower:	54,850CV	56,900CV	n/a	57,810CV	54,911CV	57,200CV
Speed:	35.27kts	35.60kts	35.59kts	35.54kts	34.20kts	36.53kts
(corrected)	(–)	(35.70kts)	(–)	(–)	(35.30kts)	(36.70kts)
Fuel consumption:	29.91t/h	29.13t/h	30.35t/h	30.96t/h	31.60t/h	27.83t/h

Notes:
1. Fuel consumption is expressed in tonnes of oil burned per hour (t/h).
2. The shaft revolution figures show the mean for the forward and after turbines respectively.
3. The figures representing the best performance for the class are underlined.
4. The torsiometers which measured the horsepower transmitted through the shafts aboard *Léopard* were not functioning on 12 May 1927.

Source: Jean Lassaque, *op. cit.*

power generated by these units was sufficient only to supply lighting and other basic functions (circuits nos.4, 6 and 7, and possibly 5).

MAIN ARMAMENT

The *avant-projet* for the 2400-tonne *contre-torpilleurs* envisaged a main armament of six or seven 130mm guns Mle 1919 in a mix of twin and single mountings. The two *Arsenaux* and the *Industrie A* ships were to have one twin (no.2 gun forward) and four single mountings, the two *Industrie B* ships two twins and three singles. In the event, trials with the twin mounting Mle 1921 aboard the sloop *Amiens* were disappointing; the layout was cramped and the loading numbers tended to get in one another's way, so the rate of fire for the twin mounting was significantly less than for two singles. It was therefore decided on 14 August 1923 that all five mountings would be of the standard Mle 1919 single type. As the weight of the twin mounting was almost twice that of the single, this would prove to be a wise decision (see Evaluation below).

Development of the 130mm Mle 1919 gun had begun shortly after the Armistice. It was a simple, robust weapon employing prewar technology, including a Welin interrupted screw breech (see table for data). It fired a heavyweight semi-armour piercing (SAP) shell weighing 32.05kg able to penetrate 8cm of cemented armour at 10,000m and 4.5cm at 18,000m; the bursting charge was 1.8kg of picric acid (*Mélinite*). There was also a high-explosive (HE) shell weighing 34.85kg, with a bursting charge of 3.6kg. However, the comparatively short barrel – adopted because it made the gun handier and lighter – meant that long-range performance was mediocre. The gun used separate ammunition, and the cased charge, comprising 7.7kg of BM9 propellant, provided a modest muzzle velocity of 734m/s. In order to maximise range the trunnions were raised to a height of 1.5 metres, permitting an elevation of 36°; however, this made loading difficult at lower angles of elevation. Loading was also slowed by the screw breech mechanism and the retention of separate ammunition, and the loading cycle was never more than six rounds per minute, even with a well-trained crew.

The 130mm Mle 1919 was already officially deemed obsolescent by September 1923, but the development of a new generation of guns was not feasible within the available time-frame, and on 10 March 1925 it was decided that the *Jaguars* would be initially armed with the 130mm Mle 1919 in order not to delay their entry into service, but that they would be retro-fitted at a later stage with a new model.[10]

The guns on the *Jaguar* and *Bourrasque* classes were on simple pivot mountings and had a lightweight shield to protect the gun crew against blast, wind and spray. The latter proved inadequate, and in 1926 Lorient dockyard developed a new 'wrap-around' model. It was trialled aboard *Panthère* in 1927 and retro-fitted to *Jaguar* and the two *Industrie A* ships; *Léopard* and *Lynx* were fitted with the shields on completion. The new shields provided much better protection for the gun crew, albeit at the cost of an additional 2.5 tonnes in topweight.

The regulation peacetime ammunition provision was 132 rounds per gun, for a total of 660 shells and 745 cased charges, of which 85 were flashless charges for night firing. The magazines fore and aft of the

---
[10] DM 527 EMG/1.

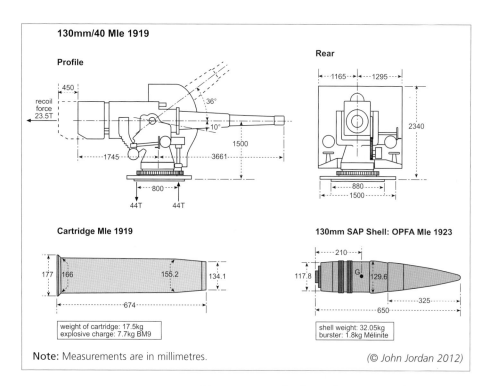

130MM/40 MLE 1919

Gun Data
Construction	not autofretted
Weight of gun	4.05 tonnes
Breech mechanism	Welin interrupted screw
Ammunition type	separate
Projectiles	OPFA Mle 1923 (32.05kg)
	OEA Mle 1923 (34.85kg)
Propellant	7.7kg BM9 in cartridge Mle 1919
Muzzle velocity	735m/s
Range at 36°	18,500m

Mounting
Designation	Mle 1919
Protection	3/5mm
Weight of mounting	12.5 tonnes
Elevation	-10° / +36°
Loading angle	not above 15°
Firing cycle	5–6rpm

Notes:
Mle	*Modèle*	Model
OPFA	*Obus de Perforation en Fonte Aciérée*	Semi-Armour Piercing (SAP)
OEA	*Obus Explosif en Acier*	High Explosive (HE)

machinery spaces had ample capacity, having been designed to accommodate the ammunition for six guns. The forward magazine, which served guns nos.1 and 2 forward of the bridge, could accommodate 398 shells and 468 charges; the after magazine, serving guns nos.3, 4 and 5, 404 shells and 418 charges. The reception posts for the electrically-powered hoists, which used a continuous chain mechanism to raise the shells and cartridges in the horizontal position (see p.46), were located behind no.2 gun and forward of no.4 gun. Shells and charges were transferred by hand either to the ready-use stowage racks or directly to the breech of the guns. There were intermediate reception positions behind no.1 gun and forward of no.5 gun. The latter were located in an enclosed ammunition lobby (see Bridge Decks drawing), whereas the upper reception trays were in the open atop their respective deckhouses, with blast shields to the sides.[11]

The French had been impressed by the British practice of providing ready-use stowage close to the guns of their destroyers. Stowage racks for 24 rounds per gun were located close to the guns for mountings nos.1, 2, 4 and 5 on the *Jaguars*. There was no midships magazine for no.3 gun, located abaft the third funnel. This gun was therefore given increased ready-use stowage of 30 rounds; the racks could be replenished from the after magazine using an overhead cable with a block and tackle, but this was not usually possible at sea and was prohibited in combat.

The ambitious original design for these ships featured a 'destroyer director' capable of providing remote training and pointing of the guns, with automatic correction for parallax and centralised firing. In the transmitting station (*PC Artillerie*) an electro-mechanical computer Mle 1923B would calculate the fire control data necessary for training and elevation and transmit them instantaneously to the guns. Unfortunately, development of this system by the DCAN[12] was protracted, and once the ships entered service it became clear that they already carried far too much topweight.

In the event all six ships were provided with a simple 3-metre coincidence rangefinder (Mle B.1926) developed by the French SOM[13] company on a lightweight pedestal of the Barr & Stroud type. They were also fitted with a mechanical fire control computer *type aviso* Mle 1919 as a temporary measure. Fire control data had to be communicated to the guns by voice-pipe or telephone and the guns were trained and laid using handwheels in the time-honoured fashion. The order to fire was transmitted by the Control Officer on the bridge and executed at the guns using an electro-mechanical device. For independent fire Homécourt sights were provided on the guns.

Although starshell was increasingly favoured as a means of target illumination during a night action because it was less likely to reveal the position of the ship, two 75cm searchlight projectors were installed atop the forward superstructure, immediately abaft the compass platform. The projectors were supplied by either BBT (Barbier, Bénard & Turenne – Arsenaux/Industrie A) or OVP (Ouvrard, Villars & Perez – Industrie B) and were remotely controlled from positions in the bridge wings. The bridge position had the advantage of excellent arcs to port and to starboard, and the projectors could also be used at reduced power for signalling. However, in service the arrangement proved less than satisfactory, as when the searchlights were switched on at night and at full power the personnel on the bridge was effectively blinded; later *contre-torpilleurs* would have a revised searchlight arrangement, and would have separate 30cm signal projectors in the bridge wings.

---

[11] In the following class of *contre-torpilleurs*, the *Guépard* class, the forward hoists were fully enclosed in a deckhouse with a curved front face.

[12] *Direction Central des Armes Navales* (Ordnance Department).

[13] *Société d'Optique et de Mécanique de haute précision.*

THE JAGUAR CLASS

75/50 MLE 1924/1922

Gun Data
Construction	autofretted barrel
Weight of gun	1.07 tonnes
Breech mechanism	Schneider concentric ring
Ammunition type	fixed
Projectiles	OEA Mle 1925 (5.93kg)
	OEcl Mle 1923
Propellant	BM5/BM7 (2.18kg)
Complete round	
weight	12.01kg
dimensions	967mm x 110mm
Muzzle velocity	850m/s
Max. range	15,000m (45°)
Ceiling	7500m (90°)

Mounting
Designation	CA Mle 1922
Weight of mounting	?? tonnes
Loading angle	–10° / +75°
Elevation	–10° / +90°
Firing cycle	15rpm theoretical
	8rpm practical

Notes:
Mle	*Modèle*	Model
OEA	*Obus Explosif en Acier*	High Explosive (HE)
OEcl	*Obus Eclairant*	Starshell

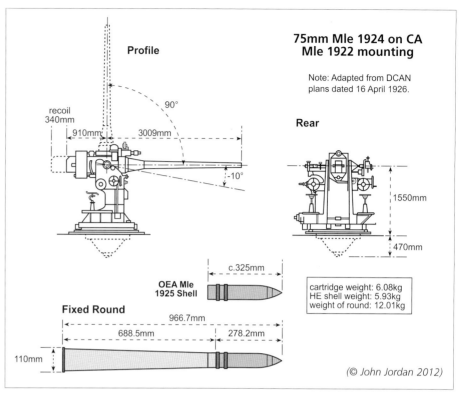

ANTI-AIRCRAFT WEAPONS

The aerial menace to ships during the 1920s remained negligible. Torpedo bombers were only just beginning to make their presence felt, and they were generally slow, low-performance aircraft requiring good weather conditions to make an effective attack. The ability to hit a moving ship with bombs dropped from altitude was still questioned in most naval quarters, and it would be a further ten years before dive-bombers began to enter service in numbers.

The anti-aircraft armament fitted in the six *Jaguar*s and the contemporary *torpilleurs d'escadre* reflected the thinking predominant at the end of the First World War. Medium-calibre guns such as the 75mm/76mm/ 3-inch and 102mm/4-inch on high-angle mountings and using time-fuzed ammunition were intended to deter – and in the event of a lucky hit shoot down – reconnaissance aircraft, and were to contribute to a long-range barrage through which torpedo-bombers would have to fly when the ships were part of a fleet or squadron formation. Light machine guns provided a modest self-defence capability against fighter aircraft

Left: *Chacal* as she appeared following her first major refit at Toulon 1927-8. The original gunshields have been replaced by the new model, and the foremast yard has been lowered. (*Leo van Ginderen collection*)

attempting to use their own MG – which were generally of 7.5mm calibre – to strafe the ship's upperworks.

Contemporary French battleships and cruisers were generally armed with four 75mm HA guns, so the two guns provided in the *Jaguar*s (one in the *Bourrasque*s) constituted an impressive armament for such small ships. Moreover, the gun was the newly developed Mle 1924 on a single mounting Mle 1922 (see table for data). In the anti-aircraft role it fired the OEA Mle 1925 high-explosive shell out to a maximum range of 15,000 metres; at the mounting's maximum elevation of 90° the ceiling was 8000m. It was also employed to fire illuminating shell during a night action. The 75mm Mle 1924 was a 50-calibre gun which proved reasonably effective in barrage fire but was over-complex in operation. The fixed round was too long to permit loading above 75°, but a firing cycle of up to 12rpm was possible with a trained crew.

The two 75mm guns were mounted on reinforcements at the sides of the upper deck just abaft the centre deckhouse (Frames 18/19). A total of 150 HE rounds plus 60 starshell rounds was provided per gun, together with a few saluting rounds. The 75mm ammunition was stowed in a magazine with a capacity of 450 rounds abaft the main 130mm magazine in the after part of the ship (see Inboard Profile and Plan drawings). The after hoists for the main guns were used to provide a ready-use supply of 30 rounds per gun, which were stowed in lockers abaft the centre deckhouse. There was no centralised fire control system for these guns, which fired through on-mount sights with automatic correction (Mle 1925a).

For self-defence against strafing aircraft there were two 8mm Hotchkiss MG Mle 1914 in single mountings; a twin mounting Mle 1926 was available from 1929. The machine guns were normally stowed below-decks, and when required were affixed to pedestal mountings on the forecastle deck abeam the bridge. In the two *Industrie B* ships they were initially installed at the forward end of the centre deckhouse, but in 1927 were relocated to the forecastle.

TORPEDOES

The *Jaguar*s, like their *torpilleur d'escadre* counterparts of the *Bourrasque* class, were equipped with two triple mountings (Schneider Mle 1920T) for the new 550mm torpedo. The tubes used compressed air for launch, each tube having a 60-litre bottle which was charged at 60kg/cm² by Sautter-Harlé compressors located in the forward engine room (upper level). A powder charge was available as back-up.

The torpedo was the 550mm Mle 1919D, developed and built by the Naval Dockyard at Toulon. The Mle 1919D was powered by a kerosene wet-heater engine, and was optimised for range (D = *Distance*) over speed.[14] It had two speed settings: a high-speed mode (GV = *Grande Vitesse*) in which the torpedo was propelled at 35 knots over a distance of 6000m; and a low-speed mode (PV = *Petite Vitesse*) for 25 knots and 14,000m. A 250kg picric acid warhead was fitted.

These were impressive figures for the day. The *Jaguar*s (and the *Bourrasque*s) were costly ships, and there was no question of their being thrown into combat at close quarters, launching their torpedoes at point-blank range in the face of a hail of shell from the secondary batteries of the enemy's battleships. Rather, the intention was that they would launch 'browning shots' against a line of battle. A division of three ships operating in formation could launch a spread of up to eighteen torpedoes at ranges in excess of 10,000–12,000 metres in the reasonable expectation of securing two or three hits. Subsequent French torpedo development would focus on exploiting the 550mm torpedo body to provide even greater speed and range, allied to a more powerful warhead (see *Guépard* class, Chapter 4).

The proposed tactical deployment of torpedoes against a distant battle line made ahead and astern fire unimportant. Both the *Jaguar*s and the *Bourrasque*s had their triple tubes mounted on the centreline, with torpedo launch limited to 30 degrees either side of the beam. No reserve torpedoes were carried, as reloading at sea was not considered a practical proposition and fleet action was in any case most likely to occur close to the ships' bases, especially in the Mediterranean. Combat warheads were not fitted in peacetime, but were stowed in the depth charge magazine beneath the stern; lockers beneath the rear end of the mountings (see drawing) were used for exercise warheads in peacetime and for combat warheads in wartime. The warheads were secured to the torpedo body, and the compressed air tanks charged, shortly before combat.

As with the main guns, the original intention had been to provide an advanced fire control system; the triple mountings were to have been remotely controlled from the bridge via electric motors without manual intervention. In the event, development was stalled. Fire control was still exercised from a station on the upper bridge (see Bridge Decks drawing) equipped with a torpedo bearing indicator and a small fire control computer, but the rangefinder for the main guns had to be employed – the later *contre-torpilleurs* had a dedicated rangefinder in its own trainable mounting for torpedo FC. Training data was transmitted to the torpedo mounting, which was equipped with a Granat 'follow-the-pointer' GD II receiver,[15] and an on-mount operator aligned the pointers to train the mounting. Depth, speed and gyroscope settings for the torpedo were set outside the tubes. The order to launch was

---

[14] A second model, designated 1919V, was optimised for high speed (V = *Vitesse*); it was shorter and could travel 2000m at 43 knots, 4000m at 35 knots.

[15] The designations of Granat transmission apparatus were based on the following symbology:
G = Granat; C = single receiver, or D = double receiver; II, III, etc. = number of circuits.

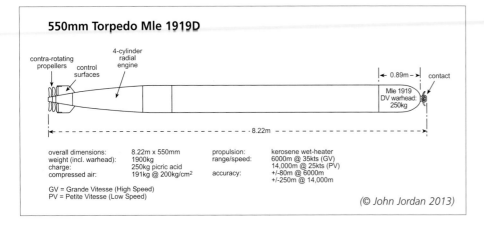

550mm Torpedo Mle 1919D

overall dimensions:	8.22m x 550mm	propulsion:	kerosene wet-heater
weight (incl. warhead):	1900kg	range/speed:	6000m @ 35kts (GV)
charge:	250kg picric acid		14,000m @ 25kts (PV)
compressed air:	191kg @ 200kg/cm²	accuracy:	+/-80m @ 6000m
			+/-250m @ 14,000m

GV = Grande Vitesse (High Speed)
PV = Petite Vitesse (Low Speed)

(© John Jordan 2013)

THE JAGUAR CLASS

given from the bridge using a lamp board which indicated 'ready' (*paré*) and 'fire' (*feu*), and executed on the mounting.

ANTI-SUBMARINE WEAPONS AND DETECTION APPARATUS

The anti-submarine armament of these ships was particularly comprehensive. Twelve depth charges were stowed in two parallel chutes directly beneath the stern, and there were four Thornycroft Mle 1918 depth charge throwers on the upper deck abeam the first funnel.

The Guiraud depth charge Mle 1922 was an exceptionally powerful weapon with an explosive charge of 200kg[16] which could be set to explode at depths of 50m, 75m or 100m. The depth charges were stowed end-to-end on a continuous chain (*chaîne Galle*) powered by an electric motor, and were laid by gravity via rails sheathed with lignum vitae to secure smooth entry into the water and keep the charges clear of the stern. Six depth charges could be launched in 27–30 seconds through stern openings which, when not in use, were sealed by sliding doors to prevent ingress of water (see schematic). Access for depth setting of the charges was from the side. In the event of failure of the electric motor, a hand-wheel could be rigged on the upper deck.

The system was original and well conceived, and had the benefit of leaving the quarterdeck free for other equipment such as minesweeping paravanes. However, it was much more complex (and costly) than the simple DC rails favoured by other navies, and in service there were instances when the tripping of the circuit breakers, or failure of the motors, resulted in the ship being unable to execute an attack when required to do so. The British Royal Navy, which had an ingrained suspicion of anything that could not be operated by 'Jack with a handle', installed simple DC rails with inclined after sections on the French ships seized in 1940 (see p.251 *Léopard* and p.253 *Le Triomphant*).

[16] The standard British depth charge of the Second World War, the Mk VII, had a 190lb (132kg) charge.

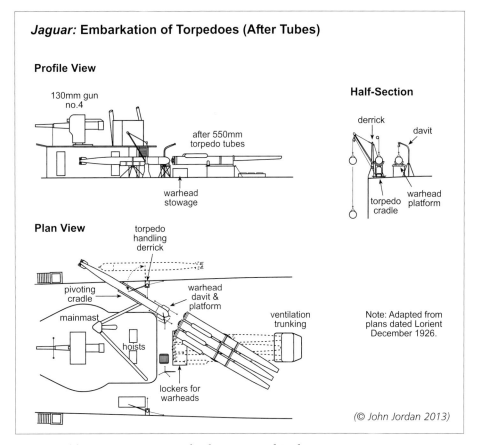

Jaguar: Embarkation of Torpedoes (After Tubes)

(© John Jordan 2013)

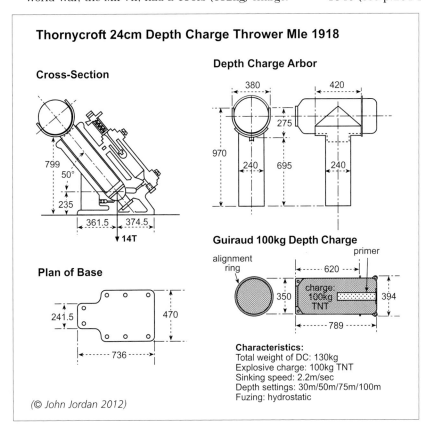

(© John Jordan 2012)

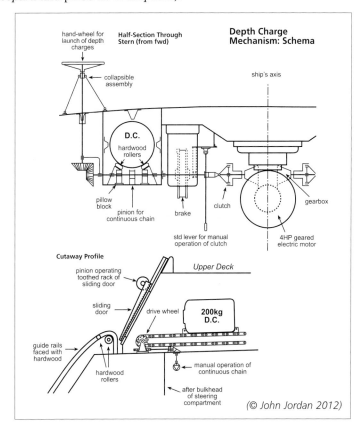

(© John Jordan 2012)

Right: *Jaguar* off Toulon on 15 July 1929. She is flying the flag of Rear-Admiral Robert, commanding the *Flotille de torpilleurs* of the 1st Squadron (Mediterranean) at the mainmast. Note the new DF office and antenna abaft no.3 gun mounting. *(Real Photographs)*

The four Thornycroft 240mm Mle 1918 depth charge throwers (see drawing), built under licence by Brandt, were in pairs on either side of the ship with a stowage rack for additional depth charges between. The thrower, which used a powder charge to project its charge some 60 metres, featured an expendable arbor. Set at a fixed elevation angle of 50 degrees, it was secured to the upper deck with eight bolts at 90 degrees to the ship's axis. It fired a smaller Guiraud depth charge (also Mle 1922) with an explosive charge of 100kg and a similar range of depth settings to the 200kg model. A block and tackle suspended from an overhead rail was used to transfer the charges from the rack to the thrower; spare arbors were stowed against the side wall of the deckhouse (for a detail drawing of the arrangements in *Verdun* see p.88).

Combat provision was calculated to permit two 'passes' each comprising six 200kg and two 100kg. Besides the twin chutes and the depth charge throwers there was a special depth charge magazine aft (see GA plan) to house reserve charges; during peacetime this was used to stow the torpedo combat warheads. Regulations when the ships were first completed stipulated twelve 200kg depth charges in the chutes plus four reserve, and thirty 100kg DC, of which four were on the throwers, twelve (six per side) in ready-use racks between the throwers, and fourteen in reserve. There were also to be two Ginocchio towed torpedoes: one on the quarterdeck and the other in the below-decks magazine. The Ginocchio torpedo (see p.49) was trialled aboard ships of the *Bourrasque* class during the late 1920s, but was subsequently abandoned, to be revived following the outbreak of war in 1939.

A compartment was provided in Section C (Frames 48–49 – see Inboard Profile) for the installation of Walser listening apparatus, which had been introduced to detect German submarines during the latter stages of the Great War. The Walser apparatus employed two 'sound lenses', 1m and 1.25m in diameter respectively, on each side of the ship; the lenses were made of steel and carried a large number of diaphragms so that they resembled the eye of a fly. Sound was focused inside the ship by a trumpet-like device connected to the listener's ears to eliminate extraneous noise. An operator could find the bearing of a submarine to within about five degrees, and could also detect whether the ship was directly above the submarine. In good weather, with the ship steaming at

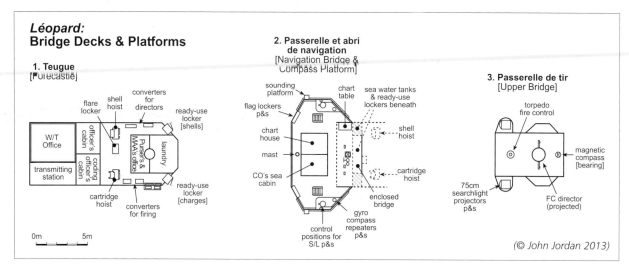

a maximum of 5 knots, a submarine could be detected at 800–2000m. Of the six *Jaguar*s, only *Panthère* was fitted with the Walser apparatus; it quickly became apparent that the system was of little use unless the ship was virtually stopped, as any signal was masked by self-noise, and there were no further installations. The Walser system was finally abandoned in 1931.

There was also provision for active submarine detection. Building on the work of French, British and American scientists in 1917–18, the French company SIF (*Société Indépendante de télégraphie sans Fil*), which specialised in wireless telegraphy, was developing an ultrasonic device housed within a 450mm-diameter tube which could be lowered through the bottom of the ship's hull. Space for the tube was provided just forward of boiler room no.1, and for a sonar room (*cabine d'écoute*) two decks above, with voice-pipe communication with the bridge. The system was trialled in units of the *Bourrasque* class (see Chapter 2), but was abandoned in September 1930. Both spaces were reserved pending future developments.

The failure of French attempts to develop an effective sensor for submarine detection meant that the extensive anti-submarine weaponry of these ships could be deployed only against a submarine sighted visually or tracked by the wake of its torpedo. On the other hand, when in 1939–40 the British made their Asdic 123/128 available, it was a comparatively easy matter to find the space necessary for installation of both the retractable dome and the monitoring console.

COMMUNICATIONS

Because the *contre-torpilleurs* were to operate as independent scouts and had a comprehensive outfit of modern weaponry, considerable attention was given to internal and external communications.

Communication between the key spaces and weapons relied primarily on a traditional network of voice-pipes. However, a combat system using Le Las or LMT (*Le Matériel Téléphonique* – on *Tigre* and the two Lorient-built ships) telephones was experimentally introduced, and its superiority over voice-pipes led to its reinforcement by telephones of the Mle 1917 'War' type. The latter were adopted to link the upper bridge (*Passerelle de tir*) with the upper guns (nos.2, 3 and 4) and the torpedo tubes.

The wireless telegraphy (W/T) equipment was distributed between two distinct spaces to provide redundancy in the event of action damage. The main W/T office, the *PC Radio*, was at the after end of the bridge block (see drawings), and was equipped primarily for long-range (strategic) communications up to 1000nm. It housed:

– an SFR (*Société Française Radio-électrique*) type D-100 1kW long-wave transmitter operating in the 600–11,000m waveband
– an SIF (*Société Indépendante de télégraphie sans Fil*) long-wave receiver operating in the 2000–12,000m waveband
– an SFR 200W 'emergency' transmitter with a range of about 50nm for bridge-to-bridge communication

The secondary W/T office was located in the after deckhouse, and was for medium-range (c.200nm radius) tactical communications with divisional units and shore stations. It housed:

– a type L-II-E-4 short-wave transmitter

Below: The two *Industrie B* ships, *Léopard* and *Lynx*, seen here in the River Penfeld at Brest in early April 1933. These two ships were virtually identical as built, having been completed at their Saint-Nazaire shipyard by A C Loire, and in this photo both have received the semi-circular rangefinder platform above the engine room access to starboard with the DF office below to port. *Lynx* is the ship moored to the quay, with *Léopard* outboard of her.

Right: *Jaguar* moored at Brest during September 1938 following summer sorties with the training school. The hull number -1 marks her out as the lead ship of the 2nd DCT, with *Chacal* (-2) and *Léopard* (-3) as her *divisionnaires*. (US Navy NH 93328, courtesy of A D Baker III)

– a CRM Mle 1918 short-wave receiver

The W/T aerials were strung between the yards of the tripod foremast and the light tripod mainmast, and between the foremast and the third funnel.

There was a space reserved for installation of a direction-finding office beneath the quarterdeck aft (port side, see GA plan). However, the contract for the equipment was placed so late that delivery post-dated the ships' entry into service (see Modifications).

BOATS

Compared to British and American destroyers, French flotilla craft of the interwar period carried a relatively large complement of boats. This reflected the frequent need to use open anchorages in undeveloped French colonial ports. As the *contre-torpilleurs* were intermediate in size between a destroyer and a cruiser, they had a more substantial boat outfit than the *torpilleurs d'escadre*. That of the *Jaguar*s when first completed was as follows:

– one 7-metre motor boat
– one 7-metre motor launch
– one 7-metre pulling cutter
– one 7-metre whaler
– two 5-metre dinghies (one motorised)

The motor boat was for use by the ship's CO or senior officers; the other boats were for ferrying members of the crew ashore (*service de rade*) or rescue at sea (*sauvetage*). When operating as a flagship the motor launch was replaced by a second 7-metre motor boat for the admiral and his staff. This would normally be painted blue with a white rubbing strake.

The whaler and the 7-metre pulling cutter were on davits abeam the second funnel. The other four boats were carried on athwartships rails abeam the first funnel with the two larger boats inboard; they were handled by twin derricks fixed to the after end of the bridge.

COMPLEMENT

The regulation peacetime complement of these ships comprised ten officers and 187 men. The function and rank of the officers were as follows:

– Commanding Officer (*Capitaine de frégate* = Commander)[17]
– First/Executive Officer (*Capitaine de corvette* = Lieutenant-Commander)
– Officers i/c Guns and Underwater Weapons (*Lieutenants de vaisseau* = Lieutenants)
– two junior officers (*Enseignes de vaisseau* = Sub-Lieutenants), one of whom was responsible for signal distribution
– one Chief Engineering Officer (*Ingénieur mécanicien de 1re classe*)
– two junior engineering officers (*Ingénieurs mécaniciens de 2e classe*)
– one Medical Officer (*Médecin de 1e/2e classe*) or Supply Officer (*Commissaire de 1e/2e classe*)[18]

Note that there were different categories of officer in the *Marine Nationale*. Officers for general sea-going and shore-based duties (*officiers de vaisseau*) were trained at the prestigious *Ecole Navale*, which from 1935 would be housed in an impressive new building at Brest; engineering officers underwent their initial training at Brest.

The crew of 187 included 22 Petty Officers, who were specialists in the various departments of the ship.

In 1928 (directive DM 2347 EMG/1) the wartime complement was fixed at twelve officers and 209 men, of whom 33 were Petty Officer grade.

When they entered service the new *contre-torpilleurs* and *torpilleurs d'escadre* would be formed into three-ship divisions. The senior officer was a *Capitaine de vaisseau* (Captain) and would command his own ship

---

[17] The equivalent Royal Navy ranks are given.
[18] There was normally one Medical Officer and one Supply Officer per three-ship division.

THE JAGUAR CLASS

as well as the division. In this role he was supported by a Chief of Staff (*Chef d'état-major - Lieutenant de vaisseau*), a Supply Officer (*Commissaire*) and a Coding Officer (*Officier du chiffre*), whose job was to encode and decipher transmissions between the divisional CO and a senior admiral afloat or ashore.

Jaguar was unique among these ships in being specially fitted out as flagship for a Rear-Admiral (*Contre-amiral*), and served in this role at the head of the torpedo boat flotillas first in the Mediterranean, then in the Atlantic from 1928 until 1937. In addition to accommodation for the admiral, quarters were provided for his staff of four officers (including one senior officer).

EVALUATION

Any evaluation of the 2400-tonne type needs to take into consideration the novelty of the design and French technological ambitions. The *Jaguars*, together with their *torpilleur d'escadre* counterparts of the *Bourrasque* class, were the first French flotilla craft to enter service since the *800-tonnes*, which dated from 1907–8. The displacement of the *Bourrasques* was almost twice that of their predecessors; the *Jaguars* were three times heavier, 50% longer and six knots faster. Both types featured new, more powerful types of gun and torpedo, and had boilers and turbines of modern design with single-reduction gearing. It is therefore unsurprising that they should have experienced technical problems when they first entered service.

Machinery

The official trials of *Jaguar* and *Tigre* began, under the supervision of Rear-Admiral Pugliesi-Conti, Vice-President of the Trials Commission (*Commission permanente des essais* or CPE), on 21 September 1925. The trials of *Tigre* began relatively smoothly, and on 3 October she achieved the impressive figure of 35.8 knots during her 8-hour trial at Washington displacement. *Jaguar*, on the other hand, suffered serious ingress of seawater into her condensers at high speed on the first day of her trials, and had to have her boilers completely retubed at Lorient; her trials were suspended for five months.

Léopard broke down on her very first sortie from the shipbuilder on 29 October 1925, and had to return to her moorings under tow for repairs to her turbines. She arrived at Lorient for her official trials on 27 November, but on the following day experienced the same condenser problems as her sister *Jaguar*, again resulting in more than five months of repairs. *Jaguar* resumed her official trials on 3 March 1926, but on the 12th two bolts in one of the ahead turbines sheared, causing extensive damage to the turbine blades and putting her into dockyard hands for a further two months.

Jaguar's problems were now at an end, but the struggles of *Léopard* continued. During speed trials on 7 June 1926 there was an explosion in a feed water tank, which again resulted in seawater entering the condensers. A complete retubing took a further five and a half months. When the ship was finally accepted by the Navy on 14 December 1926 she had missed her contract date by two years. *Jaguar*'s Lorient-built sister, *Panthère*, experienced problems with a shaft, then with one of the cruise turbines, delaying her deployment to Toulon. All six ships had been commissioned by June 1927, but it would be five more months before the Industrie B ships, *Léopard* and *Lynx*, would enter service.

Taken individually, none of these problems was unusual in a new ship with new machinery. Rather, it was the extent and the persistence of the problems which were unanticipated, even though most were eventually resolved to the satisfaction of the Navy.

More serious in the longer term was the lateral instability which plagued the ships throughout their service lives, hampered the installation of their planned armament, and thwarted attempts to improve their military capabilities.

Stability problems

The raised forecastle with its prominent flare and sheer made the *Jaguars* excellent sea-boats, able to sustain high speed in a head sea with minimal pitching. However, despite being fitted with two 40-metre bilge keels, lateral stability was poor; beam was insufficient and topweight excessive – due in part to the size of the bridge and the height of the two masts. The result was:

- excessive heel under the effect of wind or rudder (a 20-degree list when turning at 35 knots with only 5–6 degrees of helm)
- a stiff, pronounced roll of up to 25 degrees in 8–10 seconds (depending on displacement) with a beam sea, which made life uncomfortable for the crew and hampered gunnery

It had initially been envisaged that the 130mm Mle 1919 gun would be replaced by the more powerful 138.6mm Mle 1923,[19] and that these guns would be controlled by the new 'destroyer director' under development. From 1925, at considerable expense, orders were placed with the relevant subcontractors for thirty

---

[19] To be mounted from the outset in the next class of *contre-torpilleurs* (see *Guépard* class, Chapter 4)

Below: *Chacal* moored at Antwerp during the summer training cruise (*corvette d'été*) of August 1936. Note the doors for the depth charge chutes and the rails, faced with lignum vitae, which took the depth charges clear of the stern. The concentration dial is painted black with 12 graduations. (*Leo van Ginderen collection*)

THE JAGUAR CLASS

138.6mm Mle 1923 (five per ship), for their ammunition, and for the larger hoists which would be required. The increase in topweight of approximately two tonnes per mounting was considered acceptable at the time. However, the ships' lateral instability, which quickly became apparent on their official trials, led to the abandonment of both these planned improvements, and much of the expenditure had to be written off.

This did not resolve the lateral instability problem; it simply avoided exacerbating it further. More would be required. On trials the ships had been found to be too heavy at the bow when the fuel tanks were full. It was decided that from 1928 the reserve depth charges (previously to be landed in peacetime) would after all be permanently embarked,[20] as their 3.2-tonne weight provided a counterweight for the forward fuel tanks. In 1929 there was even a proposal to shorten the cables for the main anchors forward,[21] but this was resolutely (and successfully) opposed by the ships' commanding officers.

On 13 August 1930 a set of remedial measures was decreed which aimed to improve sea-keeping performance:[22]

- oil fuel capacity was to be limited; as a consequence the regulation speed runs at 8/10 power were to be restricted to a few hours once per year
- the two 75mm HA guns were to be replaced by the lighter 37mm Mle 1925 – this would also bring the ships into line with the latest *contre-torpilleurs*
- the tripod mainmast was to be replaced by a simple pole mast

Neither of these last two measures was implemented, in part for reasons of cost, although the 75mm guns would eventually be removed and replaced by lightweight Hotchkiss machine guns (see below).

In 1929 the Ginocchio torpedoes were disembarked. The 910kg reserve anchor was landed in 1930, and in 1936 the 910kg stern anchor was disembarked and replaced by the 570kg anchor previously to port. From 1932 the Thornycroft depth charge throwers, which had in any case not been a conspicuous success in the their original location, were disembarked;[23] this saved around 5.5 tonnes of topweight. Other weight savings, involving the removal of all equipment deemed inessential by the ships' officers, were officially encouraged. Before the war it was unusual for all six torpedoes to be embarked, except for the period when the ships were attached to the torpedo training school (EALM – see Chapter 10).

MODIFICATIONS 1926 TO 1939

Frustrated in its attempts to replace the 130mm Mle 1919 with the 138.6mm Mle 1923 and to develop a lightweight 'destroyer director', the Marine Nationale had to settle for less radical, incremental improvements.

Main guns

During the late 1920s an automatic loading tray was fitted to the guns to improve the firing cycle, and a

---

[20] DM 2490 EMG/1 dated 23 December 1927.
[21] DM 1496 EMG/1 dated 30 July 1929.
[22] DM 1436 EMG/1.
[23] DM 166 EMG/1 dated 28 January 1932.

Opposite: The 2nd DCT, *Jaguar*, *Chacal* and *Léopard*, open to the public at a port on the west coast of France in 1938-9 (precise date and location unknown). Despite efforts at standardisation in the postwar *contre-torpilleurs*, the multitude of differences in individual units is readily apparent in this photograph. Note in particular: the positions of the crow's nests and the concentration dials, the configuration of the topmasts and the voice tubes, the layout of the galley pipes, and the 1-metre rangefinder atop the engine room access on *Chacal* (centre). *(US Navy NH 86562, courtesy of A D Baker III)*

raised circular platform provided for the loading numbers to compensate for the excessive height of the trunnions.

From 1927 a '1st Stage Fire Control' system was retro-fitted in the first four ships, and *Léopard* and *Lynx* were so fitted on completion. It comprised the electro-mechanical computer Mle 1923 Type B originally planned, which was installed in the transmitting station, and a Granat GD II (elevation/deflection) system with receiving dials on the mountings. In 1929 it was decided that director control would be fitted for training only,[24] and Granat GD III (angle of train) receivers were duly fitted from 1931.

Although development of the planned director was abandoned, and the ships received only a 3-metre coincidence rangefinder in an open mounting on completion (see above), this was subject to successive upgrades. In 1931 it was replaced by a stereoscopic model with the same base-length, the OPL[25] E.1926 or E.1927; and from 1937 this was in turn replaced by a 5-metre OPL stereo model (PC.1936). Plans in 1931 to provide a second rangefinder on the after deckhouse were abandoned once it was decided to retain the mainmast. Powerful binoculars were provided on either side of the upper bridge between 1934 and 1939.

For fire in formation, concentration dials were fitted from 1929 onwards, the prototypes being trialled aboard *Léopard* and *Lynx*. They enabled the range of the target to be transmitted visually using 'hands' on a 'clock face', either from the leader to the other ships of the division, or from a ship able to range on the target to one whose vision was hampered by smoke. The early dials were trainable; in later years they were generally fixed to the face of the upper bridge and the after side of the mainmast. The early models had a white 'clock face' numbered 1–12 with black 'hands'; later models were painted with white or yellow numbers on black and with a double pointer for increased precision, and the numbering system was variously 0–9, 0–11, or 1–12. On the latter dials each 'hour' represented a range of 1500 metres, and each 'five minutes' 125 metres, thus enabling ranges in excess of 18,000m to be transmitted. A sailor posted behind the dial with a telephone link to the fire control position (upper bridge) moved the pointers to the required positions using a simple handle mechanism.

When VHF radio became available for tactical bridge-to-bridge communications during 1938–9 the concentration dials became increasingly redundant, and they were generally removed during the winter of 1939.

In 1938 it was proposed that the elderly 130mm Mle 1919 be replaced by a modern dual-purpose weapon. A directive dated 10 April 1939[26] approved the installation of two twin 100mm mountings Mle 1931 per ship. This proposal was never implemented due to production problems with the otherwise successful 100mm CAD mounting. Instead the *Jaguar*s were issued with a variant of the original 130mm shell (OPfK Mle 1925) with a colorant that served to distinguish the shell splashes of the individual ships of each division. The colour generally denoted the position of the ship within the division: red for the lead ship, green for the second ship, and white (later yellow) for the third.

Air defence

In 1932 it was decided that the ships' stability problems precluded the provision of fire control for the two 75mm HA guns, which were therefore of little military value. A directive dated 6 February 1932[27] prescribed the following measures:

– replacement of the 75mm HA and the 8mm MG guns by a uniform close-range AA armament comprising eight 13.2mm Hotchkiss MG Mle 1929 on twin mountings (CAD) Mle 1931; they would use the same reinforced seatings
– provision of a 1-metre stereoscopic rangefinder (OPL J.1930) on the centre-line close to the after mountings, atop the access housing for the engine rooms
– provision of 15 rounds of starshell per 130mm gun to replace the 75mm starshell rounds

The necessary modifications were implemented at Brest and Toulon during 1933–4, and had the added benefit of weight savings of 12 tonnes, of which 8 tonnes were high in the ship. The 13.2mm MG were intended to engage attacking aircraft approaching to within 3500m of the ship. They proved to be of limited value against modern high-performance aircraft during the engagements of 1940.

Anti-submarine warfare

In 1925 the regulation provision of 100kg depth charges was reduced from thirty to twelve, in recognition of the slow firing cycle of the Thornycroft depth charge throwers. The twelve DCs were stowed in racks close to the throwers, and the space freed up in the magazine aft was used to stow four additional 200kg DCs, for a total of twenty; three full passes each of 6 x 200kg and 4 x 100kg were now possible.

However, by the early 1930s it had become increasingly apparent that the location chosen for the depth charge throwers was not ideal; they increased the weight in the forward part of the ship, and firings using shallow settings were sufficiently close to the hull to

Below: The bridge of *Chacal* in 1935, showing the wheel and the order transmitters for the engines.

---

[24] DM 346 EMG/1 dated 12 February.
[25] *Optique de Précision Levallois*.
[26] DM 481 EMG/3.
[27] DM 250 EMG/1.

cause leaks in seams and in the packing boxes around the shafts. A ministerial directive of early 1932[28] prescribed that they be removed, but that the reinforced seatings be retained for installation of a future model with improved characteristics.

Communications
An SCAM[29] ultrasound depth sounder was fitted in all ships in 1927.

The 75cm searchlights proved impractical for intership communications, and in 1928–9 the *Jaguars* had 30cm signalling lamps fitted in the bridge wings. A proposal to relocate the two 75cm S/L on the centre-line atop the bridge and atop the ammunition distribution station abaft the third funnel was not implemented due to the cost.

The medium-frequency direction-finding (MF/DF) apparatus was finally delivered in 1929–30. The aerial was initially installed atop the access ladders for the engine rooms, but when this became the preferred location for the small AA rangefinder fitted in 1933–4, it was relocated above the DF office on the quarterdeck (except in *Léopard* and *Lynx*, which were given tiered platforms on the centre-line at Frame 18).

The W/T outfit was progressively modernised during the 1930s, the most significant addition being that of an SFR Mle 1937 VHF (*ondes très courtes* or OTC) tactical radio for bridge-to-bridge voice communication in 1937.

MODIFICATIONS 1939 TO 1940
Anti-submarine warfare
Following the outbreak of war, Note CM 6273 CN/6 (8 October 1939) prescribed the restitution of the ships' anti-submarine capabilities, notably the re-embarkation of two of the original four Thornycroft depth charge throwers.

Concerns remained about the stability of the ships, and only six 200kg depth charges were to be carried in the chutes, with a further six in the magazine aft. These were to be supplemented by eight 100kg depth charges: two on stowage racks close to the throwers with six in reserve.

The two depth charge throwers were installed not in their original location, but on the seatings for the 75mm guns in place of the 13.2mm Hotchkiss, which were relocated atop the platform for no.3 gun; the latter was landed, for a saving of 11 tonnes. A board with 'ready' and 'fire' lamps was provided close to the DCTs.

These modifications were carried out between October and December 1939 except for *Léopard* and *Lynx*, which were refitted in early 1940. October also saw the first deliveries of Asdic 123 from the Royal Navy. Redesignated Alpha by the French, this equipment was fitted as a priority to the *Jaguars* and the *L'Adroit* class (see Chapter 3 for a full account). Installation of the sonar and its associated listening room (*cabine d'écoute*) was relatively straightforward, as space (for Walser) had been reserved in the original design. The equipment was fitted as follows:

Tigre: Brest early November 1939
Chacal: Brest mid-November 1939
Lynx: Toulon January 1940
Léopard: Cherbourg February 1940
Jaguar: Brest March 1940

The last ship, *Panthère*, was to have received hers during a refit at Toulon in the summer of 1940, but due to circumstances this was not carried out.

Refuelling and demagnetisation
Escort duty quickly revealed the lack of endurance of these ships, and in March 1940 it was decided to install pipework between the forecastle and the forward (athwartships) fuel tank to enable the ships to conduct astern refuelling from a tanker. This work was, however, deemed not to be a priority; it was to take place during the ships' next refit, and in the event only *Panthère* was so fitted.

Demagnetisation became a priority with the

---

[28] DM 166 EMG/1 dated 28 January 1932.
[29] *Société de Condensation et d'Applications Méchaniques.*

Below: View from the crow's nest of either *Panthère* or *Tigre* onto the bridge and forecastle, probably 1938 or late 1940. Note the 5-metre stereo rangefinder (PC.1936) atop the bridge. Bearing indicator stations equipped with powerful binoculars have been fitted to port and to starboard, and there is a magnetic compass (also for bearing) on the centre-line. The small 1-metre portable rangefinder to starboard is for concentration fire; it measured the angle of parallax between the ships of the division. (*Marc Saibène collection*)

Jaguar May 1940

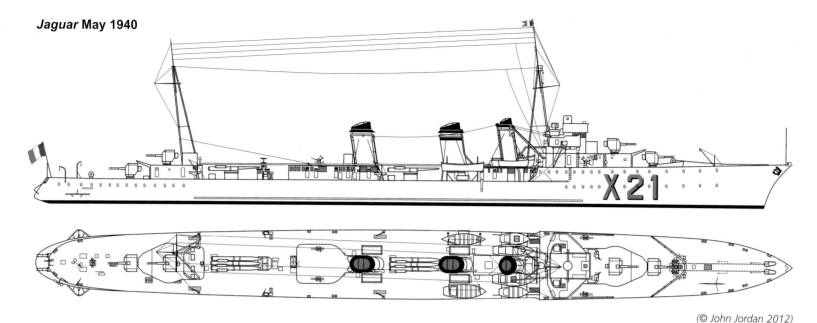

Jaguar as she appeared in the spring of 1940. During the mid-1930s the two 75mm HA guns fitted on completion were replaced by twin 13.2mm Hotchkiss MG, and two additional 13.2mm CAD were mounted on the forecastle. In 1937 the original 3-metre coincidence rangefinder was replaced by a 5-metre stereo model in a protective housing. In late 1939 *Jaguar* was fitted with two fixed Thornycroft depth charge throwers in place of the after 13.2mm CAD mountings, which were relocated atop the centre deckhouse, no.3 gun being landed. The tactical number was painted brick red with black shadowing. (© John Jordan 2012)

discovery of German magnetic mines in the ports and estuaries of the North Sea. The ships all passed through a degaussing range as a preliminary measure, and were to have been fitted with a degaussing cable as the next step. Only *Jaguar* received hers, at Brest in April 1940, before the Armistice.

Air defence

The encounters with German aviation in the North Sea in the spring of 1940 made it clear that current AA batteries were inadequate. In May 1940 Toulon Naval Dockyard, which was due to undertake the refit of *Panthère*, proposed the removal of the mainmast and the fitting in its place of a platform for a twin 37mm Mle 1933 mounting, with 300 rounds in ready-use stowage adjacent to the mounting and a further 300 stowed in cases below and hoisted manually.[30] The W/T aerials were to be re-affixed to antenna supports fitted on the after funnel.

Only *Panthère* received this modification, although *Tigre* and *Lynx* both had their mainmast removed when they returned to Toulon in July 1940. No further modifications would be made to any of the surviving ships of the class which remained in French hands after June;[31] as France's oldest *contre-torpilleurs*, they went into care & maintenance (*gardiennage*), and their light AA weapons were transferred to active ships.

---

[30] Note 3524 R of 16 May.
[31] For *Léopard*, which was seized by the British and subsequently operated with the FNFL, see pp.251-2.

Right: *Tigre* in August 1940, while serving as lead ship of the 4th DCT at Toulon. Note the 13.2mm CAD atop the former no.3 gun platform abaft the third funnel. (Marc Saibène collection)

CHAPTER 2

THE *BOURRASQUE* CLASS

INTRODUCTION

The *torpilleur d'escadre* proposed in April 1920 (see Introduction) had a normal displacement of 1350 tonnes, a designed speed of 33 knots, and was to be armed with four 100mm guns and six 550mm torpedoes in three twin or two triple mountings. Following the adoption of the larger and heavier 130mm gun displacement rose to 1455 tonnes, the other characteristics remaining the same. Twelve *torpilleurs* of the new type would be authorised on 18 April 1922 in the same programme as the six *contre-torpilleurs*. In contrast to the latter ships, none would be built in the naval dockyards. Orders for the twelve ships would be distributed among seven private shipyards, all of which had previous experience of building ships of destroyer size (see map). The Channel ports of Dunkirk, Le Havre and Caen were prominent, together with the established shipyards of the Loire and the Gironde. Of the three ships ordered from F C Gironde, *Trombe* would be built at their Honfleur shipyard – opened only in 1917 opposite Le Havre – and towed after launch to Bordeaux for fitting out.

As with the four *Jaguar*s built in private yards, the contracts would not be signed until February/March 1923. On 10 April the selected shipyards received a directive from the Navy Minister outlining the rules for standardisation, which in future would take precedence over shipyard initiative in all but small points of detail. The Minister stressed the importance of creating a uniform class of ships with identical performance characteristics. This, however, would prove more difficult to achieve than anticipated, due to the different types of turbine and auxiliary machinery which would be installed.

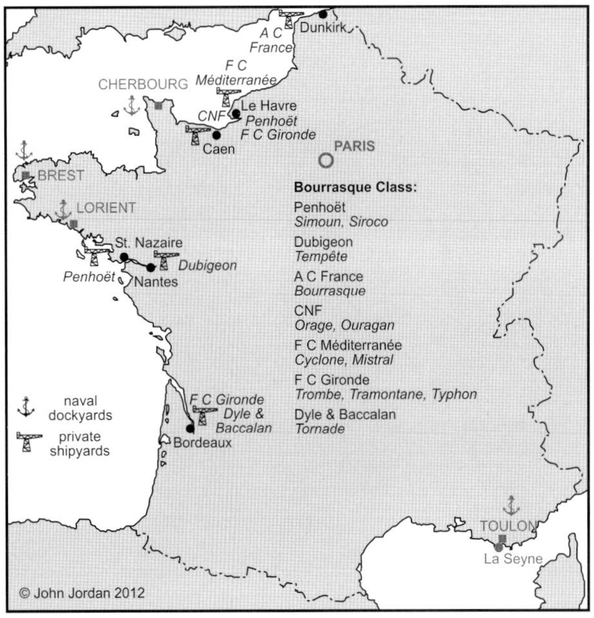

The development of a common boiler would be entrusted to Penhoët, who would be responsible for the Parsons turbine installations in the two ships built by them, *Simoun* and *Siroco*, and also the *Tempête*, built by Dubigeon at Nantes. *Bourrasque* (A C France, Dunkirk) and the two ships built by F C Méditerranée at Le Havre, *Cyclone* and *Mistral*, would be similarly fitted. However, *Orage* and *Ouragan* (CNF, Caen) would have Rateau turbines, and the four 'T's built at Bordeaux would receive a Zoelly-Schneider model.

The twelve ships of the first series were named after winds or other weather phenomena. The designated *ports d'armement*, to which the ships were to be delivered following their builders' trials, were as follows:

– Cherbourg: *Bourrasque*, *Orage*, *Ouragan*, *Cyclone*, *Mistral*, *Trombe*.
– Lorient: *Simoun*, *Tempête*, *Siroco*.
– Toulon: *Typhon*, *Tramontane*, *Tornade*.[1]

HULL AND GENERAL CONFIGURATION

While there were significant differences in layout between the *Bourrasque*s and the larger *contre-torpilleurs*, the two designs had much in common. They were fitted with guns and torpedoes of the same model and had almost identical equipment for internal and external communications. The major difference between the two types related to the propulsion

---

[1] Marc Saibène (*op. cit.*) suggests that *Typhon*, and possibly *Tornade*, were originally to assigned to the naval dockyard at Rochefort, and that they were reassigned due to the impending closure of Rochefort (1927).

GENERAL CHARACTERISTICS

Displacement:	1320 tons standard; 1455 tonnes normal*; 1820 tonnes full load
Dimensions:	Length 99.3m pp, 105.6m oa; beam 9.7m; draught 3.5m
Machinery:	Three Du Temple small-tube boilers, 18kg/cm² (216°) Two-shaft geared steam turbines 31,000CV for 33kts (designed)
Oil fuel:	360 tonnes; radius 3000nm at 15kts
Armament:	Four 130mm/40 Mle 1919 in single mountings (110rpg) One 75mm/50 Mle 1924 HA (180 rounds + 120 starshell) Two 8mm Hotchkiss MG Mle 1914 in single mountings Six 550mm torpedoes Mle 1919D in two triple mountings Two DC chutes each for six 200kg depth charges (+ 4 reloads)
Complement:	8 officers + 134 men peacetime 9 officers + 153 men wartime

* designed; normal displacement on completion was around 1590 tonnes.

BUILDING DATA

Name	*Simoun*	*Siroco*	*Tempête*	*Bourrasque*	*Orage*	*Ouragan*
Programme	1922	1922	1922	1922	1922	1922
Prog. no.	10	11	12	13	14	15
Project no.	–	–	–	–	–	–
Builder	Penhoët St-Naz	Penhoët G Que.	Dubigeon Nantes	ACF Dunkirk	CNF Caen	CNF Caen
Order	4 Apr 1923	4 Apr 1923	5 Mar 1923	5 Mar 1923	13 Mar 1923	13 Mar 1923
Laid down	8 Aug 1923	15 Mar 1924	3 Dec 1923	19 Nov 1923	20 Aug 1923	7 Sep 1923
Launched	3 Jun 1924	3 Oct 1925	21 Feb 1925	5 Aug 1925	30 Aug 1924	6 Dec 1924
Sea trials	1 Jun 1925	21 Jul 1926	20 Sep 1925	15 Aug 1925	1 Aug 1925	1 Dec 1925
Manned for trials	30 Sep 1925	13 Aug 1926	25 Feb 1926	16 Dec 1925	23 Oct 1925	25 Mar 1926
Commissioned	1 Jan 1926	15 May 1927	20 Jul 1926	10 Jul 1926	1 Sep 1926	1 Oct 1926
Completed	29 Apr 1926	1 Jul 1927	28 Sep 1926	23 Sep 1926	1 Oct 1926	19 Jan 1927
Entered service	Aug 1926	5 Feb 1928	Sep 1926	23 Sep 1926	19 Jan 1927	15 Sep 1927

Name	*Cyclone*	*Mistral*	*Trombe*	*Tramontane*	*Typhon*	*Tornade*
Programme	1922	1922	1922	1922	1922	1922
Prog. no.	16	17	18	19	20	21
Project no.	–	–	–	–	–	–
Builder	FCM Graville	FCM Graville	FC Gir Harfleur	FC Gir Bordeaux	FC Gir Bordeaux	D&B Bordeaux
Order	5 Mar 1923	5 Mar 1923	5 Mar 1923	5 Mar 1923	5 Mar 1923	5 Mar 1923
Laid down	29 Sep 1923	28 Nov 1923	5 Mar 1924	29 Jun 1923	Sep 1923	25 Apr 1923
Launched	24 Jan 1925	6 Jun 1925	27 Dec 1925	29 Nov 1924	22 May 1925	12 Mar 1925
Manned for trials	15 Mar 1926	1 Aug 1926	1 Jun 1926	25 Jan 1926	20 Jan 1927	1 Aug 1926
Acceptance trials	1 Sep 1926	30 Dec 1926	12 Nov 1926	30 Mar 1926	25 Nov 1927	7 Jul 1927
Commissioned	15 Mar 1927	5 Apr 1927	1 Jun 1927	15 May 1927	15 Feb 1928	1 Oct 1927
Completed	31 May 1927	1 Jun 1927	27 Oct 1927	15 Oct 1927	27 Jun 1928	10 May 1928
Entered service	25 Jun 1928	21 Jan 1928	21 Dec 1927	1 Jan 1928	22 Oct 1928	21 May 1928

machinery: that of the *Bourrasque*s delivered only three fifths of the power of that of the 35-knot *Jaguar*s, and this dictated a different internal division of the hull and a modified layout above decks.

There were only two boiler rooms (vs. three) and a single engine room (vs. two). The forward boiler room housed only a single boiler; the after boiler room had two boilers face to face. The French could have opted for one slim and one broad funnel (combining the uptakes from the two boilers in the after BR, as in the *Jaguar*s), but chose instead three slim funnels with funnels 2 and 3 closely spaced, giving these ships their distinctive appearance.[2] Because the turbines delivered less power both sets could be accommodated in a

---

[2] They were often referred to as *les trois-tuyaux* (lit. the 'three-pipes'). The tall original funnels would later be shortened.

The *Torpilleur d'Escadre Bourrasque* 1927

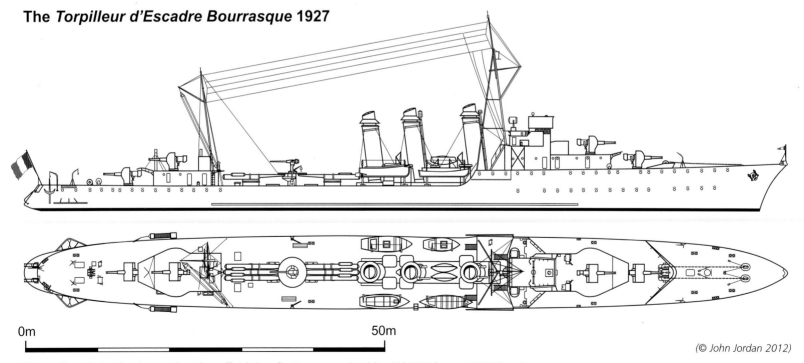

(© John Jordan 2012)

The profile and plan drawings are based on official plans for *Bourrasque* dated Dunkirk 17 February 1927. They show the ship as completed, with a 3-metre base rangefinder atop the bridge. Note the tall funnels, which were reduced in height after completion, and the single 75mm HA gun perched atop the access housing for the engine room.

THE *BOURRASQUE* CLASS

Bourrasque: General Arrangement Plans

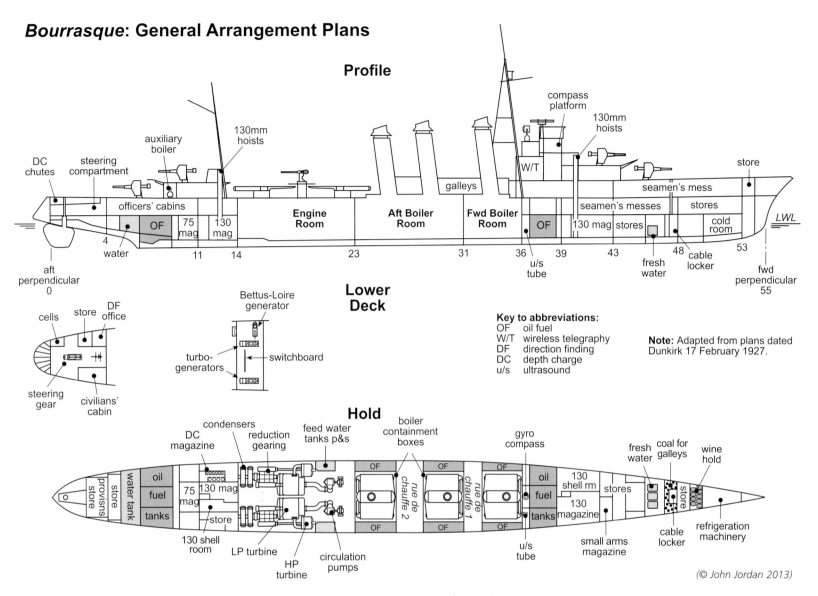

(© John Jordan 2013)

single engine room, although even a cursory look at the accompanying plan reveals just how tight a squeeze it was, with minimal room for access and maintenance.

Longitudinal framing was employed for the construction of the hull, as in the *contre-torpilleurs*. The 55 transverse frames had a standard spacing of 1.8 metres (vs. 2.1m), except in the bow and the stern, where it was reduced to approximately one metre. There were ten main transverse bulkheads (*cloisons principales*) extending from the ship's bottom to the upper deck, dividing the hull into eleven watertight compartments designated A–K (see drawing).

There were nine pumps rated at 100 tonnes per hour (t/h) and two rated at 30t/h, disposed as follows:

- Compartment A: 1 × 30t/h
- Compartments B/C and D/E: each 1 × 100t/h
- Compartments F, G and H: each 2 × 100t/h
- Compartments I/J: 1 × 100t/h
- Compartment K: 1 × 30t/h

The double bottom extended for most of the ship's length. There was insufficient breadth for the continuous longitudinal bulkheads outboard of the machinery spaces which were a feature of the *Jaguar*s, and the only lateral fuel tanks were abreast the boilers. The principal fuel tanks were disposed athwartships abaft the forward and after magazines.

Although the hull had many of the characteristics of the larger ships, the *Bourrasque*s were designed for moderate speeds and had a length/beam ratio of only 10.2:1 (vs. 10.8:1 in the *Jaguar*s). They had the same prominent raised forecastle (*Teugue*) with pronounced sheer and flare, combined with a 'clipper' bow. The Main Deck (*Pont Principal*) was the only continuous deck apart from the Hold (*Cale*) and was the strength deck; abaft the forecastle it was the weather deck. The Lower Deck (*Pont des Logements*) was interrupted by the three large machinery compartments, which extended to the Main Deck. At its forward end were the messes for seamen and petty officers, while the officers' cabins were located in the after part of the ship, forward of the steering compartment (see Inboard Profile). Additional messes for seamen and petty officers were located in the forecastle, together with the sickbay and the washplaces and heads for the crew.

The large, capacious bridge structure was similar in configuration and layout to that of the *Jaguar*s (q.v.), and housed the compass platform, chart house, main W/T office and signal distribution centre. It is difficult to see how it could have been much reduced in size; these were the first French destroyers to have superimposed guns forward,[3] and the height of the bridge had to be increased accordingly. It nevertheless contributed to the topweight problems of both the *Bourrasque*s and the *Jaguar*s.

Abaft the break in the forecastle there were only two deckhouses (vs. three in the *Jaguar*s) and this had implications for the layout of the triple torpedo tube mountings, both of which were located abaft the funnels, above the engine room. The centre deckhouse

---

[3] Superimposed mountings had been trialled in the *Enseigne Gabolde*, but the gun was the smaller, lighter 100mm model and the bridge structure altogether narrower.

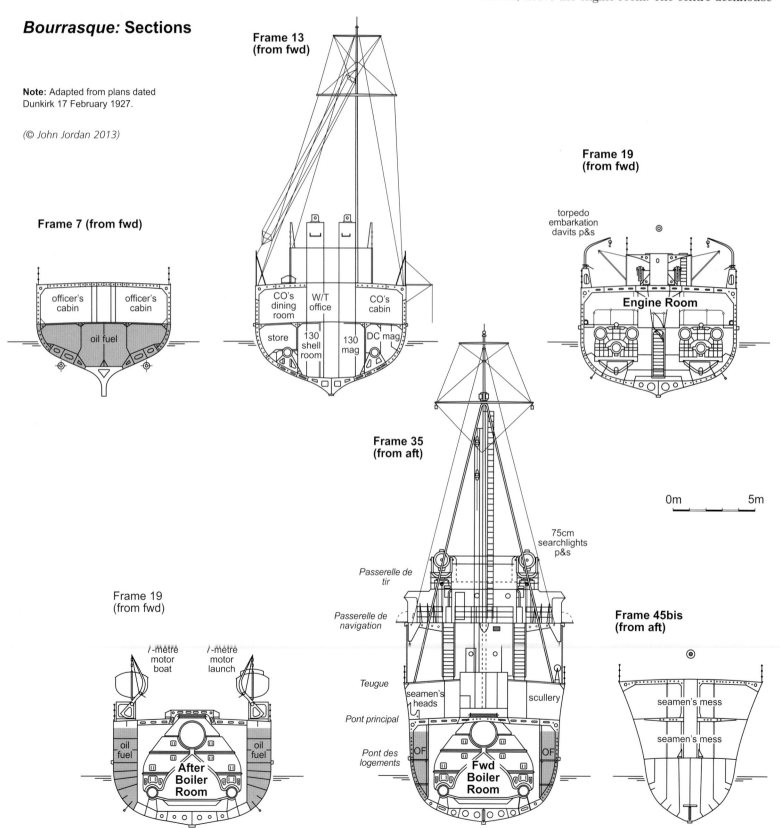

Bourrasque: Sections

Note: Adapted from plans dated Dunkirk 17 February 1927.

(© John Jordan 2013)

(*roof milieu*)[4] housed the uptakes and ventilation trunking for the two boiler rooms, the machinery workshop, the bakery and the main galleys; the after deckhouse (*roof arrière*) housed the officers' galley, the Purser's office, the after ammunition hoists and the auxiliary boiler. The ship's boats were suspended on davits abeam the forward deckhouse. The two masts were at the same 7.5-degree angle as the funnels. The tripod foremast was similar in configuration to that of the *Jaguar*s, whereas the mainmast, which was offset to port, was a simple wooden pole. The main W/T aerials were suspended between the yards of the masts.

The *Bourrasque*s were of riveted steel throughout. The thickness of the hull plating varied between 5mm and 10mm. The decks were generally constructed of 5–7mm plates, increasing to 12mm over the boilers. The original bilge keels were 32.4m long, but following trials, *Sirocco* had hers extended over a length of 36m and reinforced, and this modification was extended to the ships still building.

GROUND TACKLE AND NAVIGATION

There were two bower anchors of the 1400kg stockless type in hawsepipes. They were handled by a 15–16CV windlass located on the forecastle. Additional 310kg anchors were provided on either side of the stern, moored by gravity. The stern capstan was rated at 3.7CV.

The single suspended, balanced rudder had a surface area of $10.14m^2$. The servo-motor was designed to turn the rudder through an angle of 32 degrees in 25–30 seconds at 30 knots (27 degrees at 30 knots, without a specified time interval).

Each of the *Bourrasque*s was equipped with a single Sperry gyro-compass located on the main deck directly beneath the bridge. Four compass repeaters were provided: one on the compass bridge, two in the bridge wings, and a fourth at the forward end of the after deckhouse.

There were also four magnetic compasses: on the compass platform (course – *compas de route*), on the upper bridge (bearing – *compas de relèvement*), at the forward end of the after deckhouse (bearing), and in the steering compartment (course).

MACHINERY

Steam for the turbine machinery was supplied by three small-tube boilers of the Du Temple type. The boilers were manufactured or sub-contracted by the shipbuilders but to a common design. Performance and steam output was similar to the boilers fitted in the *contre-torpilleurs*. The boilers were rated at a conservative $18kg/cm^2$ (260psi), giving a saturated steam temperature of 216°C. Each boiler, together with its auxiliaries, weighed approximately 73 tonnes. However, the boiler adopted for the *Bourrasque*s had slightly different dimensions to that of the *Jaguar*s: the latter was 6.8m wide and 5.15m long; the boiler fitted in the *Bourrasque*s was slightly narrower and longer, 6m x 5.45m. These dimensions were better suited to the *torpilleurs d'escadre*, which had less beam but greater available length because of the reduction from five to three boilers. Despite the height of the boilers being only 5.66m (vs. 5.85m in the *Jaguar*s) the reduction in the depth of the hull meant that the centre part of the upper deck directly above the boiler rooms had to be raised approximately 60cm to accommodate them (see Inboard Profile and Section views).

The three boilers were disposed in line on the ship's axis in two boiler rooms. Boiler Room 1 (Section F) housed a single boiler, with the exhaust uptakes being led into the first of the three funnels. Boiler Room 2 (Section G) housed two boilers face to face, with a single *rue de chauffe* between them; each of the uptakes exhausted through its own funnel (see Inboard Profile). As in the *Jaguar*s, each of the boilers was housed within its own gas-tight containment box. There were fuel oil tanks outboard of each of the boilers, and up to 95 tonnes of reserve feed water in tanks in the double bottom beneath. Two feed tanks each with a capacity of 10 tonnes of distilled water were located at the sides of the engine room.

The turbine machinery was arranged side by side in a single engine room, so the shafts were of equal length. Each set of turbines was completely independent of the other, with its own pumps and other auxiliary machinery, and comprised a single high-pressure (HP) reaction/impulse turbine and a low-pressure (LP) reaction cruise turbine with an integral reverse turbine. The HP turbine was outboard of the LP turbine and both drove the shaft via single-reduction gearing. Each set of turbines, including gearing and auxiliaries, weighed 119.3 tonnes. Each shaft was fitted with an outward-turning four-bladed propeller of high-resistance brass with a diameter of 3.0 metres.

The turbine machinery was the one area in which the Marine Nationale was unable to impose standardisation. Different shipyards were licensed to build a

---

[4] In the *Jaguar*s this was termed the *roof avant*, and the deckhouse which formed the lower tier of the bridge the *roof supérieur avant*.

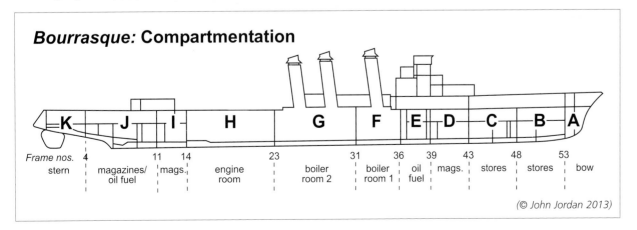

Bourrasque: Compartmentation

(© John Jordan 2013)

particular type of turbine, and these licences had to be respected for legal and economic reasons. The six ships built by Penhoët, A C France, Dubigeon and F C Méditerranée were fitted with Parsons reaction turbines; the two ships built by CNF had Rateau impulse turbines, while the four ships built by F C Gironde and Dyle & Baccalan had Zoelly-Fives-Lille and Zoelly-Schneider turbines.

All six ships attained their designed maximum speed of 33 knots on trials. *Mistral* was the fastest with 34.8 knots, and *Tramontane* sustained 34.1 knots on her 8-hour trial at an initial displacement of 1505 tonnes.[5] In service all ships could comfortably sustain the desired 30 knots.

The two large transverse fuel tanks fore and aft, together with the six side tanks abeam the boilers, held a total of 360 tonnes of furnace fuel oil. Following trials, endurance was calculated at between 3686nm and 4384nm at 15 knots on cruise turbines, although 3000nm was a more realistic estimate. In service even this proved optimistic – in war conditions little more than 1500nm was achieved, even with a full load of fuel. Endurance at the maximum speed of 32.7–33 knots was calculated as between 764.5nm and 861nm, depending on the ship.

As with the *Jaguar*s, the engine room was on two levels, with a platform at the upper level at the forward or after end, depending on the type of turbines installed and the disposition of the associated condensers. The platform was occupied by the two 50/66kW Fives-Lille turbo-generators, the oil-fuelled generators (for use when alongside and in an emergency) and the main switchboard. It was originally intended to fit only a single Bettus-Loire GM9 oil-fuelled generator rated at 15/18kW, but a note dated 16 June 1927[6] stipulated the installation of a second unit of the same type (see also *Jaguar* class). The auxiliary boiler, which provided steam for the capstans and the steering motor, and services for the crew, was located in the after deckhouse.

MAIN ARMAMENT

The *Bourrasque*s were fitted from the outset with four 130mm guns Mle 1919 in single mountings superimposed fore and aft. This was an unusually heavy gun for a destroyer of the period, and accounted for much of the 200-tonne increase in displacement over the April 1920 proposal. However, four guns had the advantage of simplifying replenishment arrangements, as the fifth gun of the *Jaguar*s was isolated from its associated magazine and had to be supplied from the after hoists.

The guns on the *Bourrasque* class were, like those of

---

[5] On the other hand, *Orage* only managed to sustain 32.57 knots over the same period.
[6] DM 1798 CN/4.

Bourrasque: Shell & Cartridge Hoists

Fwd Shell Hoist   Fwd Cartridge Hoist

Note: Adapted from plans dated Dunkirk 17 February 1927.

(© John Jordan 2012)

Right: *Siroco* on her sea trials in late 1926. Like her sisters, she was completed with three tall funnels. The 75mm HA gun has yet to be fitted between the torpedo tubes aft. (US Navy NH 110741, courtesy of A D Baker III)

THE BOURRASQUE CLASS

the *Jaguar*s, on simple pivot mountings. The original lightweight shield to protect the gun crew against wind and spray was superseded by the new 'wrap-around' model developed by Lorient dockyard. This was fitted in *Siroco* and *Typhon* on completion (early 1928), and retro-fitted to the other ships of the class during 1928–9.

The regulation ammunition provision in peacetime was 110 rounds per gun, for a total of 440 shells and 462 cased charges; 68 practice rounds were also provided, distributed between the fore and after magazines. The electrically-powered hoists, which were identical to the ones fitted in the *Jaguar*s, used a continuous chain mechanism to raise the shells and cartridges in the horizontal position (see drawing). They were located behind no.2 gun and forward of no.3 gun. Shells and cartridges were transferred by hand either to the ready-use stowage racks or directly to the breech of the guns. There were intermediate reception positions behind no.1 gun and forward of no.4 gun. The latter were located in an ammunition lobby (see Bridge Decks drawing), whereas the upper reception trays were in the open atop their respective deckhouses, with blast screens to the sides which could be covered with canvas awnings. Ready-use stowage was provided for 24 rounds per gun, as in the *Jaguar*s.

All twelve ships were provided with a simple 3-metre SOM coincidence rangefinder (Mle B.1926), which was fitted on a lightweight pedestal atop the upper bridge. The rangefinder was used to provide range and bearing data for not only the main guns but also for the torpedoes. In service it proved less than satisfactory, as smoke was drawn onto the upper bridge and the rangefinders were also subject to severe vibration at certain speeds. When the planned fire control equipment was finally installed from 1927 to 1931, data was processed in the *PC Artillerie* by a Mle 1923B electro-mechanical computer; elevation, deflection and training data were then transmitted directly to the mountings, which were fitted with Granat GD II and GD III receivers (see Chapter 1).

As in the *Jaguar*s, the two 75cm searchlight projectors were installed atop the forward superstructure, immediately abaft the compass platform. They were remotely controlled from positions in the bridge wings.

ANTI-AIRCRAFT WEAPONS

The *Bourrasque*s were initially fitted with a single 75mm Mle 1924 on a single mounting Mle 1922 (see Chapter 1 for data). It was not easy to find a suitable location for the mounting as it had to be fitted on the centre-line. In the event it was decided to mount the gun on a circular platform above the access ladders for the engine rooms, between the two triple torpedo mountings. This had the advantage of clear firing arcs on both beams; however, arcs were obstructed on forward bearings by the third funnel, and on after bearings by the mainmast and its stays. Arcs were 62 degrees forward of the beam and 70 degrees abaft the beam on either side of the ship, so blind arcs were 56 degrees forward and 40 degrees aft. There was no provision for remote HA fire control, and no telephone link with the upper bridge.

There was a magazine for HE rounds to starboard and one for starshell rounds to port on either side of the ship's axis abaft the 130mm magazines for the

Above: A splendid starboard quarter view of *Bourrasque* early in her career, on 21 January 1927. The 75mm HA gun is in place between the torpedo tubes. Tactical numbers roughly half the height of the forecastle were painted on the hulls of the first three ships during late 1926, and from the end of January these would be enlarged to extend from the waterline to the deck. (*Marius Bar*)

main guns. Saluting rounds were carried in the powder magazine. The regulation outfit was 180 HE shells Mle 1925 and 120 illuminating shell; practice rounds comprised 24 HE, 32 starshell and 25 ballasted rounds. The rounds were stowed in cases of three, and were brought up from the magazine and transferred to the gun manually. Ready-use stowage on either side of the mountings comprised ten cases (five per side) containing 30 rounds.

As in the *Jaguar*s, two 8mm Hotchkiss MG Mle 1914 were embarked for self-defence against strafing aircraft; a twin mounting Mle 1926 was available from 1929. The machine guns were normally stowed below-decks, and when required were affixed to pedestal mountings on the forecastle deck abeam the bridge. A total of 20,500 combat rounds and 2400 practice rounds could be carried in the small arms magazine forward.

TORPEDOES

The *Bourrasque*s, like the *Jaguar*s, were equipped with two triple mountings (Schneider Mle 1920T) for the 550mm torpedo Mle 1919D (for data see Chapter 1). The mountings and the tubes were supplied by the Société des chantiers de la Loire (Saint Denis). In the stowed position they were disposed facing one another above the engine room. They could be trained 30 degrees either side of the beam. Sleeves with a diameter of 450mm could be inserted in the centre tubes for practice firings using the previous generation of torpedoes.

The torpedo warheads were normally stowed in the depth charge magazine aft, which was to port outboard of the 130mm magazine. The torpedo bodies were hoisted aboard using a derrick and a pivoting cradle which could be aligned with each of the individual tubes (see drawing Chapter 1).

The torpedoes used the same fire control system as the main guns. Training data was transmitted to the torpedo mounting, which was equipped with a Granat GD II receiver, and an on-mount operator aligned the pointers to train the mounting. Depth, speed and gyroscope settings for the torpedo were set outside the tubes. The order to launch was given from the bridge and executed on the mounting.

ANTI-SUBMARINE WEAPONS AND DETECTION APPARATUS

The original design of the *Bourrasque*s featured an anti-submarine armament on a par with the *Jaguar*s: twelve 200kg depth charges in two parallel chutes directly beneath the stern and four Thornycroft Mle 1918 depth charge throwers.[7] However, the DCTs were suppressed following a ministerial decision of 25 September 1924.

The stern depth charge chutes were identical to those of the *Jaguar*s (see the accompanying drawing). The regulation depth charge outfit was twelve (2 x 6) in the stern chutes plus four in reserve, stowed in the DC magazine aft (see General Arrangement plan). The depth charges were generally embarked only in time of war or for exercises, their place in the magazine being taken by the torpedo warheads in peacetime.

Two Ginocchio towed torpedoes were also to be embarked: one on the quarterdeck and the other in the below-decks magazine. However, the deck installation was not fitted on completion, and trials of the torpedo began only in 1928, first on *Trombe* then on other ships of the class.

The Ginocchio torpedo was an Italian concept dating from the First World War. The 'torpedo' was lowered over the stern close to a submarine contact and towed at the estimated depth of the submarine in the hope/expectation that it would strike the hull or conning tower, thereby triggering the large explosive warhead. The contact fuze mechanism worked by inertia, as was the case with many mines of the period; the impact activated the spring-loaded striker, which struck the detonator and set off the charge (see drawing).

The French developed two models of Ginocchio torpedo:

– a 'medium' model, which was towed at a depth of

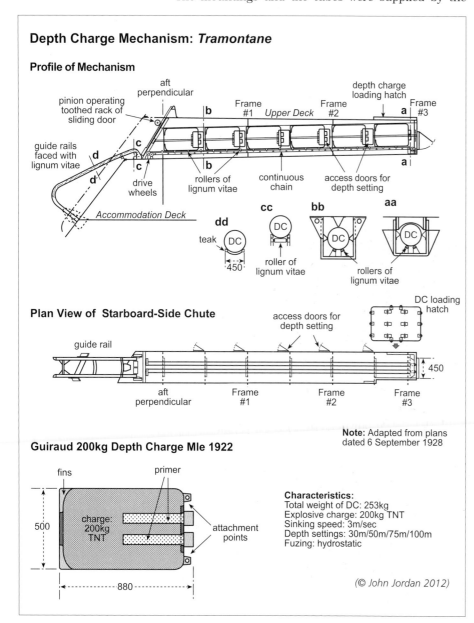

Depth Charge Mechanism: *Tramontane*

Profile of Mechanism

Plan View of Starboard-Side Chute

Note: Adapted from plans dated 6 September 1928

Guiraud 200kg Depth Charge Mle 1922

Characteristics:
Total weight of DC: 253kg
Explosive charge: 200kg TNT
Sinking speed: 3m/sec
Depth settings: 30m/50m/75m/100m
Fuzing: hydrostatic

(© John Jordan 2012)

---

[7] The arrangement on the succeeding *L'Adroit* class suggests that these would have been fitted at the after end of the forecastle beneath the overhang of the bridge wings, not abeam the first funnel as in the *contre-torpilleurs*. The boats of the *torpilleurs* were exclusively on davits, effectively precluding the latter option.

between 15 to 37 metres; length was 1.62m, weight 62kg with a 30kg TNT explosive charge
- a 'depth' model, which could be towed to a depth of up to 53 metres; length was 1.72m, weight 75.5kg with a 30kg TNT explosive charge

The depth of immersion depended on the length of the tow and the speed of the towing ship. During the trials of the late 1920s depth-keeping was found to be a problem, and the Ginocchio torpedoes were progressively disembarked. The project was formally suspended in 1933 pending resolution of the depth-keeping problem, but was revived briefly following the outbreak of war in 1939 (see *Le Hardi* class, Chapter 9).

There was provision, as in the *Jaguar*s, for the active ultrasound underwater detection device being developed by SIF (see Chapter 1). The compartment for the tube was located below the gyro-compass to starboard, between the transverse fuel tanks and the forward boiler room. The *cabine d'écoute* was two decks above and had direct voice-pipe communication with the bridge. Fitting of the equipment was begun in 1929 but abandoned the following year;[8] the incomplete installations were removed, but the spaces reserved pending future developments.

Siroco trialled a passive hydrophone system in 1930, the *cabine d'écoute* being located in the general store between frames 44 and 45. There were two sensors, but they were found to be capable of determining only whether the vessel detected was to port or to starboard; no precise bearing was possible. Again the system was abandoned.

Operational underwater sensors began to be fitted to these ships only in 1940, the French-developed SS1 (see Modifications below) being superseded by the superior British Asdic.

COMMUNICATIONS

The *Bourrasque*s had a similar, albeit less comprehensive, communications outfit to the *Jaguar*s.

The wireless telegraphy (W/T) equipment was distributed between two spaces to provide redundancy in the event of action damage. In keeping with contemporary French practice, the bulkheads of each of these spaces were lined with felt and deal panelling for sound isolation. The main W/T office, the *PC Radio*,

[8] Directive 30189 CN/4 dated 3 September 1930.

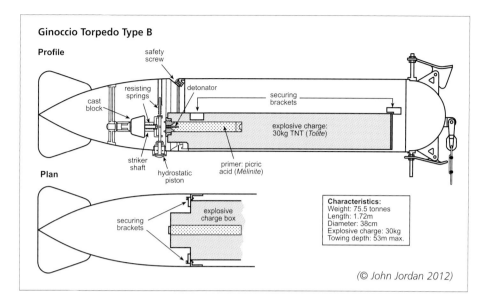

was at the after end of the bridge block (see drawings), and was equipped primarily for long-range (strategic) communications up to 1000nm. It housed:

- an SFR (*Société Française Radio-électrique*) type D-100 1kW long-wave transmitter operating in the 600–11,000m waveband
- an SFR 200W 'emergency' transmitter with a range of about 50nm for bridge-to-bridge communication

The secondary W/T office was located on the Lower Deck aft, in the centre of the CO's suite of apartments, and was for medium-range (c.200nm radius) tactical communications with divisional units and shore stations. It housed:

- a Mle E20 short-wave transmitter

The W/T aerials were strung between the yards of the tripod foremast and the light pole mainmast, and between the foremast and the third funnel.

There was a space reserved for installation of a direction-finding office beneath the quarterdeck aft, to port of the steering compartment (see GA plan). However, as with the *Jaguar*s this equipment was generally installed after the ships entered service (see Modifications).

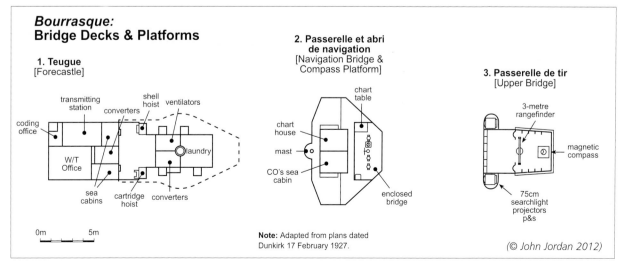

BOATS

The complement of boats when the ships were first completed was as follows:

– one 7-metre motor boat
– one 7-metre motor launch
– one 7-metre whaler
– one 5-metre motor dinghy

There was also a 3.6-metre non-collapsible canvas 'Berthon' and a 3-metre punt. All were supplied by the Navy except for the motor boat, which was by one of two sub-contractors: Maisons Conink & Cie and Jouët. The main boats were carried on davits abeam the forward deckhouse. The original davits, which were of cast steel, proved defective and would later have to be replaced. The boats had to be raised and lowered by hand, which was a long, arduous process.

COMPLEMENT

The regulation peacetime complement comprised eight officers and 134 men. The detailed breakdown was as follows:

- Commanding Officer (normally *Capitaine de corvette* = Lieutenant-Commander)
- six junior officers (*Lieutenants/Enseignes de vaisseau* = Lieutenants/Sub-Lieutenants)
- one Chief Engineering Officer (*Ingénieur mécanicien de 1re classe*)
- one Chief Petty Officer (*Premier maître*)
- six Petty Officers (*Maîtres*)
- seventeen Petty Officers 2nd class (*Seconds maîtres*)
- 111 seamen

The regulation wartime complement was nine officers and 153 men. The commanding officer had his own suite comprising a day cabin, a sleeping cabin, a bathroom and a pantry (see drawing). The junior officers were berthed in single cabins on the Lower Deck aft, and had their own wardroom and pantry plus a separate bathroom. The Chief Petty Officer was accommodated in an individual cabin forward, on the port side of the forecastle; opposite was the mess for the Petty Officers, for whom tiered bunks were provided. The mess for the Petty Officers 2nd class was farther forward, with a second mess for the PO Mechanicians on the deck below. The lower ranks were accommodated in two small and one large open-plan messes on two levels in the bow. The lowest-grade Petty Officers and the seamen ate and slept in these communal spaces, and all slung hammocks. The captain's personal chef and the steward who waited on his table were generally civilians, and had their own twin-berth cabin in the after part of the ship.

All the officer accommodation in the after part of the ship was lined with insulating material, but there was no air conditioning. French ships of the period were generally regarded as comfortable when operating in a European climate, but when serving in West and North Africa during the summer months the stifling conditions below meant that the men often slept in the open, on deck.

The *torpilleurs d'escadre* were not intended to be used as flagships and had no special accommodation for a flag staff. The commanding officer of a three-ship division would generally be of *Capitaine de frégate* (Commander) rank, and would command his own ship as well as the division. He flew a triangular tricolore pennant from the foremast top as a mark of his status (see Chapter 10).

EVALUATION

These were large, powerful ships which made a considerable impact abroad. They were ten metres longer and some 250 tonnes heavier (normal displacement) than the late-war British Modified 'W' class, which provided the template for many post-war destroyers. Indeed,

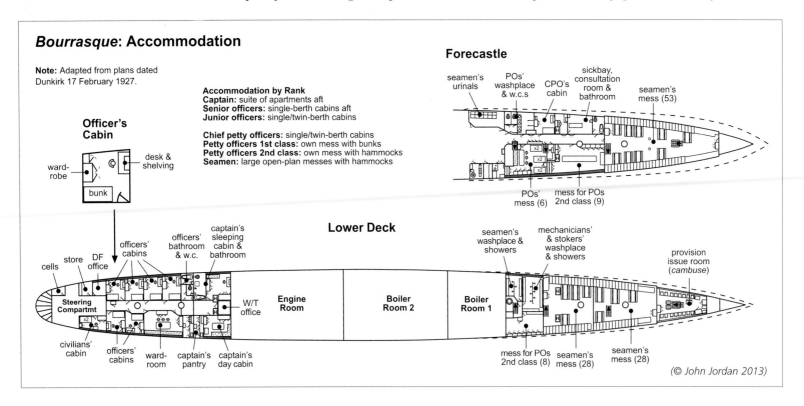

THE BOURRASQUE CLASS

Left: *Siroco* (53) during 1930–1, when she was serving with the 1st Squadron in the Mediterranean. Note the 3-metre coincidence rangefinder atop the bridge and the single 75mm HA gun between the torpedo tubes. *(René Bail collection)*

displacement was closer to that of the large British 'flotilla leaders' of the *Scott* and *Shakespeare* classes. The *Bourrasques* mounted heavier guns (130mm vs. 120mm) and more powerful torpedoes (550mm vs. 533mm) than their British counterparts. In size and power they easily outclassed the first post-war Italian destroyers of the *Sella* class (length 85 metres, normal displacement 1280 tonnes, three 120mm guns, and four 533mm torpedo tubes in twin mountings). However, the *Bourrasques* were not as fast as their contemporaries; they were 130 tonnes overweight on completion, and in service were found to have similar defects to the *Jaguars*, particularly with regard to their machinery and stability.

Below: *Bourrasque* (14) off the southern coast of France c.1930. The funnels have been reduced in height, and the new-style hull number extends from the waterline to the forecastle deck. The year 1927 saw the transfer of all the modern destroyers to the Mediterranean. Note the single 75mm HA gun under canvas between the torpedo tubes. *(A D Baker III collection)*

Right: *Siroco* docked at Toulon, where she was in refit from September 1932 to August 1933. Note the single 37mm Mle 1925 guns which have replaced the single 75mm HA, and the white-painted trainable concentration dial on a platform extending from the mainmast. *(Marc Saibène collection)*

Below: *Cyclone* (56) in 1932; the 75mm HA gun has been landed, but neither the 37mm Mle 1925 mountings nor the 1-metre rangefinder have yet been fitted in its place. In the background is the 10,000-ton cruiser *Colbert*. *(Marc Saibène collection)*

Machinery

Despite attempts by the Navy to ensure uniformity of propulsion machinery, the adoption of three different types of turbine from three different manufacturers inevitably resulted in divergences in performance which, although less dramatic than had been the case with the prewar *800-tonnes* type, remained a concern when ships with different machinery operated in the same division. The Rateau turbines were more responsive but consumed more fuel than the Parsons turbines. Some ships of the class were more economical at high speed, others at cruise speed. There were also teething problems with all three models, but particularly with the Zoelly turbines, which tended to strip their blades and gave trouble well into the 1930s. By the Second World War the more serious of these

THE BOURRASQUE CLASS

problems had been resolved and the performance of the turbines in service was considered satisfactory; however, they would remain fragile and prone to breakdown.

The steering machinery proved insufficiently robust and the servo-motor underpowered. It took 25–30 seconds to turn the rudder to its maximum angle of 32 degrees, and a further 30 seconds to bring it back to 0 degrees. However, the turning circle of just over 500m at 20 knots – it varied from ship to ship – was an improvement on the *Jaguar*s, which suffered from their high length to beam ratio.

Stability problems

The *Bourrasque*s had similar sea-keeping qualities to the *Jaguar*s, and coped well with a head sea. However, lateral stability was equally deficient, as both two types suffered from excessive topweight.

During her trials on 23 September 1927, which took place in a Force 8 gale, *Mistral* rolled 43 degrees – 17 degrees to port, 26 degrees to starboard – with a roll period of only just over five seconds. It was subsequently found that the metacentric height (GM) of the class was only 0.35–0.37 metres as compared to a designed GM of 0.45m. This not only made the ships unsteady gunnery platforms but threatened their survival if holed beneath the waterline.

An experiment was undertaken to determine the most appropriate countermeasure. *Siroco* was fitted with enlarged bilge keels, while her sister *Mistral* embarked 20 tonnes of keel ballast. An observation by a third ship of the class, *Cyclone*, established that keel ballast was much the more effective option, and

all the ships of the class would be similarly modified.

Keel ballast almost certainly resulted in a slight reduction in speed and endurance. However, even as the ships were entering service the Navy was already giving serious consideration to reductions in topweight similar to those contemplated with the *Jaguar*s (see Chapter 1). As a first step, the three funnels were reduced in height: the fore-funnel by 1.5 metres, the second funnel by 1.8 metres and the third funnel by 2 metres. This work was carried out between 1929 and 1930. The reduction in the height of the funnels had the added benefit of reducing the silhouette.

Above: *Ouragan* c.1933–4, wearing the hull number '13'. The 75mm HA gun has been landed and replaced by single 37mm guns mounted on the upper deck abeam the after deckhouse. *(US Navy NH 110 740, courtesy of A D Baker III)*

Below: *Orage* at Le Havre on 10 July 1936, during the summer manoeuvres of the 2nd Squadron. *(Philippe Caresse collection)*

MODIFICATIONS 1926 TO 1939
Main guns

During the late 1920s an automatic loading tray was fitted to the guns to improve the firing cycle, and a raised circular platform provided for the loading numbers to compensate for the excessive height of the trunnions.

For fire in formation, concentration dials were fitted from 1930 onwards (see Chapter 1). The forward dial was affixed to the face of the upper bridge; the after dial was installed on a platform above the after 130mm hoists, and could be trained manually.

An EMG directive of 28 November 1934 stated that the original 3-metre coincidence rangefinder was to be replaced by a stereoscopic model with a 4-metre base, with priority being given to the lead-ships of the divisions, then to the *contre-torpilleurs* of the *Jaguar* class. It was estimated that this would enable fire to be opened at 12,500m in good visibility; the new rangefinder would also be able to provide range data for aerial targets. This measure was implemented as the new rangefinders became available during the late 1930s. A proposal in 1936 to upgrade the rangefinder to a 5-metre stereo model in a protective trainable housing in all the early *torpilleurs* and *contre-torpilleurs* (see Chapter 3) was not extended to the *Bourrasque*s due to topweight problems.

In 1938–9 the *Bourrasque*s were issued with a variant of the 130mm SAP shell (OPfK Mle 1925) with a colorant that served to distinguish the shell splashes of the individual ships of each division. The colour generally denoted the position of the ship within the division: red for the lead ship, green for the second ship, and yellow for the third. In July 1939 the regulation ammunition outfit was 300 OPfK Mle 1925, 100 OEA Mle 1923 plus 80 starshell.

Air defence

In 1931 it was decided that the 75mm HA gun would be disembarked and replaced by two 37mm Mle 1925 single mountings (CAS), disposed as in the *L'Adroit* class (see Chapter 3). This measure had the added advantage of further reducing topweight, as the 37mm CAS was a much lighter gun and would be mounted on the upper deck. A 1-metre stereoscopic rangefinder was fitted behind the after concentration dial from 1933 onwards.

The original 75mm magazine was modified to house 500 37mm rounds per gun. As the 75mm was now no longer available to fire illuminating shell, an additional 60 starshell rounds were provided for the main guns and distributed between the fore and after magazines.

Anti-submarine warfare

Following a decision of 9 November 1938, installations for minesweeping paravanes and for Ginocchio torpedoes were to be made aboard certain destroyers of the 1500-tonne type. However, this modification does not appear to have been implemented on all ships, and deployment of the Ginocchio torpedo was finally abandoned in October 1939.

Communications

The W/T outfit was progressively modernised from 1934. In 1937–8 *Orage* and *Bourrasque* had a direction-finding (DF) office installed forward of the bridge,

Left: *Cyclone* and *Siroco* of the 5th DT representing the Marine Nationale at the *Fête vénitienne* at Cannes in March 1932. Note the white concentration dials aft and the illuminated identification letter on the stern of *Cyclone*. (Marc Saibène collection).

Right: One of the later ships of the class, *Tornade*, off the southern coast of France during 1935, when she was serving with the 1st Squadron (Mediterranean); her hull number marks her out as the third ship of the 3rd DT. The original 75m HA gun has been replaced by two 37mm guns, and there is a small 1-metre rangefinder for AA fire behind the concentration dial aft. Note the unusual gantry structure between the torpedo tubes. *(A D Baker III collection)*

Below: Tramontane at Brest during the summer of 1938. Note the long-base 4-metre stereo rangefinder (painted white) atop the bridge, and the Spanish Civil War neutrality colours on the shield of no.2 gun. *(Marc Saibène collection)*

the antenna being mounted stop the voice-pipes for no.2 mounting with a supporting arm.

MODIFICATIONS 1939 TO 1940
Main guns and torpedoes
Operations during the winter of 1939–40 highlighted the stability problems of the ships. Directive 3822 CN/6 of 30 January 1940 decreed the disembarkation of one of the after 130mm gun mountings. The removal of gun no.3 would have had the greatest impact on topweight, but in the event it was decided to land gun no.4, thereby freeing the quarterdeck for additional depth charge throwers. The measure was implemented during February and March 1940, except for *Cyclone*, *Siroco*, and *Tempête*.

Anti-submarine warfare
In order to boost anti-submarine capabilities, it was decided in to reinstall two Thornycroft Mle 1918 depth charge throwers at the after end of the forecastle, an

instruction being issued on 8 October 1939. There was to be a 100kg charge readied on the thrower with a reserve charge stowed close by. In the event it proved impossible to implement this due to a shortage of DCTs, which were much in demand for the plethora of auxiliary vessels mobilised after the outbreak of war. A total of 136 had been purchased from the UK in 1918, and orders for a further 50, then 150 were placed during the autumn of 1939, to be delivered to Cherbourg. However, only the *Tempête*, *Trombe* and *Tramontane* had been so fitted before the Armistice of June 1940.

In early 1939 it was decided to fit a passive hydrophone system designated 'Multispot' in all ships of the class. Development work continued on an ultrasonic underwater detection system designated SS1, and in May 1939 sixteen Asdic 123 devices were ordered from Britain. Before the latter could be delivered, Toulon announced its satisfaction with the initial trials of the French SS1, and it was duly installed in four of the five 'T's, which were serving in the Mediterranean, during January/February 1940. However, trials of SS1 aboard *Tramontane* would ultimately be unsuccessful; although results were comparable to those obtained with Asdic, the French system proved unreliable and prone to failure, and installations were halted.

In April 1940 it was decided that the quarterdeck space freed up by the removal of no.4 gun should be used to accommodate two Thornycroft DCTs; stowage was be provided for three reserve charges per thrower on the rear wall of the after deckhouse. Again this could not be implemented before the Armistice, and as an interim measure racks for lightweight 35kg depth charges were fitted above the stern. The regulation DC provision was now:

- 12 x 200kg depth charges in the stern chutes
- 2 x 100kg depth charges on the DCTs with six (2 x 3) in stowage racks
- 3 x 200kg, 4 x 100kg, and 10–20 x 35kg depth charges in the magazine aft

In order to compensate for the added weight of the new anti-submarine weapons and sensors, first one, then two torpedoes were disembarked from the centre tubes.

Refuelling
Wartime escort duties highlighted the limited endurance of these ships, and in the spring of 1940 it was decided that pipework would be installed between the forecastle and the forward (athwartships) fuel tank, as in the *Jaguar*s, to enable them to conduct astern refuelling from a tanker. The work was never carried out, and by December 1940 opinion was shifting in favour of alongside refuelling, which would require quite different arrangements.

Air defence
From May 1938 the naval dockyard at Brest began work on plans to replace the 8mm MG on the forecastle by 13.2mm Hotchkiss twin mountings (CAD). Installation high in the ship was rejected because of the adverse effects on the ships' stability, and in the end it was decided that they would be mounted on the forecastle in the same position as the 8mm guns.

Above: As completed, the 1455-tonne destroyers were found to have inadequate stability; metacentric height (GM) was only 0.35–0.37 metres as compared to a designed GM of 0.45m. They had a pronounced roll in adverse sea conditions and heeled badly with a cross-wind. This late view of *Simoun*, taken during the winter of 1944–5 when she was serving with the French Naval Task Force, illustrates the conditions in the Atlantic swell. *(René Bail collection)*

However, a shortage of the Hotchkiss CAD mountings led to division leaders being prioritised, the first installations being made from March 1939; even so, some ships had to wait until May 1940.

The regulation provision of 13.2mm ammunition was for 2400 rounds, of which no fewer than 1500 were stowed in ready-use lockers close to the guns. The overall provision was doubled in July 1939, and the same instruction decreed the doubling of the combat provision of the 37mm mountings to 1000 rounds per gun. Due to the shortage of 13.2mm mountings, many ships were fitted with additional single or twin 8mm MG on the quarterdeck.

In May 1940 *Mistral*, which was operating in the Dunkirk sector, appears to have had the port-side 37mm CAS replaced by a 37mm twin mounting Mle 1933 (CAD); this is confirmed by a report of the bombing of the port on 29 May.

MODIFICATIONS 1940–42
Of the eight ships which survived the early part of the war, two (*Ouragan*, *Mistral*) were seized by the British in July 1940,[9] while five remained in service with the navy of Vichy France:

- Casablanca:
  6th DT: *Simoun*, *Tempête*
- Bizerte:
  7th DT: *Tramontane*, *Typhon* and *Tornade*

The eighth ship, *Trombe*, was placed in care & maintenance (*en gardiennage*) at Toulon under the terms of the Armistice.

On 11 February 1941 CV Dornon, head of the 1st bureau of the *Forces Maritime Françaises* at Vichy, issued a circular on behalf of the French Admiralty in

---

[9] Due to a shortage of volunteers for the FNFL, *Ouragan* recommissioned with Polish crew, while *Mistral* was manned by the Royal Navy. Both ships were rearmed with British 4.7in guns in place of the French 130mm. The modifications made while in Royal Navy hands are outside the scope of this section of the book.

Right: *Typhon* (72) and *Tornade* (73) dressed overall during a port visit to Funchal (Madeira) from 28 May to 2 June 1938. At that time they formed, together with *L'Adroit* (71), the 7th DT of the 2nd Squadron. *(Yannick Iffinger collection, courtesy of Marc Saibène)*

Below: *Tornade* photographed from the cruiser *Foch* during a replenishment exercise off Toulon 18–20 February 1941. The ship is still missing her after 130mm gun. Note the paravanes and their handling davits on either side of the seating for the gun. *(Marc Saibène collection)*

which a number of important changes to the ships' armament were proposed, and the roles of the *Bourrasque* and *L'Adroit* class were redefined, the latter being oriented toward anti-submarine warfare while the former would become fast fleet minesweepers. The main gun armament of all the surviving *torpilleurs* was to be restored, and anti-aircraft capabilities enhanced within the constraints imposed by the terms of the Armistice.

Main guns

The ships of the 7th DT had no.4 gun reinstated at Toulon in March 1941, although it was June before the release of the necessary breeches was authorised by the Armistice Commission. *Simoun* had hers replaced in July during a major refit at Bizerte.

Air defence

In December 1940 it was decided that all light anti-aircraft guns would be removed from ships in care & maintenance at Toulon and reallocated to active units. A trickle of new AA gun mountings – in particular the Hotchkiss single 25mm Mle1939–40 and the 13.2mm Browning MG (see Chapter 9 for data) – was being delivered to the fleet. In February 1941 it was therefore proposed to equip each of the *Bourrasque*s in French service with a single 25mm Hotchkiss mounting and two 13.2mm Browning MG, to supplement the existing 37mm Mle 1925 CAS and 13.2mm Mle 1929 CAD.

Simoun, which was due to be refitted at Bizerte from July to September 1941, was selected for the prototype installation. The pole mainmast was removed, and supports for the W/T aerials fitted to the third funnel. A platform for a single 25mm Hotchkiss flanked by two 13.2mm Brownings was then constructed atop the hoists for the after guns. Two twin 8mm MG were fitted in the bridge wings, and the 13.2mm Hotchkiss CAD on the forecastle were mounted on a tripod to improve their ability to follow fast-moving aircraft. These modifications were subsequently extended to *Tramontane* (November 1941), *Typhon* (March 1942) and *Tornade* (April 1942), also at Bizerte. *Tempête*, which was refitted at Algiers in November 1941, was similarly modified except that the 13.2mm MG were mounted on a platform amidships, above the engine room access ladders.

Tramontane 1942

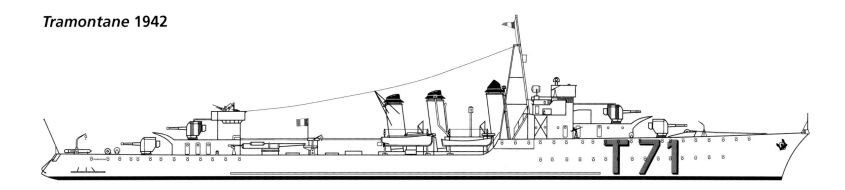

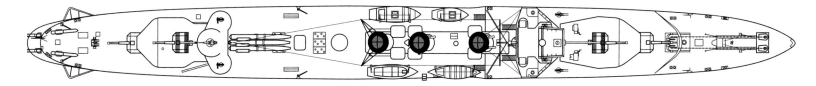

Tramontane as she appeared in early 1942, following her refit at Bizerte. No.4 gun has been reembarked but the forward triple torpedo mounting landed as weight compensation. A platform has been constructed atop the hoists for the after guns for a single 25mm Hotchkiss Mle 1939 and two 13.2mm Browning MG; the mainmast has been suppressed and the W/T antennae refixed to outriggers on the third funnel. Of the original close-range AA guns, the 37mm CAS Mle 1925 have been retained abeam the after deckhouse, and the twin 13.2mm Hotchkiss guns on the forecastle have been remounted on a tripod mount better suited to AA fire against a fast-moving target. Note the reduced tripod foremast and the C6 minesweeping paravanes on the stern. *(© John Jordan 2012)*

Weight-saving measures

In compensation for the reinstallation of no.4 gun and the enhanced anti-aircraft battery the two Thornycroft depth charge throwers previously embarked in *Trombe*, *Tempête* and *Tramontane* were landed, leaving them with only the two stern chutes for 200kg depth charges. Studies by the Sidi-Abdallah Dockyard at Bizerte suggested that further weight-saving measures were necessary to counter-balance the new AA platform; *Typhon* and *Tramontane* lost their forward torpedo tube mounting, and *Typhon* also lost the centre tube of her after mounting. Both mountings were retained on the other surviving units, but metacentric height in all ships of the class was now between 0.20m and 0.22m, less than half the designed GM.

Minesweeping paravanes

The three ships of the 7th DT (*Tornade*, *Typhon* and *Tramontane*) were fitted with two C6 minesweeping paravanes, which had been removed from ships of the *L'Adroit* class. A channel 164 metres wide could be swept at a speed of 20 knots; the cables were 230m long and the paravanes were towed at a depth of 15 metres.

Appearance

During late 1940 and early 1941 a prominent cowling was fitted to the fore-funnel to keep exhaust gases clear of the upper bridge and improve rangefinder observations. The topmast was also reduced in height (see photo of *Simoun* at Casablanca p.239).

Left: *Typhon* off Toulon during February 1941; her hull number, painted in brick red with black shadowing, marks her out as the second ship of the 7th DT, and tricolore recognition markings have been painted on the shields of guns nos. 2 and 3. She has a new cowling on the first funnel; no.4 gun mounting has yet to be replaced. *(Leo van Ginderen collection)*

CHAPTER 3
THE *L'ADROIT* CLASS

INTRODUCTION

The Navy had hoped to secure a ten-year programme in the form of a new *Statut Naval* in the wake of Washington. In the current atmosphere of *détente*, with France taking the lead in arms reduction initiatives at the League of Nations, the French parliament was unwilling to commit to a fixed, long-term programme, and preferred to vote on the Navy's proposals year by year. However, there was considerable all-party support for the Navy following France's perceived humiliation at the Washington Conference, and in the event virtually all the ships in the original programme would be authorised, albeit in successive one-year *tranches*.

To remedy its chronic shortage of modern destroyers the Navy proposed to follow the *Bourrasque*s with a slightly modified design that became the *L'Adroit* class. In comparison with the earlier ships, the new *torpilleurs d'escadre* were some 50 tonnes heavier (hence their designation by the Marine Nationale as *les 1500 tonnes*) and a metre and a half longer; the additional length was in the bow, creating more space for accommodation and stores. There was also a new, improved 130mm gun (Mle 1924) and a revised AA armament; beyond that, there were only small differences of detail in the official plans, which once again were drawn up by the 'small ships' section (*Section des petits bâtiments*) of the STCN, with some revisions by *Ingénieur Général* Antoine.

Six ships were authorised under the 1924 estimates, four under the 1925 estimates, and the final four under the 1926 estimates. The 1924 estimates also included the two 'treaty' cruisers of the *Duquesne* class, while the 1925 and 1926 estimates each included a single 'treaty' cruiser (*Suffren/Colbert*) plus three *contre-torpilleurs* of a new design (the *Guépard* class – see Chapter 4), armed with a new 138.6mm gun which was essentially the 'big brother' of the 130mm Mle 1924 to be installed in the *L'Adroit* class. After this, the pressure on France's limited naval infrastructure, and the resulting bottlenecks in production, would be such that the Navy would be compelled to halt the building of *torpilleurs d'escadre* altogether in order to prioritise the construction of the larger, faster *contre-torpilleur* type; three classes of six, together with a single 'treaty' cruiser, would be authorised in three of the following four years.[1] Even so, by the time the final ship of the *L'Adroit* class was completed in 1931, the Marine Nationale would have twenty-six large, modern destroyers capable of holding their own against any in the world.[2]

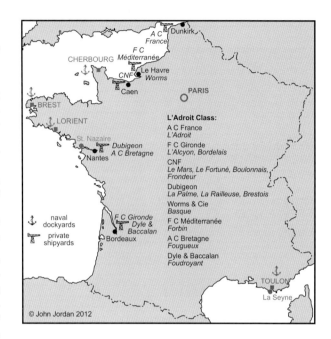

As with the *Bourrasque*s, all the ships of the *L'Adroit* class would be built in private shipyards. Most were ordered from the same yards that had built the *Bourrasque*s, the two newcomers being the A C Bretagne yard, currently building the *contre-torpilleur Tigre*, and Ateliers et Chantiers de la Seine Maritime at Le Havre. The only yard excluded was the Penhoët shipyard at Saint-Nazaire; however, Penhoët would continue to be closely involved in the programme, being responsible for the installation of Parsons turbines in no fewer than eight of the fourteen ships, and in 1926 would secure a prestigious Navy order in the form of the training cruiser *Jeanne d'Arc*, the first modern French cruiser to be ordered from a private shipyard, as well as an order for the new *contre-torpilleur Valmy*. The ships authorised under the 1924 estimates were ordered in November of the same year, the 1925 ships January-May 1926, and the four 1926 ships in April 1927.

Whereas the *Bourrasque*s, which were authorised as part of the same programme, had been named after wind and weather phenomena, the names allocated to the *L'Adroit* class had three different 'themes' which corresponded to the year of authorisation:

- The six ships authorised under the 1924 estimates bore the names of the ships commanded by the famous privateer Jean Bart: *L'Adroit, L'Alcyon, Le Mars, Le Fortuné, La Palme, La Railleuse* (note that the definite article was part of the name for these ships).
- The four ships of the 1925 estimates were given the names of inhabitants of French provinces beginning with the letter 'B': *Brestois, Boulonnais, Basque, Bordelais*.

---

[1] The original 1928 estimates were delayed by a year in order to give a 'breathing space' (see Chapter 6).
[2] During the same period the British completed twenty new destroyers ('A' and 'B' classes, plus two prototypes and two 'leaders') and the US Navy none.

THE L'ADROIT CLASS

BUILDING DATA

Name	L'Adroit	L'Alcyon	Le Mars	Le Fortuné	La Palme	La Railleuse
Programme	1924	1924	1924	1924	1924	1924
Prog. no.	48	49	50	51	52	53
Project no.	–	–	–	–	–	–
Builder	ACF Dunkirk	FC Gir Bordeaux	CNF Caen	CNF Caen	Dubigeon Nantes	Dubigeon Nantes
Order	25 Nov 1924	25 Nov 1924	21 Nov 1924	21 Nov 1924	21 Nov 1924	21 Nov 1924
Laid down	26 Apr 1925	May 1925	8 Jul 1925	11 Sep 1925	18 May 1925	1 Aug 1925
Launched	1 Apr 1927	26 Jun 1926	28 Aug 1926	15 Nov 1926	30 Jun 1926	9 Sep 1926
Manned for trials	30 Apr 1927	1 Mar 1928	10 Apr 1927	10 Jul 1927	1 Feb 1927	1 May 1927
Acceptance trials	10 Jun 1927	17 Aug 1928	12 May 1927	10 Aug 1927	13 Apr 1927	30 Jun 1927
Commissioned	1 Jan 1929	10 Apr 1929	15 Oct 1927	1 Dec 1927	1 Aug 1927	15 Oct 1927
Completed	1 Jul 1929	15 Jul 1929	20 Jan 1928	1 Feb 1928	6 Feb 1928	15 Mar 1928
Entered service	Oct 1929	17 Dec 1929	20 Apr 1928	20 Apr 1928	20 Apr 1928	20 Apr 1928

Name	Brestois	Boulonnais	Basque	Bordelais
Programme	1925	1925	1925	1925
Prog. no.	64	65	66	67
Project no.	–	–	–	–
Builder	Dubigeon Nantes	CNF Caen	Worms Le Trait	FC Gir Bordeaux
Order	27 Apr 1926	5 Jun 1926	1 Jun 1926	1 May 1926
Laid down	17 May 1926	4 May 1926	18 Sep 1926	19 Nov 1926
Launched	19 May 1927	1 Jun 1927	25 May 1929	23 May 1928
Manned for trials	1 Nov 1927	1 Jan 1928	1 Aug 1929	1 Apr 1929
Acceptance trials	7 Dec 1927	27 Feb 1928	10 Sep 1929	20 Jun 1929
Commissioned	1 Apr 1928	1 May 1928	20 Jan 1930	1 Dec 1929
Completed	15 Jun 1928	25 Jun 1928	5 Mar 1931	8 Apr 1930
Entered service	9 Dec 1928	13 Aug 1929	7 Mar 1931	19 Apr 1930

Name	Forbin	Frondeur	Fougueux	Foudroyant
Programme	1926	1926	1926	1926
Prog. no.	81	82	83	84
Project no.	T1	T2	T3	T4
Builder	FCM Graville	CNF Caen	ACB Nantes	D&B Bordeaux
Order	14 Apr 1927	21 Apr 1927	3 May 1927	21 Apr 1927
Laid down	29 Jun 1927	9 Nov 1927	21 Sep 1927	28 Jul 1927
Launched	17 Jul 1928	20 Jun 1929	4 Aug 1928	24 Apr 1929
Manned for trials	1 May 1929	1 Apr 1930	20 Apr 1929	1 Jan 1930
Acceptance trials	7 Aug 1929	12 Nov 1930	28 Jun 1929	3 Mar 1930
Commissioned	20 Jan 1930	30 Jun 1931	15 Nov 1929	15 Jun 1930
Completed	1 May 1930	20 Oct 1931	15 Jun 1930	10 Oct 1930
Entered service	12 Dec 1930	30 Oct 1931	4 Jul 1930	24 Oct 1930

– The four ships of the 1926 estimates were to have been given historic adjectival names beginning with 'F': *Flamboyant*, *Frondeur*, *Fougueux* and *Foudroyant*. However, at the last moment, it appears that an officer who knew Toulon well pointed out that *Flamboyant* was the name of a well-known local brothel, and the name *Forbin* was substituted.[3] Claude de Forbin-Gardanne (1656–1733) was a famous French seaman who fought against the English alongside Jean Bart and notably at the Battle of Beachy Head (Fr. Bévéziers) in 1690 during the Nine Years War.

The designated *ports d'armement*, to which the ships were to be delivered following their builders' trials, were as follows:

- Cherbourg: *L'Adroit*, *Le Mars*, *Le Fortuné*, *Boulonnais*, *Basque*, *Forbin*, *Frondeur*.
- Lorient: *L'Alcyon*, *La Palme*, *La Railleuse*, *Brestois*, *Bordelais*, *Fougueux*, *Foudroyant*.

The hull of *L'Alcyon* was launched on 26 June 1926 at the Harfleur shipyard of F C Gironde, and then towed to Bordeaux for fitting out. She would be the last ship built at the Harfleur yard, which subsequently closed.

HULL AND GENERAL CONFIGURATION

There were only small differences in external appearance and internal layout between the *Bourrasque*s and the *L'Adroit* class as designed. Indeed, the six ships of the 1924 estimates were completed with the three tall funnels that were a feature of the *Bourrasque*s as designed. They would subsequently be reduced in height using the same formula.

Externally, the most obvious identification feature was the absence of the 75mm HA gun on its raised platform between the tubes, the two single 37mm AA being mounted abeam the after deckhouse (see below). The last sub-group (the four 'F's) also had their two searchlights on the centre-line (see below).

There were a number of adjustments to the internal layout outside the machinery spaces. The most significant change aft was that the magazine for reserve depth charges, which in the *Bourrasque*s had been located to port of the 130mm magazine for the main guns, was moved to the centre-line aft, the water tank which formerly occupied this compartment being

---

[3] The anecdote appears in Saibène (*op. cit.*).

GENERAL CHARACTERISTICS

Displacement:	1380 tonnes standard; 1515 tonnes normal*; 2000 tonnes full load
Dimensions:	Length 100.9m pp, 107.2m oa; beam 9.9m; draught 3.5m
Machinery:	Three Du Temple small-tube boilers, 18kg/cm^2 (216°) Two-shaft geared steam turbines 31,000CV for 33kts (designed)
Oil fuel:	386 tonnes; radius 3000nm at 15kts
Armament:	Four 130mm/40 Mle 1924 in single mountings (110rpg + 60 starshell) Two 37mm/60 Mle 1925 AA in single mountings (500rpg) Two/four 8mm Hotchkiss MG Mle 1914 in single mountings Six 550mm torpedoes Mle 1919D in two triple mountings Two DC chutes each for six 200kg depth charges (+ 4 reloads) Two Thornycroft depth charge throwers Mle 1918
Complement:	8 officers + 134 men peacetime 9 officers + 153 men wartime

* designed; normal displacement on completion was around 1650 tonnes.

Below: *La Railleuse* making 33.6 knots on speed trials on 17 April 1928. She was built by the Nantes shipyard of Dubigeon. She has her original tall funnels, but the 130mm guns are fitted with the modified shield. *(Chantiers de la Loire-Dubigeon, courtesy of Marc Saibène)*

divided into two (see General Arrangement plan). This arrangement had the advantage of placing the magazine directly below the DC chutes, so that depth charges could be lifted directly from the magazine and transferred to the twin loading hatches for the chutes by the same davit. The water tanks on either side served to isolate and protect the magazine.

The bulkhead for the forward boiler room was at Frame 36 in both types, and the additional 1.5 metres length of the *L'Adroit* class was used to extend the bow, thereby creating additional space for accommodation and stores, and providing greater buoyancy forward. In the *Bourrasque*s the main transverse watertight bulkheads forward were at Frames 39, 43, 48 and 53; in the *L'Adroit* class they were at Frames 40, 45, 49 and 53 *bis*.

With regard to construction, thicknesses and grades of steel were as for the *Bourrasque*s. Riveting was again employed throughout.

GROUND TACKLE AND NAVIGATION
Ground tackle, the rudder and its associated machinery, and compass provision were identical to the *Bourrasque*s.

MACHINERY
Steam for the turbine machinery was supplied by three small-tube boilers of the Du Temple type, as in the *Bourrasque*s. Again, the boilers were manufactured or sub-contracted by the shipbuilders but to a common design. In their overall dimensions, steam conditions and output they were identical to those fitted in the earlier ships.

The turbine machinery was also similar. Eight of the ships were fitted with Parsons turbines: four from the first sub-group, and two from each of the 2nd and 3rd sub-groups. Four ships (*L'Alcyon*, *Bordelais*, *Fougueux* and *Frondeur*) received Zoelly-Schneider turbines, and *L'Adroit* a Zoelly-Fives-Lille model. One ship of the 2nd sub-group, *Basque*, was fitted with a new type of Rateau turbine designed by the Chantiers Bretagne, which was to prove far more successful than the model installed in *Orage* and *Ouragan*.

Performance on trials was on a par with the *Bourrasque*s, and all ships of the class comfortably sustained 30 knots in service. However, despite modifications to the gearing, it proved impossible to achieve the designed endurance of 3000nm at 15 knots. The best figures obtained were for the *Fougueux* of the 1926 estimates: 2010nm at 15 knots and 2138nm at 13 knots.

The production of electricity was as in the *Bourrasque*s, but with two Bettus-Loire generators fitted from the outset.

MAIN ARMAMENT
The new 130mm gun Mle 1924 incorporated a number of modifications with a view to improving on the

THE L'ADROIT CLASS

The *Torpilleur d'Escadre L'Adroit* 1927

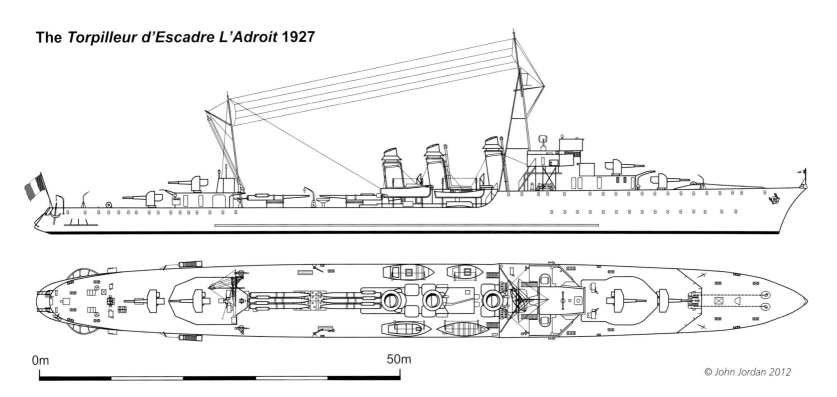

The profile and plan drawings are based on official plans for *L'Adroit* dated Dunkirk 16 November 1929. They show the ship with cut-down funnels; as completed she had the taller funnels which were a feature of the *Bourrasques*. Note the single 37mm Mle 1925 abeam the after deckhouse which replaced the single 75mm gun of the earlier ships, and the Thornycroft depth charge throwers Mle 1918 at the after end of the forecastle.

performance of the earlier Mle 1919. It was essentially a scaled-down version of the 138.6mm Mle 1923 developed for the next generation of *contre-torpilleurs*; indeed the drawings of the two guns in the CAA documentation are identical in every respect save overall dimensions.

The automatic loading tray retro-fitted to the Mle 1919 during the late 1920s (see Chapters 1 and 2) was fitted from the outset, and the trunnions of the gun were lowered by 16cm, making it easier to load at low angles of elevation. However, many of the less advanced features of the original mounting, in particular the Welin interrupted screw breech, were retained, and the addition of new safety locks meant that the designed firing cycle of 8–9rpm was never achieved. The first of the new generation of destroyer guns with a sliding breech influenced by German practice would be the 138.6mm Mle 1927 installed in the *contre-torpilleurs* of the *Aigle* class (see Chapter 5). Only then would a firing cycle in excess of 5–6rpm become a realistic proposition.

The guns on the *L'Adroit* class had an improved 'wrap-around' gunshield to shelter the gun crew from the elements and to provide some protection from shell splinters. It was the third shield of its type, and was enlarged in comparison with the shields fitted in the *Bourrasques*.

The regulation ammunition provision in peacetime was 110 rounds per gun, for a total of 440 shells and 462 cased charges, as in the *Bourrasques*. Following the decision to replace the 75mm HA gun with the lighter 37mm, 60 starshell rounds were provided, distributed between the fore and after magazines; there were also 70 practice rounds. The electrically-powered hoists were identical to the ones fitted in the *Bourrasques*, with the upper reception trays behind

Left: View aft from the crow's nest of *Frondeur* during fitting out. Note the square anti-slip steel plates welded to the deck amidships. From the 37mm mountings to the stern the deck was covered with red linoleum. *(Yannick Iffinger collection, courtesy of Marc Saibène)*

L'Adroit: General Arrangement Plans

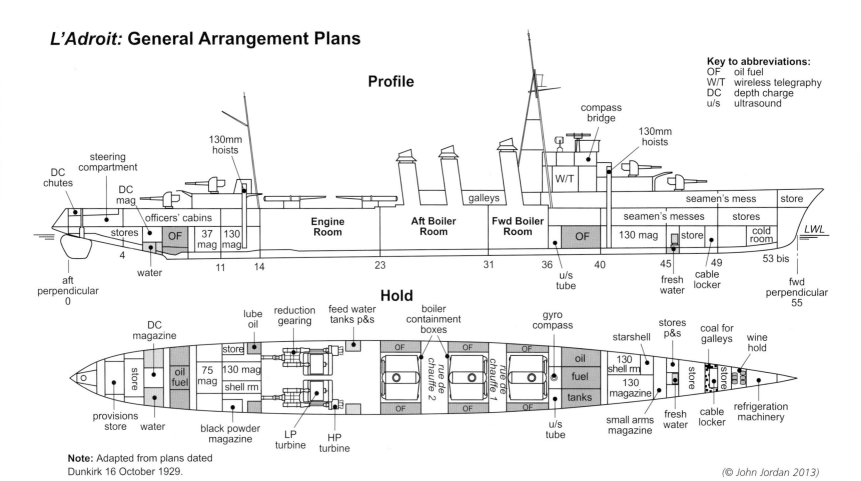

Note: Adapted from plans dated Dunkirk 16 October 1929.

(© John Jordan 2013)

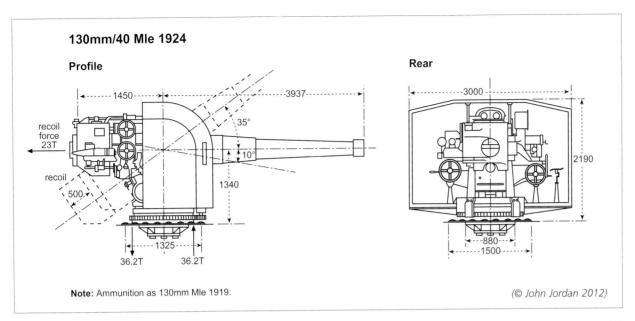

(© John Jordan 2012)

no.2 gun and forward of no.3 gun, and intermediate distribution positions behind no.1 gun and forward of no.4 gun. Shells and cartridges continued to be transferred by hand either to the ready-use stowage racks or directly to the breech of the guns, but the French were already experimenting with the brass ammunition chutes (*gouttières*) which would be a feature of the later *contre-torpilleurs*. Ready-use stowage was provided for 24 rounds per gun, as in the *Bourrasques*.

Fire control arrangements were also identical to the *Bourrasques*. All fourteen ships were provided with a simple 3-metre SOM coincidence rangefinder (Mle B.1926), fitted on a lightweight pedestal atop the upper bridge. Data was processed in the Transmitting Station (*PC Artillerie*) by a Mle 1923B electro-mechanical computer; elevation, deflection and training data were then transmitted directly to the mountings,

which were fitted with Granat GD II and GD III FTP receivers (see Chapter 1).

The 1924 and 1925 ships had their two 75cm searchlight projectors installed atop the forward superstructure, as in the *Bourrasques*. However, by the time the ships of the third sub-group had been laid down this arrangement was recognised as unsatisfactory, and the last four ships of the class had the searchlights realigned fore and aft on the centre-line. The forward searchlight was mounted on a platform projecting from the tripod foremast, the after searchlight above the engine room access ladders, between the torpedo tubes. This layout proved far superior in service.

ANTI-AIRCRAFT WEAPONS

In place of the single 75mm HA of the *Bourrasques*, the *L'Adroit* class was fitted with two single 37mm Mle 1925 guns, which were mounted directly on the upper deck abeam the after deckhouse. For its time the

130MM/40 MLE 1924

Gun Data
Construction	autofretted built-up
Weight of gun	3.81 tonnes
Breech mechanism	Welin interrupted screw
Ammunition type	separate
Projectiles	OPFA Mle 1923 (32.05kg)
	OEA Mle 1923 (34.85kg)
	OEcl Mle 1925
Propellant	7.7kg BM9 in cartridge Mle 1919
Muzzle velocity	725m/s
Range at 35°	18,750m

Gun Mounting
Designation	Mle 1924
Protection	3/5mm
Weight of mounting	12.7 tonnes
Elevation	–10° / +35°
Loading angle	not above 15°
Firing cycle	5–6rpm

Notes:
Mle	*Modèle*	Model
OPFA	*Obus de Perforation en Fonte Aciérée*	Semi-Armour Piercing (SAP)
OEA	*Obus Explosif en Acier*	High Explosive (HE)
OEcl	*Obus Eclairant*	Starshell

37/50 MLE 1925

Gun Data
Weight of gun	158kg
Ammunition type	fixed
Projectiles	OEA Mle 1925 (0.73kg)
	OI Mle 1924 (0.73kg)
Propellant	BM2 in cartridge (0.3kg)
Complete round	
weight	2.8kg
dimensions	408mm x 61mm
Muzzle velocity	810m/s
Max. range	8000m theoretical
	5000m effective

Mounting Data
Mounting designation	CAS Mle 1925
Weight of mounting	470 kg
Elevation of guns	–15° / +80°
Firing cycle	20rpm

Notes:
Mle	*Modèle*	Model
OEA	*Obus Explosif en Acier*	High Explosive (HE)
OI	*Obus Incendiaire*	Incendiary shell
CAS	*Contre-Avions Simple*	AA single mounting

Opposite: A fine starboard quarter view of *Boulonnais* at sea in October 1930, shortly after completion, when she was serving as lead ship of the 1st DT (hull number: 11) in the 1st *Escadrille* of the 1st Squadron (Mediterranean). The funnel bands and the *cartouche* with the ship's name are blue. Note the white-painted concentration dial aft. (*Marius Bar*)

37mm Mle 1925 was a useful weapon, capable of engaging attacking aircraft out to 5000m. It had a sliding breech and was fed from magazines of six rounds. However, the practical rate of fire was limited to 20rpm, which meant that it would be outclassed as an AA weapon when higher-performance aircraft began to appear during the mid-1930s. There was also no initial provision for remote fire control, and the guns fired through open sights.

The 37mm magazine was abaft the after 130mm magazine – it was formerly the 75mm magazine in the *Bourrasque*s (see GA plans). The peacetime allocation was 500 rounds per gun, of which 150 (i.e. 25 magazines) were stowed in ready-use lockers close to each of the two mountings.

As in the *Bourrasque*s, two 8mm Hotchkiss MG Mle 1914 were embarked for self-defence against strafing aircraft; a twin mounting Mle 1926 was available from 1929. The machine guns were normally stowed below decks, and when required were mounted on pedestals on the forecastle deck abeam the bridge. A total of 20,500 combat rounds and 2400 practice rounds could be carried in the small arms magazine forward.

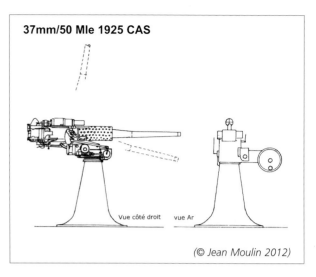

(© Jean Moulin 2012)

TORPEDOES
The torpedo armament and fire control arrangements were identical to those of the *Bourrasque*s.

ANTI-SUBMARINE WEAPONS AND DETECTION APPARATUS
The *L'Adroit* class had two stern chutes each for six 200kg Guiraud depth charges. Like the *Bourrasque*s, they were also to have been fitted with four Thornycroft depth charge throwers Mle 1918, but whereas in the former these were suppressed before the ships were completed, in the *L'Adroit* class a decision was made (9 May 1927) to install two out of the four DCTs. The rationale for this decision is unclear, but it may have been related to the installation of the 37mm light AA guns in place of the 75mm HA, which resulted in topweight savings; the greater theoretical buoyancy of the bow may also have been a factor. The two depth charge throwers were installed at the after end of the forecastle, and three 100kg depth charges per thrower were provided.

There was provision for an active ultrasonic device, the 450mm tube being located between the transverse fuel tanks and the forward boiler room, as in the *Bourrasque*s (see GA plans). Indeed the compartment in which the tube was to be housed was enlarged. However, the equipment was never fitted following the unsuccessful trials aboard the *Bourrasque*s (see Chapter 2).

COMMUNICATIONS
The communications outfit was identical to that of the *Bourrasque* class.

BOATS
The complement of boats was identical to that of the *Bourrasque* class.

COMPLEMENT
The regulation peacetime complement of these ships comprised eight officers and 134 men, as in the *Bourrasque*s. Likewise, the regulation wartime complement was nine officers and 153 men.

There was one small change in the layout of the accommodation. In the *Bourrasque*s the CO's sleeping cabin was right next to the after bulkhead of the engine room (see drawing p.50), which was undoubtedly the subject of much adverse comment when the

Below: *Basque* at her moorings at Brest during 1936, when she carried the hull number '42'. Note the colours of the province of Navarre flying from the foremast top. No.1 gun is trained to port at full elevation. *(Marc Saibène collection)*

Bottom: *Frondeur* shortly after her completion. She joined the 11th DT (3rd *Escadrille*, Mediterranean) wearing the hull number '119' on 1 November 1931, and the photo probably dates from this period, as the hull number was changed to '115' shortly afterwards. *(US Navy NH 55990, courtesy of A D Baker III)*

THE L'ADROIT CLASS

early ships entered service. In the *L'Adroit* class the CO's apartments were so arranged that the sleeping cabin was insulated from the engine room bulkhead by the captain's bathroom.

EVALUATION

The destroyers of the *L'Adroit* class had similar qualities to their predecessors and in many respects were a marked improvement. The designed metacentric height of 0.57m (vs. 0.45m) was generally met, and the slightly broader beam (all ships) and the longer bilge keels of the ships of the 1925 and 1926 estimates made them steadier sea-boats. Once the initial problems with the Zoelly turbines had been satisfactorily resolved they could sustain high speeds for long periods. The main guns were easier to operate than the Mle 1919, although the instability of the platform meant that they could still be fired only as the ship passed through the horizontal, which in practice slowed the rate of fire.

However, like their predecessors of the *Bourrasque* class, they were 130 tonnes overweight on completion; they rolled heavily when the sea was running from the stern quarter, and heeled dramatically when the rudder was activated at high speed. The hulls were too lightly built, and the plating was easily damaged by any contact when coming alongside. The auxiliary machinery was unreliable and prone to regular breakdown, as were the breeches of the guns. Fuel consumption on cruise turbines remained excessive, a problem which would come to the fore during the early war period, when the ships were employed on convoy escort duties.

The designed service speed of 30 knots of the *L'Adroit* class would be more than adequate when operating with the elderly dreadnoughts which still formed the core of the French battle fleet throughout the 1920s. However, their speed margin over the 29-knot *Dunkerque* and *Strasbourg* would prove to be totally inadequate, and during the 1930s the three-funnelled *Bourrasque* and *L'Adroit* classes would give way to a radically new type of *torpilleur d'escadre*, the 36-knot *Le Hardi* class (see Chapter 9).

MODIFICATIONS 1926 TO 1939
Main guns

Concentration dials were fitted from 1930 onwards (see Chapter 1). The forward dial was affixed to the face of the upper bridge; the after dial was installed on a platform above the after 130mm hoists, as in the *Bourrasques*.

An EMG directive of 28 November 1934 stated that the original 3-metre coincidence rangefinder was to be replaced by a stereoscopic model with a 4-metre base. The *Bordelais* was equipped with the new RF in 1935, followed by *Le Mars* and *L'Adroit* in January 1936. The

Below: An unusual aerial view of *Frondeur*, the last of the 1500-tonne type to enter service. Note the revised layout of the searchlight projectors in the four ships of the 1926 estimates, with the forward searchlight on a circular platform projecting from the foremast and the after projector above the engine room access ladders between the torpedo tubes. (*SHD Marine, courtesy of Marc Saibène*)

Above: *L'Adroit* (42) moored alongside the *contre-torpilleur Valmy* (3-) at Brest in January 1935. Note the marked difference in size between the two ships.

Right: *Bordelais* (112) in 1934, when she was serving as the lead ship of the 11th DT. The swallow-tailed pennant of the commanding officer 3rd *Escadrille* of the 1st Squadron (Mediterranean) is flying at the foremast. In the background is her sister *Fougueux* (114). *(Marc Saibène collection)*

four ships of the 1926 estimates were subsequently fitted with the new 5-metre S rangefinder (PC.1936): *Foudroyant* received hers in November 1936, and her three sisters in April 1937. The foremast searchlight platform was modified to enable the rangefinder to train through 360 degrees.

In 1935 Cherbourg Dockyard was tasked with the design of a light rangefinder turret to be retro-fitted in all the early *torpilleurs* and *contre-torpilleurs*.[4] It appears that *L'Alcyon* was the first ship of the class to be so fitted during repairs at Toulon which lasted until 21 January 1936. *Frondeur* and *Le Mars* received theirs in 1936, followed by *La Palme* in April 1937 and *Le Fortuné* in early 1938. By the outbreak of war in September 1939 all ships of the class had been so equipped.

In 1938–9 the *L'Adroit* class, like the *Bourrasque*s, were issued with a variant of the 130mm SAP shell (OPfK Mle 1925) with a colorant that served to distinguish the shell splashes of the individual ships of each division.

Air defence
In October 1933 it was decided that a 1-metre stereoscopic rangefinder was to be fitted behind the after concentration dial, as in the *Bourrasque*s, to provide range and bearing data for the 37mm CAS. At the same time it was proposed to replace the original 8mm MG on the forecastle by the new twin 13.2mm Hotchkiss MG, but a shortage of mountings made this impossible to implement until the late 1930s (see below). However, a telephone network linking the 37mm and 8mm mountings with the rangefinder was installed

Anti-submarine warfare
Three successive Notes dated April 1931 to June 1933 proposed the fitting of the *torpilleurs* of the *L'Adroit* class as fast minesweepers to clear a path ahead of the battle fleet. *Basque* was the first to be fitted in 1933, followed by *Bordelais* and the four ships of the 1926 estimates in 1934; the remaining ships of the class were modified 1935–6.

The installation comprised two C6 paravanes. A channel 164 metres wide could be swept at a speed of 20 knots; the cables were 230m long and the paravanes were towed at a depth of 15 metres.

Following a decision of 9 November 1938, installations for Ginocchio torpedoes were to be made aboard certain destroyers of the 1500-tonne type, but the measure was not implemented; deployment of the

---
[4] It was subsequently decided not to fit this in the *Bourrasque*s due to topweight problems (see Chapter 2).

THE L'ADROIT CLASS

Ginocchio torpedo aboard these ships was finally abandoned in October 1939.

Communications
The W/T outfit was progressively modernised from 1934. The D-100 long-wave transmitter was modified, and the V-28 transmitter replaced by a type 1934 600W medium-wave transmitter. An E-20 500W short-wave transmitter was fitted for tactical communications. Around 1938 the ships received a combined short/medium-wave transmitter.

MODIFICATIONS 1939 TO 1940
Although stability was superior to the *Bourrasque*s, it remained a concern for the *torpilleurs* of the *L'Adroit* class. First one, then two torpedoes were disembarked to compensate for the weight of proposed additions, and in January 1940 it was proposed to land gun

Right and below: Two views of a 130mm Mle 1924 being installed aboard a destroyer of the *L'Adroit* class: the view of the left-hand side shows the trainer's seat and the hand-wheels for training and elevation; the view of the right side, the seat for the gunlayer and the hand-wheel for elevation. Note the Granat GD II dials for tangent elevation and deflection. In the view of the left side of the mounting, note the five expendable arbors for the Thornycroft Mle 1918 depth charge throwers stacked on the deck edge. *(SHD Marine, courtesy of Marc Saibène)*

THE L'ADROIT CLASS

Left: Loading a 130mm Mle 1924 gun on board a destroyer of the *L'Adroit* class. The trainer can be seen seated at left, inside the shield. A cartridge is being loaded by hand into the breech. *(SHD Marine, courtesy of Marc Saibène)*

no.4, and to replace it with two additional Thornycroft depth charge throwers. The gun was disembarked from eight of the fourteen ships, but retained on *Brestois*, *Foudroyant* and *Boulonnais* of the 5th DT, which had been detached to Dunkirk, on *Fougueux* and *Frondeur* of the 2nd DT, and on *Forbin* of the 9th DT. The depth charge throwers would never reach the dockyards, and none was installed; racks for light 35kg depth charges were installed as an interim measure (see also Chapter 2).

ANTI-SUBMARINE WARFARE

In early 1939 it was decided to fit the 'Multispot' passive hydrophone system in all ships of the class, and at least six ships are reported to have received this by the end of February of the same year. The French-developed ultrasonic underwater detection system designated SS1 was trialled in *La Palme*, *La Railleuse* and *Le Mars* (together with *Tornade* of the *Bourrasque* class, q.v.), and on 10 May 1939 sixteen Asdic 123 devices were ordered from Britain. Admiral Darlan, C-in-C of the French Navy, attempted to acquire a second, more substantial batch of Asdics, but British industry could barely furnish sufficient for the Royal Navy's own requirements, and it was October before the Admiralty was prepared to agree a new order of fifty: twenty-five Asdic 123 plus twenty-five of the improved Asdic 128.

The first delivery took place at Cherbourg during the second half of August 1939, and other deliveries then followed at a rate of two per month in conditions of the greatest secrecy. The boxes were addressed to the British Consul in Cherbourg, and despatched from there to the British consuls at Toulon, Brest, Lorient, Casablanca and Oran; for security reasons the equipment destined for French service was rechristened 'Alpha' in October 1939.

The first Asdic 123 was fitted in the *contre-torpilleur Tigre* at Toulon. The remaining systems were fitted in the other five *Jaguars* (see Chapter 1) and in nine ships of the *L'Adroit* class. Dates of installation were as follows:

Brestois	Cherbourg	Oct 1939
Boulonnais	Cherbourg	Dec 1939
Foudroyant	Cherbourg	Jan 1940
L'Alcyon	Oran	Dec 1939
Bordelais	Oran	Dec 1939?
Fougueux	Lorient	Mar 1940
L'Adroit	Lorient	Jan 1940?
Frondeur	Lorient	Feb 1940
Forbin	Toulon	Feb 1940[5]

The second batch of Asdics ordered in October 1939 was to have equipped the 18 *contre-torpilleurs* of the *Guépard*, *Aigle* and *Vauquelin* classes, nine anti-submarine sloops, and the remaining five ships of the *L'Adroit* class, four of which had been fitted with the French SS1 system. Installation was programmed to fit in with the delivery dates of the equipment and the scheduled refits of the ships in question.

All the mechanical and electrical elements of the Asdics, together with spares, were delivered by the British. The French dockyards simply had to provide the necessary cable runs and the 'sleeve' through which the sonar dome was lowered and retracted. This was a relatively simple task, as space had been provided in the designs for the eventual installation of a tube for an ultrasonic device. However, although

---

[5] Source: Marc Saibène, *op. cit.*

Right: A fine aerial overhead view of the forecastle, forward 130mm guns and bridge of *Bordelais* (T81), taken during mid-/late-1939. Note the black-painted concentration dial with its 12 graduations. *(US Navy NH 110750, courtesy of A D Baker III)*

Below: View from above of the no.1 (forecastle) mounting of *Fougueux*. The tricolore recognition markings painted on the gun shield suggest that the photo was taken some time between 1940 and 1942. *(Marc Saibène collection)*

many ships were readied to receive the equipment, the slow speed of delivery and the rapidly-deteriorating military situation meant that neither the Asdic dome nor the associated listening console was installed before the Armistice.

Refuelling
The same modifications were planned as for the *Bourrasque*s, but again no work was carried out before the Armistice.

Air defence
As in the *Bourrasque*s, 13.2mm Hotchkiss twin mountings (CAD) began to replace the 8mm MG on the forecastle from March 1939. The shortage of Hotchkiss CAD mountings led to division leaders being prioritised, and some ships had to wait until 1940.

The regulation provision of 13.2mm ammunition was for 2400 rounds, of which no fewer than 1500 were stowed in ready-use lockers close to the guns. The overall provision was doubled in July 1939, and the same instruction decreed the doubling of the combat provision of the 37mm mountings to 1000 rounds per gun.

During the preparations for the deployment of the 5th DT to Norway in April 1940, *Brestois* had a 37mm twin mounting Mle 1933 (CAD) fitted at Cherbourg. The twin mounting did not replace either of the single mountings (as in *Mistral* – see Chapter 2), but was installed in a tub atop the small housing between the torpedo tubes.

Finally, following their participation in the battles off Dunkirk in June 1940, *Fougueux* and *Frondeur* received the first of the new 25mm Hotchkiss Mle 1939 guns in the course of their repairs at Cherbourg. The single mounting was installed in a tub atop the after ammunition hoists. The mainmast was disembarked, in part to clear arcs for the gun but also to compensate for the added topweight; the W/T aerials were fixed to antenna supports on the third funnel. This paved the way for similar modifications that were made to the surviving ships of the class during 1940–2.

THE L'ADROIT CLASS

MODIFICATIONS 1940–2

Of the eleven ships which survived the early part of the war, eight were available to the Navy under the Vichy government:

- At Toulon:
  1st DT: *Bordelais*, *Le Mars*, *La Palme*
- At Casablanca:
  2nd DT: *Fougueux*, *Frondeur*, *L'Alcyon*
  5rd DT: *Brestois*, *Boulonnais*

The three ships of the 3rd DT, *Le Fortuné*, *Forbin* and *Basque*, were immobilised at Alexandria and could not be upgraded

On 11 February 1941 CV Dornon, head of the 1st bureau of the *Forces Maritimes Françaises* at Vichy, issued a circular on behalf of the French Admiralty in which a number of important changes to the ships' armament were proposed, and the roles of the *Bourrasque* and *L'Adroit* class were redefined, the latter being oriented toward anti-submarine warfare while the former would become fast fleet minesweepers. The main gun armament of all the surviving *torpilleurs* was to be restored, and anti-aircraft capabilities enhanced within the constraints imposed by the terms of the Armistice.

Main guns

Some ships had retained all four guns. It remained to reinstate no.4 gun in only the following ships:

- *Le Mars:* April 1941
- *La Palme:* July 1941
- *Bordelais:* August 1941
- *L'Alcyon:* September 1941

As in the case of the *Bourrasque*s, the release of the necessary breeches was authorised by the Armistice Commission only in June.

Air defence

It was proposed to fit each of the ships with a single 25mm Hotchkiss mounting Mle 1939/40 and two 13.2mm Browning MG (see Chapter 9 for data), to supplement the existing 37mm Mle 1925 CAS and 13.2mm Mle 1929 CAD.

Bizerte dockyard was tasked with implementing the proposal, and the arrangements in all except *Brestois* and *Boulonnais* would be modelled on that of the *Simoun* (see Chapter 2), the inspiration for which was the modifications to *Fougueux* and *Frondeur* at Cherbourg in June 1940.

The first ship taken in hand, *Boulonnais*, was fitted with a 37mm Mle 1933 CAD in a tub atop the engine room access ladders between the torpedo tubes, as in *Brestois* (see above). In order to clear arcs for the gun, the pole mainmast was disembarked and supports for the W/T aerials fitted to the third funnel. A platform for two single 13.2mm Browning MG was installed atop the after hoists. *Brestois*, which had initially retained her mainmast, was similarly modified at Bizerte and Algiers from July 1941.

The other ships would be fitted with a single 25mm Hotchkiss in a tub atop the after hoists with two single 13.2mm Browning MG on the quarterdeck (details differed from ship to ship).

Of the 2nd DT, only *L'Alcyon* remained to be modified, and she received her 25mm Hotchkiss and two 13.2mm Browning (on an improvised twin mounting) at Algiers in a refit from July to September 1941. Of the 1st DT, *Le Mars* and *La Palme* were modified at Bizerte in February/March and April/May respectively, although they would have to wait until June before the 25mm mountings were 'released' by the

Below: *La Palme* (T13) off Toulon on 25 August 1941, shortly after her refit at Bizerte. The mainmast has been suppressed and a new AA platform constructed atop the after hoists, although the 25mm Hotchkiss gun has yet to be fitted. Note the four Thornycroft depth charge throwers mounted on the stern. *(Marius Bar)*

Fougueux 1942

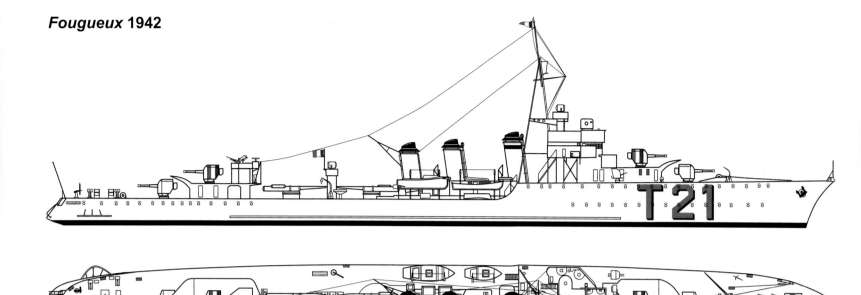

Fougueux as she appeared after March 1941. A platform for a 25mm Hotchkiss Mle 1939 gun and a 1-metre base HA rangefinder has been constructed atop the hoists for the after 130mm guns; the mainmast has been suppressed and the W/T antennae refixed to outriggers on the third funnel. Shielded 13.2mm Hotchkiss CAD are mounted on the forecastle, and these are complemented by two 13.2mm Browning MG on the quarterdeck. Four Thornycroft DCT Mle 1918, together with depth charge stowage, have also been installed on the quarterdeck.

(© John Jordan 2013)

Armistice Commission. *Bordelais* received all three guns directly during her refit July–September. In these three ships the original 37mm Mle 1925 CAS were replaced by the Mle 1933 CAD.

The 25mm Hotchkiss fitted during the 1941 refits was the improved Mle 1940, which had a significantly higher rate of fire than the Mle 1939 (350–400rpm vs. 250–300rpm theoretical).

The 25mm ammunition was in magazines containing 15 rounds. The regulation provision was for 800 rounds per gun, of which 150 rounds (10 magazines) were close to the gun in ready-use lockers, the remainder being stowed in the 37mm magazine aft.

The 13.2mm Hotchkiss twin mountings fitted during the early part of the war were retained unmodified except for the provision of shields in *Fougueux* and *Frondeur*. Some 8mm MG were also retained.

Anti-submarine warfare

Of the eight available ships, only *La Palme* and *Le Mars* had not been fitted with Asdic/Alpha prior to the Armistice. The installations aboard *Tigre* and *Panthère*, now in care & maintenance, were duly removed and refitted in the two *torpilleurs* in April 1941 at Bizerte and Toulon respectively.

The minesweeping paravanes on the quarterdeck were removed and transferred to the surviving ships of the *Bourrasque* class. The two Thornycroft depth charge throwers mounted at the after end of the forecastle were relocated to the stern, and two additional DCTs were paired with them. The regulation depth charge outfit was now:

- twelve 200kg DCs (2 x 6) in the chutes, plus three in reserve (magazine)
- four 100kg DCs on the throwers, four reloads in racks alongside, and twelve reserve (magazine)

The necessary work was undertaken at the same time as the AA modifications above.

Complement

On 28 August 1940, faced with punitive restrictions on the size of crews permitted by the Armistice Commission even for active ships, the French naval staff created a new corps of civilian personnel to perform 'hotel' and 'secretarial' functions on board ship and keep complements at wartime levels. Paid by the Navy while pursuing their respective careers without constraint, bakers, cooks, stewards, cobblers, tailors, secretaries and supply personnel were enlisted and kitted out in naval uniforms, distinguishable only by their ivory-coloured buttons (which gave them their nickname of *les corozos*). They formed part of the complement of the *torpilleurs* until November 1942.

CHAPTER 4
THE *GUÉPARD* CLASS

INTRODUCTION

Following the authorisation of the six *Jaguar*s in 1922, it would be three years before the next class of *contre-torpilleurs* featured in the French naval estimates. This allowed time to review the progress of the *Jaguar* design and to introduce a number of new features.

The development of a new, heavier gun with a calibre of 138.6mm was begun shortly after the failure of the twin 130mm mounting. It was envisaged that this would be fitted from the outset in the new ships and retro-fitted in the *Jaguar*s. The 138.6/40 Mle 1923 was successfully trialled in 1925, and subsequently went into production. However, the thirty guns ordered for the six *Jaguar*s would not be installed due to the design's topweight problems (see Chapter 1).

There was also dissatisfaction with the 75mm HA gun, which was heavy and relatively slow-firing, and for which no adequate system of fire control could be provided. On the new class of *contre-torpilleurs* it was originally to have been replaced by a 40mm 'pom-pom' gun similar to the Vickers models adopted in the UK and by the Italian *Regia Marina*. In the event a new single 37mm gun (Mle 1925) of French design and manufacture was adopted, as in the *L'Adroit* class; there would be four 37mm CAS (replacing two 75mm Mle 1924) in the *contre-torpilleurs*, and two (replacing a single 75mm) in the *torpilleurs* (see Chapter 3).

The adoption of a heavier main gun implied a larger hull, and the length of 119.5m (between perpendiculars) of the original *avant-projet* soon became 123.1m. There was a corresponding increase in beam, from 11.09m in the *Jaguar*s to 11.53m, to provide the necessary stability. Displacement increased accordingly, to 2690 tonnes, requiring a substantial increase in horsepower (from 50,000CV to 64,000CV) to provide a similar top speed.

There was a further new factor which would have a major impact on the design. France's first 'treaty' cruisers of the *Duquesne* class featured a 'unit' layout of the propulsion machinery, with alternating boiler rooms and engine rooms. This arrangement had the advantage of dividing the propulsion machinery into two completely independent groups of boilers and turbines, and minimised the risk that a single torpedo hit would immobilise the ship. It was particularly well-suited to a ship with minimal conventional armour protection, so the principle was equally applicable to the fast, lightly protected early 'treaty' cruisers and to the fast, totally unprotected *contre-torpilleurs*. It would be adopted for all subsequent ships of the latter type, and would be extended to the later *torpilleurs d'escadre* of the *Le Hardi* class (see Chapter 9).

Three *contre-torpilleurs* of the new design were authorised under the 1925 naval estimates.

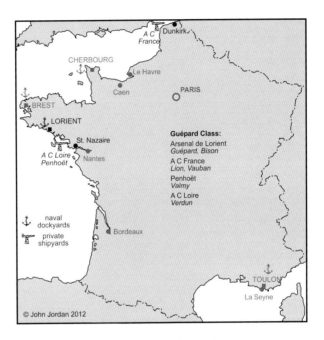

Consideration was then given to arming the next three ships (1926 estimates) with six 138.6mm guns in two single and two twin mountings – the twin mountings would have been superimposed fore and aft, thereby avoiding the isolated mounting amidships. The development of a twin mounting would then make possible an armament of eight 138.8mm (i.e. four twins) for the following ships of the 1927 estimates. It was estimated that six guns would require a ship displacing 2850–3000 tonnes, while an eight-gun ship would displace around 3500 tonnes. However, the failure to develop a satisfactory twin mounting led to the abandonment of both these projects – at least until the *Mogador* of 1932 (see Chapter 8). The three ships of the 1926 estimates would be virtually identical to the 1925 ships, and the six ships of the 1927 estimates (*Aigle* class – see Chapter 5) would also retain the same basic armament and layout.

The new *contre-torpilleurs* were initially costed at 28 million French francs per ship, a slight increase over the *Jaguar*s (26m FF). This would prove to be an underestimate; the final figure would be closer to 32m FF. As with the *Jaguar*s, the first two ships of the class were allocated to Lorient Naval Dockyard, which would be responsible for drawing up the working plans, and the remaining four hulls ordered from private shipyards. Two were ordered from Ateliers et Chantiers de France (Dunkirk), which was completing the *torpilleur d'escadre Bourrasque*, and which had been allocated the name-ship of the *L'Adroit* class the previous year. The fifth ship was allocated to Penhoët-

DISPLACEMENT

FOR NAVAL CONSTRUCTORS 'NORMAL' (or 'Legend') displacement was the measurement used as the basis for key calculations such as draught, speed, stability and endurance. For the Marine Nationale it included a fuel load which was roughly one third of capacity.

Practices differed between navies, so during the discussions on naval arms limitation at the Washington Conference of 1921–2 a new standard way of calculating displacement was proposed. The United States lacked the network of overseas bases available to the major colonial powers, and its ships needed to carry more fuel and distilled water reserves for the boilers. The US delegation argued strongly that it should not be penalised for this, and it was agreed that neither fuel nor reserve feed water would be included. The new displacement, calculated in either 'long tons' (2240lb = 1016kg) or metric tons (1000kg), would be referred to as 'standard' or 'Washington standard'.

Washington standard displacement – often abbreviated in French sources to 'tW' – was a purely theoretical displacement useful only for establishing comparability between the ships of different nations and for drawing up legal clauses relating to naval arms limitation. Ships could not sail without fuel, leading to a number of practical issues.

Prior to Washington, financial incentives – and penalties – for contractors had often been tied to the achievement of high speed on trials. Shipbuilders therefore often ran these trials at light displacement and without heavy items of equipment (such as guns) on board in order to secure the bonus stipulated in the contract. After Washington this practice changed: French warships now ran their speed trials at (or close to) their standard displacement so that the results for the different ships of a class were comparable. This became even more important following the London Conference of 1930; not only were 'destroyers' now included in the qualitative and quantitative limitations,[1] but basic characteristics including speed had to be reported to the other contracting powers.

French destroyer and submarine classes were generally referred to in official Navy documentation by their displacement rather than by the name of the lead ship (US Navy) or by the letter with which all the names began (UK). This often causes confusion, as reference is sometimes made to the designed (i.e. 'normal' or 'Legend') displacement and at others to the Washington standard displacement; moreover, the latter is sometimes expressed in long tons, and sometimes in metric tonnes. Thus the *Jaguar* class began life as *les contre-torpilleurs de 2400t*, but after Washington were frequently referred to in official documentation as *les contre-torpilleurs de 2126tW*. Sometimes 't' and 'tW' were replaced by the word *tonnes*, which only added to the confusion.[2]

The Washington standard displacement calculated for the *Guépard* class was 2436tW, so these ships frequently also came to be referred to as *les contre-torpilleurs de 2400 tonnes*, despite the fact that they were almost 300 tonnes heavier than their predecessors. Their official designation in the documentation of the period was *les contre-torpilleurs de 2690t*[3] (occasionally simplified to 2700t). Somewhat confusingly, their successors of the *Aigle* and *Vauquelin* classes are referred to in the official documentation as either *les contre-torpilleurs de 2480 tonnes* (their standard displacement expressed in metric tons) or as *les contre-torpilleurs de 2441 tonnes* (long tons)!

---

[1] The French failed to sign up to total tonnage allocations, but agreed the clauses on maximum displacement and gun calibre.
[2] Strictly, long tons should be *tonneaux*, but French practice is very 'loose' in this respect.
[3] In reference books of the period their standard displacement is given as 2436tW (long tons).

Saint Nazaire, which had built *Chacal* of the first series; the sixth to Ateliers et Chantiers de la Loire, which had built *Léopard* and *Lynx*. Following the problems experienced with the Rateau, Breguet and Zoelly turbine machinery of the first series, which were ongoing, the STCN requested that all the ships be fitted with Parsons turbines. However, this did not prove possible for contractual reasons, and the two ships built by A C France had Zoelly turbines built by Fives-Lille.

The ships of the 1925 estimates were given the names of wild beasts: *Guépard* ('Cheetah'), *Bison* and *Lion*.[1] However, in a break from previous practice, the three ships of the 1926 estimates were given 'historical' names beginning with 'V': *Vauban, Valmy* and *Verdun*.[2] Vauban (1633–1707) was a Marshal of France under Louis XIV, and was responsible for the design of a large network of land and coastal fortifications; Valmy (1792) was France's first major victory during the wars which followed the French Revolution; and Verdun (1916) was the greatest land battle of the First World War. The ships of the 1926 estimates were allocated not only a PN (*programme naval*) hull number, but new alphanumerical designations: D (later amended to Da) plus numbers 1–3.[3] Lorient was again to be the *port d'armement* for all six units of the class.

Each of the ships took some three years to build. The two units allocated to Lorient, *Guépard* and *Bison*, were laid down on the same day, on slipway no.7 and slipway no.5 respectively (see map p.22). However, the construction of *Guépard*, which was to be the lead ship of the class, was then prioritised and she would be launched a full six months before her sister.

Other differences in the timing of the various stages of construction (see table) were more closely related to shipyard practices. A C France was unusual in launching its ships almost fully fitted out, with shafts and machinery in place. Both *Lion* and *Vauban* were manned for trials one month before launch, and *Vauban* even had her boilers lit when she left the slipway! However, both these ships suffered serious problems with their Zoelly turbines during trials (see below) which delayed their entry into service.

HULL AND GENERAL CONFIGURATION

There were significant differences in layout between the *Guépards* and their predecessors of the *Jaguar* class. The arrangement of the main guns and the torpedo tubes was similar. However, the revised layout of the propulsion machinery dictated a different internal division of the hull and a modified layout above decks.

There were only two boiler rooms (vs. three), separated by the forward engine room in a 'unit' arrangement. Each of the boiler rooms housed two boilers face to face. As in the contemporary *torpilleurs d'escadre*

---

[1] Note that the two *contre-torpilleurs* proposed in April 1920 were to have been named *Guépard* and *Lion* (see Introduction).
[2] The split between the two estimates and the naming system has often led to these ships being referred to as the *Guépard/Valmy* class in reference books; however, all six ships were built to the same design, and detail differences between individual ships as completed were no greater than between the six *Jaguars*.
[3] In the same estimates, the 10,000-ton cruiser *Colbert* received the designation C1, the training cruiser *Jeanne d'Arc* the designation E1 ('E' for *école*) and the fleet torpedo boat *Forbin* the designation T1; submarines had the prefix 'Q'.

THE GUÉPARD CLASS

each of the boilers exhausted through its own slim funnel; the result was four funnels in two widely separated pairs, which gave these ships and their immediate successors of the *Aigle* and *Vauquelin* classes their distinctive appearance.[4]

The steam turbine machinery, which was designed to deliver 64,000CV (an increase of 28%) was significantly bulkier than that fitted in the *Jaguar*s, and required boiler rooms and engine rooms which individually were approximately two metres longer, so little was saved by dispensing with the third boiler room, and the machinery spaces as a proportion of the ship's length were roughly the same.

The construction methods employed for the hull were unchanged. The transverse frames again had a standard spacing of 2.1 metres, except at the stern and in the area of the machinery spaces, where it was reduced to approximately 1.6 metres. There were eleven main transverse bulkheads extending from the ship's bottom to the upper deck, dividing the hull into twelve watertight compartments designated A–L (see drawing).

The double bottom extended for most of the ship's length. Abeam the machinery spaces a continuous longitudinal bulkhead rose from the double bottom to the Main Deck, as in the *Jaguar*s, to enclose the oil fuel and feed water tanks and to provide some protection against flooding for these large compartments. There were additional transverse fuel tanks forward and aft of the machinery spaces.

The bridge structure was similar in layout to that of the *Jaguar*s, but there were variations in configuration which served to distinguish individual ships. The Upper Bridge of *Guépard*, *Valmy* and *Verdun* was broadly rectangular, whereas in *Bison*, *Lion* and *Vauban* it was rounded (see Bridge Decks drawings). The three 'V's also had a narrower face to the compass

---

[4] This series of eighteen ships was informally referred to as *les quatre-tuyaux* (lit. 'the four-pipers').

Below: *Valmy* being fitted out at the Penhoët shipyard of Saint-Nazaire. The forward 550mm torpedo mounting has just been lowered into place and is trained to starboard. The photo was taken from the bridge on 30 January 1929. *(CAA, Châtellerault)*

BUILDING DATA

Name	Guépard	Bison	Lion	Vauban	Valmy	Verdun
Programme	1925	1925	1925	1926	1926	1926
Prog. no.	68	69	70	78	79	80
Project no.	–	–	–	Da 1	Da 2	Da 3
Builder	Lorient	Lorient	ACF Dunkirk	ACF Dunkirk	Penhoët St-Naz.	ACL St-Naz.
Ordered	9 Oct 1925	9 Oct 1925	18 Aug 1926	25 Mar 1927	25 Mar 1927	25 Mar 1927
Laid down	14 Mar 1927	14 Mar 1927	27 Jul 1927	25 Mar 1929	5 May 1927	10 Aug 1927
Launched	19 Apr 1928	29 Oct 1928	5 Aug 1928	1 Feb 1930	19 May 1928	4 Jul 1928
Manned for trials	1 Oct 1928	1 July 1929	1 Jul 1929	1 Jan 1930	15 Feb 1929	1 May 1929
Acceptance trials	9 Feb 1929	17 Dec 1929	19 Oct 1929	22 Apr 1930	12 Apr 1929	18 Jul 1929
Commissioned	1 Jul 1929	15 Apr 1930	1 Dec 1930	1 Dec 1930	1 Aug 1929	1 Nov 1929
Completed	13 Aug 1929	10 Oct 1930	21 Jan 1931	9 Jan 1931	1 Jan 1930	1 Apr 1930
Entered service	16 Aug 1929	24 Oct 1930	5 Feb 1931	5 Feb 1931	26 Jan 1930	19 Apr 1930

platform with only three windows instead of seven.

There were three deckhouses abaft the break in the forecastle: the forward deckhouse (*roof avant*) housed the uptakes and ventilation trunking for the forward boiler room, as well as the bakery and the main galleys;[5] the centre deckhouse (*roof milieu*) the uptakes and ventilation trunking for the after boiler room, the machinery workshop and the emergency generators, as well as the galleys for the senior and junior officers; the after deckhouse (*roof arrière*) the secondary W/T office and the after ammunition hoists. The motor boat and motor launches were grouped around the forward deckhouse, but because the deckhouse was shorter than in the *Jaguars* the two boats on davits were relocated abeam the after deckhouse.

Originally there were to have been two light tripod masts, as in the *Jaguars*. However, in February 1928, by which time five out of the six ships had been laid

---
[5] *Bison* trialled oil-firing for galleys; traditionally, French galleys were fuelled by coal, the bunker being located in the bow around the cable locker (see Inboard Plan).

Below: Another view of *Valmy* being fitted out at the Penhoët shipyard. The photo, taken from the quayside on 29 March 1929, shows the after gun deck, with the blast screen and ready-use stowage for the after hoists already in place. Note the upper and lower chutes for the projectiles and cartridges; the lower projectile chute has been fitted, while the chutes for the gun platform are lying loose. *(CAA, Châtellerault)*

THE GUÉPARD CLASS

down, it was decided to replace the mainmast by a simple wooden pole, as in the contemporary *torpilleurs d'escadre*. The pole mainmast, like the foremast, was on the ship's axis.

The six ships of the *Guépard* class were of riveted steel throughout. The thickness of the hull plating varied between 9mm at the bow to 14mm over the machinery spaces. The decks were generally constructed of 6mm plates, increasing to 12mm over the boilers. The bilge keels were 48 metres long. The weight of the hull was between 960 and 965 tonnes, approximately 35% of normal displacement.

GROUND TACKLE AND NAVIGATION

There were two bower anchors in hawsepipes. These were of the 2360kg Hall stockless type, and were attached to seven shackles of 42mm chain cable, as in the *Jaguar*s. They were handled by a 30CV windlass located on the forecastle.

The kedge anchors were reduced in size and weight to enable them to be moored by a 7-metre launch, although the launches were poorly designed to perform this task. The weight of the anchors was 510t, 400t and 300t respectively. They were initially stowed flat on the upper deck close to the torpedo reload derricks, but were found to impede movement and were relocated shortly after the ships' completion to the after ends of the forecastle, where they were stowed vertically. The largest of the three anchors was disembarked from 1937. Because these anchors were lighter than those in the *Jaguar*s, it was possible to reduce the power of the stern capstan from 7.2CV to 5.4CV.

The single rudder was of the suspended, balanced type. The 50CV servo-motor could turn the rudder 32 degrees in 25–30 seconds. At a speed of 18 knots, and with 25 degrees of rudder, the turning circle was just under 700m.[6]

---

[6] Figures from trials of *Guépard* 22 March 1929.

GENERAL CHARACTERISTICS

Displacement:	2436 tons standard; 2690 tonnes normal; 3220 tonnes full load
Dimensions:	Length 123.1m pp, 130.2m oa; beam 11.5m; draught 4.3m
Machinery:	Four Du Temple small-tube boilers, 20kg/cm^2 (215°) Two-shaft geared steam turbines 64,000CV for 35.5kts (designed)
Oil fuel:	572 tonnes; radius 3000nm at 14.5kts, 750nm at 36kts
Armament:	Five 138.6mm/40 Mle 1923 in single mountings (100rpg + 85 starshell) Four 37mm/50 Mle 1925 AA in single mountings (500rpg) Four 8mm Hotchkiss MG Mle 1914 in twin mountings Six 550mm torpedoes Mle 1923DT in two triple mountings Two DC chutes each for eight 200kg depth charges (+ 8 reloads) Four Thornycroft depth charge throwers Mle 1918
Complement:	10 officers + 200 men peacetime 12 officers + 224 men wartime

Lion) housed in a compartment on the ship's axis on the Lower Deck directly beneath the bridge, with four repeaters. Six magnetic compasses were also fitted: one on the compass platform and one in the steering compartment (course), the others on the upper bridge, in the bridge wings, and at the forward end of the after deckhouse (bearing).

Ultrasonic depth sounders were fitted in at least four of the ships: a CET 31 model on *Verdun* in September 1931 and on *Guépard* in June 1936, a CET 32 on *Valmy* in October 1936, and a CET 32 as modified in 1935 on *Lion* in September 1936. The latter gave particularly good results: up to 200 metres at a speed of 17 knots.

MACHINERY

As with the *Jaguar*s, much of the internal hull of the ships was occupied by their powerful propulsion machinery; the machinery compartments again occupied 50% of the ships' length (pp), although due to advances in technology the weight of the propulsion machinery (804 tonnes) accounted for only 30% (vs. 35%) of standard displacement. This was a mixed

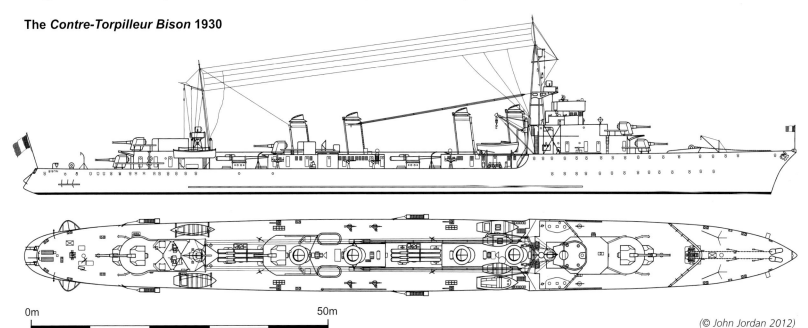

The *Contre-Torpilleur Bison* 1930

(© John Jordan 2012)

The profile and plan drawings are based on 'as fitted' plans for *Guépard* and *Bison* drawn up by the STCN and dated Lorient 23 October 1930. They show *Bison* as completed with the rounded upper bridge, and with four Thornycroft depth charge throwers plus stowage abeam the first two funnels. Note the early configuration of the ammunition chutes outboard of the 138.6mm gun mountings.

Guépard: General Arrangement Plans

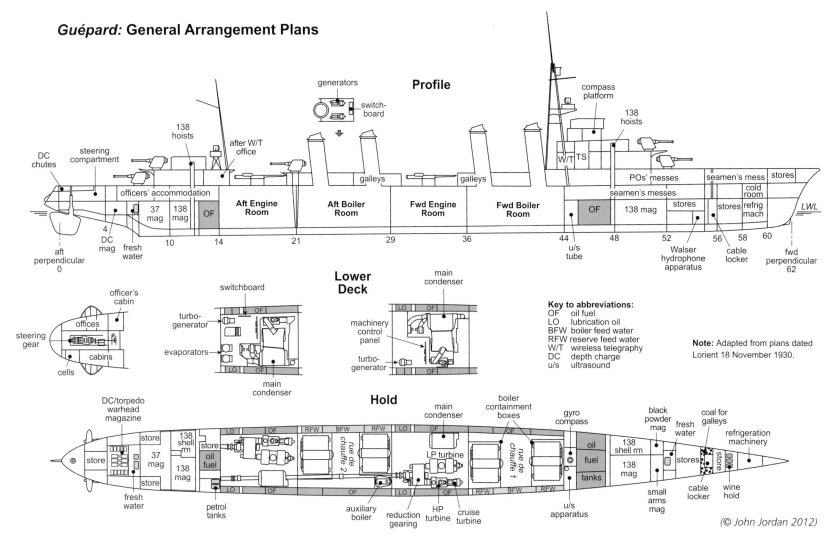

blessing, as in theory weights low in the ship reduced the height of the centre of gravity (CG), and the *Guépard*s mounted heavier guns and torpedoes than their predecessors, which had the effect of raising the CG.

Steam for the turbine machinery was supplied by four small-tube boilers of the Du Temple type of a common design. The main contractors and sub-contractors for the boilers and the turbines are listed in the accompanying table. The boilers operated at a higher steam pressure than those in the *Jaguar* and the *Bourrasque/L'Adroit* classes, 20kg/cm^2 (vs. 18kg/cm^2), and despite a significant increase in output, dimensions were similar to the boilers fitted in the *Bourrasque*s.

The four boilers were divided between two boiler rooms, each of which housed two boilers face to face with a single *rue de chauffe* between them. The two boiler rooms were separated by the engine room for the forward turbines. As in the earlier postwar destroyer and cruiser designs, each boiler was housed within its own gas-tight containment box. The adoption of a unit machinery arrangement had implications for the layout of the boilers. In order to allow the shaft for the forward turbines to be run to starboard of the boilers in the after boiler room, these two boilers were offset to port (see inboard plan); this was only possible by keeping the width of the boilers to 6.23m (vs. 6.8m in the *Jaguar*s) and by increasing the beam of the ship to 11.5m. In order to compensate for the asymmetry of the weight distribution, boiler no.2 in the forward boiler room was offset to starboard of the ship's axis (see General Arrangement plans).

The turbine machinery was in two engine rooms separated by the after boiler room. Each set of turbines

MACHINERY CONTRACTORS

	Builder	Turbine type	Main contractor	Sub-contractor
Guépard	Lorient	Parsons	F C Méditerranée	boilers: Penhoët fwd turbines: F C Méditerranée (Le Havre) aft turbines: A C Loire
Bison	Lorient	Parsons	Indret	boilers: Indret (to FCM plans) turbines: Indret (to FCM plans)
Lion	AC France	Zoelly	[shipyard]	boilers: ACF turbines: Fives-Lille
Vauban	AC France	Zoelly	[shipyard]	boilers: ACF turbines: Fives-Lille
Valmy	Penhoët	Parsons	[shipyard]	boilers: Penhoët main turbines: Penhoët cruise turbines: Compagnie Electromécanique
Verdun	A C Loire	Parsons	[shipyard]	2 boilers: F C Méditerranée (La Seyne) 2 boilers + turbines: A C Loire (St.-Nazaire/Nantes/St Denis)

THE GUÉPARD CLASS

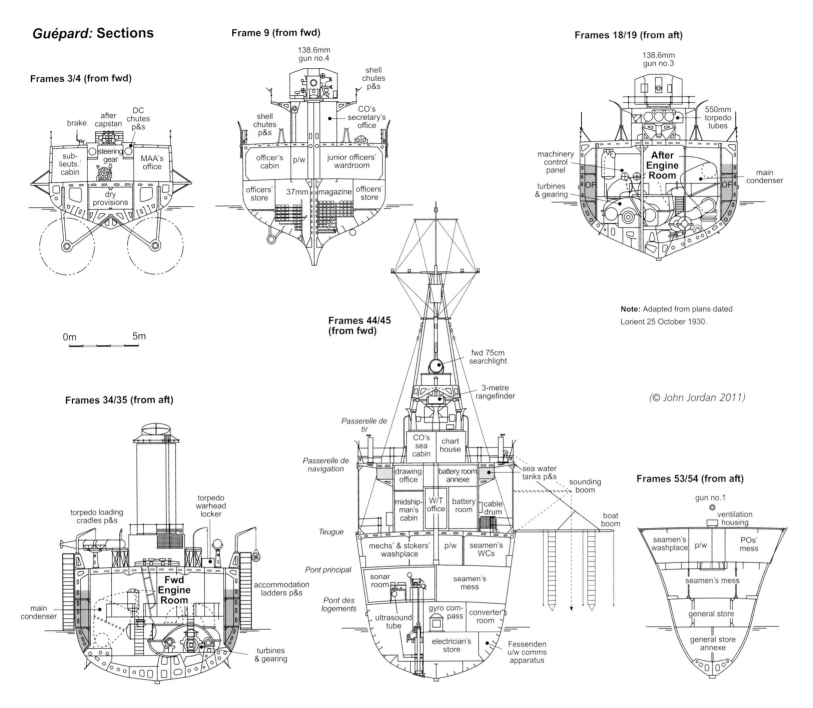

(© John Jordan 2011)

Note: Adapted from plans dated Lorient 25 October 1930.

was completely independent of the other, with its own pumps and other auxiliary machinery, and comprised a single high-pressure (HP) and a low-pressure (LP) turbine operating in series, with a separate cruise turbine clutched to the shaft of the HP turbine; the reversing turbine was on the shaft for the LP turbine and housed within the same casing. The HP turbine was outboard of the LP turbine; both drove the propeller shaft via single-reduction gearing. The forward set of turbines (Section G) powered the starboard shaft; the after set (Section I) the port shaft. When going ahead, steam was admitted to the cruise turbines up to approximately one tenth of maximum power (one twelfth in the two Zoelly-powered ships); steam was then admitted first to the HP, then to the LP turbines. The maximum power available for going astern was 16,000CV.

The starboard shaft had a length of 53.13m, the port shaft only 24.74m – hence the need to offset the boilers to balance the ship. Each shaft was fitted with a three-bladed propeller of bronze or high-resistance brass (*Valmy*, *Verdun*) with a diameter of 3.7 metres or 3.8 metres. *Valmy* initially experimented with a four-bladed propeller, but when she failed to achieve the required speed performance on trials these were replaced by three-bladed propellers of the type fitted in *Bison*, which proved particularly successful (they were also retro-fitted in *Verdun*).

The Parsons turbines proved robust and reliable and gave few problems on trials. However, the Zoelly turbines, which were fitted in *Lion* and *Vauban* (both built by A C France) and had also been installed in four ships of the *Bourrasque* class and four of the *L'Adroit* class (q.v.), suffered frequent breakdowns – deformation of the rotors, cracked turbine blades – which delayed the ships' entry into service and required

Above: *Verdun* is launched at the ACL shipyard on 4 July 1928. *(CAA, Châtellerault)*

MAXIMUM NORMAL POWER AND FULL POWER TRIALS

The trials were to be run at a mean displacement of 2,690 tonnes; adjustments were made for ships which displaced in excess of this figure at the start of the trial.

	Guépard	*Bison*	*Lion*	*Vauban*	*Valmy*	*Verdun*
Date of trial:	29 Mar 1929	20 Dec 1929	24 Sep 1930	6 Jun 1930	1 Jun 1929	26 Jun 1929
Displacement:	2694t	2662t	2794t	2779t	2975t	2926t
Average over 8 hours						
Shaft revolutions:	342rpm	346rpm	340rpm	341rpm	352rpm	352rpm
Horsepower:	69,120CV	64,990CV	66,258CV	56,018CV	69,580CV	72,120CV
Speed:	35.91kts	36.38kts	36.10kts	36.54kts	37.05kts	36.71kts
(corrected)	(–)	(36.23kts)	(35.47kts)	(36.25kts)	(37.01kts)	(36.80kts)
Fuel consumption:	28.47t/h	28.11t/h	30.63t/h	28.66t/h	28.41t/h	28.00t/h
Average 9th hour						
Shaft revolutions:	n/a	n/a	356rpm	352rpm	370rpm	365rpm
Horsepower:	n/a	n/a	70,148CV	59,235CV	76,948CV	76,240CV
Speed:	n/a	n/a	37.60kts	37.28kts	38.53kts	37.80kts
Fuel consumption:	n/a	n/a	33.45t/h	31.89t/h	31.28t/h	30.82t/h

Notes:
1. The date is that of the final trial, by which time some ships had replaced their propellers.
2. *Guépard* and *Bison* did not undertake the full power trial, so no figures are available.
3. The figures representing the best performance for the class are underlined.

Source : 9DD[1] series, SHD Vincennes.

THE GUÉPARD CLASS

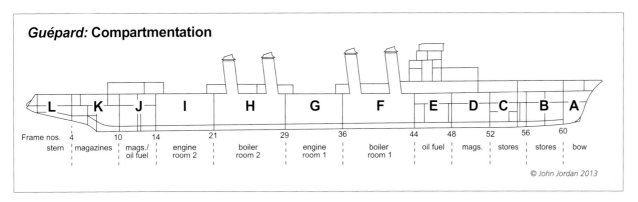

regular attention thereafter. *Lion* underwent several months of repairs following damage to her turbines and one of the shafts, while *Vauban* experienced condenser problems when she left for Lorient, and subsequently needed two months of repairs to one of her HP turbines.

All six ships sustained speeds in excess of 36 knots with 56,200–72,000CV at normal displacement over their 8-hour trials and a mean average of around 36.5 knots with forced draught over the ninth hour (see table). *Lion* was the fastest, with an impressive 38.5 knots on 77,000CV. On 8 February 1930 *Bison* recorded a speed of 40.6 knots with 81,000CV on her trials at Washington displacement

Peacetime fuel bunkerage was 360 tonnes, a figure which rose to 590 tonnes at deep load. Thirty-five tonnes of lubrication oil were carried, plus 126 tonnes of reserve feed water for the boilers, in side and bottom tanks. There were also 12 tonnes of fresh water for sanitation and 4 tonnes of drinking water for the crew in separate tanks fore and aft (see plan). Five hundred litres of petrol for the boats was stowed in tanks on deck, and 2280 litres of light oil were provided for the Bettus generators (see below). Following trials, endurance was calculated as 3450nm at 14.5 knots on cruise turbines alone with two boilers lit. As for other contemporary French flotilla craft, these figures would prove to be unduly optimistic. During the 'Phoney War' *Valmy* achieved only 2500nm at 7 knots on cruise

Below: *Verdun*, in an advanced state of completion, is dwarfed by the big cantilever crane serving the fitting-out quay in the Bassin de Penhoët. *(CAA, Châtellerault)*

turbines with one boiler on line and a second lit. It was estimated that at the maximum practical group speed of 31 knots, range was effectively 650nm.

As in the *Jaguars*, the engine rooms were on two levels, with platforms at the upper level at the after end of the engine rooms – the main condensers were directly above the LP turbines at the forward end of the engine rooms (see GA plans). The 'unit' arrangement adopted for the main turbine machinery was reflected in the layout of the turbo-generators, which instead of being grouped together were divided between the two engine rooms, with the main switchboard in the after room. The turbo-generators were rated at 80kW (106kW max.).

The auxiliary boiler, which supplied steam for the capstans and the steering motors, and also provided services for the crew, was located in the after boiler room, to starboard of boiler no.3, above the shaft for the forward turbines. Like the main boilers, it was rated at 20kg/cm^2.

To provide power when alongside and in an emergency, two oil-powered generators were provided. Each comprised a Bettus-Loire Type OCI 4 four-stroke motor and a Schneider U 110 dynamo and was rated at 22kW (26.5kW max.). As in the *Jaguars*, the emergency generators were located above-decks in the centre deckhouse.

MAIN ARMAMENT

Development of the 138.6mm Mle 1923 gun began shortly after the failure of the 130mm twin mounting (Mle 1921). The 138.6mm calibre – often referred to as 14cm during the immediate postwar period – was well-established in French naval service. The 14cm Mle 1910 was the secondary gun of the French dreadnoughts of the *Courbet* and *Bretagne* classes, and had proved particularly successful in service. However, this was an exceptionally long-barrelled gun for the period (55 calibres); it was too heavy and insufficiently 'handy' for a destroyer, and the Mle 1923 was kept to 40 calibres, the same length as the 130mm Mle 1919 which preceded it.

The French were not yet confident enough to move to a German-style sliding breech, and the 138.6/40 Mle 1923 was of conventional design, with a Welin interrupted screw breech. Problems were experienced with the extraction of the empty charge cases and with the rammer, which was underpowered. The first problem was quickly resolved, but the rammer problem persisted, particularly when the ship rolled in excess of 15 degrees. The gun shields were lightly constructed and – as designed – provided little protection for the gun crew, but did at least permit the fitting of the firing order receivers, lamps and telephones. Photographs of the ships on trials suggest that new 'wrap-around'

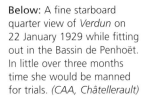

Below: A fine starboard quarter view of *Verdun* on 22 January 1929 while fitting out in the Bassin de Penhoët. In little over three months time she would be manned for trials. *(CAA, Châtellerault)*

138.6MM/40 MLE 1923

Gun Data
Construction	autofretted built-up
Weight of gun	4.1 tonnes
Breech mechanism	Welin interrupted screw
Ammunition type	separate
Projectiles	OPFA Mle 1924 (39.9kg)
	OEA Mle 1928 (40.4kg)
	OEcl Mle 1925 (30kg)
Propellant	9kg BM7 in cartridge Mle 1910
Muzzle velocity	700m/s
Range at 28°	18,200m

Mounting Data
Designation	Mle 1924
Protection	3mm
Weight of mounting	13.1 tonnes
Elevation	–10° / +35°
Loading angle	not above 15°
Firing cycle	5–6rpm

Notes:
Mle	*Modèle*	Model
OPFA	*Obus de Perforation en Fonte Aciérée*	Semi-Armour Piercing (SAP)
OEA	*Obus Explosif en Acier*	High Explosive (HE)
OEcl	*Obus Eclairant*	Starshell

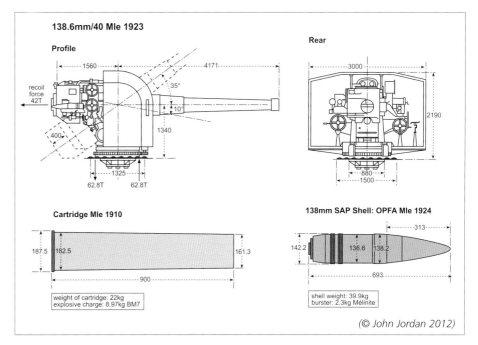

(© John Jordan 2012)

shields similar to those retro-fitted in the *Jaguar*s and the *Bourrasque*s were fitted on completion.

Maximum elevation of the 138.6mm Mle 1923 was 35 degrees, which gave a theoretical range of 18,200m, although it was difficult to spot fall of shot beyond 13,000m with the original 3-metre coincidence rangefinder. The 40kg shell was close to the limit for manual loading, and had to be transferred manually from the hoists to the breech of the guns. This was particularly difficult on a fast-moving, bucking ship, especially in heavy weather conditions when the loading numbers were exposed to the elements.[7] The French therefore devised ammunition chutes in the form of brass 'guttering' that ran from a position close to the hoists to the sides of the gun mountings. The port-side chutes were for shells, and the starboard-side chutes for cartridges. The chutes for the three upper guns ran along either side of their respective gun decks; those for no.2 gun began inboard of the forward hoists, those for no.4 gun outboard of the after hoists, which were more closely spaced. The chutes for no.1 gun began inside the upper forward deckhouse close to the hoists (see Bridge Decks drawing), while those for no.5 gun had to be located outboard of the after deckhouse, beneath the overhang of the gun deck (see accompanying drawing). The chutes for no.5 gun created an obstruction for movement around the deckhouse and the quarterdeck, and were rigged only when action was imminent; they were then dismantled and stowed. The chutes were so configured that they could supply the gun with ammunition when the gun was trained on the beam; later classes of *contre-torpilleur* would have all-round chutes that supplied ammunition when the gun was trained on extreme bearings.

---

[7] However, note that the *Guépard*s were the first postwar destroyers to have the forward hoists fully enclosed in a new deckhouse forward of the bridge; the hoists on the after deckhouse, which was less exposed to the seas, remained in the open with blast shields to the sides.

Below: *Verdun* on her Washington displacement trials on 21 September 1929, during which she briefly touched 40.20 knots; she as yet lacks her main guns, fire control apparatus and searchlight projectors. *(SHD Marine, courtesy of Marc Saibène)*

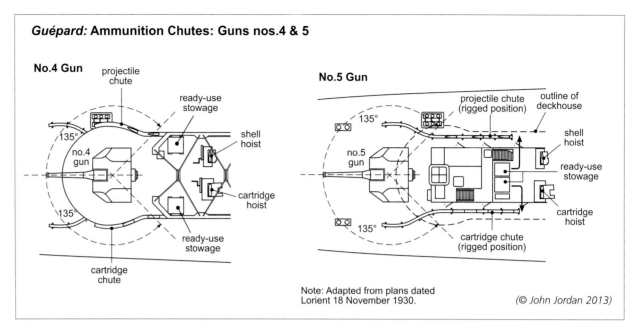

The regulation peacetime ammunition provision was 100 combat rounds per gun, for a total of 500 shells plus 85 starshell. The magazines were located fore and aft of the machinery spaces, as in the *Jaguar*s. Stowage racks for 24 rounds per gun were located close to the guns for mountings nos.1, 2, 4 and 5. The overhead cable intended to supply shells and charges to no.3 gun proved virtually unusable, and ammunition was generally moved to the gun manually along the upper deck and hoisted onto the centre deckhouse using block and tackle to replenish the ready-use racks, which housed 48 rounds.

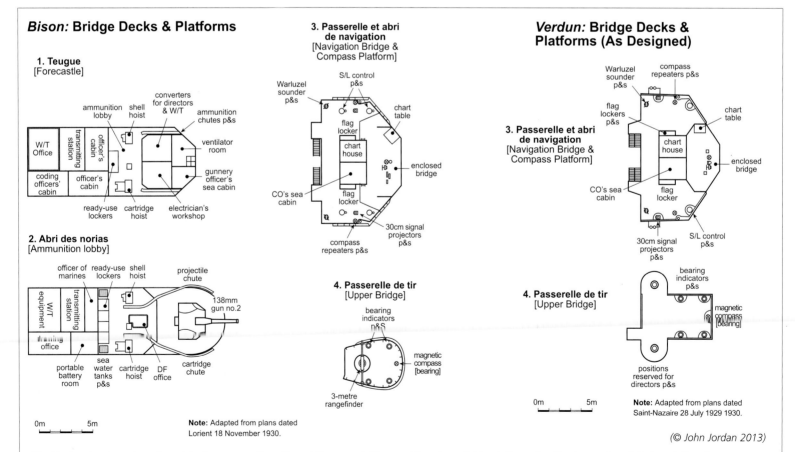

The *Verdun* drawings show the original square configuration of the upper bridge, and the planned side platforms for directors port and starboard. The director was never developed and the side platforms were suppressed. *Bison* was the first ship of the class to have the rounded face to the upper bridge. *Guépard* and *Valmy* (completed 1929 and 1930 respectively) had the square upper bridge of *Verdun*; *Lion* and *Vauban* (completed 1931) had the rounded upper bridge of *Bison*. Note the difference in the configuration of the navigation bridge of the three ships of the 1926 estimates ('V' sub-group); it had only three windows (vs. seven) on its face.

THE GUÉPARD CLASS

Left: An early view of *Verdun* shortly after entering service. As yet she has no hull number or funnel bands. *(Marc Saibène collection)*

Below, left: A single 37mm Mle 1925 gun on board one of the later four-funnelled *contre-torpilleurs*. This was the standard anti-aircraft gun mounted in French destroyers from 1928 to 1939, when the first examples of the twin Mle 1933 began to enter service. The device attached to the barrel is for firing a line across to a vessel coming alongside; a similar device can be seen attached to the barrel of one of the 37mm mountings on board the other ship. *(US Navy NH 110757, courtesy of A D Baker III)*

Below: *Bison* at Brest c.1933–4, when she was flagship of the *contre-torpilleur* group of the 2nd Squadron (Atlantic). *(Leo van Ginderen collection)*

In a Note dated 16 February 1929[8] it was proposed that all of the *contre-torpilleurs* of the 1925–1928 estimates be fitted with a director system for train and elevation of the main guns (*télépointage complet*). However, this would not be ready for some years,[9] and the six *Guépards* would have to make do initially with the 3-metre coincidence rangefinder (SOM Mle B.1926) fitted in the *Jaguars*, allied to the standard Mle 1923B electro-mechanical computer, which had only just entered service.

There were two 75cm BBT searchlight projectors. These were fitted fore and aft, as in the final series of 1500-tonne destroyers: the forward projector was on a platform projecting from the tripod foremast, the after projector on its own short tower abaft the mainmast. In *Guépard* four remote control positions were fitted so that the fore and after searchlights could be directed from the bridge wings on either side of the ship; the forward control was for the forward projector, the after control for the after projector (see Bridge Decks drawing). The BBT searchlight projectors were highly regarded; in a night exercise which took place in late November 1930, *Verdun* illuminated *Valmy* at 7000 metres. Separate 30cm signal projectors were fitted in the bridge wings.

ANTI-AIRCRAFT WEAPONS

In place of the two 75mm HA of the *Jaguars*, the *contre-torpilleurs* of the *Guépard* class were fitted from the outset with four single semi-automatic 37mm Mle 1925 guns, mounted directly on the upper deck abeam the third funnel. The location was not ideal; fore and after arcs were poor and only two guns were able to fire on each beam. However, topweight was a continuing consideration, and there was no space on the centre-

---
[8] 0346 EMG/1.
[9] The prototype system was first installed on the *Le Fantasque*s of the 1930 estimates (see Chapter 7).

Above: *Lynx* moored outboard of *Bison* at Brest in 1933. Note the heavier build of the new ships, which were a significant step up in size and power largely due to the increase in gun calibre.
(A D Baker III collection)

line unless the guns were mounted above the fore and after ammunition hoists.[10]

The 37mm magazine was abaft the after 138.6mm magazine. Stowage was provided for 600 rounds per gun, although the initial peacetime allocation was little more than half that (1250 rounds); 150rpg (i.e. 25 boxes) were stowed in ready-use lockers close to each of the four mountings.

Two twin 8mm Hotchkiss MG Mle 1914 were embarked for self-defence against strafing aircraft. The machine guns were normally stowed below-decks, and when required were affixed to pedestal mountings on the forecastle deck abeam the bridge. They would be replaced by 13.2mm Hotchkiss mountings from 1933.

[10] These would be the favoured locations during the Second World War, but anything heavier than a light machine gun would require weight compensation in the form of the suppression of the mainmast, and sometimes other heavy items of equipment such as rangefinders and torpedoes.

TORPEDOES

The *Guépard* class, like the *Jaguar*s and the *Bourrasque/L'Adroit* classes, was fitted with two triple mountings for 550mm torpedoes. However, the torpedo was a faster, more powerful model, the Mle 1923DT, and it was launched from a new triple mounting, the Mle 1924T. The tubes again used compressed air for launch, which was supplied by Sautter-Harlé compressors located in one of the two engine rooms, with a powder charge as back-up. In service they proved overly complex and were difficult to maintain.

The torpedo Mle 1923DT[11] (see illustration) was developed and built by the Naval Dockyard at Toulon. It was powered by a Brotherhood 4-cylinder radial engine built by Schneider; it was fuelled by alcohol, and had two speed settings. In the high-speed (GV) mode the torpedo had an impressive range of 9000m at 39 knots; even in the low-speed (PV) mode it could run for 13,000m at 35 knots. The AG-329 warhead fitted in the destroyer version of the torpedo[12] comprised 308kg of TNT with a 1.5kg detonator of picric acid.

The triple torpedo mountings were controlled from stations in the bridge wings equipped with a torpedo bearing indicator linked to a small central fire control computer, but the rangefinder for the main guns again had to be employed. Training data was transmitted to the torpedo mounting, which was equipped with a Granat GC II receiver, and an on-mount operator aligned the pointers to train the mounting. Depth, speed and gyroscope settings for the torpedo were set outside the tubes, and the order to launch was given from the bridge and executed on the mounting.

ANTI-SUBMARINE WEAPONS AND DETECTION APPARATUS

There were two chutes for Guiraud 200kg depth charges in the stern, as in the earlier French destroyers. However, the increase in size of the *Guépard* class made it possible to extend the chutes forward beneath the quarterdeck to accommodate an additional two depth charges on each side; each chute housed eight depth charges, and eight reserve charges were stowed in the below-decks magazine, which was substantially enlarged.

There were also four Thornycroft Mle 1918 depth

[11] D = *Distance*; T = *Torpilleur*
[12] There was a cruiser version with a more powerful 415kg warhead.

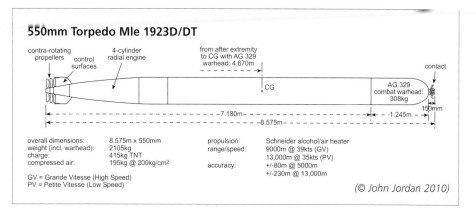

550mm Torpedo Mle 1923D/DT

overall dimensions:	8.575m x 550mm
weight (incl. warhead):	2105kg
charge:	415kg TNT
compressed air:	195kg @ 200kg/cm²
propulsion:	Schneider alcohol/air heater
range/speed:	9000m @ 39kts (GV)
	13,000m @ 35kts (PV)
accuracy:	+/-80m @ 5000m
	+/-230m @ 13,000m

GV = Grande Vitesse (High Speed)
PV = Petite Vitesse (Low Speed)

(© John Jordan 2010)

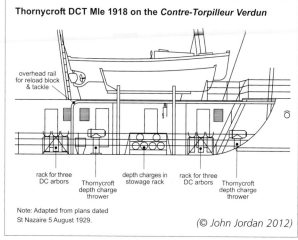

Thornycroft DCT Mle 1918 on the *Contre-Torpilleur Verdun*

Note: Adapted from plans dated St Nazaire 5 August 1929.

(© John Jordan 2012)

charge throwers on the upper deck abaft the break in the forecastle, disposed in pairs on either side of the ship with a stowage rack for six Guiraud 100kg depth charges between. A block and tackle suspended from an overhead rail was used to transfer the charges from the rack to the thrower; the expendable arbors were stowed against the sides of the deckhouse (see drawing of the arrangements in *Verdun*).

In a Note dated 19 October 1929 the Naval General Staff requested the installation of Walser listening apparatus aboard these ships. *Guépard* was duly fitted, the equipment being installed in the space reserved in compartment C (see GA plans); the other ships of the class were to have received it on completion. However, it quickly became apparent that the system was of little use above a certain speed because any signal was masked by self-noise, and installation was subsequently abandoned. The planned ultrasonic active device, for which space was provided forward of the machinery spaces, was also abandoned.

COMMUNICATIONS

The main W/T office, the *PC Radio*, was at the after end of the bridge block (see drawings), and was equipped primarily for long-range (strategic) communications up to 1000nm. It housed:

- an SFR type D-100 1kW long-wave transmitter operating in the 600–11,000m waveband
- an SIF long-wave receiver operating in the 2000–12,000m waveband
- an SFR 120W 'emergency' transmitter

The secondary W/T office was located in the after deckhouse, and was for medium-range (c.200nm radius) tactical communications with divisional units and shore stations. It housed:

- two E-20 short-wave tactical transmitters
- an OC 500W short-wave receiver

There were two E-20 receivers (one spare) in the Transmitting Station.

A space was reserved for a direction-finding office beneath the quarterdeck on the port side aft. However, this location proved unsuitable, and the DF office was later relocated to the bridge structure; the associated aerial was fitted forward of the compass platform.

BOATS

The boat outfit was similar to that of the *Jaguar*s, and comprised:

- one 7-metre motor boat
- one 7-metre motor launch
- one 7-metre pulling cutter
- one 7-metre whaler
- two 5-metre dinghies (one motorised)

There was also a 3.6-metre non-collapsible canvas 'Berthon' and a 3-metre punt.

On *Guépard* and *Bison*, which served as flagships for the destroyer flotillas, the 7-metre pulling cutter was replaced by a second motor launch. When *Verdun* served as a flagship, she embarked a second motor boat.

The whaler and the 7-metre pulling cutter were on davits abeam the after deckhouse. The other four boats were carried on athwartships rails between the first two funnels with the two larger boats outboard; they were handled by twin derricks fixed to the after end of the bridge.

The boats, which were sub-contracted to civilian pleasure-boat builders, were generally regarded as poorly designed and not well-suited to naval service, and the cylindrical engines of the motor launches were difficult to start. The twin derricks, which were powered by a single 24CV motor on the centre-line, failed to achieve their designed 5cm/sec, and 10–12cm/sec was the minimum speed at which boats could be lowered; braking resulted in jolting of the boats and was considered dangerous.

COMPLEMENT

The regulation peacetime complement of these ships comprised up to ten officers and 198 men. The function and rank of the officers were as follows:

- Commanding Officer (*Capitaine de frégate* = Commander)
- First/Executive Officer (*Capitaine de corvette* = Lieutenant-Commander)
- Officers i/c Guns and Underwater Weapons (*Lieutenants de vaisseau* = Lieutenants)
- two junior officers (*Enseignes de vaisseau* = Sub-Lieutenants)
- one Chief Engineering Officer (*Ingénieur mécanicien de 1re classe*)
- two junior engineering officers (*Ingénieurs mécaniciens de 2e/3e classe*)

If the ship was a division leader, the CO was a *Capitaine de vaisseau*, a *Capitaine de corvette* (or a *Lieutenant de vaisseau* with a staff qualification) was added as Chief of Staff, and the junior officer in charge of signal distribution (*Officier du chiffre* – coding officer) was a *Lieutenant de vaisseau*. On the other two ships of the division the other junior officer was replaced by a lieutenant of marines, and they embarked a Medical Officer (*Médecin de 1e classe*) and a Supply Officer (*Commissaire de 1e/2e classe*)

The crew, as of December 1930, comprised one Chief Petty Officer (engineer), eight Petty Officers, 25 POs 2nd class, who were specialists in the various departments of the ship, and 164 men.

Below: *Verdun* moored at the Milhaud piers at Toulon c.1932. The no.1 on the hull marks her out as the lead ship of the newly formed 7th DCT of the 1st Squadron (Mediterranean).

The wartime complement was fixed at twelve officers (+ one Medical Officer per division) and 224 men, of whom 34 were Petty Officer grade.

EVALUATION

The *Guépard* class had superior sea-keeping qualities to the *Jaguar*s, but some of the defects of the latter remained unresolved. The designed metacentric height was 0.68m, but GM as measured on trials was found to be only 0.56m. Tight turns or a strong crosswind resulted in a large angle of heel, and the ships had a pronounced roll, although this was longer and steadier than in the *Jaguar*s. They manoeuvred well due to the flexibility of their turbine machinery, but were particularly sensitive to the wind when manoeuvring at low speed. Their high silhouette was held to be responsible, and was much criticised by their commanding officers, who felt that with their four funnels and tall masts they presented too large and distinctive a target, particularly at night.

Initial problems with the turbine machinery were largely resolved during the early years of service, but the Navy continued to be unhappy with the Zoelly turbines, which would never again be fitted in French destroyers.

The 138.6mm gun was a solid, dependable weapon, despite its disappointingly slow rate of fire. During gunnery trials with the three ships of the 1926 estimates on 6 July 1930, the fire of *Valmy* was deemed to be well controlled, with tightly-grouped salvoes. The fire of *Vauban* was also rated excellent and well-controlled, despite a failure of the firing device in no.1 gun; dispersion was sometimes a problem. However, aboard *Verdun* a key component of the Granat receiver was dislodged by the concussion of firing and fell overboard. She lost all centralised elevation control, and the necessary data had to be communicated by radio. Because of this the group assessment was downgraded from 'excellent' to 'satisfactory'.

Fire control provision was still generally considered rudimentary and inadequate. Smoke drawn onto the upper bridge remained a problem, making rangefinder observations difficult in certain conditions; the rounded configuration of the upper bridge in three of the ships (see above) appears to have had little effect, and the problem was thought to be aggravated by the placing of the forward searchlight, which stopped a free flow of air to the forward funnel. The single 3-metre coincidence rangefinder initially fitted had inadequate base-length for long-range fire, and on after bearings was obstructed by the tripod foremast with its prominent searchlight platform. Although the proposed director system would not materialise in time for these ships, there would be constant upgrades to their rangefinder outfit during the 1930s.

The 550mm Mle 1923DT was a significantly more powerful weapon than the Mle 1919, and would arm all the subsequent classes of *torpilleur d'escadre* and *contre-torpilleur*.

MODIFICATIONS 1930 TO 1939
Main guns

Following trials aboard the *Vauquelin* class (see Chapter 6), the ammunition chutes were modified to improve supply, with the chutes for the upper guns (nos.2, 3 and 4) being extended to encircle the mounting. The modifications were made to *Valmy* and *Verdun* in 1936, *Lion* in 1937, and *Bison* in 1938; the remaining two ships may have been modified after 1939.

Fire Control

In August 1931[13] it was proposed to fit a second

---

[13] Note 1386 EMG/1 dated 26 August 1931.

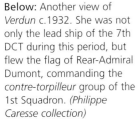

Below: Another view of *Verdun* c.1932. She was not only the lead ship of the 7th DCT during this period, but flew the flag of Rear-Admiral Dumont, commanding the *contre-torpilleur* group of the 1st Squadron. *(Philippe Caresse collection)*

THE *GUÉPARD* CLASS

Guépard 1942

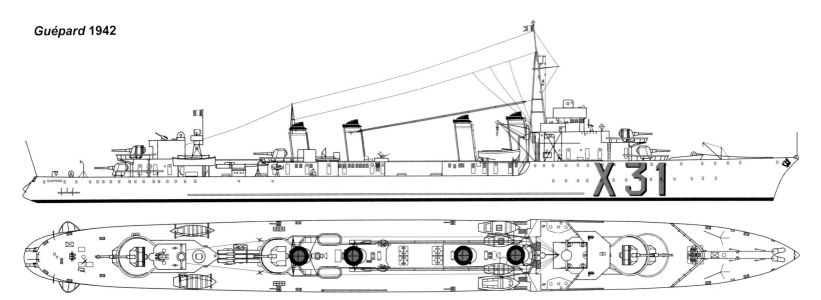

Guépard as she appeared following her refit at Toulon from September to November 1941. A platform for a 37mm CAD Mle 1933 mounting and two 1-metre HA rangefinders has been constructed atop the after 138.6mm hoists. The mainmast has been suppressed and the W/T antennae refixed to outriggers on the fourth funnel. Two 13.2mm Browning MG have been fitted in place of the 13.2mm Hotchkiss CAD forward of the bridge, and the latter mountings have been relocated to the forward end of the centre deckhouse. Only the after searchlight projector remains in place. The after fire control position, with its 4-metre base rangefinder, has been retained and integrated into the AA platform atop the hoists, but the forward triple torpedo mounting has been landed as weight compensation. (In the later four-funnelled *contre-torpilleurs* the torpedo tubes would be retained and the after fire control position suppressed.)

© John Jordan 2012

rangefinder aft to cover the 'blind' arcs astern of the main RF, at a cost of 150,000 FF per ship. A second Note dated 6 February 1932[14] proposed that the second rangefinder be fitted forward of no.4 gun, and that two 1-metre rangefinders be fitted for the light AA amidships, at the forward end of the centre deckhouse. A further Note of 23 November 1932[15] requested a study for the fitting of two 4-metre stereo rangefinders in place of the original 3-metre coincidence model. The after rangefinder, fitted with a protective hood, was subsequently trialled on *Bison* in December 1933. In August 1934 there was a ministerial directive to fit a secondary fire control position.[16]

The final installation for these ships, implemented during refits from 1936, was:

– an OPL 5-metre S rangefinder forward, in a light turret capable of accommodating two men
– an OPL 4-metre S rangefinder aft, forward of no.4 gun
– two 1-metre S rangefinders amidships

Fixed concentration dials were fitted from completion, located on the forward face of the bridge and abaft the mainmast respectively; in December 1932 it was proposed that the after dial be made trainable. With the fitting of short-wave radio from 1937 (see below) the concentration dials became redundant; they would be removed from the surviving ships of the class during the winter of 1941.

Air defence

From 1933 all six ships were fitted with two twin 13.2mm Hotchkiss machine guns (CAD). In *Bison, Lion* and *Vauban* they were initially installed on the forecastle abeam the deckhouse for no.2 gun mounting in place of the obsolescent 8mm MG, but on *Guépard*, *Valmy* and *Verdun* they were fitted on the upper deck, directly abaft the single 37mm guns.

During 1938–9 the 13.2mm CAD would be relocated to a platform forward of the bridge, atop the forward 138.6mm hoists.

Left: A tampion for one of the 138.6mm guns of *Verdun*. (Marc Saibène collection)

---
[14] Note 250 EMG/1.
[15] Note 2179 EMG/1.
[16] DM 16877 CM/4 dated 13 August 1934.

Anti-submarine warfare

In November 1931 the rear-admiral commanding the 2nd Squadron requested that the four Thornycroft depth charge throwers be disembarked to improve stability and sea-keeping (see also the remarks in Chapter 1). In a directive dated 28 January 1932[17] the Naval General Staff confirmed that the DCTs were to be removed from all the early *contre-torpilleurs*, but that the seatings should be retained for installation of a future model with improved characteristics.

Communications

The W/T outfit was upgraded during the late 1930s, the most significant addition being that of an SFR Mle 1937 VHF tactical radio for bridge-to-bridge voice communication in 1937. A medium-frequency direction-finding aerial was fitted forward of the bridge, and a DF office installed in the bridge structure.

MODIFICATIONS 1939 TO 1940
Anti-submarine warfare

Following the outbreak of war, Note CM 6273 CN/6 (8 October 1939) prescribed the restitution of the ships' anti-submarine capabilities, notably the re-embarkation of two of the original four Thornycroft depth charge throwers. These were duly fitted during the winter of 1939–40.

Bison also received an Asdic 128 during the lengthy repairs at Lorient (February to November 1939) which followed her collision with *Georges Leygues* (see Chapter 11), but she was the only ship of the class to be so fitted before the Armistice.

MODIFICATIONS 1940 TO 1942

Of the six ships of the class, only *Guépard*, *Valmy* and *Verdun* (3rd DCT) remained in service after the Armistice;[18] *Bison* had been lost during the Norwegian campaign, while *Lion* and *Vauban* were placed in care & maintenance for the duration.

---

[17] DM 166 EMG/1 dated 28 January 1932.

[18] Only two of the three were generally in commission at any one time.

Air defence

The three active ships received a major upgrade to their anti-aircraft capabilities during refits which took place at Toulon in 1941. The pole mainmast and the 37mm CAS mountings were suppressed, and a platform for a twin 37mm Mle 1933 mounting and two 1-metre HA rangefinders was constructed above the after hoists. The W/T aerials were re-affixed to supports fitted on the after funnel, and the after (4-metre) rangefinder and the after searchlight projector were raised to compensate for the height of the platform; the forward projector was suppressed altogether.

The 13.2mm Hotchkiss CAD were relocated from their current position above the forward hoists to the forward end of the centre deckhouse (the position vacated by the 1-metre RF). In their place atop the forward hoists, two 13.2mm Browning single mountings (CAS) were fitted.

Guépard lost the forward torpedo mounting, and *Valmy* the after mounting; *Verdun*, which was the first to be refitted, retained not only both sets of tubes but also the forward searchlight projector. *Guépard* and *Valmy* were fitted with Alpha 128 around this time, and this may have prompted the removal of the torpedo tubes as weight compensation.[19]

These modifications were carried out as follows:

Verdun: April–May 1941
Guépard: September–November 1941
Valmy: October–December 1941

Other modifications

The concentration dials were removed during the winter of 1941. *Valmy*, the last of the three to be refitted, had a distinctive cowling fitted to her forefunnel – the only ship of the four-funnel series to have this modification.

---

[19] The Alpha installations aboard the two ships operated at different frequencies to avoid mutual interference: 19,000Hz for *Guépard* and 14,000Hz for *Valmy*.

Below: *Guépard* at Toulon on 11 May 1942, as lead ship of the 3rd DCT of the *Forces de Haute Mer*. She underwent a major refit in the dockyard during the autumn of 1941. The original mainmast was removed, and a new AA platform for a twin 37mm Mle 1933 mounting was constructed atop the after hoists. The 13.2mm Hotchkiss CAD were relocated to the forward end of the centre deckhouse, and replaced on the platform forward of the bridge by 13.2mm Browning MG. The forward torpedo mounting was removed as weight compensation, but the after (auxiliary) rangefinder was retained. (*Marius Bar*)

CHAPTER 5
THE *AIGLE* CLASS

INTRODUCTION

The 1927 naval estimates featured another 'treaty' cruiser (*Foch*), six *contre-torpilleurs*, five fleet submarines of the *1500-tonnes* type, and the minelaying submarine *Rubis*; for the first time since 1922 there was not a single *torpilleur d'escadre*. The 1928 and 1929 estimates would follow the same pattern.

The six *contre-torpilleurs* of the *Aigle* class would essentially be repeats of the *Guépard* class, with a slightly modified hull-form and, more significantly, a new 138.6mm gun. The 138.6/40 Mle 1927 would be the first French medium-calibre gun with a German-pattern sliding breech; it would also be the third different gun installed in the *contre-torpilleurs*.[1]

Two of the six ships would again be ordered from Lorient Naval Dockyard, but due to production bottlenecks in the naval dockyards it was decided that the orders would be postponed, and that the ships would be laid down and completed in parallel with the *Vauquelin* class of the 1928 (subsequently 1929) estimates. It was subsequently decided that they would be demonstrators for superheated steam technology. They would also adopt the modified hull-form and revised characteristics of the *Vauquelin* class, so although their building data is published in the current chapter, these two ships have been grouped with the *Vauquelins* (see Chapter 6) for the purposes of technical description and analysis.

Orders for the four remaining ships were placed with traditional private destroyer builders. Ateliers et Chantiers de France (Dunkirk), which had previously built the *torpilleurs Bourrasque* and *L'Adroit*, and was currently occupied with the construction of the *contre-torpilleurs Lion* and *Vauban* of the 1925 and 1926 estimates, received the order for the first ship. The second was placed with Forges et Chantiers de la Méditerranée (TE *Cyclone*, *Mistral* and *Forbin*), to be laid down at their Graville yard, near Le Havre; the third with Ateliers et Chantiers de la Loire (CT *Léopard*, *Lynx*, *Verdun*) at their Nantes shipyard;[2] and the fourth with Ateliers et Chantiers de Bretagne, Nantes (CT *Tigre*, TE *Fougueux*). As with previous classes of *contre-torpilleur*, Lorient was again to be the *port d'armement* for all six units of the class.

The contracts were for 46 million French francs per ship, a significant increase over the *Guépard* class (32m FF) but one which reflected the current high rate of inflation rather than additional or more advanced equipment, which apart from the new gun was virtually identical to that installed in their immediate predecessors.

The ships of the 1927 estimates reverted to earlier practice in being named after predators, in this case

---

[1] In contrast, virtually all the British destroyers completed during the interwar period were armed with the same gun, the 4.7in (120mm) Mk IX.

[2] The previous three ships had been built at Saint-Nazaire

BUILDING DATA

Name	Aigle	Vautour	Albatros	Gerfaut	Milan	Epervier
Programme	1927	1927	1927	1927	1927	1927
Prog. no.	101	102	103	104	105	106
Project no.	Da 4	Da 5	Da 6	Da 7	Da 8	Da 9
Builder	ACF Dunkirk	FCM Graville	ACL Nantes	ACB Nantes	Lorient	Lorient
Ordered	18 Oct 1928	18 Oct 1928	18 Oct 1928	18 Oct 1928	1 Jul 1929	1 Jul 1929
Laid down	8 Oct 1929	21 Feb 1929	30 Jan 1929	13 May 1929	1 Dec 1930	18 Aug 1930
Launched	19 Feb 1931	28 Aug 1930	28 Jun 1930	14 Jun 1930	13 Oct 1931	14 Aug 1931
Manned for trials	20 Feb 1931	1 July 1931	15 Nov 1930	15 Jan 1931	1 Jun 1932	1 Jun 1932
Acceptance trials	16 Jun 1931	23 July 1931	20 Feb 1931	26 Mar 1931	4 Jul 1933	6 Oct 1932
Commissioned	1 Sep 1932	1 Dec 1931	4 Sep 1931	5 Sep 1931	31 Dec 1933	31 Dec 1933
Completed	10 Oct 1932	2 May 1932	25 Dec 1931	30 Jan 1932	20 Apr 1934	1 Apr 1934
Entered service	1 Nov 1932	1 Jun 1932	25 Jan 1932	15 Mar 1932	18 May 1934	18 May 1934

Aigle Class:
Arsenal de Lorient – Milan, Epervier
A C France – Aigle
A C Bretagne – Gerfaut
A C Loire – Albatros
F C Méditerranée – Vautour

GENERAL CHARACTERISTICS

Displacement:	2441 tons standard; 2660 tonnes normal; 3140 tonnes full load
Dimensions:	Length 122.4m pp, 128.5m oa; beam 11.8m; draught 4.4m
Machinery:	Four Du Temple small-tube boilers, 20kg/cm^2 (215°) Two-shaft geared steam turbines 64,000CV for 36kts (designed)
Oil fuel:	540 tonnes; radius 3650nm at 18kts, 765nm at 39kts
Armament:	Five 138.6mm/40 Mle 1927 in single mountings (100rpg + 85 starshell) One 75mm/50 Mle 1925 HA in a single mounting (100 rounds – see text) Four 37mm/50 Mle 1925 AA in single mountings (500rpg) Four 8mm Hotchkiss MG Mle 1914 in twin mountings Six 550mm torpedoes Mle 1923D in two triple mountings Two DC chutes each for eight 200kg depth charges (+ 8 reloads) Four 100/250mm depth charge throwers Mle 1928
Complement:	10 officers + 198 men peacetime 10 officers + 217 men wartime

birds of prey: *Aigle* ('Eagle'), *Vautour* ('Vulture'), *Albatros*, *Gerfaut* ('Gerfalcon'), *Epervier* ('Sparrowhawk') and *Milan* ('Kite'). The names of the last two would continue to distinguish them from their near-sisters of the *Vauquelin* class, which were named after famous French seamen (see Chapter 6).

Each of the ships took approximately three years to build. *Aigle*, in common with other ships built by A C France, was launched almost complete. *Vautour*, built by F C Méditerranée at Graville, had a difficult launch during which the bow grounded on the slipway, resulting in bent plates; it was 36 hours before the hull could be towed off, and it was then docked for repairs. The lead-ship, *Aigle*, suffered problems with her starboard turbines on trials and had to have a gearbox replaced,[3] which delayed her entry into service. Trials

[3] The gearbox was reassigned from *Le Chevalier Paul*, building at A C France (see Chapter 6).

of the other three ships proceeded relatively smoothly, and *Gerfaut*, built by A C Bretagne, distinguished herself not only by the remarkably high speeds achieved (see below), but in passing every hurdle during her formal trials at the first attempt, without a single interruption.

HULL AND GENERAL CONFIGURATION

In their general layout and appearance the four ships of the *Aigle* class closely resembled the *Guépard*. The designs for both types were drawn up under the supervision of *Ingénieur général* Antoine, head of the 'small ships' section (*Section des petits bâtiments*) of the STCN. However, there were a number of small changes, not all of which are evident in photographs of the ships.

All of the previous types of destroyer had emerged from the shipyards slightly overweight – although the French could not begin to compete with the Japanese in this respect. Weight saving was therefore an important consideration when the design for the *Aigle*s was drawn up. There was a small but significant use of electric welding for the non-strength elements of the hull and superstructures, and this resulted in moderate savings of 50–60 tonnes. The designed metacentric height (GM) was 0.80m (vs. 0.68m in the *Guépard* class).

The hull-form was also slightly modified. There was a reduction of 0.70 metres in the length between perpendiculars and 1.70 metres in length overall. The *Aigle* class had a slightly deeper hull (+0.11m) with less freeboard than the *Guépard* (see schematic of the respective hull sections at Frame 35): the height of the forecastle at deep load was 6.67 metres (vs. 7.09m), and the main deck was 3.8 metres (vs. 4.20m) above the waterline.

The construction methods employed for the hull were unchanged except for the limited employment of

The *Contre-Torpilleur Aigle* 1933

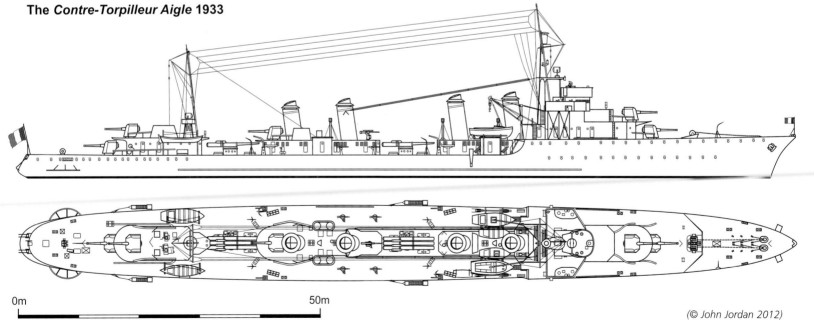

(© John Jordan 2012)

The profile and plan drawings are based on plans of *Aigle* dated Dunkirk 26 January 1933. They show *Aigle* as designed with the single 75mm HA Mle 1925 forward of the third funnel and four of the new Mle 1928 depth charge throwers abeam the first two funnels. The 75mm gun would be fitted briefly in *Albatros* and *Gerfaut* before being landed, and the DCTs would be removed from all four ships shortly after completion to reduce topweight. The ammunition chutes outboard of the 138.6mm gun mountings are similar to those of the *Guépard* class; the chutes for the shells emerged to port of the guns and those for the cased charges to starboard.

THE AIGLE CLASS

Aigle: General Arrangement Plans

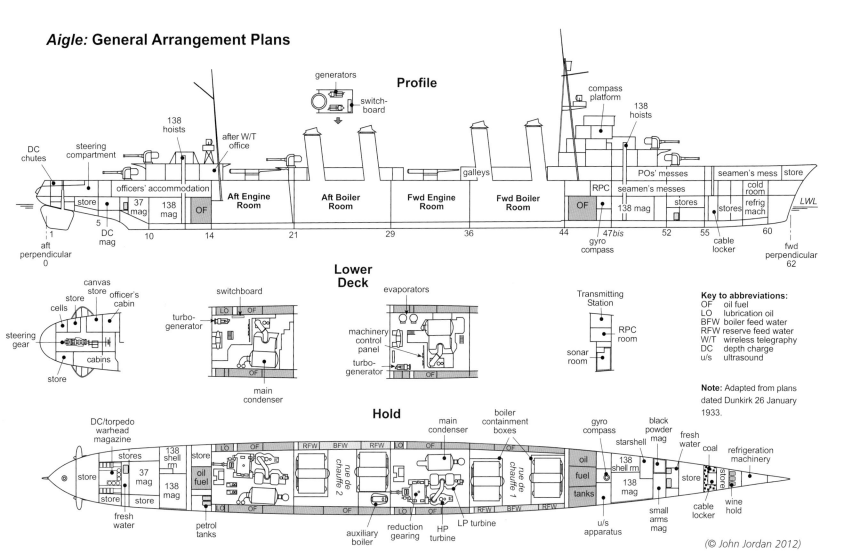

(© John Jordan 2012)

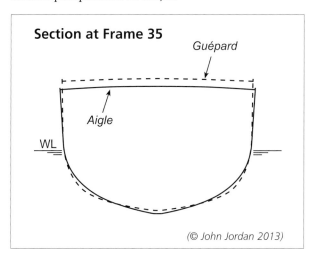

(© John Jordan 2013)

welding. The transverse frames had a standard spacing of 2.1 metres, but an additional watertight bulkhead was inserted close to the stern (Frame 1 – see General Arrangement plans); the twelve main transverse bulkheads extended from the ship's bottom to the upper deck and divided the hull into thirteen watertight compartments designated A–M. There were pumps rated at 100t/h in sections B–E and J–L, and these were doubled up in the main machinery spaces (F–I); the two narrow end compartments (A, M) had smaller pumps rated at 30t/h.

The bridge structure had a similar configuration to the later ships of the *Guépard* class (1926 estimates), with a narrow face to the compass platform and a rounded upper bridge. The layout of the deckhouses above the main deck was unchanged, as was that of the boats and searchlights. There was a light tripod foremast and a pole mainmast, as in the earlier ships.

GROUND TACKLE AND NAVIGATION

Ground tackle was as in the *Guépard* class. The rudder was of similar design, but there were minor differences in the surface area for each of the ships: in *Aigle* it was 15.52m², in *Albatros* and *Gerfaut* 14.3m².

The Sperry gyro-compass was the improved Mk VIII; compass provision was otherwise as in the *Guépard* class.

All four ships were initially fitted with a CET 31 ultrasonic depth sounder; this was replaced during the mid-1930s by a CET 32 Mod.1935 (see Chapter 4 for performance details).

MACHINERY

Despite the apparent similarities between the propulsion machinery of the *Guépard* and *Aigle* classes, the machinery of the latter was considered to be a major improvement on that of their predecessors: more robust, reliable, and economical, and with much greater flexibility of operation.

The four Du Temple boilers were of the same basic

type as for the *Guépard* class; they were disposed in similar fashion and had similar dimensions and characteristics. The two (separated) boiler rooms were linked by a 300mm steam line which enabled any of the boilers to supply steam to either set of turbines.

Aigle, *Vautour* and *Albatros* had Parsons reaction turbines; *Gerfaut*, built by A C Bretagne, had Rateau-Bretagne impulse turbines. The Zoelly turbines which had given so much trouble in *Lion* and *Vauban* were not considered for the *Aigle* class.

The Parsons turbines of the first three ships comprised a single high-pressure (HP) and a low-pressure (LP) turbine working in series, with a separate cruise turbine clutched to the shaft of the HP turbine; the reversing turbine was on the shaft for the LP turbine and housed within the same casing. The HP turbine was rated at 14,000CV and the LP turbine at 18,000CV; the astern turbine was rated at 4000CV. When going ahead, steam was admitted to the cruise turbine up to approximately one tenth of maximum power (3200CV), then to the HP turbine and finally to the LP turbine. The ship could steam at up to 18 knots on cruise turbines alone; the turbine could be declutched at low speeds, but it could be clutched to the shaft only when the ship was at rest.

Aigle following her launch at Ateliers et Chantiers de France, Dunkirk, on 19 February 1931. Ships built by ACF were launched in a far more complete condition than ships built by other shipyards. The propulsion machinery and propeller shafts were generally fitted, and the ship was often able to move under her own power immediately after launch – note the smoke from the second funnel.

THE AIGLE CLASS

Left: *Albatros* makes her first sortie into the River Loire from the ACL shipyard at Nantes on 17 February 1931. She still lacks her guns and fire control apparatus.

The Rateau-Bretagne turbines installed in *Gerfaut* were arranged differently (see schematic). There were two separate cruise turbines (designated CR1 and CR2) on each shaft, one operating at high pressure, the other at low pressure. The cruise turbines had their own separate gearing, which was clutched not to the shaft of the main HP turbine, but to the shaft of the main LP turbine. The HP cruise turbine was rated at 730CV, the LP cruise turbine at 1390CV. The astern turbine, which as in the Parsons ships was housed in the casing of the main LP turbine, could deliver 8000CV. The reduction gearing for both the main and the cruise turbines was supplied by Power Plant.

Each of the two shafts was fitted with a three-bladed propeller of high- or very high-resistance brass with a diameter of 3.67–3.7 metres.

The maximum speeds achieved on trials were remarkable. During the 8-hour Maximum Normal Power (PMN) trial, which was undertaken at normal displacement, all four ships sustained speeds in excess of 37 knots; *Gerfaut* was the fastest with a corrected speed of 40.02 knots on 80,045CV, and 41.46 knots on 83,436CV with forced draught over the ninth hour (see table).

Peacetime fuel bunkerage was 360 tonnes, a figure which rose to 540 tonnes (usable) at deep load. Provision of reserve feed water for the boilers was 128 tonnes, carried in side and bottom tanks. There was the customary 12 tonnes of fresh water for sanitation, plus 4 tonnes of drinking water for the crew in 500-litre tanks fore and aft (see plan). Following trials, endurance was calculated at 4700nm at 15 knots and 3600nm at 18 knots on cruise turbines alone with two boilers lit.[4] Much less would be achieved in wartime.

The auxiliary boiler, which again was located to starboard of boiler no.3, had slightly greater capacity; heated surface area was 59m^2 (vs. 52m^2 for the model fitted in the *Guépard*s).

The two turbo-generators, each rated at 80kW (106kW max.), were distributed between the forward and after engine rooms, as in the *Guépard* class. The two 22kW (26.5kW max.) Bettus-Loire emergency generators were identical to those fitted in the earlier ships, and were again located in the centre deckhouse.

MAIN ARMAMENT

Work on the 138.6mm/40 Mle 1927 gun began in 1926. Proving trials were successfully concluded in

[4] Figures for *Albatros*.

MAXIMUM NORMAL POWER AND FULL POWER TRIALS

The trials were to be run at a mean displacement of 2,634 tonnes; adjustments were made for ships which displaced in excess of this figure at the start of the trial.

	Aigle	*Vautour*	*Albatros*	*Gerfaut*
Date of trial:	18 May 1932	29 Aug 1931	30 Apr 1931	30 Apr 1931
Displacement:	2650t	2644t	2641t	2643t
Average over 8 hours				
Shaft revolutions:	358rpm	346rpm	369rpm	380rpm
Horsepower:	69128CV	68072CV	33850CV	80,045CV
Speed:	37.15kts	37.75kts	39.13kts	40.31kts
(corrected)	(37.2kts)	37.77kts	(39.15kts)	(40.02kts)
Fuel consumption:	28.14t/h	28.32t/h	27.60t/h	28.40t/h
Average 9th hour				
Shaft revolutions:	374rpm	362rpm	382rpm	393rpm
Horsepower:	76,906CV	75608CV	36409CV	83,436CV
Speed:	38.60kts	39.28kts	40.44kts	41.46kts
Fuel consumption:	30.81t/h	31.82t/h	30.66t/h	28.40t/h

Notes:
1. The measurements relating to horsepower for *Albatros* could be taken only at the starboard shaft.
2. The figures representing the best performance for the class are underlined.

Source: 9DD^1 series, SHD Vincennes.

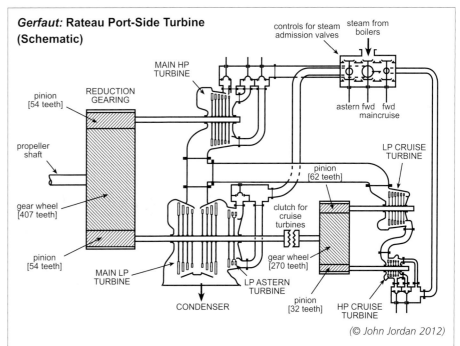

Gerfaut: Rateau Port-Side Turbine (Schematic)

(© John Jordan 2012)

March 1927, but manufacture of the production guns was protracted, and all four ships of the *Aigle* class ran their sea trials without the mountings on board. The gun itself was an advance on the Mle 1923 which armed the *Guépard* class in a number of respects. The most significant innovation was the German-style semi-automatic sliding breech, which was much faster in operation than the interrupted screw breech of earlier French destroyer guns.[5] The theoretical firing cycle was up to twelve rounds per minute – twice that of the Mle 1923.

A further modification which has attracted less comment was the lowering of the trunnions from 1.34m to 1.25m, making the gun easier to load at low angles of elevation. In order to achieve this it was necessary to sacrifice range. The maximum elevation of the Mle 1927 was only 28 degrees (vs. 35 degrees), and maximum range, using the same ammunition as the Mle 1923, was only 16,600m compared with 18,200m for the earlier gun. However, early trials with

[5] During trials with the 15cm guns of the ex-German *Amiral Sénès* (see Introduction), a firing cycle of eight rounds per minute was achieved.

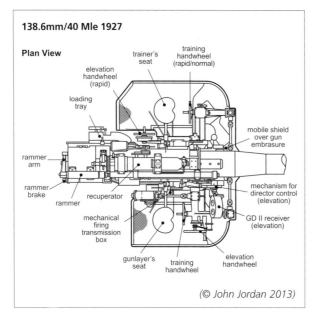

(© John Jordan 2013)

138.6MM/40 MLE 1927

Gun Data
Construction	monobloc autofretted barrel
Weight of gun	4.8 tonnes
Breech mechanism	horizontal sliding block
Ammunition type	separate
Projectiles	OPFA Mle 1924 (39.9kg)
	OEA Mle 1928 (40.2kg)
	OEcl Mle 1925 (30kg)
Propellant	9kg BM7 in cartridge Mle 1910
Muzzle velocity	700m/s
Range at 28°	16,600m

Gun Mounting
Designation	Mle 1927
Protection	3mm
Weight of mounting	13.0 tonnes
Elevation	–10° / +28°
Loading angle	any angle
Firing cycle	8–12rpm

Notes:
Mle	*Modèle*	Model
OPFA	*Obus de Perforation en Fonte Aciérée*	Semi-Armour Piercing (SAP)
OEA	*Obus Explosif en Acier*	High Explosive (HE)
OEcl	*Obus Eclairant*	Starshell

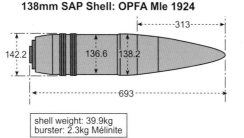

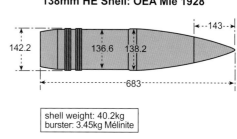

(© John Jordan 2012)

THE AIGLE CLASS

the Jaguars, equipped with the basic 3-metre coincidence rangefinder, had shown that effective fire control was only possible to 12,000–13,000 metres, beyond which dispersion was in any event excessive for these relatively short-barrelled guns. In adopting the 138.6mm Mle 1927, with its reduced elevation and sliding breech, the French had effectively come down on the side of weight of shell at moderate range at the expense of the occasional lucky hit at extreme range.

The regulation peacetime ammunition provision was unchanged at 100 combat rounds per gun, for a total of 500 shells plus 85 starshell. The electric hoists were likewise unchanged; each was capable of supplying a maximum of twenty rounds per minute for each pair of guns,[6] which meant that they were barely able to keep pace with the firing cycle. The *Aigle* class therefore depended even more heavily than previous classes on ready-use racks during the early stage of an action. There was sufficient ready-use stowage for just over two minutes of continuous fire (four minutes for no.3 gun), during which time the racks would need to be topped up from the magazine hoists. The *contre-torpilleur* concept was therefore moving inexorably in the direction of high-speed raids and rapid intervention rather than sustained combat.

There was provision in the design for full director control with remote power control (RPC) – see General Arrangement plans. In the event there was only director control for training; director control for elevation and RPC for training had to be abandoned. The four ships of the *Aigle* class were fitted on completion with a single SOM 3-metre coincidence rangefinder Mle B.1926 allied to the standard Mle 1923B electromechanical computer. Angle of train was transmitted to the mounting via a Granat GD III receiver and the trainer, who was seated on the left of the mounting, aligned the pointers.

The two 75cm BBT searchlight projectors were fitted fore and aft, as in the *Guépard* class, with the after searchlight installed atop its own short tower abaft the mainmast; the control positions were fitted in the bridge wings (see Bridge Decks drawing).

ANTI-AIRCRAFT WEAPONS

The *Aigle* class was originally intended to be armed with a single 75mm HA gun and two 37mm single

---

[6] The hoists could operate only when the ship was heeling less than 20 degrees.

Above: *Albatros* at sea during her trials. The single 75mm Mle 1925, which was embarked only briefly, is visible forward of the third funnel. Her main guns have just been fitted with shields, which are as yet unpainted. (*Pierre Boucheix collection*)

mountings of a new fully-automatic type with 2000 combat rounds plus 400 exercise rounds. The latter gun failed to materialise, however, and all four ships were completed with four single semi-automatic 37mm CAS Mle 1925, mounted as in the *Guépard* class.

The 75mm HA gun was not the 50-calibre Mle 1924 fitted in the *Jaguars* and the *Bourrasques*, but the older 35-calibre 'Army' model 1897–15 on a newly designed Mle 1925 mounting which could elevate to 70 degrees. A total of 100 HE rounds and 40 exercise rounds were provided, stowed in ready-use racks close to the mounting and in the 37mm magazine aft.

The 75mm Mle 1925 was fitted only briefly in *Albatros* and *Gerfaut*, and following trials on *Albatros* was disembarked in late 1932; the two remaining ships of the class, which entered service during the second half of that year, never received it. The location chosen for the single mounting was not ideal; arcs fore and aft were poor, and the isolation of the mounting from its magazine would have been a considerable handicap in action. In the end it was probably decided that the dubious military benefits of the gun did not compen-

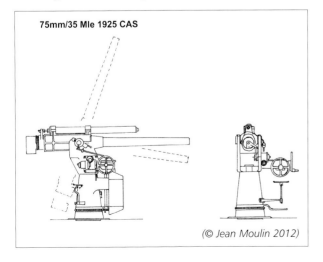

75mm/35 Mle 1925 CAS

(© Jean Moulin 2012)

75/35 MLE 1925

Gun Data

Construction	autofretted barrel
Weight of gun	?? tonnes
Breech mechanism	concentric ring
Ammunition type	fixed
Projectiles	OEA Mle 1917 (6.18kg)
Propellant	BM? (??kg)
Complete round	
weight	??kg
dimensions	649.5mm x 86.8mm
Muzzle velocity	570m/s
Max. range	??m (??°)
Ceiling	??m (??°)

Mounting Data

Designation	CAS Mle 1925
Weight of mounting	?? tonnes
Loading angle	n/a
Elevation of guns	–10° / +70°
Firing cycle (per gun)	15rpm theoretical

Notes:

Mle	*Modèle*	Model
OEA	*Obus Explosif en Acier*	High Explosive (HE)

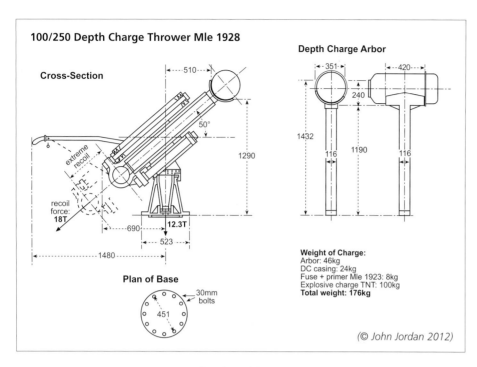

(© John Jordan 2012)

Below: A fine view of *Gerfaut*, probably during 1935, when she was serving as the lead ship of the 7th DL. Note the swallow-tailed pennant of the senior officer flying from the foremast top, and the single white band on the third funnel. She is unmodified since completion. *(Pierre Boucheix collection)*

sate for the additional topweight involved.

There was provision in the original plans for the customary 8mm Hotchkiss MG Mle 1914, to be mounted on pedestals on the forecastle. However, with the impending entry into service of its more effective replacement, the 13.2mm Mle 1929 Hotchkiss CAD, these guns were probably never embarked.

TORPEDOES
The torpedo outfit, which comprised two triple axial mountings for six 550mm Mle 1923DT torpedoes, was identical to that of the *Guépard* class.

Two of the new Mle 1929 fire control positions, linked to a Mle 1924 central fire control computer (*type Patrie*), were located in the bridge wings. The rangefinder for the main guns was again employed to provide range and bearing data. The Mle 1920 control position on the torpedo mounting was equipped with a Granat GC II receiver, and an on-mount operator aligned the pointers to train the mounting.

ANTI-SUBMARINE WEAPONS AND DETECTION APPARATUS
There were two depth charge chutes each with eight depth charges as in the *Guépard* class, and four depth charge throwers on the upper deck abaft the break in the forecastle.

The depth charge thrower was not the Thornycroft Mle 1918, but a new model designated the 100/250 Mle 1928. The Mle 1928 was of French design and manufacture, and its theoretical performance was well in advance of the ageing Mle 1918. It was significantly larger, but had a slimmer barrel; the expendable arbor had a diameter of only 116mm as compared with 240mm for that of the Mle 1918, so it was lighter, and the reduced diameter of the barrel meant greater pressure for a similar explosive charge. Range with the standard 100kg Guiraud depth charge Mle 1922 was fully 250 metres, and the time in the air was six seconds.

The depth charge throwers were disposed as in the *Jaguar* and *Guépard* classes, in pairs on either side of the ship beneath the boat rails. They were trained on forward bearings for reloading, but were normally fired on or abaft the beam. The plans for *Aigle* show an overhead rail above the throwers on either side of the ship secured to the underside of the athwartships rails for the boats. This suggests a block and tackle was used to move the charges to the throwers, as in the earlier ships.

THE AIGLE CLASS

Eight reserve 200kg depth charges were stowed in the below-decks magazine, and there was a total of twelve 100kg depth charges for the throwers, of which four were to be carried on the throwers, four in nearby racks, and four in the magazine. This allowed for three attacks each of two passes: each pass would deliver four 200kg depth charges from the chutes plus two 100kg depth charges from the throwers.

The Mle 1928 depth charge thrower does not appear to have been particularly successful; it proved to be less robust and reliable in service than the Thornycroft Mle 1918, and was presumably heavier – few details have been published in French sources. Because of this the DCTs would be removed shortly after the ships of the *Aigle* class entered service. The next class of *contre-torpilleurs* would have only two Mle 1928 DCTs, and these would be fitted amidships and would have different reloading arrangements (see Chapter 6).

COMMUNICATIONS

The W/T outfit as completed was identical to that of the *Guépard* class. The main W/T office, the *PC Radio*, was at the after end of the bridge block (see drawings), and the secondary W/T office was located in the after deckhouse.

BOATS

The boat outfit was identical to that of the *Guépard* class (q.v.), and was disposed in similar fashion on athwartships rails between the first two funnels and on davits abreast the after deckhouse. However, the arrangement of the boats was slightly modified in *Vautour*, *Albatros* and *Gerfaut*, which had the motor boat and motor launch inboard of the two 5-metre dinghies. The relative positions of the two boats on davits were also reversed in these three ships: the 7-metre whaler was to port and the 7-metre pulling cutter to starboard.

COMPLEMENT

The regulation peacetime complement comprised ten officers and 198 men. For the function and rank of the officers and a breakdown of the crew see Chapter 4 (*Guépard* class). A directive dated 10 May 1933 established the wartime complement as ten officers and 217 men: two CPOs, eight POs, 25 POs 2nd class, 179 seamen, and three civilians. The requirement to provide individual cabins for two Chief Petty Officers dictated a small revision in the layout of the accommodation. Whereas in the *Guépard* class there was a single cabin on the port side of the upper deck, adjacent to the sick bay, in the *Aigle* class two cabins were provided at the base of bridge structure (see Bridge Decks drawing).

The accommodation on these ships was highly regarded: mess-decks were spacious and well-ventilated.

EVALUATION

The modifications made to the hull-form and the increased attention paid to stability resulted in a much steadier ship with better transverse stability. Compared to the *Guépard* class the angle of heel under the helm and in a cross-wind was much reduced. This made life on board more pleasant for the crew and made the *Aigle* class a better gunnery platform.

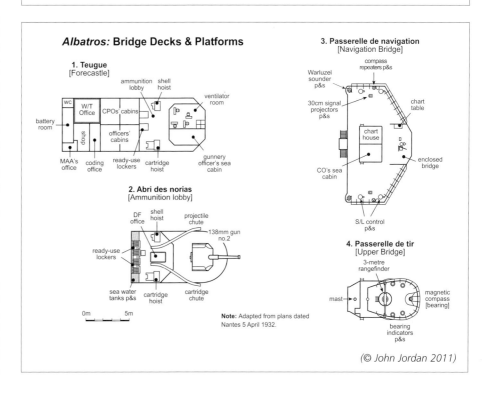

(© John Jordan 2012)

(© John Jordan 2011)

Nevertheless, concerns were raised about the lightness of their construction.

The propulsion machinery, in particular the Parsons and Rateau turbines, represented a marked improvement on the earlier ships, and the Navy was pleased both with its reliability and with its flexibility. The ships manoeuvred well, although the turning circle remained excessive for a 'small ship' – a function of the comparatively high length to beam ratio and an underpowered rudder servo-motor.

The new 138.6mm Mle 1927 gun performed exceptionally well in service. The sliding breech was a success, and the gun had the high rate of fire the Navy had long aspired to for its fast flotilla craft. It would prove to be the most reliable of all the *contre-torpilleur* guns developed during the interwar period. It would arm not only the six *Aigle*s, but also the following *Vauquelin* class, the minelaying cruiser *Pluton* (1925 estimates) and the new colonial sloops of the *Bougainville* class (first two units 1927 estimates).

Unfortunately, fire control provision still lagged some way behind; major technological advances would have to wait until the *Le Fantasque* class of the 1930 estimates. In the interim attention would increasingly focus on longer-base rangefinders and the provision of a second RF aft (see Modifications below).

MODIFICATIONS 1932 TO 1939
Main guns
The ammunition chutes for the 138.6mm guns were modified during the mid-1930s, the projectile chutes for guns nos.1–4 being extended to fully encircle the mounting. The chutes for no.5 gun continued to be stowed in the broken-down condition.

Below: *Aigle* in Toulon roads in late 1932. She had recently joined the 5th Light Division of the 1st Squadron (Mediterranean), which was formed with three out of the four ships of the class and was led by *Gerfaut*. (Charles Limonnier collection)

THE AIGLE CLASS

Concentration dials were fitted in the *Aigle* class from 1933, in response to a directive dated 7 October. The dials were initially painted white, becoming black in 1936. The arrangement adopted in the *Aigle* class was a departure from previous practice. In place of the single after dial (initially fixed, then trainable), which in earlier ships had been fitted atop a platform abaft the mainmast, there were two fixed to the after ends of the bridge wings, which were extended and angled at 45 degrees to accommodate the dials and their winding machinery. This proved to be a far better solution, and the practice was extended to all subsequent classes of *torpilleur* and *contre-torpilleur*.

From December 1935 *Gerfaut* trialled a 4-metre stereo rangefinder in a weather-proof turret aft. The rangefinder turret was located at the after end of the protective bulwarks for the after hoists, and was similar in configuration to the one due to be installed in the *Le Fantasque* class. The remaining three ships would also be fitted with a 4-metre S rangefinder in this position during the mid/late 1930s, but with a lighter protective housing, and from 1937 all four ships would receive the new 5-metre stereo rangefinder turret forward (see Chapter 4), in place of the original 3-metre model.

Air defence

From 1933 all four ships were fitted with two twin 13.2mm Hotchkiss machine guns (CAD). These were initially fitted on the upper deck, directly abaft the single 37mm guns, and 1-metre stereo rangefinders were located at the forward end of the centre deckhouse to supply range and bearing data to both the 37mm CAS and the 13.2mm MG. In 1939 the 13.2mm

Right: An unusual view aft from the crow's nest of *Gerfaut*. The four single 37mm Mle 1925 guns and the torpedo reloading davits are prominent on what is otherwise an uncluttered upper deck. *(US Navy NH 79656, courtesy of A D Baker III)*

Opposite: *Albatros* in December 1939. Twin 13.2mm Hotchkiss MG have been installed on platforms forward of the bridge, the original 3-metre coincidence rangefinder atop the bridge has been replaced by a 5-metre stereo model, and she has been fitted with a 4-metre stereo rangefinder aft. *(Charles Limonnier collection)*

THE AIGLE CLASS

CAD would be relocated to a platform forward of the bridge, atop the forward 138.6mm hoists.

Anti-submarine warfare
The four depth charge throwers were disembarked from late 1932. Two would be replaced following the outbreak of war in 1939.

Communications
The W/T outfit was upgraded during the late 1930s, the most significant addition being that of an SFR Mle 1937 VHF (OTC) tactical radio for bridge-to-bridge voice communication in 1937. A medium-frequency direction-finding aerial was fitted forward of the bridge, and a DF office installed in the bridge structure.

MODIFICATIONS 1939 TO 1940
Anti-submarine warfare
Two depth charge throwers are reported to have been reinstalled during late 1939, although these may have been removed after the Armistice; they were not on board *Albatros* at Casablanca in November 1942. At the same time, *Vautour* was fitted with an Asdic 128 during her immobilisation at Toulon October–December 1939. *Gerfaut* received hers while under repair at Cherbourg March–May 1940, while *Albatros* is thought to have had an Asdic 128 installed between June and September 1940, possibly at Oran. *Aigle* had yet to receive hers when she was placed in care & maintenance under the terms of the Armistice in October of the same year.

MODIFICATIONS 1940 TO 1942
Following the Armistice only *Albatros* remained in continuous commission; she would be detached to Casablanca in December 1941 to form a three-ship division with *Milan* and *Epervier* (see Chapter 6). *Aigle*, *Vautour* and *Gerfaut* would be placed in care & maintenance from late 1940 until July 1941, when the Armistice Commission agreed to the recommissioning of four additional *contre-torpilleurs* to allow the Marine Nationale to respond to the British attack on Syria. *Gerfaut* would now be a part of a newly reconstituted 7th DCT; however, *Vautour* would rejoin this formation only after her refit of June/July 1942 and *Aigle* would remain *en gardiennage* until she was scuttled in November 1942.

Above: *Albatros* in heavy weather during the late 1930s. Although an improvement on the early *contre-torpilleurs*, sea-keeping remained a problem, particularly in the Atlantic. *(Bernard Bernadac collection)*

Above: *Vautour* as leader of the 7th DCT in 1939. She has two white bands painted on her second funnel. *(Pierre Boucheix collection)*

Below: Part view of *Gerfaut* during the late 1930s, with *Albatros* beyond her. A 4-metre stereo rangefinder has been fitted above the after ammunition hoists.

Air defence

During 1941–2 all four ships received the standard upgrade to their anti-aircraft capabilities. The pole mainmast and the 37mm CAS mountings were suppressed, and a platform for a twin 37mm Mle 1933 mounting and two 1-metre rangefinders was constructed above the after hoists (see also Chapter 4). The W/T aerials were re-affixed to prominent supports fitted on the after funnel, and the after (4-metre) rangefinder was raised by 0.75m to compensate for the height of the new platform. Two of the four 37mm CAS were landed as weight compensation.[7]

In contrast to the *Guépard* class both 75cm searchlight projectors were to be retained, but they were relocated to a raised platform forward of the third funnel, as in the *Vauquelin* class. In *Albatros* a third, smaller 60cm projector was fitted on the foremast platform.

The 13.2mm Hotchkiss CAD were relocated from their current position above the forward hoists to the forward end of the centre deckhouse, the position vacated by the 1-metre RF. In their place atop the forward hoists, two 13.2mm Browning single mountings (CAS) were fitted.

There were differences in the way these modifications were executed. *Aigle*, which had been in care & maintenance since October 1940 and which had been taken in hand only in June 1942, never received the 37mm CAD or the 13.2mm Browning CAS before being scuttled. *Vautour*, which was refitted June–July 1942, lost all four of her 37mm CAS. *Albatros*, which was in refit at Oran 11 June–5 September 1941, retained her 13.2mm Hotchkiss CAD above the forward hoists, and had her 13.2mm Browning CAS fitted in the bridge wings.

Gerfaut underwent two refits during this period. In the first, July–August 1941, the mainmast was landed and the platform for a 37mm CAD installed, and two single Browning CAS were fitted in the bridge wings (as in *Albatros*). In the second, begun 15 September 1942 and incomplete at the time of the scuttling, she had platforms fitted forward of the third funnel for the searchlights but the latter were not reinstalled.

---

[7] Technically, under the terms of the Armistice anti-aircraft capabilities could be revised but not significantly enhanced, so the two 37mm CAS had also to be removed as compensation for the addition of a 37mm CAD mounting.

THE AIGLE CLASS

Gerfaut 1941

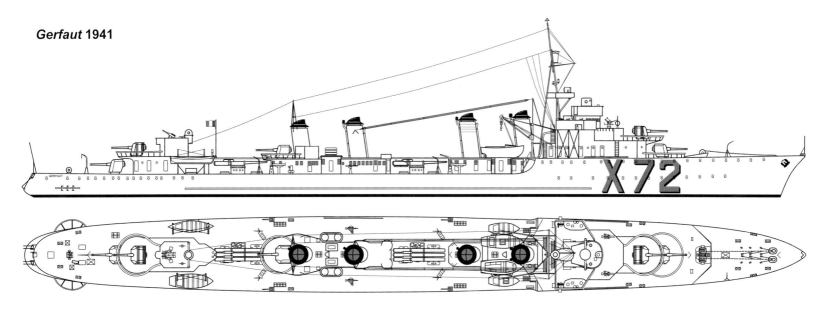

(© John Jordan 2012)

Gerfaut as she appeared in late 1941, following her refit at Toulon July/August. A platform for a 37mm CAD Mle 1933 mounting and two 1-metre HA rangefinders has been constructed atop the after 138.6mm hoists. The mainmast has been suppressed and the W/T antennae re-affixed to outriggers on the fourth funnel. The after pair of 37mm CAS Mle 1925 has been retained due to a shortage of twin mountings. The 13.2mm Hotchkiss CAD remain in place forward of the bridge, and two 13.2mm Browning MG have been added in the bridge wings. The after fire control position, with its 4-metre base rangefinder, has been retained (see also *Guépard* p.91), but both torpedo mountings remain in place. Both searchlights have been landed; in a later refit, begun in September 1942, a platform forward of the third funnel similar to that of the *Vauquelin* class was to have been constructed and the searchlights reinstated, but the work was incomplete when the ship was scuttled in November 1942.

Below: A fine bow view of *Gerfaut* on 9 October 1941, immediately after her AA refit at Toulon. *(Marius Bar)*

CHAPTER 6
THE *VAUQUELIN* CLASS, *MILAN* AND *EPERVIER*

INTRODUCTION

The six *contre-torpilleurs* of the 1928 estimates were to have been repeats of the *Aigle* class. The *avant-projet* featured not only the single 75mm gun and the twin 8mm MG, but two triple torpedo mountings on the centre-line and a Ginocchio torpedo. In accordance with previous practice, two ships were to have been built by Lorient Naval Dockyard and four by private shipyards. However, the delays now being experienced at Lorient due to work overload led the Navy Minister, Georges Leygues, to reconsider the allocation of the contracts. With the construction of the *torpilleurs d'escadre* coming to an end, the private shipbuilders had spare capacity, and also had greater flexibility than the dockyards when it came to expanding or contracting their respective workforces. In November 1928 it was therefore decided that all six ships of the 1928 estimates would be contracted to private yards. The two ships of the 1927 estimates allocated to Lorient, *Milan* and *Epervier*, would be built alongside them. The 1928 estimates would again feature a single 'treaty' cruiser (*Dupleix*), six *contre-torpilleurs*, six fleet submarines of the *1500-tonnes* type, and a minelaying submarine, the *Diamant*.

There would, however, be no authorisations by the French parliament in 1928. The 1928 estimates were postponed until 1929, and the 1929 estimates – which were to mark the completion of the six-year programme begun in 1924 – until 1930. This delay allowed a breathing space during which a review of the characteristics of the new ships took place. In October 1928 it was decided that the two ships of the *Aigle* class to be built at Lorient would be demonstrators for superheated steam technology (see Machinery below). At around the same time[1] a new disposition of the torpedo tubes and modifications to the stern would be proposed.

Previously it had been envisaged that torpedoes would be launched at long range against a formed enemy battle line during a daylight surface action. Axially-mounted torpedo tubes had therefore been preferred in order to maximise the number of tubes which could fire on either beam; the restricted arcs of the tubes (30 degrees either side of the beam) was not an issue. However, during scouting and screening operations in conditions of reduced visibility (including night action), a *contre-torpilleur* could suddenly find itself in close proximity to a major enemy unit. Wing-mounted torpedo tubes were considered, but were rejected because they would be unable to fire on the opposite beam, thereby halving the broadside. A compromise was finally adopted whereby the forward torpedo tubes were in two twin mountings on the beam, able to launch within 20 degrees of the ship's axis, and the after triple mounting was retained on the centre-line. As weight compensation – and also to clear

---

[1] Note 23677 CN/4 dated 21 November 1928.

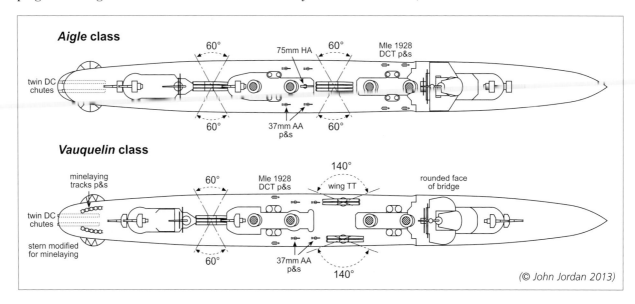

(© John Jordan 2013)

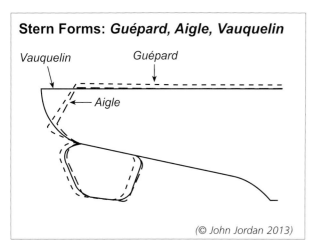

Stern Forms: *Guépard*, *Aigle*, *Vauquelin*

(© John Jordan 2013)

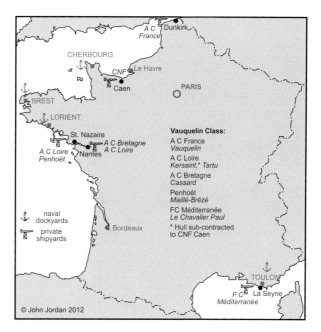

forward arcs for the twin tubes – two of the four depth charge throwers were landed and the number of 100kg depth charges embarked halved.

In the same year, 1928, the Naval General Staff decided that no more large minelayers would be built.[2] In the summer of 1928 designs for a 500kg mine with an 80kg explosive charge, capable of being laid by 'small ships' (*bâtiments légers*) were requested from Harlé, currently the exclusive suppliers of mines to the Marine Nationale, and from Breguet. Each of the new *contre-torpilleurs* was to accommodate forty mines on deck. A three-ship division would proceed at high speed to an area off the enemy coastline where the water had a maximum depth of 100 metres. A total of 120 mines would be laid in the course of a few hours at night to form a minefield 3.5nm long and 50 metres wide, thereby blockading the enemy in harbour or compelling him to take a wide detour when exiting. The stern of the *Guépard* and *Aigle* classes was poorly suited to minelaying, so a new configuration was adopted (see below).

When the time came for orders to be placed, two ships were assigned to Ateliers et Chantiers de la Loire, but with the stipulation that the hull of one was to be built by CNF Caen, which had previously only built *torpilleurs d'escadre* and would soon be short of work. The remaining four ships were allocated to Ateliers et Chantiers de France (Dunkirk), Ateliers et Chantiers de Bretagne (Nantes), Penhoët-Saint Nazaire, and Forges et Chantiers de la Méditerranée. The latter company was currently building the *contre-torpilleur Vautour* at its Graville yard, near Le Havre; however, the new ship would be built at La Seyne, opposite the dockyard at Toulon. As a further indication of monetary inflation, the contracts were for 57 million French francs per ship, an increase of 24% over the *Aigle* class (46m FF). Lorient was again to be the *port d'armement* for all six units of the class.

In December 1930 the names of the new ships were announced. In a break with earlier practice, all were named after famous French seamen of the seventeenth and eighteenth centuries:[3]

- Jean Vauquelin (1728–1772) was the captain of the frigate *Atalante*, who fought against the British during the siege of Quebec and distinguished himself by his personal bravery.
- Guy-François de Kersaint de Coëtnempren (1703–1759) forced the British blockade of Louisbourg (Ile Royale, French Canada) in 1746, and took part in campaigns in the Antilles and the Indies before his death in the Battle of Quiberon Bay.
- Jacques Cassard (1679–1740) conducted a *guerre de course* against the British 1708–10.
- Jean-François de Tartu (1751–1793) was a veteran of the Battle of Ushant (1778) and the naval battles of the American war of independence; he died in combat with the British HMS *Thames*.
- Jean de Maillé, duc de Brézé (1619–1646) was victorious in a number of battles against the Spanish. The ship which bore his name was originally to have been simply the *Brézé*, but this was subsequently changed to *Maillé-Brézé*.
- Jean-Paul de Saumeur (1598–1669) was a knight (Fr. *chevalier*) of Malta, then Commander of the Fleet under Cardinal Richelieu; he fought in the Mediterranean against the Spanish and against the Barbary pirates. He gave his name to the *Le Chevalier Paul*.[4]

There were precedents for the first four names in the Marine Nationale, but the last two ships were the first to bear these particular names.

The bottlenecks in industrial production which were a direct consequence of France's rapid naval expansion during the 1920s, and in particular the large programme of flotilla craft and submarines, now began to have a major impact on construction times. It might have been anticipated that a succession of orders for similar types of ship, with each class showing only small, incremental improvements over the last, placed with the same elite group of private shipyards, would

---

[2] Originally it had been envisaged that *Pluton* (1925 estimates) would be the first of a series.

[3] In some way this was perhaps a recognition that the missions of these ships were those of small fleet cruisers; French cruisers of the period, even those of the 10,000-ton type, also bore the names of famous seamen.

[4] Note that the '*Le*' is part of the name of this ship; in English-language sources she has often been referred to (incorrectly) as *Chevalier Paul*.

BUILDING DATA

Name	Vauquelin	Kersaint	Cassard	Tartu	Maillé Brézé	Le Chevalier Paul
Programme	1929	1929	1929	1929	1929	1929
Prog. no.	120	121	122	123	124	125
Project no.	Da 10	Da 11	Da 12	Da 13	Da 14	Da 15
Builder	ACF Dunkirk	ACL/CNF Caen	ACB Nantes	ACL Nantes	Penhoet St-Naz.	FCM La Seyne
Ordered	1 Feb 1930	1 Feb 1930	1 Feb 1930	1 Feb 1930	1 Feb 1930	1 Feb 1930
Laid down	13 Mar 1930	19 Sep 1930	12 Nov 1930	14 Sep 1930	9 Oct 1930	28 Feb 1931
Launched	29 Sep 1932	14 Nov 1931	8 Nov 1931	7 Dec 1931	9 Nov 1931	21 Mar 1932
Manned for trials	5 Nov 1932	1 Sep 1932	15 Jul 1932	1 Jul 1932	1 Sep 1932	16 Oct 1933
Acceptance trials	13 Dec 1932	8 Nov 1932	10 Aug 1932	29 Jul 1932	13 Sep 1932	27 Nov 1933
Commissioned	1 Jun 1933	20 Sep 1933	1 Nov 1932	1 Oct 1932	31 Dec 1932	1 Jun 1934
Completed	3 Nov 1933	31 Dec 1933	10 Sep 1933	31 Dec 1932	6 Apr 1933	20 Jul 1934
Entered service	28 Mar 1934	14 Jan 1934	7 Oct 1933	8 Feb 1933	23 Apr 1933	24 Aug 1934

have resulted in more rapid and trouble-free construction. In the event only one ship of the six (*Tartu*, built by Penhoët) was three years from laying down to completion; the other ships took from three and a half to four years to complete. The last ship, *Le Chevalier Paul* (F C Méditerranée), had one of her two main gearbox trains reassigned to *Aigle* (see Chapter 5), which effectively delayed her entry into service until August 1934.

The differing practices between the respective shipyards were again apparent. *Vauquelin*, built by A C France, was 96% complete when launched, as compared with figures of 63–64% for the other yards. *Cassard* experienced serious problems with her main gearing which resulted in six months of repairs. *Kersaint* also needed repairs to her main gearing, and later stripped blades on her starboard LP turbine. *Maillé-Brézé* experienced early problems with her port-side turbines, had to wait two weeks for a graving dock to be freed before embarking on her speed trials, and subsequently wrapped the chain of a buoy around a propeller while coming alongside at Lorient. *Vauquelin*'s trials began well, but she developed severe vibrations in a shaft which were traced to a badly damaged propeller; she then struck a rock when entering Lorient and had to have hull plating replaced over a length of 40 metres, delaying her entry into service by several months.

Below: The launch of *Vauquelin* at the Dunkirk shipyard of Ateliers et Chantiers de France (ACF). Due to bottlenecks at the Lorient Naval Dockyard, all six ships of this class were built in private shipyards. As was customary for ships built at ACF, *Vauquelin* was in a relatively advanced state of completion when launched.

THE VAUQUELIN CLASS, MILAN AND EPERVIER

Left: *Cassard*, complete except for her guns and fire control apparatus, leaves Nantes under tow on 9 August 1932. She would begin her acceptance trials the following day.

Taken individually, none of these problems was beyond what would normally be expected with a brand-new ship. However, the cumulative impact was substantial and contributed to long delivery times for all but one (*Tartu*) of the six ships. As the problems occurred during official trials it was the *port d'armement*, Lorient, which had to undertake the repairs, and the pressure on both the workforce and on docking capacity were considerable.

HULL AND GENERAL CONFIGURATION

The hull-form and general layout of the *Vauquelin* class were virtually identical to those of the *Aigle*. The most striking difference was the configuration of the stern, which was optimised for minelaying (see drawing). The form of the stern was described as *en cul-de-poule* (lit. 'hen's arse'), and would be adopted for the fast minelaying cruiser *Emile Bertin* and the succeeding class of *contre-torpilleurs* of the *Le Fantasque* class

Left: *Le Chevalier Paul*, built by F C Méditerranée, had one of her two main gearbox trains reassigned to *Aigle*, which effectively delayed her entry into service until August 1934. She is seen here on the slipway just prior to launch in early 1932. Note the large 3-bladed propellers and the prominent bilge keel.

GENERAL CHARACTERISTICS

Displacement:	2441 tons standard; 2635 tonnes normal; 3120 tonnes full load
Dimensions:	Length 122.4m pp, 129.3m oa; beam 11.8m; draught 4.4m
Machinery:	Four Du Temple small-tube boilers, 20kg/cm^2 (215°)
	Two-shaft geared steam turbines
	64,000CV for 36kts (designed)
Oil fuel:	585 tonnes; radius 3000nm at 14kts, 800nm at 34kts
Armament:	Five 138.6mm/40 Mle 1927 in single mountings (100rpg + 75 starshell)
	Four 37mm/50 Mle 1925 AA in single mountings (500rpg)
	Four 13.2mm/76 Mle 1929 Hotchkiss MG in two twin mountings (2400rpg)
	Seven 550mm torpedoes Mle 1923DT in one triple and two twin mountings
	Two DC chutes each for eight 200kg depth charges (+8 reloads)
	Two 100/250mm depth charge throwers Mle 1928
	Twin rails for 40 Breguet B4 500kg mines
Complement:	12 officers + 201 men peacetime
	12 officers + 220 men wartime

WEIGHTS: *MILAN* 1934

Hull:	913.19t	37%
Hull installations:	195.95t	8%
Machinery:	862.41t	35%
Guns and hoists:	86.32t	3%
Torpedo tubes:	31.39t	1%
Mines/DCs:	5.12t	0%
Consumables:*	391.88t	16%
Normal displacement:	2486.26t	100%

* includes 108.92t OF + 64t water (55t RFW)

Opposite: Maillé-Brézé fitting out in graving dock no.3 in the Penhoët Basin at Saint-Nazaire in the spring of 1932. The funnels have just been embarked and are as yet unpainted.

(both 1930 estimates). It effectively extended the quarterdeck aft, so that while length between perpendiculars was identical to that of the *Aigle*, length overall was greater (129.3m vs. 128.5m).

The other major external difference lay in the shape of the bridge structure, which was streamlined to improve air flow and prevent smoke from the first two funnels being drawn onto the upper bridge. Not only was the upper bridge rounded, as in the *Aigle* class and three of the *Guépard*s, but the face of the compass platform and the bridge wings were given completely smooth contours (see Bridge Decks drawing).

The use of electric welding for the non-strength elements of the hull and superstructures was extended, and much use was made of duralumin for deckhouses and partitions. This further reduced topweight and enabled designed displacement to be kept to 2525–2600 tonnes (normal) in the six *Vauquelin*s, and 2485 tonnes in the Lorient-built *Milan* and *Epervier*. The weight of the hull in the latter ships was 913 tonnes as against 979 tonnes for the *Aigle* class – a saving of 6.5%. The designed metacentric height (GM) was again 0.80m at deep load, and although this was not always met, GM on completion was in excess of 0.83m at normal displacement and 0.70m at deep load for all ships; for *Milan* and *Epervier* it rose to 0.98m at normal displacement. Twin bilge keels with a length of 49 metres contributed to the steadiness that distinguished them from their predecessors (see Evaluation).

The construction methods employed for the hull were unchanged except for the more extensive use of welding. There were twelve main transverse bulkheads extending from the ship's bottom to the upper deck, as in the *Aigle* class, and these divided the hull into thirteen watertight compartments designated A–M.

The layout of the deckhouses above the main deck was unchanged, but the arrangement of the boats and depth charge throwers had to be modified in order to accommodate the twin torpedo tubes. There was also a completely new arrangement of the searchlights: the two main (combat) 75cm projectors were located on a platform which also served as the auxiliary conning

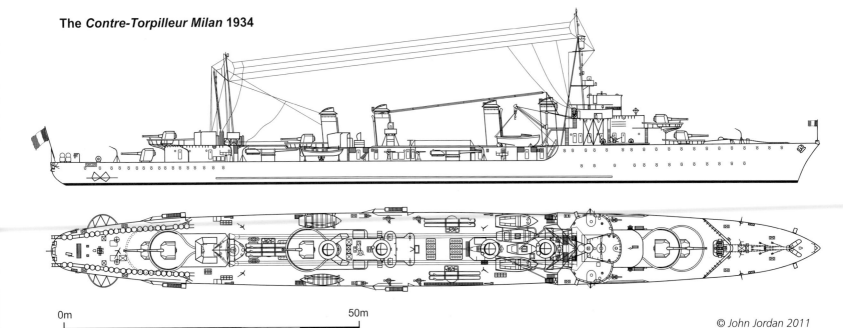

The *Contre-Torpilleur Milan* 1934

© John Jordan 2011

The profile and plan drawings are based on plans of *Milan* and *Epervier* dated Lorient 1 August 1934. They show the ships as completed, with circular ammunition chutes and two 13.2mm Hotchkiss CAD on the forecastle. There are two of the new Mle 1928 depth charge throwers amidships, and mine rails for a total of 40 B4 mines on the stern; except for the fixed after section (for 2 x 5 mines) these rails were not normally embarked. The positions of the boats and the reloading gear for the after torpedo tubes were reversed in the otherwise similar *Vauquelin* class. Note the searchlight platform on the third funnel which was a common feature of both classes. Note also the additional 7-metre motor launch to port, which was unique to *Milan*.

THE VAUQUELIN CLASS, MILAN AND EPERVIER

Vauquelin: General Arrangement Plans

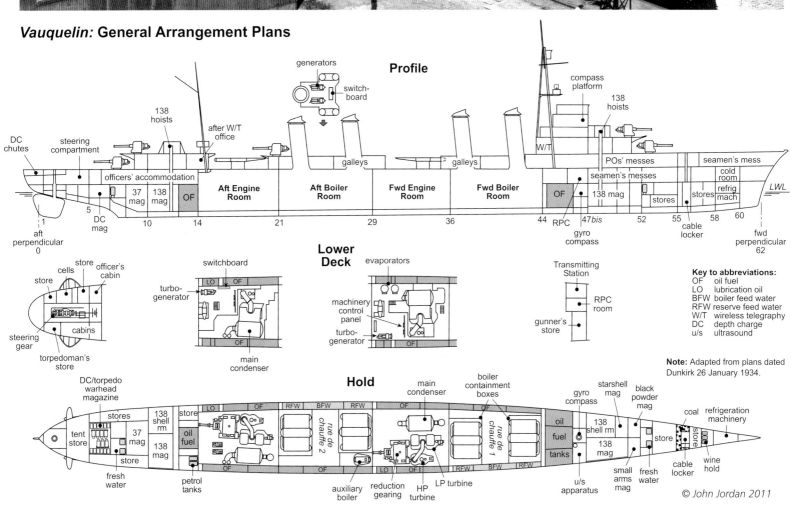

Key to abbreviations:
OF oil fuel
LO lubrication oil
BFW boiler feed water
RFW reserve feed water
W/T wireless telegraphy
DC depth charge
u/s ultrasound

Note: Adapted from plans dated Dunkirk 26 January 1934.

© John Jordan 2011

position at the base of the third funnel, and there was now a third light 45cm projector for navigation (*projecteur de manoeuvre*) on a platform at the base of the tripod foremast.

GROUND TACKLE AND NAVIGATION

Two bower anchors of the 2360kg Hall stockless type were in hawsepipes forward, as in the *Guépard* and *Aigle* classes. Three kedge anchors were provided, of which two (600kg and 300kg) were stowed against the after end of the forecastle and handled by the boat derricks; the third (400kg) was stowed against the port wall of the after deckhouse and was handled by the derrick for torpedo embarkation. The 600kg anchor would subsequently be disembarked (from 1937 onwards) to reduce topweight.

The gyro-compass was an Anschütz model, located as in the earlier ships. There were four magnetic compasses: two for bearing (upper bridge and secondary conning position) and two for course (compass platform and steering compartment).

Tartu received a CET 31 ultrasonic depth sounder,

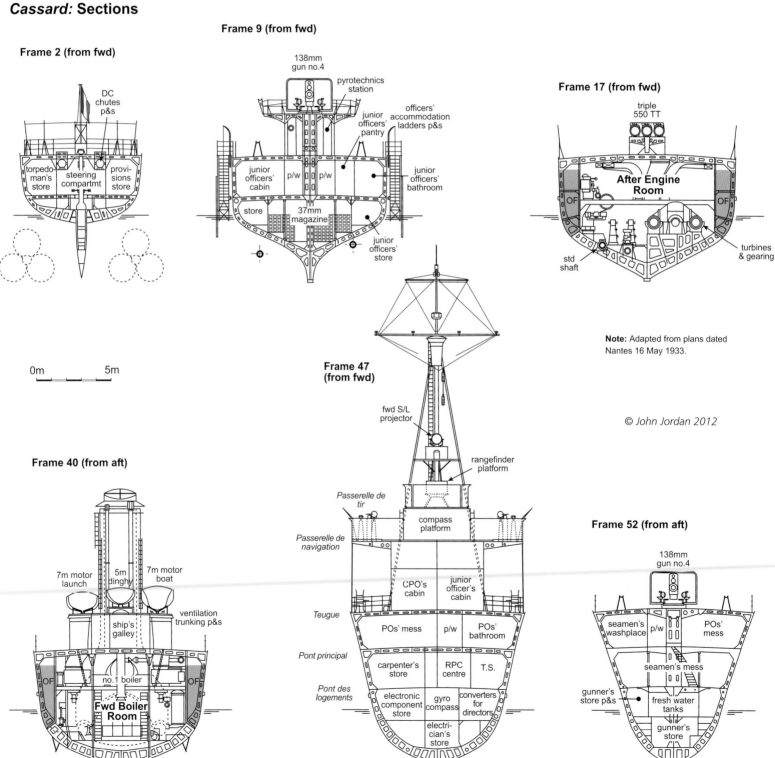

Cassard: Sections

Note: Adapted from plans dated Nantes 16 May 1933.

© John Jordan 2012

the remaining ships a CET 32. On *Vauquelin* this was replaced by a Langevin-type SCAM model.

MACHINERY: *VAUQUELIN* CLASS

The six ships of the *Vauquelin* class were the last to have saturated steam machinery; all subsequent *torpilleurs d'escadre* and *contre-torpilleurs* would have superheated steam, which would be trialled in *Milan* and *Epervier* (see below). The propulsion machinery adopted for the *Vauquelins* was virtually identical in configuration and performance to that installed in the *Aigle* class. Consideration was given to combining the uptakes for the forward and after boiler rooms into two broad funnels, but in the event the distinctive four-funnel silhouette was retained.

Cassard (A C Bretagne) and *Kersaint* (CNF, Caen) had the Rateau-Bretagne impulse turbines which had been such a conspicuous success in the *Gerfaut* (see Chapter 5); the other four ships had Parsons reaction turbines. A C Loire, Penhoët, and F C Méditerranée (all Parsons) built their own turbines; the turbines for the other three ships were contracted out to other suppliers (see accompanying table).

The Parsons turbines comprised a high-pressure (HP) and a low-pressure (LP) turbine working in series, with a separate cruise turbine clutched to the shaft of the HP turbine; the reversing turbine was on the shaft for the LP turbine and housed within the same casing. The HP turbine was rated at 14,000CV and the LP turbine at 18,000CV. When going ahead, steam was

MACHINERY CONTRACTORS

	Builder	Turbine type	Main contractor	Sub-contractor
Vauquelin	AC France	Parsons	(shipyard)	fwd boilers: AC France aft boilers: Babcock & Wilcox turbines: Fives-Lille
Kersaint	AC Loire/CNF	Rateau-Bretagne	(shipyard)	fwd boilers: CNF aft boilers: AC Gironde turbines: Schneider
Cassard	AC Bretagne	Rateau-Bretagne	[shipyard]	boilers: AC Seine-Maritime turbines: Constructions Mécaniques
Tartu	AC Loire	Zoelly	[shipyard]	fwd boilers: AC Loire aft boilers: Augustin Normand turbines: AC Loire
Maillé-Brézé	Penhoët	Parsons	[shipyard]	fwd boilers: Penhoët aft boilers: AC Gironde turbines: Penhoët
Le Chev. Paul	FC Méditerranée	Parsons	[shipyard]	fwd boilers: F C Méditerranée aft boilers: Augustin Normand turbines: F C Méditerranée

Below: *Tartu* on her trials in the spring of 1932. The first of the class to be completed, she retains the half-chutes for projectiles and cartridges with which she and her sisters were designed. *(Philippe Caresse collection)*

admitted to the cruise turbine up to approximately one seventh of maximum power (4500CV), then to the HP turbine and finally to the LP turbine. The cruise turbine could be declutched at low speeds, but it could be clutched to the shaft only when the ship was at rest.

The Rateau-Bretagne turbines were arranged as in *Gerfaut* (see text and schematic p.97). The two cruise turbines (designated CR1 and CR2), one operating at high pressure, the other at low pressure, had a combined output of 4800CV. They had their own separate gearing, which was clutched to the main HP turbine.

Each shaft was fitted with a three-bladed propeller of very-high-resistance bronze with a diameter of 3.69 metres (4.18m in *Cassard*). The single suspended, balanced rudder had a surface area of around 14.25m^2.

The maximum speeds achieved on trials were again impressive (see table for full power trial results). *Cassard* made 42.9 knots over three hours on her Washington displacement full power trial, beating the record established by *Gerfaut* the previous year (see Chapter 5). During the 10-hour Maximum Normal Power (PMN) trial, which was undertaken at normal displacement, all four ships sustained speeds in excess of 37 knots, and between 38.5 knots and 41 knots with forced draught; the figure of 37 knots was subsequently adopted as the maximum speed in formation.[5]

Peacetime fuel bunkerage was 360 tonnes, a figure which rose to 540 tonnes (usable) at deep load. Provision of reserve feed water for the boilers at deep load was 129 tonnes, carried in side and bottom tanks. There was the customary 12 tonnes of fresh water for sanitation, plus 4 tonnes of potable water for the crew in 500-litre tanks fore and aft (see plan). The endurance of the Rateau-Bretagne ships was marginally greater at high speed (800nm approx. at 34 knots), but on cruise turbines there was little to choose between the Parsons and the Rateau ships: following trials it was estimated to be some 3000nm at 14 knots.

Electricity generation was as in the *Guépard* and *Aigle* classes, with two 80kW (106kW max.) turbo-generators distributed between the forward and after engine rooms, and two 22kW (26.5kW max.) Bettus-Loire emergency generators in the centre deckhouse (see Inboard Profile and Plan).

MACHINERY: *MILAN* AND *EPERVIER*

The theoretical attraction of superheated steam was that it provided greater power with lower fuel consumption. Turbines using superheated steam technology for generating electricity were already in widespread use on land,[6] but considerable redesign was necessary to develop machinery sufficiently light and compact to be accommodated on board ship.

During the mid-1920s both the Royal Navy and the Italian *Regia Marina* had laid down destroyers using the new technology, and the *Marine Nationale* was keen not to be left behind. The 'aviation transport' *Commandant Teste* was the first French warship design to feature superheated steam, but total horse-power was little more than 20,000CV, and steam conditions relatively conservative at 20kg/cm^2 and 290°C. For the contemporary British destroyers of the 'A' class, the figures were 21kg/cm^2 and 315°C, and one ship (*Acheron*) had an experimental installation rated at 35kg/cm^2 and 450°C. The Italian destroyer *Francesco Nullo*, which ran trials in 1926 using Yarrow superheated steam machinery built under licence, achieved 37.4 knots and yet proved exceptionally economical.

In October 1928 it was decided that the two delayed ships of the *Aigle* series, *Milan* and *Epervier*, would be prototypes for superheated machinery using British technology under licence. The machinery for *Epervier* was ordered from A C Bretagne on 29 October 1929,

---

[5] 'Raiding speed' (*vitesse pratique de raid*) was fixed at 34 knots; combat speed, which took into consideration vibration and the need for a steady gunnery platform, was fixed at 30/31 knots.

[6] Pressures of 80-100kg/cm^2 were being achieved, and temperatures of 400-450° Celsius.

Opposite: *Le Chevalier Paul* as completed in 1934. She was fitted from the outset with the new circular projectile chutes. Note the platform for the two 75cm searchlight projectors that was a distinguishing feature of this class. As completed these ships had the traditional 3 metre coincidence rangefinder in an open mounting atop the bridge.

MAXIMUM NORMAL POWER AND FULL POWER TRIALS

The trials were to be run at a mean displacement of 2,690 tonnes; adjustments were made for ships which displaced in excess of this figure at the start of the trial.

	Vauquelin	Kersaint	Cassard	Tartu	Maillé-Brézé	Le Chev. Paul
Date of trial:	7 Apr 1933	28 Jul 1933	26 Aug 1932	24 Aug 1932	5 Oct 1932	3 Mar 1934
Displacement:	2633t	2628t	2626t	2636t	2618t	2623t
Average over 8 hours						
Shaft revolutions:	358rpm	348rpm	307rpm	359rpm	357rpm	360rpm
Horsepower:	72,891CV	64,625CV	69,725CV	69,976CV	66,821V	65,415CV
Speed:	38.20kts	37.03kts	39.64.10kts	38.59kts	39.20kts	37.77kts
(corrected)	(–)	(37.01kts)	(39.49kts)	(38.47kts)	(38.90kts)	(37.73kts)
Fuel consumption:	27.92t/h	28.25t/h	28.57t/h	28.56t/h	28.82t/h	28.02t/h
Average 9th hour						
Shaft revolutions:	375rpm	365rpm	391rpm	372rpm	367rpm	375rpm
Horsepower:	79,846CV	70,997CV	76,833CV	72,970CV	69,362CV	70,575CV
Speed:	39.73kts	38.41kts	41.03kts	39.90kts	40.37kts	39.13kts
Fuel consumption:	30.54t/h	31.62t/h	32.10t/h	32.10t/h	30.29t/h	32.31t/h

Notes:
The figures representing the best performance for the class are underlined.

Source : 9DD^1 series, SHD Vincennes.

and that for *Milan* from A C Loire on 12 November 1929.

Epervier had two Thornycroft-type boilers (subcontracted to Penhoët, who held the licence) in the forward boiler room, and two Du Temple/Normand boilers (subcontracted to F C Méditerranée) in the after boiler room. Each of the four boilers was fitted with a Thornycroft-type longitudinal superheater.

Milan had two Du Temple-type boilers of different design in the forward boiler room (again subcontracted to F C Méditerranée), and two Yarrow-type boilers in the after boiler room. Each of the four boilers was fitted with a Yarrow-type transverse superheater.

The boilers installed in both ships were rated at 27kg/cm^2 and 325°C (225° saturated + 100° superheated steam).[7] They therefore operated at far higher pressure than those using saturated steam technology and proved very delicate in operation. A steam leak led to a much greater loss of distilled water than with a conventional boiler, so the evaporators had a crucial role in keeping the reserve feed water tanks topped up.

Epervier had Rateau-Bretagne impulse turbines, with HP, IP and LP turbines working in series, and two cruise turbines with independent gearing clutched to the shaft for the IP turbine. *Milan* had Parsons reaction turbines, with a single cruise turbine clutched to the IP turbine. Both the Rateau and the Parsons turbines had a reverse turbine inside the housing for the LP turbine. The two three-bladed propellers, which were of very-high-resistance brass, had a diameter of 3.69m.

On the Washington displacement trial *Epervier* was marginally faster with a speed of 43.05 knots (corrected to 41.95 knots) with 83,026CV; *Milan* achieved 42.46 knots (corrected to 41.58 knots) with 79,796CV. Both trials took place in favourable weather conditions

Bunkerage was similar to the *Vauquelin* class. However, the greater fuel economy of the superheated steam machinery meant that endurance was margin-

---

[7] At maximum power *Epervier* achieved a temperature of 370°C.

MAXIMUM NORMAL POWER AND FULL POWER TRIALS

The trials were to be run at a mean displacement of 2,690 tonnes; adjustments were made for a ship which displaced in excess of this figure at the start of the trial.

	Milan	*Epervier*
Date of trial:	2 Aug 1933	20 Apr 1933
Displacement:	2587t	2624t
Average over 8 hours		
Shaft revolutions:	381rpm	379rpm
Horsepower:	72,518CV	<u>75,826CV</u>
Speed: (corrected)	38.72kts	<u>39.73kts</u>
Fuel consumption:	26.75t/h	<u>25.20t/h</u>

Notes:
1. *Milan* and *Epervier* did not undertake a full power trial directly after the 8-hour PMN trial.
2. The figures representing the best performance for the class are underlined.

Source: 9DD[1] series, SHD Vincennes.

WASHINGTON TRIALS

The trials were to be run at a 'standard' displacement of 2441 tonnes; adjustments were made for a displacement in excess of or below this figure at the start of the trial.

	Milan	*Epervier*
Date of trial:	30 Aug 1933	2 May 1933
Displacement:	2268t	2370t
Shaft revolutions:	420rpm	411rpm
Horsepower (corrected):	79,796CV	<u>83,026CV</u>
Speed (corrected):	42.46kts	<u>43.05kts</u>
Fuel consumption:	32.21t/h	<u>28.00t/h</u>

Notes:
The figures representing the best performance for the class are underlined.

Source: 9DD[1] series, SHD Vincennes.

ally greater than for the *Vauquelins*: 900nm at 34 knots, and 3100nm at 15 knots.

MAIN ARMAMENT

The *Vauquelin* class was armed with the same 138.6mm/40 Mle 1927 gun which equipped the *Aigle* class. Peacetime ammunition provision was

unchanged at 100 rounds per gun, with stowage for 24 ready-use rounds close to guns nos.1, 2, 4 and 5, and 48 rounds for gun no.3; there was sufficient magazine capacity to double this figure to 200rpg in wartime. The forward magazines also held 75 starshell rounds for gun no.2.

The official plans of the *Vauquelin* class all show the ammunition chute arrangement adopted for the *Guépard* and *Aigle* classes, with separate chutes for shells and charges emerging alongside the guns. However, those for the Lorient-built *Milan* and *Epervier* show a radically different arrangement trialled on *Cassard* in 1933, with short, paired chutes running from the charge hoist to behind the breech of the gun, emerging to port and to starboard respectively (see Bridge Decks drawing), and a circular shell chute enveloping the mounting itself. Using this arrangement, shells could be fed from the hoist or the ready-use racks so that they emerged to port or to starboard of the gun. The arrangement was logical, in that the cartridges, which were comparatively light and easily manhandled, had minimal exposure, while the shells, each of which weighed 40kg and which were unlikely to be detonated by enemy shell, could be transferred close to the breech at any angle of train.

The fire control system of the *Vauquelin*s represented an advance on that of the earlier ships, although a 'full director control' system (*télépointage complet*) using remote power control (RPC) was as yet out of reach. The rangefinder fitted in the *Vauquelin*s was the standard SOM 3-metre coincidence model (Mle 1926), but *Epervier* and *Milan* received the more advanced OPL 3-metre stereo Mle 1927.[8] The rangefinder provided range and bearing data for a new electro-mechanical fire control computer designated Mle 1929, which could supply both training and elevation data directly to the guns via a Granat transmitting system; the gun layer had a GD II receiver, and the trainer a GD III receiver, both with follow-the-pointer (FTP) dials.[9]

In the absence of remote power control, the guns could be fired only when the ship passed through the horizontal. This meant that the rate of fire that could be sustained depended as much on sea conditions as on the theoretical firing cycle of the gun.

By the time the *Vauquelin*s were fitting out, group firing by the three ships of a division against a single target (*le tir groupé centralisé par division*) had been practised regularly and formalised, with the leader of the division becoming the *bâtiment directeur de tir*. Transmission of fire control data was via a 5-metre antenna suspended from the masts, with E-20 receivers located in the respective transmitting stations. Range data could also be transmitted visually via concentration dials, which were fitted from the outset in these ships. There was a single concentration

---

[8] The *Manuel du Télémétriste 1929* gives this as the Mle 1926.

[9] In the *Aigle* class, equipped with the older FC computer Mle 1923B, only angle of train (*circulaire*) was transmitted directly.

Right: *Vauquelin* (left) and *Tartu* at Monte Carlo in 1935; they were present at the International Regatta of the Côte d'Azur, which took place from 21 to 24 March. Although French ship design was in theory centralised, the private shipyards were permitted considerable latitude in executing the plans. Note the lower position of the hawsehole in *Vauquelin*, and the different configuration of the breakwater. Both ships retain their original 3-metre coincidence rangefinder atop the bridge. (US Navy NH 88535, courtesy of A D Baker III)

dial on the face of the upper bridge, and two angled at 45 degrees fixed to the after ends of the bridge wings; the new arrangement worked well and was extended to the *Aigle* class. A portable rangefinder with a 1-metre base measured the angle of parallax between the ships; there was a support in each of the bridge wings to enable the rangefinder to be mounted to port or to starboard, depending on the position of the ship within the formation.

A new arrangement was also adopted for the searchlights to resolve the problems experienced in the earlier *contre-torpilleurs*. The two 75cm BBT searchlight projectors were fitted on a raised platform built around the third funnel; the remote control positions continued to be located in the bridge wings so that the searchlights could be operated without the bridge personnel being blinded. A smaller 45cm searchlight (*projecteur de manoeuvre*) was located on the foremast platform. This could be used at night to illuminate other ships at close range.

ANTI-AIRCRAFT WEAPONS

The *Vauquelin* class, like the *Aigle* class, was originally intended to be armed with a single 75mm Mle 1925 HA gun, located on the centre-line forward of the third funnel. The gun was removed from *Albatros* and *Gerfaut* in late 1932 (see Chapter 5) and was never fitted in their successors, which were completed with only the four single semi-automatic 37mm CAS Mle 1925, mounted abeam the centre deckhouse.

However, by the time the *Vauquelin*s were completed in 1933–4, the 13.2mm Mle 1929 Hotchkiss twin mounting (CAD) was coming off the production lines, and two of these were fitted in place of the earlier 8mm Hotchkiss MG. Originally the Hotchkiss CAD were to have been located on the upper deck amidships, with OPL 1-metre stereoscopic rangefinders (Mle J.1930) sited atop the forward end of the centre deckhouse to supply range and bearing data for both the 37mm and the 13.2mm guns. However, it was subsequently decided to relocate the 13.2mm CAD to the forecastle to cover forward arcs. Whereas the range/bearing data for the 37mm was supplied via a voice link, which tended to be drowned out by the noise of the ventilators for the after boiler room, for the 13.2mm the combat telephone system was used, which proved far more effective.

The 13.2mm CAD was a reasonably effective weapon against the relatively slow-moving biplane aircraft of the early 1930s. It had a range in excess of 2000m and could deliver 450 rounds per gun per minute. However, the 30-round magazine provided only four seconds of fire before it needed to be replaced, whereas twelve seconds of continuous fire was reckoned to be necessary in order to disable an aircraft approaching at 600k/h at 2000m. Moreover, the mounting had a slow response that made it fundamentally unsuited to engaging dive-bombers.[10]

Custom and practice for anti-aircraft fire for light guns during the period was for the guns to open fire

---

[10] A new mounting would be improvised for some of the 1455-tonne destroyers during 1941-2 by the Sidi-Abdallah dockyard at Bizerte (see Chapter 2).

13.2/76 HOTCHKISS MLE 1929

Gun Data

Weight of gun	30kg
Ammunition type	fixed
Projectiles	AP and HE (50gm) tracer
Propellant	52g
Complete round	
weight	122g
dimensions	135mm x 13.2mm
Muzzle velocity	800m/s
Max. range	3500m theoretical
	2500m effective

Mounting Data

Designation	CAD on R4
Weight of mounting	1.16t
Elevation of guns	−15° / +90°
Firing cycle (per gun)	450rpm theoretical
	250rpm practical

Notes:

Mle	*Modèle*	Model
CAS	*Contre-Avions Double*	AA twin mounting

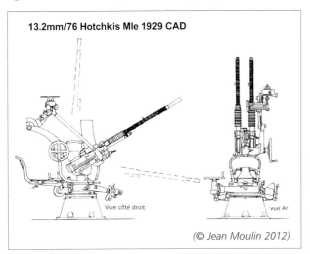

13.2mm/76 Hotchkis Mle 1929 CAD

(© Jean Moulin 2012)

Below: The *Vauquelin* class was the first to be designed from the outset with the twin 13.2mm Hotchkiss mounting Mle 1929. When sufficient mountings became available they were initially fitted at the after end of the forecastle deck. With the advent of fast, high-performance monoplane aircraft the 13.2mm was of limited use, even with the new Le Prieur sight fitted from 1939.

ahead of an approaching aircraft so that the latter had to pass through a curtain of fire (*le tir en grappes*). Once the aircraft had passed through the barrage the range was again shifted ahead of the target.

TORPEDOES

In contrast to earlier *contre-torpilleurs*, the Vauquelin class were armed with seven 550mm Mle 1923DT torpedoes, which were fired from one triple and two twin mountings. The triple mounting aft was a Mle 1928T (T = *triple*) built by A C Loire; the forward paired mountings were a new Mle 1928D (D = *double*) manufactured by the Compagnie Française de Constructions Mécaniques.

The triple mounting could launch torpedoes 30 degrees either side of the beam, as in earlier ships. However, the twin tubes could launch 70 degrees either side of the beam, i.e. within 20 degrees of the ship's axis; this made it possible to respond quickly to ships encountered on forward bearings in conditions of poor visibility or at night. Fire control for the torpedoes was as in the *Aigle* class.

ANTI-SUBMARINE WEAPONS AND DETECTION APPARATUS

There were two depth charge chutes each with eight depth charges as in the *Guépard* and *Aigle* classes, but in order to compensate for the additional weight of the torpedoes and their mountings, the number of depth charge throwers was reduced from four to two.

The four 100/250 Mle 1928 depth charge throwers fitted in the *Aigle* class would be disembarked shortly after completion, essentially to improve lateral stability. However, topweight was less of a concern in the Vauquelin class, so the two DCTs were fitted as planned. In order to free up the arcs for the twin torpedo mountings on forward bearings, the depth charge throwers were fitted on the upper deck abeam the centre deckhouse, just abaft the 37mm CAS. In *Milan* and *Epervier*, which had the two boats on davits amidships, they were farther forward than on the six Vauquelins, which had the 7-metre whaler and cutter abeam the after deckhouse. The plans of the Vauquelins show a more elaborate arrangement, with a stowage rack for three spare charges forward of the DCTs, both the rack and the DCT being served by a derrick seated on the centre deckhouse (see accompanying drawing of arrangements in *Cassard*).

There was provision for eight reserve 200kg depth charges to be stowed in the below-decks magazine in wartime, in place of the torpedo warheads, and for twelve 100kg depth charges for the DCTs: two on the throwers, six on stowage racks, and four in the magazine. This allowed for three attacks each of two passes: each pass would deliver four 200kg depth charges from the chutes plus two 100kg depth charges from the throwers. Two complete attacks could be carried out without having to bring up reserve charges from the magazine.

Milan and *Epervier* were fitted experimentally with a Nandillon underwater detection system based on two active transmitters (*cloches*) and two microphones. The equipment again proved of limited value.

MINE RAILS

Two Décauville 25-metre tracks were provided, each for 20 mines. The after sections, for five mines per side, were fixed and overhung the stern; the other sections were normally in storage on land, and were embarked specifically for a minelaying operation. They could be stowed below decks, and took some six hours for the crew to assemble.

The Breguet B4 mine, *type torpilleur*, had an all-up weight of 530kg and a 80kg TNT charge, and was laid manually over the stern; the length of the mine cable was preset on board ship. The additional 21.4 tonnes of weight could be compensated by the disembarkation of 138.6mm ammunition from the after magazines. The fixed 5-metre sections were used for the regulation annual minelaying exercise, which involved the laying of ten exercise mines; the mine rails would never be used in wartime.

The Vauquelin class was fitted for, but not with minesweeping paravane gear.

COMMUNICATIONS

The respective functions of the two W/T offices were revised in the Vauquelin class. The main W/T office, the *PC Radio* (after end of the bridge block – see GA and Bridge Decks plans), now monitored all communications and housed all the main receivers:

- an SIF long-wave (2000/12000m) receiver for strategic communications
- two Radio-Industrie D-29 medium-wave receivers (one 300/3000m, the other 100/1500m) for tactical group communications
- two David short-wave receivers

There were also two La Précision Electrique E-20 short-wave receivers in the transmitting station.

Depth Charge Throwers: Cassard

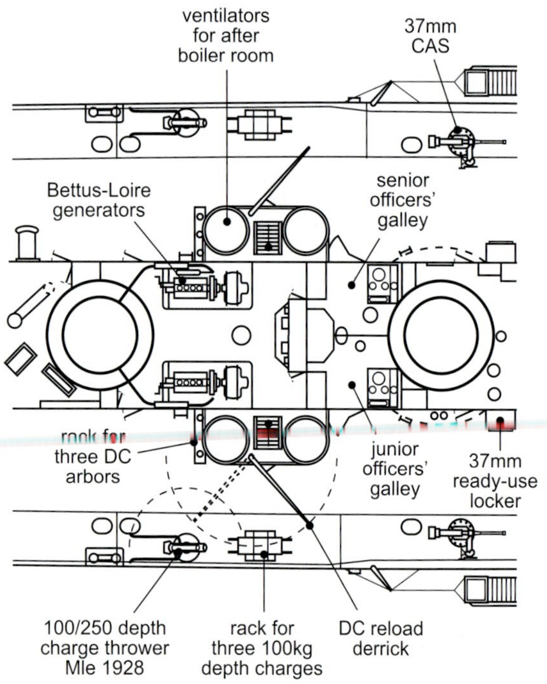

Note: Adapted from plans dated Nantes 16 May 1933.

© John Jordan 2013

THE VAUQUELIN CLASS, MILAN AND EPERVIER

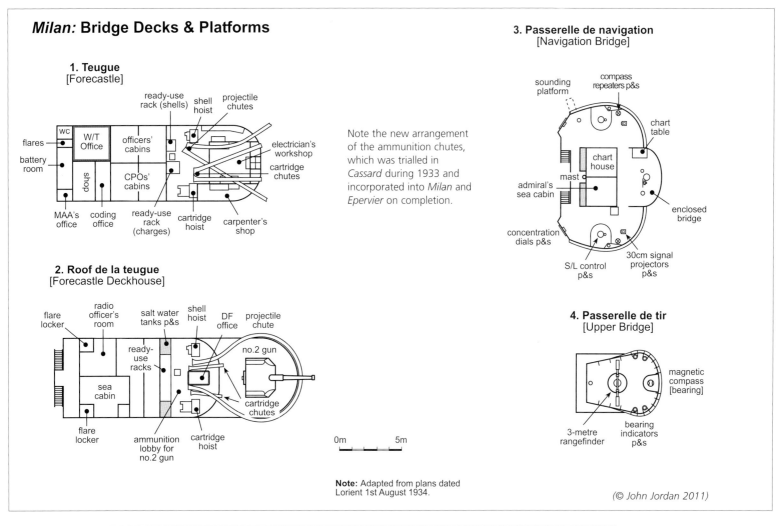

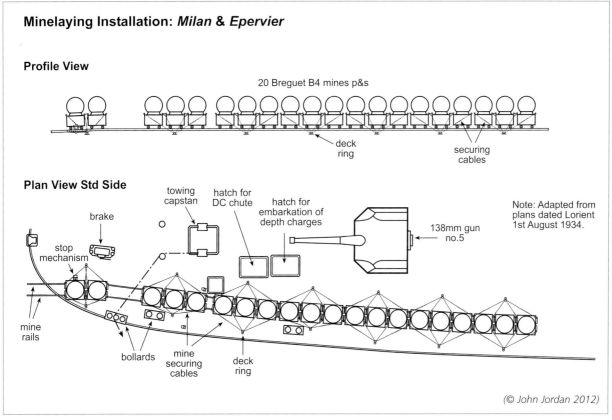

Above: *Tartu* flying the flag of Rear-Admiral Ollive, commanding the *contre-torpilleur* group of the 1st Squadron (Mediterranean) during 1935–6; she was simultaneously the leader of the 5th Light Division. *Tartu* is unmodified except for the rangefinders for the main guns: a 4-metre stereo RF in an open mounting has replaced the original 3-metre model, and the latter has been relocated to the base of the mainmast.

The secondary W/T office (after deckhouse) housed all the transmitters:

- an SFR D-100 long-wave transmitter (500/1200m)
- a Radio-Energie V-28 medium-wave transmitter
- a 500W short-wave transmitter
- two 50W E-20 short-wave transmitters

The direction-finding office was located between the hoists for the forward guns, with the antenna directly above.

Much of the radio equipment was dated; indeed some of it had been recycled from decommissioned vessels in order to save money. It was quickly acknowledged that this was unsatisfactory for ships intended to scout for the fleet, a task which required reliable, secure communications. Almost as soon as the ships were completed a modernisation programme was decreed.[11]

BOATS

The complement of boats was slightly reduced in order to free up the training arcs for the forward torpedo tubes. The 7-metre motor boat and motor launch were disposed as in *Vautour*, *Albatros* and *Gerfaut* of the *Aigle* class, on rails abeam funnels 1 and 2, but there was only a single 5-metre (motor) dinghy, and it was located between the larger boats on the centre-line. *Milan* was fitted from the outset as a flagship and had a second 7-metre motor boat forward, to port of the motor launch.

The arrangements for the 7-metre whaler and the 7-metre pulling cutter, which were on davits, varied between ships. In the six ships of the *Vauquelin* class these two boats were located abeam the after deckhouse, as in the *Guépard* and *Aigle* classes. *Vauquelin* had the whaler to starboard and the cutter to port, the respective positions being reversed in the remaining five ships. In *Epervier* and *Milan* these two boats were relocated amidships, abeam the centre deckhouse; they were effectively switched with the torpedo embarkation cradles and derricks, which were abeam the after deckhouse.

---

[11] DM 17023 CN/10 dated 30 March 1934.

COMPLEMENT

The regulation peacetime complement of these ships comprised ten officers and 201 men. The function and rank of the officers and the breakdown of the crew was as for the *Aigle* class (see Chapter 5). In wartime the number of petty officers and seamen would increase to 220.[12]

Milan was specially fitted out as flagship for a rear-admiral and his staff. The latter comprised three senior officers (a *capitaine de frégate* as chief of staff, a senior supply officer, and a senior MO), together with a *lieutenant de vaisseau* to assist the chief of staff. The supply officer and the MO were generally accommodated on board the other ships of the division.

EVALUATION

The *Vauquelin*s were considered to be excellent sea-boats, which performed even better in the broad swell of the Atlantic than in the confined waters of the Mediterranean. The reduction in topweight through extensive use of welding and duralumin in their superstructures was particularly beneficial, and they had a gentle roll of 6–10 seconds duration (depending on loading) which made them steady gunnery platforms. However, their high silhouette caused them to take on a marked angle of heel in a cross-wind, and their slim hull-form and relatively small rudder, both of which were designed for high 'straight-line' speed, gave them a large turning circle which made them poorly suited to anti-submarine and escort work. The turning circle as measured on trials was in excess of 600 metres to starboard (less to port) at 15 knots; at 30 knots it rose to 1100–1300 metres, and at 32+ knots to 1500–1600 metres.

All the early French *contre-torpilleurs* were heavy in the bow at deep load, when the forward transverse fuel tank (150 tonnes) was full, and this remained a problem in the *Vauquelin* class; it was custom and practice to use the fuel in this tank first.

The extensive use of duralumin for superstructures was much criticised once the ships entered service. The superstructures were easily damaged by blast, particularly when the guns were fired on extreme bearings, and the duralumin quickly became pitted and corroded if exposed to the elements, and needed constant maintenance.

The reduction in the number of boats became an issue when the ships deployed to Brest. At Toulon there were sufficient berths for every one of the *contre-torpilleurs*; however, at Brest there were sufficient only for the two divisional leaders, the other ships generally having to moor with their sterns to the south jetty (see map p.206).

The superheated steam machinery of *Milan* and *Epervier* gave considerable problems from the outset, but this is unsurprising given the novelty of the technology. Of greater consequence was the delay in completing the ships, which meant that their prototype machinery was still being trialled long after the orders for their successors of the 1930 estimates (*Le Fantasque* class – see Chapter 7) had to be placed, with the result that the latter ships initially experienced problems which were every bit as serious as with *Epervier* and *Milan*.

---

[12] Ships fitted with Alpha would have a supplement of four men.

MODIFICATIONS 1933 TO 1939
Main guns and fire control
In 1933 *Cassard* trialled new circular ammunition chutes for the 138.6mm guns. They proved particularly successful and directive 11481 CN/4 of 25 October 1933 stipulated that they be retro-fitted in all the *contre-torpilleurs* armed with the Mle 1927 gun during 1934–5.[13]

The rangefinder provision in these and the earlier *contre-torpilleurs* had been criticised as inadequate from the outset, and the *Vauquelin*s as completed had a circular platform around the base of the mainmast to accommodate an after rangefinder. When the OPL 4-metre stereo rangefinder Mle E.1930 became available in 1934 it replaced the original 3-metre coincidence model (SOM B.1926) atop the bridge, and the latter was relocated to the platform aft. A data link enabled range and bearing data to be sent directly to the transmitting station for processing.

At the same time the E-20 receiver in the transmitting station was replaced by an OCSE (*ondes courtes de sauvegarde de rade*) receiver which was constantly tuned to the 'artillery' frequency. *Tartu* also received, in 1934, a prototype OTC very-short-wave radio for bridge-to-bridge voice communication; it employed a 40W magnetron and operated in the 3.6/4-metre waveband. Results were promising, with ranges of up to 10nm being achieved.

Further rangefinder upgrades took place from 1935. The 4-metre rangefinder atop the bridge was replaced by the new 5-metre stereo model (OPL E.1935) in a two-man turret, and the 4-metre rangefinder replaced the 3-metre coincidence model aft; a new turret for the latter, seated around the mainmast, was developed by SAGEM, and a mechanical computer Mle 1919 was located in the base of the turret to provide a secondary fire control position. It was *Cassard* which again trialled these modifications during 1935, the other ships being progressively modified 1935–6.

In 1935, despite the weight penalties involved, a network of Granat transmitters and receivers was installed to link the three concentration dials with the transmitting station.

Shell colorants (*dispositif K*) were introduced in the late 1930s for the Mle 1924 SAP shell. Instruction DM 6154 Art./1 of 23 July 1936 assigned colours to the various ships: for the 5th and 9th DCT (*Vauquelin* class) the lead ships would fire red, the second ships green, and the third ships white. A further instruction of 29 June 1937 decreed that white be replaced by yellow, which could be seen more clearly at long range.

In 1939 the 1-metre portable rangefinders used to determine parallax in group firing (bridge wings) were replaced by a single fixed 1-metre stereo rangefinder (OPL J.1930) which replaced the compass at the forward end of the upper bridge; the new rangefinder could also be used in AA fire to supply range and bearing data for the 13.2mm Hotchkiss CAD, which were currently being relocated from the forecastle to a platform above the forward ammunition hoists (see below).

Air defence
A new Le Prieur sight with correction for deflection intended for high-speed targets was ordered in 1936, but not all ships were fitted with it before September 1939.

---

[13] Similar ammunition chutes feature in the official plans of *Milan* which are dated 1st August 1934 (see Bridge Decks drawings).

Below: A port quarter view of *Cassard* departing Toulon on 22 June 1938. She has now been fitted with a 5-metre stereo rangefinder atop the bridge, and the 4-metre model it has displaced is now in a trainable turret at the base of the mainmast. Note the distinctive *cul de poule* stern, and the tricolore neutrality markings on the shields of guns nos. 2, 3 and 4. *(Marius Bar)*

A ministerial circular dated 12 August 1938[14] proposed the replacement of the 37mm CAS with the 37mm CAD Mle 1933. However, delays in the delivery of the twin mounting prevented implementation before the outbreak of war, priority being given to the cruisers. The same circular stipulated that the 13.2mm CAD mountings were to be relocated from the forecastle to a platform above the forward hoists. This improved bow and vertical arcs, making it possible to engage aircraft approaching at higher altitudes (within the limitations of the gun and its mounting). Range and bearing data for the guns were to be provided by the 1-metre OPL stereo rangefinder fitted for group firing (see above). As this modification was given a low priority, it was implemented only in the three ships of the 5th DCT before the war, during early 1939.

The spring of 1939 saw the abandonment of the *tir en grappes* procedure; the guns were now to be aimed at the target and to follow the aircraft throughout the engagement. In order to provide continuous fire from the 13.2mm Hotchkiss MG studies were undertaken of continuous feed belts to replace the 30-round magazines. However, the main issue was the shortage of light AA mountings. The Mle 1929 was no longer in production for Hotchkiss at their Levallois factory, where work was now concentrated on anti-aircraft gun mountings for the Army. The Navy therefore turned to the Fabrique Nationale d'Herstal (Belgium), which was producing the American Browning 0.5in (12.7mm) machine gun under licence. A contract for 361 guns with the firing chamber modified to accommodate the standard French SFM 13.2mm round was signed on 10 July 1939, with delivery of the first guns specified for January 1940. At the same time, 500 mountings and sights were ordered from Italy. The Browning MG used continuous feed belts, and in theory could deliver up to 1000 rounds per minute – more than twice the rate of fire of a single 13.2mm Hotchkiss gun. It would become available in increasing numbers in 1941, when many mountings would be fitted in French destroyers and cruisers during refits at Toulon and in North Africa.

Torpedoes and anti-submarine warfare

During the latter half of 1936 Mle 1933 sights for torpedo fire control were fitted in the bridge wings.

Although topweight was less problematic than in the preceeding classes of *contre-torpilleur*, there were inevitable weight gains as a result of the provision of rangefinder turrets and the addition of other items of equipment.[15] Moreover, anti-submarine warfare was no longer regarded as a primary mission of these ships, so the two depth charge throwers were disembarked during 1936 (*Vauquelin* class) and 1937 (*Milan/Epervier*). The additional space available in the

---

[14] CM 13941 CN/6.

[15] By the late 1930s metacentric height was down from 0.8m (designed) + to around 0.62m.

Below: *Tartu* at Malta in the summer of 1939. The 5-metre rangefinder atop the bridge is now in a trainable turret, and the 13.2mm Hotchkiss mountings have been relocated from the after end of the forecastle to the platform atop the forward hoists.

magazine aft was used to accommodate a larger number of 200kg depth charges.

Communications

The W/T outfit was modernised and upgraded during 1935–6. The long-wave and medium-wave receivers were replaced by:

- an SFR Mle 1934 long-wave receiver covering the 1800/20,000m waveband
- two SFR Mle 1934 medium-wave receivers covering the 1200/2400m waveband

Of the original transmitters, only the D-100 was retained. The new transmitters were:

- an SFR 600W medium-wave transmitter Mle 1934 (120/1200m)
- an SFR 500W short-wave transmitter Mle 1934 (15/120m)
- an SFR 75W short-wave transmitter Mle 1934 (13/120m)
- an OCSR 120W short-wave transmitter Mle 1934 operating on the emergency waveband (350/800m)

The original direction-finding receiver was replaced by an SFR medium-wave Mle 1935 monitoring transmissions in the 300/3000m waveband.

From January 1936 the prototype OTC radio equipment for bridge-to-bridge voice telephone communication was replaced by a production model, the SIF Mle 1935, operating in the 3.5/5.5m waveband with a range of 5nm. From early 1939 this would be superseded by the much-improved OTC Mle 1937, which had an SIF transmitter allied to an SFR receiver and operated in the 3.5/7m waveband.

MODIFICATIONS 1939 TO 1942: VAUQUELIN CLASS

Main guns and fire control

The lack of a device able to compensate for the heel of the ship when firing was considered a major handicap, as it slowed the firing cycle. This led to a directive in late 1939[16] for optical correctors to be investigated. Two types of Cuny binocular sights ('A' to correct deflection and 'B' to correct gunlaying for each mounting) plus a simple Simonin list compensator were trialled aboard the three ships of the 5th DCT (*Tartu*, *Vauquelin* and *Kersaint*) in the autumn of 1941. The Cuny optical correctors were found to be superior.

During the winter of 1939–40 the unreliability of the ammunition hoists prompted the crews to ignore safety procedures and to stow additional ready-use rounds close to the main gun mountings. After the actions off Syria in mid-1941 this practice was formalised by the provision of additional ready-use stowage in the ammunition lobbies behind the guns.

The systematic attribution of shell colorants was steadily eroded as ships transferred between divisions. *Cassard* was issued with non-K (i.e. 'white') shells when she joined the 5th DCT in June 1940, then with 'green' K-shells when she joined the 7th DCT following her refit in late 1941.

The major AA modernisations of 1941 saw the removal of the secondary fire control position aft as

---

[16] 12985 Art./1 dated 26 November 1939.

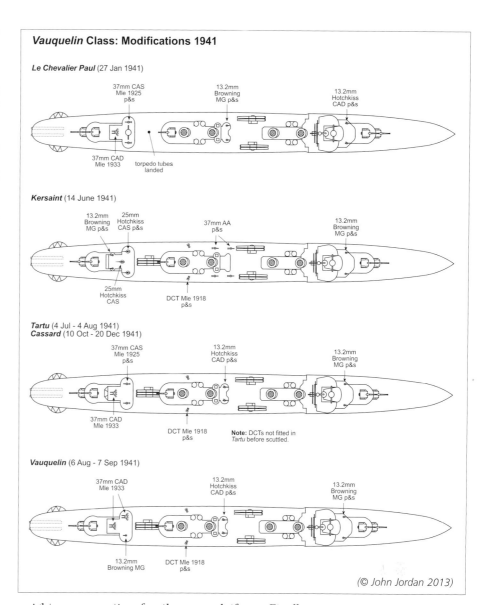

Vauquelin Class: Modifications 1941

(© John Jordan 2013)

weight compensation for the new platform. Finally, during 1941–2 the concentration dials and their Granat transmission network were removed, their function having been superseded by OTC bridge-to-bridge voice communication.

Anti-submarine warfare

Directive 172 FMF/3 (S) of 28 September 1939 established the full complement of depth charges for these ships at 48 x 200kg DC, of which 32 were stowed in the magazine aft. Each attack was now to comprise eight depth charges, so the figure of 48 allowed for six attacks.

However, while the employment of eight depth charges extended the length of the killing zone from 240m to 480m, it remained too narrow at only 60m. The only solution was to reembark two depth charge throwers, as in the earlier *contre-torpilleurs*, and these were to be of the older Thornycroft Mle 1918 type, which had proved more reliable than the Mle 1928. They were to be installed close to the position formerly occupied by the Mle 1928 and to be angled 27 degrees aft of the beam. Two 100kg depth charges would be carried on the throwers, with four reloads (together with their arbors) close by and six in reserve in the magazine aft. At the same time the number of 200kg charges was reduced to 24; each pass would now comprise four 200kg charges from the stern chutes and two 100kg from the DCT – a reversion to the practice established around 1930 (see graphic Chapter 5).

The mortars were installed as follows:

Cassard: Toulon May 1940
Vauquelin: Toulon June 1940
Kersaint: Toulon May/June 1941

Availability problems meant that there were serious delays in implementing this measure; despite subsequent proposals to double the provision to four depth charge throwers, by the spring of 1942 *Tartu* had still not received her first two. As an interim measure, each of the *contre-torpilleurs* received two rails above the stern for light 35kg depth charges; there were three charges on each of the rails and ten reserve charges in the magazine aft.

The *Vauquelin* class was also intended to receive Asdic, but availability was again a problem, and in April 1940 it was decided that *Vauquelin* and *Kersaint*, scheduled to be refitted at Toulon, would be the only ships of the class to be so fitted. *Kersaint* received her Alpha 128 in May 1940; *Vauquelin* in the autumn. *Le Chevalier Paul* could not be fitted with Alpha before her loss in June 1941, but the other two ships eventually received Alpha 128s removed from other ships during late 1941: *Tartu* at Toulon in October, *Cassard* at Oran in December.

Torpedoes

Protective shields were fitted to the torpedo tubes in 1940. In compensation for the AA platform aft *Le Chevalier Paul* disembarked her after torpedo mounting in 1941, much to the displeasure of C-in-C *Forces de Haute Mer* (FHM), who protested that this halving of the torpedo armament resulted in a minimal increase in metacentric height (0.019m). All three torpedo mountings were retained when the other ships received their AA modernisations later that year; instead the after rangefinder was disembarked.

Air defence

With the prospect of the increased availability of 37mm CAD Mle 1933 mountings during 1940 it was proposed to replace some or all of the 37mm CAS mountings. *Vauquelin* had her single guns replaced by two twin mountings at Toulon during May 1940, while *Kersaint* lost only two of her four single guns, the after pair being replaced by twin mountings in November 1940. In both ships provision was made for a total of 4000 37mm rounds (1000rpg); ready-use lockers were provided on either side of the centre deckhouse for 260 rounds, and there were 60 additional rounds (2 x 30) in cabinets on either side of the mounting itself.

A circular dated 13 June 1940[17] proposed the installation of a third CAD Mle 1933 on a new platform to be built atop the after hoists; the mainmast was to be suppressed and the W/T antennae re-affixed to outriggers on the fourth funnel. A subsequent proposal, first implemented in *Le Chevalier Paul* during her refit at Toulon in late 1940, was for the platform to be extended to the sides so that the second and third (currently upper-deck) CAD could be accommodated in the 'wings' of the platform. The after rangefinder was to be replaced by a fire control position for the light AA guns, and the after torpedo mounting landed as weight compensation.

When she left the dockyard in February 1941, *Le Chevalier Paul* had a 37mm CAD in the centre-line position, but the 4-metre rangefinder turret remained in place and two of the original four 37mm CAS were mounted in the wings of the platform. There were six

---

[17] 2642 EMG/1 (S).

Below: *Kersaint* on 21 July 1941. She has just completed her major AA refit at Toulon and has a platform atop the after hoists for three single 25mm Hotchkiss and two 13.2mm Browning MG. The after rangefinder has been landed, but all three torpedo tube mountings and all four 37mm single mountings have been retained. *(Marius Bar)*

THE *VAUQUELIN* CLASS, *MILAN* AND *EPERVIER*

Milan 1942

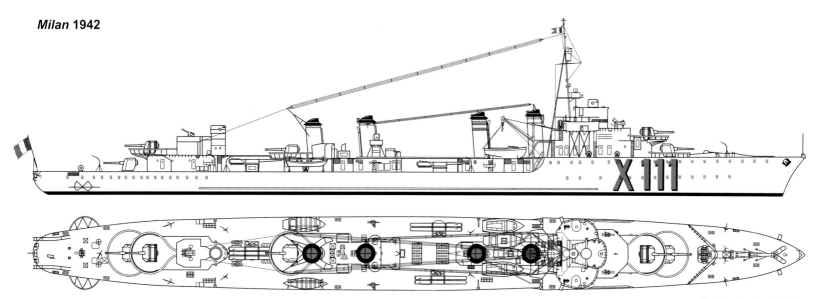

Milan and *Epervier* remained in North Africa 1940–2 and were not as extensively modified as their half-sisters of the *Vauquelin* class, which remained at Toulon. The drawing shows *Milan* as she appeared in late 1942. A platform for a 37mm CAD Mle 1933 mounting has been constructed atop the after 138.6mm hoists; however, the 13.2mm Hotchkiss CAD remain in place forward of the bridge, and the two 1-metre HA rangefinders at the forward end of the centre deckhouse. The mainmast has been suppressed and the W/T antennae refixed to outriggers on the fourth funnel. The after pair of 37mm CAS Mle 1925 has been retained, and two 13.2mm Browning MG have been added in the bridge wings. The after fire control position, with its 4-metre base rangefinder, has been retained, but raised by one metre to clear the 37mm CAD mounting; all three torpedo mountings remain in place.

(© John Jordan 2012)

ready-use lockers each with 400 rounds on the platform, three each with 260 rounds in the upper ammunition lobby directly below, and four lockers each with 360 rounds on the main deck.

This increase in AA capabilities immediately aroused the opposition of the Italian representatives on the Armistice Commission, and it was only after the Syrian crisis of June 1941 that consent was obtained. Similar modifications would subsequently be made to *Tartu*, *Kersaint* and *Vauquelin* during July and August at Toulon, and to *Cassard* during October/November at Oran. However, there were three alternative arrangements due to shortages of the CAD mounting (see accompanying schemas); only *Tartu* and *Cassard* were identical, while *Kersaint* received three 25mm Hotchkiss as a temporary measure – she retained her original 37mm CAS guns. All four ships lost their after rangefinder as weight compensation, but retained all three torpedo mountings.

Delivery of the 13.2mm Browning machine guns

Tartu 1942

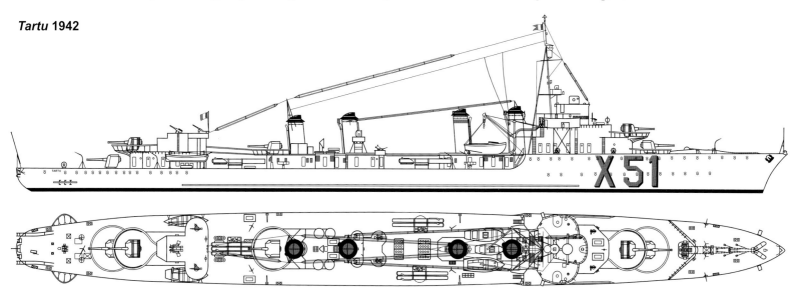

Tartu, like her sisters of the *Vauquelin* class, received a much more complete modernisation than *Milan* and *Epervier*. She is shown here following her refit at Toulon July–August 1941. There is a platform atop the after hoists for a 37mm CAD Mle 1933 mounting, with extensions to the sides for two of her four original 37mm CAS Mle 1925 guns. The mainmast has been suppressed and the W/T antennae refixed to outriggers on the fourth funnel, as on *Milan*, but the secondary fire control position has also been landed as weight compensation for the larger AA platform. Two 13.2mm Browning MG have been fitted in place of the 13.2mm Hotchkiss CAD forward of the bridge, and the latter mountings have been relocated to the forward end of the centre deckhouse. *Tartu* was the only surviving ship of her class not to receive two fixed Thornycroft Mle 1918 depth charge throwers amidships before she was scuttled.

(© John Jordan 2012)

Right: *Epervier* at Djibouti in January 1939, when she was serving with the *Division Navale du Levant* (DNL). She is moored at the Fontainebleau Quay, which was built on the site of the wreck of the liner of the same name, which sank on 11 July 1926 following a fire. *Epervier* was the first ship to moor at the quay. She and her sister *Milan* as completed were virtually indistinguishable from the six *Vauquelin*s except for the position of the boats on davits, which were abreast the centre deckhouse. In this view she has been retro-fitted with the new rangefinders. Unusually, she has tricolore identification markings on the shields of guns nos.2 and 4, but not that of no.3.

ordered in July 1939 was delayed by the need to replace the mountings and sights, which were originally ordered from Italy, with new models manufactured in France. The first was fitted in *Cassard* at Toulon in May 1940. Two were allocated to each ship and various locations were tried[18] before it was decided that they would replace the 13.2mm Hotchkiss CAD on the platform forward of the bridge, the latter mountings being relocated to the forward end of the centre deckhouse (see schemas for *Kersaint* and *Cassard*).

MODIFICATIONS 1939 TO 1942: *MILAN* AND *EPERVIER*

It was January 1940 before *Milan* and *Epervier* received 'K' shells with splash colorants; the modifications were carried out at Dakar. When the Armistice was signed in June 1940, the ships were in Africa, and there they would remain until the end of 1942; in consequence the possibilities for modernisation were restricted.

Anti-submarine warfare

Both ships had been slated to receive Alpha 128 Asdic and two Thornycroft Mle 1918 depth charge throwers. With priority for Alpha being accorded to *contre-torpilleurs* employed as convoy escorts, neither ship had been fitted with either Alpha or the DCTs before the Armistice. Indeed, there was such an acute shortage of DCTs that when in March 1941 the dockyard at Casablanca finally fitted two in *Epervier* in response to the October 1939 directive, it was instructed to remove them forthwith.

Epervier finally received Alpha 128 during her long

---

[18] *Vauquelin* and *Tartu* had theirs atop the after hoists, while in *Cassard* they were mounted on the quarterdeck.

refit at Oran in 1942; *Milan*, which was due to be refitted 1942–3, never received hers; neither ship appears to have received the Mle 1918 DCTs.

Air Defence

Milan and *Epervier* received the standard allocation of two 13.2mm Browning MG during mid/late 1940. It was initially envisaged that they would receive an AA modernisation similar to that of the *Vauquelin*s, with the four 37mm CAS replaced by two CAD Mle 1933 and a third CAD atop a platform on the centre-line aft; the 13.2mm Hotchkiss CAD would be retained in their current location forward of the bridge, and the 13.2mm Browning would be mounted in the bridge wings.

When the Armistice Commission opposed this increase in AA capabilities it was decided to install only the centre-line 37mm CAD Mle 1933 mounting, and to compensate for this by landing two of the four 37mm CAS. However, the after rangefinder and both sets of torpedo tubes would be retained. In the interim the two Brownings were mounted atop the after hoists, as in *Vauquelin* and *Tartu*.

Milan was the first to be modified. A platform was fitted above the after hoists for a 37mm CAD mounting, and the after rangefinder raised by one metre. The after pair of 37mm CAS guns was retained, the forward pair landed, and the 13.2mm Brownings were relocated as planned to the bridge wings.

Epervier had a slightly different arrangement. She had the same platform for the 37mm CAD, but the two 37mm CAS were relocated to tubs abeam this platform, at the level of no.4 gun. One of the 1-metre stereo rangefinders for AA fire control – originally at the forward end of the centre deckhouse – was mounted atop the 4-metre rangefinder turret, which was subsequently raised as in *Milan*; the other 1-metre rangefinder was mounted at the forward end of the upper bridge to cover forward arcs.

THE ART OF JEAN BLADÉ

Surgeon General Jean Bladé was formerly *Directeur Central du Service de santé des Armées*. Previously he served in the Marine Nationale as Medical Officer aboard the frigate *La Confiance*, the fast escorts *Le Béarnais*, *Le Basque* and *Le Lorrain*, the escort sloop *Commandant Bourdais*, the cruiser *Colbert* and the helicopter carrier *Jeanne d'Arc*. His passion for the sea, and in particular for the Marine Nationale, is expressed in the many superlative paintings, both watercolours and oils, which he has produced over the years; these currently total 3600 and cover the period 1922 to 1965. In this eight-page colour section we reproduce a small sample of his watercolours of the interwar *contre-torpilleurs*. Jean Bladé's painting of the *Volta* in 1939 graces the jacket of this book.

Left: *Chacal* in 1931, when she was serving with the 5th Light Division (DL) in the Mediterranean. *Panthère* (5) was the lead ship of the division, *Tigre* (6) the second ship. Exercises and port visits accounted for most of the year's activity.

Left: *Léopard* during a visit to Le Havre in late July 1934. The original 75mm HA guns have been replaced by 13.2mm Hotchkiss twin mountings. Note the semi-circular tub for a 1-metre rangefinder above the engine room access ladders; the MF/DF aerial is to port.

Left: *Chacal* running the gauntlet of German Heinkel 111 bombers during the Battle for France. On 21 May 1940 the 2nd DCT was put at the disposal of *Amiral Nord*, and *Chacal* would be assigned to the Calais sector. She conducted shore bombardments in support of the army before being struck by four bombs on the night of 23/24 May and beached; she was a constructive total loss (see Chapter 12).

Right: *Léopard* moored alongside the colonial sloop *Savorgnan de Brazza* at Portsmouth in mid-July, following their seizure in Operation 'Catapult'. *Léopard* retains her X22 hull number, soon to be painted out; she would be recommissioned by the Free French naval forces (FNFL) in early September.

Right: *Verdun* moored at Toulon shortly after her completion in 1930.

Left: *Bison* alongside *Léopard*, moored close to the mouth of the River Penfeld at Brest in January 1935. In the background is *Léopard*'s sister *Chacal*.

Above: When the Germans entered the dockyard at Toulon on 27 November, *Lion* was undergoing maintenance in Missiessy dock no.2; only her guns were sabotaged. The cruiser *La Galissonnière*, which had been scuttled in the entrance to dock no.3, can be seen beyond her. This area of the dockyard was shrouded in smoke from the fires raging in the cruiser *Dupleix*, which was moored in the adjacent Missiessy basin.

Right: An aerial bow view of *Maillé-Brézé* at Les Salins d'Hyères in 1935. At this time she was serving as the lead ship of the 9th Light Division in the 1st (Mediterranean) Squadron with the hull number 7.

Right: *Epervier* at Beirut in 1938, when she was serving with the *Division Navale du Levant* (DNL). Note the distinctive *cul-de-poule* stern and the rails for the twin depth charge chutes.

Left: *Aigle* during 1940. Together with her half-sisters *Vauban* (X11) and *Lion* (X12) she was part of the 3rd Squadron based at Toulon until placed *en gardiennage* in October.

Right: A fine study of *Gerfaut* on 9 October 1941, immediately after her AA refit at Toulon. The mainmast has been landed, and a platform for a twin 37mm Mle 1933 mounting constructed atop the after ammunition hoists; the after rangefinder has been raised 0.75m to clear the platform. The 13.2mm Hotchkiss mountings have been retained forward of the bridge, but single 13.2mm Browning MG have been fitted in the bridge wings. The 75cm searchlight projectors remain in their original positions.

Right: *Le Malin* in early 1937, soon after her entry into service. Note the hyphen after the number '9', which marks her out as belonging to the 2nd (Atlantic) Squadron. At this time *Le Malin* was serving as the second ship of the 8th Light Division (subsequently DCT).

Left: *Le Triomphant* as she appeared in the summer of 1941, when she was serving with the FNFL in British waters. A British 4-inch Mk V HA gun has replaced mounting no.4, and the torpedo rangefinder turret at the base of the foremast has been removed and replaced by a crow's nest. Single 2pdr pom-pom guns have been fitted in the tubs abreast gun no.2, and the ship is wearing an Atlantic-style dark grey livery.

THE ART OF JEAN BLADÉ

Left: *Le Fantasque* as she appeared in 1944-5, by which time she had exchanged hull numbers with her sister *Le Terrible*. She is wearing the standard US Navy Measure 22 paint scheme (Navy Blue hull and Haze Gray upperworks), and she has now received the prominent funnel cowling trialled on *Le Terrible*. Note the lattice foremast topped by the antennae for the SA air surveillance and the SF surface surveillance radars.

Right: *Le Triomphant* alongside the battleship *Richelieu* during a transfer in September 1945, when both were serving in the Indian Ocean. She is wearing a British Admiralty Standard deceptive camouflage scheme, with a medium blue lozenge on the lower hull and light grey upperworks.

Right: *Mogador* as she appeared in February/March 1939, following repairs and modifications at Lorient. She is flying the flag of Rear-Admiral Lacroix, commanding the 2nd Light Squadron at Brest. In April her hull number would change from '4-' to 'X61'. Following her spell in Lorient dockyard the fore-funnel has been fitted with a prominent cowling to keep smoke clear of the upper bridge, and the twin 13.2mm Hotchkiss mountings have been re-sited atop a new deckhouse forward of the bridge.

Below: *Mogador* at Le Havre on 14 November 1938. Five days previously, she had joined the 2nd Light Squadron at Brest, and on 14 November she would take part in exercises with the new fast battleship *Dunkerque* in the Baie de Seine. The after (twin) 550mm torpedo tubes and the after 5-metre rangefinder tower are particularly prominent in this view; the fore-funnel has yet to receive its prominent cowling.

CHAPTER 7
THE *LE FANTASQUE* CLASS

INTRODUCTION

Had the six-year naval programme embarked on in 1924 proceeded as planned, the six ships of the 1929 estimates would have been virtually indistinguishable from the *Vauquelin*s. The *contre-torpilleur type 1929* would have had four slim funnels, two inclined masts, and an identical hull-form (see preliminary sketch). The key improvements requested by the Naval General Staff were a new long-range gun and superheated steam machinery.

The long-range gun requirement was dictated by developments in the Italian *Regia Marina*, which in 1927 had begun the construction of a series of fast light cruisers armed with 152mm guns, the 'Condottieri'. The new cruisers were specifically designed to catch and out-punch the French *contre-torpilleurs*; designed for a speed of 37 knots, they mounted eight 152mm guns in twin power-operated turrets with director control; the 152/53 gun had a theoretical range of 28,500m at its maximum elevation of 45 degrees. The French Naval General Staff remained confident that a division of *contre-torpilleurs* using coordinated fire could successfully take on a single Italian cruiser, but wanted an increase in range to 20,000m for the new gun, with provision for full director fire control and remote power control (RPC) to ensure a high rate of fire. The new gun, which was a 50-calibre weapon but was otherwise similar in conception to the successful Mle 1927, was approved in February 1929.[1]

The adoption of superheated steam machinery was likewise dictated by developments abroad (see Chapter 6). It was hoped to have the two competitive prototype machinery installations – Rateau-Bretagne turbines with Thornycroft superheaters, and Parsons turbines with Yarrow superheaters – in service on *Milan* and *Epervier* of the 1927 programme before orders needed to be placed for the machinery of the 1929 ships, but in the event the delayed completion of *Milan* and her sister made this impossible, and decisions on the machinery had to be made on a purely theoretical basis.

The definitive project was duly approved by the Comité Technique on 28 June 1929 under the designation *contre-torpilleur de 2610 tonnes type 1929*. It was then delayed by two years.

The first setback was a direct result of the production bottlenecks which had led the orders for the *Vauquelin*s to be put back by one year (see Chapter 6). The *Vauquelin*s were eventually authorised under the 1929 estimates, and the next block of six ships were submitted under the 1930 estimates, which were approved on 12 January 1930; the ships were to be laid down between 1 April 1930 and 31 March 1931. The vote took place just nine days before the first session of the London Conference on naval arms limitation.[2] Although France failed to commit to the quantitative restrictions placed on 'auxiliary vessels' (now formally categorised as 'cruisers', 'destroyers' and 'submarines', etc.), it did agree to impose a 6-month moratorium on construction while bilateral talks with Italy took place, and this further delayed the laying down of the *contre-torpilleurs*, which would henceforth be referred to as the *type 1930*.

These delays inevitably led the Navy to consider further improvements to the design. The NGS wanted endurance increased to 4000nm at 15 knots. Serious

---

[1] Note 1672 Art./3 dated 27 February.

[2] The French were anxious to have their 1930 programme already 'on the table' when the conference began, to lay down a marker and to give their delegation the necessary leverage in the negotiations.

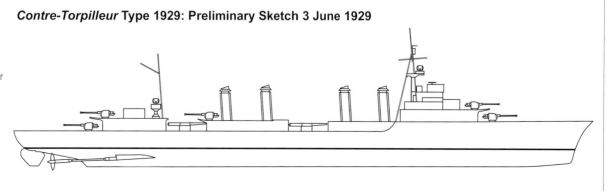

Contre-Torpilleur Type 1929: Preliminary Sketch 3 June 1929

Profile of the *contre-torpilleur type 1929*. As originally conceived, this class of *contre-torpilleurs* differed from their immediate predecessors of the *Vauquelin* class only by the longer Mle 1929 gun. Note the searchlight arrangement, which repeats that of the *Guépard* and *Aigle* classes. In the *Vauquelin*s the searchlights would be relocated to a platform forward the third funnel, and the new arrangement would also be a feature of the *Le Fantasques*.

(© John Jordan 2013)

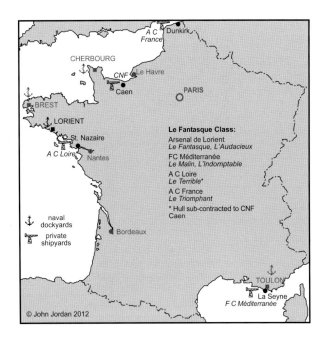

consideration was also given to a twin 138.6mm mounting, but the development of a suitable replenishment system would prove problematic, and a prototype twin mounting would be ready only in time for the following class of contre-torpilleurs (see Chapter 8).

In late 1930 two significant modifications were made to the original design. In order to take the smoke from the fore-funnel clear of the upper bridge, where it hindered rangetaking and created unpleasant conditions for the personnel stationed there, the fore and after pairs of uptakes were combined into two broad funnels. The location of no.3 gun abaft the after funnel had never been liked because it complicated the supply of ammunition, so it was now to be grouped with guns nos.4 and 5 on the after deckhouse, where it could be served directly by the after hoists. However, this posed a problem for the location of the pole mainmast, which was considered essential to the provision of the necessary W/T aerial runs. Initially it was to have been moved, but in January 1934 it was suppressed altogether and replaced by aerial supports on the after funnel. In the interim, in July 1933 it had been decided to replace the tripod foremast by a pole mast around which the forward director was to be seated. These modifications radically changed the silhouette of the ships.

After 1930, anti-surface capabilities were increasingly prioritised and anti-submarine capabilities progressively downgraded. A directive dated 27 February 1932[3] prescribed the suppression of the two 100/250 Mle 1928 depth charge throwers which were a feature of the original design; at around the same time it was decided that the two twin wing torpedo mountings would be boosted to triples for a total of nine (vs. seven) 550mm torpedoes.

Orders for the two ships due to be built at Lorient naval dockyard (Da-16 and Da-17) were placed in late June 1930, and the first steel was cut the following November. However, Lorient was as yet in no position to begin keel laying. Slipways nos.6 and 7 were still occupied, and it would be a further year before the necessary building facilities and labour force would become available; the hulls would eventually be laid down side by side on 16 November 1931 in the large covered dock known as the Forme de Lanester (see map p.22).[4]

The other orders were placed in May 1931, with Forges et Chantiers de la Méditerranée, La Seyne (Da-18 and Da-21), Ateliers et Chantiers de la Loire, Saint-Nazaire (Da-19) and Ateliers et Chantiers de France, Dunkirk (Da-20). As with *Kersaint* of the *Vauquelin* class, the hull of the ship ordered from A C Loire would be built at the CNF shipyard at Blainville, near Caen. Each ship was budgeted to cost 73 million French francs, an increase of 28% over the *Vauquelins*. In common with previous practice, Lorient was to be the *port d'armement* for all six units of the class.

At the height of the Depression, and with many of the shipyards facing financial difficulties, the orders for the propulsion machinery were distributed among no fewer than eleven different sub-contractors. (See Machinery section.)

The names of the new ships were announced by the Minister, Charles Dumont, in September 1931. They revived the names of famous ships of the Revolutionary Wars of the late eighteenth century:

Le Fantasque (launched 1758) was commanded by Suffren during the Antilles campaign of 1779.
Le Triomphant (1779) played a key part in the Antilles campaign of Admiral Guichen during the following year.

---

[3] DM 430 EMG/1.
[4] Built between 1913 and 1923, the Forme de Lanester was built on the site of the former *Fosse aux mâts*, and was one of the most advanced facilities of its kind in Europe; dimensions were 245m by 51m, which enabled two cruiser-sized ships to be built side by side. The first major unit to be laid down in the Forme de Lanester was the cruiser *Lamotte-Picquet*, which was launched on 24 March 1924.

BUILDING DATA

Name	Le Fantasque	L'Audacieux	Le Malin	Le Terrible	Le Triomphant	L'Indomptable
Programme	1930	1930	1930	1930	1930	1930
Prog. no.	142	143	144	145	146	147
Project no.	Da 16	Da 17	Da 18	Da 19	Da 20	Da 21
Builder	Lorient	Lorient	FCM La Seyne	ACL/CNF Caen	ACF Dunkirk	FCM La Seyne
Ordered	17 Nov 1930	17 Nov 1930	23 May 1931	20 Jun 1931	22 May 1931	18 Aug 1931
Laid down	16 Nov 1931	16 Nov 1931	16 Nov 1931	8 Dec 1931	28 Aug 1931	25 Jan 1932
Launched	15 Mar 1934	15 Mar 1934	17 Aug 1933	30 Nov 1933	16 Apr 1934	7 Dec 1933
Manned for trials	1 Sep 1934	1 Sep 1934	15 Dec 1934	1 Oct 1934	1 Jul 1934	1 Oct 1934
Acceptance trials	24 Nov 1934	5 Dec 1934	14 Jun 1935	6 Dec 1934	29 Jan 1935	21 May 1935
Commissioned	15 Nov 1935	1 Aug 1935	20 Dec 1935	15 Apr 1935	31 Dec 1935	15 Nov 1935
Completed	10 Mar 1936	27 Nov 1935	1 May 1936	1 Oct 1935	25 May 1936	10 Feb 1936
Entered service	1 May 1936	7 Dec 1935	8 Jun 1936	5 Feb 1936	24 Jul 1936	15 Apr 1936

THE LE FANTASQUE CLASS

Le Malin (1781) took part in two campaigns in the Antilles 1782–6.

Le Terrible (1780), *L'Audacieux* (1784) and *L'Indomptable* (1790) were part of the French squadron of Admiral Villaret de Joyeuse which successfully lured the British Admiral Howe away from an important grain convoy from North America in 1794; all three ships survived the action, and *L'Indomptable* subsequently distinguished herself during the Battle of Algeciras in 1801.

When the ships were finally laid down in late 1931/early 1932 construction initially proceeded relatively smoothly. However, the period between first sea trials and entry into service was unduly protracted due to various technical problems. Most of these problems related to the advanced propulsion machinery. *Le Triomphant* (A C France), *Le Terrible* (A C Loire) and *L'Indomptable* (F C Méditerranée) all stripped turbine blades, leading to lengthy repairs, *Le Malin* (F C Méditerranée) was unable make the transition from cruise to main turbines during her maiden voyage, and *L'Audacieux* (Lorient) suffered from defective brickwork in her boilers, which had to be completely rebuilt. *Le Fantasque* then grounded when entering Lorient, causing serious damage to her propellers and keel. The number of incidents prompted the Minister to despatch the *Ingénieur général des machines* to Lorient to lead an investigation.

Subsequently Lorient discovered defects in the steel of the deck seatings supplied to the four private shipyards for the main guns – a problem which could have had serious consequences due to the enormous recoil forces of the long-barrelled Mle 1929 gun. These had to be replaced, resulting in a further delay of 5–6 months. In the end the ships averaged four and a half years between laying down and completion, an unimpressive building time for what was essentially a large destroyer, even one as technically advanced as this.

However, there were compensations. The ships made a huge impression with their low, racy profile, and when the machinery was working well it delivered stunning results. On 22 January 1935 *Le Terrible* established the world record for a displacement vessel during her Washington trials. On 30 January 1935 she ran three lengths of the Glenans-Penmarch range, achieving 45.42 knots on her second run with 94,353CV at 419.78rpm. Following a correction made for displacement (Washington standard displacement was 2615.99t), speed was corrected to 45.07 knots. (For a detailed breakdown of the performance of *Le Terrible* and the other ships of the class on their trials see the table p.144.)

HULL AND GENERAL CONFIGURATION

In order to accommodate the changes in armament and the more powerful propulsion machinery, the hull of the *Le Fantasque*s was lengthened by three metres

WEIGHTS

Hull:	957.77t
Protection:	1.31t
Guns:	218.24t
Torpedoes:	60.66t
Mines/DCs:	12.50t
Machinery:	1016.38t
Weight related to displacement:	191.18t
Weight related to machinery:	95.56t
Special fittings:	34.73t
Margin:	20.85t
Washington standard displacement:	2609.00tW
Oil fuel:	120.00t
Reserve feed water:	43.00t
Consumables:	10.00t
Ammunition:	58.00t
Normal diplacement:	2840.00t
Oil fuel (for 360t):	240.00t
Reserve feed water:	85.00t
Ammunition:	13.00t
Various:	2.00t
Load displacement:	3180.00t
Oil fuel (for 580t):	220.00t
Ammunition (wartime):	17.00t
Deep load displacement:	3417.00t

Above: *Le Triomphant* is launched at the Dunkirk shipyard of Ateliers et Chantiers de France (ACF) on 16 April 1934. *(CAW courtesy of Jaroslaw Malinowski)*

Below: *Le Triomphant* being fitted out at ACF, Dunkirk. She was launched, in the tradition of the shipyard, in a fairly advanced state of completion, with machinery and propeller shafts in place. She is now almost ready for trials, lacking only her guns and fire control equipment. *(Stephen Dent collection)*

GENERAL CHARACTERISTICS

Displacement:	2570 tons standard; 2840 tonnes normal; 3417 tonnes deep load
Dimensions:	Length 125.4m pp, 132.4m oa; beam 12.0m; draught 4.5m
Machinery:	Four small-tube boilers with superheating, 27kg/cm² (325°) Two-shaft geared steam turbines 74,000CV for 37kts (designed)
Oil fuel:	580 tonnes; radius 2900nm at 15kts, 900nm at 35kts
Armament:	Five 138.6mm/50 Mle 1929 in single mountings (100rpg + 85 starshell) Four 37mm/50 Mle 1933 AA in twin mountings (500rpg) Four 13.2mm/76 Mle 1929 Hotchkiss MG in two twin mountings (2400rpg) Nine 550mm torpedoes Mle 1923DT in three triple mountings Two chutes each for eight 200kg depth charges (+ 12 reloads) Twin rails for 40 Breguet B4 500kg mines
Complement:	11 officers + 221 men peacetime 11 officers + 254 men wartime

and broadened by 20cm. Hull-form and internal layout were similar to the *Vauquelin* class, although the Lorient-built *Le Fantasque* and *L'Audacieux*, intended to operate as flagships, had some adjustments to their accommodation (see Complement below).

Frame spacing was 2.1 metres forward, reducing to 1.87–1.97m amidships in the area of the machinery spaces, and to 1.8m aft. There were twelve main transverse bulkheads extending from the ship's bottom to the upper deck, as in the *Aigle* and *Vauquelin* classes, and these divided the hull into thirteen watertight compartments designated A–M. Pumps were provided as follows:

– two pumps rated at 100t/h in sections E–J
– single pumps rated at 100t/h in sections B–C
– single pumps rated at 30t/h in sections A and L
– a single pump rated at 10t/h in section K

This represented an advance over the four-funnelled *contre-torpilleurs*, with pump capacity doubled in the sections housing the fore and after magazines as well as in the main machinery spaces.

The hull and main deck were of 6–14mm steel plate with a resistance of 50kg/mm², and were again of riveted construction. Concerns had been expressed regarding the extensive use of the light alloy duralumin for the superstructures of the *Vauquelin* class. The external panels of the bridge structure and deckhouses of the *Le Fantasque* class were of steel, and were reinforced where exposed to blast from the main guns; duralumin was used only for partitioning within the superstructures. These improvements were possible because of the considerable weight saved by reducing the height of the superstructures, masts and funnels. Metacentric height as designed was an impressive 0.90m; this figure was almost achieved in the two Lorient-built ships, *Le Fantasque* and *L'Audacieux* (0.88m), while the four 'industry'-built ships all had a GM of 0.76–0.84m on completion

For the first time in a *contre-torpilleur* it was possible to provide light protection for the magazines, but the weight allowed for this was only 1.3 tonnes. The effect was negligible, but these ships were not intended to withstand sustained heavy fire; according to the

Below: Le Terrible in the locks at Ouistreham, at the exit of the Caen canal, on 22 November 1934, following her completion at the Blainville yard of CNF. She would be the last ship to be built there before the shipyard was closed. The ship is manned for trials but still lacks her armament and fire control directors. (Philippe Caresse collection)

THE *LE FANTASQUE* CLASS

The *Contre-Torpilleur Le Fantasque* 1936

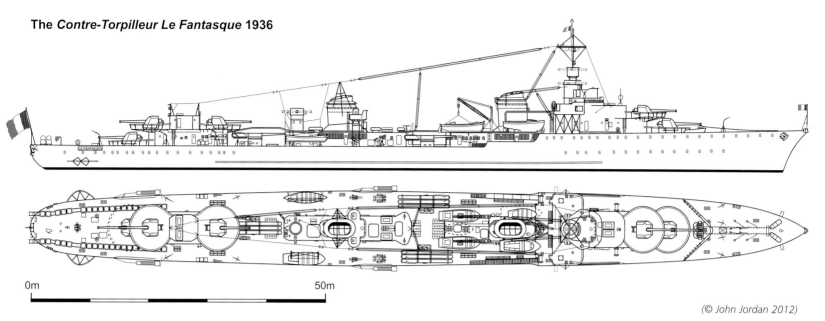

(© John Jordan 2012)

The profile and plan drawings are based on official plans for *Le Fantasque* and *L'Audacieux* dated Lorient 5 November 1936. They show the planned 37mm CAD Mle 1933 and 13.2mm Hotchkiss CAD Mle 1929 mounted on the upper deck abeam the centre deckhouse. Note the reload lockers for 550mm torpedoes abeam the break in the forecastle. The torpedoes were lifted onto the reloading cradles by the boat cranes.

tactical instructions devised for their employment, if faced with heavily armed cruisers they were to get off several rapid salvos and make their escape before the enemy could acquire the range. In practice their light construction would be an advantage, as heavy armour-piercing 203mm (and in one instance 406mm!) shell tended to pass straight through their hulls without detonating.

The layout of the deckhouses above the main deck had to be modified as a result of the decision to move no.3 gun to the after deckhouse. In the latter position it effectively displaced the after W/T office, which was

Le Fantasque: General Arrangement Plans

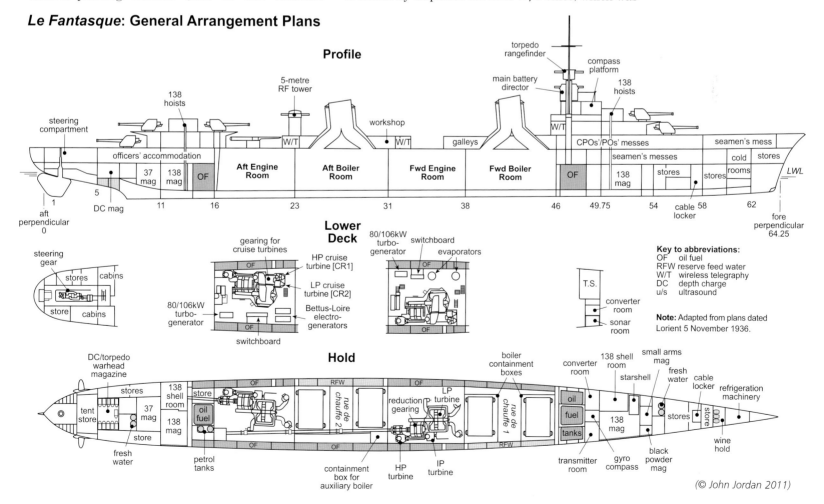

(© John Jordan 2011)

relocated to the after end of the centre deckhouse. The Bettus-Loire emergency generators, which had previously been located in the centre deckhouse, were moved down to the platform deck in the after engine room (see General Arrangement plans). The wing torpedo tubes were retained (and boosted to triple mountings – see above), so the layout of the boats was modified to accommodate the merging of the forward two funnel uptakes. Two boats were on crutches outboard of the first funnel, with the other two on the end of the deckhouse abaft the funnel (see Boats section); there were free-standing boat cranes to port and starboard between them. The two boats on davits were moved forward to a position abeam the centre deckhouse, as in *Milan* and *Epervier*. The suppression of the depth charge throwers meant a less cramped arrangement on the upper deck amidships, and had the boats been located abeam the after deckhouse they would have sustained damage when no.3 gun was fired.

The *Le Fantasque*s were easily distinguished from their predecessors not only by their two broad, relatively short funnels but by the arrangements adopted for mast and rangefinders. The pole foremast was vertical and rose some 23 metres above the waterline at normal loading. Two yards each 8.5 metres long were fixed at 90 degrees to one another in the form of a cross at about two-thirds the height of the mast. They carried the halyards for signal flags, and the W/T aerials were attached and carried aft by prominent supports on the second funnel.

At the base of the pole foremast, and seated around it, was the director for the main guns, and there was a separate rangefinder turret for torpedo fire control

Le Malin: Sections

Note: Adapted from plans dated Lorient 5 November 1936.

(© John Jordan 2011)

above it that could be trained independently. Abaft the second funnel, in the position formerly occupied by no.3 gun, was a secondary fire control position featuring the heavy rangefinder turret trialled in the *Guépard* (see Chapter 4) with a mechanical computer beneath. Similar arrangements were by this time being adopted for the four-funnelled *contre-torpilleurs*, but the delays in the construction of the *Le Fantasque*s enabled these to be built into the final design rather than retro-fitted on an *ad hoc* basis, and the additional topweight involved could be taken into account when making the stability calculations.

For the searchlight projectors an arrangement similar to that of the *Vauquelin*s was adopted, with two 75cm S/L on a raised platform forward of the second funnel. However, the light 45cm projector forward (*projecteur de manoeuvre*) could not be located on the foremast, as this position was now occupied by the torpedo rangefinder, so 45cm projectors were located in the wings of the upper bridge on either side of the ship (see Bridge Decks drawing).

GROUND TACKLE AND NAVIGATION

Arrangements were again similar to the *Vauquelin* class, but the two bower anchors were heavier to take account of the increased displacement of the ships: 2540kg vs. 2360kg. The three kedge anchors were of 600kg, 400kg and 300kg respectively, and were stowed on the forward deckhouse, where they were handled by the boat cranes. As in the earlier ships, the 600kg anchor would subsequently be disembarked (from 1937 onwards) to reduce topweight.

The gyro-compass was the Anschütz Type III FMK, located as in the earlier ships, and there were six Bianchetti magnetic compasses for course and bearing distributed between the bridge decks, the secondary conning position, which was on the searchlight platform forward of the second funnel, and the steering compartment.

All six ships were fitted with a CET 32 Mle 1934 ultrasonic depth sounder and the traditional Warluzel Mle 1914 mechanical sounder.

MACHINERY

Despite the increase in propulsive power from 64,000CV to 74,000CV, the machinery spaces were virtually identical in length to those of the *Vauquelin*s: the double boiler rooms were 15.5–16m (eight frames) long, the engine rooms 13–13.5m (seven frames) long. The machinery layout broadly followed that of *Milan* (Parsons) and *Epervier* (Rateau-Bretagne). Three ships (the Lorient-built *Le Fantasque* and *L'Audacieux*, and the ACL-built *Le Terrible*) had Rateau-Bretagne impulse turbines; the remaining three had Parsons reaction turbines.

The boilers in the forward and after boiler rooms were sub-contracted to different manufacturers, with the solitary exception of *Le Terrible*, whose hull was built by CNF Caen but whose boilers were built exclusively by A C Loire at their Saint-Nazaire shipyard (see table for details). The latter ship was the only one to employ Yarrow-Loire superheaters, which had 411 tubes as compared with 284 in the Thornycroft model. The superheated boilers had a theoretical rating similar to those trialled in *Milan* and *Epervier*: 27kg/cm^2 and 325°C (225° saturated + 100° superheated steam); in practice temperatures of 360/370° were attained during trials. Despite the merging of the funnels, the uptakes for each of the four boilers were completely separate, two uptakes being housed in each funnel envelope.

The composition and layout of the turbines was as in *Milan* and *Epervier*. There were HP, IP and LP turbines working in series. The Rateau-Bretagne ships had two cruise turbines (CR1 HP and CR2 LP)[5] with independent gearing clutched to the shaft for the IP turbine, while the Parsons ships had a single cruise turbine with reduction gearing as in the Rateau-Bretagne ships clutched to the LP turbine. Both the Rateau and the Parsons turbines had their reverse turbine inside the housing for the LP turbine. In the Rateau-Bretagne ships steam was fed into the cruise turbines up to a speed of 21 knots, then admitted to the main HP

---

[5] CR = *croisière* (cruise).

MACHINERY CONTRACTORS

	Builder	Turbine type	Main contractor	Sub-contractor
Le Fantasque	Lorient	Rateau-Bretagne	(dockyard)	fwd boilers: AC de la Seine Maritime aft boilers: AC Bretagne turbines: AC Bretagne
L'Audacieux	Lorient	Rateau-Bretagne	(dockyard)	fwd boilers: AC de la Seine Maritime aft boilers: Schneider turbines: Schneider
Le Malin	FC Méditerranée	Parsons	[shipyard]	fwd boilers: Augustin Normand aft boilers: F C Méditerranée turbines: FC Méditerranée
le Terrible	AC Loire	Rateau-Bretagne	[shipyard]	boilers: AC Loire aft boilers: AC Loire turbines: AC Bretagne
Le Triomphant	AC France	Parsons	[shipyard]	fwd boilers: Babcock & Wilcox aft boilers: AC France turbines: Fives-Lille
L'Indomptable	FC Méditerranée	Parsons	[shipyard]	fwd boilers: F C Gironde aft boilers: AC de la Seine Maritime turbines: AC Loire

Above: Le Terrible on the first of her sorties de vérification on 10 May 1935. (US Navy NH 86548, courtesy of A D Baker III)

The three ships with Rateau turbines were slightly faster than the Parsons ships, and they were grouped accordingly for operational purposes: the Rateau ships formed the 10th DCT and the Parsons ships the 8th DCT. *Le Terrible* failed to maintain the speed advantage she established on trials once she entered service, but all six ships comfortably sustained 43 knots on trials and more than 40 knots in service. 'Formation speed' was established as 40 knots for the Rateau ships, and 38/39 knots for the Parsons ships, and once the ships entered service with the 2nd Light Squadron (Brest) in 1937, the 'raiding speed' of the latter formation was raised from 35 knots to 38 knots. Combat speed, however, was significantly lower: 28 knots – it was found that between 26 knots and 30 knots not one of the six was affected by the vibrations which disturbed gunnery and rangefinder observations.

The request for a larger operating radius dating from 1929 (4000nm at 15 knots) dictated an increase in fuel bunkerage to give a total of 580 tonnes of oil in load condition and 640 tonnes at deep load. There were between ten and twelve fuel tanks (depending on the ship), and these were not completely symmetrical in layout, which posed problems; at deep load *Le Malin* had a slight but permanent list to starboard. There were 175 tonnes of feed water, of which 47 tonnes were in the system and 128 tonnes in reserve, and 12 tonnes of fresh water for the crew. The superheated evaporators proved particularly efficient, so provision of fresh and distilled water was rarely a problem.

turbine, the cruise turbines being declutched at 25 knots. In the Parsons ships steam was fed into the single cruise turbine up to 40% of normal power (29,600CV), then admitted to the HP turbine.

The two three-bladed propellers, which were of very-high-resistance (VHR) bronze, had a diameter of 3.80m. Initially, all six ships were fitted with propellers supplied by the builder of the turbines. From 1935 these were replaced by a standard propeller developed by the Navy using a test tank; the new propellers were designed to reduce the number of revolutions per minute at maximum power. However, the exceptional performance of *Le Terrible* on trials led to the adoption of propellers with a similar configuration for all ships of the class in 1936.[6]

The Parsons ships were more economical at high speed (1900/2200nm vs. 1500/1700nm at 24/25 knots), but neither type of turbine delivered the required endurance at cruise speed, despite the increase in fuel capacity: 2700/2900nm at 15 knots was standard. A further concern was the time it took to raise steam pressures in these and other contemporary French flotilla craft, particularly under wartime conditions. It took eight minutes to work up to 27 knots, 28 minutes to attain 36 knots and 46

[6] Ironically, *Le Terrible* was the only ship to retain the shaft supports fitted in the *Vauquelin* class; the other five ships had supports of a new 'improved' design!

MAXIMUM NORMAL POWER AND FULL POWER TRIALS

The trials were to be run at a mean displacement of 2,840 tonnes; adjustments were made for ships which displaced in excess of this figure at the start of the trial.

	Le Fantasque	L'Audacieux	Le Malin	Le Terrible	Le Triomphant	L'Indomptable
Date of trial:	11 Jul 1935	8 May 1935	28 Aug 1935	22 Jan 1935	26 Nov 1935	26 Jul 1935
Displacement:	n/a	2819t	2844t	2853t	n/a	2843t
Average over 8 hours						
Shaft revolutions:	388rpm	372rpm	385rpm	329rpm	395rpm	385rpm
Horsepower:	92,364CV	93,802CV	89,663CV	86,343CV	<u>95,522CV</u>	90,429CV
Speed:	40.49kts	41.42kts	41.49kts	42.92kts	42.12kts	40.99kts
(corrected)	(41.53kts)	<u>(43.00kts)</u>	41.04kts			
Fuel consumption:	n/a	31.83t/h	32.50t/h	n/a	n/a	n/a
Average 9th hour						
Shaft revolutions:	399rpm	407rpm	402rpm	403rpm	409rpm	403rpm
Horsepower:	96,773CV	97,448CV	97,956CV	90,868CV	<u>98,529CV</u>	96,112CV
Speed:	41.35kts	42.43kts	42.26kts	<u>43.78kts</u>	43.12kts	42.33kts
(corrected)	(42.80kts)					
Fuel consumption:	n/a	33.78t/h	n/a	n/a	n/a	n/a

Notes:
1. The full power trial for *Le Malin*, which was abandoned on 28 August, took place on 9 September 1935 at a mean displacement of 2678t.
2. The figures representing the best performance for the class are underlined.

Source: 9DD[1] series, SHD Vincennes.

THE LE FANTASQUE CLASS

minutes to reach the formation speed of 39 knots.

Electricity generation was as in the four-funnelled *contre-torpilleurs*, with two 80kW (106kW max.) turbo-generators distributed between the forward and after engine rooms, and two 22kW (26.5kW max.) Bettus-Loire emergency generators. The latter were, however, relocated from the centre deckhouse to the after engine room, with the forward engine room housing the evaporators and the air compressors for the torpedoes (see GA plans).

MAIN ARMAMENT

The 138.6mm/50 Mle 1929 gun was derived from the successful Mle 1927 which had armed the *Aigle* and the *Vauquelin* classes. The maximum angle of elevation was increased from 28° to 30°,[7] but the principal difference lay in the much longer barrel (50 calibres vs. 40 calibres) and the more powerful combat charge (12.1kg of BM11 propellant vs. 9kg of BM7), which combined to give a much greater muzzle velocity (800m/s vs. 700m/s). This resulted not only in increased range (20,000m vs. 16,600m) but also in much-reduced dispersion at longer ranges, with tightly grouped salvoes. The only significant drawback was the considerable recoil force (57 tonnes vs. 43.5 tonnes), which placed a huge load on the deck structure, and the increase in blast pressure, which meant that superstructures had to be reinforced and care taken with the placing of boats and light AA weapons (see Hull and General Configuration above and Anti-aircraft Weapons/Boats below).

The ammunition hoists were of a new design inspired by those of the 152mm guns developed for the light cruiser *Emile Bertin* of the same 1930 programme. Whereas the hoists in all previous French destroyers were of the continuous chain 'dredger' type, the shells and cased charges being raised in the horizontal position and offloaded onto delivery trays at one of the two reception points, the *Le Fantasque*s had Sautter-Harlé electrical 'pusher' hoists, in which both the shells and the cartridges were raised vertically, and then tipped over to the horizontal into the reception trays (see drawing). The pusher hoists were lighter than the dredger hoists and had a much smaller cross-section, so occupied less internal volume as they passed through the intervening decks. However, their

---

[7] Trunnion height remained unchanged at 1.25m.

Above: *Le Triomphant* shortly after her completion in 1936. *(Philippe Caresse collection)*

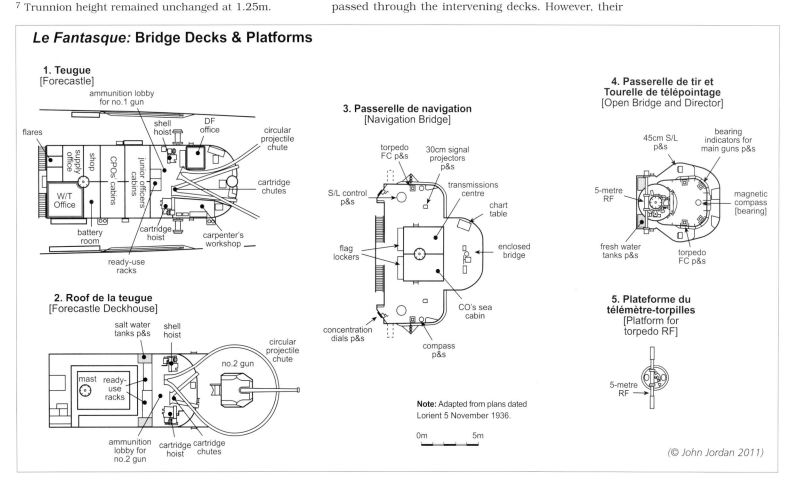

(© John Jordan 2011)

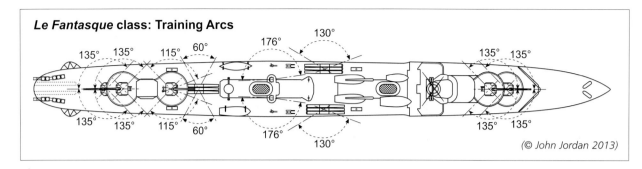

theoretical delivery cycle of approximately 20 rounds per minute was no better than the earlier hoists, and the change in orientation of the shell or cartridge at the reception trays frequently resulted in jams – a problem exacerbated by the split-level reception stations; it was not unknown for shells to fall back down the return section of the tube.

Ammunition provision was as in the four-funnelled *contre-torpilleurs*: 500 shells and 525 charges (25% flashless for night firing) plus 75 starshell rounds with 80 charges. In wartime this figure would be doubled to 200 rounds per gun. There were racks for 24 ready-use rounds close to each of the mountings, including no.3 gun, and given the unreliability of the hoists, these and the shell/charge chutes would frequently be overloaded prior to combat, in breach of safety regulations. The projectile chutes were circular and the chutes for the cartridges linear, as in *Milan* and *Epervier*.

The fire control system of the *Le Fantasque*s was a major advance on earlier ships, with full director control (*télépointage complet*) and an embryonic remote power control system (*télécommande*). The main director, which was seated around the pole foremast, housed a 5-metre base stereoscopic rangefinder (OPL/SOM SJ.1). Cued by 8 x 50 target designation binoculars located on the upper bridge, which transmitted the target bearing directly using a Granat transmission system, the director locked onto the target using a Hele-Shaw electro-hydraulic drive system. Target bearing and range were then continuously transmitted, after correction for parallax, to the Transmitting Station (*PC Artillerie*), where they were fed into the same electromechanical Mle 1929 computer that equipped the *Vauquelin*s. The elements of the fire control solution were then transmitted to the gun mountings, each of which had a GD II receiver for tangent angle and deflection to the right of the gun (see drawing), and a GD III receiver for angle of train to the

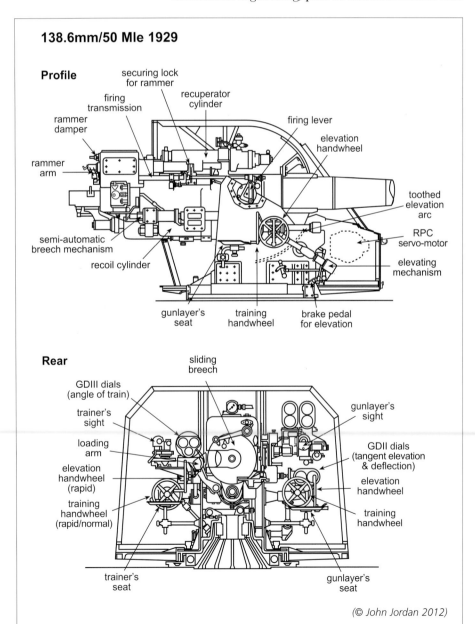

138.6MM/50 MLE 1929

Gun Data

Construction	monobloc autofretted barrel
Weight of gun	4.28 tonnes
Breech mechanism	horizontal sliding block
Ammunition type	separate
Projectiles	OPFA Mle 1924 (39.9kg)
	OEA Mle 1928 (40.2kg)
	OEcl Mle 1925 (30kg)
Propellant	12.1kg BM11 in cartridge Mle 1910
Muzzle velocity	800m/s
Range at 30°	20,000m

Mounting Data

Designation	Mle 1929 (single)
Protection	5mm
Weight of mounting	11.6 tonnes
Elevation	−10° / +30°
Loading angle	any angle
Firing cycle	8–12rpm

Notes:

Mle	*Modèle*	Model
OPFA	*Obus de Perforation en Fonte Aciérée*	Semi-Armour Piercing (SAP)
OEA	*Obus Explosif en Acier*	High Explosive (HE)
OEcl	*Obus Eclairant*	Starshell

left. The gun layer (right) and trainer (left) used hand wheels to elevate and train the gun until the pointers on the dials were aligned. The gun was then ready for firing, which was normally initiated centrally by the Control Officer (*Officier de tir*) in the director using a hand pistol with electro-mechanical transmission. (For rapid fire the gun could be set to fire automatically when the breech closed.) In the event of a director failure, fire could be controlled centrally from the secondary FC position abaft the second funnel, which was equipped with a 5-metre stereo rangefinder and a mechanical Mle 1919 computer, the elements of the fire control solution being transmitted by voice telephone using the combat telephone network.

RPC

From the late 1920s remote power control (RPC) became something of a 'holy grail' for the Marine Nationale. Before the advent of RPC rapid, accurate fire had required a steady ship. Ships of battleship and cruiser size had a natural advantage in this respect; a fast, bucking *contre-torpilleur*, on the other hand, was inherently incompatible with accurate gunfire, as even with good fire control solutions and firing cycles the guns were constantly thrown out of line by the often violent movements of the platform. The solution was seen to lie in providing sensors that could measure platform movement allied to servo-motors on the

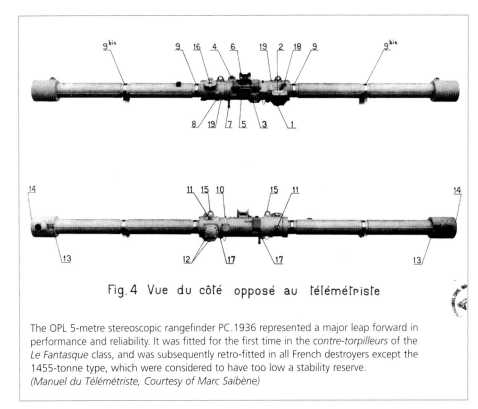

Fig. 4 Vue du côté opposé au télémétriste

The OPL 5-metre stereoscopic rangefinder PC.1936 represented a major leap forward in performance and reliability. It was fitted for the first time in the *contre-torpilleurs* of the *Le Fantasque* class, and was subsequently retro-fitted in all French destroyers except the 1455-tonne type, which were considered to have too low a stability reserve.
(*Manuel du Télémétriste*, Courtesy of Marc Saibène)

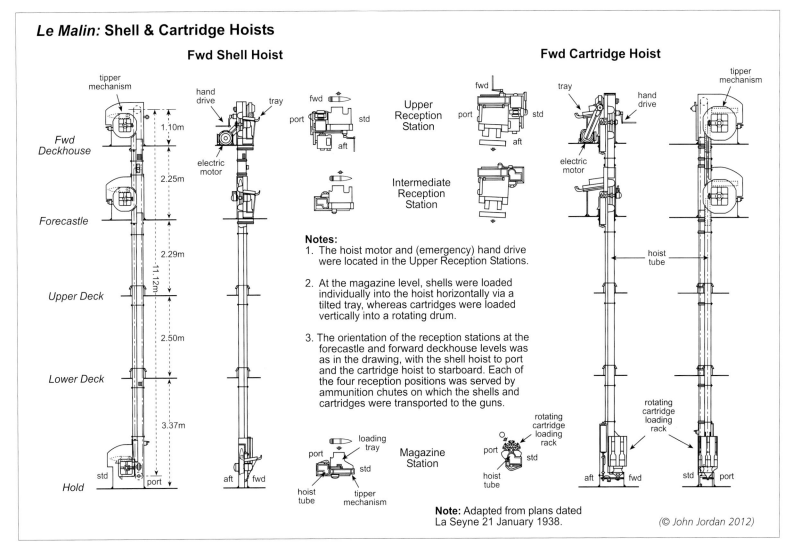

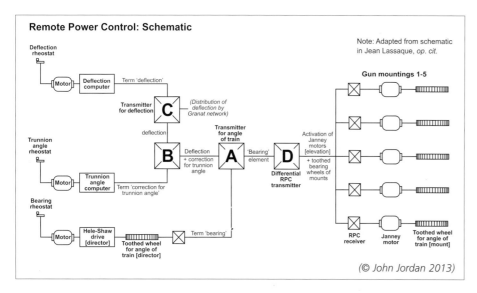

(© John Jordan 2013)

mountings which could keep the guns on the target, making possible continuous rapid fire without having to wait until the ship passed through the horizontal.

The Le Fantasques were the first ships of their type to have a prototype RPC system for their main guns. Once engaged by the Control Officer using a mechanical clutch, converter groups each comprising a 26kW LMT (*Le Matériel Mécanique*) constant-speed motor generated a variable-voltage electric current which powered two Janney motors (one for training, one for elevation) on each of the mountings as well as the Hele-Shaw electro-hydraulic power train on the director. Three variable resistors (rheostats) were operated manually and related to the three key elements of the fire control solution affected by platform movement: target bearing, deflection and correction for trunnion angle. The operator for the bearing rheostat was stationed in the director, where he simply kept his sight on the target; the other two operators were stationed in the *PC Artillerie*, where they used the constantly changing computer outputs for deflection and correction of trunnion angle respectively. These three movements were coordinated by a differential transmitter that controlled the Janney motors on the mountings (see schematic).

The system was not a success. The bearing rheostat was insufficiently sensitive to small movements, with the result that any correction tended to throw the director off the target and with it the guns. The employment of motors with different characteristics also proved problematic in that corrections of the same value for movement in the opposite direction did not always cancel out. Similar problems were experienced with the elevation part of the system, and these were of a more serious nature. In heavy seas, any attempt to correct for violent rolling of the platform caused the circuit breakers to activate, thereby putting the system out of service when in theory it should have been most useful.

Four of the six ships entered service with prototype RPC systems, and two (*Le Terrible* and *L'Indomptable*) without. In service only the bearing element of the systems installed in *Le Fantasque* and – to a lesser degree – *Le Malin* showed promise. RPC for elevation was a conspicuous failure, and the equipment would be progressively removed.

ANTI-AIRCRAFT WEAPONS

In the original Type 1929 design there were to have been four 37mm CAS, as in the *Vauquelins*. When the design became the Type 1930 it was envisaged that the ship would be fitted with two automatic 37mm guns of new design. However, development of the automatic weapon was protracted, and it was decided to fit two 37mm CAD Mle 1933 (approved 1931).

Production of the 37mm CAD was delayed, and the *Le Fantasques* were completed with two 37mm CAS as a temporary measure. Each of the 37mm CAS mounts was initially provided with the regulation 500 rounds, with lockers for 144 rounds per gun (24 x 6) close to the mounting. There was, however, sufficient capacity in the magazine aft for 2520 rounds (420 x 6) in anticipation of the twin mounting.

Two 13.2mm Mle 1929 Hotchkiss CAD were to be fitted on completion, but the forecastle position was deemed unsatisfactory because of its exposure to blast from the main guns. The adoption of the 37mm CAD mounting effectively freed up the position occupied by the after 37mm CAS in earlier ships, so the 13.2mm CAD were mounted on the upper deck immediately abaft the 37mm mountings. There were 2400

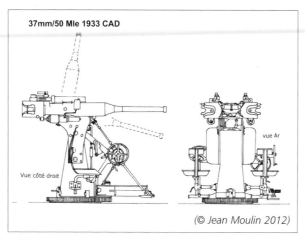

(© Jean Moulin 2012)

37/50 MLE 1933

Gun Data
Weight of gun	300kg
Ammunition type	fixed
Projectiles	OEA Mle 1925 (0.73kg)
	OI Mle 1924 (0.73kg)
Propellant	BM2 in cartridge (0.2kg)
Complete round	
weight	2.8kg
dimensions	408mm x 61mm
Muzzle velocity	810m/s
Max. range	8000m theoretical
	5000m effective

Mounting Data
Designation	CAD Mle 1933
Weight of mounting	N/A
Elevation of guns	-15° / +80°
Firing cycle (per gun)	30rpm theoretical
	15–21rpm practical

Notes:
Mle	*Modèle*	Model
CAS	*Contre-Avions Double*	AA twin mounting
OEA	*Obus Explosif en Acier*	High Explosive (HE)
OI	*Obus Incendiaire*	Incendiary

13.2mm rounds, of which half were stowed in ready-use lockers close to the mountings.

The 37mm CAD and 13.2mm CAD on the same side were grouped together for fire control purposes. Two 1-metre stereo rangefinders (OPL Mle J.1930) were mounted atop the forward corners of the centre deckhouse, and the gunnery officer was connected to the rangefinders and the two section commanders by a Mle 1917 G (*Guerre*) telephone system; voice communications, however, tended to be drowned out by the noise of the ventilators for the after engine room.

TORPEDOES

The torpedo armament of the *Le Fantasque*s was significantly enhanced at the expense of the two depth charge throwers originally projected. Not only were there nine torpedo tubes, the wing tubes being boosted to triple mountings Mle 1928T, but two reloads for the forward tubes were stowed in lockers immediately abaft the break in the forecastle, and protected by a raised bulwark (see plans). They could be lifted onto the reloading cradles by the boat cranes and from there transferred to the tubes, although it was envisaged that this operation would executed in harbour or in a sheltered anchorage rather than at sea during a pause in combat.

In peacetime there were seven Mle 1923DT torpedoes in the tubes plus two in the upper deck lockers, and two Mle 1924V submarine torpedoes modified for employment as exercise torpedoes in the centre tubes of the wing mountings. In wartime the latter were to be replaced by two additional Mle 1923DT torpedoes, which during peacetime were in storage ashore. Exercise warheads were provided for all the torpedoes in peacetime, the combat warheads being stowed in the depth charge magazine aft. In wartime the combat warheads were fitted, their place in the magazine aft being taken by additional 200kg depth charges. As in earlier classes, the compressed air tanks of the torpedoes were filled only prior to combat (or before an exercise); the two air compressors, again supplied by Sautter-Harlé, were installed in the forward engine room, to port of the turbines.

The wing torpedo mountings could launch torpedoes within 20 degrees of the ship/s axis as in the *Vauquelin* class, but their proximity to the light AA guns meant that on after bearings their arcs were reduced by 10 degrees, to 60 degrees abaft the beam (see Training Arcs drawing).

For the first time in a ship of the *contre-torpilleur* type there was a dedicated rangefinder for torpedo fire control, housed in a trainable turret above the main battery director. The rangefinder was an OPL/SOM 5-metre stereo model capable of transmitting the bearing, distance, estimated course and speed of the target directly to the fire control position, which was equipped with a modified Mle 1933 fire control computer. There were two additional FC positions in the bridge wings. Angle of train was transmitted directly by a Granat system to the mounting, and the on-mount personnel aligned the pointers and waited for the instruction to launch. Remote power control for the torpedo mountings was considered for these ships, but was not seriously pursued due to the technical complexity and cost.

Early trials revealed the need for protection from the elements for the personnel on the mounting, particularly in the case of mounting no.2 (port forward), where the platform was directly above the sea on forward bearings. These and later French destroyers with wing tubes would have a protective housing added to the control positions on the mountings.

Below: A fine starboard quarter view of *Le Triomphant* underway, taken on 30 May 1938.

A stern quarter view of *Le Terrible* entering Portsmouth on 21 March 1939, when she escorted the President of the Republic, Albert Lebrun, on a state visit to Britain. She would carry the hull number '12-' until the end of the month, when it would be replaced by 'X102'. *(Wright & Logan)*

A fine close-up of the midships section of *Le Fantasque* entering Portsmouth on 21 March 1939; she is flying the swallow-tailed pennant of the newly appointed officer commanding the division, CV Still. She retains the single 37mm Mle 1925 guns abreast the centre deckhouse, but the 13.2mm Hotchkiss CAD have been moved to the platform atop the forward hoists, forward of the bridge. *(Wright & Logan)*

THE LE FANTASQUE CLASS

ANTI-SUBMARINE WEAPONS AND DETECTION APPARATUS

There were two depth charge chutes each with eight 200kg Guiraud Mle 1922 depth charges as in earlier *contre-torpilleurs*. In wartime, when the torpedo combat warheads normally stowed in the magazine aft were fitted, there was sufficient capacity for an additional twelve depth charges.

Although it had been envisaged at the outset that Walser passive submarine detection apparatus would be fitted, this was abandoned in September 1931 and no alternative was fitted, although a space was reserved to starboard, forward of the transverse fuel tanks (see GA plans).

MINE RAILS

The minelaying arrangements for the class were as in the *Vauquelin*s. Two Décauville 25-metre dismountable tracks were provided, each for 20 mines. Apart from the regulation annual minelaying exercise, when the fixed section of rails was used to lay ten practice mines, this capability would never be exploited.

As with the *Vauquelin* class, the *Le Fantasque*s were fitted for, but not with minesweeping paravane gear.

COMMUNICATIONS

The suppression of the mainmast, which in earlier ships carried the main radio antennae, dictated a radical revision in the arrangement of the W/T offices. The main W/T office, the *PC Radio*, was at the after end of the bridge block; it monitored all communications and housed all the main receivers. The transmitters, however, were divided between two secondary offices located at the forward and after end of the centre deckhouse respectively.

The main W/T office housed:

- an SFR Mle 1933 long-wave (1800/20,000m) receiver for strategic communications
- two SFR Mle 1934 medium-wave receivers (120/2400m) for tactical group communications
- one/two[8] SFR Mle 1934 short-wave receiver/s (13/120m) for tactical group communications
- two SFR Mle 1934 OCSR short-wave receivers

---

[8] Division leaders had two receivers.

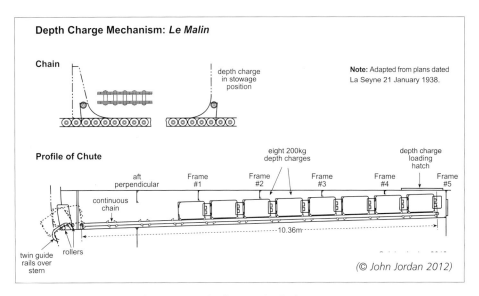

Depth Charge Mechanism: *Le Malin*

Note: Adapted from plans dated La Seyne 21 January 1938.

(© John Jordan 2012)

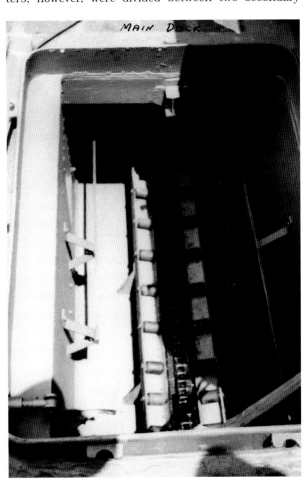

Far left: A rare view through the reload hatch for the depth charge chutes dating from *Le Fantasque*'s refit at the Charlestown Navy Yard, Boston, in the spring of 1943. The continuous chain is in the centre, flanked by the two rows of hardwood (lignum vitae) rollers on which the depth charges moved. The angle bars at the sides are to keep the depth charge from becoming displaced in a seaway. On the side wall top left is the aperture through which the depth charge could be set for depth manually, prior to being 'laid' through the stern. (*US Navy Official, courtesy of Norman Friedman*)

Left: Guiraud 200kg depth charges on the main deck of *Le Fantasque* at Boston in the spring of 1943. On the right-hand end of the nearest charge can be seen the attachment points used for handling, and the twin fuzes with the depth settings. (*US Navy Official, courtesy of Norman Friedman*)

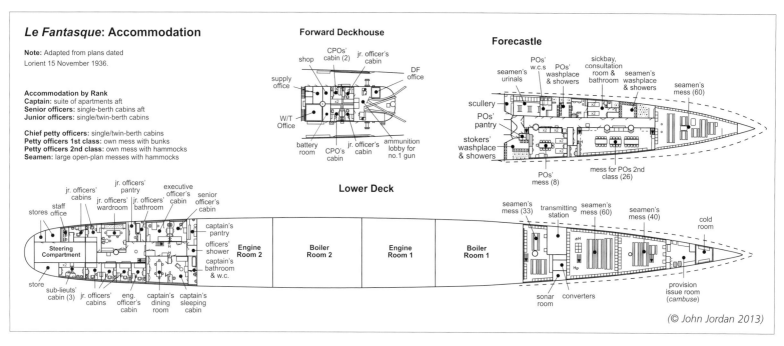

(20/120m) for bridge-to-bridge tactical communications and use in an anchorage
– an SIF Mle 1935 OTC very-short-wave receiver (3.5/5.5m) for bridge-to-bridge voice communication

The secondary W/T office (forward end, centre deckhouse) housed the transmitters for strategic communications, and the after W/T office the transmitters for medium- and short-wave communications.

The direction-finding office was located in the ammunition lobby on the forecastle deck (see Bridge Decks plan), with the antenna directly above, in front of the compass platform; it was equipped with an SFR Mle 1935 receiver (300/3000m).

From the summer of 1939 the OTC Mle 1933 equipment was superseded by the much-improved Mle 1937, which employed an SIF transmitter allied to an SFR receiver and operated in the 3.5/7m waveband.

BOATS

When completed, all six ships of the *Le Fantasque* class joined the Atlantic Squadron at Brest. The outfit

Below: *L'Indomptable* moored by the stern to the Quai Lamoune at Oran on 6 April 1940.

THE LE FANTASQUE CLASS

The three photos on p.153-4 are from a series taken on board the *Le Triomphant* while serving with the FNFL during the autumn of 1940.

Left: A view from the forecastle onto the bridge showing the bulwarks fitted around the upper main gun platforms to protect the gun-crews from green seas; these would serve as a recognition feature for this ship even after her modernisation in the USA. Note the 13.2mm Hotchkiss MG to starboard, and the 1-metre rangefinders at the sides of the upper bridge. The ship is relatively unmodified since her seizure by the British, and the torpedo rangefinder turret remains in place.

of boats provided for the *Vauquelin*s had proved inadequate when they were based there, and the *Le Fantasque*s were given an enhanced complement that included a second 7-metre motor boat (*canot de service*) for use in the anchorage. The new arrangement was made possible by the merging of the forward funnel uptakes, which freed up the after end of the forward deckhouse; the 7-metre motor boat and the 5-metre dinghy were on rails abeam the funnel, with the two 7-metre motor boats at the after end of the deckhouse. All four boats were handled by two cranes mounted on the deckhouse abaft the funnel.

The 7-metre whaler and the 7-metre pulling cutter, which were on davits, were amidships abeam the centre deckhouse so that they were not exposed to blast from the after guns. There were also eight Brest-type metal life rafts, each of which could accommodate sixteen men. Two were mounted forward of the bridge and six (2 x 3) on the centre deckhouse when the ships were first completed.

COMPLEMENT

The regulation peacetime complement of these ships comprised eleven officers, 35 petty officers and 186 men. The function and rank of the officers were as follows:

- Commanding Officer (*Capitaine de frégate* = Commander)
- First/Executive Officer (*Capitaine de corvette* = Lieutenant-Commander)
- Officers i/c Guns and Underwater Weapons (*Lieutenants de vaisseau* = Lieutenants)
- Officers i/c Signal Distribution and Landing Party (*Enseignes de vaisseau* = Sub-Lieutenants)
- Officer of the Deck (*EV de 2e classe*)
- Gunnery Second Officer - i/c AA guns (*EV de 2e classe de réserve*)
- one Chief Engineering Officer (*Ingénieur mécanicien principal*)
- two junior engineering officers (*Ingénieurs mécaniciens de 2e classe*)

Left: The 37mm Mle 1933 AA guns and the port-side torpedo tubes manned and trained for action. Note the newly fitted shield for the control platform of the torpedo tubes.

A ship acting as division leader had the same supplementary staff as earlier classes (see Chapter 4).

The Lorient-built *Le Fantasque* and *L'Audacieux* were specially fitted out to accommodate an admiral and his staff. Two additional cabins for junior officers were provided on the port side aft in place of the cells, with an adjacent Staff Office (see Accommodation plan). There was also an additional cabin for the CO or the admiral's chief of staff, the admiral taking over the CO's day cabin. Curiously, neither ship was employed as a flagship, and *L'Audacieux* was always subordinated to *Le Fantasque* in the 10th DCT before her loss.

EVALUATION

The *Le Fantasque* class was in many respects a remarkable design, let down in part by inadequacies in French industrial technology and defects in manufacture. The ships proved to be excellent sea-boats, with insignificant roll and only 6–7.5 degrees heel with 25 degrees of rudder. They therefore proved to be relatively steady gunnery platforms, and their low silhouette also made them less sensitive to wind. However, smoke and funnel gases were still drawn onto the bridge at high speed, and prominent cowlings would be fitted from 1942 onwards.

A more serious problem was their vulnerability to damage in heavy seas due to the lightness of their hull scantlings, a problem which came to the fore during the winter of 1939–40. The three ships of the 8th DCT sustained structural damage in the Bay of Biscay in November 1939, and this experience was repeated with *Le Fantasque* in 1943. The steel used in their construction was often of poor quality, and an inspection of the hull of *L'Indomptable* in January 1940 (when the ship had been in service less than four years) revealed pitting to a depth of 8mm.

The superheated steam propulsion machinery gave the ships outstanding high-speed performance. The well-known sweep of the Skagerrak by the 8th DCT in April 1940 during the Norwegian campaign was conducted at a sustained formation speed of 36 knots, and even higher speeds were maintained by individual ships throughout their service lives. However, some

Below: View from the bridge looking aft. The starboard-side tubes are prominent, with the twin 37mm mounting beyond.

THE LE FANTASQUE CLASS

Le Fantasque 1942

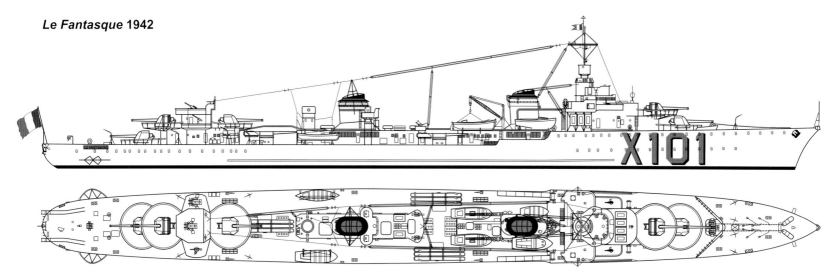

Le Fantasque as she appeared in 1942, following the upgrade to her close-range AA armament. Single 13.2mm Browning MG have been fitted in the tubs extending from the sides of the bridge structure in place of the 13.2mm Hotchkiss CAD, which have been relocated to the forward end of the centre deckhouse. A platform has been fitted on the centre-line atop the after 138.6mm hoists, and further platforms extending to the sides at the level of the after deckhouse. One of the two 37mm CAD Mle 1933 has been relocated to the centre-line platform, and the second to the lower platform to port; a 37mm CAS Mle 1925 has been fitted on the platform to starboard as an interim measure. The two small 1.5-metre rangefinders formerly fitted at the forward corners of the centre deckhouse have been reinstalled at the forward end of the upper platform. Le Fantasque received these modifications during a major refit at Oran which took place from August to December 1941.

(© John Jordan 2012)

ships (notably *Le Terrible*) experienced regular and on-going problems. Even when the initial problems had been resolved their machinery remained fragile, and it proved difficult to keep the ships in action for sustained periods.

Although full director control of the guns was an undoubted advance, the attempt to add remote power control was over-ambitious in a ship which was in essence still a large destroyer. The motors, converters and control systems for RPC required considerable internal hull volume, and the increased requirement for electrical power was not matched by a comparable upgrading of the generating systems. The two 80/106kW turbo-generators – the power rating was identical to that of the *Jaguar* class – proved inadequate during combat, and the low-voltage (115/118V) electrical supply was incompatible with the requirements of RPC.[9] It would have been difficult to install more powerful generators given internal volume constraints.

The internal communications systems were outdated, and were much criticised by the ships' commanding officers during the war. Although the mess decks were considered spacious and well-lit, there was never sufficient accommodation for the designed complement, resulting in a decision to 'double-up' on certain crew functions.[10]

---

[9] Contemporary French cruisers had a 230-235V system.
[10] The guncrew for no.5 gun manned the 13.2mm Hotchkiss CAD on the engaged side when the air alert was sounded.

Left: *Le Terrible* departs Toulon for post-refit trials on 18 May 1942. A new AA platform for a twin 37mm Mle 1933 has been constructed by the dockyard, and there are platforms extending from the deckhouse below for a second twin 37mm mounting (to port) and a single 37mm Mle 1925 (visible to starboard). The 13.2mm Hotchkiss CAD have been relocated to tubs at the forward end of the centre deckhouse, and in their place forward of the bridge there are single 13.2mm Browning MG. The prominent funnel cowling, intended to take the smoke from the fore-funnel clear of the bridge, was fitted experimentally in this ship; the modification was extended to the surviving ships only in 1944–5. *(Marius Bar)*

MODIFICATIONS 1935 TO 1939

When war broke out in September 1939 the six ships of the *Le Fantasque* class had been in service for little more than three years, and during that period there were only a few small upgrades to their equipment.

Main guns and fire control

In late 1936 at Lorient the Mle 1929 fire control computers were upgraded to provide an automated graphic for range and were redesignated Mle 1929M36.

In 1939 the small rangefinder located on the upper bridge and employed for group firing was replaced by a 1-metre stereo model (OPL J.1930), which could also provide range/bearing data for the 13.2mm Hotchkiss CAD (see below).

Air defence

The 37mm CAD Mle 1933 was trialled aboard *L'Audacieux* in April 1936, but the mounting was subsequently removed and despatched to Toulon to arm the minelaying cruiser *Pluton*. During the same month an order for 44 production mountings was placed with the Cail (guns), Salmson (mountings) and La Précision Moderne (sights) companies, for delivery between April and December 1937. In the event delivery commenced only in the autumn of 1938, with priority given to the new battleships and the cruisers. It would be the second half of 1939 before they would be fitted in the *contre-torpilleurs*.

During the refits that took place in 1937 the ships had their 1-metre AA rangefinders amidships replaced by 1.5-metre stereo models (OPL J4.1935). In order to overcome communication problems between the rangefinder and the gun mountings (see above) a board was fitted on either side of the deckhouse to provide visual data: the upper section had a horizontal scale for the speed of the target with a movable cursor; the lower section had a clock-face for range which worked on a similar principle to the concentration dials for the main guns.

In 1938 it was proposed that the 13.2mm Hotchkiss CAD mountings be relocated atop the forward hoists. However, in these ships, which had a lower bridge structure than the earlier classes of *contre-torpilleur*, they would have obstructed the view from the bridge, so during December 1938/January 1939 (10th DCT) and April 1939 (8th DCT) platforms with a prominent curved screen were built out to the sides from the forward end of the bridge wings. The planned shields for these guns had to be abandoned because they were incompatible with the new platforms.

The COs also wanted additional Hotchkiss CAD to be fitted on the upper deck amidships in place of the original mountings, but Hotchkiss had by this time ceased production of the Mle 1929 mountings, and the ships would eventually receive Browning 13.2mm MG (see below).

This page, opposite & overleaf: These four previously unpublished images date from 22 February 1943, shortly after *Le Fantasque*'s arrival at the Charlestown Navy Yard, Boston. She has been stripped of her light AA guns and her boats, and is about to undergo an inclining test. *(Official US Navy Photos, Charlestown Navy Yard NPS Park Collection, Boston, MA, courtesy of Rick E Davis)*

Below: The forward guns and the bridge. The torpedo rangefinder would be removed during modernisation, and the Brest life rafts replaced by US Navy models – see pp.268-75. *(Photo 11086 691)*

THE LE FANTASQUE CLASS

Torpedoes and anti-submarine warfare
In July 1938 it was decided that the *Le Fantasque*s would be fitted with Multispot low-frequency passive submarine detection gear derived from the Walser equipment developed during the First World War. Trials were disappointing; it was concluded that Multispot would be of use only at night in an anchorage.

MODIFICATIONS 1939 TO 1940
Main guns and fire control
The ammunition hoists of *Le Fantasque*, which had given constant problems, were modified in the course of a 1940 refit at Lorient. The intermediate reception stations were suppressed, and at Dakar in September of the same year *Le Fantasque* fired 250 rounds without a single jam.

The final attempt to install a working remote power control system for angle of train, incorporating an electro-magnetic clutch for the converter group, was made on board *L'Indomptable* in December 1939. Results were disappointing.

The provision of OTC radio meant that the concentration dials became increasingly redundant. In March 1940 *Le Malin* had hers converted for use as bearing indicators for the light AA guns.

Anti-submarine warfare
Following the outbreak of war the provision of 200kg depth charges was increased to 48, of which 32 were stowed in the after magazine. The *Le Fantasque*s also received two racks each for three light 35kg depth charges on the quarterdeck, a further 15 DCs being stowed below-decks; in compensation the mine rails (normally carried in wartime) were landed.

The *Le Fantasque*s were slated to be fitted with the French SS6 ultrasonic underwater detection device currently under development, with delivery scheduled for June 1940. However, the failure of the SS1 and the success of the British Asdic/Alpha led to the abandonment of these plans.

Air defence
The 37mm Mle 1933 CAD mountings were finally delivered and fitted at Lorient and Toulon between January and May 1940 – three years late! They were installed amidships on the upper deck as planned, so there were blind arcs of 60 degrees forward and 70 degrees aft. A total of 4000 rounds were provided, of which 3000 were 'day' rounds and 500 were tracer for night firing. There were 260 ready-use rounds in lockers close to each of the mountings and 60 (2 x 30) in on-mount stowage.

In May/June new sights (Mle 943 *bis*) were fitted to the 13.2mm Hotchkiss CAD; these were capable of following aircraft with a speed of 170m/s.

MODIFICATIONS 1940 TO 1942
The maintenance of these ships following the Armistice

Below: A close-up of the second funnel, the searchlight projectors, and the after fire control position with its turreted rangefinder. The funnel retains its two green bands. Note the massive ventilation trunking abreast the funnel, and the davits for the ship's 7-metre whaler; these would be relocated abeam the forward funnel during modernisation. *(Photo 11086 694)*

Below: An excellent view of the after deckhouse, with its axial and wing platforms for 37mm CAD Mle 1933 mountings (removed at Dakar); these were constructed during the ship's 1941 refit at Oran. The angled smoke pipe is for the officers' galley. Note the enclosed local control position for the centre-line torpedo tubes, which was added shortly after the ship's completion, and the original smoke screen generators on the main deck abeam the tubes. *(Photo 11086 695)*

was complicated by the fact that the entire stock of spare parts was at Brest, now in the occupied zone.

Main guns and fire control
Following the Armistice the RPC systems were rarely used – ironically only in calm/moderate seas when platform movements were slight! – and the converter groups were progressively disembarked to save weight. In June 1941 modifications were made to the ammunition hoists of *L'Indomptable*; pinions of new design slowed the reloading cycle but prevented jams, so the effective rate of replenishment actually improved.

Of the three concentration dials, only the forward dial was disembarked following the directive of November 1941, the after dials being used to provide bearing data for the light AA guns.

Anti-submarine warfare
In 1942, having first obtained authorisation from the Armistice Commission, the French embarked on the manufacture of Alpha-2 underwater detection apparatus, derived from the British Asdic 128, and a decision was made during the spring of 1942[11] to equip the four *Le Fantasque*s remaining in French service with the first systems delivered. The equipment was to

[11] Directive 383 FMF/1 dated 15 April 1942.

be stowed broken down in cases on board until the preliminary work (sonar dome) had been completed. It could then be installed without arousing the ire of the Italians during a subsequent maintenance period.

Le Terrible sailed for Dakar in May 1942 with the cased equipment for herself and for her sisters *Le Fantasque* and *Le Malin* on board.[12] *L'Indomptable* received hers at Toulon, where it was to have been installed during a maintenance period in 1943.

Air defence
Before they left for Dakar in September 1940, *Le Fantasque*, *L'Audacieux* and *Le Malin* all received a single 13.2mm Browning MG (2500 rounds), which was installed either atop the after ammunition hoists (*Le Malin*) or on the quarterdeck. Due to the haste with which the guns were installed there was no centralised fire control; the mountings fired independently. At the same time two twin 8mm MG Mle 1926 were fitted atop the after hoists.

During October/November 1940 at Toulon, *L'Indomptable* and *Le Terrible* were fitted with two 13.2mm Browning guns on the quarterdeck, and the latter ship also had her 13.2mm Hotchkiss replaced by Brownings – at the insistence of her CO, who refused

[12] It would be assembled and fitted during their modernisation in the USA in 1943.

Above: The after guns and quarterdeck of Le Fantasque. Athwartships rails for a weighted 'railway wagon' have been specially fitted for the inclining test, which was normally done with the ship alongside, in still water, and free of mooring restraints to achieve accuracy. Metacentric height (GM) was determined by moving weights transversely to produce a known overturning moment in the range of 1-4 degrees. The restoring properties (buoyancy) of the vessel were known from its dimensions and floating position, so by measuring the equilibrium angle of the weighted vessel the GM could be calculated. (Photo 11086 696)

to have the Hotchkiss CAD on board any longer.

A further delivery of fourteen 13.2mm Browning MG was made to the dockyard at Dakar in February 1941, enabling a second Browning to be fitted (atop the hoists) in *Le Fantasque* and *Le Malin*. In the general reorganisation of the light AA which took place 1941–2 the two Brownings were relocated to the platforms forward of the bridge, and the 13.2mm Hotchkiss were moved to the forward end of the centre deckhouse. The two 8mm twin MG were transferred to the quarterdeck, and 8mm single MG were located on the forecastle, with 7.5mm single MG in the bridge wings. The two 1.5-metre stereo RF were also moved to the bridge wings.[13]

From June 1940 a third 37mm CAD Mle 1933 mounting to cover after arcs was being proposed, and this proposal was developed during the winter of 1940/41.[14] There was to be a platform for a twin 37mm mounting atop the after hoists, with wing platforms at the level of guns 3&4 for two further twin mountings. Due to a continuing shortage of twin mountings, a 37mm CAS mounting would be fitted in one of the wing positions as a temporary measure. The work was duly carried out as follows:

L'Indomptable: during her 1941 refit at Toulon
Le Fantasque: during her 1941 refit at Oran
Le Terrible: during her 1942 refit at Toulon
Le Malin: during her 1942 refit at Casablanca

The 1.5-metre rangefinders were relocated to the centre platform atop the after deckhouse. Ammunition provision for the 37mm guns was boosted to 300rpg ready-use and 850rpg in the after magazine.

The modifications involved 30 tonnes of additional topweight, resulting in a slight change of trim. The platform atop the hoists also obstructed the after rangefinder for the main guns when it was trained close to the ship's axis. In *Le Malin* the rangefinder housing was raised by 0.5m during her 1942 refit.

The light AA guns were removed from the Dakar-based ships before they left for the USA in 1943.

---

[13] These modifications were not carried out on *L'Indomptable*, which remained at Toulon.

[14] Note 5260 R DCN/Toulon dated 23 November 1940, approved by the Admiralty in Note 121 FMF/1 dated 9 February 1941.

CHAPTER 8
THE *MOGADOR* CLASS

INTRODUCTION

With the completion of the six ships of the *Le Fantasque* class, the Marine Nationale would have thirty modern *contre-torpilleurs* and twenty-six modern *torpilleurs d'escadre* in service, and the six-year programme of flotilla craft embarked upon in 1924 would be complete. February 1932 would mark the end of the ten-year 'battleship holiday' decreed by the Washington Treaty. This would require both a change in focus and a redirection of funding. The French were now firmly wedded to the *contre-torpilleur* concept, but new ships of this type would be ordered in smaller numbers, initially as replacements for the ageing ex-German destroyers which still padded out the flotillas. To follow the *Le Fantasque*s there were to have been two ships of the same Type 1929 design in the 1931 estimates and a third (to make up a three-ship division) in the 1932 estimates.

Two events intervened to halt this programme in its tracks. The first was the London Conference of 1930, at which France refused to accept quantitative limits for the newly created 'cruiser', 'destroyer' and 'submarine' categories but agreed a self-imposed six-month moratorium on construction to enable bi-lateral naval arms limitation talks to take place with Italy. The second was the Great Depression, which began to have a severe impact on French government finances from late 1930. There would be no *contre-torpilleur* in the 1931 estimates, funding being directed instead to a fast battleship (CC-1: *Dunkerque*) to counter the German *Panzerschiffe*[1] and two new 'category (b)' cruisers armed with 152mm (6-inch) guns.

The first of the new *contre-torpilleurs* would appear in the 1932 estimates, alongside a prototype *torpilleur d'escadre* intended to escort the new generation of fast battleships (see *Le Hardi* class, Chapter 9) and a further four category (b) cruisers. The *contre-torpilleur* was to be an 'improved *Le Fantasque*' designated Type 1931; it would be armed with six 138.6mm guns in a newly developed twin mounting and would be a replacement for the ex-German *Amiral Sénès*. The estimates were duly approved on 31 December 1931, and the ships were to be laid down between 1 April and 31 December 1932. The *contre-torpilleur*, designated Da-22, to be built at Lorient, was to be named *Mogador* to commemorate the bombardment and seizure of the fort in Morocco of the same name in 1844.[2]

However, the continuing bilateral talks between France and Italy led the French parliament to suspend all naval construction until 1934 – there would be no 1933 estimates. This gave a breathing space during which the design of *Mogador* could be reconsidered. Following further studies, on October 1932 the STCN presented an *avant-projet* for a ship of 2670tmW standard[3] and 2890 tonnes at normal displacement. The design was for an enlarged *Le Fantasque* with the same propulsion machinery but armed with eight 130mm; the twin mounting was the one adopted for the prototype *torpilleur d'escadre* of the same programme.

THE TWIN MOUNTING

Proposals for a 138.6mm twin mounting began in 1929, and a formal study was commissioned in connection with the Type 1931 *contre-torpilleur*, which initially was to have had a twin mounting forward with two superimposed mountings aft. The advantages of this arrangement were stated to be:

– a reduction in the ship's silhouette due to the lowering of the bridge
– a reduction in topweight (one superimposed twin mounting versus three single mountings)
– a reduction in blast damage from the guns in the forward mounting, which could be located well clear of the bridge structure

An *avant-projet* for the mounting, which was to use the 50-calibre 138.6mm Mle 1929 gun which armed the *Le Fantasque*s, was ready by the spring of 1930.[4] The lessons of the failed 130mm twin mounting (Mle 1920 – see Chapter 1) were incorporated in the design. However, the primary issue of replenishment remained difficult to resolve. If the ammunition were supplied using conventional hoists and chutes, the diameter of the chutes would be such as to preclude their installation on the after deckhouse, while those for the lower mountings would be close to the deck

---

[1] Although the London Treaty extended the 'battleship holiday' for a further five years, France and Italy were permitted the equivalent of 70,000 tons of new capital ships to replace their oldest dreadnoughts.

[2] There had been one previous *Mogador* in the French Navy: a frigate of 1848.

[3] Although a 'Washington standard' displacement had been calculated retrospectively for the earlier classes of *contre-torpilleurs*, the *Mogador*s would be the first ships of their category to be officially designated by their standard (as opposed to 'normal') displacement. Even though France had failed to agree quantitative limits at the London Conference it was still subject to the qualitative category limits established by the resulting treaty. Ships under 3000 tons could be replaced after 16 years; ships above 3000 tons after 20 years, so it was advantageous to keep standard displacement below this figure.

[4] Note 663 EMG/1 dated 14 April.

edge and would be a major obstruction to movement around the upper deck.

The Comité Technique was of the opinion that the only effective means of replenishment was by hoists that were an integral part of the mounting platform and turned with it, as in a conventional turret. However, a turret would be heavy, would be slow to train, and would require large deck penetrations.

These demands were incompatible with a fast, lightly-built *contre-torpilleur*. The Naval Ordnance Department (DCAN) proposed a conservative solution in which 12 rounds per gun would be carried in ready-use racks on the mounting with a further twelve stowed in an ammunition lobby behind the mounting, which would be open at its after end to receive ammunition. However, this was not liked, and in the end it was decided to adopt the twin 130mm 'pseudo-turret' proposed by Saint-Chamond for the new *torpilleur d'escadre*, which featured a fixed central ammunition trunk and employed fixed ammunition (see Main Guns below). The reduction in calibre was to be compensated by an increase in the number of mountings from three to four.

A CHANGE OF MISSION

In early 1933 the primary mission of the *Mogador* changed. In the context of operations to hunt down the German *Panzerschiffe*, a requirement was established for a light vessel capable of operating in company with the new fast battleship *Dunkerque* (CC–1) to provide scouting in the open waters of the North Atlantic. This was a demanding mission requiring a strong hull, the ability to get off a few well-placed rounds and torpedoes quickly, and a good turn of speed to enable the lighter ship to make its escape before the enemy could acquire the range.

A new type of boiler currently under development would ensure that the horsepower necessary for a larger hull could be provided without any increase in machinery weight. It was initially proposed that a centre-line catapult be fitted for a 2000kg floatplane fighter,[5] but this had to be abandoned because of fears that stability would be compromised when the catapult was trained on the beam. However, a further increase in firepower was considered essential to provide support for the battleship in an engagement, so gun calibre was once again increased to 138.6mm; it was envisaged that the guns would be mounted in a twin pseudo-turret developed from the Saint-Chamond 130mm model using fixed ammunition. The STCN offered two options:

- a ship of 2670/2890 tonnes (standard/normal) with six 138.6mm (3 x II) guns and a designed speed of 39 knots;
- a ship of 2770/2990 tonnes (standard/normal) with eight 138.6mm (4 x II) guns and a designed speed of 38.3 knots

The latter option was adopted; the ship was now 200 tonnes heavier than the *Le Fantasque*. Protection of the superstructures by 22mm plating and even a cruiser-type conning tower were considered, but both these solutions would have cost 100 tonnes and resulted in a reduction in stability.

Lorient dockyard, which was to build *Mogador*, began work on the detail plans in late 1933, and placed the necessary advance orders for construction materials. The final design, which was for a ship displacing 2880 tons standard (2930tmW), was approved by the Technical Committee on 15 March 1934, subject to the following improvements:

- an increase from 100rpg to 150rpg for the 138.6mm guns to take account of the need for sustained combat
- the replacement of the triple torpedo mounting aft by two twin wing mountings

A further important modification to the plans would be made during construction, when it was decided to fit the 37mm ACAD automatic twin mounting currently under development (see below) atop the after deckhouse, the associated director replacing the secondary FC position with its turreted rangefinder abaft the second funnel.

With the German *Panzerschiff* programme continuing apace[6] it was decided that a second fast battleship (CC-2, later *Strasbourg*) would be ordered under the 1934 estimates, and that a second *Mogador* to accompany her would feature in the same programme. The necessary credits were approved in June/July 1934, and the ships were to be laid down by the end of the year. In August the new *contre-torpilleur* (designated Da-23) was named *Volta*, after the inventor of the electric battery, Alessandro Volta (1745–1827).[7] The order was to be placed with Ateliers et Chantiers de Bretagne at Nantes; at 137 metres overall *Volta* would be the longest ship ever built at the shipyard. The plans, drawn up by the STCN under the supervision of *Ingénieur en chef* Dieudonné, were completed in the late summer in anticipation of the hull being laid down in December 1934. Trials were to begin on 1 May 1937 for *Volta* and on 1 October 1937 for *Mogador*.

CONSTRUCTION AND TRIALS

Construction of the two ships was protracted. Although preparatory work at Lorient and ACB was begun in December 1934, *Volta* was not laid down until the summer of 1935, while the keel of *Mogador* was laid in the Forme de Lanester only in October. Construction then proceeded quickly, aided by the widespread adoption of welding, with *Volta* 28% complete and *Mogador* 24% complete by 1 January 1936. However, 1936 was a year of social unrest for France, with regular and prolonged industrial disputes all but halting production. The boilers for *Mogador* were delivered in September, but remained at the dockside for several months. On 1 April 1937 *Volta*, which had been launched in November the previous year, was 78% complete, and *Mogador*, which was to

---

[5] Almost certainly the Loire 210 developed for the cruisers of the *La Galissonnière* class, which would have an all-up weight of 2140kg. (See *French Cruisers 1922-1956* by the same authors.)

[6] The third ship, *Admiral Graf Spee*, was laid down in October 1932.

[7] She would be the fourth ship of that name to serve in the French Navy. The sloop *Volta* (1867) was the flagship of Rear-Admiral Courbet at the Battle of Fuzhou during the Sino-French war; 23 August 1934 marked the 50th anniversary of the battle.

Below: The launch of *Volta* at the Nantes shipyard of Ateliers & Chantiers de Bretagne on 26 November 1936. *Volta* was launched more than six months before her sister *Mogador*, which was built at Lorient Naval Dockyard, but was in a less complete state; both ships were manned for trials in August 1937. *(CAW courtesy of Jaroslaw Malinowski)*

Bottom: *Volta* fitting out at Ateliers & Chantiers de Bretagne during 1937. The ship's main armament is not yet on board. *(US Navy NH 86547/NH 86561, courtesy of A D Baker III)*

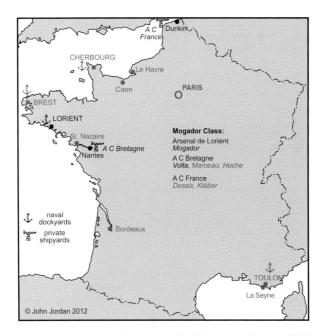

be floated out in June, was 76% complete. Final fitting out was slowed by the effects of the new labour legislation, which introduced maximum working hours and paid holidays.

With the international situation fast deteriorating, trials were conducted over an exceptionally short period. Machinery trials were successful; on 5 February 1938 *Mogador* attained 41 knots with 109,000CV, and on her Washington displacement trial on 3 March she reached a top speed of 43 knots. However, the gunnery trials were a total failure: only half the rate of fire stipulated in the contract was achieved and there were frequent jams and failures of the loading mechanisms. On 14 March 1938 the Navy despatched Rear-Admiral Collin, head of the *bâtiments en construction* section to investigate, and a series of firing trials involving a total of 160 rounds was conducted. Modifications initially achieved little, and on 27 January 1939 the Navy, forced to accept that it was the conception of the mounting which was defective rather than the work of the contractor, took the unusual step of signing off on the turrets before the problems were resolved. *Mogador* and *Volta* finally arrived at their base port, Brest, at the end of March – six months late – and it would take a further six months to resolve the problems with the loading mechanisms (see Armament below). The regulation long endurance cruise (*traversée de longue durée*) was replaced by a period of intensive work-up.

HULL AND GENERAL CONFIGURATION

In appearance and layout, *Mogador* and *Volta* broadly resembled the *Le Fantasque*s, with twin pseudo-turrets superimposed fore and aft in place of the single mountings. However, there were a number of important differences in their layout and construction.

The hull was more than five metres longer and had 0.6m greater breadth. Part of this increase was accounted for by the more powerful turbines, although a more important factor was the much greater length of the 138.6mm shell rooms and magazines, capacity being increased by 50%. Despite being fitted for minelaying, *Mogador* and *Volta* reverted to the traditional destroyer stern, which would also be a feature of the new *torpilleurs d'escadre* (see Chapter 9).

The other significant difference lay in the height of the bridge structure, the compass platform having to be raised by one deck in order to provide good views forward over the more substantial pseudo-turret. This gave the ships a heavier, more built-up appearance, particularly when viewed from the bow.

Unusually, the bow was given a rounded fore foot. This was not a conspicuous success; at speeds above 28 knots it threw up a considerable amount of spray that made movement on the forecastle hazardous. A directive of 28 March 1938[8] prescribed the fitting

[8] 9252 CN/4.

WEIGHTS: *MOGADOR* 1939

Hull:	1215.90t	37%
Fixed installations:	273.00t	8%
Machinery:	1042.40t	32%
Guns and hoists:	234.30t	7%
Underwater weapons:	55.40t	2%
Consumables:	452.00t	14%
Normal displacement:	3273.00tW	100%

THE *MOGADOR* CLASS

BUILDING DATA

Name	*Mogador*	*Volta*	*Marceau*	*Desaix*	*Kléber*	*Hoche*
Programme	1932	1934	1938 *bis*	1938 *bis*	1938 *bis*	1938 *bis complém.*
Prog. no.	180	190	282	283	284	285
Project no.	Da 22	Da 23	–	–	–	–
Builder	Lorient	ACB Nantes	ACB Nantes	ACF Dunkirk	ACF Dunkirk	ACB Nantes
Ordered	16 Aug 1934	1 Aug 1934	–	–	–	–
Laid down	28 Dec 1934	24 Dec 1934	–	–	–	–
Launched	9 June 1937	26 Nov 1936	–	–	–	–
Manned for trials	10 Aug 1937	20 Aug 1937	–	–	–	–
Acceptance trials	24 Jan 1938	5 Apr 1938	–	–	–	–
Commissioned	1 Jun 1938	15 Sep 1938	–	–	–	–
Completed	8 Apr 1939	6 Mar 1939	–	–	–	–
Entered service	6 Apr 1939	21 Mar 1939	–	–	–	–

of a false fore-foot as in the *Le Hardi* class.

The longer hull, which was designed to operate in the swell of the North Atlantic, was of much stronger construction than in earlier ships of the type. Transverse frame spacings were 1.8m throughout (vs. 2.1m for earlier *contre-torpilleurs*), and all the key components of the hull girder (sides, double bottom, main deck and transverse bulkheads) were of high-tensile 60kg/mm^2 steel, the remainder being of standard 50kg mild steel. In order to compensate for the weight of the turrets and the higher bridge structure, all internal partitions and external screens were of duralumin. Welding was used for everything except the hull, which was riveted. Despite these measures, there was an increase in topweight compared to their immediate predecessors: the metacentric height as completed was a mere 0.64m as compared with 0.78–0.88m for the *Le Fantasque*s. This was on the edge of what was deemed acceptable.

There were twelve main transverse bulkheads extending from the ship's bottom to the upper deck, as in the *Le Fantasque* class, and these divided the hull into thirteen watertight compartments designated A–M. Pumps were provided as follows:

– two pumps rated at 100t/h in sections F–I
– single pumps rated at 100t/h in sections B–E and J
– single pumps rated at 30t/h in section A and L

The layout of the funnels, deckhouses, boats/cranes and searchlight projectors broadly followed the pattern established by the *Le Fantasque*s. However, despite the increase in hull size, accommodation was cramped, and this problem was exacerbated by a decision to fit both ships as flagships, requiring a suite of apartments for an admiral aft and additional cabins for his staff. The solution was to relocate a substantial proportion of the officer accommodation to the base of the bridge structure, which no longer needed to house the ammunition lobby for no.1 gun; whereas the *Le Fantasque*s had cabins for two junior officers and three Chief Petty Officers in the lower bridge, in *Mogador* and *Volta* there were cabins for four CPOs and no fewer than four junior officers (see Bridge Decks drawing).

GROUND TACKLE AND NAVIGATION

The bower anchors and their cables had to be reinforced to take account of the increased displacement of the ships. There were two 2790kg Byers-type bower anchors with seven shackles of 46mm chain cable. However, only two kedge anchors were provided; these were 380kg and 320kg in *Mogador*, and 420kg and 320kg in *Volta*. They were stowed on the forward deckhouse and handled by the boat cranes.

An Anschütz gyro-compass was fitted, together with ten repeaters, and six magnetic compasses for course and bearing were distributed between the bridge decks

Below: An unusual overhead view taken from a crane during the fitting out of *Volta* at Ateliers & Chantiers de Bretagne in 1937. Note the cylindrical bases for the four torpedo tube mountings amidships. *(US Navy NH 86547/NH 86561, courtesy of A D Baker III)*

GENERAL CHARACTERISTICS

Displacement:	2880 tons standard; 3100 tonnes normal; 4026 tonnes full load
Dimensions:	Length 131.0m pp, 137.5m oa; beam 12.6m; draught 4.6m
Machinery:	Four Indret boilers with superheating, 35kg/cm^2 (385°) Two-shaft geared steam turbines 92,000CV for 39kts (designed)
Oil fuel:	710 tonnes; radius 3350nm at 15kts, 1100nm at 35kts
Armament:	Eight 138.6mm/50 Mle 1934 in twin pseudo-turrets Mle 1935 (140rpg + 85 starshell) Two 37mm/50 Mle 1933 AA in one twin mounting (750rpg) Four 13.2mm/76 Mle 1929 Hotchkiss MG in two twin mountings (2400rpg) Ten 550mm torpedoes Mle 1923DT in two triple and two twin mountings Two DC chutes each for eight 200kg depth charges (+ 16 reloads) 40 Breguet B4 500kg mines
Complement:	12 officers + 228 men peacetime 12 officers + 233 men wartime (+11 as flagship)

and the secondary conning position, which as in the *Le Fantasque*s was on the searchlight platform forward of the second funnel.

Both ships were fitted with a CET 32 ultrasonic depth sounder and the traditional Warluzel Mle 1914 mechanical sounder.

MACHINERY

The boilers for *Mogador* were ordered from Indret; those for *Volta* were contracted to the shipyard, A C Bretagne, which opted to sub-contract two of the four to Babcock & Wilcox, Cherbourg. They were of unusual design, with a 'V'-shaped vaporiser at the front end; the boiler was remarkably compact for its weight, and more efficient than the model fitted in the *Le Fantasque*s. This meant that it could be accommodated in double boiler rooms of the same length as those of their predecessors while supplying sufficient steam for turbines that produced 10% more horsepower. The boilers in the *Mogador*s were rated at 35kg/cm^2 and operated at a temperature of 385°C (235° saturated + 150° superheated steam). The total weight of the boilers and their associated auxiliary machinery was 456 tonnes – 15% of Washington standard displacement.

Boilers nos.11 and 12 were located in the forward boiler room (Section F) and boilers nos.21 and 22 in the after boiler room (Section H). The uptakes from each pair of boilers were led into a single broad funnel, as in the *Le Fantasque*s. Shortly after completion both ships had a prominent cowling fitted to the fore-funnel to prevent funnel gases being drawn onto the bridge at high speed.

The Rateau-Bretagne turbines had a nominal rating of 92,000CV and were to be capable of 120,000CV with forced draught. There were four main turbines operating in series: an HP turbine, an IP turbine and two LP turbines designated BP1 and BP2.[9] There was a reverse turbine in the housing of each of the two LP turbines. Two cruise turbines, CR1 and CR2, operated in series via their own reduction gearing and a Vulcan clutch.

Up to 15 knots, steam was admitted to CR1 and from there was admitted in turn to CR2, the IP turbine and low pressure turbine BP1. From 20 knots a second steam valve to CR1 was opened, and from 23 knots a third. When the main turbines were engaged, the cruise turbines continued to operate but steam was admitted directly to the HP turbine. It was only from 26 knots that the cruise turbines were declutched. In practice the cruise turbines were uneconomical beyond 22 knots and the Vulcan clutch never worked well, which led some commanding officers to propose the suppression of the cruise turbines in future *contre-torpilleur* installations.

The forward set of turbines drove the starboard shaft, and the after set the (shorter) port shaft. Both shafts were fitted with VHR brass three-bladed

---

[9] BP = *basse pression* (low pressure).

The *Contre-Torpilleur Mogador* 1939

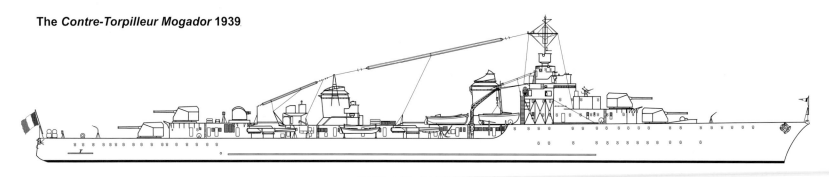

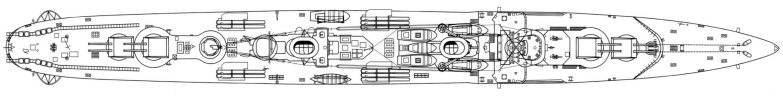

(© John Jordan 2012)

The profile and plan drawings are based on official plans for *Mogador* and *Volta* dated Nantes 17 November 1939. They show the twin 37mm ACAD Mle 1935 mounting atop the after deckhouse and a fire control platform abaft the second funnel equipped with two rangefinders: one with a 5-metre base for the main guns, the other a 2-metre stereo model for the ACAD mounting. Neither would be fitted on completion; the 37mm ACAD would be replaced by the semi-automatic CAD Mle 1933, and the dual-purpose FC platform by a conventional secondary fire control position equipped with a 5-metre RF in a tall cylindrical housing, as in the *Le Fantasque*s. The plans show the new funnel cowling and the 13.2mm atop the platform forward of the bridge, but not the distinctive side pods of the pseudo-turrets added to house the RPC motors.

Mogador: General Arrangement Plans

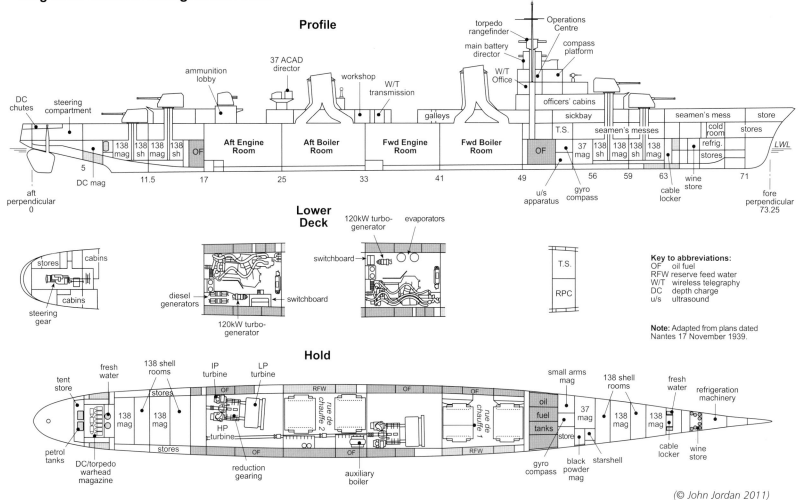

(© John Jordan 2011)

propellers with a diameter of 3.94m.

The turbine machinery, together with the associated auxiliaries, weighed 561.5 tonnes, 18% of standard displacement. The *PC machines*, in which all machinery controls were centralised, was located in the forward engine room.

A major drawback with high-pressure steam was the high temperatures in which the engine room personnel had to work. On 26 January 1939, with an outside air temperature of 11.5° Celsius, a temperature of 28°C was recorded on the engine room floor of *Mogador*, and the temperature at the turbo-fans reached 40°. It would be even more unpleasant when the ships operated in North Africa during the summer of 1940.

On trials at Washington standard displacement both ships attained in excess of 43.5 knots, which was a world record for ships of this size. In service they could comfortably sustain the *vitesse pratique de raid* of 34 knots.

The large radius required for raider-hunting operations in the North Atlantic meant a significant increase in the capacity of the fuel tanks. At deep load displacement *Mogador* and *Volta* carried 710 tonnes of oil fuel, of which 350 tonnes was carried in the large transverse tanks fore and aft. Feed water at deep load was 197 tonnes, of which 55 tonnes was in the boiler circuits and 94 tonnes in side tanks. Diesel for the boats and the electrical generators totalled 4.8 tonnes, and there were 26.2 tonnes of lubricating oil.

The consumption figures achieved on trials were disappointing. On cruise turbines alone with two boilers lit *Volta* made 3350nm at 15 knots; on patrol (same machinery profile) she made 2630nm at 20 knots; and on main turbines with all boilers lit and 8/10 power she made 1086nm at 35 knots and 887nm at 39 knots. This was an advance on the figures achieved by earlier *contre-torpilleurs*, but not by much. The time taken to raise steam pressure was again criticised: it took 52 minutes to increase speed to 40 knots and one hour ten minutes to work up to full power.

The adoption of twin power-operated pseudo-turrets required a significant increase in electrical generating capacity. There were two Alsthom turbo-generators rated at 120kW – those in earlier ships delivered 80kW.

MAXIMUM NORMAL POWER AND FULL POWER TRIALS

Mogador was the only ship for which data was recorded. The trials were to be run at a mean displacement of 3,100 tonnes; adjustments were made for a displacement in excess of this figure at the start of the trial.

Mogador

	2-hour PMN	FP/Washington
Date of trial:	16 Feb 1938	3 March 1938
Displacement (mean):	3175t	3098t
Shaft revolutions:	390rpm	402rpm
Horsepower (corrected):	109,831CV	118,320CV
Speed:	42.71kts (uncorrected)	43.45kts
Fuel consumption:	34.92t/h	37.2t/h

Source: Jean Lassaque, *op. cit.*, and CAA.

Even this proved inadequate, and the training of the pseudo-turrets was slow. During trials there was criticism of the decision to retain the standard 'destroyer' 115-Volt circuit when the ships really required a 230V cruiser configuration. The Bettus-Loire generators of earlier *contre-torpilleurs*, which had proved underpowered and unreliable, were superseded by 44kW (52kW) diesel generators. These provided sufficient power for basic services when the ships were alongside, but if the turrets were to be trained for maintenance the boilers had to lit. The turbo-generators were distributed between the two engine rooms, and the diesel generators, which could be coupled together, were side by side in the after engine room close to the main switchboard (see General Arrangement plans).

MAIN ARMAMENT

The twin pseudo turrets were contracted to les Forges et Aciéries de la Marine[10] and built at Saint-Chamond, with the exception of the after two turrets of *Mogador*, which were contracted to Schneider & Cie and built at Le Creusot. The guns were supplied by the Naval Ordnance Department of the Navy (DCAN) and manufactured at their works at Ruelle.

The 138.6mm Mle 1934 gun, which was of monobloc construction, was derived from the Mle 1929 which equipped the *Le Fantasque*s, and used separate ammunition. The standard SAP shell was the same OPf Mle 1924 fired by earlier *contre-torpilleurs* armed

---

[10] Contract dated 12 December 1934.

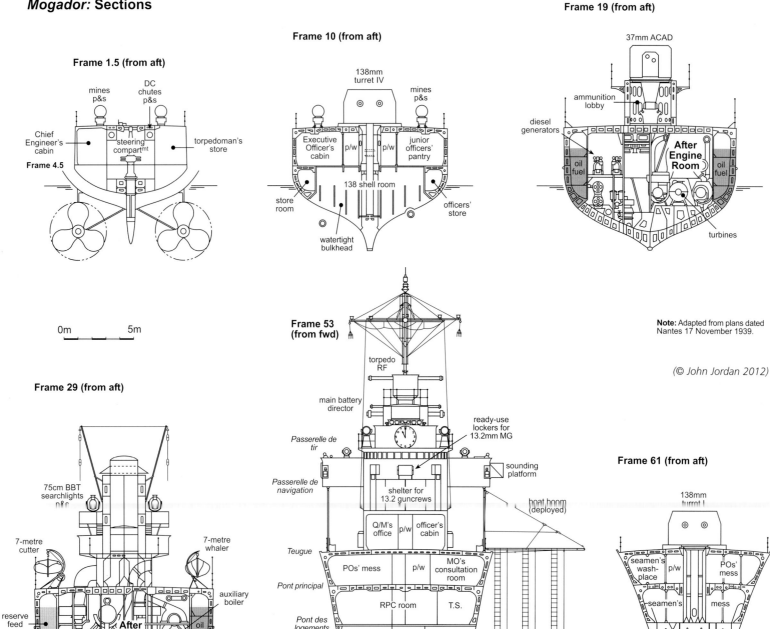

Mogador: **Sections**

Note: Adapted from plans dated Nantes 17 November 1939.

(© John Jordan 2012)

THE *MOGADOR* CLASS

with the 138.6mm gun, but a high-explosive shell (OEA Mle 1932) of more recent design was supplied; it weighed 40.2kg, marginally less than the OEA Mle 1928. The combat charge remained unchanged, so muzzle velocity was 800m/s and maximum range at 30° elevation was 20,000m. The OEcl Mle 1925 illuminating shell, of which 85 were provided and housed in the magazines for turret II, used a smaller propellant charge of 7.5kg BM7.

The Mle 1934 gun had a modified breech which was supposed to be an improvement on its predecessor but which proved seriously defective. Poor design, which often resulted in an incorrect presentation of the shell when loaded into the breech, was compounded by poor manufacturing standards. There were frequent jams, which had to be unblocked manually. On acceptance trials the rate of fire rarely exceeded 3–5 rounds per minute, less than half the figure stipulated in the contract.

The Saint-Chamond pseudo-turret

The Saint-Chamond 138.6mm pseudo-turret Mle 1935 was of the base-ring type. A fixed circular base supported the toothed training wheel and the ball race. A circular seating of cast steel which rested on the ball bearings was topped by a platform on which the gun mountings and the protective shield were mounted. The latter was of 50kg steel with a thickness of 10mm; it was open at the rear to facilitate the disposal of empty shell cases, the opening normally being closed by a canvas curtain.

The turret was derived from the 130mm model under development for the new *torpilleurs d'escadre* of the *Le Hardi* class (see Chapter 9). The latter, which employed an axial trunk for the hoists, was designed to handle fixed ammunition. This was theoretically feasible for a 130mm round, but a fixed 138.6mm round proved a step too far; it would have been too

long and too heavy for the complex reloading mechanism, which involved tipping the shell from the vertical to the horizontal when it arrived in the gunhouse. The pseudo-turret designed for *Mogador* and *Volta* therefore employed separate projectiles and cartridges, which introduced additional complexity.

The ammunition trunk around which the turret turned housed four pusher hoists, two for projectiles and two for cartridges, and emerged between the guns. The trunk was fixed between the magazine/shell room and the gunhouse, and fed a rotatable tipping drum called a *barillet de reception*. When a set of two shells and two charges arrived in the *barillet* they compressed

Above: *Mogador* during her inclining in the River Penfeld at Brest in early 1939. Note the famous Transporter Bridge (demolished at the end of the Second World War) in the background. *(Philippe Caresse collection)*

138.6MM/50 MLE 1934

Gun Data
Construction	monobloc autofretted barrel
Weight of gun	4.28 tonnes
Breech mechanism	horizontal sliding block
Ammunition type	separate
Projectiles	OPFA Mle 1924 (40.6kg)
	OEA Mle 1932 (40.2kg)
	OEcl Mle 1925 (30kg)
Propellant	12.1kg BM11 in cartridge Mle 1910
Muzzle velocity	800m/s
Range at 30°	20,000m

Mounting Data
Designation	twin pseudo-turret Mle 1935
Protection	10mm
Weight of mounting	34.6 tonnes
Distance apart gun axes	1.33m
Elevation	–10° / +30°
Loading angle	any angle
Firing cycle	8–12rpm theoretical
	5–6rm practical

Notes:
Mle	*Modèle*	Model
OPFA	*Obus de Perforation en Fonte Aciérée*	Semi-Armour Piercing (SAP)
OEA	*Obus Explosif en Acier*	High Explosive (HE)
OEcl	*Obus Eclairant*	Starshell

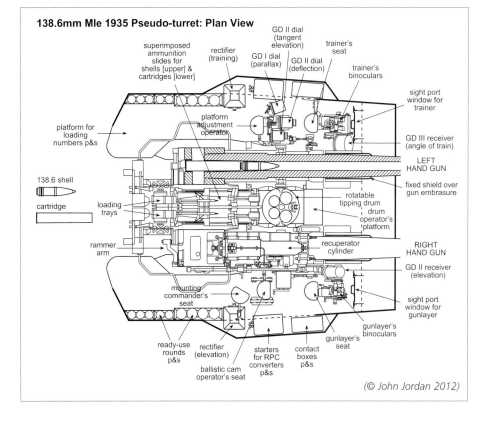

138.6mm Mle 1935 Pseudo-turret: Plan View

(© John Jordan 2012)

a set of springs. The *barillet* was then rotated to conform with the angle of train of the guns, and tipped over to the horizontal. There were superimposed twin slides (*couloirs*), the upper for shells, the lower for cartridges, running from the *barillet* to the breech of the gun. When the springs in the *barillet* were activated, they propelled the shells and the cartridges along the horizontal slides onto the loading trays. When the shell arrived at the loading tray the latter pivoted through 180 degrees to face the breech, and the catapult rammer for the gun, which had been coiled when the gun last fired, propelled the shell into the breech. The tray, relieved of its load, sprang up into its waiting position and the cartridge was loaded manually. The breech mechanism was then activated and the cartridge-loading tray sprang back into its waiting position. The gun was now ready to fire.

The reloading system was over-complex, and the possibilities for malfunction of the various (and inter-dependent) elements were endless. Moreover the slides between the *barillet* and the loading trays were virtually inaccessible due to the layout of the mounting, the stations for the personnel being exclusively on the periphery, outside the guns (see drawings).[11] In order to reduce the disruption to the firing cycle, five complete rounds per gun were stowed in racks in the after part of the turret (see side view).

Despite the attempts at automation, the number of personnel required to operate each pseudo turret was considerable. There was a turret commander, two gunlayers (for training and elevation), a platform adjustment operator, an operator for the tipping drum – for whom a special platform was provided at the forward end of the turret – two loading numbers, and a seaman who disposed of the empty charge cases. This made a total of eight, to which was added a ballistic cam operator in independent control mode (see below) and a section commander for turrets I and IV.

Before the ships were accepted into service numerous modifications were made to the breech mechanism, the catapult rammers and the loading trays.[12] Following these modifications the gun was officially known as the Mle 1934 R1938.[13]

On 21/22 July 1938 *Mogador* achieved nine successful reloads out of ten at a moderate angle of elevation with turret II, and it was decided to extend the changes to the other mountings. However, the improvement was considered acceptable only in the short term, and Saint-Chamond was commissioned to develop a new system of split loading trays for the shell and the cartridge, to be delivered within 10–12 months. This would be fitted directly into *Volta*, while *Mogador* was to be upgraded during a subsequent refit.

Ammunition provision in wartime was 1440 combat rounds (180 per gun) plus 85 starshell; 1590 charges were provided. The shells and cartridges were stowed separately in magazines fore and aft, and there was a separate magazine for starshell which supplied turret II (see GA plans).

Fire control
The fire control system of *Mogador* and *Volta* was essentially the same as in the *Le Fantasque*s. The 5-metre rangefinders in the main battery director was upgraded to the most recent model, the OPL Mle PC.1936, and a similar rangefinder equipped the

---

[11] In the Royal Navy's contemporary 4.7in Mk XX mounting ('L' and 'M' classes), which had a similar central trunk with pusher hoists for separate ammunition, the guns were given an exceptionally wide separation and the loading numbers worked between the guns, the shells and charges being transferred manually between the hoists and the loading trays (see p.196).

[12] The rammers, which had previously failed to propel the shell into the breech at any positive angle of elevation, were strengthened, and the loading tray was split into two elements to facilitate correct presentation of the shell to the breech.

[13] R = *révisé* (revised).

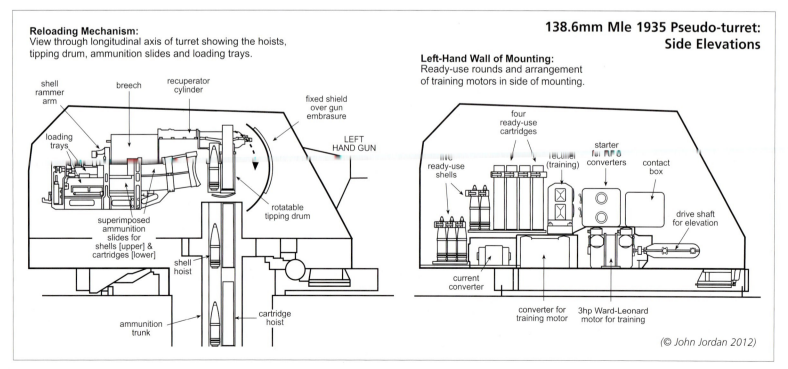

Reloading Mechanism:
View through longitudinal axis of turret showing the hoists, tipping drum, ammunition slides and loading trays.

138.6mm Mle 1935 Pseudo-turret: Side Elevations

Left-Hand Wall of Mounting:
Ready-use rounds and arrangement of training motors in side of mounting.

(© John Jordan 2012)

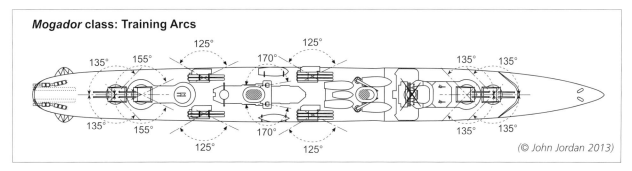

Mogador class: Training Arcs

(© John Jordan 2013)

secondary fire control position which replaced the ACAD FC director on completion.[14]

In addition to the customary Granat GD II (tangent angle/deflection) and GD III (angle of train) receivers, a GD I receiver was provided on the mountings for parallax. If the turrets were firing independently (i.e. without director control), tangent angle and deflection were received via the GD II dials, and the corrections for barrel wear and platform angle were effected by operators seated behind the gunlayers (see plan view of pseudo-turret).

The mountings were powered in train and elevation by 3CV Ward-Leonard electric motors with mechanical drive as back-up. The motors were underpowered, and the mountings turned slowly. The guns were in a common cradle and elevated together. Firing was normally by two-gun salvo and was centralised by the Control Officer stationed in the director using a hand pistol with electro-mechanical transmission; for local control there was a mechanical on-mount firing device.

Mogador and *Volta*, like the *Le Fantasque*s (q.v.), were to have been fitted with remote power control for their main guns; the necessary motors and converters were to have been housed in prominent side pods on the mountings. However, the problems experienced with the *Le Fantasque*s delayed installation of the equipment, and RPC was finally abandoned in 1942 when it became clear that there was insufficient on-board electrical power for an effective system.

ANTI-AIRCRAFT WEAPONS

The *avant-projet* had two single automatic 37mm guns (ACAS) of a type under development during the early 1930s; designed to fire 100 rounds per minute, the gun was to have been fed by twelve-round magazines. According to a report of the Technical Committee of May 1932, successful trials of the gun took place on 25 April 1933. However, because of the difficult fiscal situation, production of this weapon was not funded; instead the *Mogador* class was to receive two twin 37mm mountings Mle 1933 of the type now slated for

---
[14] The instruction to implement this modification was made in directive 2250 CN/4 dated 13 April 1937.

Below: *Mogador* at Le Havre on 14 November 1938. Five days previously, she had joined the 2nd Light Squadron at Brest, and on 14 November she would take part in exercises with the new fast battleship *Dunkerque* in the Baie de Seine. She is flying the flag of Rear-Admiral Lacroix from the foretopmast. *(Courtesy of Robert Dumas)*

Opposite: A close-up of the bridge structure, showing the massive twin 138.6mm pseudo-turrets forward. Note the shielded 13.2mm Hotchkiss twin mounting on the forecastle. It would soon be relocated atop a new deckhouse forward of the bridge – the shield would be removed. *(René Bail collection)*

the *Le Fantasque*s. Subsequently, on 13 February 1935 the Technical Committee proposed fitting a new automatic twin mounting (ACAD) aft, taking advantage of the space on the after deckhouse freed up by the adoption of twin pseudo-turrets for the main guns.

The ACAD Mle 1935 was technically very advanced, with a rate of fire of 200rpg. The installation featured an associated director with a two-metre stereo rangefinder and remote power control (see drawing and caption). The gun was to have been mounted at the forward end of the after deckhouse, and the director in place of the secondary fire control position abaft the second funnel. Both still feature in the official plans of the ships drawn up at Nantes and dated 17 November 1939 (see Profile and Plan of *Mogador* p.164). The ACAD Mle 1935 was to have been replenished from an ammunition lobby in the after deckhouse directly beneath the mounting, and the latter would have been resupplied from the magazine during pauses in combat. The magazine was located abaft the main 138.6mm magazines forward with an electric hoist which emerged on the Main Deck to starboard of the ship's axis; the rounds were then moved horizontally aft to the ammunition lobby. This was not ideal, but because of the enlargement of the 138.6mm magazines there was insufficient space to locate the 37mm magazine in the stern section as in earlier classes.

Development of the new gun was protracted, and by the time the ships were nearing completion it was accepted that it would not be ready until late 1940 at the earliest. It was therefore decided to fit a 37mm CAD Mle 1933 as a temporary measure. The mounting was fitted in the same position and provided with 1500 rounds, of which 250 rounds were stowed in ready-use lockers and the remainder in the 37mm magazine; the latter had been proportioned to supply the ACAD

37mm Mle 1935 ACAD Air Defence System

The French 37mm ACAD mounting was one of the most advanced light AA guns in the world at the time of its conception in 1935. Requirements for the new gun were for a rapid rate of fire, a high-speed projectile to minimise 'dead time' (implying a high muzzle velocity), and a highly-sensitive contact fuze for instant detonation with as powerful a burster as possible to ensure maximum damage to the aircraft. These demanding – and partially conflicting – requirements proved extremely difficult to meet.

For a high sustained rate of fire it was important that the rapid fire possible with a single six-round magazine be matched by a fast, reliable continuous replenishment system. This was realised in the Mle 1935 gun by inserting the magazine into the breech horizontally via the trunnion axis [see drawing]. Continuity was achieved by using a continuous-belt hoist capable of rapid replenishment located beneath the rotating mounting and emerging on either side of the guns. Loaders in the ammunition lobby transferred magazines from a ready-use rack to a feed which replenished the hoist. Loaders in the gunhouse then transferred the magazines to the horizontal feed for the breech.

A problem experienced with the older-model 37mm guns was that the flash and vibration of rapid firing made aiming using the on-mount sights difficult. For continuous fire against a fast-moving target the mounting ideally needed to be controlled remotely from a separate position in which the personnel were isolated from the effects of firing. This was achieved by locating a director equipped with a 2-metre rangefinder close to the mounting and linking the two by a remote power control (RPC) system driven by Sautter-Harlé electric servo-

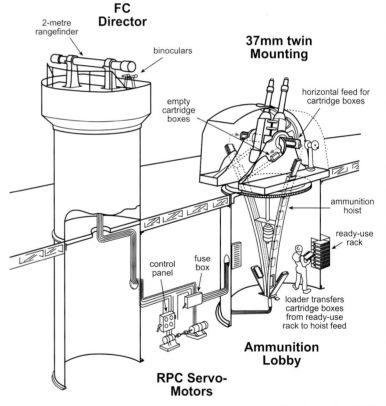

(© John Jordan 2008)

37/70 MLE 1935

Gun Data

Weight of gun	1450kg
Ammunition type	fixed
Projectiles	OEA Mle?? (0.816kg) tracer
Complete round	
weight	0.816kg
dimensions	N/A
Muzzle velocity	825m/s
Max. range	8000m theoretical

Mounting Data

Designation	ACAD Mle 1936 (prototype)
Weight of mounting	8070kg
Elevation of guns	–10° / +85°
Firing cycle (per gun)	165–172rpm theoretical

Notes:

Mle	*Modèle*		Model
ACAD	*Automatique Contre-Avions Double*		AA twin mounting
OEA	*Obus Explosif en Acier*		High Explosive (HE)

motors. The director had a five-man crew: the control officer, a director layer, a director trainer, a cross-levelling operator and a rangetaker. The gun mounting itself was power-controlled in training but not in elevation. A complete 37mm ACAD installation, as exemplified in the accompanying drawing, comprised the twin mounting, its ammunition lobby and the director. Note that the director differs from the model depicted in the 1939 plans for *Mogador* and the 1942 plans for *Foudroyant* (see Chapter 9); the upper platform is less broad and does not feature the 5-metre base rangefinder for the main guns.

The 37mm ACAD mounting was built at Ruelle. Very high rates of fire were achieved with the prototype single gun, and a prototype ACAD mounting, designated Mle 1936, was trialled aboard the sloop *Amiens* from 1939; it was used, apparently successfully, during the evacuation of Dunkirk. However, the high muzzle velocity and the comparatively heavy projectile combined to create a firing pressure of around 3000kg/cm^2, and this resulted in rapid barrel wear. The delay in the 37mm ACAD's entry into service was largely attributable to continuing efforts to resolve this problem.

THE MOGADOR CLASS

Mle 1935 mounting and had a capacity of 2500 rounds.

Two 13.2mm Mle 1929 Hotchkiss CAD were fitted on either side of the forecastle on completion, and were served by the hoist for the 37mm guns. During 1939 they would be relocated atop a new deckhouse forward of the bridge which also served as a shelter for the gun crews (see Bridge Decks drawing). There were 2400 13.2mm rounds per gun, of which 480 (16 magazines each of 30 rounds) were normally stowed in ready-use lockers close to the mountings.

Fire control for the light AA guns was centralised on the bridge. Initially the two 0.8m stereo rangefinders in the bridge wings used for concentration fire provided range and bearing. Both ships received in addition a 1.5m Zeiss stereo rangefinder specially designed for aerial targets together with two supports, but this does not appear to have been fitted due to lack of space.

TORPEDOES

Mogador and *Volta* had two triple torpedo mountings Mle 1928T forward and two twin mountings Mle 1928D aft. They carried ten 550mm 1923DT torpedoes in the tubes, one more than in the *Le Fantasque*s, but dispensed with the two reloads. The principal advantage of the new layout was that all torpedoes could be fired close to the ship's axis: 65 degrees forward of the beam and 60 degrees abaft the beam for both sets of wing tubes (see Training Arcs drawing). The control platforms on the torpedo mountings were fitted with shields from the outset to provide protection from the elements.

For torpedo fire control there was a dedicated 5-metre stereoscopic rangefinder in a trainable housing above the main director, linked to a Mle 1933 FC computer, as in the *Le Fantasque*s.

ANTI-SUBMARINE WEAPONS AND DETECTION APPARATUS

There were two depth charge chutes each with eight 200kg Guiraud Mle 1922 depth charges as in earlier *contre-torpilleurs*. In wartime, when the torpedo combat warheads normally stowed in the magazine aft were fitted, there was sufficient capacity for sixteen reserve charges. This made possible four attacks of two passes, each of four 200kg depth charges.

No submarine detection apparatus was fitted, but a

Below: *Volta* in Quiberon Bay on 14 March 1939, during trials of her main armament; she is flying the flag of Rear-Admiral Collin, of the Small Ships Section of the Naval General Staff.

space for a future installation was reserved to starboard, just forward of the transverse fuel tanks (see GA plans).

MINE RAILS
The minelaying arrangements for the class were as in the *Vauquelin*s and the *Le Fantasque*s. Two Décauville 25-metre dismountable tracks were provided, each for 20 mines. *Mogador* and *Volta* were also fitted with D6 minesweeping paravanes, which could be towed at up to 30 knots.

COMMUNICATIONS
The layout of the W/T offices was broadly similar to the *Le Fantasque*s. The main W/T office, which was located at the after end of the bridge block, monitored all communications and housed all the main receivers. Equipment was as follows:

- an SFR Mle 1935 long-wave (1800/20,000m) receiver for strategic communications
- two SFR medium-wave receivers; an SFR Mle 1934 (120/2400m) and an SFR Mle 1935 (120/2700m) on *Mogador*; two Mle 1935 on *Volta*
- an SFR Mle 1935 short-wave receiver/s (13/120m) for tactical group communications
- an SFR Mle 1934 OCSR short-wave receiver (20/120m) for group gunnery communications and use in an anchorage
- an SIF Mle 1935 OTC very-short-wave receiver (3.5/5.5m) for bridge-to-bridge voice communication

The secondary W/T offices, which were located at the forward and after ends of the centre deckhouse, housed all the transmitters.

The direction-finding office was located opposite the main W/T office on the starboard side of the bridge (see Bridge Decks plan), with the antenna atop the deckhouse in front of the compass platform; it was equipped with an SFR Mle 1935 receiver (300/3000m).

BOATS
The outfit of boats included an additional 7-metre motor boat for the admiral; it was otherwise as in the *Le Fantasque*s. The two motor boats were stowed on either side of the fore-funnel – the blue-painted admiral's barge was normally to starboard. The two 7-metre motor boats, for service duties in an anchorage, were at the after end of the forward deckhouse, with the 5-metre dinghy between them. All these boats were handled by cranes of new design (also in the *Le Hardi* class, see Chapter 9) mounted on the deckhouse abaft the fore funnel.

The 7-metre whaler and the 7-metre pulling cutter, which were on davits, were amidships abeam the centre deckhouse, as in the *Le Fantasque*s. They were relocated slightly forward to the position occupied by the light AA guns in the latter ships in order to improve arcs for the after wing tubes. *Mogador* had the pulling cutter replaced by an 8.5-metre boat for a landing party. There were also five/six Brest-type metal life rafts, each of which could accommodate sixteen men, on the centre deckhouse.

COMPLEMENT
The complement of these ships was limited by the available accommodation, and there was some doubling up of crew functions (for example, main guns/AA guns) as in the *Le Fantasque*s (q.v.).

The function and rank of the officers were as follows:

Below: *Volta* arrives at Portsmouth with Admiral Darlan on board for a conference with his Royal Navy counterparts on 8 August 1939. The funnel cowling was fitted at Lorient before the ship entered service. *(Wright & Logan)*

- Commanding Officer (*Capitaine de frégate* = Commander)
- First/Executive Officer (*Capitaine de corvette* = Lieutenant-Commander)
- Officers i/c Guns, Underwater Weapons, Signal Distribution and Landing Party (*Lieutenants de vaisseau* = Lieutenants)
- Officer of the Deck and Gunnery Second Officer - i/c AA guns (*Enseignes de vaisseau* = Sub-Lieut-enants)
- one Chief Engineering Officer (*Ingénieur mécanicien principal*)
- two junior engineering officers (*Ingénieurs mécaniciens de 1e/2e/3e classe*)

The only significant change from the *Le Fantasque*s was that the officers in charge of signal distribution and the landing party were full lieutenants.

The regulation peacetime complement comprised 38 petty officers (two CPOs, eight POs and 28 POs 2nd class) and 190 men, a total of 228. However, there was sufficient accommodation for only 221: 36 petty officers (1/8/28) and 185 seamen. This figure had to include the non-commissioned personnel of the flag staff, who were therefore allocated a combat role.[15]

Both *Mogador* and *Volta* were specially fitted out as flagships. There was an extensive suite of apartments immediately abaft the after engine room for the admiral, his chief of staff and the ship's commanding officer; the first officer's cabin was adjacent to that of his CO (see plan).

EVALUATION

In service *Mogador* and *Volta* proved to be excellent

---

[15] For example, the admiral's chef was tasked with picking up empty charge cases in one of the 138.6mm turrets.

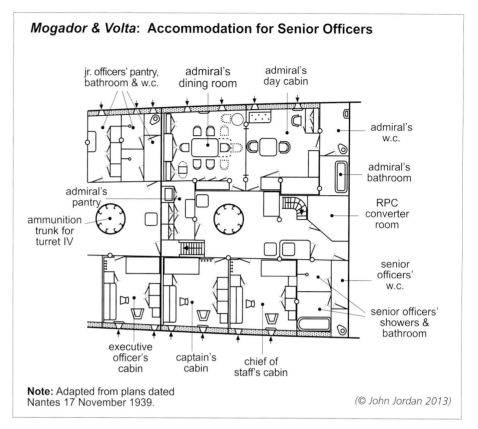

sea-boats, with a robust hull that coped well with even severe weather in the stormy waters of the North Atlantic. They were easily able to sustain 35 knots in sea state 4, and 40 knots with a 200-metre swell. Pitch was moderate, although like earlier *contre-torpilleurs* they were heavy in the bow when the forward fuel tanks were full. Despite the increase in topweight,

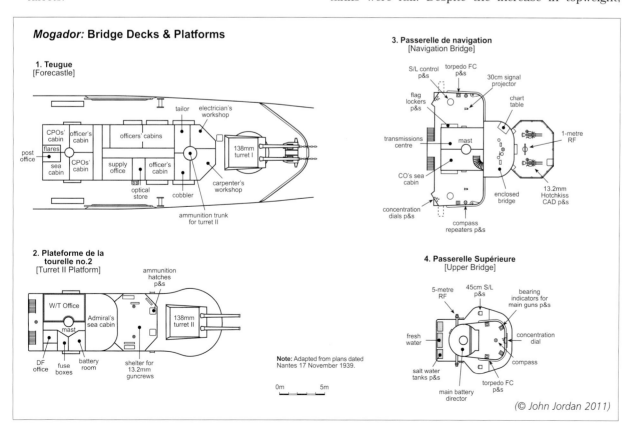

Right: *Mogador* in late December 1939, when she took Admiral Darlan to Portsmouth, UK, for a further conference. Note the dark grey hull and light grey upperworks; the hull number is still painted white with black shadowing. *(US Navy NH 86543, courtesy of A D Baker III)*

stability in the undamaged condition was adequate, and the moderate 7-second roll made them steady gunnery platforms. Heel was very slight even under full rudder, in part due to the 43-metre bilge keels: only 7–8 degrees at 43 knots. However, their excessive turning circle made manoeuvres in formation difficult.

The ships were undoubtedly fast, and the criticisms made concerning the lack of flexibility of the machinery and, in particular, the time taken to raise steam, were not borne out by experience in combat: at Mers el-Kebir, *Volta* worked up to 40 knots in four and a half minutes without any problems. However, the resistance of the materials used to manufacture the propellers was insufficient to cope with the high speeds demanded of the ships, due largely to the backwardness of French metallurgy. During their acceptance trials both ships experienced severe erosion of the propellers due to cavitation, with cavities up to 15mm deep. The propellers of these and earlier *contre-torpilleurs* – and also the fast cruiser *Emile Bertin* – had to be redesigned and replaced regularly in the years preceding the Second World War.

The problems with the main armament have been described in detail. They were all the more serious because the highly automated 138.6mm twin mountings were the primary *raison d'être* of these ships. *Mogador* and *Volta*, magnificent though they were, were evidence of just how far the French had strayed from the principles of robustness and reliability that were the cornerstone of the *Note sur les destroyers* of 1919 (see Introduction). The *contre-torpilleur* as a type was becoming a victim of the traditional French vice of constant incremental improvements, all of which pushed the state of the technology to its limits. In theory the new pseudo-turrets, allied to an elaborate system of director fire control with RPC, should have delivered a witheringly accurate hail of fire. In practice, the guns were subject to constant jams and the electrical power generating systems, feeding a 'destroyer'-type 115-Volt circuit, would have been unable to cope with the demands of RPC even if a functioning system had been developed.

The accommodation problems outlined above were again a result of trying to pack the capabilities of a cruiser into a large destroyer. The main reason *Mogador* and *Volta* – and their immediate predecessors of the *Le Fantasque* class – were unable to accommodate their designed complements was the substantial hull volume given over to reception and dining facilities for the senior officers. The admiral's apartments alone accounted for 42m^2 of deck area, and the cabins and bathrooms for the other three senior officers (Chief of Staff, CO and First Officer) for a further 52m^2. This does not take into account the additional cabins required for the junior officers on the flag staff, nor the practice of providing separate galleys for senior and junior officers and for 1st class and 2nd class petty officers. Given that the standard space allocations for junior ranks were about 2m^2 for a seaman and just under 3m^2 for a petty officer 2nd class, it is clear that the accommodation problems of the ships could have been resolved with a more judicious – and equitable – allocation of the available space.[16]

The rationale for flag accommodation is unclear

---

[16] The Americans did just this when they refitted *Le Malin* in late 1943 (see Chapter 13). The ship received a more comprehensive modernisation than her sisters *Le Fantasque* and *Le Terrible*, and the US Navy plans show a large mess with twin bunks, probably for petty officers, taken off the original senior officers' accommodation.

[17] *Volta* effectively replaced *Mogador* as flagship of the light squadron in the Mediterranean following the crippling damage suffered by the latter at Mers el-Kebir.

Below: *Volta* in the late autumn of 1940; she was now serving as flagship of the 3rd Light Squadron in the Mediterranean, comprising three 2/3-ship divisions of *contre-torpilleurs* (5th/7th/8th DCT) plus a single division of *torpilleurs d'escadre* (1st DT). She is as yet unmodified. (Marius Bar)

Left: *Volta* during 1941. Platforms for two single 13.2mm Browning MG have been fitted to the sides of turret III, and the tricolore identification markings have been transferred to turret IV. *(Courtesy of Robert Dumas)*

given the original North Atlantic scouting mission, with each of the ships being assigned as consort to one of the fast battleships, which would presumably have accommodated the admiral commanding the force and his staff. Both *Mogador* and *Volta* served as flagship of the 'light squadrons' in the Atlantic and the Mediterranean, but never at the same time.[17]

MODIFICATIONS 1938 TO 1940

Mogador and *Volta* entered service barely six months before the outbreak of war in Europe, and the only modifications made at the time of their completion were the fitting of a cowling to the fore-funnel and the construction of a deckhouse forward of the bridge for the 13.2mm Hotchkiss CAD, which were relocated from the forecastle. The 13.2mm CAD were originally fitted with prominent shields to protect the gun crew from spray, but these were unnecessary once the mountings were raised, and were removed.

Constant service after September 1939 gave little opportunity for further modifications beyond revised paint schemes. However, *Volta* had the loading arrangements for her main guns upgraded as planned during November of that year. These were an undoubted improvement; during trials in May 1940 nine rounds per minute was achieved, although the average was 5–6rpm. The underpowered rammers, which had been replaced only in *Mogador*, remained a problem.

During refits at Lorient and Brest respectively in early 1940 *Mogador* and *Volta* finally received their OPfK shells with splash colourant, and the canvas curtains fitted on the rear of the mountings were replaced by metallic rolling shutters. A screen was fitted around the platform for the 13.2mm Hotchkiss CAD, and three twin 8mm Hotchkiss MG were installed on the quarterdeck to cover the after arcs. The W/T equipment was upgraded: one of the SFR Mle 1935 short-wave receivers was replaced with an SIF Mle 1937, and OTC Mle 1935 by an SIF Mle 1937.

The D6 paravanes were replaced by the C6 model. It was also planned to fit the ships with the French SS6 underwater detection system, but the failure of the SS1 led to this measure being delayed, then abandoned.

MODIFICATIONS 1940 TO 1942

The severe damage sustained by *Mogador* at Mers el-Kebir meant that from June 1940 the two ships went their separate ways.

Mogador

Mogador lost her entire stern to a depth charge explosion set off by a 15in (380mm) shell at Mers el-Kebir (see Chapter 12). The bulkhead for the after engine room held and, remarkably, the propellers were undamaged, although one of the shafts was bent. Turret IV was destroyed, but turret III was repaired in the dockyard at Oran, which also shored up the after bulkheads and fitted an emergency wooden rudder. The ship was ready to return to Toulon by 24 August provided weather and sea conditions were favourable. She finally made the crossing on 1 November and was towed into Missiessy no.3 dock on 22 November, having first disembarked all ammunition and her torpedoes.

Repairs began officially on 15 May 1941, when the dockyard at Toulon undertook studies for her reconstruction. The proposals were approved in October 1941,[18] and the work was allocated to the La Seyne shipyard of F C Méditerranée, which was opposite the dockyard. In addition to the reconstruction of the after part of the ship, the following work was to be executed:

- Turret III was to be relocated to the position formerly occupied by turret IV, and raised to clear obstructions
- The magazine and shell room for turret III were to be replaced by an additional fuel tank
- Three 37mm CAD Mle 1933 AA mountings were to be installed atop the after deckhouse (one axial, two wing), each with 300 ready-use rounds plus 1000 rounds in the magazine
- Two 25mm CAS Hotchkiss and two 13.2mm CAS Browning were to be fitted forward of the bridge as in *Volta* (see below)

Subsequent modifications to this programme included

---

[18] Note 8274 IN/5 dated 25 October 1941.

Right: A close-up of *Volta* at Toulon taken in the spring of 1942. The AA platform forward of the bridge has been extended to the sides and now accommodates two single 25mm Hotchkiss Mle 1939/40. *L'Indomptable* and a destroyer of the *Le Hardi* class are beyond her, and the battleship *Strasbourg* can be seen in the background. *(Courtesy of Robert Dumas)*

installation of a degaussing cable[19] and Alpha 128 u/w detection apparatus,[20] and further additions to the light AA: six 25mm Hotchkiss CAS (two on the forecastle, four on the main deck amidships), and two 13.2mm Browning CAS (forward end of the centre deckhouse).[21]

In the event, repairs began only on 20 February 1942 due to a shortage of steel, with completion being progressively postponed. By October 1942 it was estimated that the ship would reenter service only in late July 1943. The following month she was scuttled.

Volta

On her return to Toulon following Mers el-Kebir, *Volta* was the largest and most modern of the French *contre-torpilleurs*. On 1 November 1940 she became flagship of the 3rd Light Division, comprising all the active *contre-torpilleurs* of the newly formed *Forces de Haute Mer* (FHM), and remained active until the scuttling of the French fleet on 27 November 1942.

In late 1940, in common with the other surviving *contre-torpilleurs* at Toulon, *Volta* received two 13.2mm Browning CAS. The dockyard opted to install these on platforms built out from the sides of turret III. The work was carried out between 20 December 1940 and 6 January 1941. The tricolore identification markings, formerly on turret III, were transferred to turret IV.

On 19 December 1940 it was proposed to fit an additional pair of 13.2mm Browning CAS and a second 37mm CAD,[22] the latter to be installed in place of the 13.2mm Hotchkiss CAD atop the deckhouse forward of the bridge. These modifications were postponed because of the shortage of light AA mountings. Instead, *Volta* received eight single 7.5mm MG as a temporary measure. However, there were now 1-metre OPL stereo rangefinders (Mle J.1930) atop the centre deckhouse. Work continued on the reloading mechanisms for the main guns, resulting in some improvements in the firing cycle without, however, resolving the fundamental issues.

During a major refit at Toulon from August to November 1941, further efforts were made to upgrade the light AA. The raised deckhouse forward of the bridge was extended to the sides to accommodate two 25mm Hotchkiss CAS Mle 1939 and two 13.2mm Browning CAS. The two 13.2mm Hotchkiss CAD displaced by the 25mm mountings were to have been mounted in tubs at the forward end of the centre deckhouse but, on the initiative of the ships' officers, were instead reinstalled on the upper deck abeam the after deckhouse. The 1.5-metre Zeiss rangefinder was finally installed in place of the two 1-metre RF at the after end of the centre deckhouse, and one of the 1-metre RF was relocated to the forward end of the upper bridge to provide range and bearing for the forward AA guns. At the same time a degaussing cable

---

[19] Note 22740 IN/7 dated 23 December 1941.
[20] Note 928 FMF/1 dated 18 September 1942.
[21] Note 1005 FMF/1 (TS) dated 7 October 1942.

[22] Note 568 FMF/1.

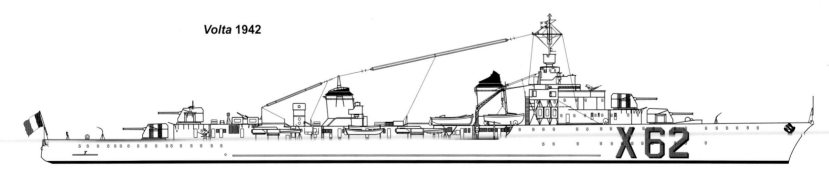

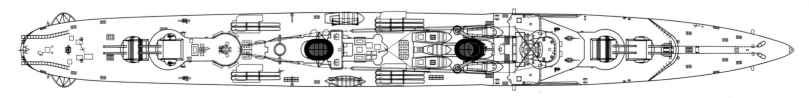

Following her refit in late 1941 *Volta* had 25mm Hotchkiss single mountings forward of the bridge, and the 13.2mm Hotchkiss CAD were relocated to the upper deck abeam the after deckhouse. Two 13.2mm Browning MG were mounted on platforms at the sides of turret III, and the tricolore neutrality markings moved from turret III to turret IV. Despite her position as flagship of the 3rd Light Squadron, *Volta* retained her original X62 tactical number. She was scuttled in this configuration at Toulon in November 1942.

(© John Jordan 2012)

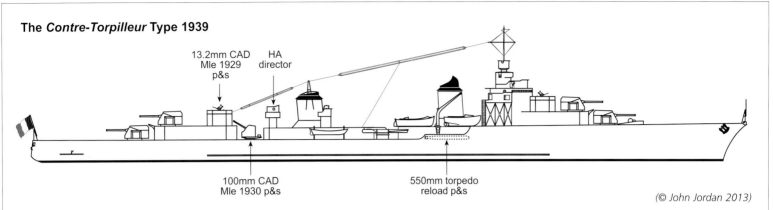

The four Mogadors authorised under the 1938 bis estimates would have been of a modified design with improved machinery and greater endurance. Two twin 100mm Mle 1930 high-angle gun mountings would have replaced the after torpedo tubes, and the secondary fire control position would have been replaced by an HA director similar to that fitted in contemporary French cruisers. The close-range anti-aircraft armament was to comprise four 13.2mm Hotchkiss CAD, the additional two mountings being fitted aft in place of the twin 37mm mounting. As part compensation for the reduction in the number of torpedo tubes, two reloads for the forward tubes would have been embarked in lockers, as in the Le Fantasques, for a total of eight torpedoes.

was installed, and blast bags were fitted to the main guns.

During 1942 the concentration dials were removed, and it was decided to install an Alpha 128 of French manufacture;[23] the latter was duly delivered but was still in cases on board when the ship was scuttled.

THE *ECLAIREURS DE 3000 TONNES TYPE 1939*

After *Mogador* (1932 estimates) and *Volta* (1934 estimates), no further *contre-torpilleurs* featured in the 1935–1938 estimates, nor in the supplementary *tranche 1938 bis*, priority instead being given to the new *torpilleurs d'escadre* of the *Le Hardi* class (see Chapter 9).

However, with a fast-deteriorating international situation, a new naval law passed on 12 April 1939 added a third ship of the *Mogador* type, to be named *Hoche*, which was to form a three-ship division with *Mogador* and *Volta*. And a few days later the Minister announced that a further three ships, to be named *Marceau*, *Desaix* and *Kléber*, would replace three destroyers of the *Le Hardi* type in the 1938 *bis* programme. The names commemorated generals of the Revolutionary Wars who fought with distinction against the Austrians and the Bavarians.

The new ships were to be of an 'Improved *Mogador*' type, with superior manoeuvring characteristics and greater endurance. Their primary mission was to scout for the fleet in all weathers and to protect it against enemy flotilla craft. They would be armed, like *Mogador* and *Volta*, with eight 138.6mm guns in the same Mle 1935 pseudo-turret, but would have two twin 100mm HA mountings in place of the after torpedo tubes. Close-in anti-aircraft fire would be provided by four 13.2mm Hotchkiss CAD (see conjectural drawing).

Subsequently, a debate took place on the Naval General Staff. Dissatisfaction with the rate of fire currently being achieved with the 138.6mm Mle 1935 mounting, and concerns regarding the additional topweight involved in mounting two 100mm CAD in place of the after torpedo tubes – 27 tonnes without taking any account of fire control or ammunition – led to a proposal for the replacement of the Mle 1935 mountings by a 130mm dual-purpose mounting employing fixed ammunition derived from the model currently being fitted in the *Le Hardi* class.

As these discussions were ongoing, only provisional orders could be placed. Lorient was notified that it would build *Marceau*, and on 23 May 1939 the other three ships were allocated to Ateliers et Chantiers de Bretagne, Nantes (*Hoche*, to be delivered 1 June 1942), and to Ateliers et Chantiers de France, Dunkirk (*Desaix* and *Kléber*, for delivery 15 May and 15 July 1942 respectively). Unusually, due to the considerable workload of the STCN, A C Bretagne was given responsibility for the aspects of redesign relating to platform performance. The allocations were formally notified on 18 August, the construction of *Marceau* being transferred from Lorient to ACB. When France declared war on Germany on 3 September only *Hoche* was on the point of being laid down, and by the end of the month all work on the ships was suspended.

During this enforced pause in construction it was decided that the new ships would be armed with four twin 130mm HA in open-backed mountings, direct replenishment having been abandoned as too complex (see also Chapter 9). The light AA was to comprise a 37mm ACAD and two 37mm ACAS automatic mountings – the latter in place of the after torpedo tubes – and either four 13.2mm Hotchkiss CAD or four 25mm Hotchkiss CAS.

An order to resume construction was issued in 15 April 1940, acceptance trials being rescheduled for September 1942 (*Marceau*), June 1943 (*Desaix*), September 1943 (*Kléber*) and December 1943 (*Hoche*). Two weeks previously, a supplementary programme for a further six ships of a modified design, Type 1940, had been passed.[24] With the defeat of France in June 1940 the orders for all these ships were cancelled.

---

[23] Note 383 FMF/1 dated 15 April 1942.

[24] The names submitted to the Navy Minister on 15 May (Circular 1138 FMF/3) were: *Bayard*, *Du Guesclin*, *D'Assas*, *La Tour d'Auvergne*, *Turenne* and *Bugeaud*. There was no time for a formal response, as the project was overtaken by events.

CHAPTER 9

THE *LE HARDI* CLASS

INTRODUCTION

In 1931 it was decided that a new type of *torpilleur d'escadre* would be needed to accompany the fast battleships of the *Dunkerque* class, which had the latest high-pressure steam machinery and were capable of 29.5 knots. A speed margin of 3–4 knots was regarded as essential for ships performing the fleet escort role, so the service speed of 30 knots of the *Bourrasque* and *L'Adroit* classes, designed to accompany an earlier generation of battleship, was completely inadequate. The first of the new *torpilleurs* featured alongside *Mogador* in the 1932 estimates, and was approved on 31 December 1931. However, construction would be delayed by the same considerations that affected the *Mogador* (see Chapter 8), giving time and space for a thorough-going review of the characteristics desired in the new design.

The Commission Permanente des Essais de la Flotte (CPE) was duly asked to make a study of the destroyers in current service[1] and to advise on the characteristics to be adopted for the new ships. It reported in June 1932, and made the following recommendations:

– a speed of 34/35 knots at normal load
– a lower silhouette, to be achieved by suppressing the mainmast, reducing the height of bridge structure, funnels and freeboard, and reducing the number of funnels
– greater initial stability (the designed GM of 0.58m of the 1500-tonne type had declined to 0.36m in the first series and 0.45 in the second)
– a reinforced bow
– improved habitability of the bridge decks
– an arrangement of the torpedo tubes which permitted launch close to the ship's axis, together with a torpedo fire control system which could cope with both prepared and quick-reaction launches
– the suppression of tripod masts, which were subject to severe vibration, and the seating of the (two) rangefinders around the base of a pole foremast
– a revised distribution of the fuel bunkerage (sea-keeping in the 1500-tonne type was adversely affected when the forward transverse fuel tank was full)

Many of these features will immediately be recognised as corresponding to the latest *contre-torpilleurs* of the 1930 type (*Le Fantasque*); they would also be features of *Mogador* and *Volta*. In addition, the CPE criticised the 130mm Mle 1919 and Mle 1924 as over-complex, with an excessive number of safety locks, and as difficult to load at angles of elevation above 15°, thereby slowing the rate of fire.[2] Mounting two single guns forward meant that the bridge had to be raised, thereby exacerbating topweight problems. Finally, the light AA was criticised as inadequate both in terms of the number of mountings and the rate of fire; the commission recommended a uniform armament of the latest 13.2mm heavy machine guns.

With regard to machinery, the commission was happy with the performance of the Parsons and the Rateau-Bretagne turbines, but recommended that the Zoelly turbines, which had given enormous problems in service, be discarded.

An *avant-projet* for the new destroyer was drawn up by the STCN during the latter part of 1932 and presented to the Comité Technique on 7 December. It

---

[1] The last ship of the *L'Adroit* class had entered service only in October 1931.

[2] The Mle 1924 was also the last French destroyer gun to have the traditional Welin interrupted screw breech; later guns would have a German-style sliding breech, which was quicker and simpler in operation.

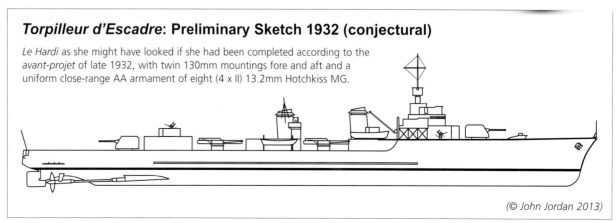

Torpilleur d'Escadre: Preliminary Sketch 1932 (conjectural)

Le Hardi as she might have looked if she had been completed according to the *avant-projet* of late 1932, with twin 130mm mountings fore and aft and a uniform close-range AA armament of eight (4 x II) 13.2mm Hotchkiss MG.

(© John Jordan 2013)

LE HARDI AND HER FOREIGN CONTEMPORARIES

	'Navigatori' (It)	Fubuki (Jap)	Le Hardi (Fr)
Built:	12 ships 1927–31	10 ships 1926–9	1932 Estimates
Displacement:	1630tW	1700tW	1770tW
Dimensions:	107m x 10.2m	118m x 10.4m	117m x 11.1m
Machinery:	2-shaft geared turbines; 50,000shp = 38kts	2-shaft geared turbines; 50,000shp = 38kts	2-shaft geared turbines; 58,000shp = 38kts
Armament:	6 – 120mm (3 x II)	6 – 127mm (3 x II)	6 – 130mm (3 x II)
	6 – 533mm TT (2 x III)	9 – 610mm TT (2 x III)	7 – 550mm TT (1 x III, 2 x II)

was for a ship displacing 1300/1400 tons standard, armed with four 130mm guns in two twin mountings – see the accompanying drawing. However, it was difficult to provide the required designed speed of 38 knots (for a service speed of 34 knots) in a ship of this size. The committee was also acutely aware of developments abroad, in particular the large destroyers of the Italian 'Navigatori' class and the Japanese 'Special Type', both of which were armed with six guns in three twin mountings as well as six/nine torpedoes (see table for characteristics). The construction of these large destroyers had effectively been 'legitimised' by the adoption of a separate 'Leader' category, with a maximum tonnage limit of 1850 tons, at the London Conference of 1930.[3] The new French torpilleur would, in its final form, be comparable to the Japanese ships in terms of firepower, and would outgun its Italian counterparts.

The final project was approved on 10 August 1934. By this time the new torpilleur d'escadre had a length overall of 117 metres and a displacement of 1772 tons (1797 metric tons) standard, and an armament of six 130mm guns in three twin pseudo-turrets and seven 550mm torpedoes in one triple and two twin mountings. The gun was the same Mle 1932 which constituted the secondary armament of the fast battleship Dunkerque, but in a low-angle mounting. The power output of the propulsion machinery was almost double that of the 1500-tonnes type, 58,000CV, for 38 knots designed and 34 knots in service; this was achieved by adopting a new type of forced-circulation boiler developed in-house by Ingéneur général Norguet. As with Mogador there were some later adjustments to the design, notably the fitting of a 37mm ACAD mounting and its associated director (see below).

The order for the first ship, to be named Le Hardi, was placed with Ateliers et Chantiers de la Loire (Nantes) on 12 November 1935, more than a year after the order for Mogador was placed with Lorient naval dockyard. In fact the delay in ordering the lead ship of the class was such that orders for two sisters, which had been approved as part of the 1935 estimates, followed on 31 December of the same year, and little more than four months later, on 4 May 1936, orders for three more ships were approved under the 1936 estimates. The first three ships were ordered from ACL Nantes, Forges et Chantiers de la Méditerranée (La Seyne) and Forges et Chantiers de la Gironde (Bordeaux) respectively, and the orders for the second group of three (1936 estimates) followed the same pattern.

The name Le Hardi (Eng: 'daring') revived one borne by four ships of the line of the seventeenth and eighteenth centuries, the last of which was a 64-gun ship that took part in the American war of independence. The ships authorised under the 1935 and 1936 estimates revived the names of early torpilleurs and contre-torpilleurs, which were generally named after military weapons and types of infantry/cavalrymen: the two 1935 ships were Fleuret ('rapier') and Epée ('sword'), while the 1936 ships were Mameluk (Turkish military slave), Casque ('helmet') and Lansquenet (mercenary foot soldier).

Six further units would be authorised under the 1937, 1938 and 1938 bis estimates (see table), and of these no fewer than four were ordered from F C Méditerranée, the orders for the remaining two being placed with F C Gironde (Bordeaux). Toulon was to be the port d'armement for the six ships built at La Seyne; the remainder, which were to be built on the Atlantic coast of France, were to run their trials from Lorient.

CONSTRUCTION AND TRIALS

Le Hardi was finally laid down on 20 May 1936, with the five ships of the 1935 and 1936 estimates following close behind. However, the delays in the design process (the lead ship, Le Hardi, was four and a half years between authorisation and laying down), together with the social and industrial disruption of 1936, meant that only Le Hardi completed every stage

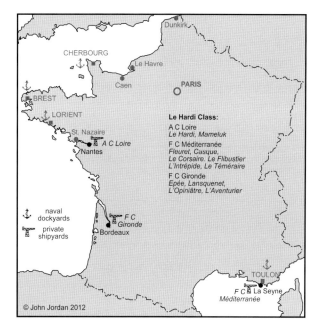

---

[3] For Britain, the USA and Japan, 'Leader' construction was limited to 16% of total destroyer tonnage. Although France was not a signatory to this part of the treaty, she could have laid down 5-6 ships of this size before the end of 1936 without being accused of 'escalation' by the other powers; in the event she authorised six ships of the Le Hardi class under the 1932-6 estimates.

BUILDING DATA

Name	Le Hardi	Fleuret[1]	Epée[2]	Mameluk	Casque	Lansquenet
Programme	1932	1935	1935	1936	1936	1936
Prog.no.	181	198	199	206	207	208
Project no.	–	–	–	–	–	–
Builder	ACL Nantes	FCM La Seyne	FC Gir Bordeaux	ACL Nantes	FCM La Seyne	FC Gir Bordeaux
Order	12 Nov 1935	31 Dec 1935	31 Dec 1935	4 May 1936	4 May 1936	4 May 1936
Laid down	20 May 1936	18 Aug 1936	15 Oct 1936	1 Jan 1937	30 Nov 1936	17 Dec 1936
Launched	4 May 1938	28 Jul 1938	26 Oct 1938	18 Feb 1939	2 Nov 1938	20 May 1939
Manned for trials	1 Jun 1939	15 Oct 1939	1 Dec 1939	20 Dec 1939	15 Dec 1939	1 Jun 1940
Acceptance trials	4 Nov 1939	16 Mar 1940	9 Apr 1940	9 May 1940	25 Apr 1940	
Commissioned	1 Dec 1939	10 May 1940				
Completed	31 May 1940					
Entered service	2 Jun 1940	11 Jun 1940	14 Jun 1940	17 Jun 1940	20 Jun 1940	[1941]

Name	Le Corsaire[3]	Le Flibustier[4]	L'Intrépide	Le Téméraire	L'Opiniâtre	L'Aventurier
Programme	1937	1937	1938	1938	1938	1938 bis
Prog. no.	226	227	265	266	267	281
Project no.	–	–	–	–	–	–
Builder	FCM La Seyne	FCM La Seyne	FCM La Seyne	FCM La Seyne	FC Gir Bordeaux	FC Gir Bordeaux
Order	24 May 1937	24 May 1937	20 Mar 1939	20 Mar 1939	20 Mar 1939	20 Mar 1939
Laid down	31 Mar 1938	11 Mar 1938	16 Aug 1939	28 Aug 1939	1 Aug 1939	4 Aug 1939
Launched	14 Nov 1939	19 Dec 1939	26 Jun 1941	7 Nov 1941	[20 Apr 1947]	
Manned for trials	1 May 1940	23 Jun 1940				
Acceptance trials	12 Aug 1940					
Commissioned						
Completed						
Entered service	01 Jul 1941	[1941]	[1942]	[1942]	[1942]	[1943]

Notes:
Fleuret renamed *Foudroyant* 1 April 1941.
Epée renamed *L'Adroit* 29 March 1941.
Le Corsaire renamed *Siroco* 1 April 1941.
Le Flibustier renamed *Bison* 1 April 1941.

of her trials. A further four ships began their acceptance trials in March/May 1940, just before the collapse of the western front, and these were hurriedly accepted into service in June 1940 with the German mobile forces fast approaching Brest and Lorient. The sixth ship, *Lansquenet*, managed to escape to Casablanca, but was placed *en gardiennage* on her return to Toulon in November 1940 and remained uncompleted. *Le Corsaire* (renamed *Siroco* on 1 April 1941) was essentially complete when placed *en gardiennage* in September 1940, while *Le Flibustier* (renamed *Bison*) was only 75% complete when manned for trials in June 1940, and remained in this state at Toulon following the Armistice; *Siroco* was scuttled with her sisters on 27 November 1942, but *Bison* was captured intact.

HULL AND GENERAL CONFIGURATION

The design of the *Le Hardi* class had many of the features of *Mogador* and *Volta*. The *torpilleurs d'escadre* were some twenty metres shorter, and had a less built-up appearance. Because there was no superimposed mounting forward, the bridge structure was on three levels rather than four, and the adoption of a single gun mounting forward and two aft, which was reflected in the magazine arrangements, had the effect of shifting the internal and external 'balance' of the ship forward. Whilst the stern section up to the after machinery bulkhead was of similar length to that of *Mogador*, the bow section up to the bulkhead for the forward engine room was significantly shorter. The reduction in the volume available for accommodation forward was acceptable because of the smaller complement, but the loss of all but one of the officer cabins on the lower level of the bridge[4] meant that virtually all the officer accommodation had to be worked in aft. Not only did the after section house the magazines for the two after mountings and depth charges, but it also accommodated the magazine for the 37mm guns, which at least had the benefit of placing them closer to the twin mounting atop the after deckhouse.

The other main difference in the internal layout of the ships was the relationship between the dimensions of the boiler rooms and the engine rooms. All the earlier French postwar destroyers featured double boiler rooms in which the two boilers, each of which occupied most of the width of the space, were located on or close to the ship's axis and faced one another. However, the new Sural boiler developed for the *Le Hardi* class (see Machinery below) had a completely different configuration to conventional boilers; it was longer and narrower, which meant that two boilers could be accommodated side by side in each of the two boiler rooms. This meant that whereas the engine rooms of *Le Hardi* were only a single frame shorter than those of *Mogador* (12.5m/7 frames vs. 13.5m/8 frames), the boiler rooms were two frames shorter (11m/6 frames vs. 15m/8 frames – a reduction of more than 25%). The external impact of this can be seen in the configuration of the funnels, which were far less broad when viewed from the side than those of *Mogador* because the exhaust uptakes came up together rather than from the opposite ends of the boiler rooms (see General Arrangement plans and compare with *Mogador* p.165).

---

[4] There was a single twin-berth cabin for two sub-lieutenants.

THE LE HARDI CLASS

The *Torpilleur d'Escadre Le Hardi*

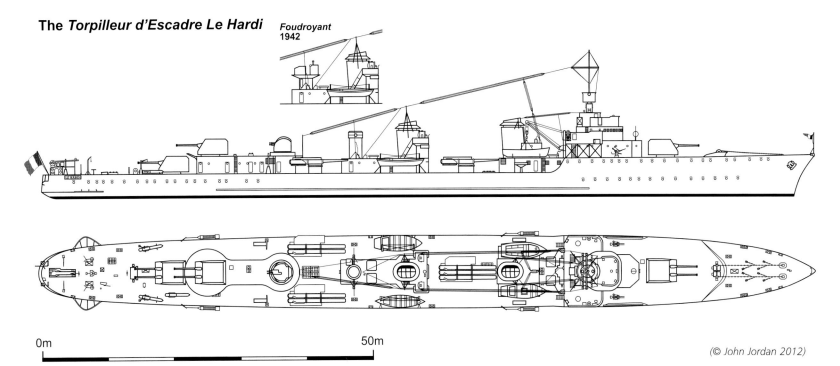

Profile and plan views of *Le Hardi* as designed. The drawings are based on the STCN plans approved in April 1936, shortly before the ship was laid down at ACL. The twin 37mm gun depicted atop the after deckhouse is the Mle 1935 ACAD, development of which had just begun; in later plans the associated director would replace the conventional secondary fire control position abaft the after funnel (see inset of *Foudroyant* 1942). Note the launch gantry for the Ginocchio towed anti-submarine torpedo above the stern. On completion the 13.2mm Hotchkiss CAD mountings on the forecastle would be relocated to the deckhouse forward of the bridge, and the boat handling derricks would be replaced by free-standing cranes.

Hull construction was similar to that of *Mogador*, with extensive use of welding and of duralumin for superstructures. Riveting continued to be used for the hull, which was sturdier than in the earlier *torpilleurs d'escadre*; despite the weight-saving measures employed in construction it accounted for 29% of trials displacement, while the machinery, which delivered almost twice the horsepower, accounted for only 33%.

There were twelve main transverse bulkheads extending from the ship's bottom to the upper deck,

Le Hardi: General Arrangement Plans

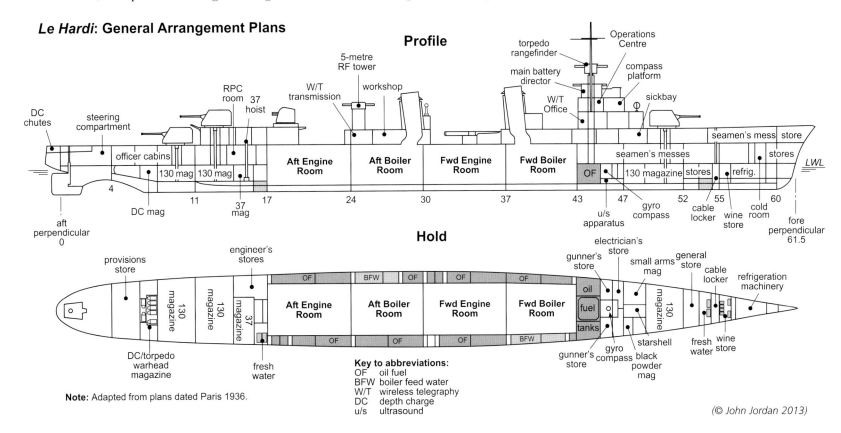

GENERAL CHARACTERISTICS

Displacement:	1772 tons standard; 1982 tonnes normal; 2577 tonnes full load
Dimensions:	Length 111.6m pp, 117.2m oa; beam 11.1m; draught 3.8m
Machinery:	Four Sural-Penhoët boilers, 35kg/cm^2 (385°C) Two-shaft geared steam turbines 58,000CV for 37kts (designed)
Oil fuel:	470 tonnes; radius 3100nm at 10kts, 1000nm at 35kts
Armament:	Six 130mm/45 Mle 1932 in twin pseudo-turrets Mle 1935 (170rpg + 60 starshell) Two 37mm/50 Mle 1933 AA in one twin mounting (1000rpg) Four 13.2mm/76 Hotchkiss MG Mle 1929 in two twin mountings (2400 rpg) Seven 550mm torpedoes Mle 1923DT in one triple and two twin mountings One/two DC chutes for eight/twelve 200kg depth charges (see text)
Complement:	10 officers + 177 men peacetime

and these divided the hull into thirteen watertight compartments designated A–M. The layout of the funnels, deckhouses, boats/cranes and searchlight projectors broadly followed the pattern established by the *Le Fantasque*s, although as with the earlier *torpilleurs d'escadre* there were two fewer boats to accommodate

GROUND TACKLE AND NAVIGATION

Due to the haste with which these ships were pressed into service, much of the usual formal documentation was not completed, and many details are lacking. The only information the authors have been able to uncover is that a windlass supplied by the Paul Duclos company was fitted. This could hoist an anchor of up to 6 tonnes (maximum capacity: 12 tonnes)

MACHINERY

The revolutionary new Sural[5] boiler was designed by *Ingénieur général* Norguet and built by Penhoët. Forced circulation and pressure firing resulted in steam production per cubic metre of volume well in excess of conventional boilers (14.4kg/m^3). This enabled overall

---

[5] Sural was an abbreviation of *Suralimenté* (= forced circulation).

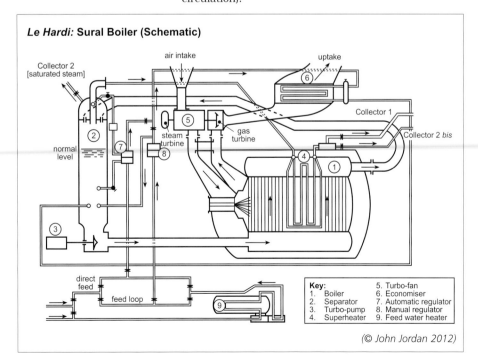

Le Hardi: Sural Boiler (Schematic)

Key:
1. Boiler
2. Separator
3. Turbo-pump
4. Superheater
5. Turbo-fan
6. Economiser
7. Automatic regulator
8. Manual regulator
9. Feed water heater

(© John Jordan 2012)

dimensions to be reduced; the outer casing of the steam generator had a broadly cylindrical configuration. This enabled two boilers to be fitted side by side in a compartment only slightly less broad than the boiler rooms of contemporary *contre-torpilleurs*, which could accommodate only single boilers in line. Approximate dimensions were: length 4.5m (vs. 5.4m in *Le Fantasque* and *Mogador*) and width – the key dimension for accommodating the boilers side by side – only 2.5m (vs. 6.50m). The boilers had a similar rating: 35kg/cm^2 (385°C).

The Sural boiler had an automatic regulation system developed by Rateau, the purpose of which was to maintain an optimum balance between the flow of oil, air and feed water at all times. It could produce 60 tonnes of steam per hour at normal power and 70t/h at overload, and proved remarkably flexible in service, making a rapid rise in steam pressure possible. However, the boilers were complex and required well-trained personnel to operate and to maintain them. Automatic regulation was also found to be an obstacle to making smoke, particularly at higher speeds; at Dakar in September 1940 independent smoke generators were provided for *Le Hardi* because of the problems she experienced making sufficient smoke to conceal the battleship *Richelieu*.

The adoption of the Sural boiler made for much shorter boiler rooms (11m/6 frames) than in other contemporary French destroyers. In the forward boiler room the boilers were located at the after end, with the *rue de chauffe* across the faces of the boilers. This meant that the forward funnel, in which the exhaust uptakes for the two boilers were combined, could be positioned well clear of the bridge. The after boiler room had the reverse arrangement, with the boilers – and the exhaust uptakes – at its forward end.

The steam turbine installation was essentially a scaled-down *Le Fantasque* plant, with a designed output of 58,000CV (vs.74,000CV in the *contre-torpilleurs*) at normal power, and 66,000CV at Washington standard displacement with forced draught. Of the twelve ships authorised, six (*Le Hardi*, *Mameluk*, *Casque*, *Le Corsaire*, *L'Intrépide* and *Le Téméraire*) had Parsons reaction turbines, and six Rateau-Bretagne impulse turbines. The type of turbine installed did not necessarily correspond to the shipyard with which the order for the hull was placed. The two A C Loire ships were fitted out with Parsons turbines and the four ships built by F C Gironde with Rateau, but four of the ships awarded to F C Méditerranée to be built at their La Seyne yard would have had Parsons and the other two Rateau.

Both types of turbine followed the pattern established by the earlier classes with superheated steam (*Milan/Epervier*, *Le Fantasque*) in having HP, IP and LP main turbines working in series and driving the propeller shaft through a large single-reduction gearbox. The reverse turbine was in the housing for the main LP turbine. The Parsons ships had a single cruise turbine clutched to the main gearbox, the Rateau ships two cruise turbines (CR1/CR2) which could be combined via their own gearbox and were clutched to the shaft for the main HP turbine (see schematic). The cruise turbines could develop a maximum power of 7500CV; 2300CV was sufficient to maintain a speed of 15 knots.

The forward set of turbines drove the starboard

THE LE HARDI CLASS

Le Hardi: Sections

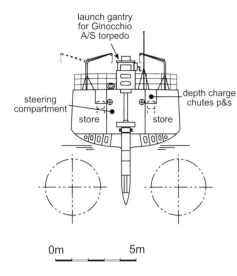

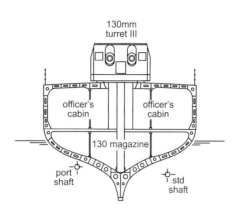

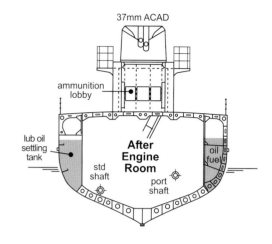

Note: Adapted from plans dated Paris 1936.

(© John Jordan 2013)

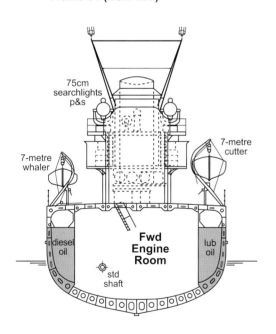

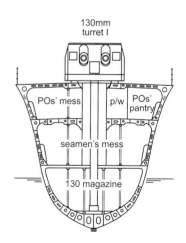

shaft, and the after set the (shorter) port shaft. Both shafts were fitted with three-bladed propellers of VHR bronze or brass with a diameter of 3.3m.

Only *Le Hardi* ran her full trials. On 6 November 1939, during her 8-hour full power (PMN) trials, with an initial displacement of 2377 tonnes, she achieved an average of 60,450CV with shaft revolutions of 378rpm; average speeds for the three standard runs were 38.56 knots, 39.09 knots and 38.69 knots respectively. These were impressive figures considering that the trials were run at load, rather than normal displacement. Of the other ships of the class, *Fleuret* achieved 40.20 knots at Washington standard displacement, and when the latter ship sailed from Casablanca to Toulon in early November 1940 she averaged 36 knots throughout the voyage.

At 38.70 knots and load displacement, fuel consumption in *Le Hardi* was calculated at 21.1 tonnes per hour. With a full load of fuel, endurance was estimated at 3100nm at 10 knots (one boiler lit), 2000nm at 16 knots (two boilers lit), 1900nm at 25 knots (two boilers), and 1000nm at 35 knots (all four boilers). These figures were a disappointment; staff requirements had specified 3000nm at 15 knots, and

Le Hardi (Parsons Turbines): Centre Machinery Rooms

In the absence of detailed plans of the machinery rooms, this drawing is necessarily conjectural, particularly with regard to the positioning of the main and the auxiliary boilers. However, the layout of the turbines and the shafts, for which plans have survived, suggests strongly that the disposition of the Sural boilers side by side, to port of the shaft for the starboard turbines, is broadly correct.

(© John Jordan 2013)

---

during wartime one would have expected the ships to operate with at least two boilers lit for safety reasons.

The electrical generating capacity was intermediate between the *Le Fantasque* and *Mogador* classes. The two turbo-generators were rated at 100kW – those in *Le Fantasque* were 80kW, the ones in *Mogador* 120kW. There were two 44kW (52kW) diesel generators, as in *Mogador* and *Volta*, for use when alongside. The increase in capacity over the *Le Fantasque*s was in part dictated by the move to twin power-operated pseudo-turrets, which made huge demands on the 115V power supply.

MAIN ARMAMENT

The 130mm Mle 1932 gun adopted for the *Le Hardi* class was essentially the same weapon employed for the secondary armament of the fast battleship *Dunkerque*. It featured a German-style sliding breech, which opened vertically in the high-angle mounting but horizontally in the low-angle mountings of the *torpilleurs d'escadre*. Unlike earlier models of 130mm it employed fixed ammunition, which theoretically simplified replenishment (using pusher hoists) and loading. However, the length (1.35m) and weight (53kg) of the round were at the upper limit for fixed ammunition, and a considerable degree of automation was necessary on the mounting to transfer the round from the hoist to the breech.

The Mle 1932 gun fired an OPFA Mle 1933 semi-armour-piercing (SAP) shell weighing 32.1kg with a 1.6kg *Mélinite* (picric acid) bursting charge; there was also an illuminating variant of the shell designated OEcl Mle 1934 weighing 30kg. Muzzle velocity for the SAP shell with a C1 combat charge was 800m/s, and maximum range at 30 degrees elevation was 19,000m. The standard allocation was 1020 SAP rounds (170rpg) and 60 starshell.

The twin pseudo-turret Mle 1935 was supplied by

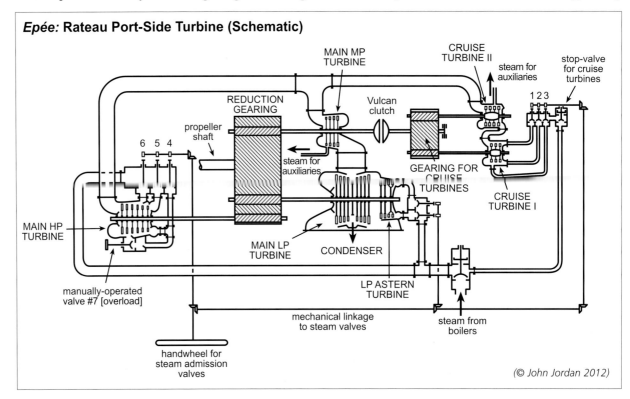

(© John Jordan 2012)

130MM/45 MLE 1932

Gun Data
Construction	monobloc autofretted barrel
Breech mechanism	horizontal sliding block
Weight of gun	3.7 tonnes
Ammunition type	fixed
Projectiles	OPFA Mle 1933 (32.1kg)
	OEcl Mle .1934 (30kg)
Propellant	8.8kg BM9
Complete round (OPFA)	
weight	53kg
dimensions	1350mm x 183mm
Muzzle velocity	800m/s
Range at 30°	19,000m

Mounting Data
Designation	Schneider Mle 1935
Protection	20mm
Weight of pseudo-turret	32.2 tonnes
Distance apart gun axes	1.3m
Elevation	−10° / +30°
Loading angle	up to +30°
Training speed	12° / sec
Elevating speed	8° / sec
Firing cycle	10–15rpm

Notes:
Mle	*Modèle*	Model
OPFA	*Obus de Perforation en Fonte Aciérée*	Semi-Armour Piercing (SAP)
OEA	*Obus Explosif en Acier*	High Explosive (HE)

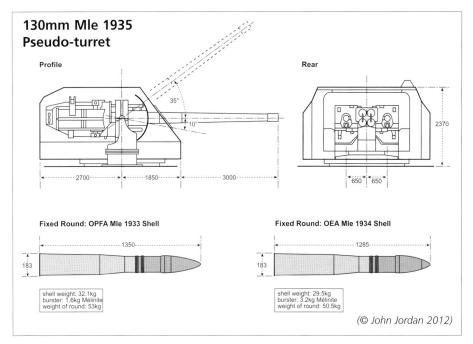

(© John Jordan 2012)

Schneider & Cie and served as the conceptual basis for the 138.6mm mounting developed for *Mogador* and *Volta* (see Chapter 8). Like the 138.6mm Mle 1935 it was a base-ring mounting with a central fixed ammunition trunk. The turret had a revolving weight of about 32.2 tonnes, slightly less than the *Mogador* turret (34.6t), but had a thicker shield of 20mm 80kg (i.e. armour-grade) steel. The turret was trained and the guns elevated by electric motors, and there was provision for remote power control (see below).

The pusher hoists in the axial ammunition trunk delivered four complete rounds (i.e. two per gun) to a rotatable tilting drum (*barillet*), as in the 138.8mm mounting. However, the loading sequence was simplified by the fixed round, which obviated the need for specially-configured slides and loading trays for the shell and the cased charge. When the rounds arrived in the gunhouse, the *barillet* was rotated to align with the angle of train of the turret, then tipped to the horizontal; springs then propelled the fixed rounds onto upper and lower loading trays from which they were power-rammed alternately into the breech. As with the 138.6mm mounting, the rammers were underpowered,

Below: *Fleuret* running her full power trials off Toulon in March 1940. A maximum speed of 40.20 knots was attained during these trials, the fastest recorded speed of any unit of the class. Note the 3-metre auxiliary rangefinder in its open mounting and the absence of a protective screen around the twin 37mm Mle 1933. (*Marius Bar*)

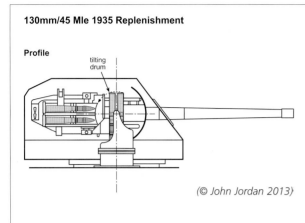

130mm/45 Mle 1935 Replenishment

A key difference between the 138.6mm and the 130mm mounting was that the latter employed fixed ammunition. This made for an extremely long round, which had to be raised base uppermost in the pusher hoists so that when tipped to the horizontal it presented in line with the breech. This was, however, a simpler arrangement than in the *Mogador* class (see previous chapter), in which the projectile and the cartridge had to be loaded separately.

(© John Jordan 2013)

and in service there were regular jams together with breakdowns in the semi-automatic loading mechanism.

With the benefit of time many of these technical problems could have been resolved, but when the early ships entered service the war had already begun. In late September 1940, following the abortive British assault on Dakar, *Fleuret* and *Epée* were dispatched, together with the older destroyers *Fougueux* and *Frondeur*, on a reprisal raid against Gibraltar. Neither ship had previously fired its guns in anger, nor had they had the opportunity to conduct gunnery practice on a firing range. During a brief and inconclusive engagement with a single British destroyer, *Epée* managed to get off 14 rounds in six minutes before all her guns broke down; *Fleuret* experienced problems with her fire control director, which was unable to track the target, and in consequence did not succeed in firing a single shot.

The performance of *Le Hardi* at Dakar the previous day provides an instructive contrast. This ship had completed thirteen sessions on gunnery ranges before the June Armistice, firing more than 700 rounds in the process. When put to the test at Dakar *Le Hardi* fired 60 shells without experiencing any breakdown, bracketing the target with her first salvo.

Fire control

The fire control system for the main guns as designed was identical to that of *Mogador* and *Volta*. Initially there was to be a secondary fire control position abaft the second funnel with a 5-metre rangefinder in a trainable turret similar in configuration to that of the *Le Fantasque*s. As with the two *Mogador*s this was subsequently superseded by a fire control director for the 37mm ACAD gun (see below) but, when the latter failed to materialise, the secondary fire control position was reinstated as a temporary measure. On completion all but *Mameluk* received a 3-metre rangefinder on a simple pedestal; the latter ship was fitted with an enclosed trainable housing of broadly square cross-section equipped with the longer-base 5-metre model.

The Mle 1935 pseudo-turrets, like those of *Mogador* and *Volta*, were to have been fitted with remote power control for their main guns, the necessary motors and converters being housed in prominent side pods on the mountings. However, following the problems experienced with the *Le Fantasque*s, RPC was finally abandoned in 1942 when it became clear that there was insufficient on-board electrical power for an effective system.

ANTI-AIRCRAFT WEAPONS

The official STCN plans dated April 1936 (see Profile and Plan of *Le Hardi* as designed) show a twin 37mm ACAD Mle 1935 mounting in the same position as in *Mogador*, atop the after deckhouse. However, these early plans show a conventional secondary fire control position abaft the second funnel, equipped with a second 5-metre stereo rangefinder. This suggests that the FC director for the ACAD gun, then at an early stage of its development, had yet to be designed. A prototype director similar to that which features in the 1939 plans of *Mogador* (see p.164) appears to have been trialled in *Le Corsaire* in the late summer of 1940

LIGHT AA GUNS

	25/60 Mle 1939/40	13.2mm Browning MG
Gun Data		
Weight of gun	147kg	31kg (40kg incl. water)
Ammunition type	fixed	fixed
Projectiles	OEA Mle 19?? (0.26kg)	AP and HE
	OI Mle 19?? (0.25kg)	tracer
Complete round		
weight	0.68kg	122g
dimensions	265mm x 25mm	135mm x 13.2mm
Muzzle velocity	900m/s	800m/s
Max. range	7500m theoretical	1500–2000m
	3000m practical	
Ceiling	5000m	
Mounting Data		
Designation	CAS Mle 1939	CAS
Weight of mounting	2.7 tonnes	178kg
Elevation of guns	–5° / +90°	–10° / +79°
Firing cycle (per gun)	250–300rpm (1939)	1000rpm theoretical
	350–400rpm (1940)	400–650rpm practical

Notes:

Mle	*Modèle*	Model
CAS	*Contre-Avions Simple*	AA single mounting
OEA	*Obus Explosif en Acier*	High Explosive (HE)
OEcl	*Obus Eclairant*	Starshell
OI	*Obus Incendiaire*	Incendiary shell

25mm/60 Hotchkiss Mle 1939/1940

CAA sketch of the 25mm Hotchkiss Mle 1939 mounting, showing the elaborate system of cams which limited the elevation and depression of the gun at certain angles of train to prevent damage to the superstructures of the ship on which it was mounted. The hoops in use in the British Royal Navy and the US Navy for the same purpose proved far simpler and were later adopted by the Marine Nationale.

Le Hardi: Bridge Decks & Platforms

1. Teugue [Forecastle]

2. Passerelle de navigation [Navigation Bridge]

3. Passerelle Supérieure [Upper Bridge]

Note: Adapted from plans dated Paris 1936.

(© John Jordan 2012)

(see photo in Salou, *op.cit.*, p.79), but the gun mounting atop the after deckhouse was the 37mm CAD Mle 1933 fitted as a temporary measure; the associated RPC would almost certainly not have been installed, so fire control data would have been transmitted by telephone.[6] A later plan of *Foudroyant* (ex-*Fleuret*) dating from 1942 (R16515, CAA archives) shows both the ACAD gun mounting and the director in place. However, with the availability of ACAD some way off when the first ships of the class were completed in the spring of 1940, the original secondary FC position was restored (see above).

In addition to the replacement of the 37mm ACAD by a 37mm CAD Mle 1933, the two twin 13.2mm Hotchkiss CAD, which in the 1936 plans were mounted on either side of the forecastle, were relocated atop the deckhouse which formed the lowest level of the bridge, abaft turret I.

A total of 2960 37mm rounds were provided. To replenish the ready-use lockers on and close to the mounting there was a magazine abaft the after engine room served by its own hoist, which brought the ammunition up to the main deck close to the mounting. Provision for the 13.2mm Hotchkiss CAD was the standard 2400 rounds per gun, of which 480 (16 magazines each of 30 rounds) were normally stowed in ready-use lockers close to the mountings.

As a temporary measure, a 1.5-metre stereo rangefinder was provided atop the after deckhouse to provide bearing and range data for the light AA.

TORPEDOES

The *Le Hardi* class had a triple torpedo mounting Mle 1928T forward, and two twin mountings Mle 1928D aft. The axial triple mounting could fire 30 degrees on either side of the beam, and the wing mountings, which were located between the second funnel and the after deckhouse, had arcs of 70 degrees forward of the beam and 60 degrees abaft the beam. As in *Mogador* and *Volta* the control platforms on the torpedo mountings were fitted from the outset with shields to provide protection from the elements.

For torpedo fire control there was a dedicated 5-metre stereoscopic rangefinder in a trainable housing above the main director, linked to a Mle 1933 FC computer, as in the *Le Fantasque* and *Mogador* classes.

ANTI-SUBMARINE WEAPONS AND DETECTION APPARATUS

The original plans show two depth charge chutes each for six 200kg Guiraud Mle 1922 depth charges as in the *Bourrasque* and *L'Adroit* classes, with a launch platform above the stern for a Ginocchio towed torpedo (see Chapter 2 for details) between them. This arrangement appears subsequently to have been modified, as

---

[6] The prototype gun mounting, together with its director, was trialled in the sloop *Amiens* from late 1939.

Below: *Epée* coming alongside the 10,000-ton cruiser *Dupleix* in the Mediterranean in the autumn of 1940. Note the single depth charge chute to port and the prominent boxes for the RPC motors on the sides of the pseudo-turrets. (*Conrad Waters collection*)

Right: *Epée* during a visit to Marseille, probably in February or early March of 1941. She is as yet unmodified. The stern of *Mameluk* can be seen in the foreground; note the twin stern chutes which distinguish her from her sisters *Epée* and *Le Hardi*.

the first three ships of the class were fitted on completion with a single DC chute with eight charges to port; the launch gantry for the Ginocchio torpedo was to have been offset to starboard and angled outboard by 30–40 degrees.

It is not clear whether the Ginocchio torpedo was ever embarked, and following further trials on destroyers of the *Bourrasque* class in late 1939 all Ginocchios were landed and put into store.[7] The later ships of the *Le Hardi* class were fitted out as planned, with two 6-charge chutes but without the gantry, and the square stern apertures for the twin chutes are a clear distinguishing feature in photographs.

The official plans also show handling gear for C6 minesweeping paravanes abeam turret III; with the suppression of the Ginocchio handling arrangements these were relocated to the stern and provided with a new type of davit.

No submarine detection apparatus was fitted, but a space for a future installation was reserved to starboard, just forward of the transverse fuel tanks (see GA plans).

COMMUNICATIONS

The W/T outfit was broadly similar to that of *Mogador* and *Volta*, but was less comprehensive. The main W/T office, which was located at the after end of the bridge block on the port side, monitored all communications and housed all the main receivers. A smaller W/T office housing the short-wave transmitters was located opposite, to starboard, and the office housing the medium and long-range transmitters was located at the after end of the centre deckhouse, abaft the uptakes for the second funnel.

Further details are lacking, but an SIF Mle 1937 very-short-wave (OTC) radio for bridge-to-bridge voice communication was almost certainly fitted on completion.

---

[7] Note 131 FMF/3 dated 18 January 1940.

BOATS

The outfit of boats comprised a 7-metre motor boat for the senior officers, a 7-metre motor launch for service duties in an anchorage, plus the standard 7-metre whaler and the 7-metre pulling cutter. The latter were on davits abeam the centre deckhouse, while the motor boat and motor launch were on crutches atop the deckhouse abeam the fore-funnel. The original plans show boat-handling derricks at the after end of the bridge structure, as on the earlier *contre-torpilleurs*. However, when completed the *Le Hardi* class were fitted with free-standing 'goose-neck' cranes similar to those which equipped *Mogador* and *Volta*.

COMPLEMENT

The designed complement of the *Le Hardi* class was ten officers, 31 petty officers and 146 men. This compared with eight officers, 24 petty officers and 111 men in the earlier *torpilleurs d'escadre*, and reflected the increased size and manpower demands of these ships.

The official plans show a large space for the two senior officers abaft the main RPC room and the transmitting station, which in contrast to earlier ships was just behind the after engine room bulkhead. There were sleeping cabins for the captain (*capitaine de frégate/corvette*) and for his second-in-command to port and starboard respectively, with adjacent bath/shower rooms and WCs, a large wardroom and a pantry. In the event of an admiral embarking, the admiral would displace the commanding officer, with the latter moving into the executive officer's cabin

Between the next two watertight bulkheads (Frames 4 and 11) was the main accommodation for junior officers, comprising five single-berth cabins, a twin-berth cabin for *enseignes de vaisseau*, a large wardroom and pantry, plus showers and W.C.s. There was an additional two-berth cabin for EVs at the forward end of the lower bridge, to port.

The accommodation for petty officers and seamen was laid out as in earlier ships. At Main Deck level in

THE LE HARDI CLASS

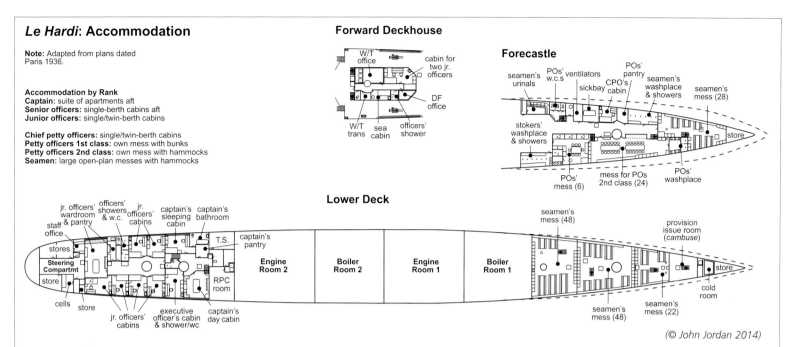

Le Hardi: Accommodation

Note: Adapted from plans dated Paris 1936.

Accommodation by Rank
Captain: suite of apartments aft
Senior officers: single-berth cabins aft
Junior officers: single/twin-berth cabins

Chief petty officers: single/twin-berth cabins
Petty officers 1st class: own mess with bunks
Petty officers 2nd class: own mess with hammocks
Seamen: large open-plan messes with hammocks

(© John Jordan 2014)

The layout of the accommodation on the *Le Hardi* class was closer in conception to the later *contre-torpilleurs* than to the earlier *torpilleurs d'escadre* (see the drawings of *Bourrasque* p.50 and of *Le Fantasque* p.152 for a comparison). The petty officer accommodation was grouped together at the after end of the forecastle; the larger crew also meant an additional seamen's mess on the Lower Deck forward. The main difference from the later *contre-torpilleurs* was that the transmitting station and RPC converter room had to be relocated from directly beneath the bridge to the longer after section of the accommodation deck. This made sense given the arrangement of the ships' main guns, but lengthened cable runs to the main directors and the forward 130mm gun mounting. In terms of the balance of the ship's complement, note the number of 'specialists' required to service the sophisticated weapons systems and machinery: 24 Petty Officers 2nd Class vs. only eight in the *Bourrasques*.

the forecastle there were separate messes for seven POs 1st class and 24 POs 2nd class to starboard, with the sick-bay and a single-berth cabin for a Chief Petty Officer to port. The seamen were accommodated in four large messes, one at the forward end of the forecastle and the remaining three on the accommodation deck below.

EVALUATION

On completion the *Le Hardi* class were, at least on paper, among the world's most impressive destroyers. In displacement, speed and power they matched the latest IJN destroyers of the *Kagero* class, with which they can be legitimately compared. Their robust hulls and low centre of gravity gave them seakeeping quali-

Le Hardi November 1940

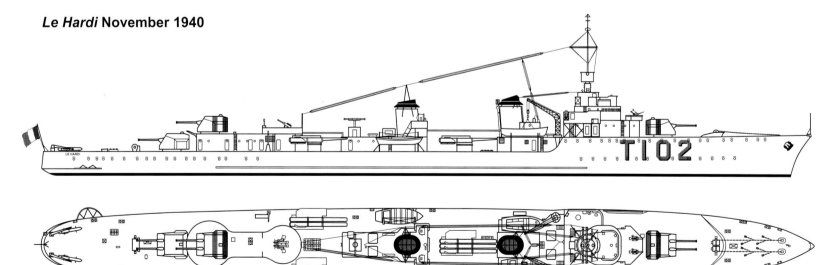

Le Hardi as she appeared in November 1940. The planned 37mm ACAD mounting atop the after deckhouse has been replaced by the Mle 1933 CAD as an interim measure, and a circular screen fitted around the mounting. The 13.2mm Hotchkiss CAD have been relocated from the forecastle to the deckhouse forward of the bridge, and a 3-metre rangefinder in an open pedestal mounting has replaced the original secondary FC position abaft the second funnel. The launch gantry for the Ginocchio torpedo has been removed, and the C6 paravanes relocated to the stern. Note the new boat cranes, which were similar to those fitted in *Mogador* and *Volta*. *Le Hardi* is shown with her new tactical number T102 and tricolore identification markings on turrets I and II.

(© John Jordan 2012)

ties which were far superior to those of the 1500-tonne destroyers built during the 1920s.

Had the Marine Nationale been allowed the necessary time to resolve the teething problems which were inevitable in a design of this complexity, they would almost certainly have proved to be excellent fighting units. The ships of the class scuttled at Toulon were coveted by both the Germans and the Italians, who made their salvage a priority. In the event, delays in the design, ordering and construction process meant that only the lead ship, *Le Hardi*, had completed her trials and work-up before the Armistice; four others were rushed into service in June 1940 in various states of completion and readiness, while two other ships, *Lansquenet* and *Le Corsaire*, escaped the clutches of the Germans but would remain incomplete until the scuttling of the fleet in November 1942.

The problems experienced by *Le Hardi* with both her artillery and her machinery suggest the same issues of over-elaboration in the pursuit of theoretical high performance that we have noted in respect of *Mogador* and *Volta*. Even if these problems had been satisfactorily resolved, it is arguable whether the concept of an exceptionally fast, technically advanced and heavily armed destroyer was correct. When conflict finally came to the Mediterranean theatre in 1940–2, it demonstrated the need for different qualities: reliability, endurance, resistance to damage, and multiple anti-aircraft guns with well-developed fire control capabilities.

MODIFICATIONS 1940–2

The destroyers of the *Le Hardi* class drifted back from North Africa to Toulon during the late summer and autumn of 1940 in various states of completion. They were formed into a 10th Torpedo Boat Division (DT), and five (all except *Casque* and *le Corsaire*) were given tactical numbers from T101 to T105. From 10 October only three ships were active, the remaining units being placed *en gardiennage*. The 10th DT was initially under regional command, but was integrated into the *Forces de Haute Mer* (FHM) from 1 November 1941.

Most of the work done on these ships during 1940–1 was related to completing and, where necessary, modifying their designed installations. During the spring of 1941 the active units received the standard allocation of two 13.2mm Browning MG, and these were initially mounted on the quarterdeck. However, in late 1941 *Le Hardi* underwent a major refit at Toulon that would become the template for modifications to the other active units of the class.

Two of the new 25mm Hotchkiss CAS Mle 1939 were fitted in place of the 13.2mm Hotchkiss CAD forward of the bridge, the latter being relocated to the quarterdeck. As on *Volta* (q.v.) platforms were built out from the sides of turret II for the two 13.2mm Browning MG mounted. There were now two 25mm guns able to fire on forward bearings, and two 37mm guns plus six 13.2mm MG aft.

These modifications were duly extended to *L'Adroit*, *Mameluk* and *Casque*, which replaced *Le Hardi* in the (active) 10th DT in May 1942. They were carried out at the dockyard during the second half of 1941 and the early months of 1942. In *Mameluk* and *L'Adroit*, the tricolore identification markings, formerly on turret II, were transferred to turret III; in *Le Hardi* and *Casque* they were retained on turret II.

Below: *Mameluk* as she appeared in April 1941. She has 13.2mm Hotchkiss CAD atop the deckhouse forward of the bridge, and single 13.2mm Browning MG on the quarterdeck. Note the 5-metre rangefinder aft in its distinctive turret, which served to distinguish her from her sisters. (*Marius Bar*)

Mameluk April 1941

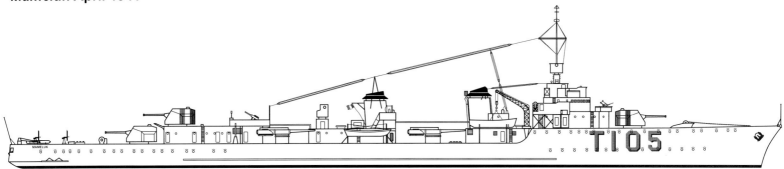

By April 1941 *Mameluk* had received two single 13.2mm Browning MG, which were mounted on the quarterdeck. Note the enclosed trainable housing for the after rangefinder; *Mameluk* was the only ship of the class to have this feature on completion. Note the depth charge chute to starboard; the first three ships of the class had only a single chute to port.

(© John Jordan 2012)

Photos of *L'Adroit* taken during 1942 show her with a conical housing at the base of the secondary rangefinder for the main guns abaft the second funnel, while *Casque* received a 4/5-metre rangefinder with a protective hood similar to that fitted aft in the *Guépard* and *Aigle* classes; this may have been removed from one of the latter ships when placed *en gardiennage*.

THE 1938 AND 1938 *BIS* SHIPS

The experience of neutrality patrols during the Spanish Civil War led the Naval General Staff to reconsider many of its previous assumptions about naval war in the Mediterranean. It now viewed dual-purpose guns as essential for ships tasked with escorting capital ships. During 1938 there were successive memos to the STCN proposing a revision of the *Le Hardi* design.[8] It was suggested that the mounting be modelled on the twin fitted in *Dunkerque* and *Strasbourg*. There was no question at this late stage of modifying the eight ships already laid down, but it was considered a practical proposition for the four ships of the 1938 and 1938 *bis* estimates, which were not due to be laid down until the summer of 1939.

The STCN duly responded on 30 November 1938.[9] It proposed a ship mounting six 130mm guns in three dual-purpose mountings and a total ammunition provision of 1350 combat rounds plus 60 starshell and 315 exercise rounds. The increase (from 1020 combat

---

[8] Notes 606 EMG/1 dated 29 June, followed by 758 EMG/3, and finally 1094 EMG/3 dated 22 November.
[9] Note 14161 CN/4.

Below: *Le Hardi* in December 1941, following a major refit, with her main guns trained and fully elevated. The photo shows clearly the single depth charge chute to port which was a feature of the first three ships of the class. Single Hotchkiss 25mm mountings (not visible) have been fitted forward of the bridge, and the Hotchkiss 13.2mm CAD relocated to the quarterdeck. Platforms for single 13.2mm Browning MG have been fitted to the sides of turret II, but note that the tricolore identification markings have been retained on this turret. *(Marius Bar)*

Right: Not a single unit of this class survived the scuttling at Toulon on 27 November 1942. The photograph shows *Foudroyant* (ex-*Fleuret*) and *Le Hardi* on the bottom of the harbour, with the incomplete *Bison* (ex-*Le Flibustier*) towering above them, at the Quai Noël. *(US Navy NH 110745, courtesy of A D Baker III)*

rounds and 193 exercise rounds) was deemed necessary because of the need to provide both SAP (for surface engagement) and HE time-fuzed rounds (for aerial engagement). There was a cost of 55 tonnes for the D-P mountings, and if other aspects of performance such as speed and endurance were to be maintained, this would require a significantly larger ship with greater installed horsepower (see table for comparison).

Alternative armaments put forward by the STCN as possibilities for a ship of this size were:

– 3 x II 130mm LA + 2 x II 100mm HA
– 4 x II 100mm HA (with 200rpg)
– 4 x II 130mm LA (this last option served to highlight the cost of fleet air defence to anti-surface capabilities)

In early 1939 consideration was given to providing the pseudo-turrets and the bridge with light plating to protect against aerial strafing with 12.7/13.2mm machine guns. As weight compensation the number of torpedo tubes would be reduced from seven to six. The light AA would be replaced by a uniform armament of three twin 23mm mountings of a type currently under study.

It was decided that three of the four 1938/1938 *bis* ships would be of the first type proposed, with three 130mm D-P mountings, while the fourth was to form a three-ship division with *Le Corsaire* and *Le Flibustier* (1937 estimates) and would be armed as follows: 3 x II 130mm LA, 2 x II 100mm HA, 4 x II 13.2mm and 2 x III TT.

These plans were thrown into confusion by the outbreak of war; construction was suspended only

L'Adroit August 1942

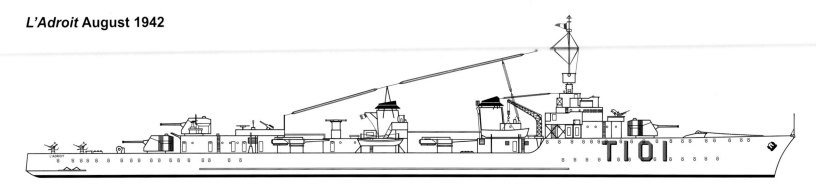

L'Adroit (formerly *Epée*) as she was in August 1942; she had been lead ship of the 10th *Division de torpilleurs* ever since it was formed on 8 August 1940. By August 1942 the 13.2mm Hotchkiss CAD had been relocated to the quarterdeck and replaced forward of the bridge by two of the new 25mm Hotchkiss CAS. Two 13.2mm Browning MG have been fitted on platforms projecting from the sides of turret II, and the tricolore identification markings have been moved to turret III. Note the cylindrical housing around the base of the 3-metre rangefinder abaft the second funnel.

(© John Jordan 2012)

THE LE HARDI CLASS

weeks after the keels had been laid.

The following March, when construction was resumed, the NGS reported to Admiral Darlan that although no destroyers of new design could be completed before 1944 it would be possible, by taking advantage of the slipways available at the La Seyne shipyard of F C Méditerranée, to have either four torpedo boats of the *Le Fier* class or three destroyers of the *Le Hardi* class ready for trials during 1943.[10]

On 28 April[11] Darlan opted for a further three destroyers of the *Le Hardi* class with the following characteristics:

- hull as original design (or the new, enlarged design if the plans were sufficiently advanced)
- speed: 35.5/36 knots max.
- endurance (wartime conditions): 1700nm at 20 knots/1300nm at 25 knots, plus six hours at 9/10 maximum speed[12]
- 2/3 x II 130mm D-P capable of an elevation of 40/50 degrees with 1200 rounds
- one 37mm ACAD mounting on the centre-line and 37mm ACAS mountings on either beam, plus four 13.2mm Hotchkiss CAD (all in shielded mountings)
- 2 x III 550mm torpedo tubes
- two DC rails each with ten 100kg depth charges, plus two fixed DCTs

Darlan stipulated that the 130mm D-P guns should be robust and simple and should have access to ready-

1938/1938 *BIS* INITIAL PROJECT

	Le Hardi	1938/1938 *bis*
Length (pp):	111.59m	118.80m
Beam (wl):	11.06m	11.88m
Depth:	6.65m	7.00m
Freeboard:	3.11m	3.38m
Displacement:		
Standard	1772t	2215t
Trial	2279t	2562t
Deep load	2577t	2929t
Horsepower:	58,000CV	62,000CV

use ammunition. He further specified that there should be *no mechanical continuity* (author's italics) between the hoist and the breech of the guns; separate ammunition was to be used and the guns were to be loaded manually. He noted that these arrangements worked well in the latest British destroyers.

In March 1940 there had been exchanges between the Marine Nationale and the Royal Navy. The French liaison officers had been shown the latest Mk XX twin 4.7in (120mm) mounting due to be fitted in the destroyers of the 'L' and 'M' classes (see accompanying illustrations).[13] Their favourable report provided a marked contrast with the reports which regularly fell on Darlan's desk of persistent and on-going problems with both the 130mm and the 138.6mm twin mountings, in which automation had been taken to an unprecedented level.

---

[10] Note 105 EMG/FC dated 27 March 1940.
[11] Note 1029 FMF/3.
[12] The new criteria allowed for both operational radius and combat.

[13] The British Mk XX mounting allowed a maximum gun elevation of 50 degrees, which almost certainly accounts for the modest elevation of 40/50 degrees requested by Darlan for its French 130mm counterpart.

Below: *L'Adroit* on 10 August 1942, showing the final configuration of these ships. There are two single Hotchkiss 25mm mountings forward of the bridge, Hotchkiss 13.2mm CAD on the quarterdeck, and 13.2mm Browning MG on platforms on the sides of turret II. In this ship the tricolore identification markings have been relocated to turret III. Note the unusual cylindrical housing around the base of after rangefinder. *(Marius Bar)*

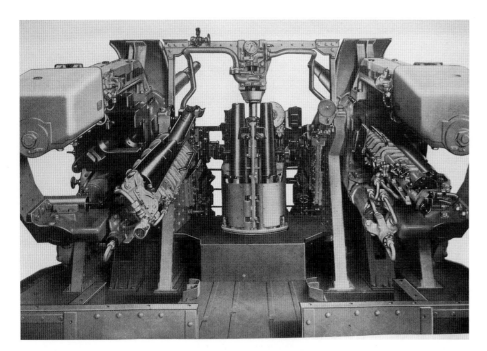

Above: Rear view of the British 4.7in Mk XX twin mounting with the shield removed. In the centre two brass cartridges are emerging from the trunk for the pusher hoists; the two pusher hoists for shells are concealed behind them. The mounting rotated around the fixed trunk. On the left is the tilting tray for the fuze setter and – nearest the camera – the loading tray with a shell and cartridge ready for ramming. Shells and cartridges were rammed hydraulically or by hand. The working space required for the fuze setters and the loading numbers was responsible for the exceptionally large size of the fully-enclosed mounting. *(Handbook BR916 1942, Courtesy of John Roberts)*

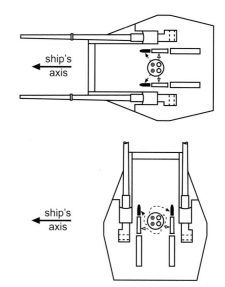

The British 4.7-inch Mk XX mounting

The arrow between the barrels indicates the fore-and-aft stowed position. The short arrows from the ammunition trunking show the passage of the shell (black) and the cased charge (white) to the tilting trays. The passage is straightforward in the upper sketch, but in the lower, with the mounting trained 90 degrees on the starboard beam, the routes from the axial ammunition trunk are extended, and become even more difficult when the mounting is trained abaft the beam.

Adapted from Peter Hodges' drawing in Hodges & Friedman, *Destroyer Weapons of WW2* (Conway Maritime Press, 1979).

(© John Jordan 2013)

Darlan recognised that the time required to develop a new dual-purpose mounting would exceed the projected building times for the ships; he therefore proposed a provisional armament of three or four 100mm HA mountings.[14]

Less than two months later France was compelled to enter into an Armistice with Germany. None of the ships of the 1938 and 1938 *bis* estimates would be completed. *L'Intrépide* and *Le Téméraire*, which were building at the La Seyne yard of F C Méditerranée outside the occupied zone, were launched in June and November 1941 respectively, but were only 20% and 15% complete when the hulls were seized by the Germans in November 1942. *L'Opiniâtre* and *L'Aventurier* were seized on the slipway at Bordeaux in June 1940, and although the former was formally inscribed on the German fleet lists as *ZF 2*, little work was done on her and her hull was partially dismantled in 1943.

Arguably the most positive thing to come out of the projects of 1939–40 was that they laid the basis for the design of the postwar 'fleet escorts' (*escorteurs d'escadre*) of the T47 series, which were initially to have been armed with six 130mm in twin D-P mountings,[15] but which had an altogether superior (and uniform) heavy AA armament of six 57mm guns.

---

[14] There is again a parallel with the British ships: four units of the 'L' class were given four twin 4-inch (102mm) Mk XIX mountings in place of the designed 4.7in Mk XX mountings as a temporary measure due to late delivery of the latter; the decision was taken in mid-March 1940, just over a month before Darlan's memo.

[15] It was subsequently decided to replace the 130mm with a 127mm gun which could use American 5-inch proximity-fuzed ammunition.

CHAPTER 10
PAINT SCHEMES AND IDENTIFICATION MARKINGS

PAINT SCHEMES
1926–1939
From April 1908, French warships normally had a blue-grey livery; the latest version was designated *gris bleu 1922*. This was superseded, following an instruction dated 8 November 1929,[1] by a light grey paint scheme designated *gris clair no.1*. From 1938 a paint with a gloss finish (*gris clair vernissé*) was applied. This made it easier to wash down the toxic residues that accumulated when the guns were fired, but the paint was reflective and in certain light conditions made the ships easier to see from the air.

The forecastle forward of the breakwater, the main deck above the machinery spaces, and the quarterdeck above the stern, which were the areas of greatest movement for the crew, had a dark grey non-slip paint applied; the *torpilleurs* had square plates welded to the deck in these areas in order to further improve grip. The after part of the forecastle and the upper deck abaft the machinery spaces were covered with red-brown linoleum secured with brass strips. From 1931 the areas of the upper deck previously painted grey were repainted in 'deck red' (*rouge pour pont*) to give them a more homogeneous appearance. Around the main guns the deck was often a dark red-brown.

The underside of the ship was painted in a red or reddish-brown anti-fouling paint. At the waterline there was a black band of bitumen-based paint (*Bitumastic*) one-metre deep to mask oil stains. The bronze (or brass) propellers remained unpainted.

The funnel caps and the upper ends of the galley pipes were not initially painted, but were coated with a mixture of soot and grease called *bouchon gras* to facilitate maintenance. They would subsequently be painted black, together with anchors, hawse holes, bollards and fairleads. The pivots of the 130mm guns on the *torpilleurs* initially had the appearance of black steel but were painted grey from 1929.

1939–1956
In late 1939 ships based in the Atlantic, notably those belonging to the *Force de Raid*, were repainted in a dark grey livery. Some ships had their superstructures painted medium grey and their masts light grey.

[1] Circular 747 CN/6.

Left: *Simoun* (12), *Orage* (13) and *Bourrasque* (14) at sea on 19 June 1927. They are in the original uniform blue-grey paint scheme common to Atlantic-based ships of the period. Note the tall funnels with which these ships were completed. (*SHD Marine, courtesy of Marc Saibène*).

Right: *Tempête* off the southern coast of France during 1930–1, when she served as leader of the 3rd *Escadrille* in the 1st Squadron. She is painted in the now-standard *gris clair no.1*, and has the classic large white hull numbers of the period with black shadowing. Note the tricolore pennant of the senior officer at the foremast top. *(A D Baker III collection)*

Several ships were given a false bow wave to create an impression of speed. At the same time camouflage schemes began to appear. In early October 1939 *Jaguar* was given a disruptive scheme which used three shades of grey and was symmetrical on both sides, probably at Cherbourg; it was painted out following the collision with HMS *Keppel* in mid-January of the following year.

When serving with the FNFL, *Léopard* received a Western Approaches-type disruptive camouflage comprising blue and light green regular panels on a white background. She wore this from May 1942 until

Right: *Le Triomphant* coming alongside a US Navy ship to take on dry stores; the photo was taken in the Western Pacific in early 1942. During this period she carried an unusual two-sided deceptive/disruptive camouflage scheme, in which the port side was painted to resemble a mercantile freighter. *(US Navy NH 81738, courtesy of A D Baker III)*

PAINT SCHEMES AND IDENTIFICATION MARKINGS

Above: *Le Fantasque* on 30 May 1936, when the 2nd Squadron was reviewed off Brest by President Lebrun. Note the hyphen before the number '10', which marked her out as an 'Atlantic' ship, and the single white band on the fore-funnel denoting the 10th Light Division. The swallow-tail tricolore pennant of the officer commanding the division is flying at the foremast top. *Le Fantasque*'s two *divisionnaires* were *L'Audacieux* (-11) and *Le Terrible* (-12). (US Navy NH 86554, courtesy of A D Baker III)

French Naval Ensigns

Marine Nationale

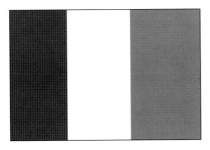

Flown from ensign staff at stern. Note the proportions, which differ from the national flag.

Marine Nationale

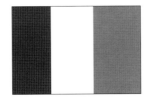

Flown from the jack staff in port and from a short mast abaft the after funnel when at sea.

FNFL

Flown from the jack staff when in port.

Flag & Divisional Command

Contre-amiral

A Rear-Admiral embarked on a contre-torpilleur would normally command a Light Squadron (*Escadre légère*) or a Destroyer Flotilla (*Flotille de torpilleurs*).

Capitaine de vaisseau: chef de division

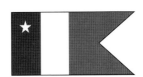

A three-ship division of *contre-torpilleurs* was commanded by a *Capitaine de vaisseau*. His two *divisionnaires* were under the command of *Capitaines de frégate*.

Capitaine de frégate: chef de division

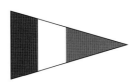

A three-ship division of *torpilleurs* was commanded by a *Capitaine de frégate*. His two *divisionnaires* were under the command of *Capitaines de corvette*.

(© John Jordan 2013)

her loss in May 1943 (see Chapter 12). Following her deployment to the Pacific in late 1941, *Le Triomphant* received an unusual two-sided asymmetrical camouflage scheme – one side represented the silhouette of a cargo ship – which she wore from December 1941 until October 1943, when she was repainted in a uniform dark grey (see Chapter 12).

From 1943 to 1950, the *contre-torpilleurs* and *torpilleurs* remaining in active service were repainted in the US Navy's Measure 22 scheme, with a Navy Blue (5-N) hull and Haze Gray (5-H) upperworks. When *Le Triomphant* deployed to the Far East in 1945 she was

Above: A photo of *Siroco* dating from late 1939. She not only has the new 'T' hull number which was introduced for *torpilleurs* on 1 April 1939, but her hull has been re-painted a darker grey with a false bow wave. *Siroco* would be lost off Nieuwport on 30 May 1940 during the evacuation of Dunkirk. *(US Navy NH110741-1, courtesy of A D Baker III)*

Opposite: *Albatros* at Casablanca in 1942, wearing the hull number 'X73'. Hull numbers were re-painted in brick red from early 1940 to reduce the visibility of the ships. In addition to the standard AA modifications *Albatros* has had her two 75cm searchlights relocated to newly constructed platforms forward of the third funnel, and a third, smaller 60cm searchlight has been fitted on the foremast platform. *(Pierre Boucheix collection)*

Tactical Numbers

Torpilleurs

Bourrasque 1930

In the Mediterranean Squadron, *torpilleurs* had a two-digit number. The first digit represented the number of the *escadrille*, and the second the position of the ship within the *escadrille*; the leader was no.1 and the remaining units were allocated numbers 2-9.

L'Adroit 1936

By the mid-1930s, *contre-torpilleurs* serving in the Mediterranean had single-digit numbers from 1 to 10, while the *torpilleurs* had two-digit numbers; the first digit represented the number of the division, the second the position of the ship within the division (1-3).

A similar system was adopted in the Atlantic from October 1934, but in order to distinguish the *contre-torpilleurs* from their counterparts in the Mediterranean, there was a hyphen abaft the number (see *Le Fantasque*).

In October 1936, when the 1st Squadron became the Mediterranean Squadron, a rationalisation took place. From that date until 1939 the two-digit system used for the *torpilleurs* was extended to the *contre-torpilleurs*.

Fougueux 1939

Fougueux 1940

Contre-torpilleurs

Contre-torpilleurs serving in the Mediterranean were allocated single-digit numbers 1-9 (see *Albatros* below). Atlantic-based ships had only their funnel bands to distinguish them.

Albatros 1936

Le Fantasque 1937

Albatros 1938

Volta 1939

Volta 1940

From April 1939 both the Atlantic and the Mediterranean Fleets adopted a uniform system of numbering imposed by Admiral Darlan. It was similar to that employed in the Mediterranean from October 1936, but the two/three-digit hull number was preceded by a 'T' for *torpilleurs* and an 'X' for *contre-torpilleurs*.

The numbers were initially painted white with black shadowing, as in the prewar period, but from early 1940 the white was replaced with brick red for reduced visibility at longer ranges.

(© John Jordan 2013)

PAINT SCHEMES AND IDENTIFICATION MARKINGS

given a Royal Navy Admiralty Standard paint scheme of light grey with a medium blue-grey lozenge on the lower part of the hull; on her return she was repainted in Measure 22. When serving under the Italian flag *Lion*, *Panthère* and *Tigre* were painted with a three-tone 'saw-tooth' disruptive pattern.

In 1951 all ships were repainted in a standard overall light grey livery.

NAVAL ENSIGNS AND COMMAND FLAGS

The French naval ensign was – and remains – proportioned differently to the national flag, the red of the fly being extended at the expense of the blue (closest to the staff); the proportions were blue 30%, white 33% and red 37%. When a ship was in port, and particularly when dressed overall, the larger ensign was flown at the ensign staff above the stern, with a smaller version at the jack staff. When the ship was at sea, the national ensign was flown from the mainmast or, once mainmasts had been suppressed during modernisations, from a short mast or yard abaft the after funnel

Funnel Bands October 1934 to August 1936: *Contre-Torpilleurs*

1ʳᵉ Escadre (Mediterranean)

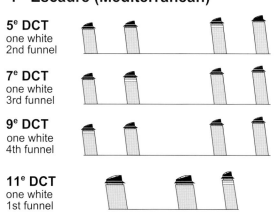

5ᵉ DCT — one white 2nd funnel
7ᵉ DCT — one white 3rd funnel
9ᵉ DCT — one white 4th funnel
11ᵉ DCT — one white 1st funnel

2ᵉ Escadre (Atlantic)

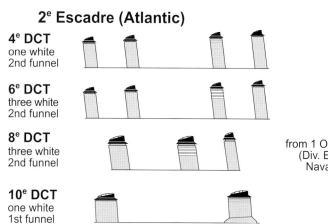

4ᵉ DCT — one white 2nd funnel
6ᵉ DCT — three white 2nd funnel
8ᵉ DCT — three white 2nd funnel — from 1 Oct 1935 (Div. Ecole Navale)
10ᵉ DCT — one white 1st funnel

Funnel Bands September 1936 to March 1939: *Contre-Torpilleurs*

Escadre de la Méditerranée

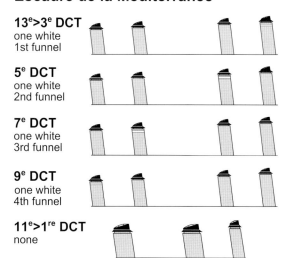

13ᵉ>3ᵉ DCT — one white 1st funnel
5ᵉ DCT — one white 2nd funnel
7ᵉ DCT — one white 3rd funnel
9ᵉ DCT — one white 4th funnel
11ᵉ>1ʳᵉ DCT — none

Escadre de l'Atlantique

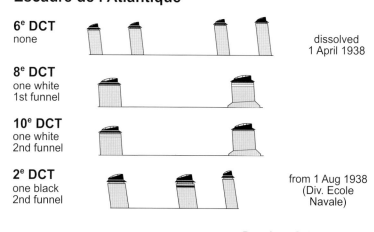

6ᵉ DCT — none — dissolved 1 April 1938
8ᵉ DCT — one white 1st funnel
10ᵉ DCT — one white 2nd funnel
2ᵉ DCT — one black 2nd funnel — from 1 Aug 1938 (Div. Ecole Navale)

Data from Guiglini, *op. cit.*

(© John Jordan 2013)

Divisions de Contre-Torpilleurs: September 1939

1ʳᵉ DCT
X11 Vauban
X12 Lion
X13 Aigle
— one white

2ᵉ DCT
X21 Jaguar
X22 Léopard
X23 Chacal
— one black

3ᵉ DCT
X31 Guépard
X32 Valmy
X33 Verdun
— one yellow

4ᵉ DCT
X41 Tigre
X42 Lynx
X43 Panthère
— one green

5ᵉ DCT
X51 Tartu
X52 Le Chevalier Paul
X53 Vauquelin
— one red

6ᵉ DCT
X61 Mogador
X62 Volta
— one blue

7ᵉ DCT
X71 Vautour
X72 Gerfaut
X73 Albatros
— two white

8ᵉ DCT
X81 L'Indomptable
X82 Le Malin
X83 Le Triomphant
— two black

9ᵉ DCT
X91 Maillé-Brézé
X92 Cassard
X93 Kersaint
— two yellow

10ᵉ DCT
X101 Le Fantasque
X102 L'Audacieux
X103 Le Terrible
— two green

11ᵉ DCT
X111 Bison
X112 Epervier
X113 Milan
— two red

Data from Guiglini, *op. cit.*   (© John Jordan 2013)

---

or atop the after deckhouse, depending on the layout of the main guns; most of the photos taken during the war show the ensign in this position.

Ships serving with the FNFL flew a modified ensign with a *Croix de Lorraine* at its centre at the jack staff (see illustration), but retained the national naval ensign when at sea.

Flagships and division leaders flew the admiral's or senior officer's colours from the mainmast, or at the foremast top in ships with only a single mast. The flag for a Rear-Admiral (commanding a light squadron or a flotilla of *torpilleurs*) was square with a white cross at its centre and two white stars in the upper blue quadrant. The Captain (*Capitaine de vaisseau*) commanding a three-ship division of *contre-torpilleurs* flew a tricolore swallow-tailed pennant with a white star at the top of the blue sector, and a Commander (*Capitaine de frégate*) commanding a three-ship division of *torpilleurs* flew a triangular tricolore pennant with no distinguishing features.

IDENTIFICATION MARKINGS

Ships operating as part of the same fleet or squadron, particularly flotilla craft, often have a similar silhouette and cannot be identified by the small differences between individual ships at long range. Identification markings were introduced into the French Navy around 1880. Several different systems were employed which used either funnel bands of various colours or letters/figures painted on the hull.

Until 1 October 1934 the markings adopted were imposed by the admiral commanding the squadron and two different systems were used: funnel bands in the Atlantic and hull symbols in the Mediterranean.

In the Mediterranean the hull marking was a letter/figure painted on the bow; funnel bands were not used until October 1934. *Torpilleurs* were normally numbered 1–10 according to their place in the *escadrille* and the division: numbers 1–3 were allocated to the first division,[2] numbers 4–6 to the 2nd division, and so on, which brought a complication when a new ship was attached to an existing division as a temporary measure pending a reorganisation. Unattached ships (*hors rang*), flagships, and ships not fully manned (*en complément*) were not allocated hull numbers.

A similar system was in force until 15 August 1936 for *contre-torpilleurs* serving in the Mediterranean, and from 1 October 1934[3] it was also adopted in the Atlantic. However, in order not to create confusion during combined exercises, a hyphen was added abaft the hull number (i.e. before the number to starboard and after the number to port). Funnel bands were used to distinguish between the different divisions.

On 15 August 1936 a general reorganisation of the *contre-torpilleur* and *torpilleur* divisions led to the adoption in the Mediterranean of a uniform system using two digits.[4] The first digit represented the number of the division, and the second the position of the ship

---

[2] Not necessarily the 1st Division, but normally the division with the lower number in its title.

[3] The date is that of the instruction. Its application depended on whether the ship was active or in refit; if a ship was at sea it could be several days before the order was executed.

[4] This had been introduced in 1935 for the *torpilleurs*.

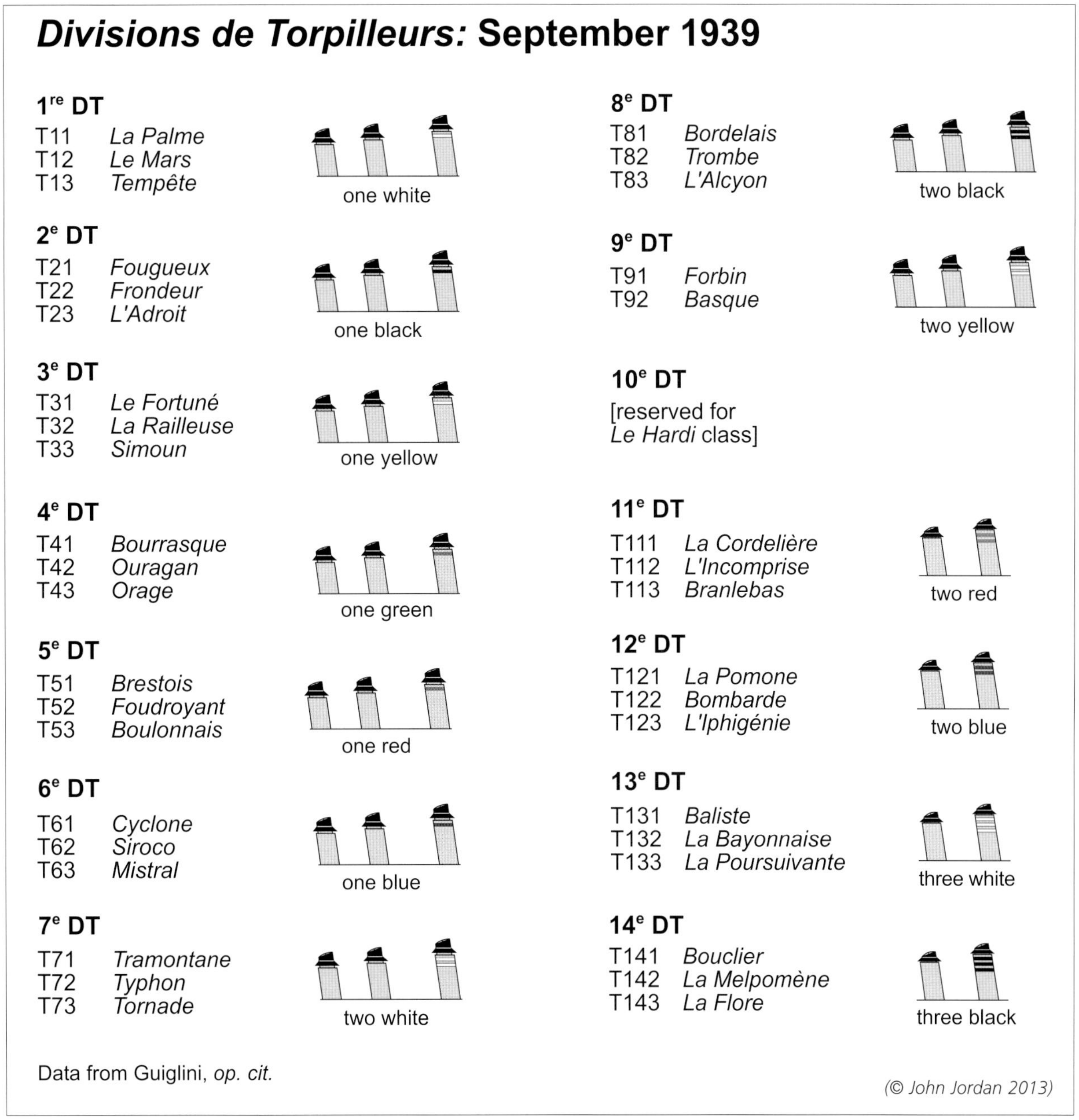

Divisions de Torpilleurs: September 1939

1ʳᵉ DT
T11 La Palme
T12 Le Mars
T13 Tempête
one white

2ᵉ DT
T21 Fougueux
T22 Frondeur
T23 L'Adroit
one black

3ᵉ DT
T31 Le Fortuné
T32 La Railleuse
T33 Simoun
one yellow

4ᵉ DT
T41 Bourrasque
T42 Ouragan
T43 Orage
one green

5ᵉ DT
T51 Brestois
T52 Foudroyant
T53 Boulonnais
one red

6ᵉ DT
T61 Cyclone
T62 Siroco
T63 Mistral
one blue

7ᵉ DT
T71 Tramontane
T72 Typhon
T73 Tornade
two white

8ᵉ DT
T81 Bordelais
T82 Trombe
T83 L'Alcyon
two black

9ᵉ DT
T91 Forbin
T92 Basque
two yellow

10ᵉ DT
[reserved for Le Hardi class]

11ᵉ DT
T111 La Cordelière
T112 L'Incomprise
T113 Branlebas
two red

12ᵉ DT
T121 La Pomone
T122 Bombarde
T123 L'Iphigénie
two blue

13ᵉ DT
T131 Baliste
T132 La Bayonnaise
T133 La Poursuivante
three white

14ᵉ DT
T141 Bouclier
T142 La Melpomène
T143 La Flore
three black

Data from Guiglini, *op. cit.*

(© John Jordan 2013)

---

within the division, which depended on the seniority of the respective commanding officers. The second digit was allocated as follows:

- No.1: the division leader, commanded by a *capitaine de vaisseau* (CV) for a *contre-torpilleur* and by a *capitaine de frégate* (CF) in a *torpilleur*
- No.2: the second ship in the formation, commanded by a *capitaine de frégate* (CF) for a *contre-torpilleur* and by a *capitaine de corvette* (CC) in a *torpilleur*
- No.3: the third ship in the formation, commanded by the senior of the two *capitaines de frégate* or *capitaines de corvette*

In principle the junior CO was therefore bracketed by the two senior officers when the ships were operating in formation. The major drawback to the system was that a change of commanding officer could bring about a change in hull number and also in the divisional orders and instructions where these related to the hull numbers.

Funnel bands were retained to distinguish one division from another until March 1939 (see graphic for details). For the *contre-torpilleurs* there was a white band on a particular funnel. This worked well enough when ships had either three or four funnels, but with the advent of the two-funnelled *Le Fantasque*s in 1935–6 black bands were allocated to some divisions.

From 1 April 1939[5] a uniform system of hull numbers and funnel bands was adopted for the entire fleet. The two/three-digit hull numbers were retained, and for the *contre-torpilleurs* the numbers were preceded by the letter 'X', while those of the *torpilleurs* were preceded by the letter 'T'. In some respects this had become necessary because of converging architectural styles; the *1500-tonnes*, with their three slim funnels, could easily be distinguished at distance from contemporary *contre-torpilleurs*; this would not be the case with the new *torpilleurs d'escadre* of the *Le Hardi* class which would enter service from 1940 and which

---

[5] Instruction 244 EMG/3 dated 27 February 1939.

Right: The destroyer *Forbin* in May 1943 during her repatriation to French North Africa following her internment in Alexandria. She retains her red brick hull number 'T32'. When repainted in the US Navy's two-tone Measure 22 scheme, the hull numbers would be reduced in size and painted in white. *(US Navy, NH110755-2, courtesy of A D Baker III)*

could easily be mistaken for ships of the *Le Fantasque* or *Mogador* classes.

Funnel bands were now of six different colours in the sequence: white, black, yellow, green, red and blue. The first six divisions (1–6) would have these colours in a single band, the following six (7–12) two bands, and the following six (13–18 – applicable only to the *torpilleurs*) three bands. *Contre-torpilleurs* would have the bands painted on the second funnel, *torpilleurs* on the first (see graphic).

The hull numbers, which were initially painted white with black shadowing as previously, would be repainted in brick red in early 1940 to make them less conspicuous,[6] and the white funnel bands would be painted out for the same reason after May 1940.[7]

After the Armistice of June 1940 it was decided that hull numbers should remained unchanged, whatever the affiliation of the ship or its position in the division; the single exception was *Milan*, which in October 1941 was renumbered X111 (formerly the number worn by *Bison*).[8] When ships changed division to replace a ship lost in action or one due to be placed *en gardiennage*, they retained their original hull number but had funnel bands painted in the colour of their new division. Thus *Le Malin*, despatched from Toulon to replace *L'Audacieux*, which had been crippled at Dakar, retained her X82 number but adopted the two green funnel bands of the 10th DCT.

This system of hull markings remained in force throughout the war, but from 1943 the tactical numbers were much reduced in size (0.64m vs. 4.3m); they were painted white with no shadowing. They straddled the line between the dark blue-grey of the hull and the light grey of the upperworks. The *Le Fantasque*s, depite being rechristened 'cruisers',

retained their 'X' prefix. The *torpilleur Basque* was unusual in having the number painted in black rather than white from September 1945.

Tricolore identification markings were carried during two distinct periods. The first was the Spanish Civil War; ships assigned to neutrality patrols carried them from April 1937 until April 1939. Bands of blue, white and red were applied to the sides and tops of the shields of guns nos.2 and 3 (2, 3 and 4 for the 5-gun *contre-torpilleurs*), with the blue to the fore. These markings were revived following the Armistice, from July 1940 to November 1942, the bands being painted on guns/turrets 2 and 3 or 2 and 4, depending on the class of ship. In addition to the tricolore turret bands, some ships sported a tricolore roundel painted on the circular roof of the rangefinder housing.

After the war, on 7 July 1948 the Navy adopted a system of permanent hull markings that was completely independent of the ship's tactical affiliation. The light cruisers (formerly *contre-torpilleurs* of the *Le Fantasque* type) retained their late-war numbers X101–104, while destroyers (whether originally classified *contre-torpilleur* or *torpilleur d'escadre*) had a number preceded by the letter 'T'.

Membership of NATO brought with it a new system that applied to the ships of all members except the US Navy, which retained the system in place since July 1920. A Note dated 23 March 1951 formally put this system in place in the Marine Nationale. There was a letter denoting the type of ship, plus a 3-digit number which identified each vessel; each country was allocated a particular sequence of numbers. The former *contre-torpilleurs*, which were designated 'destroyers' in the Anglo-Saxon navies, were allocated the letter 'D' and numbers in the '600' series. The former *torpilleurs*, assimilated to the British 'frigate' or ocean escort categories, were allocated the letter 'F' and numbers in the '700' series. In France the NATO pennant number was initially painted white then, following an instruction dated 3 June 1952, black.

---

[6] Instruction 22683 CN/4 dated 6 January 1940.
[7] Instruction 1165 FMF/3 dated 19 May 1940.
[8] *Milan* and her *divisionnaire*, *Epervier*, also exchanged the original serifed '1' in their tactical numbers (X111/X112) for simple vertical bars.

PAINT SCHEMES AND IDENTIFICATION MARKINGS

APPENDIX A: THE 610-TONNE TORPEDO BOATS

THE LONDON TREATY OF 1930 INTRODUCED QUALITATIVE and quantitative restrictions for every class of naval vessel above 600 tons (610 metric tons) standard. Below this figure there were to be no limits on gun calibre, torpedo armament, maximum speed or numbers. All but one of the signatories to the treaty took advantage of this to build ships in the antisubmarine escort or torpedo boat categories.

From 1937 the Marine Nationale commissioned a series of twelve small torpedo boats of the La Melpomène class with a Washington standard displacement of 610 tonnes; they had an overall length of 80.7 metres and displaced 708 tonnes at normal loading. Turbine machinery gave them a top speed of 34 knots. Armament was two single 100mm LA guns, two twin 13.2mm Hotchkiss AA, a twin 500mm torpedo mounting and a quarterdeck rail for 10 depth charges. Endurance was limited to 1800nm at 10 knots. Initially classified as 'escorts' (escorteurs), they were redesignated torpilleurs de 610 tonnes in October 1936.

The twelve ships formed four 3-ship divisions which were shared between the Atlantic and the Mediterranean. The Atlantic ships distinguished themselves in the evacuation of Dunkirk then, having taken refuge in English ports, were seized by the British following the armistice. The torpedo boats recommissioned by the Royal Navy or by the Free French (FNFL) were restricted to local escort or secondary missions; deemed to be insufficiently robust,[1] they were soon decommissioned.

The Mediterranean ships undertook escort missions, then became part of the Vichy fleet at Toulon. Three were scuttled at Toulon on 27 November 1942, and three were seized at Bizerte by the Germans on 8 December 1942, ceded to the Italians and finally destroyed by the Allies. None of the survivors was recommissioned after the war.

The 610-tonne type was to be followed by the 1010-tonne Le Fier class. Fourteen were ordered, of which three were launched before the armistice and three subsequently for the Germans; none was completed.

---

[1] Branlebas foundered in a gale off the southwest of the UK on 14 December 1940.

Upper, right: The 610-tonne torpilleur Branlebas on her speed trials in the summer of 1937. She has yet to receive her armament. (A D Baker III collection)

Lower, right: The 610-tonne torpedo boat Branlebas at anchor in late 1939. The pendant number marks her out as the third ship of the 11th DT. She has two red bands on her first funnel.

BUILDING DATA

Name	Shipyard	Laid down	Launched	Trials	In service	Assigned (1938)
La Bayonnaise	ASM S.O., Bordeaux	18 Oct 1934	28 Jan 1936	15 Nov 1936	1 Jul 1938	13th DT (Toulon)
La Cordelière	Normand, Le Havre	16 Aug 1934	2 Sep 1936	15 Sep 1936	11 Jan 1938	11th DT (Cherbourg)
La Poursuivante	AC France, Dunkirk	13 Aug 1934	3 Aug 1936	1 Sep 1936	3 Dec 1937	13th DT (Toulon)
L'Incomprise	Worms, Le Trait	20 Oct 1934	14 Apr 1937	1 Jul 1937	3 May 1938	11th DT (Cherbourg)
La Melpomène	AC Bretagne, Nantes	13 Dec 1933	24 Jan 1935	20 Aug 1935	27 Jan 1937	12th DT (Bizerte)
La Flore	AC Bretagne, Nantes	26 Mar 1934	4 May 1935	20 Dec 1935	27 Jan 1937	12th DT (Bizerte)
La Pomone	AC Loire, Nantes	22 Nov 1933	25 Jan 1935	1 Aug 1935	27 Jan 1937	12th DT (Bizerte)
L'Iphigénie	AC Loire, Nantes	14 Dec 1933	18 Apr 1935	1 Dec 1935	27 Jan 1937	12th DT (Bizerte)
Branlebas	Normand, Le Havre	27 Aug 1934	12 Apr 1937	1 May 1937	3 May 1938	11th DT (Cherbourg)
Bombarde	AC Loire, Nantes	12 Feb 1935	23 Mar 1936	15 Aug 1936	16 Aug 1937	13th DT (Toulon)
Bouclier	Worms, Le Trait	18 Oct 1934	10 Aug 1937	15 Oct 1937	1 Oct 1938	11th DT (Cherbourg)
Baliste	AC France, Dunkirk	21 Sep 1934	17 Mar 1937	1 Jan 1937	27 Jun 1938	13th DT (Toulon)

CHAPTER 11
THE PERIOD 1926–1939

THE FRENCH *CONTRE-TORPILLEURS* BUILT after the Great War of 1914–18 were unusual in having a displacement significantly greater than that of contemporary destroyers, which generally displaced 1300–1500 tons. Their classification would be the subject of much discussion during the international naval arms limitation conferences. The Treaty of London of 22 April 1930 defined a 'destroyer' as a ship with a maximum displacement of 1850 tons carrying guns with a maximum calibre of 5.1in (130mm). France refused to sign up to the part of the treaty (Part III) which allocated a maximum tonnage for cruisers and destroyers, because this would have compelled her to classify all her *contre-torpilleurs* as cruisers. In order to resolve this problem the following treaty, signed in London on 25 March 1936 and ratified by France, introduced a single category of 'light surface vessels' that embraced both the former 'cruiser' and 'destroyer' categories. This was then subdivided into three categories, of which (c) was defined as a vessel displacing between 100 tons and 3000 tons carrying guns with a maximum calibre of 6.1in (155mm); all current types of destroyer, torpedo boat and *contre-torpilleur*, including the latest French CTs of the *Mogador* class, fell into this new sub-category.

The French *contre-torpilleurs* were designed specifically to combat the Italian fleet in the Mediterranean. They were to accompany the battle fleet to sea and to provide scouting and screening. During combat, which assumed the traditional scenario of battle lines on parallel courses, the *contre-torpilleurs* would be placed on the non-engaged side but with their guns just in range of the enemy. Their task was to prevent any envelopment of the line, frustrate enemy torpedo attacks and attack the enemy line with torpedoes, especially at night. It was envisaged that a division of three *contre-torpilleurs* would be able to successfully take on a single cruiser of the Italian '*Condottieri*' type.

The 1500-tonne *torpilleurs d'escadre* of the 1922–1926 estimates were expected to perform a similar role to their foreign counterparts. They were to attack the enemy line with torpedoes and protect their own line against enemy torpedo boats with their guns; when steaming with the fleet they were expected to stay close to the battleships to protect them from enemy surface craft and submarines; they were not tasked with scouting and screening.

ORGANISATION

Traditionally, naval forces based in France were organised as two large formations; one at Brest on the Atlantic coast, the other at Toulon in the Mediterranean.

The naval force based at Brest (informally known as the Western Squadron – *Escadre du Ponant*) was successively named The Naval Division of the Channel and the North Sea (15 September 1921), the Second Squadron (1 February 1927), the Atlantic Squadron (15 August 1936) and the Atlantic Fleet (10 June 1939).

The naval force based at Toulon (known as the Eastern Squadron – *Escadre du Levant*) was successively named the Mediterranean Squadron (20 July 1921), the First Squadron (1 February 1927), the Mediterranean Squadron (15 August 1936) and the Mediterranean Fleet (10 June 1939).

(© John Jordan 2011)

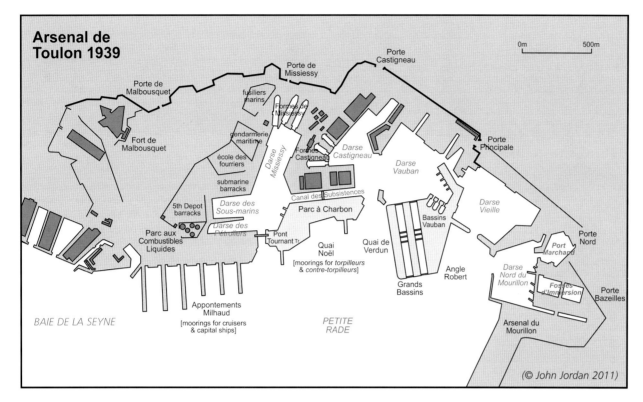

Each of these two squadrons comprised one or several divisions of major surface vessels (battleships and/or cruisers), sometimes a 'light squadron' with cruisers and/or *contre-torpilleurs*, light forces with *contre-torpilleurs* and *torpilleurs* and, usually, a formation of large submarines. Coastal submarines, sloops, auxiliaries and units deployed or stationed overseas were generally under local (*vice* squadron) command.

Changes in the assignment of the *contre-torpilleurs* and the *torpilleurs d'escadre* were relatively frequent, with active deployment to either the Atlantic or the Mediterranean squadrons, inactivity due to refit or repair, and periods in care & maintenance or *groupe de complément* (see below).

The *contre-torpilleurs* based in the Atlantic formed a 2nd Light Squadron (*2e Escadre légère*) on 4 October 1932, a *Contre-torpilleur* Group (*Groupe de contre-torpilleurs*) on 6 November 1934, reverting to 2nd Light Squadron on 15 September 1936. Those based in the Mediterranean formed a *Contre-torpilleur* Group on 15 April 1931, then a 3rd Light Squadron on 15 September 1936. The basic tactical unit was the division, initially termed *Division légère* (DL) then, from 12 April 1937, *Division de contre-torpilleurs* (DCT). A division was normally made up of three ships, occasionally of four (particularly when new ships joined immediately before a reorganisation).

The *torpilleurs d'escadre* were initially formed into 'mini-squadrons' (*escadrilles*) of six ships. In the Mediterranean and Oceanic Squadrons, three *escadrilles* made up a flotilla (*flotille*). From October 1927 the number of ships in each *escadrille* was reduced to four.

On 1 March 1929 the *escadrilles* became 'divisions' (*Divisions de torpilleurs* or DT), the flotilla became an *escadrille* and a flotilla group became a flotilla (*Flotille de torpilleurs* or FT). The 1st FT was formed with the 1st, 2nd and 3rd *escadrilles* each with between six and nine *torpilleurs*. On 1 September 1932 the number of ships in each division was reduced to three. On 15 September 1934 the *escadrilles* disappeared altogether.

Both the *contre-torpilleurs* and the *torpilleurs* rotated between active service and care & maintenance (*disponibilité armée* or DA), a status which was intermediate between 'active' and 'reserve'. Ships in DA had a reduced complement sufficient for maintenance, and occasionally undertook training sorties for reservists. A ship in refit could also be placed in *disponibilité armée*. There were seven *torpilleurs* in DA in 1931. With the composition of the divisions revised downwards to three units, there were sufficient ships with reduced crews to form a Supplementary Group (*Groupe de complément*.)

A *Groupe de complément* was constituted on 16 December 1932 with all the *torpilleurs* in good material condition not assigned to active units; these ships had only 60% of their full complement, and left harbour only for the training of reservists or for port visits.

From 1936, because of the demands of the Spanish Civil War, all the *contre-torpilleurs* and *torpilleurs*, with the sole exception of those in refit, were fully manned.

THE *ANNÉE D'INSTRUCTION*

The greater part of ships' activities were devoted to training and work-up. There was a significant changeover in personnel during the summer, and training then began again, starting with individual manoeuvres, then proceeding quickly to divisional manoeuvres and exercises with larger formations.

The training cycle, which generally ran from October to September of the following year, was termed the *année d'instruction*. Its course was frequently interrupted by missions such as rescue at sea and showing the flag, and in particular by the Civil War in Spain, which involved the evacuation of civilians and maritime surveillance.

In the natural order of things, the first individual

Above: The 1500-tonne destroyer *Boulonnais* in 1935–6 during divisional manoeuvres in the Mediterranean. *(Philippe Caresse collection)*

training sorties were followed by divisional, then fleet or squadron manoeuvres. From January or February, sorties lasting several days took place employing all available ships of the squadron. These manoeuvres were generally conducted off Toulon and Brest, and were often broken by overnight visits along the coast. A major sortie termed the Winter Cruise (*croisière d'hiver*), often involved a deployment of one or other of the squadrons to the African coasts. The cycle generally ended with the Summer Cruise (*croisière d'été*), which took place between May and July, and often involved manoeuvres with the combined squadrons from Brest and Toulon after a cruise which took the ships either to the eastern Mediterranean or to the waters off West Africa, often with visits to the ports of Algeria and Tunisia.

In 1932, for example, the 1st Squadron embarked on a cruise between 15 April and 25 June as far as the eastern Mediterranean. The Mediterranean Squadron returned to the same waters in May/June 1938. The Winter Cruise of the Second Squadron of 15 January to 26 February 1937 took the 2nd Light Squadron as far south as Conakry, the capital of Guinea.

The ships of the Marine Nationale were often open to the public during visits to the main holiday resorts of the Atlantic coast in August – the 'tour of the casinos' – and during the Nice Carnival in the Mediterranean in February, when there was a naval sail-past along the coast.

SHOWING THE FLAG

The first of the new generation of ships to enter active service were the *contre-torpilleur Tigre* on 7 February 1926 and the *torpilleur d'escadre Simoun* in August of the same year.

Right: The ships of the 2nd (Atlantic) Squadron moored at Casablanca, probably during the visit of the Second Squadron (Brest) 15–17 February 1937. Ships present include *L'Indomptable* (-7), *Jaguar* (flagship of the 2nd Flotilla of destroyers), the four-funnelled CT *Vauban* (in transit from Lorient to Toulon), and the battleship *Bretagne* (two white bands on the second funnel). A second ship of the *Bretagne* class and other *contre-torpilleurs* of the *Le Fantasque* class can be seen in the background. *(US Navy NH86551, courtesy of A D Baker III)*

THE PERIOD 1926-1939

Above: Port visit to Naples, 8–14 May 1935. In the foreground is the Italian cruiser *Zara*. At right are six *contre-torpilleurs* of the 2400-ton type moored with their sterns towards the harbour breakwater: the 5th DL with *Tartu* (no.1), *Albatros* and *Chevalier Paul*, and the 7th DL with *Gerfaut*, *Aigle* and *Vautour*. There is a second Italian heavy cruiser alongside the breakwater in the left distance. (*US Navy NH86446, courtesy of A D Baker III*)

The Navy was anxious to put its new ships on display to showcase the rebirth of the fleet following the Great War. Special missions, many of which involved 'showing the flag', followed closely on top of one another from June 1926, using ships which had often yet to be accepted into active service.

Shortly after her arrival at Toulon on 7 February 1926, *Tigre* was moored in the roads at Villefranche 12–17 February for the Nice Carnival. *Chacal* conducted her first 'show-the-flag' mission between 25 June and 15 July of the same year, representing France at the Hanko Regatta in Finland. The same ship then formed a light division with her sister *Jaguar*, the destroyer *Simoun* and the submarines *Marsouin* and *Souffleur* for a cruise in the Baltic from late August to late September.

Between late November and late December 1926 there was a cruise in the eastern Atlantic involving the newly completed cruisers *Lamotte-Picquet* and *Duguay-Trouin*, the *contre-torpilleur Chacal*, the destroyers *Tempête*, *Simoun*, *Bourrasque*, and the submarines *Souffleur* and *Narval*. The *Jaguar* went to Dakar (capital of Senegal) and the *torpilleurs* as far as Conakry.

Representative missions continued with a visit by *Jaguar* to Seville in mid-April 1927. A group comprising the cruisers *Lamotte-Picquet* and *Duguay-Trouin*, the CTs *Tigre*, *Chacal* and *Jaguar*, and the TEs *Bourrasque*, *Orage* and *Ouragan* escorted the cross-channel ferry *Invicta*, on which the President of the

Republic was embarked, during an official visit to Great Britain in late May/early June 1927. *Jaguar* then accompanied *Lamotte-Picquet* on a cruise to Dakar and Buenos Aires between 9 June and 22 September 1927.

On 17 January 1930 *Panthère* and the new *contre-torpilleur Guépard* embarked on a cruise with *Lamotte-Picquet* and *Primauguet* that took them to the French West Indies (Antilles); they returned on 30 April. On 5 April 1930 the President of the Republic, Gaston Doumergue, embarked at Nantes on the CT *Verdun*, which had just completed her trials, for a passage to Saint-Nazaire, where he would lay the first stone of the Joubert Dock (later known as the Normandie Dock after the famous liner built there, and the target of the British raid of 28 March 1942).

Tigre and *Chacal* accompanied the cruiser *Primauguet* to the west coast of Africa on a cruise which lasted from 13 January to 10 April 1931.

From 5 August to 23 September 1934 the new CT *Vauquelin* embarked on six-week cruise which took her to Saint Pierre et Miquelon, Halifax and Quebec to commemorate the 400th anniversary of the landing of Jacques Cartier in Canada. This would be the only transatlantic mission conducted by a four-funnelled *contre-torpilleur*.

The CT *L'Audacieux*, the first of her class to be completed, represented the Navy at the ceremonies marking the 300th anniversary of the attachment of the Antilles to France. She left Brest on 4 December 1935, was admitted into active service on the 7th during the passage to Ponta Delgada (Azores), and arrived in the Antilles to join the cruiser *Emile Bertin* and the submarine cruiser *Surcouf*, visiting Pointe-à-Pitre and Fort de France.

The last important representative mission before the war was undertaken by the CT *Volta*, on which Admiral Darlan embarked for a visit to Portsmouth on 7 August 1939.

Right: *Jaguar* at the Quai des Quinconces, Bordeaux, on 11 May 1936. She is dressed overall for the festival of Joan of Arc. Behind her is a destroyer of the 2nd Flotilla; *Jaguar* was flagship of the 2nd Flotilla from 5 July 1935 to 6 September 1937.

NAVAL REVIEWS

The period between the two world wars was marked by several naval reviews which allowed the Navy to show off its new ships to the media and the general public.

On 27 April 1927, the 1st Squadron moored in the Estaque roads at Marseille. It was reviewed by the President of the Republic, Gaston Doumergue, who had come to the city for the inauguration of the Rove tunnel on the canal connecting Marseille to the Rhône. The TEs *Orage* and *Bourrasque* escorted the President's boat into the port of Marseille.

Below: *Chacal* attends the inauguration of the port of Douala (Cameroon) in early February 1931. *(Marc Saibène collection)*

Left: *Lion* is open to the public during a port visit to Marseille which took place 20–24 November 1936. At that time *Lion* was serving at Toulon as flagship of the *1re Flotille des sous-marins*, and seven of her 'brood' accompanied her on the visit. *(US Navy NH88525, courtesy of A D Baker III)*

Right: *Le Terrible* during the review of the 2nd Squadron by the President of the Republic on 30 May 1936 at Brest. *(US Navy NH 86550, courtesy of A D Baker III)*

Left: *Volta* is seen here arriving in Portsmouth in August 1939. On board was Admiral François Darlan, who was due to attend a joint conference with his counterpart in the Royal Navy to discuss naval dispositions in the event of a war against Germany. Note the flag of Admiral of the Fleet – a tricolore with crossed anchors in the centre – flying from the foremast top. *(US Navy NH86544, courtesy of A D Baker III)*

Following combined manoeuvres by the Brest and Toulon squadrons, there was a major naval review off Le Havre on 3 July 1928 by the President of the Republic, who embarked on the CT *Jaguar*, followed by the destroyers *Orage* and *Simoun*. Moored in the La Carosse roads were the CTs *Panthère*, *Tigre*, *Chacal*, *Léopard* and *Lynx*, and the TEs *Tempête*, *Bourrasque*, *Tornade*, *Trombe*, *Tramontane*, *Siroco*, *Cyclone*, *Mistral*, *Le Mars*, *Le Fortuné*, *La Palme* and *La Railleuse*.

The centenary of the first French landing in Algeria on 13 June 1830 was the occasion for a major naval review off Algiers on 10 May 1930 involving the combined First and Second Squadrons. Destroyers of the 1st Squadron taking part were the CTs *Panthère*, *Verdun*, *Guépard* and *Jaguar*, and the TEs *L'Adroit*, *Bourrasque*, *Brestois*, *Ouragan*, *Orage*, *Tornade*, *Typhon*, *Tramontane*, *Cyclone*, *Mistral*, *Simoun*, *Le Mars*, *Tempête*, *Le Fortuné*, *La Palme*, and *La Railleuse*.

The inauguration of the new Ocean Terminal at Cherbourg on 20 July 1933 was the occasion for a review of the Second Squadron by the President of the Republic, Albert Lebrun, who embarked on the *Vauban*. Moored in the Cherbourg roads were the cruiser *Lamotte-Picquet*, the CTs *Lynx*, *Léopard*, *Lion*, *Maillé-Brézé* and *Bison*, the TEs *Bourrasque*, *Orage* and *L'Adroit*, and twelve submarines.

On 27 June 1935 the Navy Minister, François Piétri, embarked on the *Gerfaut* for a naval review in Douarnenez Bay following combined manoeuvres of the Brest and Toulon squadrons. *Gerfaut*, followed by *Aigle* and *Vautour*, steamed past 55 ships moored in five lines. Destroyers participating in the review were the CTs *Tartu*, *Albatros*, *Le Chevalier Paul*, *Maillé-Brézé*, *Vauquelin*, *Kersaint*, *Jaguar*, *Milan*, *Epervier*, *Valmy*, *Lion* and *Vauban*, and the TEs *Tramontane*, *Trombe*, *Tornade*, *Cyclone*, *Simoun*, *Mistral*, *La Palme*, *La Railleuse*, *Brestois*, *Forbin*, *Orage*, *Ouragan*, *Bourrasque*, *L'Adroit*, *Basque* and *Foudroyant*.

On 30 May 1936 President Lebrun, attended the inauguration of the prestigious new building for the *Ecole Navale* at Brest, which was built on the Quatre Pompes plateau overlooking the harbour (see map). The inauguration was followed by a review of the Second Squadron in the outer anchorage; the President embarked for the occasion on the battleship *Provence*. Present were the newly completed CTs *Le Fantasque*, *Le Terrible*, *L'Audacieux* and *L'Indomptable*, and the TEs *Fougueux*, *Bordelais*, *Frondeur*, *L'Adroit*, *Basque*, *Foudroyant*, *Cyclone*, *Mistral* and *Siroco*.

Finally, on 27 May 1937, off Brest, the fleet was reviewed by the Navy Minister, Alphonse Gasnier-Duparc, who was embarked in the newly completed battleship *Dunkerque*. The destroyers present were the CTs *Le Fantasque*, *L'Audacieux*, *Le Terrible*, *L'Indomptable*, *Le Malin*, *Le Triomphant*, *Maillé-Brézé*, *Cassard*,

Below: French destroyers at Brest. Closest to the camera are four units of the *Le Fantasque* class, including the three ships of the 10th DCT, and beyond them are ships of the *1500-tonnes* type. The photo probably dates from 1936; tricolore identification markings have yet to be painted on the gunshields. *(US Navy NH 86552, courtesy of A D Baker III)*

THE LIGHT SQUADRONS 1 OCTOBER 1936

2nd Light Squadron (Brest)
Flagship: *Emile Bertin* (CA Odendhal)
  6e DL: *Milan* (-4), *Epervier* (-5)
  8e DL: *L'Indomptable* (-7), *Le Triomphant* (-8), *Le Malin* (-9)
  10e DL: *Le Fantasque* (-10), *L'Audacieux* (-11), *Le Terrible* (-12)

3rd Light Squadron (Toulon)
Flagship: *Tartu* (CA Ollive)
  5e DL: *Tartu* (51), *Vauquelin* (52), *Le Chevalier Paul* (53)
  7e DL: *Gerfaut* (71), *Albatros* (72), *Vautour* (73)
  9e DL: *Maillé-Brézé* (91), *Kersaint* (92), *Cassard* (93)
  13e DL: *Guépard* (31), *Valmy* (32), *Verdun* (33)

Notes:
1. In the 2nd Light Squadron only two divisions were active; the third (6th DL) was *en complément* (DA).
2. In the 3rd Light Squadron only three divisions were active at any one time; the fourth (initially 13th DL) was *en complément* (DA).
3. The hull number anomaly of the 13th DL was resolved the following year when the division was renamed the 3rd DCT.

Kersaint, Guépard, Valmy, Verdun and *Jaguar*, and the TEs *Bourrasque, Ouragan, Orage, Tornade, Trombe* and *Tramontane*.

TACTICAL ORGANISATION: *CONTRE-TORPILLEURS*

When they entered service, the six *contre-torpilleurs* of the *Jaguar* class would form two three-ship divisions: one in the Mediterranean, the other in the Atlantic. Insufficiently robust, they would be rapidly worn out by intensive service; from 1935 they were no longer regarded as first-line vessels and would be used for training.

The first *contre-torpilleurs* were assigned to the *1re division de contre-torpilleurs* (1st DCT) of the 1st Squadron at Toulon. *Tigre* joined on 7 February 1926, *Chacal* on 23 December of the same year, and *Panthère* in January 1927. In early 1927 the 1st DCT became the *5e division légère* (5th DL). On 15 November 1927 the 4th DL was formed, with *Léopard, Lynx* and *Jaguar* (until April 1928) and assigned to the Second Squadron at Brest.

The next series of *contre-torpilleurs*, the four-funnelled ships ('*les quatre-tuyaux*'), after a 'settling-in' period which lasted until 1935, were formed into homogeneous divisions each of three units. Eleven of the eighteen *quatre-tuyaux* were assigned to the Mediterranean as soon as they entered service; they would be joined by a further six ships between October 1934 and October 1937.

The first *quatre-tuyaux* to enter service were the *Guépard* and *Valmy*, arriving on 22 September 1929 and 15 February 1930 respectively and joining the 5th DL alongside *Panthère, Chacal* and *Tigre*. On 1 May 1930 a new 7th DL was formed at Toulon with *Verdun* (arrived 18 April), *Guépard*, and *Valmy*; *Albatros* joined on 25 January 1932 and *Gerfaut* on 15 March, but *Guépard* left the division. The 5th DL now comprised only the three ships of the *Jaguar* class (see above).

The last of the eighteen *quatre-tuyaux*, *Le Chevalier Paul*, arrived at Toulon on 21 August 1934. Subsequently all the four-funnelled ships except *Bison* were grouped together at Toulon. *Maillé-Brézé, Kersaint* and *Vauquelin* arrived in October 1934 to form the 9th DL; *Lion* arrived from Brest in October 1936, *Vauban* in February 1937, and *Milan* and *Epervier* in October of the same year.

Seven of the eighteen *quatre-tuyaux* were initially based in the Atlantic. *Bison* arrived at Brest on 15 November 1930. On the 19th she replaced the cruiser *Mulhouse* (ex-German *Stralsund*) as flagship of the Second Squadron, flying the flag of the newly appointed commanding officer, Rear-Admiral Jean de Laborde. Besides *Bison*, the squadron comprised the *2e escadrille de torpilleurs* (the *Mécanicien Principal*

Below: *Verdun* leading the *Groupe des contre-torpilleurs* of the First Squadron. She wore the tactical number '1' during the period 30 May to September 1933.

THE PERIOD 1926-1939

Above: The Quai Noël at Toulon in late 1933. In the foreground are the 1500-tonne destroyers *Frondeur*, *L'Alcyon*, *Foudroyant* and *Forbin*. Behind them can be seen *contre-torpilleurs* of the *Jaguar* class and, in the background, other ships of the *1500-tonnes* type.

Lestin + the twelve 'Japanese' torpedo boats), the *4e escadrille de sous-marins* (four former U-boats), and four auxiliaries. The *contre-torpilleur Lion* arrived on 8 February 1931 and formed a 4th DL with *Léopard* and *Lynx*. *Bison* remained at Brest until 1939, serving successively as flagship of the Second Squadron, the 2nd Light Squadron, the *Contre-torpilleur* Group of the Second Squadron, the 2nd Flotilla of Submarines, and finally the 2nd Torpedo Boat Flotilla.

Lion arrived at Brest on 8 February 1931. She served with the 4th DL, then the 6th DL, and left for Toulon in late September. Her sister *Vauban* arrived on 5 September 1931 and replaced the *Lynx* in the 4th DL. She remained at Brest with the 4th DL, then with the 6th DL until August 1936, leaving for Toulon in February 1937 following a major refit.

Maillé-Brézé, *Kersaint* and *Vauquelin* arrived at Brest between April 1933 and March 1934. They formed the 6th DL which, when transferred to Toulon in October 1934, became the 9th DL. *Milan* and *Epervier* arrived on 18 May 1934. They were incorporated into the 4th DL, then the 6th DL, transferring to the Mediterranean in October 1937.

The six units of the *Le Fantasque* class all entered service at Brest between December 1935 and July 1936. They constituted the newly formed 8th and 10th DL (subsequently DCT).

Mogador arrived at Brest on 6 November 1938. She was joined by her sister *Volta* on 21 March 1939, and on 25 March the two ships formed the 6th DCT.

TACTICAL ORGANISATION: *TORPILLEURS D'ESCADRE*

As soon as they entered service, the new *torpilleurs d'escadre* were all incorporated into the Toulon squadron. The first to arrive was *Orage*, on 27 January 1927. She was joined in March by *Tempête* and *Simoun*, then by *Bourrasque*. On 1 October 1927 these four ships formed the 1st *escadrille* of the 1st Flotilla.

THE TORPEDO BOAT FLOTILLA OF THE 1st SQUADRON 1 OCTOBER 1930

Flotilla Leader: *Jaguar* (CA Drujon)

1re Escadrille: *Amiral Sénès* (11)
    5e DT: *Cyclone* (52), *Siroco* (53), *Simoun* (54), *Basque* (55)
    9e DT: *Boulonnais* (96), *Brestois* (97), *Forbin* (98), *Foudroyant* (99)

3e Escadrille: *Tempête* (31)
    7e DT: *Le Mars* (72), *La Railleuse* (73), *La Palme* (74), *Le Fortuné* (75)
    11e DT: *L'Alcyon* (116), *Bordelais* (117), *Fougueux* (118), *Frondeur* (119)

Torpedo Boat Group in Care & Maintenance:
    1re DT: *L'Adroit* (12), *Ouragan* (13), *Bourrasque* (14), *Orage* (15)
    3e DT: *Tornade* (36), *Trombe* (37), *Typhon* (38), *Tramontane* (39), *Mistral*

The last of the new destroyers to arrive at Toulon was *Frondeur* on 30 October 1931.

The great manoeuvres of the summer of June 1928 were the largest since the war. They involved the combined squadrons of Toulon and Brest, and eleven of the new destroyers took part. The manoeuvres culminated in the review at Le Havre (see above). The 1st Squadron left Toulon on 30 May and returned on 4 August.

During the 1920s, the Navy was organised with a view to a possible conflict with Italy, and the Mediterranean Squadron was assigned all the most modern units. From 1931, with German rearmament in prospect – the *Panzerschiff Deutschland* was launched on 18 May 1931 – the Atlantic Squadron began to receive reinforcements.

The first destroyer at Toulon to be transferred to the Atlantic was *L'Adroit*, which was previously in reserve. She arrived at Brest in October 1931 and became leader of the 2nd escadrille, which at that time comprised two divisions of 'Japanese' torpedo boats. She was joined at Brest on 18 February 1932 by *Bourrasque*, and the two *torpilleurs* then formed the 1st DT, the Japanese-built ships having been decommissioned. *Orage* arrived at Brest in early July and

THE TORPEDO BOAT FLOTILLAS
1 NOVEMBER 1936 TO 31 OCTOBER 1937

Mediterranean Squadron
1st Flotilla
    1re DT: *La Palme* (1), *Le Mars* (2), *Forbin* (3)
    3e DT: *Le Fortuné* (4), *La Railleuse* (5), *Simoun* (6 – from 1 Apr 1937)
Unattached: *Tempête*

Atlantic Squadron
2nd Flotilla
Leader: *Jaguar* (CA Brohan)
    2e DT: *Fougueux* (21), *Frondeur* (22), *Basque* (23)
    4e DT: *Bourrasque* (41), *Ouragan* (42), *Orage* (43)
    5e DT: *Brestois* (51), *Foudroyant* (52), *Boulonnais* (53)
    6e DT: *Cyclone* (61), *Siroco* (62), *Mistral* (63)
    7e DT: *L'Alcyon* (71), *Typhon* (72), *Tornade* (73)
    8e DT: *Bordelais* (81), *Trombe* (82), *Tramontane* (83)
En complément, then Morocco: *L'Adroit*

THE PERIOD 1926-1939

Left: *Bison* moored in the anchorage at Brest. Between late 1930 and 1934 she served first as flagship of the 2nd Light Squadron, and then as flagship of the *contre-torpilleur* group of the 2nd Squadron. Note the Rear-Admiral's flag flying at the mainmast.

Ouragan in late September 1932. They were followed by *Foudroyant* on 21 April 1935 and *Basque* on 3 May 1935. *Cyclone*, *Mistral* and *Siroco* (5th DT) transferred to the Atlantic on 5 July 1935, where they constituted a new 6th DT.

On that same date, 5 July 1935, the 2nd T-B Flotilla was formed with the 2nd DT (*Orage*, *Ouragan*, *Bourrasque*), 4th DT (*L'Adroit*, *Basque*, *Foudroyant*) and the 6th DT (*Cyclone*, *Mistral*, *Siroco*). *Fougueux*, *Bordelais* (both 27 July 1935) and *Frondeur* (17 September) were then incorporated into the Second Squadron at Brest, forming the 2nd DT on 1 October.

On 15 February 1936 *L'Alcyon* was also transferred to the Second Squadron; *Typhon* and *Tornade* left the Mediterranean in August, and following a short period of maintenance at Brest formed a new 7th DT with *L'Alcyon*. *Brestois* and *Boulonnais* left Toulon for Brest on 15 August of the same year, forming the 5th DT with *Foudroyant* on 1 October. *Trombe* (from the Levant) and *Tramontane* (from Toulon) followed in September and October respectively.

Brest was unable to accommodate all these ships. *Orage*, *Bourrasque*, *L'Alcyon* and *Foudroyant* were based at Cherbourg in June 1936; the 6th DT was despatched to Lorient until September. By the end of 1936, only seven of the twenty-six 1500-tonne destroyers remained in the Mediterranean.

In early 1938 *Basque* and *Forbin* were detached to Morocco, and in October the 7th DT (*Tramontane*, *Typhon*, *Tornade*) left Brest for Toulon, where they were attached to the Mediterranean training squadron.

Finally, in late August 1939, the 8th DT (*Bordelais*, *Trombe*, *L'Alcyon*) deployed from Brest to Oran, where they formed part of a new Sixth Squadron.

THE TRAINING SHIPS

The entry into service of newer *contre-torpilleurs* made it possible to assign the *Jaguar*s to secondary duties.

At Toulon the Torpedo Training School (*Ecole d'application du lancement à la mer*, or EALM), which belonged to the training division of the First Squadron, was responsible for training torpedomen. On 1 October 1932 *Tigre*, *Panthère* and *Chacal* formed a 9th DL attached to the EALM. In practice, only one or two ships would be permanently available, the others being in refit or care & maintenance. Training took place in the anchorage at Les Salins d'Hyères, to the east of Toulon. *Chacal* left in 1933, to be replaced by *Lynx* in 1935. The 9th DL would become the 11th DL on 1 October 1934, the 1st DCT on 12 April 1937 and finally the 4th DCT on 15 September 1938.

From 15 July 1935 the Atlantic-based *Chacal* and *Léopard* (8th DL) were attached to the *Ecole Navale* at Brest. They would form the 2nd DCT from 12 April 1937, being joined by *Jaguar* in September of that year. Their role was to conduct short training cruises (*corvettes*) for the officers under training at the *Ecole Navale*, the longest of which took place at the end of the training year (July/August) and included visits to the ports of northern Europe.

With the expansion of training in the late 1930s, *Lion* and *Vauban*, forming a 1st DCT, would also serve with the EALM from 15 September 1938 to 1 June 1939.

Finally, *Tramontane*, *Typhon* and *Tornade* would be attached to the training squadron in the Mediterranean in October 1938.

THE FLAGSHIPS

Some of the *contre-torpilleurs* were specially fitted out to accommodate an admiral and his staff.

The first was *Jaguar*, which on 1 May 1928 became flagship for the Group of Torpedo Boat Flotillas, which became the 1st T-B Flotilla on 1 March 1929, then of the 2nd Flotilla until late 1937. *Jaguar* was flagship of

Opposite: A grouping of training ships at Villefranche between 16 and 22 February 1939. The 2400-tonne type *Vauban* (no.12, foreground) was at the time assigned to the *Ecole d'application du lancement à la mer* (EALM) as part of a newly-created 1st DCT; her division leader was *Lion* (11). Beyond her in the picture are the cruiser *Duguay-Trouin* (right) and the old battleship *Courbet* (left). Together with the battleship *Paris* (flagship of Vice-Admiral Devin) these ships formed the new Training Squadron (*Escadre d'instruction*) tasked with boosting the number of trained personnel. (*US Navy NH110742, courtesy of A D Baker III*)

the 1st Flotilla from 1 May 1928 to 15 September 1931, then from 10 October 1932 to 13 September 1933 and from 11 September 1934 to 5 July 1935. *Guépard* alternated with her as flagship of the 1st Flotilla from 15 September 1931 to 10 October 1932 and from 13 September 1933 to 11 September 1934. *Jaguar* then became flagship of the 2nd Flotilla at Brest from 5 July 1935. She was replaced by *Bison* on 26 September 1937, but when the latter was under repair following a collision with the cruiser *Georges Leygues* on 8 February 1939 (see below), *Jaguar* returned as flagship from 1 March to 22 June of the same year.

The *Contre-torpilleur* Group of the First Squadron (which on 15 August 1936 became the 3rd Light Squadron), was led in succession by *Verdun* (from 15 April 1931), *Tartu* (from 29 September 1933) and *Maillé-Brézé* (from 12 October 1938).

Bison was flagship of the Second Squadron at Brest from 19 November 1930 and, when replaced in this role by the cruiser *Lamotte-Picquet* on 3 October 1932, became flagship of the *Contre-torpilleur* Group of the Second Squadron. She was replaced in this role by first *Milan* (25 September 1934), then by the fast minelaying cruiser *Emile Bertin* (1 September 1935). The latter ship remained at the head of this formation when it became the 2nd Light Squadron on 15 September 1936. On 9 August 1938 *Emile Bertin* was replaced by *L'Audacieux* while awaiting the arrival of *Mogador*, which became flagship on 7 November 1938.

The flag staffs of the submarine flotillas (*Flotilles de sous-marins*, or FSM) were embarked in a surface ship from 1934. The flagship of the 2nd FSM at Brest was normally the submarine depot ship *Jules Verne*, but when the latter was in refit from 1 October 1936 to 27 February 1937 she was replaced by *Bison*. The 1st FSM (Mediterranean) was led by *Lion* from 2 October 1936 and by *Aigle* from 15 August 1938. The 1st FSM, which was transferred to Bizerte, became the 4th FSM on 10 May 1939. *Aigle* remained flagship of this formation except for the period 2 June to 2 August, when she was in refit; she was replaced by *Epervier*.

FOREIGN INTERVENTION
The Levant
After the end of the Great War, France was granted a Mandate for Syria and the Lebanon by the newly-formed League of Nations. From that time a small naval force, the Naval Division of the Levant (*Division navale du Levant*, or DNL), was based at Beirut. It was reinforced during the 1930s by the semi-permanent detachment of a *contre-torpilleur* from Toulon on a rolling 6-month deployment cycle. *Epervier*, serving with the DNL, was deployed to Djibouti (Horn of Africa / Red Sea) in January and February 1939 to counter a possible Italian aggression on the coast of French Somalia.

Spanish Civil War
The Spanish Civil War began on 18 July 1936. The Marine Nationale initially ensured the safe evacuation of French citizens, and was subsequently engaged in monitoring maritime traffic.

An agreement between 27 European states signed on 20 April 1937 permitted limited checks on merchant ships headed for Spanish ports. The French, British, German and Italian Navies set up patrols outside the ports of both sides. Illegal attacks by submarines, later acknowledged to be Italian, against republican merchant ships led to new international conferences resulting in the Nyon (14 September 1937) and Paris (30 September 1937) Agreements, which aimed to eradicate 'piracy'. The Mediterranean was divided into seven surveillance zones assigned to France, Britain and Italy. France had responsibility for Zones 2 (centre of the western Mediterranean), 5 (Greek waters) and 8 (eastern part of the eastern Mediterranean) – see map for Zones 1–3. French naval deployments in support of these operations were referred to as the *Dispositif spécial en Méditerranée* (DSM).

The first DSM deployment, from 22 July 1936, was by the cruiser *Duquesne*, the CTs *Kersaint*, *Cassard*, *Albatros*, and the TEs *Le Fortuné* and *Brestois*. The CT *Maillé-Brézé* deployed to Tangier (Morocco). From 24 September most of the French ships based in the Mediterranean, both *contre-torpilleurs* and destroyers, deployed on a monthly rotation to provide a permanent presence in Spanish waters and to monitor maritime traffic in the zones assigned to France.

There were a number of attacks, generally by 'unidentified' aircraft, on French ships. On 18 January 1937 *Maillé-Brézé* was leaving Spanish coastal waters having identified insurgent ships off Barcelona when a Government aircraft dropped four bombs, which missed. On 9 August 1938, the destroyers *Fougueux* and *Frondeur* were attacked while on patrol by four Government aircraft, ten or so bombs falling 4000m from the ships. The Spanish Civil War lasted for three years and ended on 1 April 1939.

Morocco
The pacification of French Morocco was achieved only in 1934, after the elimination of the last centres of resistance in the High Atlas mountains. In 1930, the ship on station was the sloop *Duperré*. She was

DEPLOYMENT OF *CONTRE-TORPILLEURS* TO THE LEVANT

	From France	Arrived Beirut	From France	Arrived Beirut
Guépard	14 Sep 1934	19 Oct 1934	03 Nov 1934	13 Nov 1934
Cassard	14 Sep 1934	22 Oct 1934	03 Nov 1934	13 Nov 1934
Verdun	14 Jan 1935	12 Feb 1935	16 Jul 1935	22 Jul 1935
Guépard	17 Aug 1935	03 Sep 1935	14 Apr 1936	26 Apr 1936
Trombe (TB)	25 Mar 1936	11 Apr 1936	26 Jul 1935	03 Aug 1936
Aigle	30/17/1936	09 Aug 1936	08 Mar 1937	23 Mar 1937
Vauban	01 Mar 1937	15 Mar 1937	18 Sep 1937	04 Oct 1937
Aigle	14 Sep 1937	03 Nov 1937	14 Mar 1938	29 Mar 1938
Vauban	15 Mar 1938	28 Mar 1938	08 Aug 1938	26 Aug 1938
Epervier	09 Aug 1938	01 Sep 1938	21 Mar 1939	28 Mar 1939
Milan	17 Jan 1939	23 Jan 1939	05 Aug 1939	11 Aug 1939
Vautour	09 Sep 1939	14 Sep 1939	18 Sep 1939	01 Oct 1939
Gerfaut	09 Sep 1939	14 Sep 1939	18 Sep 1939	24 Oct 1939
Vauban	09 Sep 1939	30 Sep 1939	02 Oct 1939	06 Oct 1939
Epervier	09 Sep 1939	30 Sep 1939	02 Oct 1939	06 Oct 1939
Verdun	08 Aug 1939	03 Oct 1939	05 Oct 1939	24 Oct 1939
Milan	18 Oct 1939	23 Oct 1939	27 Oct 1939	26 Feb 1940
Aigle	20 Jan 1940	25 Jan 1940	30 Jan 1940	07 Feb 1940
Vauban	20 Jan 1940	25 Jan 1940	30 Jan 1940	07 Feb 1940
Guépard	04 Nov 1940	11 Nov 1940	29 Jun 1941	22 Jul 1941
Valmy	04 Nov 1940	11 Nov 1940	29 Jun 1941	22 Jul 1941
Le Chevalier Paul	11 Jun 1941	[Sunk 16 Jun 1941 off Syria]		
Vauquelin	16 Jun 1941	21 Jun 1941	29 Jun 1941	22 Jul 1941

THE PERIOD 1926-1939

Left: *Vauban* off Beirut in 1937–8; during her deployment to the Levant she wore no hull number. *(Philippe Caresse collection)*

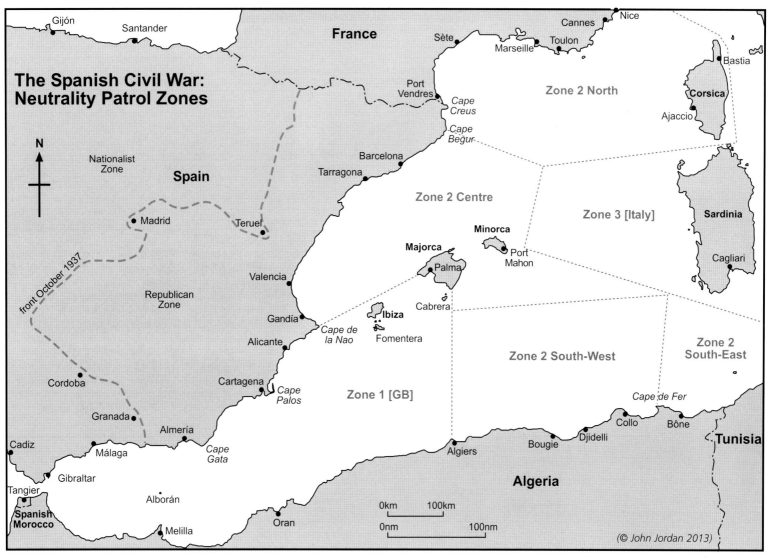

Above: Mistral following her grounding during the night of 1/2 July 1930 on the Sardinaux Bank, at the entrance to the Gulf of Saint-Tropez. *(Service Historique de Toulon, courtesy of Philippe Caresse)*

replaced by the sloop *Mondement*; subsequently one of the 1500-tonne destroyers was detached and stationed there, normally for a period of six months.

The first destroyer deployed to Morocco was *Typhon*, from February to July 1935. She would be replaced by *Fougueux*, then by *Simoun*, *Tempête* (February to September 1936), *La Railleuse*, *L'Adroit* (until October 1937) and *Basque*.

On 1 April 1938 a 9th DT was formed with *Basque* (91) and *Forbin* (92), which had just arrived from Brest. The two destroyers were based at Casablanca. They were tasked with a permanent patrol in the Tangier sector, which was placed under a 'permanent neutrality' regime. This sector was particularly sensitive because of the continuing Spanish Civil War, the proximity of the Strait of Gibraltar, the concentration of Spanish, British, German and Italian (and often French) warships in these waters and the open designs of the Spanish nationalists on the neutral zone of Tangier. In the end, Tangier would be seized by the Spanish on 14 June 1940, when the French and British were fully occupied elsewhere. The two destroyers relieved one another every fortnight on a patrol which took in the Gibraltar Strait and the anchorage at Tangier.

ACCIDENTS

There was no radar before the war, and night exercises were increasingly common. In the circumstances, accidents were inevitable, often resulting from a technical problem such as failure to receive an order in the engine room or from the poor judgement of the officer of the watch. There follows an account of the best-known incidents, the most serious being that of the CT *Bison* in February 1939.

On 4 January 1927 *Tramontane* ran aground to the east of the Tour Royale (also known as the *Grosse Tour*) at Toulon when attempting to moor at a buoy. Once

refloated, the destroyer was docked with damage classified as 'minor'.

On 2 July 1930 *Mistral* ran aground on the Sardinaux Bank near Sainte-Maxime (opposite Saint-Tropez). When she was refloated she was found to have suffered serious damage (twisted hull, turbines out of alignment), and she was fit for sea again only in August 1933.

On the night of 5/6 June 1931 *Simoun* and *Siroco* were involved in a collision off Algiers. *Siroco* lost ten metres of her stern plating to starboard (see photo).

On 29 June 1932, *Ouragan* ploughed into the Quai Noël at Toulon (see map p.207) to a depth of four metres. Repairs to her bow took until September.

On the night of 22/23 June 1933, *Maillé-Brézé* collided with the aviation transport *Commandant Teste* when changing her moorings in the Bay of Quiberon. The *contre-torpilleur* was virtually undamaged, but *Commandant Teste* sustained a large hole in her port side forward.

On 6 August 1933 *Le Fortuné* collided with the old battleship *Jean Bart* as she left the Quai Noël at Toulon. The stern of the destroyer was damaged.

On 27 October 1933 *Ouragan* collided with the stern of *Orage* at night. The two destroyers were docked, and *Ouragan* was immobilised until July 1934.

On 16 November 1933, *Vauquelin* was entering Lorient when she struck the *roche du Pot* opposite the citadel of Port Louis. The officer of the watch had been deceived by the masking of a shore light by a new crane in the newly constructed Keroman fishing port. When refloated, the ship was found to have hull damage over 40 metres. Repairs were made at Lorient at the same time as the machinery inspections that marked the final stage of her trials (see Chapter 6).

On 11 January 1934 *La Palme* collided with *Guépard* off Saint-Tropez. The *contre-torpilleur* sustained only light damage to her upperworks, and *La Palme* bent her bows.

On 11 June 1936 *Foudroyant* lost her steering and collided with the battleship *Lorraine*. Her damaged bow was repaired at Cherbourg.

On 27 July 1938 *Basque* collided with the freighter *Villiers* while transiting the Strait of Gibraltar with two submarines she was escorting. The freighter lost her engines and went aground. The destroyer was temporarily patched up at Gibraltar, returned to Toulon for full repairs, and re-entered service in November 1938.

A night exercise during the night of 7/8 February 1939 involving the 4th Cruiser Division and the 1st T-B Flotilla was marked by a major collision between *Bison* (leading the flotilla) and the cruiser *Georges Leygues*. The bow of the *contre-torpilleur* was completely severed forward of the bridge by the bow of the cruiser. The latter sustained only minor damage, but the *contre-torpilleur* had to be towed into Lorient for construction of a new bow; she was fit for sea again only in December 1939. Eighteen men were lost and gun no.2, together with the gun-crew, ended up on the forecastle of the cruiser.

Left: *Bison* following her collision with the cruiser *Georges Leygues* during the night of 7/8 February 1939, off Penmarch (Brittany).

Right: The forecastle of the cruiser *Georges Leygues* on the morning of 8 February 1939, with the D/F office and gun no.2 of *Bison*.

Opposite, bottom: *Siroco* in port following the collision with *Simoun* off Algiers on 6 June 1931. The damage allows us to see the internal arrangement of the stern section. In the foreground is the starboard depth charge chute, which has been almost completely torn away. Note the regularly-spaced access doors used for setting the depth charges. Inboard of them is the steering compartment. *Simoun* is still moored alongside; she will soon sail for Toulon, while *Siroco* will remain at Algiers for repairs. *(Marc Saibène collection)*

CHAPTER 12

THE PERIOD 1939–1943

FRANCE DECLARED WAR ON 3 SEPTEMBER 1939. The Navy's organisation for war had been drawn up one week previously, on 27 August.

The Atlantic Fleet comprised the *Force de raid* with two battleships, three cruisers and the eight most modern *contre-torpilleurs* (see accompanying table); the other ships, including the twelve destroyers of the 2nd Flotilla, were placed under orders of the *Forces maritimes de l'Ouest*, a major command located at Brest under Vice-Admiral Jean de Laborde (*Amiral Ouest*) covering the Atlantic theatre.

In the Mediterranean, the ships of the Mediterranean Fleet formed the *Forces de haute mer* with the Second and Third Squadrons at Toulon, and a Fourth Squadron (*Forces légères d'attaque*) at Bizerte; the remaining ships were attached to the local commands. Escort forces were placed under the command of Admiral South (VA Estéva) from 7 September for the escort of convoys in the Mediterranean. The neutrality of Italy would make it possible to detach numerous warships from the Mediterranean to the Atlantic.

THE INDEPENDENT COMMANDS 3 SEPTEMBER 1939

Force de raid (Brest)
    1re DL: *Dunkerque* (VA Gensoul), *Strasbourg*
    4e DC: *Georges Leygues, Montcalm, Gloire*
    2e escadre légère:
    6e DCT: *Mogador* (CA Lacroix), *Volta*
    8e DCT: *L'Indomptable, Le Malin, Le Triomphant*
    10e DCT: *Le Fantasque, L'Audacieux, Le Terrible*

Forces de haute mer (Toulon)
2e escadre:
    Provence (VA Ollive)
    2e DL: *Lorraine* (CA Vallée), *Bretagne*
    1re flottille de torpilleurs:
    1re DT: *La Palme, Le Mars, Tempête*
    3e DT: *Le Fortuné, La Railleuse, Simoun*
    7e DT: *Tramontane, Typhon, Tornade*

3e escadre:
    1re DC: *Algérie* (VA Duplat), *Dupleix, Foch, Colbert*
    2e DC: *Duquesne* (CA Kerdudo), *Tourville*
    3e escadre légère:
    5e DCT: *Tartu, Le Chevalier Paul, Vauquelin*
    7e DCT: *Vautour, Gerfaut, Albatros*
    9e DCT: *Maillé Brézé, Cassard, Kersaint*

Forces légères d'attaque (Bizerte)
    3e DC: *Marseillaise* (CA Marquis), *Jean de Vienne, La Galissonnière*
    Emile Bertin
    1re DCT: *Vauban, Lion, Aigle*
    3e DCT: *Guépard, Valmy, Verdun*
    11e DCT: *Bison, Epervier, Milan*

The Mediterranean Theatre

In the Mediterranean, the *Forces de haute mer* covered a troop convoy from Marseille to Ajaccio (Corsica) on 31 August, and the Third Squadron departed Toulon for Oran on 3 September. The *contre-torpilleurs* of the Third Squadron were then placed under the orders of Admiral South.

The reinforcement of French forces in the Levant at the beginning of the war resulted in a series of escorted convoys between North Africa and Beirut. During the night of 21/22 September convoy L1, escorted by *Vautour* and *Gerfaut* (returning from Beirut), passed convoy L3 escorted by *Guépard*, which was headed in the opposite direction, to the north of the island of Linosa (near Sicily). Collisions between the two groups of ships were narrowly avoided, but *Vautour* was struck by the passenger ship *El Djézaïr*, and two other passenger ships (*Chenonceaux* and *Mariette Pacha*) also collided. A dozen men died or were missing, presumed dead, including a crew

ESCORT FORCES (MEDITERRANEAN)

Escort Forces early Oct 1939
    1re DCT: *Vauban, Lion, Aigle*
    7e DCT: *Vautour, Gerfaut, Albatros*
    9e DCT: *Maillé Brézé, Cassard, Kersaint*
    11e DCT: *Epervier, Milan*

Group G1: *La Palme, Le Mars, Greyhound* (GB)
Group G2: *Tramontane, Tornade, Glowworm* (GB)
Group G3: *Tigre, Tempête, Typhon.*

Patrols in the Western Mediterranean 31 Dec 1939
1re DT: *La Palme, Le Mars, Tempête*
3e DT: *Le Fortuné, Simoun*
7e DT: *Tramontane, Typhon, Tornade*
8e DT: *Bordelais, Trombe, L'Alcyon*
A command ship (yacht *Cyrnos*) + 6 auxiliary patrol vessels

Patrols in the Western Mediterranean 1 May 1940
1re DT: *La Palme, Le Mars, Tempête*
3e DT: *Le Fortuné, Simoun*
7e DT: *Tramontane, Typhon, Tornade*
8e DT: *Bordelais, Trombe, L'Alcyon*
9e DT: *Forbin, Basque*
13e DT: *Baliste, La Bayonnaise, La Poursuivante*

Patrols in the Western Mediterranean 10 June 1940
1re DT: *La Palme, Le Mars, Tempête*
3e DT: *Le Fortuné, Simoun*
5e DT: *Brestois, Boulonnais*
7e DT: *Tramontane, Typhon, Tornade*
8e DT: *Bordelais, Trombe, L'Alcyon*
9e DT: *Forbin, Basque*
13e DT: *Baliste, La Bayonnaise, La Poursuivante*
8 sloops, 6 auxiliary patrol vessels

member of *Vautour*, but material damage was limited.

From 20 January to 7 February 1940, *Vauban* and *Aigle* escorted the cruiser *Tourville* which was transporting a consignment of gold to Beirut, and carried out checks on maritime traffic on their return.

Convoying in the Mediterranean was abandoned in November, and the escort forces were first reduced in size, then suppressed altogether in mid-December with the organisation of patrols of the western Mediterranean conducted by ships operating from Toulon, Oran and Bizerte (see table).

THE ATLANTIC THEATRE

In the Atlantic, the *Force de raid* made its first sortie – the only occasion on which it was at full strength – from 2 to 6 September following an (erroneous) report that the German surface forces had left port. Broken down into various components, the force would subsequently take part in the pursuit of surface raiders, and the *contre-torpilleurs* would undertake a number of escort missions, notably for British convoys bringing materiel to France.

Force X (Dakar)

A Force X was constituted on 10 October 1939 to hunt for German raiders in the South Atlantic; French ships from both the Atlantic and the Mediterranean fleets operated in conjunction with British forces from Dakar. The CTs *Le Fantasque*, *L'Audacieux* and *Le Terrible* were assigned to Force X from 10 October to 18 November; they were relieved by *Cassard* (12 November–21 January), *Milan* (12 November–13 February), *Bison* (30 December–13 February) and *Epervier* (19 January–13 February). On 25 October *Le Fantasque* and *Le Terrible* stopped and seized the German freighter *Santa Fe* (see map).

Maillé-Brézé and *Vauquelin* escorted the cruisers *Algérie* and *Dupleix* from Toulon to Dakar on 14 October, but left on the 19th with convoy SL5.

Escort missions in the Atlantic

Until April the *contre-torpilleurs* and *torpilleurs d'escadre* would be dispersed for escort duties. The French ships, particularly the 1500-tonne destroyers, formed part or all of the escort for 29 British convoys from Gibraltar to Britain (HG), 27 from Britain to Gibraltar (OG), 117 convoys from Brest or Le Verdon to Casablanca (BS), and 219 convoys from Casablanca or Oran to Brest (KF and KS). These small convoys, comprising between one and fifteen merchant ships, were generally escorted by one, two or perhaps three destroyers or sloops, sometimes reinforced by a patrol vessel. In principle the convoys left from Casablanca, and the merchantmen left the convoy off the Gironde for Le Verdon, Bordeaux and La Pallice or off the Loire for Saint-Nazaire and Nantes. Out of 2700 ships escorted only four were lost.

The destroyers from Brest also escorted major warships during their sorties from and returns to Brest. The organisation of all these operations was the responsibility of the Ocean Patrol command (*Patrouilles de l'océan*, or PATOC), created on 20 November 1939 – although the 2nd Flotilla was assigned to it only from 1 January 1940.

Some ships were detached to perform particular escort missions, such as battleships or cruisers in transit (especially to Dakar) and convoys involving the transport of precious cargo. Gold was transported from France to Canada on major warships which, when they returned to Casablanca, had arms manufactured in North America (particularly aircraft) embarked.

Le Fantasque and *Le Terrible* escorted *Strasbourg* and *Algérie* when they left Dakar on 21 November 1939. They were joined by the CTs *Guépard*, *Verdun*, *Valmy*, and *Lion* and the TE *La Railleuse* on the 24th. The group divided shortly afterwards, the ships returning to Casablanca, Brest or Toulon.

Force Z (the battleship *Lorraine*, and the cruisers *Marseillaise* and *Jean de Vienne* from Toulon), which transported gold to Canada, returned to France escorting four freighters loaded with American planes for the French forces. The convoy was joined at sea by the CTs *Maillé-Brézé*, *Kersaint*, *Vauban*, *Albatros* and *Bison* on 22 December 1939, then by the TEs *Tempête*, *Typhon* and *Tornade* the following day. The force divided off Casablanca, with the freighters, *Bison* and the destroyers entering the port, and the other ships proceeding to Toulon.

On 13 February 1940, the returning cruisers *Dupleix* and *Foch* and three freighters loaded with American planes were joined by the CTs *Maillé-Brézé*, *Vautour* and *Albatros*, then on 14 February by the TEs *Le Fortuné*, *Simoun* and *Basque*. The freighters entered

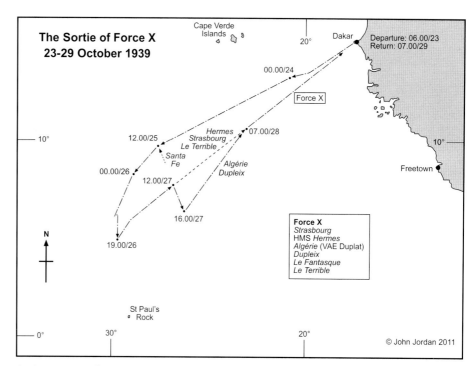

Left: *Volta* in late 1939.
(US Navy NH 86546, courtesy of A D Baker III)

Right: *Le Malin* coming alongside the fast battleship *Dunkerque* during an underway replenishment exercise on 22 March 1940. (Philippe Caresse collection)

Casablanca with *Maillé-Brézé*, *Le Fortuné*, and *Basque*, the other ships proceeding to the Mediterranean.

When they left Toulon, the cruiser *Algérie* and the battleship *Bretagne* were escorted until 14 March by the Mediterranean-based CTs *Vauban*, *Aigle* and *Maillé-Brézé*, then joined in the Atlantic by the TEs *La Palme*, *Le Mars* and *La Railleuse*. When this force returned from North America, reinforced by the cruiser *Colbert*, the armed merchant cruiser *Victor Schoelcher* and two freighters with American planes on board, it was met by the CTs *Aigle*, *Valmy* and *Verdun* on 6 April, then by the TEs *La Palme*, *Le Mars* and *Forbin* the following day. The freighters and the destroyers entered the port of Casablanca on 8 April.

Operations against the U-boats

The destroyers often had to deal with enemy submarines, and claimed several sinkings following attacks with depth charges, the submarine having been sighted on the surface prior to diving, never to surface again. In reality, because the crews of the escorts had never experienced a depth charge attack they often mistook the blackish explosion of a depth charge in poor light conditions for a blackish hull in the process of sinking.

On 17 October 1939, *Cyclone* and *Mistral* were on their way to reinforce the escort of a convoy when *Cyclone* saw what she thought to be the conning tower of a diving submarine. She attacked with depth charges without any visible result.

On 28 October *Chacal*, while escorting convoy OG4, spotted the wake of a torpedo, and *Mistral* dropped depth charges at the spot from where the torpedo was thought to have been fired.

On 31 October convoy K20, escorted by *Ouragan* and the sloop *Commandant Rivière*, was attacked by *U-25* (Type IA), which sank the freighter *Baoulé*. As it was unclear where the torpedo had been fired from, the destroyer stayed with the convoy while the sloop rescued the freighter's crew.

On 2 November, *Siroco* was despatched to a position 8nm from Guernsey (Channel Is.), where a submarine had been sighted. The next morning the destroyer detected propeller noises and the Canadian destroyer *Assiniboine* dropped depth charges, but without success.

On 15 November convoy 27KS, comprising 18 merchantmen escorted by the TEs *Siroco*, *Frondeur*, *Trombe* and the sloop *Chevreuil*, was off Lisbon, Portugal. A seaplane, directed to the area following the detection of a radio transmission, detected a suspect wake, and dropped a flare. *Siroco* headed for the spot and dropped depth charges, and the crew of the destroyer saw what they thought to be a submarine sinking. In the event *U-53* (Type VIIB) not only escaped, but continued to shadow the convoy for three days. The following day, 16 November, *Frondeur* dropped depth charges in an area where the presence of a submarine was suspected, but without success. And on 20 November *Siroco* sighted a submarine and attacked with depth charges. On this occasion the bow of the submarine was seen to break the surface. However, *U-41* (Type IXA) suffered only damage to her gyro-compass and returned to Wilhelmshaven on 7 December. *Siroco*, convinced she had sunk two submarines, was subsequently the subject of several news reports and her exploits were much fêted; there were nevertheless reservations on the part of the general staff about the veracity of her claims, due to the lack of any concrete evidence such as debris on the surface.

On 21 November, *L'Adroit* was escorting three ships out of Casablanca when a submarine was sighted dead ahead. She attacked with depth charges, reported seeing a yellow stain on the surface, then rejoined her convoy.

On 16 December, convoy 40KS was being escorted by *Siroco*, *La Railleuse* and the auxiliary patrol vessel (APV) *Jutland*, and was due to be joined by the sloop *Commandant Bory* with a second group of ships. A seaplane dropped a flare to signal the presence of a possible submarine. *Siroco* (again!) headed for the area and dropped depth charges. Again a surfacing submarine was sighted.

On 14 January 1940 *Fougueux*, the sloop *Gazelle*, the APVs *Heureux* and *Vaillant* were escorting convoy 20BS. The sighting of the feathered wake of a periscope was followed by a depth charge attack by *Fougueux*, without any apparent result.

On the night of 16/17 January 1940, *Jaguar* was on her way to meet a convoy from Morocco when she was rammed by the British destroyer *Keppel* in the Bay of Biscay. The bow of the *Keppel* penetrated as far as the centre-line of the *contre-torpilleur* to starboard in compartment D. A junior petty officer was killed. The ship managed to make it back to Brest, entering the harbour on 19 January; she was towed into no.3 dock for repairs which lasted until early May.

On 24 January, convoy 56KS was being escorted by *Fougueux* and *Heureux*. The freighter *Alsacien* was torpedoed and sunk. *Fougueux* attacked the estimated torpedo launch position with depth charges, but *U-44* (Type IXA) escaped; she would sink a straggler from the convoy, *Tourny*, the following day.

On 25 January convoys 22S and 30XS, which had been merged the previous day, were being escorted by *Basque*, the sloop *Annamite* and the trawler *Hardi II*. *Basque* carried out two depth charge attacks based on periscope sightings by *Annamite*.

On 30 January convoy OG16 was attacked by *U-55* (Type VIIB), which sank the British tanker *Vaclite* and the Greek freighter *Keramiai*. The CT *Valmy* joined the convoy just as the British sloop *Fowey* (L15) obtained an Asdic contact and began dropping depth charges. The destroyer *Whitshed* (D77) joined in the attacks. *Fowey* sighted a submarine on the surface. Hindered by the foggy conditions, she opened fire but the submarine proved difficult to follow. A Sunderland flying boat belonging to 228 Squadron dropped a bomb on the submarine, and signalled to *Valmy* the presence of a submarine bearing 210. The *contre-torpilleur* increased speed to 18 knots then to 24 knots, and sighted the submarine at 15.01 at a range of 13,000 metres. *Valmy* fired 13 rounds before the submarine disappeared with its propellers out of the water. However, a short while before, *Fowey* had seen five men in the water, then a raft with 36 men from the submarine. The survivors were rescued. The French at first thought they were responsible for sinking the submarine, but they had at best prompted the crew to abandon ship, the depth charge attack of the *Whitshed* having forced *U-55* to the surface and into range of first *Fowey*, then the Sunderland and then *Valmy*.

On 14 February 1940, the convoy formed by the merging of convoys 27BS and 34XS was escorted by the destroyer *Frondeur*, the sloop *La Capricieuse*, and the APVs *La Bônoise*, *La Sétoise* and *Cap Fagnet*. The sighting of a periscope, followed by the wake of a torpedo, led to two depth charge attacks by *Frondeur*, without result.

On 18 February 1940 the destroyer *Bourrasque*, the sloop *Chevreuil* and the APV *Léoville*, escorting convoy 65KS, could not prevent the torpedoing of freighter *PLM 15* by *U-37* (Type IXA).

On 23 February, *Simoun* was escorting the transports *Austral* and *Golo* from Gibraltar to Brest before being relieved by *Forbin*. She was returning to Casablanca when the sighting of a periscope prompted three depth charge attacks, followed by a violent shock close to the stern. The destruction of *U-54* (Type VIIB) was long attributed to *Simoun*, but it is more likely that drifting tree trunks were responsible.

On 29 March, convoy 76KS was being escorted by *Fougueux*, the sloop *Chevreuil*, and the APVs *l'Ajaccienne* and *La Toulonnaise*. *Fougueux* obtained a contact on her Asdic set and attacked with depth charges, but the contact was almost certainly a submerged wreck.

On 31 March *Mistral* and the sloop *Annamite* were escorting a convoy headed for the Mediterranean, when *Annamite* sighted a periscope. The two escorts attacked with depth charges, but without success.

On 15 May *Orage*, escorting convoy 95KF, carried out an unsuccessful depth charge attack 60nm to the north-west of Cape Finisterre.

Casablanca
Casablanca in French Morocco became an important naval base following the outbreak of war; the *Groupe des sous-marins du Maroc* and a minesweeping section were based there. The 9th DT was already at Casablanca with *Basque* and *Forbin*. The latter was replaced by *Trombe* from 2 to 22 November, then by *La Railleuse* which arrived on 17 November. *Le Fortuné* and *Simoun* arrived at Casablanca on 6 February. *Basque* left Morocco on 16 January, and *Le Fortuné* followed on 29 February. They were replaced by *Le Mars* (arrived 1 March) and *La Palme* (8 March). *Simoun* left on 21 March, replaced by *Trombe* on 29 March.

La Railleuse was lost in an accident that took place on 23 March 1940. She was on guard duty in the port of Casablanca at the head of the anchorage when a torpedo exploded. The ship was cut in two; 28 men died and a further 24 suffered serious injuries. The 130mm guns were salvaged and installed as a coast defence battery at Safi, south of Casablanca.

The wreck was sold for breaking up in April 1942.

Tramontane, *Typhon* and *Tornade* (7th DT) arrived in Morocco 12 April. With the intentions of Italy becoming increasingly uncertain, the destroyers based at Casablanca left Morocco between 13 and 26 April and were transferred to the Mediterranean.

THE NORTHERN THEATRE
In the northern theatre, light forces were assigned to the admiral commanding the *Forces maritimes du Nord* (VA Castex), who had his HQ at Dunkirk.

Initially he had under his command the 11th DT with three 610-tonne torpedo boats and a few sloops. On 7 September, in anticipation of a German offensive against Belgium, he received reinforcements in the form of the 2nd DCT with the elderly *contre-torpilleurs Jaguar*, *Léopard* and *Panthère*. On 10 September *Panthère* ran aground in misty conditions, but was quickly refloated without major damage to her hull or propellers. The *contre-torpilleurs* proved to be too large and unhandy for operations in the shallow waters off the Pas de Calais and in the North Sea. On 9 October *Panthère* was struck by a Belgian trawler and returned to Cherbourg for repairs. *Léopard* returned to Brest on 17 October and *Jaguar*, which ran aground off Boulogne on the night of 28/29 October, followed on 1 November. The *contre-torpilleurs* were replaced by the 5th DT: *Boulonnais* arrived on 15 October (but left again for docking on the 31st), and *Foudroyant* on 2 November.

Attached to the *Forces maritimes de l'Ouest* (Brest), *Léopard*, *Chacal*, *Tigre*, *Panthère*, *Jaguar* and *Lynx* participated in the escort of 18 convoys between Brest and Gibraltar and three between Casablanca and Le Verdon between October 1939 and May 1940.

The destroyers *Bourrasque* and *Ouragan* left Brest on 10 November for Dunkirk. Fearing an attack by the German fleet on the Pas de Calais, the forces in the North were reinforced by the powerful *contre-torpilleurs Mogador* and *Volta*, which were at Cherbourg from 12 to 22 November. *Brestois* would also be despatched to Dunkirk.

The *Forces maritimes du Nord* were reinforced following an alert by the CTs *Guépard* and *Verdun*, which arrived at Dunkirk on 15 January 1940 and by

Above: *Le Terrible* with the 4th Cruiser Squadron in North Africa in the spring of 1940: the cruiser with three green bands on her first funnel is the *Gloire*; beyond her, with a single green band, is *Georges Leygues*. (Pradignac & Léo collection)

Chacal and *Léopard*, which however remained at Cherbourg.

A reconnaissance off the Dutch coast was undertaken on the night of 13/14 January by the CTs *Guépard* and *Verdun* and the TEs *Brestois*, *Bourrasque* and *Ouragan*. The same ships sailed on an identical mission on the evening of 16 January, but *Guépard* ran aground on Hill Bank. She was quickly refloated, at the cost of a damaged propeller, but it was decided that *contre-torpilleur* operations in this area would end. *Verdun* left Dunkirk on 22 January and *Guépard*, following rudimentary repairs, on 7 February.

On 17 February, having just returned form the Dutch coast, *Brestois* again sortied after detecting an underwater contact on her Asdic. She attacked with depth charges, then opened fire on a 'surfaced submarine'; the latter turned out to be the sloop *Amiral Mouchez*, which was struck by a 130mm shell; four members of her crew died.

THE NORWEGIAN CAMPAIGN

On 5 April a Force Z was formed in anticipation of an intervention in Norway, which was precipitated by the German invasion of that country on 9 April. The main task of the *contre-torpilleurs* and *torpilleurs d'escadre* would be to escort transports between Scotland and Norway.

The transports carrying French troops were escorted from Brest to Greenock by the CTs *Bison*, *Milan*, *Epervier*, *Valmy*, *Vautour*, *Albatros*, *Verdun*, *Valmy*, *Léopard* and *Guépard*, and the TEs *Cyclone*, *Mistral*, *Orage* and *Tempête*.

FORCE Z (NORWAY) 5 APRIL TO 27 MAY 1940

Cruiser: *Emile Bertin* (replaced by *Montcalm* 23 April)
5e DCT: *Tartu*, *Le Chevalier Paul*, *Maillé Brézé*
11e DCT: *Bison*, *Epervier*, *Milan*
5e DT: *Brestois*, *Foudroyant*, *Boulonnais*
A transport group, including 6 auxiliary cruisers
A supply train

On 9 April the cruiser *Emile Bertin*, and the CTs *Tartu* and *Maillé-Brézé* were operating with a British formation off Bergen when they were attacked by German bombers, the bombs falling between 300m and 2000m from the French ships. All Allied ships approaching the Norwegian coast had to expect to face bombing by German aircraft, and these attacks revealed the full extent of the inadequacy of their anti-aircraft armament.

Convoy FP1 from the Clyde to Namsos was escorted by the CTs *Tartu*, *Le Chevalier Paul*, *Maillé-Brézé* and *Epervier*; it arrived on 19 April after a torpedo attack by a submarine which was depth-charged by *Maillé-Brézé* (see illustration).

On 13 April *Milan*, while returning from Greenock to Brest, collided with the British trawler *Glamorgan Coast*. Damage was relatively minor, but one of the 37mm guns was replaced at Greenock 7–10 May.

On the night of 23 April, the 8th DCT with *L'Indomptable*, *Le Malin* and *Le Triomphant* conducted a high-speed raid into the Skagerrak against German shipping headed for Norway. The French ships, increasing speed to 34 then to 36 knots, intercepted

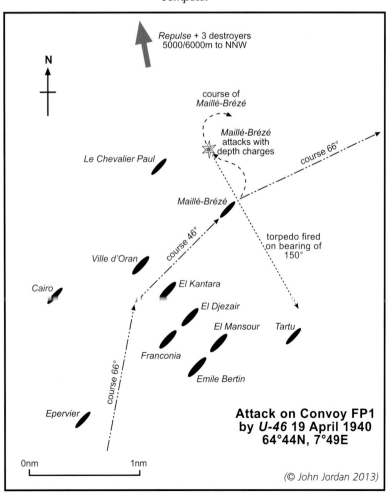

(© John Jordan 2013)

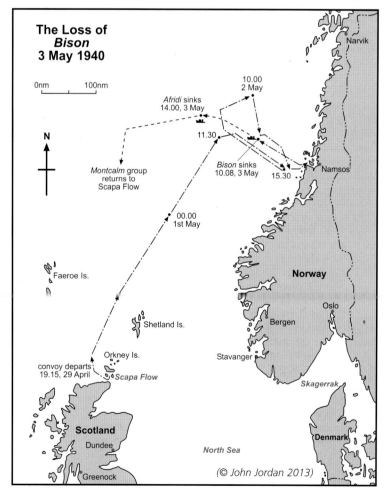

(© John Jordan 2013)

the auxiliary patrol vessels *VP-702* and *VP-709* and damaged the former. They also fired on two S-boats, whose torpedoes they managed to avoid. The French believed they had sunk one of the S-boats, but they were mistaken. A boiler turbofan failure on board *Le Malin* compelled her to reduce speed to 32 then to 30 knots. The division then became the focus of German air attacks, and *Le Triomphant* was near-missed by three bombs, one of which landed 30 metres from the after boiler room. The force just failed to locate a German convoy, and on 30 April *Le Triomphant* returned to Lorient for repairs to a misaligned port shaft.

Convoy FS1, escorted by the TEs *Brestois* and *Boulonnais*, arrived at Namsos on 26 April.

On 30 April, *Maillé-Brézé* was about to get underway in Greenock roads, when a torpedo was accidentally launched from the port forward tubes and exploded in the after end of the forecastle. A fire broke out in the forward part of the ship and the *contre-torpilleur* eventually sank. Casualties were six dead, 31 missing, presumed dead, and 47 wounded. The wreck was raised for breaking up only in 1954. An enquiry established that the torpedo had been fired in error during maintenance on the tubes, which would not have been possible had a planned safety modification been made.

The evacuation of Namsos was carried out on the night of 2/3 May. The convoy was attacked as it left Namsos by Stuka dive-bombers from I./StG 1, of which one managed to drop its bomb just forward of the bridge of *Bison* at about 10.08. There was an explosion and the bow separated from the rest of the ship and sank. Her AA guns continued to blaze away at the attackers even as the fire spread aft. The crippled *Bison* was sunk at 12.07 by the British destroyer *Afridi*, which picked up the survivors (see map). *Afridi* would be sunk in her turn an hour later. The French destroyer lost 139 men.

On 3 May a raid on the coast of Norway was carried out by the French *Tartu*, *Le Chevalier Paul*, and *Milan*, and the British 'Tribal' class destroyers *Sikh* and *Tartar*. The target was a German convoy, which the Allied force attempted to intercept. Sailing was delayed by last-minute technical problems and speed was then limited to the 30-knot maximum of the British destroyers; in consequence the mission was a failure

The campaign continued in the north of Norway. *Foudroyant* operated with the British destroyer *Somali* in the Mo region 13–14 May, undertaking a fire support mission on the 14th. She was damaged by a near-miss during an air attack on the morning of the 15th.

Milan operated in the Narvik area and was engaged in fire support missions in Rombaksfjord on the 18th and in Ofotfjord on 19 May. She suffered minor damage from two near-misses on 22 May, and was later repaired at Brest.

THE BATTLE FOR FRANCE

The battle for France opened on 10 May 1940. The Navy, notably the 2nd T-B Flotilla commanded by CV de Portzamparc, played a major part in operations in the North. *Foudroyant*, *Frondeur*, *L'Adroit*, *Cyclone*, *Siroco*, and torpedo boats of the 610-tonne type escorted troops to Walcheren (Netherlands). They undertook fire support missions in support of the land forces up to the evacuation of Vlissingen on 18 May,

which was carried out under heavy air attack. The Germans eventually encircled the British Expeditionary Force (BEF) and the remnants of the French armies in a pocket centred on Dunkirk, which served to resupply Allied forces pending their evacuation. The evacuation again took place under heavy attack from the air by German bombers.

L'Adroit was wrecked in the Dunkirk roads on 21 May, shortly after midnight; she was struck by one bomb and further damaged by two near-misses from a Heinkel 111. She was beached at Malo-les-Bains and suffered a number of further explosions, including one in the forward magazine which broke her in two (see photo). Remarkably, there were no losses among her crew.

The 2nd DCT returned to the northern theatre on

Above: *Maillé-Brézé* on fire and sinking at Greenock, Scotland, after the accidental launching of one of her torpedoes into the bridge structure. Note the extensive damage resulting from the explosion of the torpedo warhead. *(US Navy NH 86537, courtesy of A D Baker III)*

Below: *Bison* minus her bow and on fire following the Ju-87 attacks off Namsos on 3 May 1940.

Above: The burnt-out hull of *L'Adroit*, beached at Malo-les-bains, Dunkirk, after being struck or near-missed by three German bombs on 21 May 1940. *(CAW courtesy of Jaroslaw Malinowski)*

the evening of 22 May, carrying demolition teams to Dunkirk (*Jaguar*), Calais (*Chacal*) and Boulogne (*Léopard*). On 23 May *Jaguar* was entering the channel for the port of Dunkirk when she was struck by a torpedo launched by a German S-boat, either *S-21* or *S-23*. The *contre-torpilleur* suffered 13 dead and 23 wounded; she too was beached at Malo-les-Bains, and was written off as a total loss.

From 22 to 24 May, the CTs *Léopard* and *Chacal*, and the TEs *Cyclone*, *Siroco*, *Mistral*, *Fougueux*, *Frondeur*, *Foudroyant*, *Bourrasque* and *Orage* took part in the defence of Boulogne, undertaking a number of fire support missions.

On the evening of 23 May, *Fougueux*, *Frondeur* and *Orage* were off Boulogne when they were attacked by German bombers. *Frondeur* was damaged by a near-miss and had to return to Cherbourg; there were 300 holes in her upperworks. *Orage*, attacked by a Ju-87 of I./StG 77, was hit by no fewer than five bombs and was burnt out. She sank during the night; 26 men were lost.

On the night of 23/24 May *Chacal* was struck by four bombs dropped by Heinkel 111 bombers. The stricken ship, which was taken under fire by German batteries, was abandoned and was eventually beached in front of the Slack dunes, between Wimereux and Ambleteuse. Shortly afterwards, on the morning of 24 May at Boulogne, *Fougueux* was struck by one bomb and near-missed by another. She returned to Cherbourg after one last fire support mission around midday.

Losses had already been heavy, and the surviving ships were now committed to operations linked with the evacuation of the Dunkirk pocket. *Epervier* was off the beaches (Dunes de Flandre) from 24 May to 5 June. Too large to take part in the evacuation of troops, she exercised control over the smaller surface vessels, and fended off enemy S-boats.

Mistral was damaged on 29 May in the course of embarking troops from the Embecquetage jetty at Dunkirk, when a bomb fell close by on the quay-side; she had to return to Cherbourg. The following day *Bourrasque*, with between 500 and 700 troops on board, was sunk off Nieuport. The cause of her loss is disputed; she was struck either by a drifting mine of French origin or by a well-placed shell from a German battery, and quickly capsized. That night, 30/31 May, *Siroco* was also sunk. She had just embarked 750 men from the jetty, and was in the West Hinder area

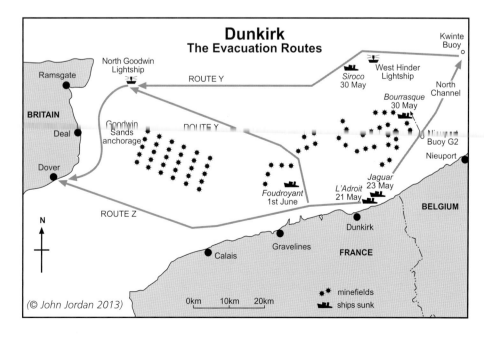

(© John Jordan 2013)

(between Dover and Ostend), when she was struck aft by two torpedoes launched by the German S-boats *S-23* and *S-26*, then by a bomb. More than 650 men were lost, including 58 of her crew.

On 31 May *Cyclone* was damaged, her bows blown off by a torpedo from the German *S-24*. Two men were missing, presumed dead. The ship returned to Dover, proceeded from there to Cherbourg and finally entered Brest on 3 June. On 1 June *Foudroyant* was struck by four Stuka bombs off Gravelines, just as she was about to enter Dunkirk. She keeled over and sank, with the loss of about twenty of her crew.

The German advance compelled the Navy to evacuate first the Channel, then the Atlantic ports. Brest was evacuated on 18 June 1940. The destroyer *Mistral* made it to Plymouth (UK) under her own steam but *Ouragan*, still under repair following a collision with the auxiliary minesweeper AD.2 *Louise-Marie* off Boulogne on 1 February, had to be towed. *Cyclone*, also under repair, was scuttled in one of the Tourville docks. The wreck would be recovered in the commercial port at Brest following the Liberation.

Fougueux and *Frondeur* escorted the battleship *Richelieu* when she left Brest on 18 June. Too short-legged to accompany her to Dakar, the destroyers put in at Casablanca. Finally, the two modern CTs *Milan* and *Epervier* escorted the 1st Division of Armed Merchant Cruisers (1re DCX), on which 1200 tonnes of gold were embarked, from Brest to Dakar.

WAR WITH ITALY

From April 1940, the increasing likelihood of Italy entering the war led to a regrouping of French naval forces in the Mediterranean, where the 3rd Light Squadron was reconstituted on 30 May 1940. *Vauban*, *Kersaint*, *Cassard* and *Vauquelin*, which had remained at Toulon, were joined on 20 April by *Aigle*, on 27 May by *Guépard*, *Verdun*, *Valmy*, *Vautour*, *Albatros*, *Tartu* and *Le Chevalier Paul*, on 24 May by *Lion*, and on 21 June by *Gerfaut*.

Operation 'Vado'

A bombardment of the Italian coast had been planned by the Mediterranean Fleet as a response to a declaration of war by Italy, which duly materialised on 10 June. The operation, which would subsequently be known by the name Operation 'Vado', after the first of its two objectives, Vado and Genoa, was executed on

Above: *Bourrasque* sinking by the stern off Nieuport (Belgium) on 30 May. She had just embarked 600 troops, who are seen here crowding the decks and cramming themselves into boats, which cannot be launched due to the rapid list of the ship. *(Leo van Ginderen collection)*

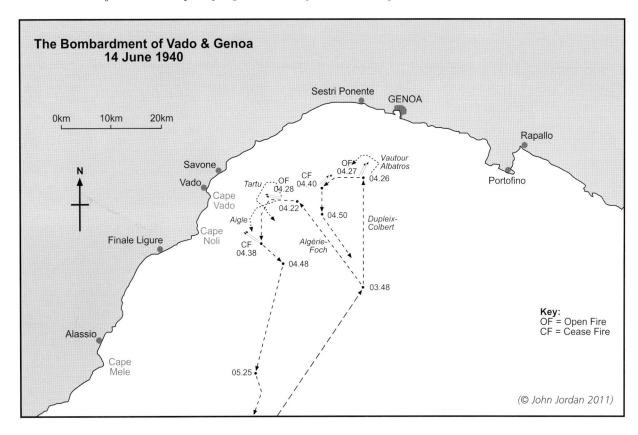

OPERATION 'VADO' 14 JUNE 1940

Vado Group:
Algérie (VA Duplat), *Foch*
1re DCT: *Vauban, Lion, Aigle*
5e DCT: *Tartu, Le Chevalier Paul, Cassard*

Genoa Group:
Dupleix (CA Derrien), *Colbert*
7e DCT: *Vautour, Albatros*
3e DCT: *Guépard, Valmy, Verdun.*

the night of 13/14 June by the 3rd Squadron based at Toulon, under the command of Vice-Admiral Duplat.

The squadron arrived at a point 20nm bearing 120 from Cape Vado at 03.48, then separated into two groups: one headed for Vado, the other for Genoa.

The 1st DCT, which was to scout for the Vado group, was formed into a line abreast 1000m across and stationed 3000m ahead of the flagship, the cruiser *Algérie*; the 5th DCT was tasked with shore bombardment. *Tartu* fired on the Nafta oil tanks, *Le Chevalier Paul* on those of Petrolea, and *Cassard* on the factories at Savone. *Aigle*, which was with the scouting division, fired at a range of 9800m on the coast defence battery at Cape Vado, which was silenced after a few minutes, then on the signalling station, the main road and a fast patrol boat. The FPBs were *MAS535* and *MAS539*, which were attempting to attack the Vado group; only *MAS539* managed to launch a torpedo. Taken under fire by *Aigle*, the cruisers *Algérie* and *Foch*, and the 5th DCT, the two FPBs returned to Savone having sustained only minor damage.

Meanwhile *Dupleix* and *Colbert*, of the Genoa group, engaged targets ashore between 04.27 and 04.40. The scouting division, the 3rd DCT, was stationed 6000m from the flagship, *Dupleix*. *Albatros* and *Vautour*, forming the bombardment division (7th DCT), were stationed 2.5nm to the north of the cruisers; Sestri Ponente was their objective. *Albatros* opened fire at 04.33 at a range of 7300m. She had a brief steering failure at 04.40, and made smoke to cover herself at 04.45. The 7th DCT was fired on by the Mameli CD battery (152mm guns) and by the Italian torpedo boat *Calatafimi*.

Albatros was struck by a 152mm shell that passed through a fuel tank and exploded in the after boiler room. Steam lines were severed and fuel leaked into the boiler room but without causing a fire. The boiler was isolated from the steam collector, and the officer in charge of the boiler room, even though seriously burned, hurled himself onto his stomach, and with the help of a junior stoker managed to shut down the burners; these two would be the only survivors of the boiler room personnel. The after turbines had to be shut down. There were a dozen casualties with steam burns in the boiler room. *Albatros* momentarily hauled out of line, then rejoined on a single shaft. The division continued its bombardment of the Ansaldo-Fossati works of Genoa-Sestri, and opened fire on the *Calatafimi* and on the FPBs *MAS534* and *MAS538*, which launched torpedoes between 04.35 and 04.40. The Italian FPBs returned to Savone with one minor casualty.

Following the bombardment by the cruisers, the French formation regrouped. At first making 26 knots, the squadron had to reduce speed to 25 knots at 05.07 because of the damaged *Albatros*, but was able to increase to 27 knots for the final run into Toulon. Two aircraft, which were quickly identified as French, were sighted at 06.15. There was also a submarine alert at 07.55. *Albatros* moored at Pier 4 (Milhaud) at 11.55. Her losses had been heavy: out of the 14 men who suffered burns, five died the same day and a further six in the days that followed.

The final results of the operation were disappointing. The French cruisers fired more than 500 203mm rounds and some 300 rounds with their secondary (90mm/100mm) guns; the *contre-torpilleurs* fired 800 rounds of 138mm. Italian losses were nine civilians killed and 34 wounded. Minor damage was inflicted on housing and on industrial buildings at Vado, Savone, Abissola, Zinola and Quiliano. In the Genoa area, the cruisers had trouble locating their

Right: Force X at Alexandria between 3 and 20 May 1940; in the foreground are the *contre-torpilleurs Tigre* (left) and *Lynx*.

targets – they fired on the Lerone Valley instead of the Polcevera Valley – but they did damage some industrial buildings, and the *contre-torpilleurs* hit the Ansaldo-Fossati works at Sestri. All the damage was repaired within a few days.

The 3rd Squadron would sortie once more on 17–18 June to cover the passage of convoy 6P, consisting of 17 ships, from Marseille to Oran.

The *Force de Raid* is transferred to the Mediterranean

In anticipation of war with Italy the *Force de raid*, later reinforced by the older battleships (returning from the eastern Mediterranean) and by the cruisers from Bizerte, was distributed between the anchorage at Mers el-Kebir (Oran) and Algiers.

Dunkerque, *Strasbourg*, *Gloire*, *Montcalm*, *Mogador*, *L'Indomptable*, *Le Triomphant*, *Le Malin* and *Le Terrible* arrived at Mers el-Kebir for the first time 5–9 April 1940. They were then transferred back to Brest when operations off Norway began.

On 27 April *Dunkerque*, *Strasbourg*, *Georges Leygues*, *Gloire*, *Mogador*, *Le Terrible* and *L'Audacieux* returned to Mers el-Kebir. They were joined on 2 May by the 3rd Cruiser Division, on 9 May by *L'Indomptable* and *Le Malin*, on 14 May by *Volta*, and on 27 May by *Montcalm*, *Provence*, *Bretagne*, *Tigre* and *Lynx*. Because the jetty and the piers under construction at Mers el-Kebir were still incomplete, the ships were distributed between Mers and Oran, except for the 4th DC and the 8th DCT, which were at Algiers.

In the eastern Mediterranean, a Force X based at Alexandria was constituted 3–20 May comprising the three older battleships, four cruisers and the CTs *Tigre* and *Lynx*. The latter two ships were replaced by the 3rd DT (*Le Fortuné*, *Forbin* and *Basque*), and joined the *Force de raid* at Mers el-Kebir, in company with the battleships *Provence* and *Bretagne*, on 27 May.

The *Force de raid*, now complete, sortied with the 5th and 7th DTs on 12–13 June. *Brestois* and *Boulonnais* depth-charged a submarine which had attacked the 3rd Cruiser Division. The 3rd DC, 8th DCT and 7th DT then returned to Algiers.

Cover for convoys evacuating personnel from metropolitan France prompted sorties by the 4th DC and the 8th DCT and, on 22 June, by the 4th DC and the 10th DCT (minus *Le Terrible*, which remained as Mers el-Kebir). Reports of Italian cruisers at sea led to the reinforcement of the 4th DC by the 3rd DC and the 8th DCT, which joined just after midnight on 24 June. They failed to find the Italian cruisers, and the French ships returned to Algiers around midday on the 24th.

In preparation for a possible evacuation of the French government, the Admiralty positioned the CTs *Tartu*, *Le Chevalier Paul* and *Cassard* at Sète 20–22 June, and the TEs *La Palme*, *Le Mars* and *Tempête* at Port-Vendres between 21 June and 3 July.

The evacuation of ships on trials or in refit

Le Hardi, the first of the new 1772-ton destroyers, entered service on 2 June 1940. She escorted the passenger ship *Ville d'Oran* from La Pallice to Casablanca, then to Brest. She left Brest on 18 June and on the morning of 19 June joined the incomplete battleship *Jean Bart*, which had escaped from Saint-Nazaire the previous night. Joined by *Mameluk* and *Epée* (see below), the ships arrived at Casablanca during the afternoon of 22 June.

Fleuret, whose admission into active service was scheduled for the end of June, left Toulon on 12 June for Casablanca, escorting the battleship *Richelieu* from Casablanca to Dakar.

Epée, which had conducted her first firing trials in early May, joined the escort of *Jean Bart* and accompanied her as far as Casablanca.

Mameluk was still undergoing her post-trials machinery inspection when she left Lorient on 17 June to join the escort of *Jean Bart*.

Casque, which had begun trials only on 25 April, left Toulon on 20 June for Oran.

Lansquenet, fitting out at Bordeaux, was manned for trials on 1 June. She left the shipyard on 24 June, despite having never previously sailed under her own steam. She was fired on by German batteries as she sortied from the River Gironde, and arrived at Casablanca on 27 June.

Le Corsaire, which was 82% complete and still without her guns, left her building yard at La Seyne on 22 June and sailed for Oran with convoy 8P, arriving on 26 June.

Le Flibustier remained at Toulon, where she began her trials on 23 June.

Of the older ships already in service *Albatros*, which had been under repair since Operation 'Vado', remained at Toulon. *Vauquelin*, in refit with only a single set of turbines available, could have left on one shaft on 23 June but also remained at Toulon. Likewise, *Panthère* could have left on one shaft but remained. However, *Kersaint*, which was in a similar situation, left Toulon on 20 June and escorted the aviation transport *Commandant Teste* to Oran, where the two ships arrived on 22 June. On 24 June she sortied in response to a submarine alert.

THE ARMISTICE AND MERS EL-KEBIR

Once the armistice with Germany and Italy came into force at 00.35 on 25 June, all French ships were immobilised.

Although the independence of the French fleet was guaranteed by the armistice, the British did not trust the Germans to respect its terms, nor did it trust the new national French government of Marshal Pétain to resist German pressure. The British Prime Minister,

POSITIONS OF DESTROYERS 25 JUNE 1940

Toulon:	CTs *Panthère*, *Guépard*, *Valmy*, *Verdun*, *Vauban*, *Lion*, *Albatros*, *Gerfaut*, *Vautour*, *Aigle*, *Tartu*, *Vauquelin*, *Cassard*, *Le Chevalier Paul*, TE *Le Flibustier*.
Port-Vendres:	TEs *Tempête*, *Le Mars*, *La Palme*.
Mers el-Kebir:	CTs *Tigre*, *Lynx*, *Kersaint*, *Le Terrible*, *Mogador*, *Volta*.
Oran:	TEs *Tramontane*, *Tornade*, *Typhon*, *Trombe*, *Brestois*, *Boulonnais*, *Bordelais*, *Le Corsaire*, *Casque*.
Algiers:	CTs *Le Fantasque*, *L'Audacieux*, *Le Malin*, *L'Indomptable*, TE *Simoun*.
Bizerte:	*L'Alcyon*.
Casablanca:	TEs *Fougueux*, *Frondeur*, *Le Hardi*, *Epée*, *Lansquenet*, *Mameluk*.
Dakar:	CTs *Milan*, *Epervier*, TE *Fleuret*.
Alexandria:	TEs *Le Fortuné*, *Forbin*, *Basque*.
Portsmouth:	CT *Léopard*.
Plymouth:	CT *Le Triomphant*, TEs *Ouragan*, *Mistral*.

Right: Mers el-Kebir on 3 July 1940: *Mogador* passes *Le Terrible* at about 14.00 to moor near the harbour entrance. *(Philippe Caresse collection)*

Far right: *Mogador*, her stern section destroyed by a 15-inch shell, is immobilised close to the pass. *(Philippe Caresse collection)*

Opposite: The stern of *Mogador*, wrecked by a combination of a British 15-inch shell and the explosion of her own depth charges. Miraculously, the propeller shafts remained virtually intact. Although *Mogador* successfully made the return crossing to Toulon in November 1940, repairs were still incomplete at the time of her scuttling.

Winston Churchill, therefore determined that the French fleet either had to come under British control or to be eliminated as a potential threat.

Those French ships which had sought refuge in British ports were forcibly seized before dawn on 3 July (Operation 'Catapult'). On the same day, an attempt by the British to persuade the *Force de raid* at Mers el-Kebir to make common cause against the Germans failed; the British Force H then opened fire on the French ships in the harbour. The old battleship *Bretagne* was sunk, and the battleships *Provence* and *Dunkerque* were beached and seriously damaged. *Strasbourg* managed to escape with the CTs *Volta*, *Le Terrible*, *Lynx*, *Tigre* and *Kersaint*, but *Mogador* was disabled as she was approaching the pass, an unlucky hit by a 15-inch (381mm) shell destroying her stern. *Strasbourg* and four of the *contre-torpilleurs* regained Toulon, followed by *Kersaint*, which could make only 20 knots on her one shaft.

The *torpilleurs d'escadre*, which were in the port of Oran, got underway shortly after the British opened fire. *Bordelais* and *Trombe* followed in the wake of *Strasbourg*. *Trombe*, joined by *Tramontane*, *Tornade*, *Typhon*, *Brestois* and *Boulonnais*, which were unable to catch *Strasbourg*, attempted to join forces with the cruisers from Algiers, and ended up entering that port. *Trombe* then sailed for Toulon, arriving 7 July. The new destroyer *Casque*, which damaged a propeller when she was getting underway, had to return to

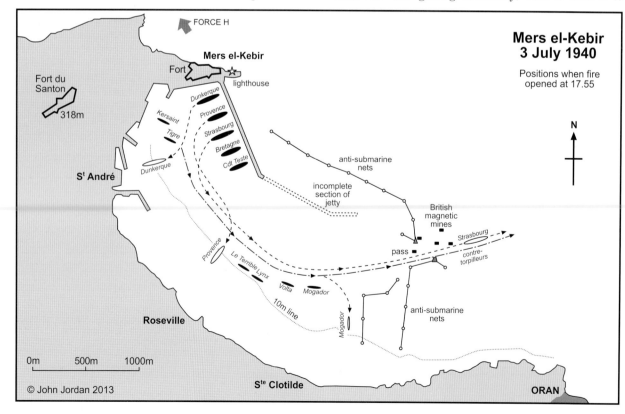

Oran; she left again on 7 July with her sister *Le Corsaire* and headed for Toulon.

The six 7600-ton cruisers and four *contre-torpilleurs* based at Algiers left in the early afternoon of 3 July and first headed for Oran, then attempted to join up with *Strasbourg* following her escape.

On the evening of 3 July the Third Squadron sailed from Toulon with the cruisers *Algérie*, *Foch* and *Colbert*, and the CTs *Vauban*, *Lion*, *Aigle*, *Guépard*, *Valmy*, *Verdun*, *Tartu*, *Le Chevalier Paul*, *Cassard*, *Vautour*, *Gerfaut* and *Albatros*. They joined up with the cruisers from Algiers and, having failed to locate the *Strasbourg*, returned to Toulon, arriving at midday on 4 July.

At Alexandria an agreement between the British Admiral Cunningham and his French counterpart, Rear-Admiral Godfroy, permitted a partial demobilisation of the French ships with reduced crews.

At Dakar, in late June, were the new battleship *Richelieu*, the CTs *Milan* and *Epervier*, the new destroyer *Fleuret*, plus some armed merchant cruisers, sloops and auxiliary vessels. After the events at Mers el-Kebir, one ship was kept on permanent alert in anticipation of a possible British attack on *Richelieu*. On 6 July, there were mutinies on board first *Epervier* then *Milan*, with certain elements refusing to carry out orders to get underway. Some of the crew of *Epervier* disembarked with their kitbags, preventing any departure.

On 8 July *Richelieu* was damaged by a torpedo dropped by a Swordfish from HMS *Hermes*. With *Epervier* temporarily immobilised, *Milan* undertook patrols off the port between 8 July and 14 August.

Epervier, having embarked replacement personnel, left Dakar on 4 August, arriving at Casablanca on the 7th. *Milan* and *Fleuret* also left for Casablanca on 17 August, escorting three passenger ships; they arrived on 23 August.

The new destroyers *Epée* and *Le Hardi* headed in the opposite direction, leaving Casablanca on 28 July for Dakar; they would return to Casablanca on 10 September and 7 October respectively.

DAKAR AND OPERATION 'MENACE'

The events at Mers el-Kebir meant that the complete immobilisation of the fleet prescribed by the armistice convention did not take place.

In the wake of the decision by the countries of French Equatorial Africa (Chad on 26 August, followed by Cameroon on the 27th and Congo on the 28th) to throw in their lot with the Free French of de Gaulle, it was decided to despatch a naval force, designated Force Y, to the Gulf of Guinea; the move was duly authorised by the armistice commission. The force comprised the cruisers *Georges Leygues*, *Montcalm* and *Gloire* (4th DC) and the *contre-torpilleurs* *Le Fantasque*, *Le Malin* and *L'Audacieux* (10th DCT);[1] it left Toulon on 9 September. The ships refuelled at Casablanca, then left immediately for Dakar on the night of 12 September to escape the pursuing battle-cruiser *Renown*, which was reported to have left Gibraltar and to be headed south, accompanied by six destroyers.

The three *contre-torpilleurs* had insufficient fuel to

---

[1] *Le Terrible* was unavailable, so was replaced by *Le Malin* of the 8th DCT.

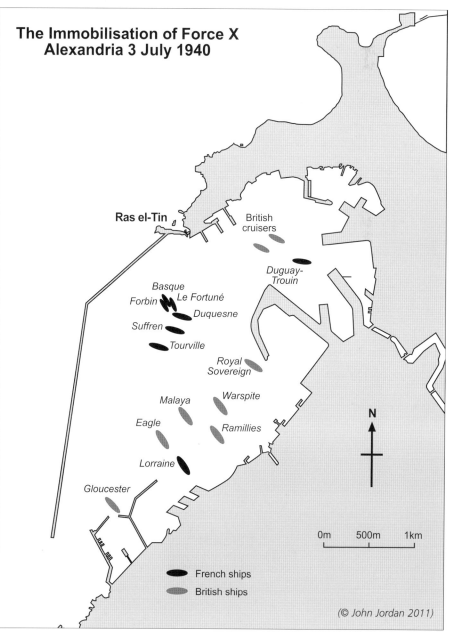

The Immobilisation of Force X
Alexandria 3 July 1940

(© John Jordan 2011)

Opposite: Two views of the wreck of *L'Audacieux*. On the first day of the action she was struck by a salvo of 8-inch shells from the cruiser *Australia*, which detonated the torpedoes in the forward tubes, causing massive fires that burned for two days. She was subsequently salvaged and partially repaired, and in August 1942 arrived at the Sidi-Abdallah Dockyard of Bizerte to be reconstructed, but with the Allied invasion of North Africa she became a constructive total loss.

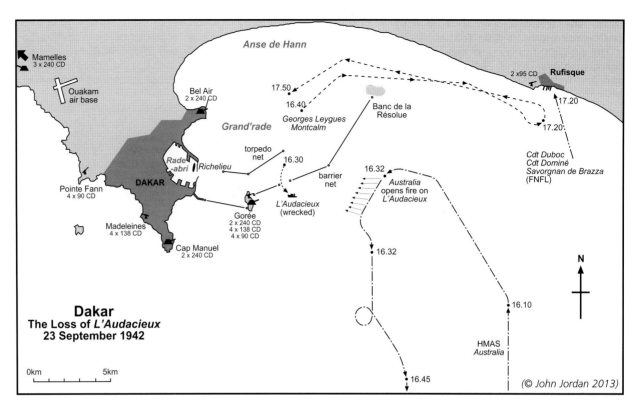

be able to reach Dakar at the 24 knots prescribed by the admiral commanding Force Y, CA Bourragué, and had to return to Casablanca. *L'Audacieux* and *Le Malin* finally reached Dakar on 19 September, and *Le Fantasque*, delayed by machinery problems, arrived the following day.

A large British naval force, accompanied by sloops and transports manned by the Free French, appeared off Dakar on 23 September. Following an abortive attempt by General de Gaulle to rally the garrison to the Free French cause, and the subsequent failure of an attempted landing of troops at Rufisque (see maps), the British force opened fire on the ships in the harbour. The French forces in Dakar resisted, and

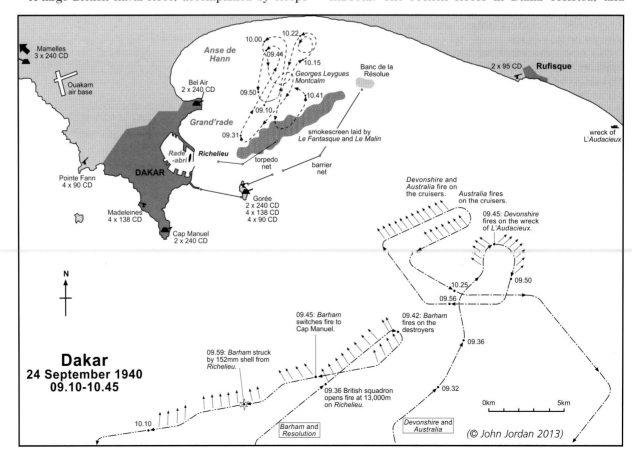

THE PERIOD 1939-1943

responded with fire from the ships in the port and the powerful coastal batteries of 240mm guns.

During the bombardment, the *contre-torpilleurs* and the destroyer *Le Hardi* were tasked with protecting the cruisers *Georges Leygues* and *Montcalm*, which were manoeuvring in the Bay of Hann, by making smoke. In the prevailing foggy conditions *L'Audacieux*, which sortied from the harbour on a reconnaissance mission, was taken under fire at close range by the cruiser *Australia*, which destroyed her bridge with 8-inch (203mm) shell and set her on fire. She lost 81 dead or missing and the wreck, drifting without power, was finally beached close to Rufisque. Meanwhile, *Le Fantasque*, *Le Malin* and *Le Hardi* continued to manoeuvre in the Bay of Hann, making smoke to cover the cruisers.

The Allied assault on Dakar ended with the withdrawal of the British and FNFL ships on 25 September, after the battleship *Resolution* had been torpedoed by the submarine *Bévéziers*.

Le Hardi left Dakar for Casablanca on 30 September. Force Y, which was redesignated the Fourth Squadron on 28 October 1940, remained at Dakar. *Le Terrible* joined the 10th DCT on 26 February 1941 as a replacement for *L'Audacieux*. The latter ship was refloated on 11 March 1941 and patched up sufficiently to undertake a passage to the Mediterranean for more permanent repairs; she left Dakar on 7 August 1942 and arrived at Bizerte on 22 August.

A rolling programme of maintenance for the *contre-torpilleurs* of the Fourth Squadron meant that one of the three ships was generally absent from Dakar. These refit periods were as follows:

Le Malin: from 27 February to 11 July 1941 at Toulon
Le Fantasque: from 20 July 1941 to 27 January 1942 at Oran
Le Terrible: from 31 December 1941 to 14 June 1942 at Toulon
Le Malin: left Dakar on 13 July 1942 for Casablanca – refit never completed (see below)

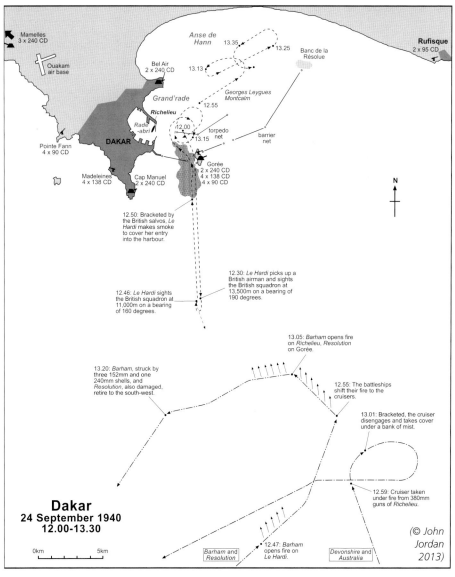

THE *FORCES DE HAUTE MER*

Discussions with the Germans and the Italians, and various proposals for the reorganisation of French naval forces, were on-going at the time of the assault on Dakar. Some ships would remain in commission overseas (at Dakar, Casablanca, Bizerte, Oran, Algiers, Beirut, Saigon, Diego Suarez and Djibouti), and a new independent squadron, designated the *Forces de haute mer* (FHM = 'High Seas Forces'), was constituted at Toulon on 25 September 1940 centred on the battleship *Strasbourg*. Ships which were not incorporated into the FHM or under the command of the local *préfet maritime* were placed in care & maintenance (*en gardiennage d'armistice*), and decommissioned with a skeleton crew. Regular maintenance and partial modernisations (which largely concerned the light AA) were undertaken, despite the limited industrial means available – most of the French weapons and munitions factories were in the occupied zone.

At Toulon the activities of the *Forces de haute mer* were limited in order to save fuel, of which limited stocks remained. In 1941 the FHM was generally restricted to one full sortie a month plus a few training exercises involving divisions or small groups. Each sortie would involve manoeuvres while underway, an overnight stay in the Les Salins anchorage, and further manoeuvres while returning to Toulon.

The first full sortie took place 16–18 October 1940, and involved *Strasbourg*, the cruisers *Algérie*, *Foch*, *Dupleix*, *Marseillaise* and *La Galissonnière*, and the CTs *Aigle*, *Guépard*, *Valmy*, *Cassard*, *Gerfaut*, *L'Indomptable* and *Volta*.

FORCES DE HAUTE MER (TOULON) 25 SEPTEMBER 1940

Strasbourg (Ad. de Laborde)
1re division de croiseurs: *Algérie* (VA Bouxin), *Foch*, *Dupleix*
3e division de croiseurs: *La Marseillaise* (CA Barnaud), *La Galissonnière*
3e escadre légère
   Aigle (CA Jardel)
   3e DCT: *Guépard*, *Valmy*, *Cassard*
   7e DCT: *Vautour*, *Albatros*, *Gerfaut*
   8e DCT: *L'Indomptable*, *Volta*

During October/November five ships of the *Le Hardi* class were despatched to Oran: *Fleuret* arrived on 15 October, *Le Hardi* on 25 October, and *Epée*, *Mameluk* and *Lansquenet* on 5 November. They sailed from Oran on 6 November as escort to the battleship *Provence*, which had been patched up after Mers el-Kebir; they arrived at Toulon on 8 November, having been met by *Strasbourg*, the cruisers *Algérie*, *Foch*, *Dupleix*, *Marseillaise* and *La Galissonnière*, and the CTs *Volta*, *L'Indomptable*, *Cassard* and *Vautour*.

The destroyers of the *Le Hardi* class were now concentrated at Toulon where the 10th DT, formed on 8 August 1940, would henceforth comprise three fully-commissioned ships; the other units of the class, which were in various states of completion, were placed *en gardiennage*.

A rolling programme of refits meant that some ships in care & maintenance were recommissioned to replace others that were undergoing refit or modernisation. *Aigle* and *Gerfaut* left the *Forces de haute mer* on 16 October 1940, followed by *Vautour* on 16 December; all three were placed in care & maintenance. They were replaced by *Tartu*, *Vauquelin* and *Le Chevalier Paul* on 15 November. *Guépard* and *Valmy* left Toulon on 4 November for Beirut. On 17 December *Albatros* left for Morocco to make up a three-ship division with *Milan* and *Epervier*.

Bordelais, *Le Mars* and *La Palme* (1st DT) were incorporated into the FHM on 10 November 1940, but left on 23 January for Bizerte, where they would receive a major AA modernisation; they were refitted in turn so that two ships were generally available at any given time. They were replaced in the FHM by *Tramontane*, *Typhon* and *Tornade* (7th DT) from 1 February to 11 April 1941.

Le Terrible, having completed a major refit, was incorporated into the FHM from 25 December 1940 to 11 February 1941 before sailing for Dakar.

During the spring of 1941, four destroyers of the *Le Hardi* class were rechristened to honour the names of ships lost in the campaign of 1940. *Epée* was renamed *L'Adroit* on 29 March, and on 1 April *Le Corsaire* was

Right: Le Chevalier Paul at Toulon with the Grands Bassins beyond her. The photo was taken before the AA modifications which began on 10 January 1941. There is a 7600-ton cruiser in one of the docks. (Pradignac & Léo collection).

renamed *Siroco*, *Fleuret* became *Foudroyant*, and *Le Flibustier* was renamed *Bison*. *L'Adroit* and *Mameluk* were detached to Morocco on 8 May; *L'Adroit* returned on 25 September, and *Mameluk* on 17 October.

Le Chevalier Paul sailed for Beirut on 11 June 1941, but was sunk by the British before she arrived. She was immediately replaced by *Vauquelin*, which left on 17 June. *Guépard*, *Valmy* and *Vauquelin* returned from the eastern Mediterranean on 19 July. *Vauquelin* rejoined the 5th DCT, and *Guépard* and *Valmy*, forming the 3rd DCT, were integrated into the FHM on 18 August.

Kersaint and *Verdun* recommissioned on 15 June 1941, and formed the 7th DCT with *Gerfaut*, which would join the division on 25 July following a major refit.

Between 30 June and 1 July 1941 the cruiser *Foch* and the CTs *Tartu* and *Cassard* transported from Algiers to Marseille a battalion of infantry destined for the Levant. *Le Hardi* escorted troops from Algiers to Marseille 3–5 July 1941.

Le Hardi was attached to the FHM on 18 August 1941. On 1 November the 1st DT (*Bordelais*, *Le Mars*, *La Palme*) was transferred to the metropolitan police division, and the 10th DT (*L'Adroit*, *Le Hardi*, *Mameluk*) took its place in the FHM. *Le Hardi* was placed *en gardiennage* on 20 May 1942. She was replaced by the newly refitted *Casque*, which was assigned on 1 May, although she was ready for service only on 1 July.

In late 1941 three *contre-torpilleurs* were despatched to Algeria to escort the battleship *Dunkerque*, which was due to return to Toulon after repairs to the damage sustained at Mers el-Kebir. *Kersaint* left Toulon for Algiers on 8 December, followed by *Tartu* on the 10th and *Vauquelin* on the 13th. They returned to Toulon with *Dunkerque* on 20 February 1942.

On 20 July 1942, *Vautour* recommissioned and replaced *Verdun* in the 7th DCT; the latter ship replaced *Valmy*, placed *en gardiennage*, in the 3rd DCT.

THE CAMPAIGN IN SYRIA

In late 1940 the Naval Division of the Levant (DNL) was reinforced by the two *contre-torpilleurs* of the 3rd DCT, *Guépard* and *Valmy*, which arrived at Beirut on 11 November.

On 8 June 1941 the British launched an invasion of Syria and Lebanon, which were held by Vichy forces. News of the British offensive had not reached the French command when *Guépard* and *Valmy* departed Beirut before dawn on 8 June to escort the freighters *Saint Didier* and *Oued Yquem* to the Greek island of Castellorizo. When the British attack was announced, the convoy was rerouted to Tripoli (Lebanon); the two *contre-torpilleurs* then searched in vain for another convoy and returned to Beirut at dawn on 9 June.

After refuelling they again got underway, executed a fire support mission against a British mobile column, then engaged the destroyers *Janus*, *Jackal*, *Hotspur* and *Isis* (see map). *Janus* was damaged and would enter Haifa under tow from the destroyer *Kimberley*, covered by the cruiser *Ajax* and the destroyer *Kandahar*. The two French ships returned to Beirut,

Left: A *contre-torpilleur* of the *Guépard* class, probably *Valmy*, in the port of Beirut in 1940. To the right of the picture: the stern of the minesweeping sloop *Elan*.

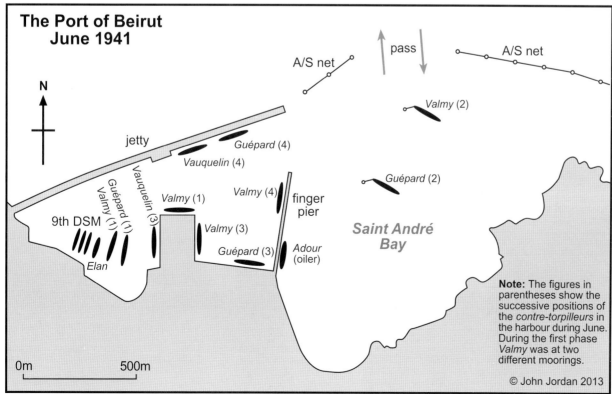

Right: *Valmy* picking up the survivors of *Le Chevalier Paul* following her loss to an aerial torpedo on 15 June.
(Collection René Bail)

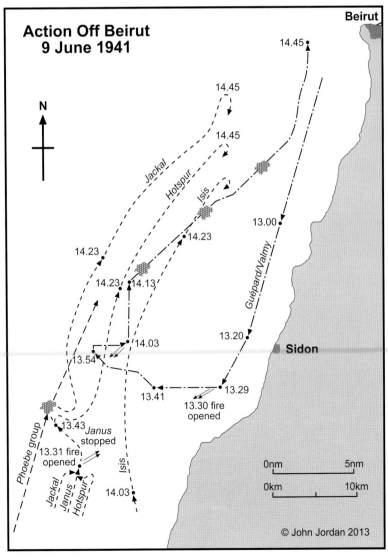

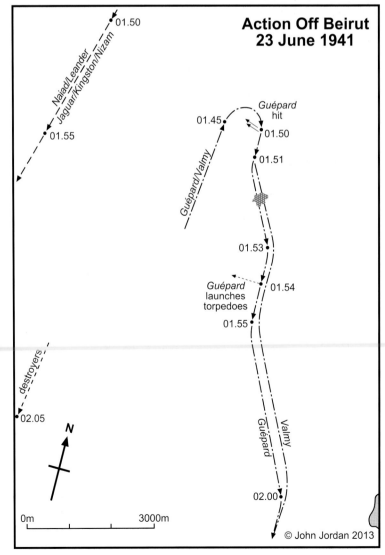

Guépard having been struck on the forecastle by a shell that exploded in seamen's mess no.1.

The French, who had no munitions storage at Beirut, had expended half their 138mm ammunition, so 800 rounds were embarked in *Le Chevalier Paul*, which left Toulon on 11 June to reinforce the DNL.

Guépard and *Valmy*, targeted by British bombers, remained in the port of Beirut or at anchor in the Bay of Djounie, sortieing only to provide fire support for the ground forces. These sorties risked encounters with powerful British naval forces, and combat was only just avoided on 14 June.

On the night of 15/16 June the two *contre-torpilleurs* were off Batroum when they sighted the British cruiser *Leander* in company with the destroyers *Jervis*, *Hasty*, *Ilex* and *Isis*. An exchange of fire was quickly broken off; the French, who were short of ammunition, broke contact and were approaching Beirut when they were ordered to assist *Le Chevalier Paul*. The latter, on her way from Toulon to Beirut with munitions, had been torpedoed by a Swordfish of 815 Squadron off Lattakia (Syria), east of Cyprus. *Guépard* and *Valmy* arrived as *Le Chevalier Paul* was sinking, and rescued the survivors (seven men were unaccounted for).

Vauquelin left Toulon on 17 June to replace *Le Chevalier Paul*. Arriving at Beirut on the 21st, she sustained moderate damage from bomb splinters during an aerial bombardment on the 22nd which left five dead, and was out of action until the 29th.

On the night of 22/23 June, an engagement took place between *Guépard* and *Valmy* and a British naval force which comprised the cruisers *Naiad* and *Leander* and the destroyers *Jaguar*, *Kingston* and *Nizam* (see map). *Guépard* was hit by two 6-inch (152mm) shells, which killed one member of her crew, and the two *contre-torpilleurs* returned to Beirut.

Guépard, *Valmy* and *Vauquelin* departed Beirut on 29 June and on 1 July arrived at Salonika, where they each embarked 150 men from a battalion of Algerian Light Infantry and 30 tonnes of materiel. They left on 5 July for Beirut, but were found by reconnaissance aircraft and reversed course except for *Vauquelin*, which was despatched to the aid of the freighter *Oued Yquem*. The three *contre-torpilleurs* returned to Salonika on the 9th, and from there made their way back to Toulon, arriving on 22 July.

CASABLANCA

After the armistice, Casablanca was the main French port in the Atlantic. Many of the ships which had escaped from the Atlantic ports of metropolitan France, notably the incomplete battleship *Jean Bart*, had fled there. The *contre-torpilleurs* and *torpilleurs d'escadre* based at Casablanca served to protect the maritime traffic between that port and Dakar, and escorted small convoys and valuable ships. Ships in transit between Dakar and the ports of the Mediterranean (see Force X above) also put into Casablanca for a long or short stay.

The period that followed the armistice was marked by several reorganisations of command. On 2 August ships based on Casablanca were placed under the orders of the Navy in Morocco (*Marine au Maroc*). On 18 April 1942, the cruiser *Primauguet* and the destroyers at Morocco would be designated the 2nd Light Squadron.

During the night of 24/25 September 1940, the new destroyers *Fleuret* and *Epée*, together with the older destroyers *Fougueux* and *Frondeur* (2nd DT), sortied from Casablanca for a raid in the Strait of Gibraltar, in retaliation for the British attack on Dakar. They exchanged fire with a British destroyer and went on to Oran. *Epée* and *Frondeur* returned to Casablanca on 30 September, and *Fleuret* on 7 October.

At Casablanca one ship remained on alert and able to get underway within six hours, and all available ships sortied for a group exercise once per month. The most noteworthy event during this period of relative calm was the recapture of the banana boat *Fort de France*, which had been seized by the British AMC *Bulolo* on the evening of 8 April 1941, when the ship was on her way to Casablanca from Martinique. *Fougueux* was sent to the rescue, followed by *Primauguet*, *Albatros*, *Simoun* and *Frondeur*. The *Fort de France* was found and retaken on 12 April, and brought into Casablanca the following morning, the British prize team having been reembarked in *Albatros*.

Above: Shell damage to the *Guépard* following the action of 23 June. She was struck by two 6-inch shells from the British cruiser *Leander* and damaged by a series of near-misses.

Below: Destroyers of the 2nd, 5th and 6th Divisions moored at Casablanca in late 1940. *Simoun* (T61) is in the foreground, sporting the modifications made in August: a shortened foremast, a cowling on the first funnel and antenna supports on the third. Beyond her is *Boulonnais* (T53), as yet largely unmodified. (Marc Saibène collection)

Above: The recently-completed destroyers *L'Adroit* (T101) and *Mameluk* at Casablanca during 1941. They were despatched from Toulon on 8 May; *L'Adroit* left Casablanca on 25 September and arrived back on 4 October, while *Mameluk* left on 17 October and arrived back on 23 October. Beyond the destroyers is the cruiser *Primauguet*, painted in the darker 'Atlantic' grey. (US Navy NH 110752, courtesy of A D Baker III)

Between August 1940 and January 1942, maritime traffic (38 return convoys in all) was reestablished between Casablanca and three of the ports of the occupied zone: Bordeaux, Nantes and La Pallice. The CTs *Milan* and *Albatros*, and the TEs *L'Adroit*, *Fleuret*, *Brestois* and *Fougueux*, together with sloops and patrol boats, played a part in escorting these convoys, generally as far north as the 40th parallel.

Composition of the naval forces at Casablanca

After the movements of ships which resulted from the British aggressions at Mers el-Kebir and Dakar, Casablanca was the base for the cruiser *Primauguet* (flagship), the CTs *Milan*, *Epervier*, *Albatros* (11th DCT) and three 2/3-ship divisions of destroyers. Maintenance was generally carried out at Casablanca, although some ships were sent to Oran or Toulon for docking and refit.

Milan, from Dakar, arrived at Casablanca on 24 August 1940. She was absent from Morocco between 14 December 1940 and 17 April 1941, when she was docked and refitted at Oran. *Epervier*, which had arrived from Dakar on 7 August 1940, left Casablanca on 8 June 1942 for Oran, and would never return. *Albatros*, from Toulon, arrived at Casablanca on 23 December 1940. She was absent from Morocco from 5 June to 25 September 1941 for a major refit which took place at Oran.

Fougueux and *Frondeur* (2nd DT) had been at Casablanca since the armistice. They would be joined on 1 November 1940 by *L'Alcyon* and *Tempête* from Toulon, and by *Brestois*, *Boulonnais* and *Simoun* from Bizerte. These ships would form the 5th and 6th DT.

L'Adroit and *Mameluk* (10th DT) were detached from Toulon to Casablanca from 8 May 1941 to 25 September and 17 October 1941 respectively.

For the *torpilleurs d'escadre*, the periods when they were absent from Casablanca were as follows:

Frondeur: refit Algiers 15 November 1940 to 24 March 1941[2]

Fougueux: refit Toulon 23 November 1940 to 18 March 1941

Brestois: major repairs at Algiers 9 March to 7 July 1941

Boulonnais: major repairs at Oran 20 March to 18 July 1941

L'Alcyon: major refit Algiers 22 June to 12 October 1941

Simoun: refit Bizerte 29 June to 5 October 1941

Tempête: major repairs Algiers 15 September 1941 to 12 January 1942

Frondeur: Oran 12 January 1942, escort of *Dunkerque* from Mers el-Kebir to Toulon 19–20 February 1942, then major refit Algiers; returned to Casablanca 18 June 1942

Fougueux: Oran 6 February 1942, escort of *Dunkerque* from Mers el-Kebir to Toulon 19–20 February 1942, then major refit Oran; returned to Casablanca 21 August 1942

Simoun: detached to Oran as guard ship 16 February to 28 April 1942

L'Alcyon: detached to Oran as guard ship 11 May to 12 June 1942

Boulonnais: detached to Oran as guard ship 18 August to 9 October 1942

Cover for the convoys in the Gibraltar area on the Mediterranean side of the strait was provided by the 7th DT (*Tramontane*, *Typhon*, *Tornade*), which left Bizerte on 15 September and arrived at Oran on 1 October 1942.

THE ALLIED LANDINGS IN NORTH AFRICA

On 8 November 1942 the Allies landed in Morocco, and in the Oran and Algiers areas.

At Casablanca the 2nd Light Squadron got underway at dawn. *Primauguet* was initially unavailable because she had been undergoing maintenance on her machinery, and the destroyers *Simoun* and *Tempête* were still under repair following a collision on 8 September. The squadron headed for the American transports anchored off Fedala with *Milan* (flying the flag of Rear-Admiral Gervais de Lafond), *Albatros*, *Brestois*, *Boulonnais*, *Fougueux*, *Frondeur* and *L'Alcyon*. They ran into the cruisers *Brooklyn* (CL-40) and *Augusta* (CA-31), which were providing fire support and protection for the transports, and the destroyers *Wilkes* (DD-441), *Ludlow* (DD-468) and *Swanson* (DD-443).

The French ships, which were later joined by the *Primauguet*, manoeuvred between the entrance of the port of Casablanca and Fedala (see map), under fire from the American cruisers and under attack from American aircraft, which dropped bombs and strafed their bridges with machine gun fire. They were also engaged by the US Navy covering group comprising the battleship *Massachussetts* (BB-59) and the cruisers *Tuscaloosa* (CA-37) and *Wichita* (CA-45).

2nd LIGHT SQUADRON (CASABLANCA)

2e escadre légère (Casablanca) 25 May 1942
Primauguet (CA Gervais de Lafond)
11e DCT: *Milan*, *Epervier*, *Albatros*
5e DT: *Brestois*, *Boulonnais*
6e DT: *Tempête*, *Simoun* (not in service – personnel manning patrol boats *L'Algéroise* et *La Servannaise*)
Detached to Oran: *L'Alcyon* (from 8 May)
Refit: *Fougueux* (Oran), *Frondeur* (Alger)

2e escadre légère (Casablanca) 8 November 1942
Primauguet (CA Gervais de Lafond)
11e DCT: *Milan*, *Albatros*
2e DT: *Fougueux*, *Frondeur*, *Alcyon*
5e DT: *Brestois*, *Boulonnais*
6e DT: *Tempête*, *Simoun* (both under repair following collision)
Detached to Oran: *Epervier*

---

[2] The first date is that of the departure from Casablanca, the second is the date of return.

THE PERIOD 1939-1943

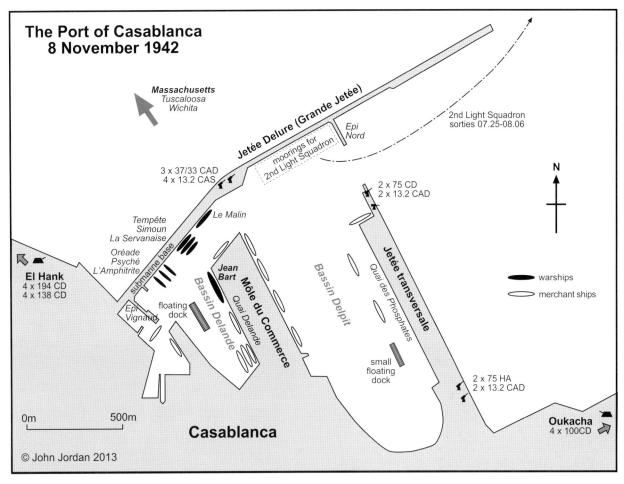

Below: The aftermath of the battle: the *contre-torpilleur* Albatros is in the foreground, with the cruiser Primauguet beyond her stern; both have been beached in the approaches to the harbour. Albatros has lost her third funnel, while Primauguet is burnt out. *(US Navy 80-G-30649, courtesy of A D Baker III)*

Above: *Le Malin* (centre) has a large hole in her side amidships, caused by a 16in (406mm) shell from the battleship *Massachusetts* which hit the edge of the quay and exploded alongside the ship. In this photo, taken a week after the event, she has been turned so that the damage is facing outboard. Extensive damage is also visible on the shore at the right of the picture. At left, the stern of *L'Alcyon*, with the bow of the APV *L'Algéroise* (W66) outboard. (US Navy 80-G-31608, courtesy of A D Baker III)

Right: The *contre-torpilleur* *Milan* beached in the approaches to Casablanca harbour. She was struck by a 16-inch shell from the battleship *Massachusetts* during the battle of 8 November, and her forward structure has been largely burnt out. The photo was taken on 16 November. (US Navy 80-G-31610, courtesy of A D Baker III)

Primauguet, hit by shells and bombs, was beached near the entrance of the port, in front of the Roches Noires. Burnt out, she was a constructive total loss. *Milan* was struck by a 16-inch (406mm) shell, then by two smaller-calibre shells. Fires raged in the fore part of the ship, which was also beached on the beach of Roches Noires; she lost 31 men. *Albatros*, hit by two SBD Dauntless bombs, managed to moor off the coast near Oukacha. She was then struck by two 8-inch (203mm) shells from *Augusta*, and was finally beached close to *Primauguet* and *Milan* (see photos); she had lost 14 men.

Of the destroyers, *Fougueux* was hit forward by a salvo from one of the cruisers[3] and sank rapidly; she lost 14 men. *Frondeur* was riddled with splinters from an 8-inch gun salvo, then struck by a shell. She began to sink but managed to return to the port with the loss of 14 men; she eventually capsized in the Delpit Basin. *L'Alcyon*, damaged by bombs which fell close to her side, was shelled by *Brooklyn* and then machine-gunned by fighters. Her four 130mm guns were put out of action, and she returned to the port, where she moored that evening; she had lost five men. *Boulonnais* was struck by six 6-inch (152mm) shells from *Brooklyn*. She capsized and sank; she lost 13 killed or missing, presumed dead. Finally *Brestois*, seriously damaged, moored at the Delure jetty with a list of 12°, and capsized that evening; nine of her crew were lost.

In the port of Casablanca, *Simoun* and *Tempête* were moored alongside the Delure jetty. *Simoun* was damaged by two bombs and was moved to the outer anchorage; she lost three men. *Tempête*, damaged by

---

[3] It has not been possible to determine whether the salvo was fired by *Massachusetts*, *Tuscaloosa* or *Augusta*. In fact it has proved impossible to determine with any degree of certainty the origin of the shells which struck the ships of the 2nd Light Squadron. However, the majority were undoubtedly fired by *Tuscaloosa* and *Wichita*.

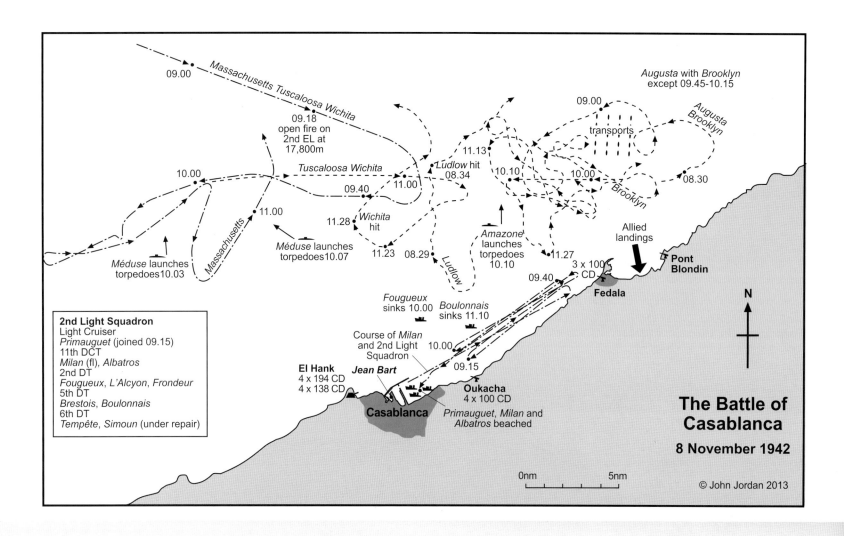

splinters, suffered the loss of five men, and sank to the bottom of the Delpit Basin on the evening of 8 November. The *contre-torpilleur Le Malin*, which was completing a major refit, was also moored alongside the Delure jetty. She was damaged by a 16-inch shell that hit the edge of the quay and exploded alongside the ship, tearing a large hole in her port side (see photo). The forward boiler and engine rooms were flooded and she lost seven men.

Meanwhile, at Oran, the escort sloops *Walney* and *Hartland* attempted to land commandos in the port. *Epervier*, which was in the final stages of a long refit, opened fire on the *Walney*, which had forced an entry into the port. *Walney* was set on fire and capsized with heavy loss of life, while *Hartland* was set on fire by the destroyer *Typhon* and blew up.

The 7th DT (*Tramontane, Typhon* and *Tornade*) then got underway to attack enemy forces in the Bay of Arzew, to the northeast of Oran. *Tornade* was in the lead but, hindered by the smoke, ploughed into the rocks at the base of the dyke and damaged her bows. *Tramontane* then came under fire from the British cruiser *Aurora*, which landed shells on first no.1, then no.2 mounting. Drifting, and on fire forward, the destroyer was extricated with the help of *Typhon* and, taken under tow by the tug *Cotentin*, was beached in the Bay of Kristel (see map).

Typhon fired two torpedoes at *Aurora*, went alongside *Tramontane* to recover survivors, then followed *Typhon* which had just sortied from Oran. The two destroyers were taken under fire by *Aurora* and the destroyer *Calpe*. *Tornade*, which launched all six of her torpedoes against *Aurora*, was hit by at least six 6-inch (152mm) shells. With ammunition running low – there were only 30 rounds remaining in her magazines – and with her rudder jammed, she drifted towards land and capsized near Cap de l'Aiguille. *Typhon*, out of torpedoes, with only half her 130mm ammunition remaining and with the survivors of the *Tramontane* on board, returned to Oran to top up her magazines.

Epervier, which was at last available for action, left with *Typhon* for Toulon the following day (9 November). However, the ships soon encountered the British cruisers *Aurora* and *Jamaica*, which outgunned them by a considerable margin. *Epervier*, which fired off almost 200 138mm rounds, sustained at least eight 6-inch shell hits. On fire, she was beached near Cap de l'Aiguille. *Typhon*, which fired on *Jamaica*, was beaten off and returned to Oran, scuttling herself in the pass the following day, 10 November.

Opposite, bottom: The *contre-torpilleur Albatros* beached off Casablanca on 16 November. She was struck by two bombs during the battle of 8 November. Her third funnel has been completely destroyed and the fourth badly damaged, and her port side is heavily stained with oil fuel. *(US Navy 80-G-31611, courtesy of A D Baker III)*

Below: The destroyer *Tempête* alongside at Casablanca. She and her sister *Simoun* had been involved in a collision on 8 September and were unable to take part in the actions of 8 November 1942. *Tempête* was near-missed by a bomb. *(US Navy 80-G-31528)*

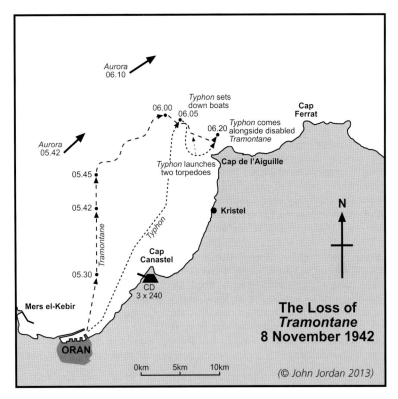

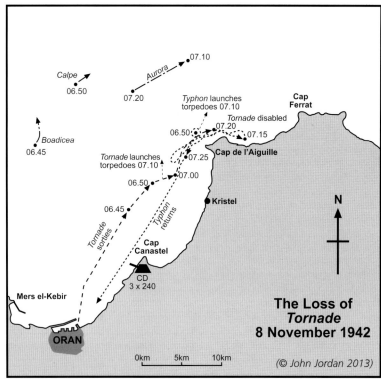

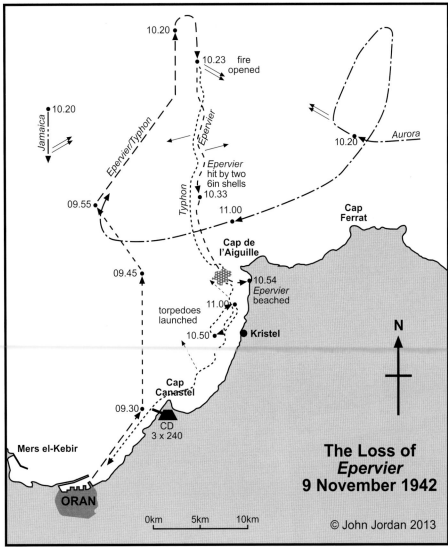

THE SCUTTLING OF THE FLEET AT TOULON

When the German columns arrived at Toulon before dawn on 27 November 1942, there were eighteen *contre-torpilleurs* and eight *torpilleurs d'escadre* in the port, of which eight *contre-torpilleurs* and six *torpilleurs* were in care & maintenance (*en gardiennage*).

The 'active' ships, with full crews on board despite some reassignment of personnel to ships serving overseas, were all scuttled. Two *contre-torpilleurs* (*Tigre* and *Panthère*) and two *torpilleurs* (*Trombe* and the incomplete *Bison*), which were in care & maintenance with only skeleton crews on board and which received the order to scuttle too late, were seized intact by the Germans, and *Lion*, which was in dock, was able to sabotage only her guns.

The fate of the ships at Toulon was as follows:

Volta: sunk at the Quai Noël (see map). Refloated on 20 May 1943, she was rated a constructive total loss. Damaged by bombing in 1944, she foundered; she was refloated in 1948 and broken up.

L'Indomptable: sunk at the Quai Noël. The Germans considered salvaging her for a time and rechristened her *SG9*, but she was damaged by the Allied bombings of 4 February, 7 March and 29 April 1944, and was rated a constructive total loss. Her bow was recovered to repair *Le Malin* in 1945. The remains of the wreck were demolished *in situ* in 1950.

Guépard: sunk at the Quai Noël. She was raised on 4 September 1943, hit by Allied bombs during the raids of 7 and 11 March 1944, and capsized and sank on the 15th. She was refloated in 1947 and scrapped.

Verdun: sunk at the Quai de l'Artillerie (see map). Raised on 29 September 1943, she was damaged by Allied bombs on 7 and 11 March 1944, and capsized. She was refloated in 1948 and broken up at Savone.

Gerfaut: undergoing refit, she was sunk in the Missiessy Basin. She was refloated on 1 June 1943, but was rated a constructive total loss. Demolition of

THE PERIOD 1939-1943

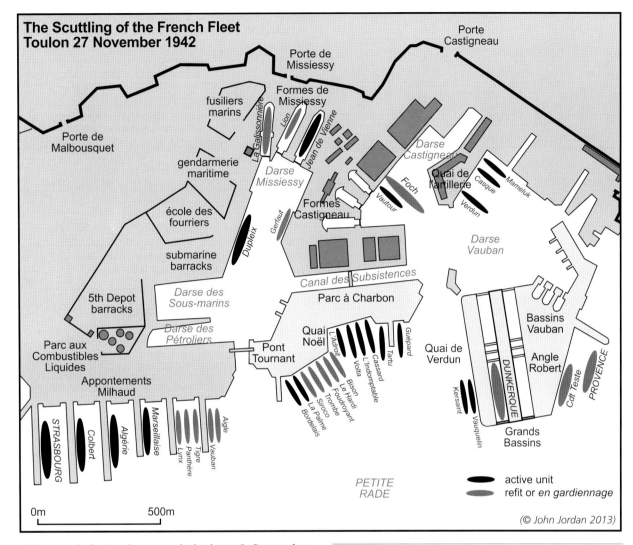

the wreck began but was halted on 9 September 1943. She was sunk by bombs on 7 March 1944, and the wreck was demolished in 1948.

Cassard: sunk at the Quai Noël. An attempted salvage, begun in late 1943, was halted. She was struck by a bomb on 7 March 1944. The wreck was demolished *in situ* in 1950.

Vautour: sunk in the Castigneau Basin. She was refloated on 17 July 1943, but sank again on 24 November and was again struck by a bomb on 23 April 1944. Demolition of the wreck *in situ* was completed in 1951.

Tartu: sunk at the Quai Noël. Attempts to refloat her were abandoned on 11 December 1943. She was then hit by bombs during the raids of 7 and 11 March and 29 April 1944, and demolished *in situ* in 1956.

Vauquelin: sunk at the West Quay of the *Grands Bassins*. Salvaging operations were quickly abandoned. She was struck by a bomb, and the wreck was demolished *in situ* in 1951.

Kersaint: moored alongside *Vauquelin*, she was also sunk at the West Quay of the *Grands Bassins*. Salvaging operations were quickly abandoned and the wreck was demolished *in situ* in 1950.

L'Adroit: sunk at the Quai Noël. She was refloated on 20 April 1943, became the Italian *FR33*, and was damaged in the Allied bombing raids of 24 November 1943 and 4 February 1944. She was again refloated in September 1945 and broken up.

FORCES DE HAUTE MER (TOULON) 8 NOVEMBRE 1942

Strasbourg (Amiral de Laborde)
1re escadre de croiseurs :
    1re DC: *Algérie* (VAE Lacroix), *Dupleix*, *Colbert*
    3e DC: *Marseillaise* (CA Bléhaut), *Jean de Vienne*
3e escadre légère :
    6e DCT: *Volta* (CA Négadelle), *L'Indomptable*
    5e DCT: *Tartu*, *Vauquelin*, *Kersaint*
    7e DCT: *Gerfaut*, *Cassard*, *Vautour*
    8e DCT: *Guépard*, *Verdun*
    10e DT: *L'Adroit*, *Mameluk*, *Casque*

Left: *Vautour*, scuttled at the Quai des Machines in the Castigneau basin.

Above: *Lion* was in Missiessy dock no.2 when the Germans entered the dockyard; only her guns were sabotaged. In the background, *La Galissonnière* is in dock no.3.

Below: *Valmy* (left) and *Mogador* scuttled at the quayside of the La Seyne shipyard.

Below, right: *Le Mars*, scuttled in the Petite Rade. She capsized to starboard and would subsequently sink. Note the pairs of depth charge throwers for 100kg DCs on either side of the stern. *(US Navy NH110743, courtesy of A D Baker III)*

Mameluk: sunk at the Quai de l'Artillerie. Salvage operations were interrupted; she was then damaged by a bomb on 4 February 1944. She was finally refloated in 1947 and broken up.

Casque: sunk at the Quai de l'Artillerie. Salvage operations were interrupted, then abandoned following damage sustained in the Allied bombing raid of 29 April 1944. The wreck was raised in 1948 and broken up at Port de Bouc.

Bordelais: sunk at the Quai Noël. Salvage work was begun in 1944 but was abandoned, and the wreck was demolished *in situ* in 1950.

Le Mars: sunk in the *Petite Rade*, near Lazaret. She was refloated on 6 March 1944 and beached at Brégaillon. She was again refloated in 1947 and broken up.

La Palme: sunk at the Quai Noël. She was refloated on 26 December 1943 and beached at Brégaillon. She was again refloated in 1947 and broken up.

Tigre: *en gardiennage*, seized intact at the Milhaud piers. She became the Italian *FR23* and left Toulon on 13 April 1943 for Taranto. She was still not operational in September 1943, and was handed back to the French Navy on 28 October 1943.

Lynx: *en gardiennage*, scuttled at the Milhaud piers. She was raised on 23 January 1944 and beached at Brégaillon. She was refloated in 1948 and broken up.

Panthère: *en gardiennage*, seized intact at the Milhaud piers. She became the Italian *FR22* and left Toulon on 23 March 1943. She was scuttled by the Italians at La Spezia on 9 September 1943.

Lion: *en gardiennage*, in one of the Missiessy docks; only the guns were sabotaged. She left the dock on 9 February 1943 and became the Italian *FR21*; she was rearmed with three 138mm guns from *Valmy*. She left Toulon for Italy on 16 April 1943, but was scuttled at La Spezia on 9 September 1943. Refloated by the Germans in 1944, she was again sunk in a bombing raid in 1944.

Valmy: *en gardiennage*, sunk at La Seyne but otherwise undamaged. She was refloated on 15 March 1943. She became the Italian *FR24*, and left Toulon under tow on 6 July 1943. Her wreck was found at Genoa in 1945.

Aigle: *en gardiennage*, sunk at the Milhaud piers. She was refloated on 10 July 1943 but was sunk again on 24 November, and was again hit by bombs on 29 April 1944. The wreck was demolished in 1952.

Vauban: *en gardiennage*, sunk at the Milhaud piers. Salvage operations were halted once her poor condition became apparent. She was further damaged by bombs on 24 November 1943 and 7 March 1944. She was raised on 12 May 1947 and broken up.

Mogador: *en gardiennage* while undergoing repairs, sunk at La Seyne. She was refloated on 5 April 1943, damaged by a bomb on 29 April, then again on 4 May 1944. She was beached at Brégaillon and refloated in 1949 for breaking up.

Lansquenet: *en gardiennage*, sunk at La Seyne. She was refloated on 24 April 1943. She left Toulon on 30 April 1943 and became the Italian *FR34* at Imperia, then the German *TA34*. Scuttled at Genoa, she was raised and towed to Toulon on 19 March 1946. She was then renamed *Cyclone*, and was stricken only on 22 September 1958 without ever having been repaired.

Le Hardi: *en gardiennage*, sunk at the Quai Noël. She was raised on 12 June 1943, became the Italian *FR37*, and was towed to Genoa on 6 September 1943. She was scuttled at Genoa on 20 April 1945.

Foudroyant: *en gardiennage*, sunk at the Quai Noël. Raised on 20 May 1943, she became the Italian *FR36*. She was damaged by a bomb on 7 March 1944, and on 17 August 1944 was scuttled in the

main pass. She was refloated in 1951 and broken up in 1957.

Siroco: *en gardiennage*, sunk at the Quai Noël. She was refloated on 16 April 1943, became the Italian *FR32* and was towed to Genoa on 10 June 1943. She was scuttled at Genoa on 20 October 1944.

Bison: incomplete, seized intact at the Quai Noël. A request by the Germans for her completion was rejected, and she became the Italian *FR35*. Utilised as a smoke pontoon by the Germans, she was damaged in an Allied bombing raid, then by a collision with a submarine on 25 June 1944. She sank at Brégaillon, was refloated in 1945 and broken up.

Trombe: *en gardiennage*, seized intact. She became the Italian *FR31* and left Toulon for La Spezia on 13 April 1943. She was then transferred to Taranto, running aground on 2 May 1943 on Ginosa beach, close to the Italian port. She was still being repaired at Taranto in September 1943.

Most of these ships were seized by the Germans, then handed over to the Italians, then again seized by the Germans on 9 September 1943. *FR21* (ex-*Lion*), *FR22* (ex-*Panthère*) and *FR23* (ex-*Tigre*) were to have formed the 21st destroyer division at Taranto to undertake rapid transport missions. In fact, despite the effort involved in their salvage and repair, not one of the French *contre-torpilleurs* and *torpilleurs* was ever fully operational with either the Germans or the Italians.

With the exception of *Tigre* and *Trombe*, which were

Left: Toulon under air attack from Allied bombers on 4 February 1944. The bombers arrived in two waves of 38 and 29 aircraft respectively. The Quai Noël is in the centre in the upper part of the photograph. *(USAF 27450, courtesy of A D Baker III)*

rearmed by the Italians and retroceded in late 1943, none of these ships would ever again serve in the French Marine Nationale.

THE FORCES NAVALES FRANÇAISES LIBRES (FNFL)

The British transferred most of the ships seized on 3 July 1940 (Operation 'Catapult') to the Free French Naval Forces (FNFL). The two *contre-torpilleurs* were refitted – both were under repair or had suffered damage – and recommissioned, not without difficulty, notably because of differences in machine tooling, materials, units of measurement and language.

Le Triomphant

Le Triomphant, which had been evacuated from Lorient, was recommissioned on 23 October 1940, but was not ready for sea until November. She was assigned to the 11th Escort Group on the Clyde, but constant problems with her machinery and shafts, together with a collision when she broke loose from her moorings at Greenock during a gale, meant that she was under near-constant repair at Glasgow and Devonport, culminating in a major refit at Devonport from May to July 1941 (see p.253). She finally left Plymouth on 31 July for the Pacific via the Panama Canal and San Diego, with a view to her eventual deployment to the Mediterranean.[4]

Le Triomphant arrived at Papeete (Tahiti) on 23 September. With the outbreak of war in the Pacific, she was assigned to the ABDA command under the C-in-C Eastern Fleet. She took part in the evacuation of Nauru on 24 February 1942, and undertook numerous escort missions in Australasian waters. Immobilised at Sydney from 19 March 1942 to 20 January 1943, when her boilers were retubed and her light AA armament upgraded, she was employed for escort missions from late January to September 1943, and underwent a further refit at Sydney from 8 September to 7 November 1943. She was finally due to deploy to the Mediterranean, and left Fremantle for Madagascar on 25 November 1943 with the oiler *Cedar Mills*. In the course of an underway replenishment, an accident with the transfer gear meant that replenishment had to be halted when the *contre-torpilleur* had only 170 tonnes of fuel in her tanks. She was therefore taken under tow to save fuel, and an *ad hoc* repair meant that she was again able to top up on 1 December. During the night of 2/3 December she was disabled by a typhoon. She had a permanent list of 15 degrees which in the heavy seas attained a maximum of 50 degrees. There was water ingress into the after boiler room and the forward boiler and engine rooms were flooded. Some of the crew were taken off, and on 5 December the ship was taken under tow with considerable difficulty by the oiler. Le Triomphant finally arrived at Diego Suarez (Madagascar) on 19 December under tow from the British cruiser *Frobisher*. Repairs sufficient to make her seaworthy were carried out at the dockyard and she sailed on 21 February 1944 for Boston, via Bizerte and Algiers, arriving on 12 April 1944. Repairs would take the best part of a year, and Le Triomphant was again ready for service only in April 1945.

Léopard

Léopard was recommissioned on 20 November 1940. She undertook convoy escort missions in the North Atlantic, then was extensively refitted from 8 May 1941 to 5 May 1942 (see p.251). She was due to join Le Triomphant in the Pacific via the Indian Ocean. Léopard was escorting a convoy from Greenock to Freetown (Sierra Leone) when she took part in the destruction of *U-136* (Type VIIC) with the British frigate *Spey* and the sloop *Pelican* to the west of Madeira. The following night, Léopard was damaged (bow stove in) when she collided with the sloop *Lowestoft*. She was repaired at Simonstown and at Cape Town in September-October. She rallied the island of La Réunion to the Free French cause on 27 November 1942, then undertook escort work in the Madagascar area.

She arrived at Alexandria on 12 May 1943 and went on to Malta, departing on 24 May with a convoy destined for Alexandria. Aerial attacks disrupted the passage of the convoy and Léopard, the escort ship stationed farthest to the south, grounded just before dawn during the night of 27 May to the northeast of Benghazi. Attempts to refloat her failed and the wreck, which broke in two on 19 June, was abandoned on 1 July.

Mistral and Ouragan

The destroyer Mistral, taken over by the Royal Navy, recommissioned on 12 November with the pendant number H03. She undertook local escort missions between the south of England and Ireland. She was taken in hand at Cardiff from 20 April to 3 May 1941, when her original armament was replaced by 4.7-inch (120mm) guns and British-model depth charge rails and throwers. She then served as a gunnery training ship. She underwent a major refit from November 1942 to December 1943 in which her armament was further modified, then escorted convoys in the Western Approaches; she was involved in a hunt for a German U-boat on 15 January 1945. She was handed back to the French Marine Nationale on 24 August 1945 at Portsmouth.

Her sister Ouragan, also seized by the British, recommissioned with a Polish crew as H16.[5] She received an armament similar to that of Mistral, but machinery problems meant that she was again ready for active service only on 2 January 1941. She joined the Western Approaches escort group, but was still handicapped by machinery problems, and she was finally transferred to the FNFL on 30 April 1941. Because of the poor state of her boilers she was employed as an accommodation ship at Portsmouth, before being placed in special reserve in December 1942. A British plan to convert her into a target ship was abandoned on 8 October 1943, and Ouragan was again handed over to the French, but never recommissioned. She was towed to Cherbourg in September 1945.

The FNFL would also man nine 'Flower' class corvettes transferred from the Royal Navy and completed between May 1941 and May 1942 (see p.265); these ships would play an important part in the Atlantic convoys.

---

[4] The reasons for this tortuous itinerary were political rather than operational.

[5] This was done with the full consent of the Free French authorities, who had insufficient willing volunteers available to man all the ships seized by the British.

APPENDIX B: *LÉOPARD* FNFL 1940–1943

IN JUNE 1940 *LÉOPARD*, TOGETHER WITH A number of other French ships in UK ports, was seized by the British. This was a difficult time for Britain. The Royal Dockyards were overloaded, and industrial output was lagging behind the country's increasingly urgent needs, so the only materiel available to equip the ship for anti-submarine duties in the Western Approaches was elderly weaponry stored in the naval depots.

Léopard entered service at Portsmouth with the FNFL on 3 September, and from that date until November 1940 the ship was docked for repairs following the bomb damage sustained during the Dunkirk evacuation and the sabotage inflicted by the ship's crew on the fire control computer in the transmitting station. The damaged hull plating was replaced, and leaks in steam collector no.1 sealed. *Léopard* had already been fitted with Asdic 128 at Cherbourg in February 1940, and as it was intended to deploy her for anti-submarine escort duties in the Western Approaches, the following modifications were now made with a view to enhancing her air defence capabilities:

- a single 4-inch Mk V gun on a Mk IV HA mounting (80° elevation) was fitted in the position origin-ally occupied by no.3 138mm gun, and currently by two of the four 13.2mm Hotchkiss CAD mountings
- two of the four 13.2mm Hotchkiss CAD mountings were relocated abeam the first funnel on platforms projecting from the sides of the forward deckhouse, the 5-metre dinghies formerly carried in the two outer positions being disembarked
- the two forecastle 13.2mm CAD were landed, and were replaced by Vickers 2pdr single Mk II pom-poms, which were installed on new platforms abeam the bridge structure. The French 1-metre HA rangefinder was moved to a platform atop the after ammunition distribution station; a third Vickers Mk II pom-pom would later occupy this position
- a degaussing cable was fitted (it is possible this had been fitted at Cherbourg in April 1940)
- the ship was initially repainted in Admiralty 516B dark grey (Home Fleet colours) with a false bow wave. In January 1941 this was replaced by a 'Western Approaches' scheme: blue and light green regular panels on a white background

Following a winter spent on convoy duties in the Western Approaches, *Léopard* was in need of serious maintenance, the limited endurance of the French ships was also highlighted by this arduous work, and from 8 May 1941 *Léopard* underwent a major refit and reconstruction at Hull. The refit was scheduled to last three and a half months; in the event it took a whole year. The boilers had to be completely retubed, and an anti-submarine conversion similar to that of the elderly 'V' and 'W' classes was carried out. The following modifications were made:

- the forward boiler and its associated funnel were removed. Compartment 'E' was thereby freed up completely for additional fuel bunkerage and accommodation for the crew. There was now a central transverse fuel bunker holding 200 tonnes of fuel oil, and conversion of half the reserve feed water (RFW) wing tanks provided a further 50 tonnes capacity. The total fuel load was now 780 tonnes, for a range of 4200nm on cruise turbines. The lower seamen's mess was extended aft beneath the main deck above the new fuel bunkers to provide additional accommodation. The complement was now 234 men (plus officers)
- the light anti-aircraft armament was enhanced and reorganised. The two Vickers 2pdr Mk II pom-poms on the platforms abeam the bridge were relocated to the upper deck amidships, using the seatings for the 75mm HA carried when first built, and a third was located atop the platform above the after hoists. Three 20mm Mk II single Oerlikons were fitted: two on the bridge side platforms, and the third on the centre deckhouse in place of the 4-inch Mk V gun. There were also two twin Vickers .5-inch Mk III machine guns on platforms either side of the forward deckhouse, two French 8mm Hotchkiss MG in the bridge wings, and two .303 Lewis MG in a twin mounting on the quarterdeck
- the original depth charge chutes aft and their associated chain mechanism, which had proved prone to electrical and mechanical failure in the severe weather conditions prevailing in the North Atlantic, were suppressed. In their place were two simple British-style rails each holding twelve Mk VIIH 'heavy' depth charges (weight 251kg; charge 132kg amatol), with a further four 'reserve' charges in the magazine aft. In order to accommodate the DC rails without obstructing the after gun and quarterdeck machinery an extension was built out above the stern (see drawing), completely altering the ship's silhouette
- four of the latest Thornycroft Mk IV depth charge throwers, which had a range of 60 metres and featured a piston-type non-expendable arbor, replaced the original pair of 240mm Mle 1918 mortars. They were located, like the French models, between the centre and after deckhouses. A total of 24 Mk VII 'light' depth charges (weight 191kg; charge as Mk VIIH) was carried: four on the mortars, twelve (4 x 3) on adjacent 'parbuckle'-type stowage racks, and eight in reserve
- the antenna for a Type 291 radar was fitted atop a shortened topmast; the radar plot was accommodated in the forward deckhouse in place of the former uptakes for BR1. Type 291 was the latest British small-ship P-Band surveillance radar; typical ranges were 9nm on a battleship, 6nm on a destroyer, 3nm on a submarine, and 15–35nm on an aircraft
- the after triple torpedo mounting was disembarked, as was the 7-metre motor launch, leaving only the 7-metre motor boat (relocated

Léopard May 1942

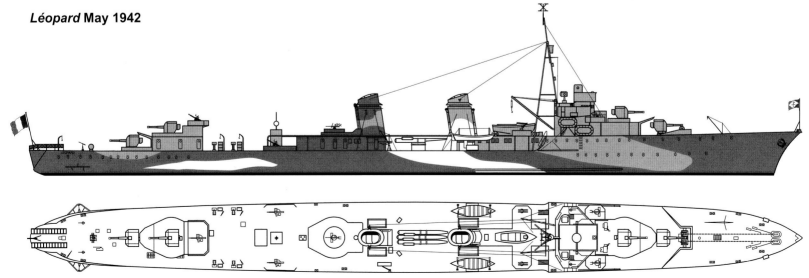

(© John Jordan 2013)

on the centreline of the forward deckhouse) and the two boats on davits. This was insufficient to compensate for the weight additions, so 100 tonnes of lead ballast was now carried in the bottom tanks to restore stability
- an Admiralty 'Disruptive, Medium' paint-scheme was applied using three tones of grey. The design appears to have been specially developed for Léopard and was symmetrical on both sides

Displacement was now 3500 tonnes in 'normal' condition, an increase of 50% over that of the ship when first completed. Despite this, Léopard achieved a maximum speed of 31.5 knots on her post-refit trials, and comfortably sustained 30 knots in service until her loss.

Above: Léopard at Hull on 6 May 1942 following her major refit in the UK. Her silhouette has changed considerably with the removal of the first funnel. She is wearing an Admiralty 'Disruptive, Medium' camouflage which is identical on both sides. *(US Navy NH 89001, courtesy of A D Baker III)*

Above: A stern quarter view of Léopard at Hull taken on the same day, showing many of the detailed modifications. The single 2pdr on a platform atop the after hoists is particularly prominent, as is the 20mm Oerlikon mounted in place of gun no.3, abaft the second funnel. In place of the after torpedo mounting there are four Mk IV DCTs with stowage racks for additional charges. Note the remodelled stern: the original depth charge chutes have been suppressed and in their place are two 12-charge rails for Mk VIIH 'heavy' depth charges. *(US Navy NH 89002, courtesy of A D Baker III)*

APPENDIX C: *LE TRIOMPHANT* FNFL 1940–1944

IN JUNE 1940 *LE TRIOMPHANT*, TOGETHER WITH a number of other French ships in UK ports, was seized by the British. Maintenance and modernisation were hampered by the same factors which affected *Léopard* (q.v.).

During a short refit at Devonport from September to December 1940 the following modifications were made with a view to enhancing anti-submarine and air defence capabilities:

- no.4 138mm gun was replaced by a single 4-inch Mk V gun on a Mk III HA mounting (80° elevation); no fire control was provided
- two .303in (7.62mm) Lewis machine guns were fitted atop the after ammunition hoists
- Asdic 128 (removed from a French *torpilleur*) was installed
- four French 240mm Mle 1918 anti-submarine mortars (from Patrol Vessels) were bolted onto the upper deck abeam the after deckhouse; there were two reloads per mortar in adjacent racks, and a further eighteen 100kg depth charges were stowed in the DC magazine in place of the original 35kg depth charges, which were disembarked. The new depth charge complement permitted six attacks each of eight 200kg depth charges (from the stern chutes) and four 100kg depth charges (from the mortars)
- the torpedo rangefinder was given a roof to protect the crew from the elements
- the ship was repainted in Admiralty 516B dark grey (Home Fleet colours); she was allocated the pendant number H02, but this was not painted on the hull and the ship's boats retained the French tactical number X83

In April 1940, when *Le Triomphant* was operating

Above: Le Triomphant at Plymouth following her refit at Devonport Naval Dockyard, May–July 1941. Note the 4-inch Mk V HA gun in place of no.4 gun, the Thornycroft depth charge throwers abeam the after deckhouse, and the two 9-charge rails for Mk VIIH 'heavy' depth charge rails above the stern. There is an aerial for a Type 296M air search radar atop the foremast, and the torpedo rangefinder has been disembarked; in its place there is a crow's nest. *(Stephen Johnston, CyberHeritage International)*

from Glasgow during the Norwegian campaign, she was given a Mountbatten Pink livery. She carried this for only a short period, as from May to July 1941 she was again refitted at Devonport, when the following modifications were made:

- a Type 286M radar was installed, with a fixed aerial at the masthead. Type 286M was an early air/surface surveillance radar derived from the ASV Mk II, and was fitted in RN destroyers from 1940 onwards. Operating on a 1.5-metre wavelength, its fixed aerial could detect ships and aircraft on forward bearings 50° either side of the ship's axis. Detection range was approximately 6–8nm for a cruiser, 4–7nm for a destroyer, 1.5–2nm for a submarine, and 15–25nm for aircraft
- Vickers 2pdr Mk II pom-poms were fitted either side of the bridge in place of the 13.2mm Hotchkiss CAD, which were relocated either side of no.2 gun mounting on the forecastle deck, using the original seatings

Le Triomphant July 1941

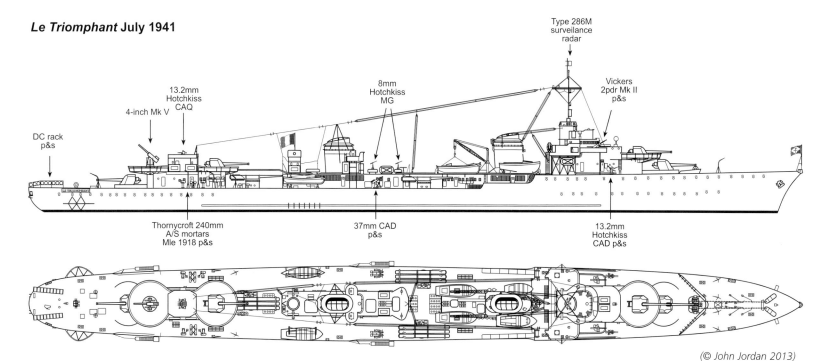

(© John Jordan 2013)

Above: One of the two Vickers 2pdr Mk II pom-poms fitted either side of the bridge in place of the 13.2mm Hotchkiss CAD.

Below: *Le Triomphant* arriving at San Diego, 25 August 1941. The photograph was taken from the USS *Saratoga* (CV-3). Note the false bow wave.
(US Navy NH 55853, courtesy of A D Baker III)

- a 13.2mm Hotchkiss Mle 1929 quadruple mounting (CAQ) removed from the old battleship *Paris* was installed on a platform atop the after ammunition hoists in place of the Lewis MG
- two British-style depth charge rails each for nine Mk VIIH 'heavy' depth charges (weight 259kg; charge 132kg amatol) were installed on the quarterdeck
- two 8mm Hotchkiss MG were fitted atop the centre deckhouse, forward of the second funnel
- the torpedo rangefinder turret was landed as weight compensation; it was replaced by a crow's nest on the forward side of the mast
- the Admiralty 516B paint scheme was reapplied, this time with a false bow wave

When the ship was at San Diego in September 1941 the Admiralty livery was superseded by a Dark Gray (5-D) overall scheme, and during 1–5 December *Le Triomphant* was again repainted at Sydney in anticipation of a deployment to the Mediterranean. The starboard side of the ship had a 'disruptive' pattern, the port side a 'deceptive' pattern which featured the silhouette of a cargo ship. A few days later the ship was committed to operations against Japan, primarily escort duty in the South Pacific region.

By March 1942 *Le Triomphant* was in desperate need of a refit due to constant steaming, and this was scheduled to take place at Garden Island, Sydney; in the event work was delayed by the

THE PERIOD 1939-1943

Above: *Le Triomphant* moored in San Diego harbour 26 August 1941. Note the British 4-inch HA gun in place of no.4 gun, the 13.2mm Hotchkiss CAQ atop the hoists, and the antenna for the Type 286M air surveillance radar atop the foremast. *(US Navy NH 81739, courtesy of A D Baker III)*

Below: *Le Triomphant* during her docking at San Diego in late August 1941. Maintenance work is taking place on the starboard propeller and shaft. *(Philippe Caresse collection)*

heavy workload at the dockyard, and it was six months before the ship was again ready to deploy. The following work was undertaken:

– the boilers were retubed

Right: *Le Triomphant* in Jervis Bay on 4 May 1943. During her refit at Garden Island, Sydney, the camouflage was reversed, with the mercantile freighter pattern to starboard and the disruptive pattern to port. (cf. the photo in Chapter 10, p.198). *(US Navy, courtesy of Rick E Davis)*

- the 13.2mm and 8mm MG were disembarked, and replaced by six single 20mm Oerlikon Mk 2 (US): two on the forecastle; one on the centre deckhouse in place of the 8mm guns; two atop the after hoists in place of the 13.2mm CAQ; and one on the quarterdeck between the depth charge rails
- the Type 286 radar was replaced by the more recent (and more effective) Type 290
- the camouflage pattern was reversed so that the 'deceptive' pattern was to starboard. It would be renewed on 23 June 1943 at Melbourne; the ship would subsequently be repainted in the US Navy's Dark Gray livery at Sydney in October 1943

Right: *Le Triomphant* at Sydney in early November 1943, following a two-month refit. She is now painted in a US standard Dark Gray livery. *Le Triomphant* was due to deploy to the Mediterranean, and left Fremantle for Madagascar on 25 November 1943. *(Courtesy of Peter Cannon)*

CHAPTER 13
THE PERIOD 1943–1945

ON 18 NOVEMBER 1942 THE FRENCH FORCES of Algeria and Morocco – the naval forces were designated the *Forces maritimes d'Afrique* or FMA – again took up arms against the Axis on the side of the Allies. They were joined by French forces in West Africa on 24 November 1942, by Force X at Alexandria on 17 May 1943, and by the ships in the Antilles on 14 July 1943. The FMA would be amalgamated with the FNFL on 4 August 1943.

At the end of 1942 the *Marine d'Afrique* had only three *contre-torpilleurs* available (*Le Fantasque* and *Le Terrible* at Dakar, and *Le Malin* at Casablanca), and only three *torpilleurs d'escadre* (*Simoun*, *Tempête* and *L'Alcyon* at Casablanca). They would later be joined by the TEs *Le Fortuné*, *Forbin* and *Basque* from Alexandria, by *Tigre* and *Trombe* (retroceded by the Italians), and by *Le Triomphant* (FNFL). *Mistral* and *Ouragan* remained in Britain: the first was manned by the Royal Navy; the second served as an accommodation ship.

Le Fantasque and *Le Terrible* left Dakar on 24 January 1943 for Casablanca, then headed for the Charlestown Navy Yard, Boston, where they arrived on 21 February to undergo a major modernisation. *Le Malin* would follow after the completion of repairs at Casablanca, arriving in Boston on 26 June. *Le Triomphant*, currently serving with the FNFL in the Pacific, was the last of the four surviving *Le Fantasque*s to be modernised; she arrived in Boston on 12 April 1944.

Of the eighteen four-funnelled *contre-torpilleurs*, not a single one was fit for service. The repair of *Albatros* at Casablanca and *Epervier* at Oran was considered, but proved to be beyond the capabilities of the respective dockyards.

The repair of the three *torpilleurs d'escadre* at Casablanca was more straightforward, and they would be formed into a new 6th DT. *Tempête* was available from early April, and underwent a partial modernisation at Bermuda Dockyard from 26 April to 7 July, returning to Casablanca on 29 July. *Simoun*, which was repaired by late June, was modernised (also in Bermuda) from 10 August to 18 October, returning to Casablanca on 31 October. *L'Alcyon* was ready for service only in early July, but did not undergo a further modernisation at this stage.

The three destroyers of Force X, *Le Fortuné*, *Forbin* and *Basque*, left Port Said on 22 June and arrived at Casablanca on 3 July. They continued to form the 3rd DT.

All six of the 1500-tonne destroyers were to be based initially at Casablanca. *L'Alcyon* would be the first in

Left: *Le Terrible* arrives at Boston on 21 February 1943 for her major refit at the Charlestown Navy Yard. All the French-model light anti-aircraft weapons have been landed in North Africa, but she is otherwise as yet unmodified. *(US Navy, courtesy of A D Baker III)*

Right: *Le Triomphant* alongside at the Charlestown Navy Yard, Boston, prior to her modernisation. *(Official US Navy photo 11085 2179, Charlestown Navy Yard NPS Park Collection, Boston, MA, courtesy of Rick E Davis)*

Below and opposite: These three previously-unpublished images show the three destroyers of Force X at Alexandria, *Le Fortuné* (T31), *Forbin* (T32) and *Basque* (T33), during their repatriation to the ports of French North Africa. Note the four 20mm Oerlikon fitted behind steel screens on the main deck forward and aft: the forward pair abeam gun no.2, the after pair in place of the original 37mm AA. The ships are otherwise unmodified. *(US Navy, NH110754/5/6, courtesy of A D Baker III)*

active service, escorting convoy K56 in early July 1943. The main task of these ships was to escort convoys between Casablanca and Gibraltar; they also escorted British-flagged ships carrying men who had fled from France across the Pyrenees, only to be arrested by the Spanish authorities, who released them after a stay in a prison or a camp.

Two of the ships seized by the Italians at Toulon were recovered at Taranto. *Trombe* was formally handed back at Bizerte on 25 October 1943. It took four months to repair her; she then sailed for Casablanca to complete her refit. She was incorporated into the 6th DT at Algiers on 10 July 1944, but was again immobilised from 22 July to mid-November following problems with her turbines.

Tigre was handed over at Bizerte on 28 October 1943. She recommissioned with a French crew on 15 December, but repairs, first at Bizerte then at Casablanca, were completed only in March 1944. She escorted convoy CAF31 from Ajaccio (Corsica) to Algiers, and was attacked on 20 April 1944 by German torpedo planes and bombers armed with the Hs 293

THE PERIOD 1943-1945

glide bomb. She was also employed as a fast troop transport[1] in June. She was placed in care & maintenance on 15 August 1944 and then underwent a repair and modernisation at Oran in which she lost her first funnel. Ready again for service on 3 February 1945, she joined the Flank Force at Toulon (see below).

THE 'LIGHT CRUISERS'

Modernisation of the four ships of the *Le Fantasque* class at the Charlestown Navy Yard, Boston, took place as follows:

Le Fantasque: 21 February to 25 June 1943
Le Terrible: 21 February to 22 May 1943

---

[1] Most French merchantmen were integrated into the Allied shipping pool, and the French retained full control over only a handful of ships for local employment. It was therefore warships which carried out the majority of short-term transport missions, particularly those involving personnel. These missions would continue until early 1947.

Right: *Le Malin* at speed on her post-refit trials in Casco Bay. Note the British Thornycroft Mk IV depth charge throwers abeam the after deckhouse. *(US Navy 80-G-208052, courtesy of A D Baker III)*

Right: *L'Audacieux* during her transit from Dakar to Bizerte in August 1942. *(Philippe Caresse collection)*

Le Malin: 26 June to 10 December 1943[2]
Le Triomphant: 12 April 1944 to 26 February 1945

The modernisation of *Le Malin* was delayed by the need for repairs following the damage suffered at Casablanca in November 1942, and that of *Le Triomphant* by the damage resulting from the typhoon of 3 December 1943 in the Indian Ocean and the lengthy transit necessary for her to reach Boston.

---

[2] *Le Malin* suffered damage in a gale that lasted for two days during her passage to New York, and underwent repairs at the Norfolk Navy Yard before leaving for Bermuda and the Azores.

L'Indomptable had been scuttled at Toulon and *L'Audacieux*, which had arrived at Bizerte on 22 August 1942, was in one of the docks at Sidi-Abdallah awaiting repair. She was not scuttled when the Germans occupied Bizerte on 8 December 1942, but was damaged by Allied bombing. The Germans sabotaged the dock gate before evacuating Bizerte, and the ship was further damaged. What was now little more than a wreck was refloated on 14 December 1943 and towed out of the dock following five months of repairs. Deemed to be a constructive total loss, *L'Audacieux* was cannibalised for spares for ships still in service. *Epervier* at Oran suffered a similar fate.

Le Fantasque, the first of the ships to return from

modernisation in the USA, arrived at Casablanca on 18 July 1943 and at Algiers on the 25th. *Le Terrible* was despatched to the Antilles just after the islands rallied to the *Comité français de libération nationale* (CFLN) at Algiers. She was in Martinique on 14 July and in Guadeloupe on the 15th. She left Martinique on 30 July, called in at Dakar 5–9 August and arrived at Algiers on 15 August. *Le Malin* left Norfolk on 19 December and arrived at La Horta (Azores) on 26 December 1943.

Le Fantasque took part in escort missions in the Mediterranean in August 1943, and on 20–21 August *Le Fantasque* and *Le Terrible* undertook their first raid, on Scalea in Calabria, where they engaged Italian MAS boats. Another raid, this time in the Bays of Naples and Gaeta, took place on 21–22 August. These operations brought home to the Allies the possibilities of these ships, which were significantly more capable than the Allied destroyers. They were duly reclassified as 'light cruisers' on 28 September 1943, which gave them priority over the former when it came to resupply and replenishment.[3]

Le Fantasque and *Le Terrible* operated with the British Force H, which was providing cover for the landings at Salerno on 9 September 1943. *Le Fantasque* took part in the shooting down of a German plane on the night of 9/10 September. The two ships were then made available to the French authorities for operations in Corsica. They made two raids on Ajaccio, departing Algiers on the 13th. *Le Terrible* was then immobilised with turbine problems. *Le Fantasque* left again for Ajaccio on 16 September (with *Tempête* and *L'Alcyon*), on the evening of the 19th (with the two destroyers and the cruiser *Jeanne d'Arc*), and on the 22nd with the cruiser *Montcalm*. She herself was then out of service for a short period after running aground in the approaches to Ajaccio a little after midnight.

Le Fantasque (X101) and *Le Terrible* (X103), which would soon be joined by *Le Malin* (X102), still formed the 10th DCT, which became the 10th DCL (*Division de croiseurs légers*) on 28 September 1943. However, their fragile propulsion machinery required regular attention and was subject to numerous breakdowns, leading to the adoption of a policy of keeping only two ships in operation while the third underwent maintenance. *Le Triomphant* would only join the 10th DCL on 1 April 1945, with the tactical number X104.

Le Fantasque and *Le Terrible*, whose turbines had now been repaired, left Oran on 17 October 1943. They headed for the Azores, where they met with the battleship *Richelieu*, which was returning to North Africa having been modernised in the USA, and escorted her to Mers el-Kebir. They then carried out two raids in the Eastern Mediterranean out of Alexandria in company with the British cruiser *Phoebe*. The first was in the Aegean on 19–20 November; they were attacked by aircraft, one of which was downed. The second was between Crete and Rhodes on 22–24 November, but the ships failed to find any targets.

On 24 December *Le Fantasque* intercepted the freighter *Nicoline Maersk*, which was transporting tungsten from Valencia to Marseille, and forced her to beach herself to avoid capture.

On 31 December *Le Fantasque* joined up with *Le Malin*, returning from her modernisation in the USA, at La Horta (Azores), and the two ships then went in search of blockade runners. The same two ships then took part in the landings at Anzio (Italy). *Le Fantasque* undertook a diversionary mission at Civita Vecchia on 22 January; she bombarded Formia and Terracina the following day.

In late February, the ships of the 10th DCL were despatched to an 'alert' anchorage at Manfredonia, north of Bari. On 27–28 February, *Le Fantasque* and *Le Terrible* carried out their first raid in the Adriatic, but found no worthwhile targets; *Le Malin* remained at Taranto. The next raid, on 28–29 February, was carried out by *Le Fantasque* and *Le Malin*, but was equally fruitless. However, the third raid, with the same two ships on the night of 29 February/1 March, encountered a German freighter with a heavy escort. The freighter *Kapitän Diederichsen* was sunk and the torpedo boat *TA37* and the corvette *Uj201* seriously damaged, while the *TA36*, *Uj205*,[4] *R188*, *R190* and *R191* suffered light damage.

Le Fantasque and *Le Terrible* left the anchorage on 2 March to intercept another convoy in the Gulf of Venice, but the operation was cancelled due to the lack of obvious targets. A new operation was undertaken in the Gulf of Trieste on the night of 4/5 March. The same ships sortied again on 7–8 March and bombarded the port of Zakynthos (Greek island). A further night patrol on 15/16 March took the two ships as far as Mljet Island (Croatia). This was followed by a night raid on 18/19 March, in which two landing craft, *SF273* and *SF274*, were sunk, and *SF270* and *F124* disabled. Eight crew members of *Le Fantasque* and one on *Le Terrible* were wounded; they were disembarked at Malta.

After a short refit, the division was again detailed for raids on Crete, operating out of Alexandria. Four raids were cancelled between 23 and 27 April; a fifth raid on the night of 28/29 April took place but the ships found nothing, while a sixth raid scheduled for the night of 30 April/1 May was cut short due to heavy seas. *Le Fantasque* and *Le Malin* patrolled between the islands of Scarpento and Kos, then bombarded the port of Kos. After a brief rest period, the complete three-ship division got underway on 22 May to attack a convoy, which failed to leave port; several similar operations were cancelled.

Following a maintenance period at Alexandria during which the port shaft of *Le Malin* was removed for repairs, *Le Fantasque* and *Le Terrible* returned to operations in the Adriatic. During the night of 16/17 June, they intercepted a convoy in the Kvarner Gulf (Croatia); they sank the small oil tanker *Giuliana*, but *R4*, *R8*, *R14* and *R15* escaped.

The last raid took place on the night of 24/25 June

---

[3] The French ships which rejoined the conflict in North Africa in 1943 had only a limited stock of munitions available (200 138mm rounds per gun was a typical figure), so orders were placed with the Americans for 152mm (cruisers), 138mm (*Le Fantasque*s) and 130mm (1500-tonne destroyers) shells and charges. Ammunition for the cruisers was prioritised, and it was only after the landings in Provence that the 130mm ammunition was delivered.

[4] *TA36* (ex-*Stella Polare*) and *TA37* (ex-*Gladio*) were former Italian torpedo boats of the *Ariete* class; *Uj201* (ex-*Egeria*) and *Uj205* (ex-*Colubrina*) were former Italian corvettes of the *Gabbiano* class.

Above: *Le Malin* at Algiers in 1944. Note the 20mm Oerlikon guns in place of the after torpedo tube mounting which were a feature of this ship.

Below: *Tigre* between March and August 1944, when she was employed as a fast transport. She has been fitted with a handful of 20mm Oerlikons as an interim measure prior to a full modernisation.

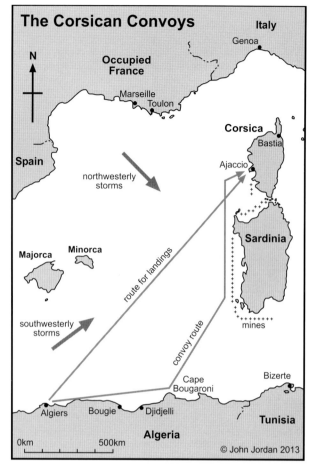

and took the ships into the Gulf of Trieste. No maritime traffic was encountered, but *Le Fantasque* experienced severe vibrations in her port shaft which restricted her to a maximum speed of 25 knots. All three ships were now suffering regular problems with their propellers and shafts which entailed repairs at Bizerte. *Le Malin*'s shaft problems were not easily resolved, the replacement of the support by one removed from *L'Audacieux* proving too time-consuming.[5]

THE LIBERATION OF CORSICA

The first major operation of the reconstituted Marine Nationale was the liberation of Corsica (operation 'Vesuvius'). The operation was launched after the announcement of the armistice with Italy, despite a lack of enthusiasm on the part of France's Anglo-

---

[5] *L'Audacieux* and *Le Malin* were built in different yards, and parts were not always interchangeable. Despite the best of intentions, standardisation proved beyond the capacity of the French Navy during the interwar period.

Saxon allies, who were nevertheless prepared to release certain ships, notably *Le Fantasque* and *Le Terrible*, to serve under French command. The submarine *Casabianca*, which had already undertaken six liaison missions with the Corsican resistance movement, landed 109 men at Ajaccio on the night of 12/13 September 1943. The first contacts between Algiers and Ajaccio were in the shape of high-speed raids by the light cruisers *Le Fantasque* and *Le Terrible* on 13–14 September. *Le Terrible* was then immobilised due to turbine problems, but *Le Fantasque* would carry out three more raids. The 1500-tonne destroyers were also involved: *Tempête* took part in three raids, *L'Alcyon* four, *Le Fortuné* two, *Basque* two and *Forbin* one. The Germans used Corsica as a transit point when they evacuated Sardinia, and eventually evacuated Corsica itself on 4 October, when the port of Bastia was recaptured.

Following the liberation of Corsica, sea links between North Africa (Algiers) and Corsica were established with small French convoys escorted principally by the 1500-tonne destroyers, which were reinforced from early 1944 by six ex-American destroyer escorts (DEs) transferred to the Marine Nationale. A total of 87 return convoys were organised between late September 1943 and August 1944. *Tempête* escorted 44 convoys (22 each way), *L'Alcyon* 36, *Le Fortuné* 20, *Basque* 32, *Forbin* 34, *Simoun* 18, *Tigre* two, *Sénégalais* two, *Algérien* ten, *Tunisien* eight, *Hova* two, *Trombe* six and *Marocain* two.

Numerous depth charge attacks were made on reported submarine contacts during these escort missions. The convoys to Corsica were also subjected

THE PERIOD 1943-1945

Left: The destroyer escort *Le Sénégalais* is towed into Algiers on 13 May 1944 after being torpedoed. She had sortied from Algiers in response to a submarine alert off the coast. *(US Navy FN-22844B SS)*

Below: *Le Terrible* at Manfredonia, Italy, in March 1944. *(Leo van Ginderen collection)*

to aerial attack by Luftwaffe bombers despatched in search of the major Allied east-west convoys from the USA to Port Said (UGS) and those proceeding in the opposite direction (GUS).

Le Fortuné was at Ajaccio on 30 September 1943 with the British tank landing ship *LST 79* when the port was attacked by ten German Dornier 217 bombers of III./KG 100 from Istres (southern France). Three Hs 293 glide bombs were launched at *Le Fortuné*, one of which fell 30 metres to starboard and two on the adjacent jetty. The destroyer was seriously damaged by bomb splinters, while *LST 79* was set on fire by another bomb and became a constructive total loss.

On the evening of 20 April 1944, sixty German aircraft (III./KG 26, I. and III./KG 77) were searching for the major convoy UGS38, which comprised 87 ships. Twelve Ju-88 torpedo planes and several Dornier 217s armed with glide bombs came across the small French convoy CAF31, which was returning from Corsica to Algiers, escorted by *Tigre*, *Tempête* and *Forbin*. *Tigre* was damaged by two near-misses and lost 140 tonnes of fuel oil, *Tempête* was missed by a bomb which landed 200–300m away, and *Forbin* managed to shoot down a glide bomb which was aimed at her. The passenger ship *El Biar* was sunk by a Ju-88 torpedo; the remaining aircraft attacked convoy UGS38, which lost three ships to torpedoes.

On 3 May 1944, an underwater attack on convoy GUS38 prompted a submarine hunt by the French *Sénégalais* and *L'Alcyon*, the American *Joseph E Campbell* (DE-70) and *Pride* (DE-323) and the British *Blankney* ('Hunt' II class). Hunted down and depth-charged, *U-371* (Type VIIC) was finally sunk, the French *Sénégalais* having played a decisive role. However, the latter ship was torpedoed and lost her stern; *L'Alcyon* came to her assistance and towed her into Djidjelli (now Jijel, Algeria).

Finally, during the night of 30/31 May *L'Alcyon*, which was escorting convoy KMS51, engaged German aircraft with her light AA and downed a Ju-88.

THE ALLIED LANDINGS IN METROPOLITAN FRANCE

The participation of the French Navy in the Normandy landings (Operation 'Overlord') was limited; the only units to take part were the Kieffer commando battalion, the cruisers *Georges Leygues* and *Montcalm*, the destroyer *La Combattante* (ex-British 'Hunt' class), the frigates *L'Aventure*, *L'Escarmouche*, *La Surprise* and *La Découverte*, and the corvettes *D'Estienne d'Orves*, *Aconit*, *Renoncule* and *Roselys*. These ships undertook convoy escort missions, while *La Combattante* (together with the cruisers) provided fire support on 6 June 1944.

In contrast, the landings in Provence (Operation 'Dragoon'), which took place on 15 August 1944, involved virtually all the ships available to the Marine Nationale. The 10th DCL comprised *Le Terrible* (now X101), *Le Malin* and *Le Fantasque* (now X103);[6] *Le Malin* had to operate on a single shaft, but was nevertheless capable of 25 knots. The 3rd DT comprised *Le Fortuné* and *Forbin*, and the 6th DT *Tempête*, *Simoun* and *L'Alcyon*. The five ex-American destroyer escorts available – *Sénégalais* was under repair at Charlestown Navy Yard – made up the 2nd and 3rd DE divisions.

The three light cruisers, together with the cruisers *Georges Leygues* and *Montcalm*, were part of Task Force 85, the support group for Force Delta, which landed the 45th US Infantry Division on the beach of La Nartelle (north of Sainte-Maxime – see map).

The destroyers and the DEs were attached to Task Group 80.6, the escort group for the convoys. Convoy TF1, for example, consisted of ten transports carrying the first echelon of Army B (the future 1st French Army) from Naples to the landing zones, escorted by *Hova*, *Algérien*, *Marocain*, *Le Fortuné*, *Forbin*, *Simoun* and the US destroyer *Hilary P Jones* (DD-427).

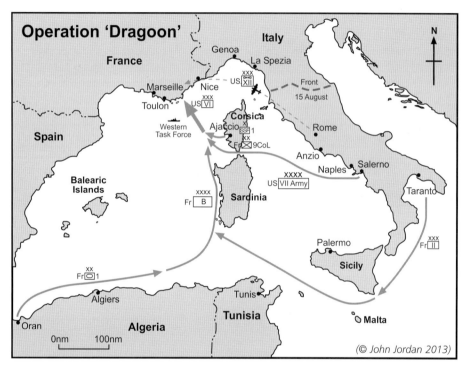

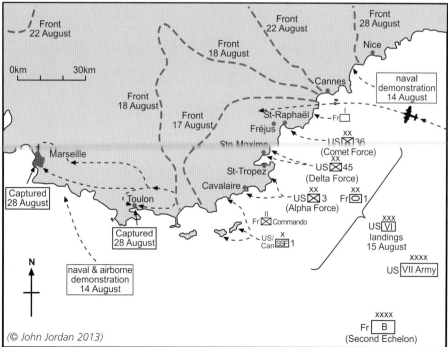

---

[6] The hull numbers were exchanged following a change in command on 8 June.

On 15 August *Le Fantasque* and *Le Malin* were in the Gulf of Saint-Tropez, firing off 280 and 80 rounds of 138mm HE shell respectively. At the same time *Le Terrible* bombarded the Saint-Aygulf area, expending 158 rounds.

During the night the light cruisers provided protection for the bigger ships and were ready to execute fire support missions during the day, but the rapid advances of the Allied troops soon put potential targets out of range. *Le Terrible* provided fire support for the advance on Cannes, and the other two ships for the advance on Toulon. On 5 September *Le Malin* was operating with the American destroyer *Ludlow* (DD-438) south of Monaco when they were attacked by a group of five German 'Marder'-type midget submarines of the 364th Flotilla. The attack failed: the submarines were engaged by the guns of *Le Malin* and depth-charged by the *Ludlow*; three were sunk and one captured. On 13 September 1944 *Le Malin* took part in the reentry of the French fleet into Toulon; she would be joined on 1 October by her sisters *Le Terrible* and *Le Fantasque*, escorting the battleship *Richelieu*.

After brief refit and maintenance periods (at Toulon and Bizerte respectively), *Le Terrible* and *Le Malin* left Bizerte for Toulon, via Naples. Shortly afterwards, a night exercise was abruptly terminated when *Le Terrible* collided with her sister, which was making 26 knots at the time. Losses were heavy: 70 killed or missing, presumed dead, of whom 62 were in the bow of *Le Malin*, which was completely severed and sank. The hull of *Le Terrible* was stove in over a length of 27 metres; there were four major breaches, and the after boiler and engine rooms were flooded.

The 1500-tonne destroyers were fully occupied with escort missions, but some ships were detached to protect the fire support ships when Toulon was retaken, and on occasion they made smoke to cover them. Shortly before the recapture of Toulon, *Simoun* embarked Admiral André Lemonnier, Chief of the French Naval General Staff, on a visit to the ships engaged against the coast defence batteries at Saint-Mandrier. The destroyer's commanding officer convinced the admiral to allow him to fire on the batteries. Taking full advantage of the opportunity presented, *Simoun* fired almost 400 rounds against the Croix des Signaux battery. As French stocks of 130mm ammunition were by now nearly exhausted, the admiral swore that he would not make any more visits to the ships off Toulon!

After the landings, the French destroyers and DEs continued to provide escort for convoys of troops sent to reinforce and expand the bridgehead, then for the Allied logistics effort, notably ships bound for Marseille.

THE FLANK FORCE

In early September 1944, the front stabilised approximately on the former Franco-Italian border. On 1 September, the naval forces that remained to support ground operations constituted Task Force 86; most of the ships assigned to this force were French. It was renamed the Flank Force and placed under French command on 4 November.

The primary missions of this force were to provide fire support for troops involved in operations near the coast, and cover against the German and Italian forces

THE ESCORTS TRANSFERRED BY THE ALLIES

French crews manned a number of ships lent or transferred by the Allies.

The *Forces navales françaises libres* (FNFL) received:

– nine corvettes of the British 'Flower' class: renamed *Mimosa, Alysse, Aconit, Roselys, Renoncule, Lobélia, Commandant Détroyat, Commandant Drogou* and *Commandant d'Estienne d'Orves*, they commissioned between 5 May 1941 and 23 May 1942. Two were sunk in 1942: *Alysse* on 8 February by *U-654* and *Mimosa* on 9 June by *U-124*
– one destroyer of the British 'Hunt' III type. Renamed *La Combattante*, she commissioned on 15 December 1942;

she was lost on the night of 23/24 February 1945 to a mine in the Humber estuary
– six frigates of the British 'River' class: renamed *La Découverte, L'Aventure, L'Escarmouche, La Surprise, Croix de Lorraine*, and *Tonkinois*, they entered service between 29 October 1943 and 15 October 1944

The *Forces maritimes d'Afrique du Nord* received:

– six escort destroyers of the *Cannon* class: renamed *Sénégalais, Algérien, Tunisien, Marocain, Hova* and *Somali*, they were transferred between 2 January and 9 April 1944

ALLIED TRANSFERS

'River' class Frigates

Name	Launched	Transferred	Stricken	Renamed
La Découverte (ex-*Windrush*)	18 Jun 1943	11 Oct 1943	13 May 1961	*Lucifer* 1967
L'Aventure (ex-*Braid*)	30 Nov 1943	21 Jan 1944	3 Nov 1976	
L'Escarmouche (ex-*Frome*)	1 Jun 1943	14 Feb 1944	8 Sep 1961	*Ailette* 1 Jan 1957
La Surprise (ex-*Torridge*)	16 Aug 1943	9 Mar 1944		*Al Maouna* (Morocco) 1964
Croix de Lorraine (ex-*Strule*)	08 Mar 1943	16 Nov 1944	8 Sep 1961	
Tonkinois (ex-*Moyola*)	27 Aug 1942	15 Oct 1944	8 Sep 1961	*La Confiance* 1953

'Cannon' class Destroyer Escorts

Name	Launched	Transferred	Stricken	Renamed
Sénégalais (ex-DE-106)	11 Nov 1943	2 Jan 1944	End 1964	*Yser* 28 Jun 1963
Algérien (ex-DE-107)	27 Nov 1943	23 Jan 1944	End 1964	*Oise* 28 Jun 1963
Tunisien (ex-DE-108)	17 Dec 1943	11 Feb 1944	4 Oct 1957	
Marocain (ex-DE-109)	1 Jan 1944	28 Feb 1944	4 Oct 1957	
Hova (ex-DE-110)	22 Jan 1944	18 Mar 1944	15 Nov 1957	
Somali (ex-DE-111)	12 Feb 1944	9 Apr 1944	end 1972	*Arago* 1968

Right: *Le Terrible* with the British Type 285P4 radar fitted to her main gunnery director during her 1945 refit.

Below: At Algiers, 1944: the TEs *Tempête*, *Basque*, *L'Alcyon*, *Forbin* and *Le Fortuné*. (Leo van Ginderen collection)

still occupying Genoa and La Spezia, who were equipped notably with German midget submarines (referred to as *la vermine* by the French sailors).

The French destroyers thus played a major part in coastal operations, undertaking fire support missions in which the range of their 130mm guns was particularly appreciated by the Allied troops. They were also involved in a number of missions as fast transports. *Forbin*, *Le Fortuné*, *L'Alcyon*, *Basque*, *Tempête*, *Simoun* and *Trombe* all served with the Flank Force at one time or another until the end of the war in Europe.

Forbin was operating with the US destroyer *Madison* (DD-425) off Menton and Cape Ferrat on 25–26 September 1944. On the first day the destroyer carried out two fire support missions in the Menton/Ventimiglia area. The following day, the two destroyers were attacked by a group of nine 'Molch'-type midget submarines of K-Verband 411 Flotilla operating out of San Remo. During the engagement which followed, none of the torpedoes launched by the submarines hit their target, whereas the depth-charging of the destroyers was so effective that not a single boat was able to return to its base. *Forbin*, which was credited with three 'kills', rescued one of the pilots.

Forbin (again) was providing protection for a group of minesweepers south of Ventimiglia and San Remo on 20 October, when she was taken under fire by an enemy battery. The destroyer, which responded by firing on the port area of San Remo, was rewarded after nine minutes of fire by a massive explosion and a large, black cloud of smoke. The exchange of fire continued for four hours, until the arrival of a US destroyer. However, the story did not end there: the Germans and the Italians were convinced that the Allied ship – *Forbin* was mistaken for a British or American destroyer – had come to bombard San Remo armed with specific intelligence. A German flotilla (K-Verband 213) with 48 explosive motor boats had arrived the previous day and been stored, together with fuel and explosive payloads, in the covered Flower Market. The French would only learn about the destruction of the German flotilla at San Remo 34 years later! *Forbin* again engaged in fire support off the coast on 30–31 October, embarked on one last fire support mission 16–19 November, then began a long refit.

Trombe and *Simoun* made a depth charge attack on a submarine contact off Toulon on 17 November. *Le Fortuné* fired on two explosive motor boats during the night of 9/10 January 1945, destroying one. On the

FNTF 15 DECEMBER 1944–MAY 1945

Battleship:	*Lorraine*
Cruisers:	*Duquesne, Gloire*
Destroyers:	*Le Fortuné, L'Alcyon, Le Basque*
Destroyer Escorts:	*Hova, Somali*
Frigates:	*L'Aventure, La Surprise*

night of 17/18 March, *Tempête* and *Basque* were engaged in the pursuit of three German ships[7] which sortied from Genoa, but it was the British destroyers *Meteor* and *Lookout* which intercepted the Germans, sinking the torpedo boats *TA24* and *TA29*.

On the night of 16/17 April, *Trombe* was patrolling south of Ventimiglia when she was shaken by a violent explosion forward, to starboard. It is possible that she was struck by a torpedo – the explanation favoured in French sources – or an MTM-type explosive motor boat (German sources) associated with a two-man motor torpedo boat, *SMA 312*. The destroyer returned to Toulon with a breach in her hull beneath the forward 130mm guns that extended from one side of the ship to the other. She lost 20 killed or missing, presumed dead. The damage was so extensive that she was never repaired.

THE FRENCH NAVAL TASK FORCE (FNTF)

Following the liberation of most of mainland France, the Germans continued to occupy the 'Atlantic Pockets' at Lorient, Saint-Nazaire, La Rochelle and Royan. A French Naval Task Force (FNTF – see table for composition) was formed on 15 December 1944 to enforce the blockade of these pockets and to take part in their recapture, which was regarded by France's Anglo-Saxon allies as a distraction from the main military thrust against Germany and was therefore accorded low priority for resources.

Three destroyers were assigned to the FNTF at one time or another. *Basque* and *Simoun*, escorting the old battleship *Lorraine*, arrived in Plymouth on 5

---
[7] These were two former Italian torpedo boats, *TA24* (ex-*Arturo*) and *TA29* (ex-*Eridano*), together with the former Yugoslavian destroyer *Dubrovnik*, which became the Italian *Premuda* then the German *TA32*.

December 1944. The two destroyers then returned to Brest, and on 13 January again left for the Mediterranean, operations against the pockets having been postponed.

Le Fortuné and *Basque* arrived at Plymouth on 4 April, and were joined by *L'Alcyon* the following day. They patrolled off the pockets with the frigates *L'Aventure* and *La Surprise*. On the night of 10 April, *Le Fortuné* detected on her radar plot a trawler, *Le Hasard*, which had been manned by the Germans for fishing on the Roche Bonne plateau in order to provide rations for the besieged troops in the La Rochelle pocket. It was the DE *Hova* which captured the trawler. The three destroyers were then assigned to escort the *Lorraine* when she carried out a bombardment of the Pointe de Grave on 15 April, also taking part in the bombardment.

The patrols off the pockets continued. *Le Fortuné* and *L'Alcyon* were again involved on 30 April, together with the cruiser *Duquesne*, during the landings on the Ile d'Oléron. *L'Alcyon* carried out a final fire support mission on 1 May.

Above: *Tigre* serving with the Flank Force in 1945, following her refit and modernisation at Oran August 1944 - February 1945. The modernisation was similar to that given to her sister *Léopard* by the British. The forward boiler room, together with the slim fore-funnel, were removed and replaced by additional fuel bunkerage and accommodation. Note the British-style depth charge racks above the stern, each of which held nine charges. There were also four (later two) Thornycroft Mk IV mortars with parbuckle reload stowage on the quarterdeck. The two centre-line 40mm (Canadian Mk I) are prominent, as are the after 20mm Oerlikon mountings on the main deck aft of amidships. *(Leo van Ginderen collection)*

APPENDIX D: *LE FANTASQUE* MODERNISATIONS USA 1943–1944

FOLLOWING THE LIBERATION OF FRENCH NORTH Africa it was decided that the most modern French naval surface units would undergo a modernisation in the United States. The battleship *Richelieu*, the cruisers *Georges Leygues*, *Montcalm*, *Gloire* and *Emile Bertin*, and the surviving four *contre-torpilleurs* of the Le Fantasque class formed a steady procession across the Atlantic from early 1943 to be rebuilt in US naval dockyards.

Of the four *Le Fantasques*, the name-ship and *Le Terrible* were in service at Dakar, *Le Malin* had sustained serious damage during the American assault on Casablanca, and *Le Triomphant*, which had been seized by the British in June 1940, was currently serving with the FNFL in the Pacific.

Le Fantasque and *Le Terrible* were inspected at Dakar by Rear-Admiral Glassford (USN) on 3 January 1943 and a list of repairs and modifications drawn up in consultation with the French. The two ships left Dakar on the night of 24 January, arriving at Casablanca on the 28th. There they joined a convoy to the USA which departed 1 February. They arrived at New York on 13 February, four days after the arrival of *Richelieu* and *Montcalm*, and moored at Pier no.33 in the Brooklyn Navy Yard. Fog delayed their departure for Boston, but on 20 February they left for the Charlestown Navy Yard, where the work was due to be undertaken.

The machinery was given a thorough overhaul, holes being cut in the deck to enable the turbines to be removed. Unreliable (and uneconomical) items of auxiliary machinery were replaced: in particular, the HP evaporators were replaced by low-pressure models powered by steam from the turbines. In *Le Fantasque* reserve feed water tanks with a total capacity of 60m³ were converted into fuel tanks to remedy the range deficiency experienced during earlier wartime operations: the additional 79 tonnes of fuel increased endurance by 17%.

The most important element of the modernisation was the upgrading of the anti-aircraft weaponry and fire control systems. Before being despatched to the United States the 37mm Mle 1933 mountings and the 13.2mm Hotchkiss and Browning machine guns had been removed from the ships. They would be superseded by eight

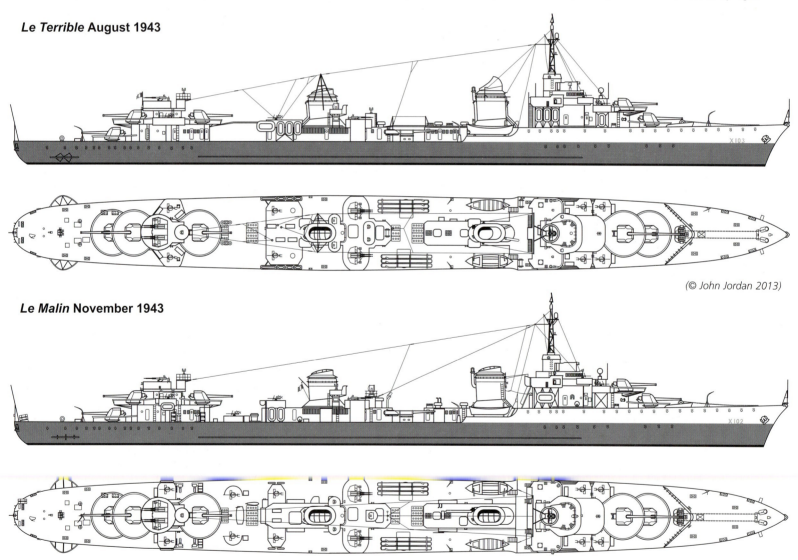

Le Terrible August 1943

(© John Jordan 2013)

Le Malin November 1943

(© John Jordan 2013)

The profiles and plans are based on the official US Navy BuShips Booklets of General Plans dated August 1943 and 9 November 1943 respectively. The major external differences between *Le Terrible* and *Le Malin* following their modernisation were the funnel cowling (fitted 1942) of *Le Terrible*, the removal of the antenna supports on the second funnel in *Le Malin*, and the four Thornycroft Mk IV depth charge throwers fitted in the latter ship abeam the after deckhouse; each of the DCTs had parbuckle stowage for further Mk VIIH 'heavy' depth charges. Note also on *Le Malin* the rear extension to the navigation bridge, the different arrangement of the midships 20mm Oerlikons, the suppression of the W/T office at the after end of the centre deckhouse (evident from the absence of W/T 'risers' abaft the second funnel), and the smoke generators on the port side of the stern. Only a single 75cm searchlight projector has been retained (reduction of topweight), and this has been relocated on a newly-built platform atop the centre deckhouse, freeing up the former searchlight positions for the two Mk 51 directors for the midships Bofors mountings.

THE PERIOD 1943-1945

Above and below: Three views of *Le Terrible* following her refit at the Charlestown Navy Yard, Boston, taken on 18 May 1943. *(Official US Navy, courtesy of A D Baker III)*

Above: *Le Terrible* received an identical modernisation to her sister *Le Fantasque*, but could be easily distinguished from her by the prominent funnel cowling she received during her 1942 refit at Toulon. Note that funnel caps post-modernisation were painted in the Haze Gray which corrresponded to the US Navy's Measure 22 paint scheme. *(Photo NH 81774)*

Below, left: In this bow view, taken for the ONI (Office of Naval Intelligence) Recognition Manual, note the US SA-1 air surveillance antenna and the thimble radome for the SF surface radar atop the foremast. Note also the four single 20mm Oerlikon guns on either side of the bridge structure. *(Photo NH 81777)*

Below, right: The stern view, also taken for recognition purposes, makes it clear that *Le Fantasque* and *Le Terrible* retained the original depth charge chutes for French Guiraud 200kg depth charges, and that British-style depth charge rails were not fitted, as claimed in some sources. Note the single 20mm Oerlikon guns in tubs abreast the after hoists. *(Photo NH 81776)*

Above, left and opposite: Four views of *Le Fantasque* taken during her post-refit high-speed trials between Cape Cod and Boston on 13 June 1943. During these trials she comfortably sustained 37 knots, despite the weight gain resulting from equipment additions. *(Official US Navy photos, 80-G-68394/97/98/99)*

THE PERIOD 1943-1945

40mm Bofors guns and eight 20mm Oerlikons.

A quadruple Bofors 40mm Mark 2 was mounted in a circular tub atop the after ammunition distribution shelter, with two twin Mark 1 mountings in semi-circular tubs forward of the second funnel. The massive tubs, which in the case of the twin mountings had a 40mm control room and a ready-use room directly beneath, were pre-fabricated and simply lifted on board and welded onto the decks and superstructures. A Mk 51 director was provided close to each of the three gun mountings.

Four of the eight 20mm single Oerlikon Mark 7 guns were on platforms fitted abeam the bridge, and there were a further four sided mountings abaft the second funnel. In *Le Fantasque* and *Le Terrible* two were mounted on platforms atop the centre deckhouse, with seatings for a further two mountings, and two were on platforms extending from the sides of the after deckhouse; there was a slightly different layout in the two later conversions (see drawings of *Le Malin*)

The original pole foremast was replaced by a light lattice mast carrying SA air surveillance and SF surface surveillance radars, and the bridge structure was modified – and in the later conversions enlarged – to accommodate the necessary radar plot. The three concentration dials were suppressed and replaced by the US Talk Between Ships (TBS) system, a low-powered voice radio for short-range tactical communications. Finally, Asdic was installed in a retractable dome – usable below 25 knots – and degaussing cabling fitted. The model fitted in *Le Terrible* was an Alpha 128, which had been on board broken down in cases since 1941; *Le Fantasque* received a newly manufactured Asdic 128D of Canadian origin.[1]

The new AA armament and electronics outfit required extensive recabling. Sacrifices also had to be made to counter-balance the increase in topweight. The after triple torpedo mounting was landed, as was the torpedo rangefinder and the

---
[1] Most French secondary sources claim that *Le Fantasque* and *Le Terrible* were also fitted with British Thornycroft Mk IV depth charge throwers, but only *Le Malin* and *Le Triomphant* had these.

5-metre auxiliary gunnery rangefinder abaft the second funnel. The original boat outfit was considered excessive by US Navy standards; the two 7-metre motor launches atop the forward deckhouse, the 7-metre pulling cutter and the 5-metre dinghy were landed. Only the 7-metre motor boat (for the officers) and the 7-metre whaler were retained (the latter was replaced in at least one of the ships by a motorised 26ft US model). These two boats were suspended on davits and relocated abeam the forward funnel. The original twin boat cranes were now superfluous and were removed, giving the modernised ships an altogether 'cleaner', leaner appearance. The boats and the original Brest-type life rafts were replaced by 15-man and 25-man rafts of US Navy design.

Following the reconstruction, stability trials of *Le Terrible* revealed that she was now 410 tonnes heavier, with a normal displacement of 3200 tonnes. The navy yard recommended that no.3 gun be landed as part-compensation, but this was strongly resisted by the French, who preferred to 'wait and see' once the ships were again in operational service.

Navigation Bridge: *Le Terrible* & *Le Malin* Post-Modernisation 1943

Plans of the navigation bridges of Le Terrible *and* Le Malin *following reconstruction. That of* Le Terrible *has received minimal modification, although the captain's sea cabin has been partitioned off and considerably reduced in size to accommodate a radar office. The original chart house/signal distribution office now accommodates upgraded communications equipment. In* Le Malin, *however, the deckhouse supporting the upper bridge has been extended aft to provide significantly enhanced command and control capabilities. The captain's sea cabin has again been reduced in size, and an Asdic control station fitted in abaft it. To port, the enlarged chart house has become a radar and communications office, with consoles for the SA and SF radars as well as for the US Navy's TBS ('Talk Between Ships') voice communications system. Externally, equipment has also been extensively upgraded, with US Navy-type 12-inch signal projectors fitted port & starboard in place of the 30cm and 45cm French models, and signal flag boards at the after end of the bridge wings.*

The first three ships to be modernised were repainted in the standard US Navy Measure 22, with the hull up to the upper deck Navy Blue (5-N), the forecastle and superstructures Haze Gray (5-H), and the upper deck Deck Blue (20-B). Lassaque claims that this was modified during 1945, with Haze Gray replaced by the slightly darker Ocean Gray (5-O), although he is almost certainly in error in describing this as a modified Measure 12 scheme.[2] *Le Triomphant* served in the Indian Ocean following her modernisation and received a British Admiralty Standard paint scheme of light grey overall with a sea blue lozenge on the lower hull.

It was decided that the ships would retain their former tactical designation as members of the 10th division of *contre-torpilleurs* (10e DCT). The lead-ship, *Le Fantasque*, retained her tactical number X101, which was repainted in small white letters straddling the Navy Blue/Haze Gray close to the bow. *Le Terrible* continued with the number X103, and the division would again be complete with the recommissioning of *Le Malin* in late 1943 (now X102). They retained the 'X' prefix even after they were redesignated 'light cruisers' in August 1943 – the 10th DCT became the 10th DCL. When *Le Triomphant* finally reentered service in 1944 she would be tacked onto the division as X104. *Le Fantasque* and *Le Terrible* would

---
[2] Jean Lassaque, *Histoire des croiseurs légers* (self-published sequel to *Les CT de 2800 tonnes du type Le Fantasque*, op. cit.).

Machinery: *Le Terrible* & *Le Malin* Post-Modernisation 1943

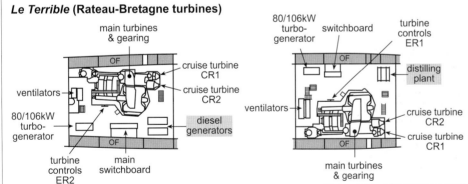
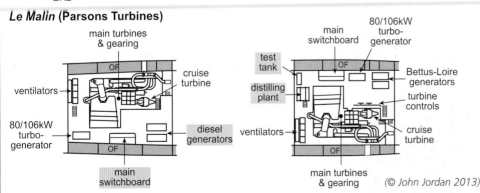

(© John Jordan 2013)

The machinery compartments of *Le Terrible* remain unmodified except for the replacement of the two Bettus-Loire generators by diesel generators of US manufacture and of the two original evaporators by a low-pressure distilling plant driven by the main turbines. The BuShips drawings of the engine rooms of *Le Malin* show more extensive changes. The two Bettus-Loire generators, which in the Parsons ships were located on the upper level of the forward engine room, have been retained, and a new upper platform has been constructed at the same level (Lower/1st Platform Deck) in the after engine room to accommodate the turbo-generator (moved from the engine room floor), two new diesel generators and a second main switchboard.

Note. The BuShips plans of *Le Malin* assume an engine room layout similar to that of *Le Fantasque* and *Le Terrible*. However, the original French plans of *Le Malin/L'Indomptable* show a completely different layout of the turbine machinery, as one would expect with a ship fitted with Parsons turbines. The author's drawing of the forward engine room follows the French plans. For the after engine room the precise configuration of the upper platform is conjectural; it assumes that the new platform was virtually a mirror-image of the one in ER1, as in the ships with Rateau-Bretagne turbines. In both drawings the revised arrangements for the auxiliary machinery follow the US Navy BuShips plans.

exchange hull numbers on 8 June 1944, when there was a change of command.

Le Terrible began her post-modernisation trials on 13 May; Le Fantasque would not begin hers for another month due to turbine problems. Once these were resolved she attained 39.5 knots in speed trials which took place on 12 June. On 19 June the two ships began working up together, in anticipation of their return to Europe. On 27 June Le Fantasque left for Casablanca, arriving on 18 July. Her complement was topped up, and on 22 July she left for Algiers via Gibraltar, arriving on the 25th. She would be joined there by her sister Le Terrible, which had been diverted to the Antilles, on 15 August. Accommodation was by this time so tight that a British liaison team assigned to Le Fantasque had to sling hammocks in the forward ammunition lobby. The other major drawback of the modernisation discovered during service in the Mediterranean was that when the ship was closed up, the gun crew for the after (quad) Bofors mounting often had to suffer the smoke and exhaust gases from the second funnel for long periods, particularly when the ship was steaming at speed.

Le Fantasque and Le Terrible would be followed into refit at the Charlestown Navy Yard by their sister Le Malin. On 8 November 1942 the contre-torpilleur had been days from completing a refit begun in July at Casablanca, when she became embroiled in the American assault on the harbour. Moored with her port side to the outer Jetée Delure she had been struck by a 16in shell ricochet from a salvo of 'shorts' from the battleship Massachusetts directed at the Jean Bart. Boiler no.3 had been disabled, and a large hole had been

When Le Fantasque and Le Terrible reentered service on the side of the Allies following their modernisation in the USA it quickly became apparent that there was a major shortage of accommodation. When a 9-man British liaison team embarked on board Le Fantasque at Algiers on 1 August 1943 the eight enlisted personnel had to be accommodated in the forward ammunition lobby, which was unheated and often wet. When the Charlestown dockyard came to refit Le Malin it was decided to implement a radical solution which involved almost halving the spaces previously allocated to the senior officers and inserting quarters for 27 enlisted men in three-tiered bunks immediately abaft the after engine room bulkhead. This had a knock-on effect on the remaining officer accommodation aft, with junior officers being accommodated in two/three-berth cabins, and multi-berth cabins for Chief Petty Officers worked in abeam the steering compartment.

(© John Jordan 2013)

Accommodation: *Le Terrible* & *Le Malin* Post-Modernisation 1943

Le Terrible

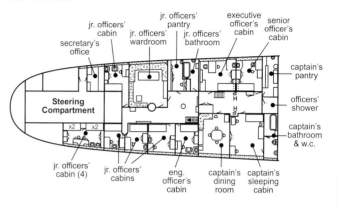

Le Malin

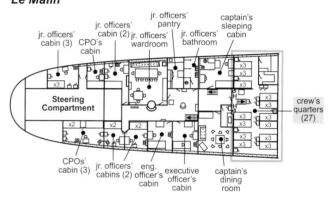

Above: A starboard quarter view of Le Fantasque on 24 June 1943, on completion of her refit at the Charlestown Navy Yard, Boston. The first funnel has its original cap. *(US Navy Official 2763/4-43 NYBos, courtesy of Norman Friedman)*

opened up in her port side, flooding the forward boiler and engine rooms. A heavy list to port was partially corrected by shoring and pumping, but the ship then had to wait in the Delande Basin for several months to be repaired due to work overload in the relatively small local dockyard. She was scheduled to leave for modernisation in the United States during the first half of May, but three months were necessary to make her seaworthy. She finally left on one set of turbines with her speed limited to 12 knots in company with a convoy, and arrived in Boston on 26 June. Work at the Charlestown Navy Yard was completed on 17 November 1943, and she left Norfolk on 19 December for the Azores, joining her divisional leader *Le Fantasque* there on the 31st.

The final unit of the class to undergo modernisation in the USA was the FNFL *Le Triomphant*, which following repairs at Diego Suarez and at the Sidi-Abdallah Dockyard, Bizerte, using parts from her sister *L'Audacieux*, joined a convoy at Gibraltar on 10 April, then sprinted for Boston at 25 knots, arriving 12 April. Repair and modernisation took the best part of a year, and *Le Triomphant* was again ready for service only in April 1945.

There were small external differences between all four units following their modernisation. *Le Terrible* had been fitted with a distinctive hooded funnel cowling during repairs at Toulon in 1942,

Right: This starboard quarter view of *Le Malin* following her modernisation provides an interesting comparison with the one of *Le Fantasque* taken from a similar angle. Note the absence of antenna supports on the second funnel – they would be replaced in 1945 – and the US Navy-type smoke generators on the stern. *(Official US Navy photo 5092-43, Charlestown Navy Yard NPS Park Collection, Boston, MA, courtesy of Rick E Davis)*

Below: *Le Fantasque* on 24 June 1943, on completion of her refit at the Charlestown Navy Yard, Boston. *(US Navy Official 2763/4-43 NYBos, courtesy of Norman Friedman)*

and similar cowlings would be retro-fitted in *Le Fantasque* and *Le Malin* during 1944–5 and in *Le Triomphant* in 1947. *Le Malin* had the W/T aerial supports removed from the second funnel to clear arcs for the 40mm quad Bofors. *Le Triomphant*, which had mounting no.4 restored (the gun came from *L'Audacieux*), retained the bulwarks fitted around the main gun mountings by the British in 1941, and had a short pole mast for a US-type HF D/F Outfit DAQ stepped abaft the second funnel. A shortage of quadruple Bofors mountings resulted in her being fitted with three twin mountings, although in part-compensation there were

eleven 20mm Oerlikon guns, the eleventh mounting being installed on the quarterdeck.

Contrary to what has been stated in a number of secondary sources, the first three ships to be modernised retained their original depth charge chutes. However, during 1944 stocks of the Guiraud 200kg depth charge in North Africa were becoming badly depleted, and during refits in 1944–5 the chain mechanisms were removed and the openings for the chutes sealed. Conventional British rails for the Mk VIIH depth charge were fitted on the quarterdeck, and the chutes used to stow additional charges.[3] From 1945 British gunnery radar Type 285P4 was installed, the distinctive yagi antennae being fitted to the main director. Gun wear was already a major problem by the spring of 1944. *Le Fantasque* and *Le Terrible* shared the 138.6mm guns salvaged from their sister *L'Audacieux* between them in April 1944, and in a refit September to December 1944 *Le Malin* had her own guns replaced by Mle 1927 models salvaged from ships beached off the North African ports (possibly *Epervier*) as a temporary measure. All three ships would receive new barrels during 1945, following the liberation of mainland France.

Further modifications during the late war period included the lowering of the director pedestal for the quad Bofors 40mm by 0.8m to reduce topweight, the fitting of funnel cowlings similar to that trialled on *Le Terrible* in *Le Malin* (1944) and *Le Fantasque* (1945),[4] and the removal of the original antenna supports in *Le Fantasque* and *Le Terrible*.

---

[3] *Le Triomphant* had already been fitted with two DC rails in the UK in 1940-1 and appears to have retained them after her 1945 modernisation.
[4] *Le Triomphant* had to wait until 1947 for this modification.

APPENDIX E: MODERNISATION OF THE OLDER DESTROYERS 1943–1945

FEW OF THE 1455-TONNE AND 1500-TONNE destroyers survived Operation 'Torch' and the scuttling at Toulon. *Tempête*, *Simoun* and *L'Alcyon* sustained moderate damage at Casablanca, *Forbin*, *Basque* and *Le Fortuné* remained immobilised at Alexandria, and *Trombe* had been seized intact at Toulon and pressed into service by the Italian Navy. It would take three to six months for the ships damaged at Casablanca to complete repairs, using the rudimentary and overloaded dockyard facilities available in French North Africa, and a similar period for the ships impounded in Alexandria to be released. The destroyer *Trombe* was formally handed over by the Italians only at the end of October 1943.

The oldest of these destroyers had been completed in 1926, so were now almost 17 years old. The Americans, with brand-new ships rolling off the building ways every day, were (understandably) unwilling to disrupt their own dockyard schedules to modernise these elderly and obsolescent vessels. The British were more sympathetic, but their own dockyards were working to capacity. It was agreed that *Tempête* and *Simoun*, following their repairs, would be taken in hand by the Royal Naval Dockyard, Bermuda, but the remaining ships would have to be modernised in French North Africa using materiel supplied by the British and the Americans.

Modernisation was complicated by philosophical and political issues. The British wanted these vessels rebuilt as anti-submarine escorts, with a complete ASW outfit and a substantial battery of defensive AA guns. However, the commanding officers, with the support of the French naval authorities, fought to retain the ships' offensive capabilities in the form of 130mm main guns and torpedoes. Inevitably, compromises had to be made which left neither party completely satisfied.

1455-tonne Type

Tempête was under repair at Casablanca until 12 April 1943, *Simoun* until 25 June 1943. At the same time both ships were prepared for their refits at Bermuda. The following work was done:

- 15mm protective plating was applied to the face and sides of the bridge (a lesson from the strafing by US naval aircraft during the battle for Casablanca)
- the tripod legs and topmast were removed, leaving a simple pole foremast
- turreted rangefinders (5-metre in *Tempête*, 4-metre in *Simoun*), removed from destroyers lost in the action off Casablanca, were fitted atop the bridge
- the two 75mm searchlight projectors were removed and replaced by a single 60m model mounted on a platform at the base of the foremast

Tempête November 1943

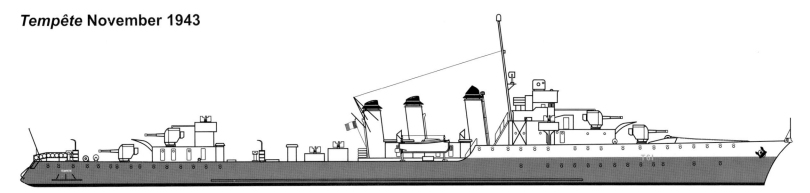

Tempête January 1945

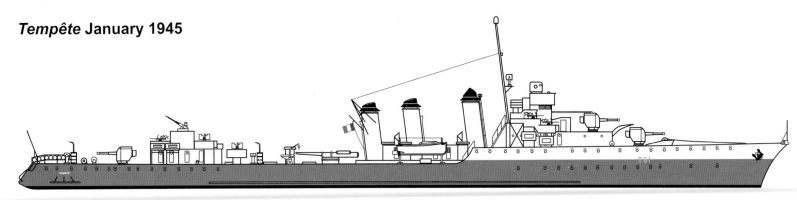

(© John Jordan 2013)

The first of the two profiles shows *Tempête* following her refit in Bermuda 16 April to 7 July 1943, and her subsequent minor refit at Algiers from October to 6 November of the same year. At Bermuda she had received five 20mm Oerlikon guns: two in an athwartships tub atop the after hoists, two in half-tubs abeam the forward end of the bridge, and a single in a tub in place of the forward torpedo tubes. Two British-style gravity rails each for ten Mk VIIH depth charges were fitted above the stern, with six reloads stowed in each of the former DC chutes. There were also four Thornycroft Mk IV depth charge throwers each with parbuckle stowage for the standard Mk VII depth charge, two on the quarterdeck and two amidships, in place of the after torpedo tubes. In addition to the depth charges on the DCTs, there were three DCs in each of the reload racks with a further three beneath, so the total number of charges embarked was 60 (2 x 10 rails, 2 x 6 chutes, 4 x 1 DCTs, 4 x 6 reloads). An Asdic 128D was installed, together with the associated sonar room, and a US Navy SF surveillance radar (atop the pole mast) with an RDF 172 radar room in an extension to the upper bridge.

A further two 20mm were installed in sided half-tubs immediately abaft the single amidships at Algiers in October/November.

The second profile shows *Tempête* following her refit at Casablanca and Toulon/La Seyne September 1944 to January 1945. The principal modifications involved the disembarkation of gun no.3 and its replacement by an elevated tub for a single 40mm Bofors. The forward triple torpedo mounting was restored, and the three 20mm guns amidships were relocated, together with a fourth mounting, to the four corners of the after deckhouse. Two further 20mm guns were installed in new tubs superimposed above the original tubs at the side of the bridge, and two more in place of the after torpedo tubes, inboard of the DCTs, for a total of of ten 20mm Oerlikons.

Above: *Tempête* at Mers el-Kebir in early 1944. The photo shows the modifications made at Bermuda April–July 1943 (see text and caption for drawing), and following her refit at Algiers in October 1943 she has two additional 20mm Oerlikon in half-tubs amidships and has been repainted in the US Navy Measure 22 two-tone colour scheme. *(Philippe Caresse collection)*

Above: *Basque*, probably during the winter of 1944/45. The last of the ships to undergo a full modernisation, she displays a full set of ten 20mm Oerlikon: four forward, four aft, and two in tubs amidships. *(Leo van Ginderen collection)*

- the motor launch and two sets of davits were landed, the launch being replaced by four Brest-type life rafts stowed abaft the third funnel; the motor boat and whaler were retained, but their davits were moved forward
- replenishment stations were installed port and starboard with a pipe connection to the forward fuel tanks
- the minesweeping paravanes and their handling gear were disembarked
- 130mm gun no.2, the two 37mm AA guns and both torpedo mountings were disembarked, and four single 20mm Oerlikons fitted as a temporary measure: two forward of the bridge (in place of no.2 gun) and two amidships
- the remaining 130mm guns were given increased elevation, to 35 degrees, and the sight ports were widened to enable them to engage aircraft at long range
- four Thornycroft Mle 1918 depth charge throwers for French Guiraud 100kg charges were fitted on the quarterdeck

Following the completion of this work, *Tempête* left Casablanca with a convoy for Bermuda, arriving on 26 April 1943 and remaining in the dockyard until 7 July. She was followed by her sister *Simoun*, which arrived on 10 August and remained in the dockyard until 18 October. Her refit benefited considerably from experience with *Tempête*.

The plans for the modernisation of the two ships had been drawn up by the DCAN at Casablanca. However, the British engineers were very unhappy with some aspects of the proposals. The stability of these vessels was already marginal by British standards, and they calculated that the weight of the equipment due to be installed was double that estimated by the French. The French continued to insist on the conservation of all four 130mm guns, and plans for two twin 40mm Bofors mountings had to be abandoned. Work was delayed by problems with delivery of the necessary components and by labour shortages, but in the end the following modifications were made:

- gun no.2 (which had to come from Casablanca) was reinstalled
- five 20mm were fitted in tubs (see accompanying drawing and caption)
- the French depth charge throwers were removed, and in their place a complete British-style anti-submarine outfit was installed: two 10-charge rails, four Thornycroft Mk IV DCTs, and an Asdic 128D (brought from Casablanca broken down in cases)
- an American SF surface surveillance radar was installed; the thimble radome was fitted atop the pole foremast, and the radar room in an extension to the upper bridge

The refit of *Simoun* at Bermuda was simplified by the loss of no.1 gun mounting, which was heavily damaged during the battle for Casablanca. No.2 gun had been moved to no.1 position at Casablanca, and no.3 gun now replaced no.2 forward of the bridge, leaving the after deckhouse free for a proper AA battery. The 25mm Hochkiss gun was retained there as an interim measure – the French were running short of ammunition for this gun in the depots of North Africa – pending installation of a single 40mm Bofors. It was flanked by two 20mm guns in tubs, and there were three further 20mm mountings disposed as in *Tempête*. The other modifications were as in *Tempête*, except that the DCTs were angled aft and *Simoun* also received a British-model medium-wave radio which facilitated her operation with Allied convoys.

Following their refits at Bermuda, *Tempête* and *Simoun* were painted in the US Navy's Measure 22, with a Blue Gray hull and Haze Gray upperworks. They still constituted the 6ᵉ *Division de torpilleurs* (6th DT), but with their respective positions reversed. The hull numbers T61 and T62 were now painted in small white letters 0.64m high which straddled the dark and light grey sections of the forecastle. *Trombe* initially became T41, in anticipation of the formation of a 4th Division, but on 16 October 1944 became T64.

Both *Tempête* and *Simoun* initially retained six 13.2mm Browning MG, but these would steadily be replaced during 1944–5 by additional 20mm Oerlikons as these became available; the final complement for both ships was ten. In late 1944 *Tempête* lost gun no.3 in favour of a single 40mm, had her forward torpedo mounting reinstated and her 20mm Oerlikons reorganised (see drawing). In mid-1945 *Simoun* had her four DCTs grouped together on the after deckhouse to clear the arcs for no.4 gun. When returned by the Italians, *Trombe* received similar modifications to her two sister ships during a refit at Bizerte which lasted until mid-March 1944.

1500-tonne Type

Of the 1500-tonne type, *L'Alcyon* was the first to be taken in hand. Damaged during the battle for Casablanca, she first had to undergo repairs in the local dockyard, and subsequently received modifications similar to those of *Tempête* and *Simoun*. An American SF radar was fitted and improved reload stowage for the existing anti-submarine mortars was provided, but she received only four 20mm as a temporary measure in place of her torpedo tubes. The 25mm Hotchkiss gun was retained for the present. She emerged from refit only in late June 1943.

The three ships immobilised at Alexandria received only the minimum modifications necessary for them to be repatriated to North Africa: the 37mm and 13.2mm mountings were replaced

Above: *Le Fortuné* in 1945 *(US Navy NH93464, courtesy of A D Baker III)*.

by four 20mm Oerlikon guns, two on the forecastle and two abeam the third funnel. They received further modifications during the second half of 1943, but these were of a piecemeal nature, and Admiral Lemonnier, Chief of the Naval General Staff, was charged with putting forward proposals which would result in greater uniformity of armament, using scheduled refit periods during 1944. These were dependent on delivery of material by the British, the French dockyards being tasked with pre-fabricating the necessary gun tubs ready for rapid installation.

The general principles adopted were as follows:

- guns nos. 1, 2 and 4 to be retained and their elevation increased; no.3 position to be used to fit a single 40mm Bofors and 2/4 20mm Oerlikon
- two 20mm Oerlikon to be fitted abeam the bridge, and a further two in a common tub amidships
- two British-style DC rails for Mk VIIH charges to be installed above the stern (the existing chutes to be used to stow reloads), and four British Mk IV DCTs with parbuckle stowage to be fitted amidships – it was subsequently decided to relocate two to the quarterdeck, as on *Tempête*; there were to be 80 depth charges divided almost equally between the 'heavy' and standard Mk VII types
- Asdic 128D and SF radar to be installed
- the only boats to be retained were the motor boat, the whaler (on davits) and a dinghy, the other boats being replaced by life rafts

It was subsequently decided to reinstall the forward torpedo mounting.

The first unit to be refitted to this standard was *Le Fortuné*, which was taken in hand at Casablanca 16 February to 21 May 1944. She was followed by *L'Alcyon*, refitted from 15 June to 5 August 1944.

Forbin had been extensively refitted at Casablanca from 22 August to 20 September 1943, but Admiral Lemonnier's report was submitted some weeks after the refit ended, and her anti-submarine and anti-aircraft outfit remained incomplete – two additional 20mm Oerlikons were installed in a common tub amidships, but she retained the original DC chutes and two of her four mortars were of the French Mle 1918 type. The work was completed at Algiers 12–17 June 1944, when two additional 20mm Oerlikon were fitted and the ASW armament brought up to British standards.

Basque received only piecemeal modifications during 1943–4, and had to wait until a major refit at Casablanca 28 May to 26 August 1944 to be brought up to the standard of the other ships. She emerged from this refit with no fewer than ten 20mm Oerlikons: four forward, four atop the after deckhouse, and two in a common tub amidships.

All four of these ships were repainted in the American Measure 22 two-tone scheme. Hull numbers were *L'Alcyon* T63 (completing the 6th DT with *Tempête* and *Simoun*), *Le Fortuné* T31, *Forbin* T32 and *Basque* T33.

CHAPTER 14
THE PERIOD 1945–1956

FOR THE MAJORITY OF FRENCH PEOPLE, the war ended with the capitulation of Germany. Participation in the final stages of the war against Japan was envisaged, but it was to be primarily naval, and even the newest warships would need to be modernised before being sent to the Indian Ocean. French plans involved the despatch of the four light cruisers of the *Le Fantasque* class, and *Le Triomphant* duly arrived at Colombo on 27 May 1945. However, the war against Japan ended on 15 August 1945, and some of the ships which it had been planned to deploy to the Far East were involved in the repossession of Indochina, and in the conflict that followed.

The end of the war in Europe was followed by the handing back of the seven surviving British corvettes and by the retirement of the more elderly French-built ships, which were now completely worn out. The four light cruisers remained in service, but the 1500-tonne destroyers and *Tigre* were quickly decommissioned. The *contre-torpilleur Albatros*, laid up at Casablanca since November 1942, was repaired and refurbished to serve as a gunnery training ship.

New ships were projected, but because of the poor state of both the French military-industrial infrastructure and the postwar economy, these could not be laid down before 1949. In the interim the Navy would have at its disposal the six ex-American destroyer escorts, the six British-built frigates, and a handful of ex-German and ex-Italian destroyers. With French membership of NATO the escort forces were reinforced by a second batch of destroyer escorts, six of which were transferred in 1950 and two in 1952.

The naval forces were reorganised according to a circular dated 1 January 1947. The ships in active service were formed into three groups: the *Richelieu* Group, the Aircraft Carrier Group, and the Cruiser Group, which comprised the 4th Cruiser Division (4e DC) and the 10th Light Cruiser Division (10e DCL). For major fleet exercises, these three groups were combined into the Intervention Force (*Force d'intervention* or FI), which was formed for the first time on 21 April 1947.

A permanent formation designated the Squadron (*l'Escadre*) was finally created at Toulon on 19 April 1949 with the Cruiser Group, the Aircraft Carrier Group, and the Anti-Submarine Action Group (*Groupe d'action anti-sous-marine* or GASM), which comprised all the escorts and the operational submarines.

INDOCHINA

Le Triomphant was the first French warship to be sent to the Far East. She arrived at Colombo on 27 May 1945. Following repairs at Diego Suarez in July she left Madagascar on 20 August and, together with the battleship *Richelieu*, covered the return of the British to Singapore. She arrived at Saigon on 3 October 1945. She provided protection for Nha Trang, alternating on station with *Le Fantasque* until February 1946, then provided cover for the landing of French forces at Tonkin. On 6 March, she was at the head of a convoy

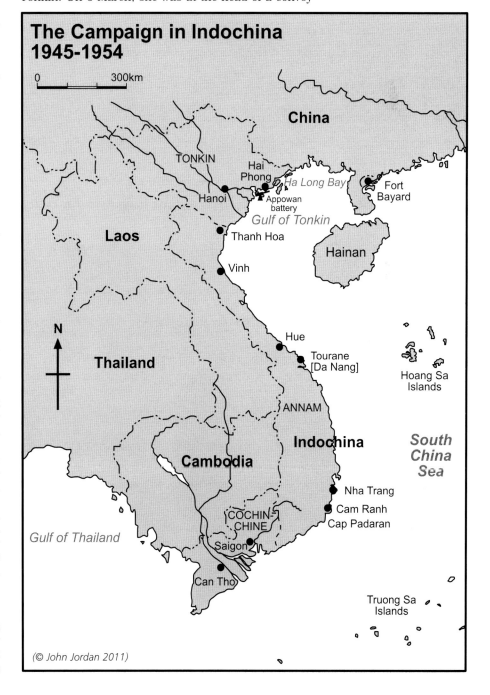

(© John Jordan 2011)

which was entering the northern port of Hai Phong when she was taken under fire by the Chinese forces whom the French were due to relieve. She was under fire for 20 minutes, and suffered eight dead, 39 wounded (of whom 19 seriously), and 439 holes in her hull and superstructures. The Chinese then ceased fire, and after talks the French were able to land.

On 24 March 1946 *Le Triomphant* took part in a small naval review in Ha Long Bay. She departed Indochina on 9 April 1946, returning to Toulon on 16 May.

Le Fantasque arrived in Saigon on 27 October 1945. She alternated with *Le Triomphant* in providing fire support for the garrison at Nha Trang, then for the Tonkin operations. She also participated in the naval review in Ha Long Bay. She embarked on a 'show-the-flag' mission to Japan, which took place in late May/early June. She left Saigon on 4 July 1946, returning to Toulon on 20 August.

Le Malin, which was reactivated to serve as an escort for the French aircraft carriers, was in Indochina with the carrier *Arromanches* from September 1951 to May 1952.

The French destroyer escorts also deployed to Indochina. Dates were as follows:

Sénégalais: October 1945 to March 1946, then October 1953 to August 1954
Somali: October 1945 to March 1946
Marocain: November 1948 to January 1949, then September 1952 to February 1953
Tunisien: April 1954 to January 1955

The frigates *Tonkinois*, *L'Escarmouche*, *Croix de Lorraine* and *La Découverte* were deployed between March 1946 and mid-1947.

The DE *Hova* was detached to Madagascar from June 1947 to December 1947.

THE LIGHT CRUISERS

Together with the three surviving 7600-ton cruisers, the four light cruisers of the *Le Fantasque* class constituted the nucleus of the French fleet during the postwar period.

Le Malin was repaired following her collision with *Le Terrible* using the bow (length 22 metres; weight 120 tonnes) cut from the wreck of *L'Indomptable*, which had been scuttled at Toulon in November 1942. She recommissioned on 5 November 1945, and undertook a number of transport missions.

Le Terrible, which had been even more extensively damaged, was repaired at Bizerte and recommissioned on 1 January 1946. The port-side twin 40mm Bofors had been damaged beyond repair in the collision, so both twin mountings were replaced by single shielded mountings. The ship returned to Toulon on 26 April. *Le Terrible* and *Le Malin* then embarked on a 'show-the-flag' mission to northern Europe as far as Narvik in May 1946.

On 1 January 1947 the 10th DCL was combined with the 4th DC, forming the Cruiser Group. On 1 January the following year the 10th DCL became the 1st DCL.

In general two of the four light cruisers were operational at any given time, the remaining two being in refit or reserve to reduce demands on trained personnel. They participated in the activations of the *Force d'intervention*, then in the activities of the Squadron when it was formed on 19 April 1949, notably in the major fleet exercises which took place between April and July of each year: *Le Malin* and *Le Terrible* in 1947, *Le Terrible* and *Le Triomphant* in 1948, and *Le Fantasque* and *Le Triomphant* in 1949.

On her return from Indochina, *Le Fantasque* was operational from March to September 1947, then underwent a major refit at Bizerte until May 1948. Weaknesses in the hull girder led to the hull being

Right: The bow of *l'Indomptable* is used for the repair of *Le Malin* at La Ciotat in July 1945.

Below: A fine port quarter view of *Le Fantasque* at Toulon on 8 May 1950, towards the end of her career. The short mast abaft the second funnel was an experimental aerial spreader; it was not a success and was not fitted to any other ship of the class. *(Marius Bar)*

Below: *Le Malin* at speed off Toulon on 1 August 1951, shortly after her major refit. On 21 August she would make 41 knots for four hours during trials. Note the restoration of the aerial supports on the second funnel and the relocation of the 20mm Oerlikons formerly on the upper deck to the centre deckhouse. *(Marius Bar)*

Above: An aerial view of *Le Terrible* following her refit of 1952–3. The twin 40mm Bofors were restored, and aerial supports similar to those in *Le Malin* were fitted to the second funnel. *(René Bail collection)*

reinforced at Bizerte from March to May, and she recommissioned with a full complement only on 12 July 1948. She then replaced *Le Terrible* and remained in active service until August 1950, and was the only (and last) light cruiser in service with the Squadron during the 1949–50 *année d'instruction*. Finally, she left for Bizerte for a major refit which was cancelled due to the poor state of the ship. She was moored at Saint-Mandrier in September 1953, was stricken in 1953 and broken up in 1958.

Le Triomphant was placed in care & maintenance on her return from Indochina, and then underwent a major refit at Bizerte from February to November 1947. She returned to Toulon on 7 November, relieving *Le Malin* on the same day. She was placed in 'normal' reserve at Bizerte on 1 November 1949, placed in reserve A in March 1953 and in 'special' reserve B on 20 July 1954. She was sold for scrap in December 1957 and broken up in 1958.

Le Malin was placed in care & maintenance on 7 November 1947. She underwent a major refit at Bizerte until October 1948, and was placed in normal reserve on 1 November 1949.

Le Terrible was placed in care & maintenance on 12 July 1948. She arrived in Bizerte on 27 April 1949 and was placed in reserve there on 15 March 1950.

The light cruisers, which were reclassified as 'escort destroyers 1st class' (*destroyer-escorteur de 1re classe*) on 1 July 1951, then as 'fast escorts' (*escorteur rapide*) in 1958, were assigned a specific mission from the beginning of the 1950s. An *escorteur rapide* was to accompany an aircraft carrier during take-off and landing operations. The commissioning of the carrier *La Fayette* (ex-*Langley*, CVL-27) in 1951, which was capable of 30 knots, led to the recommissioning of an escort fast enough to accompany the carrier.

Le Malin duly recommissioned on 1 July 1951. On 21 August, she made 41 knots for four hours. On 28 August she departed Toulon in company with the carrier *Arromanches* (ex-*Colossus*). The two ships operated off Indochina from September 1951 to May 1952, but *Le Malin* also undertook some missions on her own. She returned to Toulon, still in company with *Arromanches*, on 13 June 1952. She left again on 23 June for Brest, where she was placed in reserve A on 1 August 1952. She served as a breakwater and as an annex to the *Ecole Navale* at Poulmic, then served as a floating jetty for the minesweepers at Laninon. She was stricken on 3 February 1964, used as a breakwater at Lorient from 1965 to 1976, and broken up in 1977.

Le Terrible underwent a major refit at Bizerte from 1 May 1952. She was due to replace *Le Malin* as a carrier escort, but arrived at Toulon only on 10 April 1953. She embarked on a cruise of the eastern Mediterranean in late May/early June, and operated with the carrier *La Fayette* from June 1953 to February 1954, then with her sister *Bois Belleau* (ex-*Belleau Wood*, CVL-24) from February to August 1954. She again accompanied *La Fayette* from September 1954 to February 1955, and *Arromanches* from February to August 1955. She was then transferred to Brest, arriving 28 August 1955. She decommissioned on 1 September, serving as an annex to the *Ecole Navale* at Poulmic. She was placed in special reserve on 1 December 1956, was stricken on 29 June 1962 and broken up at Brest in 1963.

THE END OF THE *CONTRE-TORPILLEURS* AND *TORPILLEURS*

Tigre was at Toulon in May 1945. She served as a troop transport in Algeria and carried out a fire support mission during the May/June riots. She deployed to Kiel and Bremerhaven in September 1945. She resumed the transport of personnel in the Mediterranean until December 1946, and was then employed as a gunnery school ship (*bâtiment-école d'application du tir à la mer*) as a temporary measure during the reconstruction of *Albatros* for the purpose. Following her decommissioning, she served as a pontoon for the Engineering School at Saint-Mandrier. She was stricken on 4 January 1954 and broken up in 1955.

Albatros, the only surviving four-funnelled *contre-torpilleur*, returned to active service on 9 September 1948. The forward pair of boilers and their associated funnels were removed, and she was armed with three 138.6mm guns and a selection of other weapons which included the German-type 105mm SKC/33 (until late 1950), the prototype French 100mm Mle 1945 (from early 1951), the older-model 75mm, and 40mm and 20mm light AA (see pp.287-91 for details). Based at Toulon, she was employed as a gunnery school ship (EATM). The decommissioning of *Albatros*, which had her complement reduced on 3 August 1956, was accelerated by Suez. She was placed in reserve A on 10 September 1956, then in special reserve B. She was stricken on 22 June, written off on 7 September 1959 and broken up.

The 1500-tonne destroyers, which from September 1945 were based at Cherbourg, were quickly decommissioned:

Trombe, which had been decommissioned at Toulon following the damage sustained on 17 April 1945 (see Chapter 13), was placed in special reserve on 3 July 1945, stricken on 12 December 1946, and put up for sale on 7 December 1950.

Tempête undertook transport missions between metropolitan France and Algeria in May/June 1945, then again in November/December. In care & mainte-

nance at Oran during 1946, she arrived at Cherbourg on 3 February 1946 to be placed in reserve. She was stricken on 17 February 1950 and put up for sale on 1 August 1951.
- *Simoun*, which was available from 28 July 1945 following repairs, returned to Toulon on 2 October, undertook a mission to Wilhelmshaven in early 1946, and returned to Cherbourg on 3 February 1946 to be placed in reserve. She was stricken on 17 February 1950 and put up for sale on 23 April 1952.
- *Basque*, following a major refit during the second half of 1945, was attached to the *Ecole Navale*. She decommissioned after taking part in the summer cruise of 1948, and was placed in special reserve on 1 January 1949. She was stricken on 10 December 1952.
- *Le Fortuné*, following a major refit at Casablanca, arrived at Cherbourg on 18 May 1946 to be placed in normal reserve. She was stricken on 31 August 1950.
- *L'Alcyon* undertook transport and trials missions. She was assigned to the *Ecole Navale* in February 1947. Having suffered damage to her starboard propeller on 11 October 1947, *L'Alcyon* decommissioned on 15 March 1948, was placed in special reserve on 20 July 1949, then stricken on 20 November 1952.
- *Forbin*, after a long refit, left Bizerte in late October 1945 and arrived at Cherbourg in early December. She visited Greenock, Wilhelmshaven, Hamburg and Bremen. She suffered weather damage while at sea; she was placed in reserve on 31 March 1946 and finally stricken on 10 November 1952.

THE EX-GERMAN SHIPS

What remained of the German fleet was distributed among the Americans, the British and the Russians following the Potsdam Conference of July 1945. Neither the British nor the Americans had any need for the ex-German ships, as they had a surplus of recently completed destroyers. Some were recommissioned for trials, and the others were broken up with the exception of a few ships ceded to the French, whose fleet had been severely depleted by the war. Some of the ships that were in French ports when France was liberated were also reactivated to serve with the Marine Nationale. In this way the French acquired five destroyers, six torpedo boats, ten submarines, 25 minesweeping sloops and 40 auxiliary vessels.

Four destroyers were handed over by the British at Cherbourg on 4 February 1946: Z5 *Paul Jacobi* was renamed *Desaix*, Z6 *Theodor Riedel* was renamed *Kléber*, Z25 was renamed *Hoche* and Z31 renamed

Below: *Albatros* during an underway replenishment exercise with the battleship *Jean Bart* off Nice in November 1955. Note the antenna for the French DRBC 11A fire control radar which has replaced the British AB/M on the main gunnery director, and the rails for illuminating rockets on the sides of the shield for no.2 gun mounting. *(Charles Limonnier collection)*

Marceau. They made up the 1st DCT at Cherbourg.

Desaix was repaired, but was worn out and would not be upgraded like the others. She ran trials in September 1946, then took part in the African cruises with the *Force d'intervention* which took place April–June 1947 and March–June 1948. She was decommissioned on 1 January 1949. Of the other three, *Kléber* was modernised 1948–51, *Hoche* 1951–3, and *Marceau* 1948–50. Following her refit *Hoche* served as a trials vessel.

The Americans transferred *Z39*, which was cannibalised for spares then served as a pontoon for the minesweepers at Brest until she was broken up in 1964. *Z23* and *Z37*, the wrecks of which were found at La Pallice and Bordeaux, proved beyond repair.

Two torpedo boats of the 1300-tonne *Elbing* class were also transferred by the British in February 1946. *T23* became *Alsacien* and *T28* was renamed *Lorrain*.[1] A third ship, *T35*, was ceded to France by the Americans in 1947 and was cannibalised for spares.

Below: *Desaix* (ex-*Paul Jacobi*, ex-*Z5*) on the occasion of her handing over to the Marine Nationale. She is still fitted with German-model 37mm Flak M/42 guns and radar. (A D Baker III collection)

Alsacien and *Lorrain* were refurbished at Cherbourg and incorporated into the fleet. American radars and 40mm Bofors guns (in place of the German 37mm) were installed, and they recommissioned only in December 1949. They were then based at Toulon, assigned to the Aircraft Carrier Group, then to GASM. *Alsacien* was decommissioned on 9 June 1954 and *Lorrain*, which was used to trial new models of torpedo tube and sonar being developed for the future fast escorts, on 31 October 1955.

The three ex-German 600-tonne torpedo boats *T11* (renamed *Bir Hakeim*), *T14* (*Dompaire*) and *T20* (*Baccarat*) were not recommissioned and were stricken in 1951.

THE EX-ITALIAN SHIPS

A peace treaty between France and Italy was signed on 10 February 1947. Article 57 stipulated that the Italians were to deliver a total of 43 ships as reparations for the seizure of 30,000 tonnes of light vessels at Toulon after November 1942. Following negotiations, an agreement was signed on 14 July 1948 and the Marine Nationale received 19 ships.

Between 14 July and 1 October 1948 the following ships arrived at Toulon: the light cruisers *Scipione Africano* and *Attilio Regolo*, the destroyers *Mitragliere* (renamed *Jurien de la Gravière*), *Velite* (>*Duperré*), *Alfredo Oriani* (>*D'Estaing*) and *Legionario* (>*Duchaffault*), and the colonial sloop *Eritrea* (>*Francis Garnier*). In the event, due to a lack of dockyard capacity and funding, the Navy recommissioned only the two light cruisers, the colonial sloop (decommissioned only in 1966), an oiler (reactivated only from April 1948 to October 1949) and a few auxiliary vessels. One of the four destroyers, *Jurien de la Gravière*, was recommissioned for trials from October 1948 to April 1949. The Navy Ministry, which had fought hard during negotiations with the Italians to recover the maximum number of ships, was naturally unhappy with this outcome.

The two light cruisers, which were renamed *Châteaurenault* (ex-*Attilio Regolo*) and *Guichen* (ex-*Scipione Africano*), recommissioned in 1949 and 1950 respectively. They formed the 2nd Light Cruiser Division (7 September 1948), then the 2nd Destroyer Division (22 March 1951), but rarely left harbour. They would be reconstructed at La Seyne, rearmed with six 105mm SKC/33, ten 57mm Mle 1951 guns and four triple anti-submarine torpedo tubes, and fitted with new radars of French design and manufacture (DRBV 20, DRBV 11, DRBV 30 and DRBC 11 and 30). *Châteaurenault* was reconstructed from 1 February 1951 to 1 May 1956 (includes trials), and *Guichen* from 14 June 1951 to 1 July 1954. Reclassified as 'fleet escorts' (*escorteur d'escadre*), they were incorporated

---

[1] There was clear political intent in the choice of names for the ex-German destroyers and torpedo boats. The names given to the destroyers, which were originally to have been used for the Improved *Mogador*s of the 1938 *bis* estimates, commemorated generals of the Revolutionary Wars who fought with distinction against the Austrians and the Bavarians; those allocated to the two torpedo boats celebrated the restitution to France of the two provinces of Alsace and Lorraine – lost to Prussia in the war of 1870-1 and then again in June 1940.

THE PERIOD 1945-1956

Left: *Guichen* (ex-*Scipione Africano*) at Malta in 1956. The Italian light cruiser was rebuilt on the pattern of the French fleet escorts between 1951 and 1953. She would pay off in April 1961. *(Leo van Ginderen collection)*

into the 1st Fleet Escort Flotilla (*flotille d'escorteurs d'escadre* or FEE).

They were subsequently modified to serve as flotilla leaders (the after 105mm mounting and two TT mountings were disembarked to provide additional accommodation): *Châteaurenault* from January 1956 to July 1957, and *Guichen* from July 1957 to November 1958. *Châteaurenault* served as flagship of the 1st FEE at Toulon from 9 April 1955 to 4 April 1961, then as flagship of the Light Squadron at Brest from 15 April 1961 to 18 June 1962. *Guichen* was flagship of the Light Squadron at Brest from 17 November 1958 to 15 April 1961.

REBUILDING OF THE FLEET

The armistice of June 1940 effectively halted all construction work in progress. Ships projected or building included the following:

– the eight destroyers of the *Le Hardi* class: five would eventually be completed and accepted into service (*Le Hardi* on 31 May 1940 and the other four, still

Below: *Hoche* (ex-*Z25*) in 1948. She retained her original twin 150mm mounting forward until refitted in 1952. *(Philippe Caresse collection)*

Above: Two of the new generation of 'fleet escorts': *Surcouf* outboard of *Forbin*. *Surcouf* was the first of twelve ships of the T47B type; *Forbin* was one of the five T53s modified as radar pickets for the control of air operations. *(Leo van Ginderen collection)*

The programmes of 1 April and 27 May 1940 envisaged ordering 24 destroyers of the *Livermore* class (referred to in French documentation of the period as the *Woolsey* class) from the United States. The Americans were contacted on 30 May 1940 – it was proposed that in order to hasten the entry into service of the destroyers, ships already in service with the US Navy would be transferred and replaced by the hulls laid down under the French contract – but the proposal was preempted by the armistice.

Following the armistice, studies continued in order to keep design staff occupied, and with a view to a rapid resumption of construction when the situation permitted. A study designated T41 (*torpilleur* 1941) displacing 1642 tonnes was followed by studies for a large fleet escort designated E42 and E43 displacing between 2767 and 3080 tonnes and with four or six 130mm guns.

During the postwar period, the priority accorded to rebuilding the merchant navy meant that concrete proposals for naval construction had to wait until the budget of 1949. Studies embarked on following the end of the war culminated in two types:

running trials, in June 1940), while the last three (*Lansquenet*, *Le Corsaire/Siroco*, *Le Flibustier/Bison*) remained incomplete up to the scuttling of November 1942
- the seven destroyers of the *L'Intrépide* class which were to have been of an Improved *Le Hardi* design displacing 2215 tons standard (see Chapter 9): two were launched at La Seyne in 1941 and one in 1947; none was completed
- the fourteen 1010-tonne torpedo boats of the *Le Fier* class (an improved 610-tonne type): three were launched prior to the armistice and four after June 1940; again, none was completed
- ten *contre-torpilleurs* of the *Marceau* class, an Improved *Mogador* design displacing 2930 tonnes standard (see Chapter 8): *Marceau*, *Desaix*, *Kléber* and *Hoche* were authorised under the 1938 *bis* and supplementary 1938 *bis* estimates, and a further six were to have been built under the programme of 1 April 1940. None was laid down

- a large fleet escort which was in effect an updated version of the prewar *contre-torpilleurs* and which would become the *escorteur d'escadre* (EE) of the mid-1950s
- a small ocean escort derived from the American DEs, primarily for ASW, which would become the *escorteur rapide*

The last *contre-torpilleurs* serving with the Marine Nationale were reclassified *destroyers-escorteurs de 1re classe* on 1 October 1951, *escorteurs rapides* in 1953, and *escorteurs d'escadre* on 17 January 1955.

The first ship of the postwar progammes to enter service was the *escorteur rapide Le Bordelais* (E50 type), on 7 April 1955. *Surcouf*, the first *escorteur d'escadre* (T47 type), entered service on 1 November 1955. Four *escorteurs d'escadre* and four *escorteurs rapides* were in service by late 1956, and took part in the Suez operation (*Opération 'Mousquetaire'*) in early November of that year.

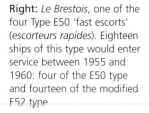

Right: *Le Brestois*, one of the four Type E50 'fast escorts' (*escorteurs rapides*). Eighteen ships of this type would enter service between 1955 and 1960: four of the E50 type and fourteen of the modified E52 type.

APPENDIX F: *ALBATROS* AS AN EATM SHIP 1948–1955

REFLOATED BY THE AMERICANS FOLLOWING THE damage sustained at Casablanca in November 1942, *Albatros* was finally repatriated to Toulon under tow in June 1946. On 20 March 1947 it was decided that she would be rebuilt to serve as a Gunnery School Ship (*Ecole d'application de tir à la mer*, or EATM). Work began in June of the same year and was completed on 8 August 1948. *Albatros* finally entered service as a gunnery school ship on 9 September, replacing the elderly *Tigre* in that role. The *Ecole de canonnage* was based on the old battleship *Lorraine*, which since 1947 had been moored at the Angle Robert close to the *Grands Bassins*. Sea-going gunnery exercises involved *Albatros*, the cruiser *Emile Bertin* and two patrol boats. Still designated a *contre-torpilleur*, *Albatros* carried the pendant number T06. Displacement following reconstruction had risen to 2607 tons standard and 3192 tonnes deep load.

She retained three of her original 138.6mm Mle 1927 guns (nos.1, 2 and 5) in her new role, but shielded 75mm Mle 1924 HA (from the armed merchant cruiser *Barfleur*) were fitted in the other two gun positions (nos.3 and 4), and the after funnel was moved one metre forward to maximise arcs for the midships mounting. The main guns were controlled by a large new director fitted with an A/BM (British Type 275) FC radar at the after end of the bridge, the 75mm guns by a cruiser-type HA director. The two boilers in the forward boiler room were removed and replaced by a cruiser-type HA plot; the director itself was located atop the forward deckhouse in place of the forward pair of funnels. Both engine rooms were now supplied with steam by the after pair of boilers, with a corresponding reduction in speed.

Initially there were to have been two 40mm Bofors twin Mk 1 mountings of US origin – the model mounted in the four surviving *contre-torpilleurs* of the Le Fantasque class – in tubs at the forward end of the centre deckhouse. In the event only one was fitted to starboard, the tub to port being occupied by a single Bofors Mk I of Canadian manufacture – the same model installed on *Richelieu* in 1945. Fire control for the twin mounting was provided by the standard US Mk 51 director. Finally, two 20mm Mk 7 single Oerlikon guns were fitted forward of the bridge, in the positions formerly occupied by the 13.2mm Hotchkiss guns.

In place of the former tripod foremast there was a lattice mast similar to that fitted in the *Le Fantasque*s, carrying the standard US small-ship air and surface surveillance radars: SA (later upgraded to SA-2) at the masthead and SF (thimble radome) on a platform below. There was also an Americal SJ-1 surface search radar atop a post forward of the bridge, and a 20m^2 combat information centre (*Central Information*, or CI) directly behind the navigation bridge. The officers' and POs' galleys were relocated from the forward to the centre deckhouse, with new galley pipes run up outside the remaining pair of funnels. The engine room workshop, which was originally in the centre deckhouse, was moved to the forward deckhouse.

The outfit of boats showed little change from the one with which the ship entered service: a 7-metre motor boat and a 7-metre cutter and two 5-metre dinghies (one motorised) on rails and crutches atop the forward deckhouse, and a 7-metre motor launch and a 7-metre whaler on davits abeam the after deckhouse.

On and around the centre deckhouse were six open rangefinders for training: two with a 4-metre base (upper deck abeam funnel no.2), two with a 2.5-metre base (between the funnels), and two with a 1.5-metre base in place of the after torpedo tube mounting – the forward TT mounting was retained.

In addition to her training function, *Albatros* was also utilised to trial new gun mountings and radars. Initially it was intended that she trial the twin 130mm dual-purpose mounting which was approved in December 1946, but this was subse-

Below: *Albatros* during her reconstruction at Toulon in the spring of 1948. The forward boilers have been stripped out, and the first two funnels removed, as have guns nos.3 and 4. A new lattice mast has been stepped abaft the bridge to support US-model surveillance radars.

FRENCH DESTROYERS 1922-1956

Above and opposite: Two part-views of *Albatros* following the completion of her first EATM reconstruction. Beyond *Albatros* are the cruiser *Suffren*, the battleship *Lorraine* and the cruiser *Emile Bertin*. In the photo above, the new HA director can be seen on the left; the HA plot is housed in the deckhouse beneath. Note the 4-metre and 2.5-metre rangefinders under canvas amidships, and the smaller 1.5-metre RF mounted on the base of the after torpedo tubes, which have been removed. *(US Navy NH 91981, courtesy of A D Baker III)*

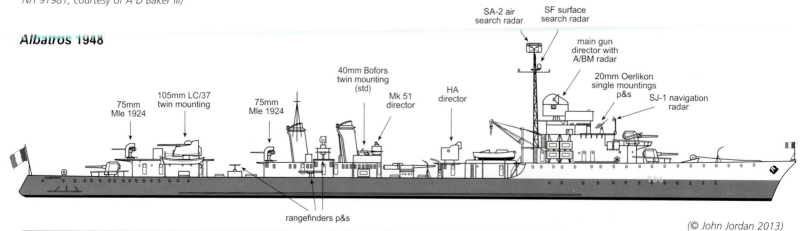

(© John Jordan 2013)

THE PERIOD 1945-1956

Above: The ex-German 105mm LC/37 twin HA gun mounting is particularly prominent in this view; it would also be fitted in the rebuilt ex-Italian cruisers *Châteaurenault* and *Guichen*. On *Albatros* it is flanked by two 75mm HA guns mounted in the former no.3 and no.4 gun positions. Between the 105mm mounting and the 75mm gun abaft the second funnel are the two 1.5-metre rangefinders mounted on the base of the after torpedo tubes. *(US Navy NH 91982, courtesy of A D Baker III)*

Albatros 1954

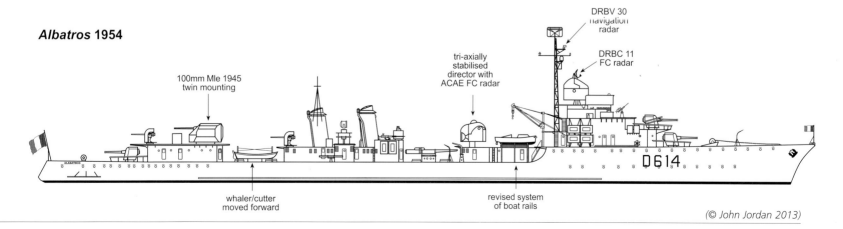

(© John Jordan 2013)

quently redeveloped as the twin 127mm Mle 1948 which armed the new fleet escorts of the T47 type. When she emerged from the dockyard in 1948 she mounted instead an ex-German 105mm LC/37 twin HA gun mounting, which was installed at the forward end of the after deckhouse; this mounting, of which the Marine Nationale inherited a number, was subsequently fitted in the two former Italian light cruisers of the *Attilio Regolo* class, which were rebuilt

Left: A close-up of the ex-German 105mm LC/37 twin HA gun mounting during installation in April 1948. *(Charles Limonnier collection)*

Below: September 1951: *Albatros* receives a German-style triaxially-stabilised director, allied with the French-developed ACAE radar, to control the new French 100mm Mle 1945 twin mounting which replaced the German 105mm LC/37. The production model of the director would be fitted in *Jean Bart* on her completion in 1953, and later in *Châteaurenault* and *Guichen*. *(DCAN Toulon, Charles Limonnier collection)*

THE PERIOD 1945-1956

Right: This photo was taken from the bridge looking aft in late 1948. In the foreground is the massive cruiser-style HA director equipped with a 4-metre rangefinder. In the larger tubs outboard of the first funnel are a US-style 40mm Bofors Mk 1 twin mounting (to starboard) and a Canadian single Bofors Mk I (to port). The smaller tub to starboard is equipped with a US Mk 51 director for the 40mm Bofors twin mounting.

1951–4 as the fast escorts *Châteaurenault* and *Guichen*.

In a refit which took place January to April 1951 the twin 105mm was replaced by the prototype for the new 100mm Mle 1945 twin mounting intended for the battleship *Jean Bart*, and at the same time the original HA director was replaced by a German-style triaxially-stabilised model, allied with the French-developed ACAE radar – the installation of the latter was completed only in September 1951. The production model of the director would be fitted in *Jean Bart* on completion to control her 152mm and 100mm guns, and later in the *Châteaurenault* and *Guichen* to control their ex-German 105mm mountings. During the same refit the opportunity was taken to reline the three 138.6mm guns and to replace the barrels of the 75mm HA guns. The ship was now classified as *escorteur de 2e classe*, and carried the NATO pendant number F 762.

In 1953 the davits for the 7-metre whaler and cutter were moved forward to protect them from the blast of the 100mm. The prototype 100mm was replaced by a production model, and the American SJ radar by the new French DRBV 30 navigation radar, which now occupied a small platform above the tiny SF thimble radome (see drawing). In place of the Canadian Bofors 40mm Mk I there was now a prototype Mle 51 hydraulic model. During the same year, *Albatros* was redesignated *escorteur rapide*, with the pendant number D 614.

In a short refit early in 1954 the 40mm Mle 51 prototype was replaced by a production model, and the A/BM FC radar by the new French DRBC 11A, the antenna for which was fitted atop the main gunnery director. Finally, in 1956, the American SF radar was removed.

Below: *Albatros* at Les Vignettes in 1954–5. The photo shows her final configuration with the production model of the 100mm Mle 1945 twin mounting aft and the triaxially-stabilised HA director atop the forward deckhouse. *(Pierre Boucheix collection)*

SOURCES

TECHNICAL

Campbell, John, *Naval Weapons of World War Two* (London: Conway Maritime Press, 1985 reprinted 2002).

Friedman, Norman, *Naval Weapons of World War One* (Barnsley: Seaforth Publishing, 2011).

Guiglini, Jean, *Les marques particulières des navires de guerre français 1900–1950* (Vincennes: Service Historique de la Marine, 2002).

Jordan, John, *Warships After Washington* (Barnsley: Seaforth Publishing, 2011).

Jordan, John, & Dumas, Robert, *French Battleships 1922–1956* (Barnsley: Seaforth Publishing, 2009).

Jordan, John, & Moulin, Jean, *French Cruisers 1922–1956* (Barnsley: Seaforth Publishing, 2013).

Lassaque, Jean, *Les contre-torpilleurs Epervier et Milan 1931–1946* (Bourg-en-Bresse: Marines Editions, 1995).

Lassaque, Jean, *Les C.T. de 2400 tonnes du type Jaguar* (Bourg-en-Bresse: Marines Editions, 1996).

Lassaque, Jean, *Les C.T. de 2880 tonnes du type Mogador* (Bourg-en-Bresse: Marines Editions, 1996).

Lassaque, Jean, *Les C.T. de 2800 tonnes du type Le Fantasque* (Bourg-en-Bresse: Marines Editions, 1998).

Lassaque, Jean, *Les C.T. de 2700 tonnes du type Vauquelin* (Nantes: Marines Editions, 2000).

Lassaque, Jean, *Les croiseurs légers: histoire des croiseurs légers 1943–1964* (Editions d'histoire navale, 2007).

Le Masson, Henri, *Histoire du torpilleur en France* (Paris: Académie de la Marine, 1967).

Moulin, Jean, *Les contre-torpilleurs type Guépard 1928–1942* (Rennes: Marines Editions, 2010).

Moulin, Jean, *Les contre-torpilleurs type Aigle 1929–1956* (Rennes: Marines Editions, 2012).

Moulin, Jean, *Dates de Construction: Bâtiments des programmes de 1922 à 1940* (self-published as booklet, 1999).

Saibène, Marc, *Les torpilleurs de 1500 tonnes du type Bourrasque* (Nantes: Marines Editions, 2001).

Saibène, Marc, *Les torpilleurs de 1500 tonnes du type L'Adroit* (Nantes: Marines Editions, 2002).

Salou, Charles, *Les torpilleurs d'escadre du type Le Hardi* (Outreau: Lela Presse, 2001).

Plans and other documentation from the Centre d'Archives de l'Armement (CAA), Châtellerault, and from the Service Historique de la Défense, département marine (http://www.servicehistorique.sga.defense.gouv.fr/02fonds-collections/banquedocuments/planbato/planbato/central.php)

HISTORICAL

Antier, Jean-Jacques, *La Flotte se Saborde: Toulon 1942* (Paris: Presses de la Cité, 1992).

Auphan, Admiral Gabriel, & Mordal, Jacques, *La Marine française pendant la seconde guerre mondiale* (Paris: Editions France-Empire, 1959).

Caroff, CV, *La compagne de Norvège 1940* (Paris: Service Historique de la Marine, 1955).

Caroff, CV, *Les débarquements alliés en Afrique du Nord* (Paris: Service Historique de la Marine, 1960).

Caroff, CV, *Le théâtre Atlantique*, 2 volumes (Paris: Service Historique de la Marine, 1958 & 1959).

Caroff, CV, *Le théâtre Méditerranéen*, 2 volumes (Paris: Service Historique de la Marine, 1960).

Cras, Hervé, *Les forces maritimes du Nord 1939–1940*, 3 volumes (Paris, Service Historique de la Marine, 1955 & 1956).

Cras, Hervé (Jacques Mordal), *Dunkerque* (Paris: France-Empire, 1960).

Guiot, Commandant, *En Syrie, combats sans espoir* (Paris: La couronne littéraire, 1950).

Le Hir, Martial, *Mers el-Kébir & Catapult* (Rennes: Marines éditions, 2005).

Lemonnier, Amiral, *Cap sur la Provence* (Paris: France Empire, 1954).

Lepotier, Commandant, *Cap sur la Corse* (Paris: France Empire, 1951).

Masson, Muracciole, Villardi de Montlaur, *La participation de la Marine française aux débarquements de Normandie et de Provence* (Paris: Service Historique de la Marine, 1969).

Meirat, Jean, *Les marins de la Tramontane* (Paris: France Empire, 1960).

Mordal, Jacques, *La campagne de Norvège* (Paris: Self, 1949).

Mordal, Jacques, *La bataille de Casablanca* (Paris: Plon, 1952).

Mordal, Jacques, *La bataille de Dakar* (Editions Ozanne, 1956).

Saibène, Marc, *Toulon et la Marine, du sabordage à la Libération* (Rennes: Marines Editions, 2002).

Varillon, Pierre, *Mers el Kebir* (Paris: Amiot Dumont, 1949).

Varillon, Pierre, *Le sabordage de la Flotte* (Paris: Amiot Dumont, 1954).

The archives of the Service Historique de la Défense:

Département marine at Vincennes, Paris (Activities/Operations);

Centre d'archives de l'armement et du personnel civil (CAA) at Châtellerault (Design/Plans).

INDEX

The main body of the index consists predominantly of names of ships, people and places. For ships the nationality and type of vessel are in parentheses; for places the location/country is given; the personalities, with the exception of national leaders, are French unless otherwise stated. Due to the broad scope of the historical section, the only place names included in the index are major ports and those associated with significant actions or campaigns. There are 'thematic' entries for the following: **formations**, **guns**, **operations**, **propulsion machinery**, **radars** and **underwater weapons & sensors**. Sections of the book which focus on a particular system, or on a particular aspect of a ship or class of ship are in **bold** type; ***bold italics*** are used for a major illustration of a ship or weapons system, and also for key maps.

A
Acheron (Br. destroyer) 116
Aconit (Fr. corvette) 264-5
Admiralty Standard (Br. paint scheme) 136, 201, 272
Afridi (Br. destroyer) 226-7
Aigle (Fr. *contre-torpilleur*) 63, 71, 75-7, **93-107**, 108-12, 115-120, 122, *133*, 137, 140, 145, 193, 202, *209*, 213, 218, 222-4, 229-31, 233, 236, 247-8
Ajax (Br. cruiser) 237
Albatros (Fr. *contre-torpilleur*) 93-9, 101, 104-6, 119, 122, 200, 202, *209*, 213, 222-3, 226, 229-33, 236, 239-41, 244-5, 257, 279, 282, *283*, **287-91** [EATM ship]
Alexandria, Egypt 73, 230-3, 250, 257-8, 261, 276-7
Algérie (Fr. cruiser) 222-4, 229-30, 233, 236, 247,
Algérien (Fr. destroyer escort) 262, 264-5
Algiers, Algeria 58, 73, 213, 219, 221, 231-3, 236-7, 240, 250, 258, 261-4, 266, 273, 276-8
Alsacien (Fr. torpedo boat, ex-Ger. *T35*) 224, 284
Alysse (Fr. corvette) 265
Amiral Mouchez (Fr. sloop) 226
Amiral Sénès (Fr. destroyer, ex-Ger. *S.113*) 18-9, 98, 160, 215
Annamite (Fr. M/S sloop) 224-5
Anschütz gyro-compass 114, 143, 163
Antilles, West Indies 109, 138-9, 210, 257, 261, 273
Antoine, Ingénieur général 60, 94
Armistice Commission 58, 73-4, 105, 127-8, 158, 233
Arquebuse (Fr. destroyer) 9
Arromanches (Fr. aircraft carrier, ex-Br. *Colossus*) 280, 282
Assiniboine (Can. destroyer) 224
Ateliers et Chantiers de Bretagne (Nantes) 14, 21, 60, 93-4, 96, 109, 115-6, 161-4, 179
Ateliers et Chantiers de la Loire (St. Nazaire) 21-2, 33, 48, 76, 80, 93, 109, 115, 117, 120, 138, 143, 181, 184
Ateliers et Chantiers de la Seine-Maritime Worms & Cie (Le Trait) 21, 60-1, 205
Ateliers et Chantiers de St. Nazaire-Penhoët 20-1, 41-2, 46, 60, 75, 77-8, 80, 109-10, 115, 117, 184
Augusta (US cruiser) 240, 242, 244
Aurora (Br. cruiser) 245-6
Austral (Fr. transport) 225
Australia (Aus. cruiser) 234-5

B
Baccarat (Fr. torpedo boat, ex-Ger. *T20*) 284
Badger (Br. destroyer) 11
Baliste (Fr. torpedo boat) 203, 205, 222
Baoulé Fr. freighter) 224
Basque (Fr. destroyer) 60-2, 66, 68, 73, 203-4, 213, 215-7, 220-5, 231, 233, 257-8, 262, 266-7, 276-8, 283
Beaver (Br. destroyer) 11
Beirut, Lebanon 219, 222-3, **236-9**
Bermuda, Royal Naval Dockyard 257, 261, 276-7
Bettus-Loire generators 23, 26, 43, 46, 62, 83-4, 97, 116, 120, 142, 145, 166, 272
Bévéziers (Fr. submarine) 235
Bir Hakeim (Fr. torpedo boat, ex-Ger. *T11*) 284
Bison (Fr. *contre-torpilleur*) 75-83, **79** [prof/plan 1930], 86-92, *131*, 204, 213-5, 217-8, 220-3, 226-7
Bison (Fr. destroyer) 182, *194*, 237, 246-7, 249, 286
Bisson class (Fr. destroyers) 9-10
Bizerte, Tunisia 8, 57-9, 73-4, 119, 205, 218, 222-3, 231, 234-6, 240, 250, 258, 260, 262, 265, 274, 277, 280, 282-3
Blankney (Br. destroyer) 264
Bois Belleau (Fr. carrier, ex-US *Belleau Wood*) 282
Bombarde (Fr. torpedo boat) 203, 205, 261, 265
Bordelais (Fr. destroyer) 60-2, 67-8, 71-4, 203, 213, 215-7, 222-3, 231-2, 236-7, 247-8
Bory (Fr. destroyer) 10
Bouclier class (Fr. destroyers) 10-11
Bouclier (Fr. torpedo boat) 203, 205
Bourragué, Rear-Admiral Pierre 234
Bourrasque (Fr. destroyer) 6-7, 20, 26-7, 30, 32-3, 35, **41-59**, 60-3, 65, 67-9, 71-5, 80, 85, 88, 93, 99, 180, 189-91, 197, 200, 203, 209, 211, 213-7, 225-6, 228-9
Branlebas (Fr. destroyer) 10, 12
Branlebas (Fr. torpedo boat) 203, 205
Breguet (Fr. manufacturer) 26, 76, 109, 112, 120-1, 140, 164
Brest Naval Dockyard 20-1, *33*, 38-41, 57, 71, 122, 158, 162, 167, 177, 182, ***206*** [map], 213, 217, 227, 229
Brestois (Fr. destroyer) 60-1, 71-3, 203, 213, 215-8, 222, 225-7, 231-2, 240, 242, 244
Brestois (Fr. fast escort) 286
Bretagne (Fr. battleship) 12, 84, 208, 222, 224, 231-2
British Expeditionary Force 227
Brohan, Rear-Amiral Gabriel 216
Brooklyn (US cruiser) 240, 242, 244
Bulolo (Br. AMC) 239

C
Calatafimi (It. torpedo boat) 230
Calpe (Br. destroyer) 245-6
Cap Fagnet (Fr. APV) 225
Casabianca (Fr. submarine) 262
Casablanca, Morocco 57, 59, 71, 73, 105, 128, 159, 185, 200, 208, 220, 223-5, 229, 231, 233-6, **239-45**, 257-8, 260-1, 268, 273, 276-9, 283, 287
Casque (Fr. destroyer L 1909) 10, 12
Casque (Fr. destroyer LD 1936) 181-2, 184, 192-3, 231-2, 237, 247-8
Cassard (Fr. *contre-torpilleur*) 109-11, 114-6, 118, 120-1, 123, 125-8, 202, 213-4, 218, 222-3, 229-31, 233, 236-7, 247
Castex, Vice-Admiral Raoul 225
Cedar Mills (Br. tanker) 250
Chacal (Fr. *contre-torpilleur*) 2-3, 20-22, 27, *29*, 34, *35*, *37-38*, 39, 76, *129-131*, 202, 209-10, 211, 213-4, 217, 224-6, 228
Chevreuil (Fr. M/S sloop) 224-5
Chantiers Dubigeon (Nantes) 21, 41-2, 46, 60-2
Chantiers Navals Français (Caen) 21, 41-2, 46, 60-1, 109-10, 115, 138, 140, 143
Charlestown Navy Yard, Boston 151, 156, 257-9, 264, 268-9, 273-4
Châteaurenault (Fr. fleet escort, ex-It. *Attilio Regolo*) 284-5, 289-91
Chenonceaux (Fr. passenger ship) 222
Cherbourg Naval Dockyard 20-1, 39, 41, 57, 61, 68, 71-3, 105, 164, 181, 198, 205, 213, 217, 221, 225-6, 228-9, 250-1, 282-4
Churchill, Winston (Br. Prime Minister) 232
Colbert (Fr. cruiser) *52*, 60, 76, 222, 224, 229-30, 230, 247

Collin, Rear-Admiral 162, 171
Commandant Bory (Fr. destroyer) 210, 212
Commandant Bory (Fr. M/S sloop) 224
Commandant D'Estienne d'Orves (Fr. corvette) 264-5
Commandant Détroyat (Fr. corvette) 265
Commandant Drogou (Fr. corvette) 265
Commandant Rivière (Fr. M/S sloop) 224
Commandant Teste (Fr. aviation transport) 116, 221, 231-2
Comité Technique 12-14, 18, 20, 137, 161, 180
concentration dials 37-8, 55, 67, 91-2, 103, 118, 121, 123, 125, 145, 156-8, 173, 189, 271
Conseil Supérieur de la Marine (CSM) 7, 17
'Condottieri' (It. cruisers) 137, 206
Corsica, western Mediterranean 219, 222, 258, 261, **262-4**
Cotentin (Fr. tug) 245
Courbet (Fr. battleship) 84, *217*
Croix de Lorraine (Fr. frigate) 265, 280
Cunningham, Vice-Admiral Sir Andrew (GB) 233
Cyclone (Fr. destroyer) 41-2, *52*, *53*, *55*, 56, 93, 203, 213, 215-7, 224, 227-9, 248

D
D'Estaing (Fr. destroyer, ex-It. *Oriani*) 284
Dakar, Senegal 128, 157-9, 184, 188, 204, 209-10, 223, 229, 231, **233-5**, 236, 239-40, 257, 260-1, 268, 292
Darlan, Admiral François 71, 172, 174, 195-6, 200, 210, 212
DCAN (Fr. ordnance department) 7, 28-9, 161, 166, 277
De Bon, Vice-Admiral Ferdinand 16, 21
De Gaulle, General Charles 233-4
De Laborde, Vice-Admiral Jean 214, 222, 236, 247
De Portzamparc, Captain Yves Urvoy 227
Décauville mine tracks 120, 151, 172
Dehorter (Fr. destroyer) 10
Delage (Fr. destroyer, ex-Ger. *H.147*) 15
Desaix (Fr *contre-torpilleur*) 162-3, 179

Desaix (Fr. destroyer, ex-Ger. *Paul Jacobi*) 283-4, 286
Deutschland (Ger. *Panzerschiff*) 216
Diego Suarez, Madagascar 236, 250, 274, 279
Dieudonné, *Ingénieur en chef* 161
dispositif 'K' (shell colorant) 123
Djibouti, Red Sea 128, 218, 236
Dompaire (Fr. torpedo boat, ex-Ger. *T14*) 284
Drujon, Rear-Admiral Charles 215
Duchaffault (Fr. destroyer, ex-It. *Legionario*) 284
Duguay-Trouin (Fr. cruiser) 20-1, 209, 217, 233
Dumont, Charles (Fr. Navy Minister 1931-2) 138
Dunkerque (Fr. battleship) 67, 136, 160-1, 169, 180-1, 186, 193, 213, 224, 231-2, 237, 240, 247
Dunkirk, northern France 71-2, 205, 225-9, 251
Duperré (Fr. destroyer, ex-It. *Velite*) 284
Duplat, Vice-Admiral Emile 222-3, 230
Dupleix (Fr. cruiser) 108, 132, *189*, 222-3, 229-30, 236, 247
Duquesne (Fr. cruiser) 60, 75, 218, 222, 233, 267
Duralumin 112, 122, 140, 163, 183
Durandal class (Fr. destroyers) 9
Dyle et Baccalan (Bordeaux) 21, 41, 46, 60

E
E42 (Fr. fleet escort design) 286
E43 (Fr. fleet escort design) 286
Ecole d'application du lancement à la mer (EALM) 37, 217
Ecole d'application du tir à la mer (EATM) 282, 287-8
Ecole Navale 4, 34, 201, 206, 213, 217, 282-3
El Biar (Fr. passenger ship) 264
El Djézaïr (Fr. AMC) 226
Elan (Fr. M/S sloop) 237
Emile Bertin (Fr. cruiser) 111, 145, 176, 210, 214, 218, 222, 226, 268, 287, *288*
Enseigne Gabolde (Fr. destroyer) 11, 14, 26, 44
Enseigne Roux class (Fr. destroyers) 10-11
Epée (Fr. destroyer) 181-2, 186, 188, *189*, 190, 194, 231, 233, 236, 239
Epervier (Fr. *contre-torpilleur*) 93-4, 106, 108, 112, 115, **116-7** [superheating], 118-125, 127-8, *132*, 137, 142-3, 146, 184, 202, 204, 213-5, 218, 222-3, 226, 228-9, 231, 233, 240, 245-6, 257, 260, 275
Estéva, Vice-Admiral Jean-Pierre 222

F
Fanion (Fr. destroyer) *10*
Fleuret (Fr. destroyer) 181-2, 185, *187*, 188-9, 194, 231, 233, 236, 239-40

Foch (Fr. cruiser) 58, 93, 222-3, 229-30, 233, 236-7, 247
Forbin (Fr. destroyer) 60-61, 71, 73, 76, 93, 203, 213, 215-7, 220, 222, 224-5, 231, 233, 257-8, 262, 264, 266, 276, 278, 283
Forbin (Fr. fleet escort) 286
Forges et Chantiers de la Gironde (Bordeaux/Harfleur) 21, 25, 41, 46, 60-1, 115, 143, 181, 184
Forges et Chantiers de la Méditerranée (La Seyne/Le Havre) 21, 41, 46, 80, 93-4, 109-11, 115, 117, 138-9, 143, 177, 181, 184, 195-6
formations (squadron and above)
  2e Escadre (2nd Squadron) 14, 201, 222
  3e Escadre (3rd Squadron) 222, 247
  2e Escadre légère (2nd EL) 207, 222, 240
  3e Escadre légère (3rd EL) 222, 236
  Armée Navale 11
  Atlantic Fleet 206, 222
  Atlantic Squadron 152, 206, 216
  Escadre d'Instruction 217
  Escadre de l'Atlantique 201
  Escadre de la Méditerranée 201
  Escadre du Levant 206
  Escadre du Ponant 206
  'Flank Force' 259, 265-7
  Force H (Br. force based Gibraltar) 232, 261
  Force X [Dakar] 223, [Med] 230, 233, 239, 257, 258
  Force Y [Dakar] 233-5
  Force Z [Norway] 223, 226
  Force d'intervention (FI) 279-80, 284
  Force de raid 197, 222-3, 231-2
  Forces de haute mer (FHM) 92, 126, 178, 192, 222, 236, 247
  Forces légères d'attaque 222
  Forces maritimes de l'Ouest 222, 225
  Forces maritimes du Nord 225
  French Naval Task Force (FNTF) 267
  Groupe d'action anti-sous-marine (GASM) 279, 284
  Mediterranean Fleet 200, 206, 222-3, 229
  Mediterranean Squadron 200, 206-8, 216
Fort de France (Fr. freighter) 239
Foudroyant (Fr. destroyer, LD 1927) 60-1, 68, 71, 203, 213, 215-7, 221, 225-9
Foudroyant (Fr. destroyer, LD 1936) 170, 182-3, 189, *194*, 247-8
Fougueux (Fr. destroyer) 60-62, *68*, 71-4, **74** [prof/plan 1942], 93, 188, 200, 203, 213, 215-8, 220, 224-5, 228-9, 231, 239-40, 242, 244
Fowey (Br. sloop) 224-5
Francesco Nullo (It. destroyer) 116
Francis Garnier (Fr. sloop, ex-It. *Eritrea*) 284
Frobisher (Br. cruiser) 250
Frondeur (Fr. destroyer) 60-3,
66-67, 68, 71-74, 188, 203, 213, 215-8, 224-5, 227-9, 231, 239-42, 244

G
Garetta, *Ingénieur général* 20
Genoa, northern Italy **229-30**, 248-9, 262, 264, 266-7
Gensoul, Vice-Admiral Marcel-Bruno 222
Georges Leygues (Fr. cruiser) 92, 218, 221-2, 225, 231, 233-5, 264, 268
Gerfaut (Fr. *contre-torpilleur*) 93-7, 99-107, **107** [prof/plan 1941], 115-6, 119, 122, *133*, 202, *209*, 213-4, 218, 222, 229, 231, 233, 236-7, 246-7
Gibraltar, western Mediterranean 219-21, 223, 225, 233, 239-40, 258, 273-4
Giuliana (It. tanker) 261
Glamorgan Coast (Br. trawler) 226
Gloire (Fr. cruiser) 222, 225, 231, 233, 267-8
Glowworm (Br. destroyer) 222
Godfroy, Rear-Admiral René-Emile 233
Golo (Fr. transport) 225
Greyhound (Br. destroyer) 222
Guépard (Fr. *contre-torpilleur*) 18, 21, 28, 30, 35, 71, **75-92**, 93-101, 106-7, 109, 112, 114, 116, 118, 120, 122, 137, 143, 193, 202, 210, 213-4, 218, 221-3, 225-6, 229-31, 233, 236-9, 247
Guichen (Fr. fleet escort, ex-It. *Scipione Africano*) 284-5, 289-91
guns
  138.6/40 Mle 1923 35, 37, 63, 79, **84-5**
  138.6/40 Mle 1927 63, 94, **97-99**, 102, 112, 117-8, 287
  138.6/50 Mle 1929 140, **145-7**, 160
  130/40 Mle 1919 22, **27-8**, 35, 37-8, 41, 46-7, 65, 84, 180
  130/40 Mle 1924 60, **62-3**, **65**, 70-1, 180
  130/45 Mle 1932 **186-7**
  4.7in Mk XX (Br.) 196
  105/45 SKC/33 (Ger.) 282, 284-5, 288-91
  100//55 Mle 1945 282-91
  75/50 Mle 1924 22, **29-30**, 37-8, 40-1, 42, 46-7, 51-3, 55, 61, 63, 65-6, 75, 77, 129, 251, 282, 287-9, 291
  75/35 Mle 1925 94, **99**, 108, 119
  40mm Bofors 267, 271, 274-8, 280, 282, 284, 287-8, 291
  37mm CAS Mle 1925 37, 52-3, 55-9, 61-3, **65-66**, 68, 72-5, 79, 87, 91-2, 94, 99, 103-4, 106-8, 112, 119-20, 124-8, 148, 150, 155, 159, 226, 258, 277
  37mm CAD Mle 1933 40, 57, 72-3, 91, 94, 106-7, 124-8, 133, 140-1, **148-9**, 153-9, 164, 169-70, 177, 179, 184, 187, 189, 253, 268
37mm ACAD Mle 1935 161, 164, 166, **170**, 179, 181, 183, 185, 188-9, 191-2, 195
37mm ACAS 169, 179, 195
25mm Hotchkiss Mle 1939/1940 58-9, 72-4, 125-7, 178-9, **188-9**, 192, 194, 277
20mm Oerlikon 251-2, 256, 258, 262, 267-99, 271, 275-8, 281, 287-8
13.2mm Hotchkiss CAD Mle 1929 38-40, 57-9, 68, 72-4, 88, 91-2, 100, 103-4, 106-7, 112, **119**, 123-5, 127-9, 133, 136, 140-1, 148-50, 153, 155-9, 164, 173, 177-80, 183-5, 189, 191-5, 205, 251, 253-4, 256, 268, 287
13.2mm Browning CAS 58-9, 73-4, 91-2, 106-7, 125-8, 133, 155-6, 158-9, 166, 170, 177-9, **188**, 192-5, 268, 277
8mm Hotchkiss MG Mle 1914 22, 30, 38, 41, 48, 57-8, 62, 66, 68, 72, 74, 79, 88, 91, 94, 100, 108, 119, 158-9, 177, 251, 253-4, 256

H
Hardi II (Fr. trawler) 224
Hartland (Br. escort sloop) 245
Hasty (Br. destroyer) 239
Heureux (Fr. APV) 224
Hermes (Br. carrier) 223, 233
Hoche (Fr. *contre-torpilleur*) 162-3, 179, 286
Hoche (Fr. destroyer, ex-Ger. *Z5*) 283-5
Hotspur (Br. destroyer) 237-8
Hova (Fr. destroyer escort) 262, 264-5, 267, 280

I
Ilex (Br. destroyer) 239
Indochina **279** [map]
Indret (Fr. naval propulsion establishment) 80, 164
Intrépide (Fr. destroyer) 15
Isis (Br. destroyer) 237-9

J
Jackal (Br. destroyer) 237-8
Jaguar (Br. destroyer) 238-9
Jaguar (Fr. *contre-torpilleur*) 6, 14, 18, **20-40**, 41-9, 51, 53, 55, 57, 71, 75-80, 84-90, 99-100, 155, 198, 202, 208-10, 213-8, 224-5, 228
Jamaica (Br. cruiser) 245-6
Janus (Br. destroyer) 237-8
Jean Bart (Fr. battleship LD 1910) 221
Jean Bart (Fr. battleship LD 1936) 231, 239, 241, 244, 273, 283, 290-1
Jean de Vienne (Fr. cruiser) 222-3, 247
Jeanne d'Arc (Fr. cruiser) 60, 76, 261
Jervis (Br. destroyer) 239
Joseph E Campbell (US destroyer escort) 264

INDEX

Jurien de la Gravière (Fr. destroyer, ex-It. *Mitragliere*) 284
Jutland (Fr. APV) 224

K

Kaba class (Fr. destroyers) 15
Kandahar (Br. destroyer) 237
Kapitän Diederichsen (Ger. freighter) 261
Kersaint (Fr. *contre-torpilleur*) 109-10, 115-6, 125-8, 138, 202, 213-5, 218, 222-3, 229, 231-2, 237, 247
Kimberley (Br. destroyer) 237
Kingston (Br. destroyer) 238-9
Kléber (Fr. *contre-torpilleur*) 162-3, 179
Kléber (Fr. destroyer, ex-Ger. *Theodor Riedl*) 283-4, 286

L

L'Adroit (Fr. destroyer LD 1925) 6, 39, 48, 58-59, **60-74**, 75, 80-1, 88, 93, 180, 189, 200, 203, 213, 215-7, 220, 224, 227-8,
L'Adroit (Fr. destroyer LD 1936) 182, 192-5, **194** [prof/plan 1942], 236-7, 240, 247, 292
L'Ajaccienne (Fr. APV) 225
L'Alcyon (Fr. destroyer) 60-2, 68, 71, 73, 203, 215, 217, 222, 231, 240, 242, 244, 257, 261-2, 264, 266-7, 276-8
L'Algéroise (Fr. APV) 240, 242
L'Audacieux (Fr. *contre-torpilleur*) 138-41, 143-4, 154, 156, 158, 202, 204, 210, 213-4, 218, 222-3, 231, 233-5, 260, 262, 274-5
L'Aventure (Fr. frigate) 264-5, 267
L'Aventurier (Fr. destroyer) 181-2, 196
L'Escarmouche (Fr. frigate) 264-5, 280
L'Incomprise (Fr. torpedo boat) 203, 205
L'Indomptable (Fr. *contre-torpilleur*) 138-9, 143-4, 148, *152*, 154, 157-9, *178*, 202, 208, 213-4, 222, 226, 231, 236, 246-7, 260, 272, 280
L'Intrépide (Fr. destroyer) 181-2, 184, 196, 286
L'Iphigénie (Fr. torpedo boat) 205
L'Opiniâtre (Fr. destroyer) 181-2, 196
La Bayonnaise (Fr. torpedo boat) 205, 222
La Bônoise (Fr. APV) 225
La Capricieuse (Fr. M/S sloop) 225
La Combattante Fr. destroyer) 264-5
La Cordelière (Fr. torpedo boat) 203, 205
La Découverte (Fr. frigate) 264-5, 280
La Fayette (Fr. carrier, ex-US *Langley*) 282
La Flore (Fr. torpedo boat) 203, 205
La Galissonnière (Fr. cruiser) 132, 161, 222, 236, *248*
La Melpomène (Fr. torpedo boat) 203, **205**
La Palme (Fr. destroyer) 60-1, 68, 71, 73-4, 203, 213, 215-6, 221
La Pomone (Fr. torpedo boat) 203, 205
La Poursuivante (Fr. torpedo boat) 203, 205, 222
La Railleuse (Fr. destroyer) 60-2, 71, 203, 213, 215-6, 220, 222-5
La Sétoise (Fr. APV) 225
La Surprise (Fr. frigate) 264-5, 267
La Toulonnaise (Fr. APV) 225
Lamotte-Picquet (Fr. cruiser) 21, 138, 209-10, 213, 218
Lansquenet (Fr. destroyer LD 1909) 11
Lansquenet (Fr. destroyer LD 1936) 181-2, 192, 231, 236, 248, 286
Le Bordelais (Fr. fast escort) 286
Le Bris, Vice-Admiral Pierre 12
Le Chevalier Paul (Fr. *contre-torpilleur*) 94, 109-11, 116, 126, 202, 213-4, 218, 222, 226-7, 229-31, 233, 236-9
Le Corsaire (Fr. destroyer) 181-2, 184, 188, 192, 194, 231, 236, 286
Le Fantasque (Fr. *contre-torpilleur*) 7, 87, 102, 111, 122, *135*, **137-59**, 160-4, 166, 168-73, 176, 179-80, 184, 186, 188-9, 191, *199*, 200, 202-4, 208, 213-5, 222-3, 233-5, 257, 259-62, 264, **268-75** [Modernisation USA], 279-81, 287
Le Fier class (Fr. torpedo boats) 205, 286
Le Flibustier (Fr. destroyer) 181-2, 194, 231, 237, 286
Le Fortuné (Fr. destroyer) 60-1, 68, 73, 203, 213, 215-6, 218, 221-5, 231, 233, 257-8, 262, 264, 266-7, 278, 283
Le Hardi (Fr. destroyer) 6, 49, 67, 75, 160, 163, 167, 172, 178, **181-196**, 203, 231, 233, 235-7, 248, 285-6
Le Malin (Fr. *contre-torpilleur*) 134, 138-9, 142-4, 147-8, 151, 157-9, 176, 202, 204, 213, 222, *224*, 226-7, 231-5, 241-2, 245-6, 257, 260-2, 264-5, **268-75** [Modernisation USA], 280-2
Le Mars (Fr. destroyer) 60-1, 67-8, 71, 73-4, 203, 213, 215-6, 222, 224-5, 231, 236-7, 248
Le Prieur gunsight 119, 123, 222
Le Téméraire (Fr. destroyer) 181-2, 184, 196
Le Terrible (Fr. *contre-torpilleur*) *135*, 138-40, 143-4, 148, *150*, 155, 158-9, 176, 199, 202, *212*, 213-4, 222-3, 225, 231-3, 235-6, 257, 259, 261-6, **268-75** [Modernisation USA], 280, 282
Le Triomphant (Fr. *contre-torpilleur*) 31, *134*, *135*, 138-9, 143-5, 149, *153*, *198*, 200, 202, 213-4, 222, 226-7, 231, 250, **253-6** [Modernisation UK]
Leander (Br. cruiser) 238-9
Lebrun, President Albert 150, 199, 213
Lemonnier, Vice-Admiral André 265, 278
Leone (It. light scout) 18, 21
Léopard (Fr. *contre-torpilleur*) 20-2, 26, 27, 31-5, *37*, 38-40, 76, 93, *130-1*, 198, 202, 213-5, 217, 225-6, 228, 231, 250, **251-2** [Modernisation UK], 253, 267
Léoville (Fr. APV) 225
Levant, eastern Mediterranean 128, *132*, 206, 217-9, 222, 237
Leygues, Georges (Fr. Navy Minister 1917-30, 1932-3) 16, 108
Lion (Fr. *contre-torpilleur*) 18, 21, 75-83, 86, 90-3, 96, *132-3*, 201-2, *212*, 213-5, 217-8, 222-3, 229-31, 233, 246-9
Livermore class (US destroyers) 286
Lobélia (Fr. corvette) 265
London Treaty 1930 9, 21, 160, 205
Lookout (Br. destroyer) 267
Lorient Naval Dockyard 20-1, **22** [map], 26-7, 31, 33, 35, 41, 47, 60-1, 71, 75-6, 78-81, 83, 86, 92-3, 108-12, 118, 121, 136, 138-43, 145, 152, 154, 156-7, 160-3, 172, 177, 179, 181-2, 208, 217, 221, 227, 231, 250, 267, 282
Lorrain (Fr. torpedo boat, ex-Ger. *T28*) 284
Lorraine (Fr. battleship) 221-3, 233, 267, 287-8
Louise-Marie (Fr. aux. M/S) 229
Lowestoft (Br. sloop) 250
LST 79 (Br. tank landing ship) 264
Ludlow (US destroyer) 240, 244, 265
Lynx (Fr. *contre-torpilleur*) 20-22, 26-7, *33*, 39-40, 76, *88*, 93, 202, 213-5, 217, 225, 230-2, 247-8
Lyon class (Fr. battleships) 12

M

M89 (Fr. destroyer) 12, 14
M90 (Fr. destroyer) 12, 14
Madison (US destroyer) 266
Maillé-Brézé (Fr. *contre-torpilleur*) 109-10, 112, 115-6, *132*, 202, 213-15, 218, 221-4, 226-7
Mameluk (Fr. destroyer) 181-2, 184, 188, 190, 192-3, **193** [prof/plan 1941], 231, 236-7, 240, 247-8
Marceau (Fr. *contre-torpilleur*) 162-3, 179, 286
Marceau (Fr. destroyer, ex-Ger. *Z31*) 284
'Marder' type midget submarine (Ger.) 265
Mariette Pacha (Fr. passenger ship) 222
Marocain (Fr. destroyer escort) 262, 264-5, 280
Marquis, Rear-Admiral André 222
Marseillaise (Fr. cruiser) 222-3, 236, 247
Marseille, southern France 190, 211-2, 219, 231, 237, 261-2, 264-5
MAS boats (It.) 230, 234, 261
Massachusetts (US battleship) 241-2, 244, 273
Measure 22 (US paint scheme) 135, 201, 269, 272, 277-8
Mécanicien Principal Lestin (Fr. destroyer)
Mélinite (explosive) 12, 27, 28, 49, 85, 98, 186-7
Mers el-Kebir, Algeria 176-8, **231-3**, 236-7, 240, 246, 261, 277
Meteor (Br. destroyer) 267
Milan (Fr. *contre-torpilleur*) 93-4, 105, 108, **112** [prof/plan 1934], 115, **116-7** [superheating], 118, 120-4, **127** (prof/plan 1942), 128, 137, 142-3, 146, 184, 202, 204, 213-5, 218, 222-3, 226-7, 229, 231, 233, 236, 240, 242, 244
Milhaud piers, Toulon 89, 207, 230, 247-8
Mimosa (Fr. corvette) 265
Mistral (Fr. destroyer) 41-2, 46, 53, 57, 72, 93, 203, 213, 215, 217, 220-1, 224-6, 228-9, 231, 250, 257
Mogador (Fr. *contre-torpilleur*) 6, 75, *136*, **160-179**, 180-4, 186-92, 202, 204, 206, 215, 218, 222, 225, 231-2, 248, 284, 286
'Molch' type midget submarine (Ger.) 266
Mondement (Fr. sloop) 220
Montcalm (Fr. cruiser) 222, 226, 231, 233-5, 261, 264, 268
Moreno (Arg. battleship) 14
Mousqueton (Fr. destroyer) 10

N

Naiad (Br. cruiser) 238-9
Nicoline Maersk (Ger. freighter) 261
Nizam (Br. destroyer) 238-9
Norguet, *Inspecteur général* 181, 184
Normandie class (Fr. battleships) 12, 292
Norway, campaign 72, **226-7**, 231

O

Odendhal, Rear-Admiral Jean 214
Ollive, Rear-Admiral (later VA) Emmanuel 122, 214, 222
Operations:
'Catapult' 130, 232, 250
'Dragoon' 264
'Menace' **233-5**
'Overlord' 264
'Torch' 274
'Vado' **229-31**
'Vesuvius' 262
OPL (Fr. manufacturer) 38, 91, 118-9, 123-4, 146-7, **147**, 149, 156, 168, 178
Orage (Fr. destroyer) 41-2, 46, *53*, 55, 62, *197*, 203, 211, 213-7, 221, 225-6, 228
Oran, Algeria 71, 105-6, 126-8, 152, 158-9, 177, 217, 219, 222-3, 226, 231-3, 235-6, 239-40, **245-6**, 257, 259-61, 264, 267
Oued Yquem (Fr. freighter) 237, 239
Ouragan (Fr. destroyer) 41-2, 53, 57, 62, 203, 209, 213-7, 221, 224-6, 229, 231, 250, 257

P

Panthère (Fr. *contre-torpilleur*) 20-2, 25, 33, 35, 39-40, 74, *129*, 201-2, 210, 213-4, 217, 225, 231, 246-9
Panzerschiffe (Ger. armoured ships) 160-1, 216
Pelican (Br. sloop) 250
Pétain, Marshall Philippe 231
Phoebe (Br. cruiser) 238, 261
Pluton (Fr. cruiser) 102, 109, 156
Pride (US destroyer escort) 264
Primauguet (Fr. cruiser) 21, 210, 239-42, 244

Propulsion machinery
Breguet turbines 26, 76, 109
Du Temple boiler 22, 41, 45, 62, 79, 80, 94-5, 112, 117
Parsons turbines 11, 13, 26, 41, 46, 52, 60, 62, 80-1, 96-7, 102, 115-7, 137, 143-4, 180, 184, 186, 272
Rateau turbines 26, 41, 46, 52, 76, 96-7, **97**, 102, 115-7, 137, 143-4, 164, 180, 184, **186**, 272
Sural boiler 6, 182, **184**, 186
Thornycroft boiler + superheater 117, 137
Yarrow boiler + superheater 116, 117, 137, 143
Zoelly turbines 41, 46, 52, 62, 67, 76, 80-1, 90, 96, 115, 180

Provence (Fr. battleship) 213, 222, 231-2, 236

Q

Quai Noël, Toulon 194, 207, 215, 221, 246-9

R

radars
A/BM gunnery fire control 287-8, 291
ACAE gunnery fire control 289-91
DRBC 11A gunnery fire control 283-4, 289, 291
DRBV 30 navigation 284, 289, 291
SA-2 air surveillance (US) 287-8
SF surface surveillance (US) 269, 271-2, 276-8, 287-8, 291
SJ-1 surface surveillance (US) 287-8
Type 285 gunnery fire control (Br.) 266, 275

Renoncule (Fr. corvette) 264-5
Renown (Br. battlecruiser) 288
Resolution (Br. battleship) 234-5
Richelieu (Fr. battleship) 6, *135*, 184, 229, 231, 233-5, 261, 265, 268, 279, 287
Rivadavia (Arg. battleship) 14
Robert, Rear-Admiral Georges 32
Rochefort Naval Dockyard 10, 12, 21, 41
Roselys (Fr. corvette) 264-5
RPC (remote power control) 8, 95, 99, 113-4, 118, 137, 142, 146, **147-8**, 155, 158, 165-70, 173, 176, 183, 188-91
Rubis (Fr. submarine) 93

S

S.113 (Ger. destroyer) 18-19
Saint Didier (Fr. freighter) 237
Saint-Chamond (Fr. armaments works) 161, 167-8
Saratoga (US aircraft carrier) 254
Sautter-Harlé (Fr. manufacturer) 30, 88, 149, 170
Schneider (Fr. manufacturer) 14-6, 29-30, 41, 46, 48, 62, 84, 88, 115, 143, 166, 187
Scott (Br. destroyer) 18, 51
Sénégalais (Fr. destroyer escort) 262-5, 280
Sidi-Abdallah Naval Dockyard, Bizerte (Tunisia) 59, 119, 234, 260, 274
Sikh (Br. destroyer) 227
Simoun (Fr. destroyer) 41-2, 57-9, 73, 197, 203, 208-9, 213, 215-6, 220-3, 225, 231, 239-42, 244-5, 257, 262, 264-7, 276-8, 283
Siroco (Fr. destroyer LD 1924) 41-2, 46-7, 49, 51-3, 55-6, 200, 203, 213, 215-7, 221, 224, 227-8
Siroco (Fr. destroyer LD 1938) 182, 237, 247, 249, 286
SOM (Fr. manufacturer) 28, 47, 65, 87, 99, 123, 146, 149
Somali (Br. destroyer) 227
Somali (Fr. destroyer escort) 265, 267, 280
Spahi class (Fr. destroyers) 9-10
Spey (Br. frigate) 250
Statut Naval 1912 12
Statut Naval 1922 60
STCN (Fr. corps of constructors) 6, 13, 16, 20, 22, 60, 76, 79, 94, 160-1, 179-80, 183, 188, 193-4
Strasbourg (Fr. battleship) 67, 161, *178*, 193, 222, 231-3, 236, 247
Suffren (Fr. cruiser) 60, 233, 288
Surcouf (Fr. submarine) 210
Surcouf (Fr. fleet escort) 286
Swanson (US destroyer) 240
Syria, campaign **237-9**

T

T41 (Fr. torpedo boat design) 286
TA24 (Ger. torpedo boat) 267
TA36 (It. torpedo boat) 261
TA37 (It. torpedo boat) 261
Tartar (Br. destroyer) 227
Tartu (Fr. *contre-torpilleur*) 109-11, 114-6, 118, 122-8, **127** [prof/plan 1942], 202, *209*, 213-4, 218, 222, 226-7, 229-31, *200*, 236-7, 247
Tempête (Fr. destroyer) 41-2, 56-9, 203, 209, 213, 215-6, 220, 222-3, 226, 231, 240, 242, 244-5, 257, 261-2, 264, 266-7, **276-8** [Modernisation Bermuda], 282
Tigre (It. light scout) 18
Tigre (Fr. *contre-torpilleur*) 20-22, 25-7, 33, 35, 39-40, 60, 71, 74, 93, *129*, 201, 202, 208-10, 213-4, 217, 222, 225, 230-2, 246-9, 257, 258, 262, 264, 267, 279, 282, 287
Tonkinois (Fr. frigate) 265, 280
Tornade (Fr. destroyer) 41-2, *56*, 57-9, 71, 203, 213-7, 222-3, 225, 231-2, 236, 240, 245-6
Toulon Naval Dockyard 8, 10, 21, 29-30, 32, 35, 38-41, 52, 57-9, 61, 68, 71, 73-4, 88-9, 91-2, 102, 105, 107, 109, 123-4, 126-8, 131-3, 155-9, 177-8, 181-2, 185, 187, 192, 194, 204-9, **207** [map], 212, 214-25, 229-33, 235-7, 239-40, 245, **247-50** [scuttling], 258, 260, 262, 264-7, 269, 274, 276, 279-85, 287-90, 292
Tourville (Fr. cruiser) 222-3, 233
Tramontane (Fr. destroyer) 41-2, 46, 48, *56*, 57-9, **59** [prof/plan 1942], 203, 213-7, 222, 225, 231-2, 236, 240, 245-6
Trombe (Fr. destroyer) 41-2, 48, 57, *59*, 71, 203, 213-8, 222, 224-5, 231-2, 246-7
Tunisien (Fr. destroyer escort) 262, 265, 280
Tuscaloosa (US cruiser) 240-2, 244
Typhon (Fr. destroyer) 41-2, 47, *56*, 57-9, 203, 213, 215-7, 220, 222-3, 225, 231-2, 236, 240, 245-6

U

U-25 (Ger. submarine) 224
U-37 (Ger. submarine) 225
U-41 (Ger. submarine) 224
U-44 (Ger. submarine) 224
U-53 (Ger. submarine) 224
U-54 (Ger. submarine) 225
U-55 (Ger. submarine) 224-5
U-136 (Ger. submarine) 250
U-371 (Ger. submarine) 264

Underwater weapons & sensors
35kg depth charge 57, 71, 126, 157, 253
100/250 DCT Mle 1928 94, **100**, 112, 120, 138
550mm torpedo Mle 1919D 22, **30**, 41, 48, 62
550mm torpedo Mle 1923D 79, **88**, 90, 94, 112, 120, 140, 149, 164, 184
Asdic 123/128 (French 'Alpha') 33, 39, 49, 57, 71-2, 74, 92, 105, 122, 126, 128, 157-8, 178-9, 224-6, 251, 253, 264, 271-2, 276-8
Breguet B4 mine 112, 120, 140, 164
C6 minesweeping paravane 59, 68, 177, 190-1
CFT depth sounder 79, 95, 114-5, 143, 164
D6 minesweeping paravane 172, 177
Ginocchio torpedo 32, 37, **48-9**, 55, 68-9, 108, 183, 185, 189-91
Guiraud 100kg depth charge 17, **31-2**, 38-9, 57, 66, 74, 89, 100-1, 109, 116, 120, 125-6, 195, 248, 253, 277
Guiraud 200kg depth charge 19, 22, 31-2, 38-9, 41, **48**, 57, 59, 62, 66, 74, 79, 88, 94, 101, 112, 120, 125-6, 140, 149, 151, 157, 164, 171, 184, 189, 253, 269, 275
Mk VII/VIIH depth charges (Br.) 31, 251-4, 268, 275-6, 278
Multispot u/w detection system 57, 71, 157,
Nandillon u/w detection system 120
SS1 u/w detection system 49, 57, 71, 157, 177
SS6 u/w detection system 157, 177
Thornycroft Mk IV depth charge thrower (Br.) 251, 260, 267-8, 271, 276-7
Thornycroft Mle 1918 depth charge thrower 22, **31-32**, 48, 56, 62-3, 66, 70, 74, 79, **88**, 100-1, 125, 127-8, 251, 253, 277-8
Walser hydrophone system 19, 23, **32-3**, 80, 89, 151
Warluzel depth sounder 86, 101, 143, 164

V

Vaclite (Br. tanker) 224
Vaillant (Fr. APV) 224
Valmy (Fr. *contre-torpilleur*) 60, 68, 75-83, 86-7, 90-2, 202, 213-4, 218, 222-6, 229-31, 233, 236-9, 248
Vandier, Captain 16
Vauban (Fr. *contre-torpilleur*) 75-83, 86-7, 90-3, 96, *133*, 208, 213-5, 217-9, 222-4, 229-31, 233, 236-9, 247-8
Vauquelin (Fr. *contre-torpilleur*) 71, 76-7, 90, 93-4, 102, 106-7, **108-28**, 137-8, 140, 143-6, 148-9, 151, 153, 172, 202, 210, 213-5, 218, 221-3, 229, 231, 236-7, 239, 247
Vautour (Fr. *contre-torpilleur*) 93-4, 96-7, 101, 105-6, 109, 122, 202, 209, 213-4, 218, 222-3, 225, 229-31, 233, 236-7, 247
Verdun (Fr. *contre-torpilleur*) 32, 75-83, 86-93, *131*, 202, 210, 213-4, 218, 222-6, 229-31, 233, 237, 246-7
VHF (OTC) tactical radio 39, 92 105
Victor Schoelcher (Fr. AMC) 224
Ville d'Oran (Fr. AMC) 226, 231
Volta (Fr. *contre-torpilleur*) 161-5, 167-73, 176, 177-80, **178** [prof/plan 1942], 182, 186-8, 190-2, 200, 202, 210, *212*, 215, 222, 223, 225, 231-2, 236, 246-7
Voltigeur (Fr. destroyer) 11
VP-702 (Ger. APV) 227
VP-709 (Ger. APV) 227

W

Walney (Br. sloop) 245
Washington Treaty 1922 20, 26, 60, **76**, 160
Whitshed (Br. destroyer) 224-5
Wichita (US cruiser) 240-2, 244
Wilkes (US destroyer) 240
Woolsey class (US destroyers) 286

Z

Zara (It. cruiser) *209*